BUSINESS ECONOMICS

Decision-making and the firm

To my parents

BUSINESS ECONOMICS

Decision-making and the firm

David Brewster

Thames Valley University,
London,
UK.

The Dryden Press
Harcourt Brace & Company Limited
London • Fort Worth • New York • Orlando
Philadelphia • San Diego • Toronto • Sydney • Tokyo.

This book is printed on acid-free paper

THE DRYDEN PRESS
24/28 Oval Road,
London NWI 7DX

Copyright © 1997 by
THE DRYDEN PRESS
Harcourt Brace & Company Limited

A catalogue record for this book is available from the British Library

ISBN 0 03-099017-3

Typeset by Florence Type Limited, Stoodleigh, Devon
Printed in Great Britain by The Bath Press, Bath, Avon

Contents

▶ *Preface*

The purpose of this book is to provide a clear and comprehensive account of how economics explains and analyses the functions and operations of the firm in a modern industrial society. It is suitable for level two (years two and three) undergraduate students who are pursuing courses with business management as an ultimate career objective. They are likely to be taking an Economics or an Accountancy degree or they may be following a more broadly-based Business Studies or European Studies course. It is also designed to suit the needs of existing managers who are undertaking a professional qualification, for example a DMS course or an MBA programme, of which business economics forms an integral part. The book can meet the needs of students studying for qualifications in particular areas, for example the hospitality and leisure industries. It may also suit some courses in industrial economics. A previous knowledge of basic economic principles, with particular reference to microeconomic concepts, and simple mathematical and statistical techniques is presumed. The book can be used for a single semester course or for a year-long programme of study.

It is certainly not the intention of the book to give a complex and highly theoretical account of business behaviour, which would probably have the effect on most management students of putting them off economics for life. However, the book does seek to combine theoretical rigour with sound application. It needs to be sufficiently rigorous in order to provide those working in a business environment with a sound knowledge of the concepts and techniques involved in understanding the behaviour of the firm. It also needs to be suitably applied so that managers and prospective managers can observe how firms have reacted to different circumstances within a dynamic competitive environment. They may then be able to apply the knowledge gained to any problems that their own companies may face.

This book is concerned with the analysis of the internal organisation of the firm and its decision-making processes. In so doing, it discusses the nature of the firm, the types of decisions made, what determines these decisions and their effects. The exposition is largely undertaken within a market structure, conduct and performance framework, although the latest theoretical developments are incorporated into the analysis wherever possible. In other words, the text employs a combination of traditional and modern theories of the firm in order to investigate its behaviour. As such, it mainly encompasses microeconomic concepts, although macroeconomic topics are also covered where applicable. The decision-making processes of the firm can apply equally to all types of business organisation, irrespective of their scale or form of ownership. However, the typical organisation for current purposes is taken as the large, privately-owned corporation that predominates in modern industrial economies. It can exert a strong influence on its environment, but separate and perhaps competing groups of interests exist within it. Comparisons are made wherever possible between the behaviour and policies of these companies in the UK and the activities of similar firms in Western Europe, the US and Japan.

▶ Acknowledgements

I would like to thank a number of colleagues at Thames Valley University for their help and advice in the writing of this book. In most cases my request for assistance was met with a positive and generous response. My thanks goes to Stephen Pyle for comments and encouragement on the early drafts, to Peter Dawson for elucidation of certain quantitative techniques and to Philip Wyatt for help and advice in the later stages. In particular, I would like to express my gratitude to Stephen Hope, for reading well over half the chapters, and to David Glen, who read the entire book, including the initial material. Their invaluable comments, support and patience, especially in coping with my numerous telephone calls, will long be remembered. I wish to thank the staff of the Learning Resources Centre at the university for dealing patiently and efficiently with my various requests for help, not the least of which involved extracting information from Business Periodicals on Disc. The sincerest of thanks goes to my father for reading through the complete manuscript and for offering many helpful suggestions on vocabulary and points of grammar. I would also like to express my appreciation to family and friends for their encouragement and also for their tolerance of my variable moods during the whole project; it probably would not have been completed without them. Of all my friends I would like to single out Kate Pittman for always offering the right words of support when most needed. Finally, I would like to extend my gratitude to Maggie Smith and Manjula Goonawardena at Dryden Press for their support and constant good humour despite my mounting paranoia as deadlines approached.

I am grateful to the following for permission to reproduce copyright material: D. Salvadori for Table 1 (D. Salvadori, The Automobile Industry in The European Challenge, edited by David G. Mayes, Harvester Wheatsheaf, 1991); Economic Review for Table 19 (Economic Review Data Supplement, Sept. 1995, Philip Allan Publishers); The Economist for Tables 25, 41 and 60 © The Economist, London, 27 March 1993, 17 October 1992 and 21 October 1995); Office for National Statistics for Figure 13 (Economic Trends 1994, Office for National Statistics, Crown Copyright 1994, reproduced by permission of the Controller of HMSO and of the Office for National Statistics); Scottish Economic Association for Tables 72 and 73 (D. Parker and S. Martin, Scottish Journal of Political Economics, Vol. 42, 1995).

CHAPTER 1

▶ *Introduction*

1.1 OVERVIEW

The basic aim of the text is to examine the *organisation* and the *decision-making processes* of the firm. The firm has a number of legal forms: the sole trader, the partnership, the private and public limited company and the co-operative. It can also vary in size from very small, defined as an organisation that employs less than 10 people, to a large organisation that has thousands on its payroll. The firm can be single or multiplant; it can operate in a narrow, localised market or as a global entity with subsidiaries worldwide. However, the main characteristic from an economic perspective is that the firm has the ability to direct and allocate resources. The prime purpose of this book is to investigate the nature and decision-making techniques of the *modern, large corporation* that operates in the private sector of the major industrialised economies of the world. In such an organisation the key decisions surrounding resource direction and allocation are often undertaken by the 'visible hand' of salaried managers who, while they may have an equity stake in the business, may also have interests at variance with the main body of shareholders.

In *neoclassical* terms the firm is viewed as an abstract unit or 'black box' restricted to the sole activity of converting inputs into output. As such, it lacks the power to undertake its own price and output decisions.[1] The problem with this view of the firm was that, even at the time of the development of the theory at the end of the nineteenth and the beginning of the twentieth centuries, there was an absence of empirical verification. The major concern of

neoclassical theory was to explain the market allocation of resources by analysing the behaviour of two groups of decision-makers, firms and households, within a unifying framework: the perfectly competitive model. The assumptions of the model (perfect information, a given set of tastes, resources and technology and given objective functions, to maximise profits in the case of firms and to maximise utility for households) meant that an analysis of the internal intractabilities of the organisation and its decision-making techniques was largely ignored. This was to facilitate a study of how the price system directs resources according to changes in demand and supply conditions and within which market forces act as an 'invisible hand' to ensure that the maximum amount of goods and services and those that are most socially useful are produced.

Thus, traditional, neoclassical economic theory established a framework for analysing resource allocation, but the firm itself had no power to direct and allocate resources into marketable output. It was simply regarded as one element in the system:

While the literature of economics is replete with references to the 'theory of the firm', the material generally subsumed under that heading is not a theory of the firm but actually a theory of markets in which firms are important actors (Jensen and Meckling, 1976:306–7).

In fact, alternatives to the perfectly competitive neoclassical view of the firm had developed since the 1930s. In 1933 Robinson and Chamberlin introduced the theory of *monopolistic competition*, incorporating the theoretical innovation of monopoly power, albeit temporary, on the part of the firm. Empirical evidence questioned both the key assumption of profit maximisation (Berle and Means, 1932) and the use of 'marginal' rules (Hall and Hitch, 1939). In 1937 Coase analysed the reasons for the existence of the firm in transactional cost terms and initiated an investigation into the role and impact of its internal structure. Other analytical insights into the behaviour of the firm were provided by the *managerial* and *behavioural* theories of the 1950s and 1960s. The former examined the effects, within a traditional optimising framework, of a divorce between ownership and control on business objectives; the behavioural model explored the nature of the firm as a collection of interest groups with competing goals operating in an uncertain environment.

Williamson (1975, 1981) developed Coase's analysis by incorporating the key features of behavioural theory into a *transaction cost* approach to the theory of the firm based on limited knowledge by economic agents and self-interested or opportunistic behaviour. A *transaction* refers to any agreement between economic agents, whether individuals, firms or the government. Transaction costs describe the costs of using the market mechanism. In traditional theory such costs do not exist because it is assumed that economic agents have perfect information and are certain about the future. However, with limited information and in an uncertain environment there may be significant costs involved in using the market; they comprise the costs of obtaining the necessary information, say by a firm in searching for prospective suppliers, and then in negotiating and possibly enforcing a contract with the chosen supplier. Transaction costs can provide a rationale for the existence of the firm: limited knowledge can lead to deceitful, opportunistic behaviour and, in situations where there are relatively few agents involved in a bargaining process and where assets are highly specific to a particular task, it may be preferable to absorb an activity, for example the supplier, into a firm. However, there may be a limit to the range of activities that a firm can undertake, in which case other firms exist and market transactions between firms will occur.

At the same time that the transaction cost view of the firm was being developed an alternative avenue was being explored, although from a similar analytical perspective: *principal–agent* analysis views the firm as a series or 'nexus' of contracts between the various stakeholders (for example, employees, creditors, shareholders, customers and suppliers) who have a direct interest in its activities. Individuals act as agents or principals and, in situations of asymmetric information and self-interested human behaviour, substantial agency costs may arise; it is argued that opposing interests can be reconciled through contractual arrangements.

The modern view of the firm, existing as a series of contracts between interested parties and based on assumptions of limited and asymmetric information, self-interested behaviour and an uncertain environment, is a far cry from the amorphous entity of neoclassical theory that operates in a certain world and in which economic agents possess perfect information. However, the recent models are essentially concerned with explanations of the existence of the firm, which is to minimise transaction costs. A predilection for a neoclassical foundation has restricted the development of an alternative unifying paradigm for analysing the behaviour of the firm; in

particular, the models lack the analytical power to predict corporate strategic behaviour. Therefore, in examining the basic decision-making processes of the firm the text takes a fairly standard approach; particular issues are examined initially from a traditional perspective and this is combined with an assessment of the modern theories where relevant. Recourse to the empirical evidence in certain instances can help to determine the relative merits of the different approaches. The *key topics* to be examined include the following:

(1) the reasons for the existence of the modern, large corporation;
(2) the nature and significance of its internal structure;
(3) an analysis of decisions concerning the quantities to produce, the production techniques to employ and the prices to charge;
(4) an exploration of the relationships between the organisation and its major stakeholders;
(5) a discussion of the firm's strategic decision-making by examining the motives for, and methods and financing implications of, its expansion;
(6) the interrelationships between the firm and the competitive and governmental environments.

1.2 OUTLINE OF THE BOOK

Chapter 2 discusses the market environment in which firms operate. The delineation of markets and industries is explained; the relationships between market structure, conduct and performance are outlined; the traditional, structuralist framework is contrasted with the views of other, more recent, schools of thought; the evidence on and the measurement and determinants of market concentration are discussed; barriers to entry are examined.

Chapter 3 undertakes an in-depth comparison of the industrial and employment structures of the UK with those in other major industrial economies. The relative importance of the manufacturing sector in the UK and elsewhere is examined. The role of the firm as an instigator of structural change is also assessed.

Chapter 4 discusses the nature of the firm in theory and in practice. It examines the reasons for the existence of the firm and explains why firms and markets co-exist as co-ordinators of resources. There is an examination of the internal organisation of the firm and the meaning of entrepreneurship. The chapter also describes the main institutional characteristics of the firm, with special emphasis on the multinational organisation.

Chapter 5 outlines several of the main concepts involved in the study of business decision-making. These include the importance of time and the need to understand the significance of incrementalism and marginalism. As such, the chapter forms the groundwork for much of the analysis that follows, at least from a traditional perspective. The problems of dealing with risk and uncertainty are also examined.

Chapters 6 and 7 examine the basic economic conditions, production and costs on the one hand and demand and revenue on the other, that underpin the resource-allocating decisions of firms and that determine the competitive environment in which they operate. In each case, the traditional approach to the topic is examined before more recent concepts and theories are discussed and the empirical evidence examined. An Appendix on isoquant and isocost analysis follows Chapter 6.

Chapter 8 investigates corporate decision-making within the theory of the firm, mainly from a traditional perspective; it explains how different market structures or competitive environments can influence such decision-making. Particular emphasis is placed on analysing the conduct of large firms that operate in oligopolistic market environments.

Chapter 9 assesses the relationship between ownership and control in large firms and the consequent effects on corporate objectives. The control of managerial behaviour is examined mainly in principal–agent terms.

Chapters 10–14 explore the strategic decision-making processes in more detail by examining the behaviour (and underlying behavioural characteristics) of firms in particular key areas: pricing, advertising and branding policies; investment and financing strategies; mergers and multimarket decisions involving diversification, vertical integration and multinational expansion (with special emphasis on transaction cost explanations); and labour market strategies.

Finally, Chapter 15 investigates the relationship between the firm and the governmental and regulatory environment by assessing the impact of public policy, with particular reference to competition policy and the privatisation debate, on corporate decision-making and performance.

Most of the chapters end with at least one case study in which the analytical concepts that have been covered are applied to particular practical examples.

1.3 USE OF THE BOOK

Naturally, it is hoped that the book could be used in its entirety, especially for year-long courses of study, but this need not be the case. There is no reason why individual chapters cannot be selected and put together to form the basis of shorter courses. This is particularly apposite given the preference in many institutions of higher education for semester-based programmes, both at the undergraduate and postgraduate levels.

Some examples of how this may be achieved may be helpful. A business economics unit for students with a sound prior knowledge of basic microeconomic theory may reasonably comprise Chapters 4,5,9,10,11,12,13 and 15; for those with only a slight prior background in microeconomic theory the unit may consist of Chapters 4,5,6,7,8,9,10 and 12. On the other hand, for students taking an industrial economics module its composition may comprise Chapters 2,3,9,10,11,12,13,14 and 15.

NOTES

1. The term neoclassical is based on the view that the originators of the so-called 'marginalist revolution' refined and developed the work of the classical school, the economic philosophy that predominated between the mid-eighteenth to the mid-nineteenth century. The mainstays of neoclassical thought were John M. Clark (1847–1938), Francis Edgeworth (1845–1926), Irving Fisher (1867–1947), Stanley Jevons (1835–82), Alfred Marshall (1842–1924), Vilfredo Pareto (1848–1923) and Léon Walras (1834–1910). Marshall synthesised the prevailing ideas into a theory of price determination in a perfectly competitive free market economy.

CHAPTER 2

▶ *The Market Environment*

In this chapter we will examine the *market environment*, or the structure of the market in which firms operate. The *market structure* consisting of its key organisational features, is said to exert a strong influence on the *conduct* or *behaviour* of firms and on the sorts of decisions that they make, whether these are concerned with price, output, objectives, mergers, personnel, R&D, or whatever else. Conduct, in its turn, affects the *performance* of firms and markets, performance being defined in terms of profits, rates of growth or rates of technological progress. This traditional structure–conduct–performance (SCP) paradigm assumes a one-way causal relationship, although it can be adapted to include other possible relationships. In order to appreciate fully the importance of and the interconnections between market structure, conduct and performance it is necessary to understand how one market can be distinguished from another.

We first examine the delineation of *markets* and how markets can be differentiated from *industries*. The relationships between market structure, conduct and performance are examined in some detail. *Alternative schools of thought* to the SCP paradigm are outlined and their implications for business decision-making are discussed. An important feature of market structure is *market concentration*. This as a summary measure is often used to distinguish between different market structures. The measurement of, and evidence on, market concentration is examined. *Barriers to entry*, a second significant structural characteristic, are also discussed. Finally, the *product life cycle* hypothesis and the dynamic approach to markets and market

structures is examined. At the end of the chapter there is a *case study* on the structure–conduct–performance relationships and the effect of changing market conditions in the UK plasterboard industry.

2.1 THE DELINEATION OF MARKETS AND INDUSTRIES

A *market* refers to those buyers and sellers of the same product or resource who are constantly engaged in its transaction. The activities of different markets are interrelated. Thus, an increase in demand for a product will lead to an increase in demand for the resources to produce that product, *ceteris paribus*, or other things being equal. An increase in demand to purchase new homes will lead to a rise in their price and an eventual addition to their stock as more resources are attracted into their production via the higher rewards (such as higher wages) that are offered to the owners of resources to work in this particular market. Alternatively, a rise in demand for a product will lead to an increase in demand for complementary goods and a fall in demand for substitutes. For example, an increase in demand for new houses will add to the demand for furnishings and fittings, while it will cause a decline in demand for rented accommodation.

Because different markets are interrelated, it is very important to distinguish between one market and the next. A firm would like to know which other organisations are its main competitors, i.e. which are most affected by its decisions, and *vice versa*. A firm's main competitors will presumably be those that operate in its particular market. However, the definition of a market is rather vague, the main problem being to decide what constitutes the same product or resource. This can be interpreted as where there is a close degree of substitution between products, although the latter is in itself extremely difficult to measure.

One solution is to apply a concept known as *cross-price elasticity of demand*. This is defined as a measure of the responsiveness of the demand for one product to a change in the price of a different product, *cet. par.* (see Section 7.5 for a more detailed description). Products are substitutes if a change in the price of one has a significant and positive impact on the demand of another. (It may be that a product's price change has a negative impact on the demand for another product, in which case the two products are complements.) If there is a significant and positive effect the two products can be viewed as belonging to the same market. However, there are problems in using cross-price elasticity of demand to define market boundaries. Firstly, it is very difficult to obtain estimates with any accuracy. Secondly, what is meant by a significant impact? In other words, when cross-price elasticities are estimated, what value is the critical cut-off point in deciding whether products should belong to the same market? A third problem is that cross-price elasticity of demand unsurprisingly only measures the degree of substitution on the demand side. If the degree of substitution on the supply side is to be taken into account, the cross-price elasticity of supply should be used. This measures the responsiveness of the supply of a product to a change in the price of another product, *cet. par.* In this instance, two products would be regarded as substitutes if the change in the price of one had a significant and negative (since firms would switch to producing the more highly priced good) effect on the supply of another. This concept is beset by the same problems as cross-price elasticity of demand. In fact, the problems are all the greater, since supply usually responds far less readily than demand to price changes.

An important factor that needs to be taken into account when defining markets is that products have a number of different characteristics, which means that they can be defined in a variety of ways: in terms of their physical nature, such as size or location, by the production processes or raw material inputs used in their manufacture, via the prices of the product, and so on. These characteristics can divide any market into distinct *segments*, in each of which groups of consumers exhibit similar tastes and preferences. Whether products are considered close substitutes will depend on which particular characteristics are used to define them. Products that are thought to be substitutes by consumers are not necessarily the same groupings from the point of view of producers. Market segmentation is often determined by the degree of *product differentiation*. This is the extent to which similar products are perceived to be different by consumers, irrespective of whether the differences are based on actual physical variations in quality or other important characteristics. The differences may be the result of advertising and other marketing techniques,

Table 1 *Segmentation in the European Car Market*

Segment	Characteristics	Principal models
1 Economy	<1100 cc Price <45,000FF[a]	Austin Mini, Citroën 2cv, Fiat Panda, Maruti 900, Renault 4, Seat Marbella, Yugo 45
2 Small	1000–1450 cc Price 45–65,000FF	Austin Metro, Citroën AX, Fiat Uno, Ford Fiesta, Honda Civic, Lancia Y10, Mazda 121, Nissan Micra, Opel Corsa, Peugeot 205, Renault 5, Seat Ibiza, VW Polo
3 Medium (lower)	1100–1600 cc Price 60–80,000FF	Alfa Romeo 33, Austin Maestro, Fiat Tipo, Ford Escort, Ford Orion, Honda Accord, Lada Samara, Lancia Delta, Mazda 323, Nissan Sunny, Opel Kadett, Peugeot 309, Renault 19, Rover 213, Seat Malaga, VW Golf/Jetta, Volvo 340, Yugo 65
4 Medium (upper)	1500–1950 cc Price 76–100,000FF	Alfa Romeo 75, Audi 80, Austin Montego, Citroën BX, Fiat Regata, Ford Sierra, Honda Prelude, Lancia Dedra, Mazda 626, Nissan Bluebird, Opel Vectra, Peugeot 405, Renault 21, Toyota Corolla, VW Passat, Volvo 440
5 Large	1600–2000 cc Price 95–160,000FF	Alfa Romeo 164, Audi 90/100, BMW 3 series, Citroën XM, Fiat Croma, Ford Scorpio, Honda Legend, Lancia Thema, Mazda 929, Mercedes 190, Mitsubishi Galant, Peugeot 605, Renault 25, Rover 820, Saab 900, Volvo 240
6 Deluxe	>2000 cc Price >160,000FF	Audi 200, BMW 5.7 series, Mercedes 200, 300, 500, Saab 9000, Volvo 740/760
7 Prestige sport, leisure	Sport Prestige Deluxe sport Offroad	Alpine, Ferrari, Porsche Bentley, Jaguar, Rolls-Royce BMW M3 M5, Audi 200 Lada Niva, Mitsubishi Pajero, Nissan Patrol, Land/Range Rover, Jeep, Toyota Land Cruiser
	Concept-van	Chrysler Voyager, Nissan Prairie/Vanette, Renault Espace

[a]Prices are given in French Francs

Source: Salvadori (1991: 33).

such as branding, that simply create or exaggerate differences in the mind's eye of the consumer.

The car market is one in which there is a high degree of product differentiation and segmentation. As Table 1 reveals, the European market can be divided into seven distinct segments based on model size. Within each segment, individual producers may offer different versions of the same model (i.e standard or deluxe models, or there may be slight variations in engine capacities) and they may undertake separate advertising campaigns for each model that they offer.

The significance of market segmentation for corporate behaviour cannot be overstated. The characteristics of the various segments can lead to very different corporate strategies (Salvadori, 1991). For example segment 1, the economy car market, is characterised by high price sensitivity. Firms are therefore likely to use pricing policies as their main strategic weapon rather than more supply-side policies such as variations in technical features or the availability of special models. Alternatively, demand in segments 2, 3, 4 and 5, which accounts for 90% of the entire market, is far more sensitive to supply factors and far less so to price. Within these segments, firms are much more likely to offer models with a range of specifications and technical features. Since customers are attracted by image and brand loyalty, advertising and other marketing policies will also be important strategies. Segments 6 and 7 are particularly sensitive to the effects of image and there are strong attachments to certain makes of car. In these sectors brand loyalty is strong. Therefore, advertising becomes an even more significant corporate strategy.

Another problem involved in accurately defining markets is that the modern, large corporation is often multiproduct or diversified in some way. The problem then is to decide into which market each firm should belong. The spatial dimensions of markets also need to be taken into account when defining them. From the consumer's point of view the market for many services comprises a town, or even a part of a town. The purchase of a hotel room for a night in London cannot be considered a substitute for a hotel night in Paris. The consumer travels to the product, the hotel room, and consumes it on the spot; production and consumption occurs at the same place, whereas goods are usually produced at one point and consumed at another. The market for utilities like gas, electricity and water is often defined by national boundaries, or at least fairly large regional areas. On the other hand, the globalisation of production for many products, both goods and some services, means

that markets are becoming increasingly international. Within each of these geographic markets, whatever their extent, others may exist, each defined by the different characteristics of the various products.

Standard industrial classifications

A further problem of defining markets is that all economic activity is classified in terms of *industries*. These are collections of firms that produce the same product. This definition again raises the question of how to define the term, 'the same'. However, despite this recurring problem, and although industries are defined solely in supply or production terms, the two concepts, markets and industries, are usually used interchangeably.

In the UK the first standard industrial classification (SIC) was introduced in 1948. Since then it has been revised in 1958, in 1968 and in 1980. The latest SIC was published in November, 1992. Revision is necessary because new products and new industries emerge and shifts of emphasis, the decline of one sector and the growth of another, occur in existing industries.

The UK SIC(92) adheres closely to the EU regulation on defining and classifying industries. This is referred to as 'Nomenclature Générale des Activités Économiques dans les Communautés Européennes', or NACE for short. The only difference is that whereas NACE is a four-digit system, the UK SIC(92) uses five digits (it includes subclasses). As Table 2, page 8, shows, at the broadest level of aggregation, SIC(92) is divided into 17 sections, listed as A–Q (some sections are divided into subsections, each denoted by the addition of a second letter, for example DB). The next breakdown is the two digit level, divisions. The divisions are then broken down into groups (three digits), then into classes (four digits) and, in several cases, into subclasses (five digits).

As in previous classifications the unit of analysis is the *establishment*. This is defined as a factory, shop, farm, hotel, restaurant or any other economic unit that carries on its business at one geographic location. It is the smallest unit that can provide the requisite information on matters like numbers of employees, costs and revenues. It should be noted that an establishment is not necessarily the same thing as a firm. The *firm* is the unit of ownership. A small firm can consist of a single establishment or *plant,* in which case it is referred to as single plant. However, many firms, and especially large firms, are likely to comprise several, or indeed hundreds, of

Table 2 *UK SIC(92)*

A	Agriculture, Hunting and Forestry
B	Fishing
C	Mining and Quarrying
D	Manufacturing
E	Electricity, Gas and Water Supply
F	Construction
G	Wholesale and Retail Trade; Repair of Motor Vehicles, Motorcycles and Personal and Household Goods
H	Hotels and Restaurants
I	Transport, Storage and Communication
J	Financial Intermediation
K	Real Estate, Renting and Business Activity
L	Public Administration and Defence; Compulsory Social Security
M	Education
N	Health and Social Work
O	Other Community, Social and Personal Service Activities
P	Private Households With Employed Persons
Q	Extra-Territorial Organisations and Bodies

Section D	Manufacturing (comprises Divisions 15–37)
Subsection DB	Manufacture of Textiles and Textile Products (comprises Divisions 17 and 18)
Division 17	Manufacture of Textiles
Group 17.4	Manufacture of Made-up Textile Articles, Except Apparel
Class 17.40	Manufacture of Made-up Textile Articles, Except Apparel
Subclass 17.40/1	Manufacture of Soft Furnishings

Source: Central Statistical Office (London, HMSO).

individual plants. They can be located both at home and abroad. In economic parlance these firms are multiplant.

In order to try to overcome the problem of into which industry to classify multiplant, multiproduct firms, SICs are usually based on a number of different factors. Establishments are grouped into industries according to various criteria, such as the similarity of techniques or processes of production, the similarity of raw materials used and the similarity of the final good or service produced. However, establishments are classified according to their main activity. Should more than one activity be undertaken (i.e. more than one product produced) at a single site this will not be obvious from the available data.

Furthermore, all the criteria used are supply considerations. Demand factors are ignored. SIC(92) and the other classifications may place firms in the same industry, but this does not necessarily put them in the same market. The problem can even be seen at the first and broadest level of aggregation, sections. Hotels and rented accommodation can be viewed as substitutes in terms of the demand created by local authority tenancies or by lengthy business trips. However, hotels are in section H and rented accommodation in section K of SIC(92). In this instance, the taking into account of consumers' judgements results in a wider classification of economic activity than is actually found in SIC(92). Since services often have a very localised demand, this would usually lead to a narrower grouping of firms into industries compared with SIC(92). All industrial classifications suffer from such problems.

2.2 MARKET STRUCTURE, CONDUCT AND PERFORMANCE

Corporate *behaviour* or *conduct* consists of the major strategies or policies that firms undertake. These policies are both influenced by, and can influence, the competitive environment, or the *market structure*, in which firms operate. The policies of firms can also affect how firms *perform*, and in particular their levels of efficiency. The performance of firms may, in its turn, have an effect on corporate behaviour and the firm's competitive environment.

Market structure is itself determined by the particular characteristics of the markets in which firms exist. The study of the relationships and interrelationships between these characteristics, firm behaviour and firm and market performance causes considerable disagreement amongst economists. It is known as the *structure–conduct–performance debate* and it has important implications for an understanding of the decision-making process.

The most popular or traditional view, alternatively referred to as the *structuralist* position and indebted in particular to the work of Mason (1939) and Bain (1959), is that any 'causation' flows mainly in one direction, from structure, which is assumed to be exogenously determined, to conduct and ultimately to performance (hence it is also known as the *SCP approach* or *paradigm*). According to this neoclassical approach, decision-makers are able to maximise their objectives on the basis of perfect knowledge of their respective environments. Firms maximise profits and

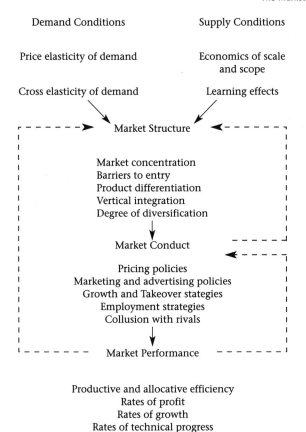

Demand Conditions Supply Conditions

Price elasticity of demand Economics of scale and scope

Cross elasticity of demand Learning effects

Market Structure

Market concentration
Barriers to entry
Product differentiation
Vertical integration
Degree of diversification

Market Conduct

Pricing policies
Marketing and advertising policies
Growth and Takeover stategies
Employment strategies
Collusion with rivals

Market Performance

Productive and allocative efficiency
Rates of profit
Rates of growth
Rates of technical progress

Figure 1 *Market structure–conduct–performance relationships.*

households maximise utility. Markets will always tend towards their equilibrium positions. Maximisation of economic welfare is based on the achievement of a Pareto-efficient allocation of resources (in the sense that it would be impossible to move to a different allocation and make one person better off without making somebody else worse off) in a perfectly competitive environment. The unidirectional relationship between market structure, conduct and performance is shown by the downward flow of the arrows in Figure 1. The possibilities for reverse causation, which can exist in this approach but are not considered essential to it, are shown by the dashed arrows. For example, should a firm make a loss, or at least not fulfil its potential, it may have to leave the industry; the firm's performance will have affected the degree of concentration and hence the structure of the industry. These interrelationships are examined more fully in Chapter 8.

The structure of a market is determined by the nature of the demand and supply conditions that exist within it. The major determining factors from the sup-

ply or cost of production point of view are the existence or otherwise of *economies of scale and scope* and *learning effects*, or the effects of experience of operating in an industry. The most important factor on the demand side is the *elasticity of demand* for the product. These concepts are dealt with more fully in Chapters 6 and 7. The key structure, conduct and performance variables are outlined in Box 2.1, page 10.

Many studies have been undertaken in order to test the relationships between market structure, conduct and performance (see Table 3, page 11). Most have concentrated on whether structure determines performance, and in particular what effect seller concentration has on profitability; some studies have also examined the concentration–price relationship. As the table shows, the results of the studies are not conclusive. This is due, at least in part, to the problems involved in adequately measuring both concentration and profitability. (The problems of measuring concentration are discussed in the next section.) The difficulties in measuring profitability are twofold: firms use different accounting procedures and alternative profit ratios can be employed in empirical investigation. Bain (1951, 1956), in one of the earliest studies, used the rate of return on shareholder's equity as a measure of profitability, whereas most of the other investigations have employed the rate of return on assets. Early work by Bain (1951, 1956) and Mann (1966) in the US found a positive, although fairly weak, association between concentration and profits. These results were supported by evidence from Collins and Preston (1968, 1969) and by Weiss (1974) in a follow-up study for the US and by Hitiris (1978) and Lyons (1981) in the UK. On the other hand, Holtermann (1973), Clarke (1984) in the UK and Berger (1995) for the US found an insignificantly negative relationship. Brozen (1971) investigated the relationship between concentration and profits over time on the basis that a positive relationship at one point in time may simply reflect a temporary disequilibrium situation. By examining the same 42 US industries as had Bain, it was found that the difference in profitability between high- and low-concentrated industries vanished over time. Evidence by Coate (1989) supported the results of the Brozen study, indicating that the effects of market power, at least in certain instances, may only be temporary.

It is because the relationships between structure, conduct and performance are complex, coupled with the fact that the empirical evidence is inconclusive, that other schools of thought have developed. The different assumptions and predictions inherent in

Box 2.1 *Market structure, conduct and performance variables*

Market structure is defined most commonly in terms of the number and size distribution of firms within a market. Together they determine the degree of *market* or *seller concentration*. This is dealt with more fully in the next section. A second important structural feature is the extent of *barriers to entry* in a market. These are obstacles to potential entrants or competitors that lie on the boundary of a market. (This topic is covered in Section 2.4.) A third key structural element is the degree of *product differentiation* in a market. Policies that involve product differentiation, specifically advertising and branding, are discussed in Chapter 11. The other main structural features of a market are the extent to which firms engage in *vertical integration* and *conglomerate integration* or *diversification*. Vertical integration refers to the extent to which firms also operate in successive markets, whether these are the upstream markets that supply their inputs (backward vertical integration) or the downstream markets that buy their outputs (forward vertical integration). Conglomerate diversification is the degree to which firms also operate in other product markets. These may be products that have some sort of link with the other product areas of firms. They may require similar technology or similar marketing methods. This is known as *lateral conglomerate diversification*. Alternatively, the product markets may have no obvious relationship with the existing product base. This is *pure conglomerate diversification*. Vertical and conglomerate diversification strategies are discussed in Chapter 13.

According to the SCP view the structure of a market influences the conduct of firms. *Market conduct* refers to the *competitive policies* or *strategies* adopted by the firms in a particular market. They include pricing policies, marketing and advertising policies, growth and takeover strategies, employment policies and the extent of competition or collusion with rivals. These topics are dealt with in Chapters 10–14. An example of the relationship that may occur between structure and conduct is that firms in a highly-concentrated market which is dominated by a few large firms (an oligopoly) are likely to collude about price but engage in a good deal of non-price competitive behaviour such as advertising.

The structure and conduct of a market can affect the performance of firms. *Market performance* is assessed in a number of ways. *Productive* or *technical efficiency* is the extent to which the firms in a market produce their outputs at the lowest possible cost. *Allocative efficiency* refers to the degree to which the market, and indeed all markets, produces an optimal allocation of products for the benefit of society. Market performance can also be assessed by examining the *profit rates* of the constituent firms and the extent to which prices exceed the true economic costs of producing the product. The degree of *technical progress* in a market can be a useful indicator of its performance. The invention and innovation of new processes, or methods of production, can lead to reduced costs of production, and the development of new products can mean improvements compared with what already exists. The faster their rate of technical progress, the more quickly will firms be able to grow. Performance can therefore be measured by inspecting the *rates of growth* of firms in a market. Market performance, and its policy implications, is examined in more detail in Chapter 15. According to the mainstream view, the higher the level of competition in a market then usually the better it will perform. In a competitive industry (i.e. one with low concentration) firms operate efficiently, they have little power to set their own prices and freedom of entry and exit means that profits above the normal are temporary. In a highly concentrated industry, on the other hand, collusive behaviour among a few large firms gives them the power to price above competitive levels and to make excess monopoly profits; barriers to entry may ensure that the excess profits persist.

---

these paradigms mean that there are significant public policy implications; they also have implications for firm behaviour. The *Chicago school*, so-called because that is where it originated in the 1970s (see, for example, Stigler, 1971; Demsetz, 1973; Peltzman, 1976), reverses the causation process completely, although it still assumes that markets automatically move towards their equilibrium positions and that maximising objectives can be attained. Its basic premise is that a firm's performance is the major determinant of market structure. If a firm is very efficient and it has lower costs of production (due, say, to economies of scale and scope and superior production techniques) and higher profits than its rivals, it will gain an ever larger market share; eventually it will dominate the market. The Chicago school assumes that the best performance is often positively related to the extent of monopoly power in a market.

Brozen (1971) had also questioned whether a positive concentration–profitability relationship reflected the greater efficiency of large firms rather than their exercise of market power. This point was taken up by Demsetz (1973) who claimed that the significantly positive relationship between concentration amd profits, especially when comparing the smallest and largest firms in an industry, indicated the superior efficiency of the latter. However, Martin (1988) found that, by allowing for productivity differences between

Table 3 *Tests of the relationship between market concentration and performance*

Study	Period	Coverage	Relationship tested	Effects
Bain (1951, 1956)	1936–40 1947–51	42 US manuf. indust.	Conc.–profit	+
Mann (1966)	1950–60	30 US manuf. indust.	Conc.–profit	+
Collins and Preston (1968, 1969)	1958, 1963 1958–63	All US 4-digit indust.	Conc.–profit	+
Brozen (1971)	1936–40 1953–57	42 US manuf. indust.	Conc.–profit	NR[a]
Demsetz (1973)	1963	95 3-digit US indust.	Conc.–profit	+
Holtermann (1973)	1963	3-digit UK indust.	Conc.–profit	−
Weiss (1974)	1958–63	All US 4-digit indust.	Conc.–profit	+
Hitiris (1978)	1965 1968	2-digit UK indust.	Conc.–profit	+
Lyons (1981)	1968	3-digit UK indust.	Conc.–profit	+
Clarke (1984)	1970–76	UK manuf.	Conc.–profit	−
Amato and Wilder (1988)	1963	95 US indust.	Conc.–profit	NS[b]
Martin (1988)	1972	185 US indust.	Conc.–profit	+
Berger and Hannan (1989)		470 US banks	Conc.–price	+
Coate (1989)	1958–62	48 US indust.	Conc.–profit	NR[a]
Marvel (1989)	1964–71	US gasoline	Conc.–price	+
Weiss (1989)	1948–80	US cement	Conc.–price	+
Berger (1995)	1980–89	4800 US banks	Conc.–profit	−

[a]No relationship over time.
[b]No significant relationship.

subgroups of differently-sized firms in various industries, the positive concentration–profit relationship remained; in other words, market power, not increased efficiency, determined the higher profitability of the more concentrated industries. Amato and Wilder (1988) were not able to replicate Demsetz's results using more disaggregated data. Weiss (1989) claimed that the positive relationship found between concentration and price provided clear evidence that the effects of market power dominated those arising from greater efficiency, given the strong theoretical relationship between increased market power and higher prices. Marvel (1989) and Berger and Hannan (1989) also reported a significantly positive concentration–price relationship. The only factor that would appear to be clear from the evidence testing the relationship between structure, in the form of market concentration, and market performance is that no clear conclusions can be drawn. It is not possible to state with any sort of certainty what kind of market structure is compatible with the best performance, however that is defined, or even in what direction the causation lies; it is also not possible to state categorically whether the higher profitability associated with more highly concentrated industries, should it occur, is the result of market power or whether it is due to the effects of superior efficiency.

Contestability theory (Baumol, 1982; Baumol *et al.*, 1982) also assumes that optimising behaviour is pursued and is attainable. The theory posits that the major factor that determines structure, conduct and performance has nothing to do with what is happening in the market itself. Instead it has everything to do with possible entry from outside. If new firms enter, or are trying to enter a market, they will determine how existing firms behave and perform. In other words, market structure is endogenously determined. A perfectly contestable market is one in which, under certain conditions, 'entry is absolutely free and exit is absolutely costless' (Baumol, 1982:3). Hence, there are no barriers to entry, although economies of scale may still be features of monopoly and oligopoly markets. Given the fact that there are no sunk costs (such as past expenditure on machinery and equipment that have no alternative use), in which case it would be costly to leave the market, monopoly profits cannot exist. If they did, new firms would be attracted into the market and prices would be driven down to the level of average cost. In the long run the performance of a perfectly contestable market is equivalent to that of a perfectly competitive market. A perfectly contestable market, however, despite being regarded as a benchmark market form, is considered to have wider applicability. Again this theory has policy implications, which presumably would be to open up markets to greater levels of competition from outside rather than to concentrate on trying to influence the behaviour of the existing firms in the market.

The other major development in the structure–conduct–performance debate that is based largely on neoclassical theory is the *new industrial organisation* theory (see Spence 1977, and Dixit 1982, in the US; Cowling and Waterson 1976, and Clarke and Davies 1982, in the UK). This approach regards conduct, which is assumed to be exogenously determined, as the main factor affecting both structure and performance. Conduct is analysed in an equilibrium context and is linked mainly to oligopolistic behaviour.

Other approaches to the debate are not so reliant on traditional neoclassical assumptions. The most extreme development is the *Austrian revival*. This is based on the works of nineteenth-century Austrian writers like Menger, but it was not developed as a formal school of thought until the late 1970s (see Littlechild, 1981; Reekie, 1984). Essentially, it adopts a free-market approach to businesses and business behaviour. Its main tenet is that competition between firms cannot be analysed very easily and certainly not by traditional structure–conduct–performance techniques. Hence, it is mainly concerned with the process by which competition is achieved within a dynamic and changing environment, of which decision-makers do not have perfect knowledge. The entrepreneur is regarded as the engine of the competitive process, ever alert to new opportunities. Profit is his or her reward and is mainly short-term. Profit does not necessarily indicate the existence of monopoly power. Any government intervention should be based on this premise.

The other two theoretical developments, transaction cost theory and principal–agent analysis are more easily applied to firm rather than market behaviour, although they both have implications for the structure–conduct–performance debate. The basic premise of the *transaction cost* approach to the theory of the firm is that firms exist to reduce transaction costs in conditions of uncertainty. It originated from the work of Coase (1937) and was later developed in particular by Williamson (1975, 1981). Asset specificity (i.e. the employment of highly specialised assets, which have lower or zero values in alternative uses) individualises firms. Imperfect information coupled with the limited ability of humans to assimilate and process the information that is available create the conditions for firms to internalise transactions that would otherwise be left to the market. Thus, a firm may decide to vertically integrate and absorb particular activities in order to minimise transaction costs; such a strategy, by creating an additional barrier to entry, could increase market concentration and hence have implications for conduct and performance.

Principal–agent analysis (see Spence and Zeckhauser, 1971; Ross, 1973; Jensen and Meckling, 1976) assumes maximising objectives can be achieved, but the existence of imperfect information and uncertainty hinder the transactions between different groups of people, who are known as principals and agents. Principals employ agents to act on their behalf. For example, the managers of a firm may act as the agents for the shareholders, who are the principals in any contract between the two groups. The objectives of the principals and the agents may differ, and so the principals draw up contracts that align their objectives more closely. Managers may be given share owner-ship or share option schemes as part of their remu-neration package, so tying their rewards more closely to the profitability of the firm and thus possibly affect-ing corporate behaviour and performance. The prin-cipal–agent and transaction cost approaches are discussed in more detail in Chapter 4.

It is not the intention here to go into detail about the pros and cons of the different theories. At the present time the arguments about their relative merits still rage. However, no theory has yet completely usurped the traditional SCP paradigm, despite its neoclassical basis. We shall adopt a fairly traditional framework for the analysis of firm behaviour. Other explanations, and particularly those like transaction cost analysis that centre on the distinctive features of the individual firm, are featured as necessary. Initially, however, two of the most important features of market structure, market concentration and barriers to entry, are discussed.

2.3 MARKET CONCENTRATION

Market concentration refers to the extent to which output (or some other indicator) in a market is domi-nated by a few firms. Other things being equal, a market is more concentrated (or less competitive) the fewer the number of firms in existence and/or the more uneven their size distribution. Market structure is usually identified by some measure of market concentration, which can also exert a considerable influence over firm behaviour and market perfor-mance. Therefore, it is worthwhile examining in some detail how it can be measured, the extent to which concentration varies within industries and between countries and what determines the levels of market concentration.

The measurement of concentration

It is not essential that concentration is measured by using output or sales figures as the *base*, although the use of different variables to assess the size distribu-tion of firms can affect the results significantly, i.e.:

(1) If sales figures are used, intrafirm transactions are ignored. The size of vertically integrated firms may be understated. Value-added figures (i.e. the difference between the cost of materials and sales revenue) may overcome this problem, although

they may be distorted by differences between industries in the raw material share of final value.

(2) Employment figures are often used as an alter-native, but capital-intensive firms, or those oper-ating in capital-intensive industries, will be automatically undervalued. Since large firms tend to be more capital-intensive than smaller ones and concentration measures are mainly influ-enced by the size of the largest firms in a market, the employment base may consistently understate the degree of concentration.

(3) The value of assets is least likely to be employed as a measure of concentration because of the prob-lems of distinguishing between historical and current values of assets, due to their continuous revaluation and depreciation. In addition, it has the opposite problem to the use of employment. The size of larger, more capital-intensive firms may be overstated by using assets as the base; hence, the extent of concentration will be overestimated.

If information exists on the relative shares of all firms in a market (admittedly a rather unlikely assumption, especially for the smallest firms) it is then possible to construct a *concentration curve* for the industry. This plots the cumulative percentage of output (or whatever other base indicator) against the cumulative number of firms starting from the largest. It shows the percentage of output controlled by any number of firms in the industry. Equally it can provide information about what number of firms control any specified percentage of output.

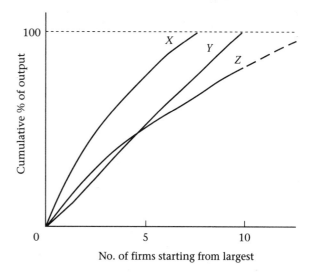

Figure 2 *The concentration curve.*

In Figure 2, page 13, the concentration curves for three industries, X, Y and Z, are shown. The concentration curve for industry X is higher than that for Y and Z at every point. Logically, it can be assumed that concentration in industry X is greater than in Y or Z and a concentration index should reflect this. However, Z lies above Y until the five-firm level, at which point the two curves coincide. For more than five firms the situation is reversed and Y lies above Z. In the case of industries Y and Z alternative measures of concentration may weight the industries differently, depending on the number of firms at which the measurement is taken. It is not immediately obvious which industry, Y or Z, is the more concentrated.

Box 2.2 *Measures of market concentration*

The most commonly used measures of concentration are the *absolute measures*, which focus on the number of firms in a market and their size disparities. The main absolute measures are:

(1) *The concentration ratio.* The most popular measure of concentration is the simple concentration ratio. At the market level it is defined as the percentage of output (or whatever base is used) accounted for by a specific number of the largest firms in the market. It is the sum of the market shares of the largest few firms in the market. Thus

$$C_r = \sum_{i=1}^{r} s_i \qquad (2.1)$$

where s_i is the market share of the ith firm; r equals any relatively small number, say 3, 4 or 5. If $r = 5$ and the five largest firms in a particular market account for 80% of total sales, then the five-firm concentration ratio, C_5, is 80.0. The UK usually uses the C_5 ratio, whereas C_3 or C_4 are more popular elsewhere.

(2) *The Herfindahl index.* A second popular measure of concentration is the Herfindahl index, which is also known as the Hirschman–Herfindahl index (Hirschman, 1964). It is a more comprehensive measure than the simple concentration ratio. It takes into account the number and the size distribution of all the firms in a market. It is given by the formula

$$HI = \sum_{i=1}^{n} s_i^2 \qquad (2.2)$$

where s_i is the market share of the ith firm and i equals 1, 2, 3, . . ., n. Therefore, HI is the sum of the squares of the market shares of all firms in an industry. If an industry has five firms with market shares of 50%, 30%, 10%, 5% and 5%, the squared market shares become 0.25, 0.09, 0.01, 0.0025 and 0.0025; HI = 0.355. The value of the index can vary between close to zero and one. It equals $1/n \rightarrow 0$ for a large number of equally-sized firms and one for a monopolist.

(3) *The Hannah and Kay index* (Hannah and Kay, 1977). The Hannah and Kay index is a more general measure of concentration, in which market shares can be raised to the power of α. The exact value of α can be decided by whoever is undertaking the research. A value in the range 0.6 to 2.5 is recommended. The index is usually defined in the form

$$HK = \left(\sum_{i=1}^{n} s_i^\alpha \right)^{1/(1 - \alpha)} \qquad (2.3)$$

There are also *relative concentration* measures which emphasise the differences in the sizes of firms and which ignore the numbers of firms in a particular market. The main relative concentration measure is the *Gini coefficient*.

Figure 3 shows a *Lorenz curve* for a particular industry. This plots the cumulative percentage of output in a particular industry against the cumulative percentage of firms. In this case the firms are arranged from the smallest to the largest. The larger the area of concentration (the shaded area A), the greater the inequality in firm size, and the further the Lorenz curve from the diagonal line.

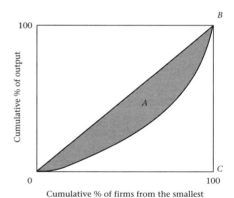

Figure 3 *The Lorenz curve.*

The Gini coefficient summarises the information shown in the Lorenz curve. It can be measured by

$$G = \frac{\text{Area of concentration}}{\text{Area below the diagonal line}} \qquad (2.4)$$

In Figure 3 this is equal to the shaded area A divided by the triangle 0BC. If all firms are of equal size the area of concentration or inequality will be zero, in which case G is equal to zero. If the industry consists of a single firm, then G is equal to one.

Market concentration measures attempt to transfer the information on the number and size distribution of firms given in the concentration curve to a single value. The main measures are summarised in Box 2.2. However, they all have drawbacks. A problem in using the concentration ratio is that the weighting of industries may vary depending on how many firms are actually included in the ratio. In Figure 2, at the C_4 level industry Z is more concentrated that industry Y, whereas at C_6 Y has the higher level of concentration. A second drawback is that, whatever the number of firms included in the ratio, it does not take into account the distribution of sales or employment within those few firms. For example, five firms may each produce 15% of the total output of an industry. In another industry, one firm may produce 35% of the total supply and four others 10% each. In both cases the C_5 is 75.0. Firm behaviour may be very different in the second industry, which one firm dominates, compared to the first industry, where the leading firms all have equal shares. The final problem with the concentration ratio is that it ignores the number and relative size of firms outside the largest group. Two industries may have similar C_5 ratios with similar distributions of output within their respective largest five firms. The remainder of the market in each case may be very different, in one case consisting of just a couple of fairly large firms and in the other comprising a fringe of numerous very small firms. Again, these differences can have important implications for corporate behaviour.

The largest firms have the greatest weighting in the Herfindahl index, which is clearly an advantage given that they are likely to have the biggest effect on market behaviour. However, the figure can give a rather misleading impression of the degree of concentration in an industry. For example, if an industry consists of three equally-sized firms, HI = 0.33, a rather low figure for what is a highly concentrated industry. Also, different interindustry size distributions of firms could produce the same, or at least a very similar, value for HI.

The Hannah and Kay index has the advantage of flexibility: it is able to attach a greater weighting to large firms by increasing the value of α. It suffers from the same drawback as the Herfindahl index in that very different size distributions may give the same, or similar, values for HK.

The main problem with the Gini coefficient is that very different market structures can have similar Gini coefficients. This is due to the fact that the Lorenz curve ignores the number of firms in a market. For example, the line of equal distribution can mean that a hundred firms have 1% of the market each or that four firms each have a 25% market share.

There is no general agreement on which measure is the best one to use, although a comparison of the different measures raises a number of issues. Hannah and Kay (1977) have listed several *criteria* that any concentration measure should fulfil. These include:

(1) *The concentration curve ranking criterion.* Concentration measures should rank one industry as more concentrated than another if its concentration curve lies entirely above the concentration curve of the other.
(2) *The sales transfer principle.* Measured concentration should increase if there is a transfer of sales from a small to a large firm.
(3) *The entry condition.* The entry of a small firm to an industry should reduce the level of concentration; the exit of a small firm should have the opposite effect.
(4) *The merger condition.* The merger of two or more firms within an industry should produce an increase in measured concentration. This criterion follows from the previous two criteria, on the assumption that a large firm in the market takes over a smaller rival. The merger can be considered as a transfer of sales from a small to a large firm; in addition there is the exit of the small firm from the industry.

The Herfindahl and Hannah and Kay indices come closest to meeting all these criteria. However, whatever method of measuring concentration is employed, all the indices suffer from a number of common drawbacks. They only take into account a single indicator of market structure, the degree of concentration in an industry. Other structural features, such as barriers to entry or the degree of product differentiation, each of which can have important implications for market behaviour, are ignored. Secondly, the necessary data may not be available or may be difficult to obtain, especially if information on all firms in an industry is required. Thirdly, indices usually only refer to domestic output. Where there is a significant amount of foreign competition in a market the extent of concentration will be overestimated. This point has been highlighted elsewhere:

In open economies (such as the UK and other members of the EC) the link between recorded concentration and market power must inevitably be weakened if foreign competition is ignored (Ferguson and Ferguson, 1994:51).

On the other hand, in industries like vehicle production and consumer electronics the domestic suppliers may also be the importers. The products may be imported from overseas branches of the domestic producers and then re-sold in the home market. In these instances, concentration indices will underestimate the actual degree of concentration in a market. A final problem facing all concentration indices is that they may understate the true level of concentration where local or regional monopolies exist. This is often the case in service industries. Nevertheless, despite such problems and given the available information, concentration indices usually provide the best and in some cases the only available measure of market structure. Whatever index is chosen usually depends on which particular aspect of market behaviour is being investigated.

The evidence on concentration

Manufacturing industries are usually the most highly concentrated, although there is evidence of increasing concentration in some service industries like food retailing and financial services. Table 4 shows the extent of concentration in various manufacturing industries, using the C_5 ratio based on both net output and employment. On average, concentration is greater in those industries characterised by a high degree of capital-intensiveness and which are classified as high-technology.

Between 1951 and 1958 it is estimated that, on average, market concentration measured in terms of employment in UK manufacturing industry grew at about 0.4% per annum. From 1958 until 1968 it increased at double that rate, partly due to an increased tendency at this time for firms to merge (Clarke, 1985). Rises in concentration also occurred in the distribution and financial services industries. Since the late 1960s, however, market concentration in manufacturing has remained fairly stable, or has even fallen, although trends vary widely between industries. Between 1980 and 1990 the five-firm concentration ratio for net output increased in iron and steel (from 73 to 96), in pharmaceuticals (from 43 to 48) and in clothing (from 12 to 17), whereas it fell in motor vehcles (from 91 to 82), motor vehicle parts (from 40 to 26), in rubber goods (from 59 to 49), telecommunication equipment (from 49 to 38) and in bread and biscuit manufacture (from 65 to 50). Whatever change in market concentration has taken place it should not be presumed that the same

Table 4 *Five-firm concentration ratios in various UK manufacturing industries, 1990*

	Net output	Employment
Tobacco	99	98
Iron and steel	96	92
Motor vehicles and their engines	82	82
Ice cream, cocoa, chocolate and sugar confectionery	74	63
Insulated wires and cables	66	62
Domestic electrical goods	56	54
Bread, biscuits and flour confectionery	50	40
Glass and glassware	50	44
Rubber products	49	42
Pharmaceuticals	48	32
Footwear	46	43
Motor vehicle parts	26	27
Printing and publishing	17	13
Clothing, hats and gloves	17	16
Leather goods	15	12
Plastic processing	10	7

Source: Census of Production, 1992, Business Monitor PA 1002.

firms comprise the three, four or five largest. The actual concentration figure may not have altered, but the identity of the largest few firms may well have.

Other evidence on changes in market concentration centres on the impact of international trade. The effect of trade on concentration is quite marked. Evidence taking the effect of international trade into account shows that average C_5 ratios in the UK fell from 41.3 in 1970 to 35.9 in 1983. The equivalent figures unadjusted[1] for the effects of international trade were 49.0 in 1970 and 50.1 in 1983 (Ferguson and Ferguson, 1994). Given the extent of import penetration in UK manufacturing (see Section 3.2) it is likely that more recent evidence on average levels of market concentration would show an even greater discrepancy between the adjusted and unadjusted trade figures.

Comparisons between levels of market concentration in the UK and other industrialised economies are difficult because of differences in coverage and in methods of measurement. Table 5 shows the comparative level of concentration in various industries in EU countries. Market concentration fell in the UK during the 1970s, stabilised in Germany, increased slightly in Italy and strongly in France (de Jong, 1993b). Unlike the UK subsidiaries are usually treated as separate firms in the rest of Europe, giving a downward bias to the measurement of concentration. However, on average, market concentration probably remains higher in the UK than in these other Western European economies. The evidence from selected industries in Table 5 tends to confirm this. According to Davies and Caves (1987) levels of market concentration in the UK are also higher than in the US. In general, market concentration appears to be inversely related to the size of a country's market, although levels in the UK are higher than the size of the market probably warrants.

An alternative method by which the growth of big business can be assessed is to investigate the rise of *aggregate concentration*, or the share of total output or employment contributed by the largest few firms in the whole economy, or in large sectors of it. Table 6, page 18, shows that by 1909 the level of aggregate concentration was already quite high in UK and US manufacturing. In the UK the largest 100 manufacturing firms accounted for 16% of total net output, whereas in the US the equivalent figure was 22%. The level of aggregate concentration grew particularly quickly in the UK in the two decades after the Second World War, mirroring the changes in market concentration. From 1949 to 1958 the share of net output of the one hundred largest manufacturing firms rose by nearly 50%, from 22% to 32%. The period to 1968 saw another sharp increase, to 41% ($C_{100} = 41.0$). Since then there appears to have been very little change in aggregate concentration. There is even some recent evidence of a slight fall in the figure for the UK. The level of aggregate concentration in the US also seems to have stabilised at about 33%. The figure for the European Union (EU) as a whole is lower due to the larger overall size of market. For most EU economies the level of aggregate concentration was fairly static during the 1950s, but it increased quite substantially in the 1960s and early 1970s (de Jong, 1988).

There is evidence of a direct relationship between changes in market and aggregate concentration. Clarke and Davies (1983) found two main reasons for the increase in aggregate concentration in the UK during 1963–68. The first reason, and by far the most significant (accounting for 90% of the increase in aggregate concentration) was the increase in concentration that took place at the industry level. The second reason was the greater likelihood of diversification by large firms, although this only contributes towards higher aggregate concentration in manufacturing if the diversification is confined to the manufacturing sector. The increased blurring of the manufacturing/services divide makes it more difficult to separate sectoral trends (see Section 3.4).

Any increase in firm size that may be implicit in rises in aggregate concentration has more probably been due to increases in the numbers of plants operated by large firms than to increases in the average size of plant. Evidence shows that, in the 40 years to 1970, the share of the one hundred largest plants in manufacturing net output remained constant at about 11% in the UK. In the US the equivalent figure for the same period was also fairly constant at about 9%. More recent evidence from the US reveals a fall in the average plant size, from 1100 employees in 1967 to 665 in 1985.[2] This may be part of a long-term trend towards smaller businesses, although it could simply mean that large firms wish to operate a greater number of smaller units.

Table 5 *Comparative levels of market concentration within selected Western European economies*

	Aerospace[a]	Food and drink[b] retailing	Textiles[c]	Pharmaceuticals[d]
UK	68	52	56	29
W.Germany	–	–	7	14
Italy	75	41	7	–
France	56	34	26	25
Netherlands	–	–	25	–

[a]C_3, 1989. [b]C_5, 1985–6. [c]C_5, 1980. [d]C_4, 1989. Figures are rounded upwards to the nearest whole.

Source: Taken from various chapters in de Jong, ed. (1993a).

Table 6 *A comparison of aggregate concentration levels in manufacturing, 100-firm concentration ratios, in the UK, the US and the EU*

Year	UK[a]	US[a]	EU[b]
1909	16	22	
1924	22		
1935	24	26	
1947		23	
1949	22		
1953	27		
1954		30	
1958	32	30	
1963	37	33	
1967		33	
1968	41		
1972	41	33	
1975	42		24
1977	41	33	24
1980	41		25
1982	41		26
1984	39		
1986	39		
1988	39		
1989	38		

[a]Shares of net output.
[b]Share of total turnover.

Sources: Prais (1976); Sawyer (1981); Ferguson and Ferguson (1994).

There has also been a growing concentration of ownership in industrialised economies. Institutional investors, mainly comprising insurance companies and pension funds, own roughly 63% of the ordinary shares of British companies. In 1957 the figure was 21%. There has been a similar trend in the US, where institutional investors now own about 45% of all ordinary stock. The degree of ownership concentration is also high in Japan where banks are significant shareholders as well as being creditors. Banks own 20% of Japanese quoted stock, with other financial institutions responsible for another 30% of the total. Banks also act as both creditors and shareholders in other Western European countries, although other financial institutions are less prominent shareholders than elsewhere (Brewster, 1993).

The determinants of concentration

The questions of why concentration is higher in one industry than in another, why concentration levels may change and why concentration may vary across countries are extremely difficult ones to answer. There is no common agreement on the determinants of concentration and so a number of the main explanations are given here.

(A) TECHNOLOGICAL AND RELATED FACTORS

The argument that technological factors, or the extent of economies of scale, are an important cause of market concentration levels is known as the *deterministic* approach and is based on the traditional SCP framework. There will be a predetermined level of concentration in a market at any point in time, the result of existing cost and demand conditions. For example, as Davies (1989) explains, if all firms in a market have access to the same technology and produce a homogenous product, then they will each face a U-shaped average cost curve as shown in Figure 4(a) page 19; costs are minimised at c^*, which is the efficient scale of output (ES) and is indicated by X. Assuming that the competitive price, $p = c^*$, prevails, all firms will produce output X. Assuming that the market size, determined by the level of demand, is denoted by Z, then an industry can accommodate Z/X firms. Thus, the larger is X relative to Z (i.e. the larger is efficient size relative to market size), the higher the level of market concentration, *cet. par.*

However, this assumes a U-shaped cost curve. As explained in Section 6.5 on an L-shaped curve, X is referred to as the *minimum efficient scale* of output (MES);[3] in Figure 4(b) a firm could produce efficiently at any point beyond MES output or along the horizontal section of the curve. In this situation Z/X defines the upper limit to the number of firms rather than the exact number of firms.

It should also be noted that the MES level of production is defined in terms of the individual plant, whereas large firms usually operate a number of plants, so economies of scale at the firm (or multiplant) level need to be investigated. The existence of barriers to entry (see next section) may further complicate the issue. Profit-maximising firms may produce at less than MES output, especially when protected by entry barriers, in order to set a price above the competitive level; the size of the market is reduced and concentration increases. On the other hand, if the higher price enables small-scale firms to survive, concentration may fall. Finally, should entry occur, concentration need not necessarily fall; if the entrant is, say, a diversifying company and entry takes place on a relatively large scale, then concentration may well increase.

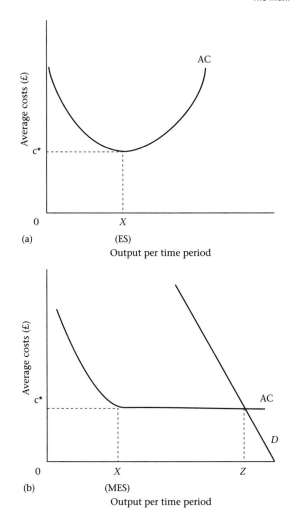

Figure 4 *Efficient scale and minimum efficient scale levels of output.*

(B) MERGERS

Mergers are regarded as an important contributory factor to increases in concentration. It is estimated that mergers accounted for between a third and all of the increases in market and aggregate concentration in the UK in the late 1950s and in the 1960s (see Hay and Morris, 1979 for a survey of the evidence). The variations in the estimates arise from differences in the time periods covered by the studies and from differences in the measurement of concentration. The Herfindahl index will always show an increase in market concentration if one of the firms in the market acquires another, whereas in the case of the r-firm concentration ratio the effect on concentration depends on whether the acquiring firm is already one of the largest r firms. If it is, then the level of concentration will increase by the extent of the acquisition. For example, if the largest five firms in an industry have market shares of 25%, 15%, 12%, 10% and 8% respectively, the C_5 ratio equals 70.0. If one of these firms acquires the next largest firm, $r + 1$, which has a market share of, say, 6% the new C_5 ratio equals 76.0. On the other hand, if the acquirer is outside the original r firms then concentration will only increase if the acquisition brings the acquiring firm into the largest r firms. In the above example, should $r + 1$ acquire a rival with a 4% market share, the C_5 ratio would rise to 72.0, because the five largest companies would then have market shares of 25%, 15%, 12%, 10% and 10% respectively.

(C) GOVERNMENT POLICY

Governments can exert an impact on concentration through their policies towards monopolies and mergers. The UK has tended to have a more lenient attitude towards horizontal mergers than, say, the US. For example, in the 1960s the UK operated a policy, under the aegis of the Industrial Reorganisation Corporation (IRC), that actively encouraged mergers and this is thought to be a contributory factor in the higher levels of concentration in the UK compared with other countries at that time. The rationale for the IRC's promotion of merger activity, while accepting the possible inherent disadvantages of large-scale businesses, was the need for the UK to have large firms in order to compete in international markets. On this basis, it employed a single performance criterion for manufacturing industry, the visible trade account of the balance of payments. Many combinations of companies were supported, the most famous, or possibly the most notorious, example being IRC'S encouragement of the then General Electric Company (GEC) in its merger with Associated Electrical Industries (AEI), which was hotly contested by the AEI board.

(D) STOCHASTIC FACTORS

Stochastic influences on market concentration emphasise the chance factors that can affect the growth rates of individual firms. This approach is concerned with actual concentration changes, in contrast to the deterministic approach which assesses the factors that determine the equilibrium level of concentration. The areas of business behaviour where chance or luck plays a part include the choice of an advertising campaign, the launch of a new product, the hiring of key executives, the success of

Table 7 *High, low and average results from 16 simulation runs of a stochastic growth process model*

	Four-firm concentration ratio at year							
	1	20	40	60	80	100	120	140
High run	8.0	21.6	23.5	42.2	47.3	64.4	73.1	76.6
Low run	8.0	17.5	27.1	28.3	30.7	39.9	37.7	35.3
Average	8.0	20.4	27.0	33.8	42.1	46.7	52.9	57.4

Source: Scherer (1980).

a merger and numerous others possibilities. These factors may mean that the actual growth rates of firms in a market will vary. Some firms will experience rapid periods of growth; once they are ahead of the others they will stay ahead, because it is assumed that all firms face the same average growth prospects.

An example should make this clearer (see Scherer, 1980). Assume there are 50 firms in a market, each with a 2% market share. The firms begin to grow. It is assumed that each firm faces the same probability distribution of proportionate growth, independent of its size. This assumption conforms to Gibrat's law of proportionate growth. In this instance, it is assumed that the probability distribution of growth rates facing each firm is normal, with a mean of 6% and a standard deviation of 16%. The growth history of each firm and the overall size distribution of the industry are then tabulated at 20-year intervals, based on various computer runs. The high and low (in terms of final levels of concentration) and average results of 16 runs (for C_4) are given in Table 7. As can be seen from the table, firms do not remain equal in size. In fact, the patterns that emerge resemble the concentration histories of many manufacturing industries in industrialised economies. Concentration increases over time, first fairly rapidly, since the larger firms grow by greater absolute amounts, and then more slowly.

Studies that test the validity of the model, or at least its basic premises, are fairly sparse. There has been some supportive evidence, mainly from the US, that the initial sizes of firms do not have a significant effect on growth rates. However, there is also evidence that smaller firms tend to have a more variable growth experience, which refutes the idea that growth rates are independent of firm size. More recently, there is growing evidence of a negative association between firm size and firm growth (Evans, 1987; Hall, 1987).

(E) CONCLUSIONS

In conclusion, cross-sectional studies suggest that the MES level of output is always an important determinant of market concentration, given the proviso that MES is difficult to estimate. Capital requirement and product differentiation barriers are also thought to be significant and there is some role for stochastic influences. Time-series studies indicate that increases in concentration have been the result of economies of scale, falls in market size, forward vertical integration and government attitudes to mergers. Mergers themselves were important determinants of increases in both market and aggregate concentration in the UK during the 1950s and 1960s.

2.4 BARRIERS TO ENTRY

The concept of *entry barriers* originated from the work of Bain (1956) on firms' pricing behaviour, in which he assessed the effect of the potential entry of new firms on the pricing strategies of existing firms in an industry. He concluded that the existence of barriers to entry, which make it more difficult or costly for a new firm to enter a market, enable existing concerns (the incumbents) to maintain their prices above the competitive level and not attract entry. The greater the *height* of the barriers (or the *conditions of entry*, as Bain calls it), the more difficult that entry becomes and the greater the likelihood of persistent monopoly profits on the part of the incumbents.

Bain identified three main *sources* of barriers to entry: product differentiation or the preference barrier, absolute cost advantages and economies of scale, although a fourth, initial capital requirements, is often accorded its own category. Structural barriers such as these are usually referred to as *exogenous*. Ostensibly, the firm has no control over them; they occur more or less naturally. Government restrictions imposed by law (such as the operation of tariffs, the issuing of licenses and the granting of patent rights or other monopoly status) may be afforded a separate category. Other definitions of, and viewpoints about, entry barriers have been advanced, although it is still pertinent to categorise them according to these three or four structural types. Thus, the main exogenous barriers are as follows:

(1) *Product differentiation.* Product differentiation can create *brand loyalty* (the allegiance to the particular combinations of characteristics inherent in a branded good) on the part of consumers. Such loyalty can be enhanced through advertising. Advertising and other selling expenses may also add to the potential costs of new firms, who may be forced to advertise their products more heavily than incumbents simply to gain recognition. Advertising is also a risky activity. There is no guarantee of a successful campaign, no matter how much is spent on it. *Brand proliferation* can also make it difficult for potential new entrants to gain a foothold in an industry. An industry may be dominated by just two or three firms, but each firm may supply several brands to the market in order to fill the 'characteristics space'. A new firm might find it difficult to establish itself in such circumstances. Examples of markets where brand proliferation occurs are beer, breakfast cereals, cigarettes and soaps and detergents.

It is very difficult to assess whether brand loyalty *per se* acts as a barrier to entry. In fact, no adequate empirical measure of product differentiation has been established. Taking advertising expenditure as a proxy the evidence of its entry-preventing properties is fairly mixed. These and other issues relating to product differentiation are discussed in Chapter 11.

(2) *Absolute cost advantages.* These confer lower average production costs on incumbents relative to new entrants. The cost advantages can arise from various sources:

(i) *Favoured access* to managerial talent, to information about suppliers and customers, to raw materials, to financial resources and to superior locations by incumbent firms, which can give them a cost advantage relative to potential new entrants.

(ii) *Patent rights*, which can give an individual or a firm sole access to superior technology or the right to supply a particular product for a specified number of years. One of the most lucrative patents issued this century was to Gilbert Hyatt of California for the microprocessor. Patents are most common in the traditionally science-based, high-technology industries, such as aerospace, chemicals, electronics and pharmaceuticals, where the pace of technical progress is such that firms are continuously needing to patent new products or processes. Glaxo Wellcome, the large UK pharmaceutical firm, makes 40% of its sales and nearly half its profits from a single patented (until 1997) drug, Zantac, an anti-ulcer treatment.

(iii) The *knowledge, experience* and an *established reputation* from working in the industry. These may stem from, or result in, favourable access to resources and the ownership of patents. These benefits of learning-by-doing accrue in particular to the first firm to supply a product, at least assuming that the product is successful, in which case they are known as *first-mover advantages*.

(iv) *Lower-cost finance* may be available to established firms. Existing firms are likely to be able to rely on internal finance as a major source of new capital. Their established reputation may mean that they are able to secure external funds, such as debt finance, at lower rates than prospective new entrants. This can be a particularly important advantage where large capital requirements are needed for entry.

(v) *Vertical integration and other vertical exclusion policies.* In the UK, vertical integration is reckoned to be most extensive in the brewing, chemical, iron and steel, petrol and pulp and paper industries. In these industries a potential entrant will have to enter at two, or more, levels in the production process. This can be both risky and costly. Vertical exclusion policies comprise those that prevent rivals from having equal access to particular inputs or to consumers. They include exclusive-dealing contracts between dominant firms and suppliers or customers, refusal to supply a rival with parts and tying the purchase of a product to the purchase of (complementary) products. Vertical integration is discussed in more detail in Chapter 13. Instances of vertical exclusion policies by firms are given in Chapter 15.

(3) *Economies of scale.* Economies of scale create lower unit costs at larger levels of output. The effectiveness of economies of scale as a barrier to entry depends particularly on the level of MES output

relative to the market as a whole (and on the relative cost disadvantage at smaller than MES outputs). For example, should the MES form a relatively large market share, a new firm will have to enter at a relatively large scale in order to compete at the same level of average costs. This will have important implications, since a large new entrant would automatically have a depressing effect on price in a market of a given size. The evidence on the significance of economies of scale in various industries is examined in Section 6.7. Lyons (1989) concludes that economies of scale are considered to be an important barrier in some industries, although their impact depends on the existence of sunk costs and the additional effects of product differentiation. In some industries the scale economy barrier can be surmounted by imports. For example, Lyons notes that many British firms imported Italian refrigerators in the 1960s and 1970s in order to add to their product ranges.

(4) *Capital requirements.* In many industries, especially in manufacturing where capital-intensive techniques are the norm, large initial capital outlays are required in order to begin production. The problem becomes all the greater if an expensive advertising campaign or large-scale R&D is required. In some consumer goods industries the nature of the product may necessitate a high advertising intensity by firms. A significant amount of R&D spending may be needed for firms to gain a foothold, especially where product design and development form a significant proportion of total costs, as in the chemical, electronics, motor vehicle and pharmaceutical industries. Evidence suggests that, of all the structural barriers, capital requirements, combined with technical knowledge, are the greatest impediments to entry (Lyons, 1989).

The fact that the Bain definition of entry barriers includes pricing strategies means that it encompasses both structural and behavioural features. Entry barriers relating to the conduct of firms, or that involve firms' strategic decisions, are referred to as *endogenous*. For example, *pricing policy* can be used as a defensive weapon by the incumbents to make entry more difficult, although only if entry barriers are high enough (i.e. if there is 'effectively impeded entry') to make entry-forestalling behaviour worthwhile. If there is no cost advantage ('easy entry'), or if the cost advantage of the incumbents is very small ('ineffectively impeded entry') they will not consider it worthwhile

pursuing entry-forestalling price tactics. On the other hand, if entry barriers are very high ('blockaded entry') the incumbents can conceivably charge any price they like and not incur entry. Assuming that effectively impeded entry exists, the incumbents can price up to the level of the new firms' costs (the *limit price*) without inducing entry. They will forgo some profit in the current period in order to achieve higher profitability in the future. Limit pricing to deter entry is discussed in greater detail in Chapter 10.

It should be noted that the dividing line between exogenous and endogenous barriers is not always distinct. Advertising and brand proliferation, both elements of product differentiation, can be used specifically to exclude potential new entrants. If so, they can be counted as endogenous barriers. Similarly vertical integration and patents, both identified as sources of absolute cost advantage, can conceivably be used as strategic weapons by incumbents to exclude entrants: hence, they will be categorised as endogenous impediments to entry.

The Bain definition of a barrier to entry has been criticised because it includes both structural and behavioural elements. Hence, other definitions have been put forward. Stigler (1968) defined an entry barrier as follows:

. . . a cost of producing (at some or at every rate of output) which must be borne by a firm which seeks to enter an industry but is not borne by firms already in the industry (Stigler, 1968:67).

In other words, the Chicago school view is that entry barriers are far less prevalent than the Bain analysis suggests. Economies of scale would not be classified as a barrier to entry according to the Stigler definition; neither may product differentiation, although the additional penetration costs of advertising in order to announce a new firm's arrival could be counted as an obstacle to entry. Von Weizsacker (1980) specifically included the social or welfare implications of entry barriers in his definition:

They thus can be defined to be socially undesirable limitations of entry, which are attributable to the protection of resource owners already in the industry (von Weizsacker, 1980:400).

The point about this definition is that it explores the possibility that entry barriers need not be regarded as intrinsically bad. Patents and the ability to secure monopoly profits, for example, provide an important incentive for investment in new products and processes. In welfare terms some kind of trade-off may be necessary between the welfare-enhancing effects of patents and the welfare-distorting effects of monopolistic output restrictions. Demsetz (1982) also examined the policy issues surrounding barriers to entry by placing particular emphasis on the legal restriction to markets, such as licences, trademarks, copyrights and patents. He points out that it is possible to place legal rights or restrictions more or less anywhere, such as the right not to burn down the factory of a competitor or not to sell the product of a rival as your own. The question is whether they have been put in the right places.

The Austrian school also views barriers to entry as less formidable than implied by the traditional, structuralist framework. It is assumed that most barriers to entry can be overcome over time. Legal barriers are regarded as the most effective impediments to entry and are thought more likely to persist. Evidence of the importance of legal barriers, specified in both structural and behavioural terms, comes from the US banking industry. Clark and Speaker (1992) found that, in the 1970s, legal entry barriers in the US interstate banking industry were likely to lead to monopolistic pricing. Rose (1992) noted that the reductions in the barriers in the 1980s and the associated increased competition produced lower costs, higher productivity and increased dividend payouts.

New industrial organisation theory has highlighted the relationship between the traditional entry barriers and the interaction of strategic behaviour by incumbents and entrants. It also stresses the importance of sunk costs in the calculations of potential entrants; entry will be deterred if it involves sunk costs and incumbents may exploit this situation by strategic investments in capacity, advertising and R&D. Such strategic behaviour is examined in more detail in Chapter 11.

In perfectly contestable markets, barriers to entry and exit do not exist, even in the presence of economies of scale. A perfectly contestable market occurs when all firms have access to the same technology, when the technology allows for economies of scale such as recoverable fixed costs but not for sunk costs and when the incumbents cannot change their prices instantly, yet consumers can react instantly to price changes. Under these circumstances, incumbents can only prevent entry by pricing at the level of average costs and by avoiding monopoly profits, or by 'behaving virtuously' as Baumol (1982) puts it. If they tried to price at a higher level they would be susceptible to 'hit-and-run entry' by new firms, keen to grab a share of the available profits and then quickly depart. As Baumol admits a perfectly contestable market is unlikely to exist in practice; in many markets the key barrier to entry may be the sunk costs previously incurred by firms.

The deregulated US internal airline market is sometimes considered to have a high degree of contestability. Early studies, such as Bailey and Panzar (1981), found some supportive evidence. Trunk airlines on long-haul routes priced competitively even when the routes were natural monopolies, whereas local airlines on short-haul routes that were natural monopolies were able to price above the competitive level, because more specialist aircraft were required. These aircraft could not be re-deployed from or onto other routes; they were more likely to represent sunk costs. More recently, Joesch and Zick (1994) noted that the overall level of market concentration increased during the 1980s as many of the post-deregulation entrants failed or were taken over, although this did not translate into an increase in average route-specific concentration in the 19 destinations that they investigated. However, it was found that the remaining carriers in the industry were able to strengthen entry barriers (such as frequent flier programmes, computerised reservation systems and control of gates at congested airports) and gain greater control of fares on those routes where there was less competition. In other words, over time the evidence points to reduced contestability in the market.

Whatever definition of a barrier to entry is adopted, it is less likely to present an obstacle to a large, diversifying firm with substantial financial resources at its disposal (the so-called 'long purse' argument) than to a small newcomer. The latter is the implicit assumption in the Bain analysis. However, even where the entrant is a large-scale diversifier, it may still be very expensive to compete with the established firms.

2.5 THE PRODUCT LIFE CYCLE HYPOTHESIS

So far it has been implicitly assumed that markets and market structures somehow simply exist. Various demand and supply conditions combine to produce a particular type of market structure, whether competitive or concentrated, and this market structure influences both market conduct and performance. In fact, markets and market structures evolve and change through time as new products (and processes) are developed and commercially implemented and then pass through varying market conditions or phases.

As a product moves through the various stages of its life, and as the market structure adjusts accordingly, so market behaviour and performance are influenced; both behaviour and performance, in turn, may have an impact on the structural conditions in the market. In other words, the process of market development is a dynamic one in which the relationships and inter-relationships between market structure, conduct and performance are continually changing over time. As Section 3.1 makes clear, new products and processes are developed and old ones decline in response to changing demand and supply conditions, both at home and abroad. As a result, industries and even whole industrial sectors (although this is rather more debatable) may also pass through some kind of life cycle procedure during which various stages of development are experienced.

In Section 2.1 it was pointed out that the European car market is very segmented. The overall market can be divided into a number of distinct segments and within each numerous models compete. What is true of the European car market is true of the world market. Widespread segmentation is a feature of a mature market, in which total sales growth in the major national markets levels off, or it may even decline. The maturity stage is just one of four major stages through which most products pass. They are shown in Figure 5.

In the *introduction* stage, total demand for the new product is small in relation to potential demand. The innovating firm of a successful product is likely to gain from first-mover advantages of being the only firm in the market and from cost reductions due to learning effects; these result in monopoly profits. Market demand increases fairly slowly during this stage and production runs are quite small, but firms (including new entrants) are likely to invest in new capacity in advance of anticipated higher demand.

Market demand increases much more quickly in the *growth* stage as the product becomes established and sales growth is rapid. The rate of new entry may increase. (The sales of individual firms will increase as long as the rate of growth of market demand continues to exceed the rate of entry of new firms.) Larger-scale production means longer production runs; profitability is likely to rise. However, some firms will grow more quickly than others and this eventually leads to increased levels of market concentration.

Eventually, as the product reaches *maturity*, the rate of growth of new sales begins to decline. Most sales simply replace old sales of the product. Market demand approaches saturation; it increases at a decreasing rate or may even fall. New firms are not attracted into the industry as profitability declines. Excess capacity arises and competition between existing firms is intense as they try to maintain their level of sales and their market shares. Price wars are likely to occur and the least efficient firms will not survive. There will be an increased tendency for cartels, mergers and co-operative agreements among the remaining firms; market concentration may increase still further. The reduced numbers of firms forces suppliers into vertical agreements with the survivors. These firms may diversify into other areas during this stage, or try to introduce new variants of the product (causing increased segmentation) in order to stave off the inevitable *decline* stage, in which both market demand and the demand facing individual firms declines rapidly and firms leave the industry at an increasing rate.

The demand for most products probably tends to follow some kind of life cycle format, although the duration of each stage probably varies from product to product. In the case of some fashion items the whole cycle could be over in a matter of months, while for others it takes much longer. The length of the product cycle for most products is probably diminishing as the pace of technological change quickens. However, there are exceptions to the product cycle rule. The demand for bicycles has increased in many countries, having once been falling rapidly, in response to the general desire for healthier lifestyles.

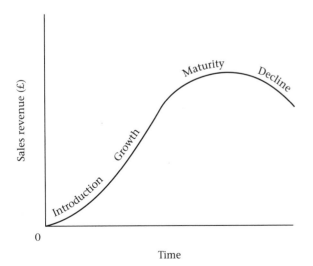

Figure 5 *The product life cycle.*

Similarly, the demand for domestic fire surrounds, new or second-hand, has increased strongly in the UK in the last decade, having seemingly been in terminal decline, as consumer taste has switched to the opening-up of previously covered fireplaces.

2.6 CONCLUSIONS

This chapter examines the market environment in which firms operate. The nature of markets and industries is discussed and the problems of defining them are considered. The traditional, unidirectional relationship between market structure, conduct and performance is examined and the evidence on the relationship between market concentration, a key structural variable, and market performance is reviewed. The alleged complexities of the structure–conduct–performance relationships and the inconclusiveness of the empirical evidence have contributed to the development of alternative schools of thought or paradigms, whose main features are outlined. Their contributions to the analysis of corporate behaviour and their public policy ramifications are both considered. Thus, the Chicago school reverses the causation process completely; by concentrating on the efficiency aspects of monopoly power it emphasises the performance–structure relationship. In addition, transaction cost theory and principal–agent analysis have provided important insights into the nature of the firm and the significance of its internal structure for corporate behaviour. However, in the absence of an alternative theoretical framework for analysing

strategic decision-making, the book adopts a fairly traditional approach to the analysis of corporate behaviour; the alternative theories are featured, and critically appraised, as necessary.

Two of the most important features of market structure, seller concentration and barriers to entry, are discussed in some depth. The problems of measuring market concentration are discussed and the evidence on market and aggregate concentration is considered. It would appear that levels of concentration are higher in the UK than elsewhere, although there is also evidence of stability or even some decline in the figures in recent years. The main determinants of concentration are outlined: market concentration can be best explained in terms of minimum efficient scale, capital requirements and product differentiation, although mergers and stochastic influences also have parts to play.

Exogenous and endogenous barriers to entry are discussed; evidence points to the importance of capital requirements and economies of scale as significant exogenous barriers to entry, although the importance of the latter depends on the existence of sunk costs and product differentiation. The Chicago and Austrian approaches view barriers to entry as less formidable than in traditional theory, although legal barriers are regarded as of potential significance. There are no barriers to entry in a perfectly contestable market, even in the presence of economies of scale; thus, incumbents are susceptible to the threat of 'hit-and-run' entry. Contestability theory raises the possibility that the most important barrier to entry in an industry may be the exit costs incurred by a firm.

Case Study: The impact of entry on structure–conduct–performance relationships in the UK plasterboard industry

---

The Monopolies and Mergers Commission (the MMC) investigated the UK plasterboard industry in 1990 (MMC, 1990). This was in response to a request by BPB Industries PLC (BPB) for release from undertakings imposed upon it by the Office of Fair Trading in 1976 and 1977 as a result of a previous investigation of the industry by the MMC. At the earlier time, BPB had virtually a complete monopoly of the market, and various measures were taken in order to try to regulate the degree of control that the company exercised. The measures included undertakings that it must quote the same ex-works prices at all its plants and that its delivered prices in Great Britain should recoup the cost of delivery. BPB felt that these measures prevented it from competing on a fair and equal basis with the new entrants to the market, Redland Plasterboard Ltd (RPL) and Knauf UK GmbH (Knauf). The report exemplifies the structuralist approach taken by the Commission. In its study of the industry it highlighted the relationships that can exist between market structure, conduct and performance and revealed a number of the ways in which a changing market structure can have an impact on corporate behaviour and performance.

Market structure

The nature of the product. Plasterboard is used widely in both domestic and commercial buildings as an internal lining for walls and ceilings. At the time of the report, 90% of plasterboard that was sold in the UK was homogenous plain or primary board, although there was a growing demand for the inclusion of additives or external coatings for extra resistance and strength and for improved visual attractiveness. The main materials used in the production of plasterboard are gypsum and liner paper. BPB controlled the supply of natural gypsum in the UK. It was also responsible for all liner paper production. RPL and Knauf imported their gypsum and liner paper requirements. Eighty to ninety percent of plasterboard sales in the UK at the time of the report were to builders' merchants.

Degree of concentration. Both RPL and Knauf began production of plasterboard in the UK in 1989. Eternit UK Ltd (Eternit) had begun importing in 1987. Prior to then, BPB supplied over 95% of the UK market by volume, the remainder being imported. The market was a single-firm monopoly providing a more or less homogenous product. With the entry of the new firms it became much more oligopolistic, consisting of several firms competing against each other, although BPB retained by far the largest market share. RPL and Knauf made rapid inroads into the market. In 1989/90, BPB had a 76.0% market share, RPL 12.2% and Knauf 6.2%. Eternit had 2.9% of the market.

On current trends it was estimated that by mid-1990 RPL would have an 18% market share, Knauf 10% and Eternit 4%. BPB's share would have fallen to 65%. The entry of RPL and Knauf into the market lowered the level of concentration, although it was still high. It had a C_4 ratio of 97.3 in 1989/90. The relevant concentration curve is shown in Figure 6.

Barriers to entry. It was estimated that the MES of production was roughly 20–25 million square metres, with an implied capital cost of about £20 million to operate a plant on this scale. Such a cost obviously did not deter RPL and Knauf from entering the market (nor did the fact that they had to import gypsum and liner paper), although they entered when demand appeared relatively buoyant. As with any large-scale manufacturing process, technical knowledge is necessary, but this could be obtained from Europe and elsewhere. There was some evidence of brand loyalty for the product of the incumbent. Certain purchasers tended to use the brand name of BPB, Gyproc, rather than the generic product name.

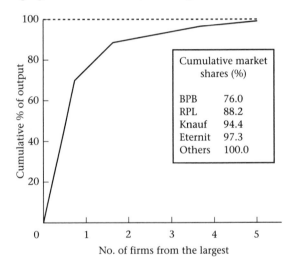

Figure 6
The concentration curve in the plasterboard industry.

After 1988/89, the recession and the consequent reduction in new house building and commercial construction led to a rapid decline in sales of plasterboard and to large-scale overcapacity in the industry. With all the plants of the new entrants operational manufacturing capacity amounted to roughly 294 million square metres, whereas annual sales in 1990/91 were running at 170 million square metres. Despite forecasts of rising demand for the product, prices fell. In these circumstances, other prospective entrants would probably find it difficult to make a return on their capital investments. Therefore, excess capacity constituted a barrier to entry for any other potential new firms, although not a strategically imposed one. As a result of the spare capacity, exit from the market would be far from costless since it would be difficult to dispose of a plasterboard plant in the UK. Therefore, significant sunk costs existed.

Market conduct

The arrival of the new entrants led to greater product differentiation in the market. There were changes in the style of the product and particularly in the quality of service as a result of the entry of the new firms. Both RPL and Knauf concentrated on improving standards of customer care and delivery in the industry. These changes were accompanied by significant marketing campaigns, which enabled the two firms to achieve their rapid growth in market shares. It was generally felt in the industry that the arrival of RPL and Knauf had improved BPB's quality of service.

The major impact of the new firms was in relation to pricing policies. The entry of the new firms into the industry, coupled with the spare capacity that the new investment created, led to significant price competition, the effect of which was to cause an average reduction in BPB's prices in real terms of 21% between 1985 and 1990.

Market performance

BPB's profits and return on capital employed from the supply of plasterboard are shown in Table 8. Profits increased from £40.4 million in 1986 to £73.7 million in 1989. In each of the four years from 1986–89 BPB earned returns on capital assets in excess of 32%. This compared with an average return on assets of just over 20% during these four years in the building materials sector as a whole and an average return of a little over 25% in the paper and packaging sector during the same period.

It was felt that BPB was able to achieve a high level of profits and a high rate of return by exploitation of its monopoly position. It

Table 8 *BPB's profits and rate of return from the supply of plasterboard, 1986–90*

Year	Profit (before interest and tax) (£ million)	Return on capital employed (year-end) (%)
1986	40.4	32.6
1987	53.4	40.0
1988	67.1	43.7
1989	73.7	38.8
1990	33.6	16.8

Source: MMC (1990).

was able to charge higher prices than if competitive conditions had existed. However, the arrival of RPL and Knauf into the industry coincided with a sharp decline in BPB's level of profitability and rate of return. Profits dropped to £33.6 million and its rate of return fell to 16.8% in 1990. This was thought to be due to a combination of the increased competition in the industry, plus the decline in demand.

Conclusions

The report stressed that the plasterboard industry was transformed by the entry of RPL and Knauf in 1989. The increased competition in the market represented a profound structural change. The arrival of RPL and Knauf coincided with a sharp downturn in demand for the product, but nevertheless the increased competition in the market had implications for both conduct and performance. It led to greater price competition and to lower profits and rates of return, respectively. Market structure had influenced firm behaviour and this, in turn, had had an impact on performance. The report concluded that, on the basis of the competitive conditions that now existed in the industry (and presumably, therefore, the improved level of economic welfare), there was nothing in the market that operated against the public interest and that the undertakings previously imposed on BPB should be lifted.

FURTHER READING

Clarke, R. (1985) *Industrial Economics* (Oxford, Basil Blackwell), Chapters 2,4.

Davies, S. and Lyons, B. with Dixon H. and Geroski, P. (1991) *Economics of Industrial Organisation* (London, Longman), Chapters 2,3.

Ferguson, P.R. and Ferguson, G.J. (1994) *Industrial Economics: Issues and Perspectives* (London, Macmillan), Chapters 2,3.

Martin, S. (1993) *Advanced Industrial Economics* (Oxford, Basil Blackwell), Chapters 7, 17–19.

NOTES

1. The trade-adjusted concentration ratio C_r is given by

$$C_r = \frac{Q_r}{Q + \dfrac{MQ}{Q - X}} \times 100$$

   where Q_r represents sales at home and abroad by the largest r domestic firms, Q is total sales in the market, X equals total exports and M total imports.

2. See *The Economist*, 11 June 1994, Management Focus, 'Size'.

3. The MES is strictly defined as that level of output where the long-run average cost curve first reaches its minimum point. It is the output where all scope for plant-level economies of scale have been fully utilised.

Questions □ □ □

2.1 Since all economic activity is classified in terms of industries why do economists consider the concept of the markets to be so significant?

2.2 The following data show sales of beer in the outdoor market (outside the home) as a percentage of total beer sales for various European countries:

Germany (West)	60%
Belgium	65%
UK	84%
France	41%
Italy	30%
Denmark	22%
Netherlands	40%
Ireland	94%

Source: de Jong (1988).

What do these figures suggest about the market segmentation of beer in the different countries? How might the variations in the figures cause differences in corporate strategies between the countries?

2.3 'The association between market structure, conduct and performance is much more complex than a simple one-way causal relationship, and empirical evidence reflects this complexity.' Discuss.

2.4 'All concentration bases are fundamentally flawed. Therefore, all concentration indices are likely to be inadequate measures of concentration.' Explain and discuss.

2.5 'Food shopping is carried out on a local basis, and on that level many areas of the country are dominated by two or three supermarket chains' (*The Guardian*, 10 January 1995). What problems does this situation present for the measurement of market concentration?

2.6 There are seven firms in an industry with market shares as follows: 25%, 20%, 15%, 15%, 10%, 10% and 5%. Calculate the C_5 ratio and the Herfindahl index for the industry. What do your answers say about the relative merits of each index as a measure of concentration?

2.7 Comment fully on the following measurements of concentration in the car market before and after adjustments for international trade:

	C_4 ratio		Herfindahl index	
	Unadjust.	Adjust.	Unadjust.	Adjust.
UK				
1970	100.0	89.2	0.338	0.260
1986	96.0	66.7	0.308	0.147
US				
1970	100.0	91.0	0.341	0.270
1986	97.2	78.4	0.383	0.235
Germany				
1970	94.5	73.7	0.345	0.182
1986	88.7	65.3	0.259	0.142
Japan				
1970	87.9	78.2	0.277	0.252
1986	86.0	89.7	0.236	0.309

Source: Ferguson and Ferguson (1994).

2.8 The C_5 ratio for the insulated wires and cables industry in the UK is 62.0%, which is almost identical to that of the ice-cream industry at 63.0%. Does this necessarily imply that the market structures of the two industries are the same?

2.9 'Market concentration will usually tend towards its equilibrium level, the result of demand and cost conditions.' Explain and discuss.

2.10 'Prospective new entrants can overcome most impediments to entry through time. Hence, barriers to entry pose a far less serious threat to potential new firms that was previously supposed.' Explain and discuss.

2.11 'Markets are fragmenting, both in size and time. Product cycles have grown shorter, making production runs smaller and reducing the time that any manufacturing system designed for a single product could be useful' (*The Economist*, 5 March 1994). Discuss the possible implications of these changes for corporate strategies.

CHAPTER 3

▶ UK Industrial and Labour Market Structure– A Comparative Analysis

This chapter examines some of the key *structural features* or characteristics of British industry and, since labour is usually the most significant input of firms, its *labour market*. In so doing it places the strategies of firms in some kind of context. Comparisons are made with other major industrialised economies wherever possible. A number of important issues are raised that are pursued and developed throughout the text. Some key macroeconomics variables that affect the behaviour of firms are also discussed.

A comparative analysis of *changes in industrial structures* is undertaken, with particular reference to the UK. This is followed by a detailed analysis of the various *hypotheses of structural change*. The importance of the role of the individual firm as an instigator of structural change is examined. *International competitiveness*, and its measurement in price and non-price terms, is discussed. *Deindustrialisation* is defined and the deindustrialisation debate is outlined. The importance of the *manufacturing sector* for the UK is examined. The *structure of the labour market* in the UK is discussed and is compared with the labour markets of other industrial countries. In the course of the discussion the relationships between the characteristics of particular industrial and labour market structures and corporate behaviour are analysed. Two *case studies* are presented at the end of the chapter. One examines the impact that certain successful firms have had on their respective industries, and hence on industrial structure. The other uses the example of Toyota to discuss briefly the effect of the exchange rate on corporate strategy.

3.1 THE UK INDUSTRIAL STRUCTURE

One of the main uses of any SIC, and a prime reason why it needs to be updated, is to analyse the nature of, and to trace changes in, a country's *industrial structure*, i.e. the relative importance of different industries in a country and the patterns of transactions between them. SICs can also be used to compare the industrial structures of different countries.

Since there are problems in defining and classifying industries *per se*, which have been discussed in Section 2.1, there are likely to be even greater problems in analysing changes in an industry over time and/or making comparisons between countries at the same point in time. Therefore, these investigations are often made at a much broader level of aggregation. Industries can be divided into three wide-ranging sectors: *primary*, which are any industries connected with natural resources, such as agriculture, fishing and mining; *secondary*, which encompasses all other goods produced by the economy, of which *manufacturing* is a major part; and *tertiary* or all *services*. The primary sector covers sections A–C from Table 2, page 8, the secondary sector sections D–F and the tertiary sector the remainder, G–Q. The term *industry* (or *production industries*) applies more or less to the secondary sector, although industry includes mining and excludes construction. The *goods* sector is the primary and secondary sectors combined.

Reasons for changes in the industrial structure

Over time, as changes occur in the relative importance of different industries, so there are changes in the relative sizes (whether measured in output or employment terms) of the particular industrial sectors. There are three main reasons for the shifts in relative importance of industries and industrial sectors through time.

(A) DEMAND FACTORS
Assuming that economic growth causes real incomes to rise, there will be a greater increase in demand for those goods and services with higher income elasticities of demand and lower increases, or even falls, in demand for other products. Income elasticity of demand measures the responsiveness of demand for a product to changes in income, *cet. par.* (see Section 7.5). Products with relatively high income elasticities

are travel and tourism and other leisure activities. Products with low income elasticities are food, clothing and footwear. For example, between 1983 and 1994 total real consumers' expenditure at 1985 prices increased by 37.4% in the UK. However, spending on 'food' during this period rose by only 12.5%, whereas spending on 'recreation, entertainment and education' increased by 61.6%. Naturally, the structure of output and employment in the economy will respond to such differences in expenditure patterns.

The age structure of the population will also affect the overall nature of demand in the country. The average age of the population in the UK is slowly rising as people live longer. In 1950, 11% of the population were aged 65 and over. In 1994 the equivalent figure was over 17%. The greater numbers forming this age-group means there will be an increased demand for the products that meet their tastes and needs, like certain types of leisure activities or healthcare services.

(B) SUPPLY FACTORS

Technological change creates both new products and new processes. Technical developments, and in particular the introduction of steam power, were instrumental in creating the rapid industrialisation in the UK in the eighteenth and nineteenth centuries. Since innovation is usually embodied in investment in capital goods, it often creates new and cheaper processes in which capital is substituted for labour. The obvious current example is the widespread use of computer technology and robots: reduced costs lead to lower prices. Technical progress also creates new and better quality products that both change and stimulate demand. As new technologies diffuse throughout society they can have similar effects on costs, prices and the pattern of demand in other industries. Technologies develop as they diffuse, so improving reliability and quality and giving the potential to reduce costs and prices still further. Technical change influences demand and the pattern of output and employment by reducing the price of existing products and by creating new products. (Both consumers and producers can benefit from these changes. The prices of video recorders, home computers, word processors and compact disc players have fallen in absolute and relative terms since they were introduced. Large firms first used computer-controlled machine tools in 1968. Some smaller firms are still waiting for their cost to fall sufficiently before introducing them.[1])

Changes in the supply of resources can also effect changes in industrial structure. The restriction in the supply of oil by OPEC, the oil producing and exporting countries, in the 1970s led to a dramatic increase in the prices of oil and complementary products. As a result, there was a fall in the consumption of oil and oil-based goods and a rise in demand and production for substitute forms of energy, such as coal and gas.

(C) FOREIGN COMPETITION

Changes in demand and in supply can also affect the British industrial structure via competition from abroad. Later in the chapter it will be seen that the UK manufacturing sector has suffered from rising *import penetration* (the ratio of imports of manufactured goods to total domestic demand for manufactures) in the last 20–25 years. This trend has been particularly severe in certain industries, like chemicals, electrical engineering and vehicle production, which has led to their relative decline in both output and employment terms in the UK. The investment decisions of multinational corporations can also have profound effects on the UK's industrial structure. UK-based multinationals may decide to reduce the scale of their investments in the UK and instead invest in other countries. At the same time, foreign-based firms may wish to initiate, or increase, operations in the UK. Either way their decisions can alter the pattern of output and demand in Britain.

Structural changes

Having discussed the reasons why structural change occurs, this subsection examines the main changes that have taken place within the major economies. Table 9 shows the estimated long-term changes in employment patterns in the major industrial sectors in the G7, the world's largest industrial nations. The data in the table should be treated with some caution, since changes occur in the definitions of sectors over time and it is difficult to compare like with like. However, the table does provide an indication of the secular trend. It reveals that in all advanced economies there has been a long-term shift in resources from the primary sector into industry and then into the tertiary sector. The process started sooner in the UK than anywhere else because of its earlier industrialisation. It then occurred in the US and by the mid-1960s these two countries had smaller

Table 9 *The long-term changes in the share of employment[a] in major sectors,[b] Selected Countries (%)*

	Late 19th C[c]			Mid-20th C[d]			1970			1992		
	P[e]	I	S	P[e]	I	S	P	I	S	P	I	S
UK	12	43	45	5	47	48	3	45	52	2	27	71
US	50	25	25	12	35	53	5	34	61	3	25	72
Germany	42	36	22	29	41	30	9	48	43	3	39	58
France	52	29	20	33	34	33	14	39	47	6	29	65
Italy	62	24	14	41	31	28	21	39	40	9	32	59
Japan	83	6	11	48	21	30	18	35	47	6	35	59
Canada	50	13	37	21	35	44	8	31	61	4	23	73

[a]Shares of the total working population. Figures may not sum to 100 due to rounding.
[b]P = primary; I = industry; S = services.
[c]UK = 1911; US = 1870; Germany = 1882; France = 1866; Italy = 1871; Japan = 1877; Canada = 1871.
[d]UK = 1951; US = 1950; Germany = 1933; France = 1950; Italy = 1954; Japan = 1950; Canada = 1950–53.
[e]Excludes mining.

Sources: Adapted from Kuznets (1959); OECD Historical Statistics 1960–90; OECD (1993).

proportions of their workforce in their primary sectors than anywhere else. They also had larger shares of employment in their tertiary sectors. It is likely that most economies follow this very general pattern of development through time, although there may be some variations in the structural changes that they experience because of differences in the supplies of factors of production or differences in the size and pattern of demand within each country.

The industrialisation process can explain the shift in resources from the primary sector to industry in the nineteenth and early twentieth centuries. However, as will be pointed out, the growth of tertiary sector employment in the second half of the twentieth century in the industrialised world has not necessarily been at the expense of employment in the industrial sector.

Table 10 analyses changes in the UK industrial structure in the last 30 years. (The years 1964, 1969, 1973, 1979 and 1989 are often used for comparative purposes because they are cyclical peaks.) The data confirm the trends noted in Table 9. The tertiary sector has become more significant, in terms of both labour and output, while the primary and industrial (or in this case the secondary) sectors have declined in relative importance. The primary sector output figures for 1979 and 1985 are inflated by the high real price for oil following the price hikes of 1973 and 1979. In 1986 the oil price was halved and UK production fell by over 20% during the next five years.

The most important constituent of either the secondary or the industrial sector is manufacturing. Table 11, page 34, shows that there has been a decline

Table 10 *The Shares of output (O)[a] and employment (E)[b] in major sectors of the UK, various years (%)[c]*

	1964		1969		1973		1979		1985		1989		1993	
	O	E	O	E	O	E	O	E	O	E	O	E	O	E
Primary	5.8	5.1	4.3	3.6	4.2	3.4	6.7	3.0	8.1	2.9	3.5	2.1	4.1	2.0
Secondary	40.8	46.9	42.0	46.8	40.9	42.4	36.7	38.5	34.0	31.2	33.5	28.9	30.0	27.2
Tertiary	53.8	47.8	53.0	49.3	54.9	54.4	56.5	58.5	57.9	65.9	63.1	68.9	66.1	70.8

[a]Shares of GDP at current factor cost.
[b]Shares of total employment.
[c]Figures may not sum to 100 due to rounding.

Sources: Calculated from CSO, *UK National Accounts Blue Book,* various years; *Economic Review Data Supplement,* 1993, 1994.

in the relative importance of manufactured goods in both employment and output terms in most industrial economies in the last 30 years, a decline which seems to have been particularly acute in the UK. The decrease in the significance of manufacturing (or of the industrial sector as a whole) is often referred to as *deindustrialisation*. However, there is disagreement about precisely what this term indicates. It has been applied to both absolute and relative changes in output, or in employment, or in both output and employment. It can also refer to the overseas trade performance of the manufacturing sector.

An important qualification of the figures in Table 11 is that the output figures are given in current prices, those for each year being in that year's prices. However, in constant price, volume or real terms a rather different picture emerges: the relative changes are much smaller. In value terms all the countries witnessed a significant fall in the manufacturing share of output. In volume terms (admittedly over a shorter period) the share of manufacturing in GDP at constant 1985 prices during 1970–90 increased in the US by 0.6% and in Japan by 2.2%. In Italy it rose by 0.2% during 1980–90. The manufacturing share fell in France during 1980–90 by 1.8% and in Germany by 1.5% during 1970–89. In the UK the manufacturing percentage of GDP in volume terms decreased by 2.8% during 1970–90, although the relative decline was much slower in the 1980s (a fall of 0.7%) compared to what happened in the 1970s (a 2.1% drop). The differences in the figures are due to variations in the rates of technical progress and productivity between sectors. There is

usually a faster rate of both technical progress and productivity growth in manufacturing than in other parts of the economy (especially services), which has the effect of lowering the prices of manufactured goods relative to non-manufactured products. Part of the fall in the share of manufacturing in GDP at current prices in all countries is due to this relative fall in prices. In constant price terms the trends tend to be more stable. Even so, in absolute terms the volume of manufacturing output in the UK in 1993 was only very slightly higher than the figure for 1973, a situation unique to the UK among the industrial nations.

During 1980–89, the share of manufacturing jobs in total in the OECD declined by about 3%, although different countries have had very different experiences. In Japan, manufacturing employment has risen in absolute terms since 1970; for example, in 1992 it was more than 10% higher than in the early 1980s. In the US manufacturing employment was higher in 1992 than in 1970, although it was lower than in 1980. In each of the four largest EU economies manufacturing employment has declined in absolute terms since 1970. It has declined most notably in the UK, at a rate of over 2% a year during 1970–90. Manufacturing employment in Britain fell by a total of 3.5 million during 1973–93, or by 44.5%, a far larger percentage decline than for any of its major competitors.

There have also been significant changes within the manufacturing sectors of OECD countries. In general, there has been a shift of resources away from 'low-tech' industries, in which there is a relatively low rate of technological progress and which tend to be characterised by relatively low wage levels. During 1980–92, employment in the textile, leather and footwear industry fell by 75%, in metal-producing by 65% and in wood products by 10% in total in the OECD. Employment in food, drink and tobacco stayed about level during the period. At the same time there has been a growth in employment and output in high- and medium-technology industries, which have relatively high levels of R&D spending as proportions of their total output and which are also relatively high-wage. They include aerospace, chemicals, communications equipment, computing, electrical machinery and scientific instruments. During the 1980s the share taken by these industries in total manufacturing value added increased by 5.6% in Japan, by 6% in the US, but by only 3.5% in the major EU economies. In the UK, employment actually fell during this period in

Table 11 *The relative importance of manufacturing output (O)[a] and employment (E),[b] selected countries (%)*

	1960		1990	
	O	E	O	E
UK	32.1	38.4	18.9	23.0
US	28.3	26.4	18.9	18.5
Germany	40.3	34.3	31.2	31.6
France	29.1	27.3	21.0	21.3
Italy	28.6	24.2	22.4	22.7
Japan	34.6	21.3	28.9	24.2

[a]Value added of manufacturing relative to GDP, in current prices.
[b]Shares of the total working population.

Sources: OECD Historical Statistics, 1960–90; OECD (1993).

virtually every manufacturing industry, although the relative decline was lower in the high-technology industries. The only industry where employment increased strongly in the period was pharmaceuticals, which accounts for 1.5% of total manufacturing employment.

3.2 HYPOTHESES CONCERNING STRUCTURAL CHANGE

Various hypotheses have been advanced about the precise causes of structural change in the UK. This section critically analyses the main arguments that have been put forward.

The stages of development hypothesis

The basis of this hypothesis is that the earlier an economy industrialises, earlier it will experience a shift from industry into services. Therefore, any fall in industrial employment will at some stage simply be taken up by the tertiary sector. Since the UK was the first country to industrialise, it has been the first country to go through the transformation process from industry to services. Resources are reallocated according to changing demand and supply condi-tions. In general, services have higher income elas-ticities of demand than goods. As incomes rise over time, then proportionately more services are demanded. There also tends to be lower labour productivity in services than in manufacturing. Even with demand unchanged, a proportionately greater number of people would need to be employed in services than in the industrial sector.

This argument is a fairly simplistic explanation of structural change; the evidence does not entirely fit such a basic analysis. The relatively high levels of unemployment that many countries, including the UK, have experienced since the mid-1970s should have meant that the growth in service sector employ-ment could have taken place without a substantial drop in industrial or manufacturing jobs. As was pointed out in the previous section the US, Japan (and Canada) had higher numbers employed in manufacturing in 1992 than they had 20 years earlier, whereas manufacturing employment fell in all other major industrial economies. If unemployment levels are put to one side, employment trends in the EU in the last 20 years would seem to fit the hypothesis. Service sector employment was 25% higher in 1992

than in 1980. In the same period almost 20% of manufacturing jobs have disappeared. However, within the European Free Trade Association (EFTA) service sector employment has actually fallen since 1990.

The 'crowding out' argument

This argument is mainly associated with Bacon and Eltis (1975) who divided the UK economy into the market sector, in which products are sold in a market at a price that generally covers costs, and the non-market sector. The market sector finances itself through its profits, whereas the non-market sector consists of activities like health and education services which are not sold in a market and that have to be financed via taxation. This distinction is virtually synonymous with the private sector/public sector division, although not completely. For example, some of the previously nationalised industries that were included in the public sector, such as British Airways, sold their products in a market in the same way as private sector companies. They would have been counted as market sector firms according to this analysis.

If it is assumed that the non-market sector and the public sector are one and the same, the crowding out argument runs as follows. Any increase in the size of the public sector leads to increases in the claims by public sector workers for the products provided by the market or private sector. The growth of the public sector can only be sustained by increases in taxation (and by higher interest rates as government borrowing rises). Higher taxes reduce the real dispos-able incomes of all workers and lessen the demand for the total marketed output, but they also lead to wage claim rises. Wage increases mean that they take up a higher proportion of total marketed output; profits and investment in the market sector fall. The greater demand coming from both sectors for the output of the market sector will mean either a lower proportion of production available for export and/or a rise in imports. In other words, it will lead to balance of payments problems. The growth of the non-market sector crowds the market sector out of both labour and, through the lower profits and higher interest rates, financial resources for invest-ment.

This argument puts the relative decline of Britain's industrial sector largely at the door of the growth of the non-market public sector. There has been a growth in the relative size of the public sector in the UK, but this has occurred in most industrial economies and not just in Britain. Government spending formed 43.2% of GDP in 1994 against 32.2% in 1960. The overall tax burden has also risen, but this too has happened in virtually all major economies. This has been despite attempts by many governments, particularly in the UK, to reduce the scale of public involvement in the economy. However, as Leslie (1993) points out, assuming that labour in the service sector is paid some kind of 'going rate' and given that that services generally have a lower rate of productivity growth compared with the industrial sector, then in a growing economy, with the state providing a fixed range of services, government spending as a proportion of GDP must rise if people wish to maintain a constant share of non-marketed services.

The high levels of unemployment since the mid-to late 1970s would make it seem unlikely that the market sector has been starved of labour. Besides, much of the increase in public sector employment has been female, often employed on a part-time basis, whereas most of the decline in manufacturing jobs has consisted of male workers. The change in the relative positions of the two sectors has mainly involved two entirely different sets of workers. Low levels of investment in private industry have probably been due more to pessimistic expectations of the future than to high interest rates. In fact, the profitability of large private sector companies has risen on average in the 1980s, especially in the second half of the decade. There is little evidence of a shortage of financial resources, at least for large firms. The evidence since the late 1970s does not offer any great support for the crowding out argument as an explanation of industrial decline in the UK.

Competition from newly industrialised economies

There is an argument that competition from abroad, and especially from the low-wage newly-industrialised economies of Asia (NIAs) like Hong Kong, Taiwan, South Korea and Singapore, has been responsible for, or has at least exacerbated, the industrial decline of the UK.

OECD projections show that the share of world export trade in manufactures of non-OECD Asian economies (including China) is expected to rise to over 20% by the late 1990s from 11.5% in 1986. The market shares of UK trade are shown in Table 12. Relative to the UK's trade with the EU, its overseas dealings with the NIAs are small. Imports from the NIAs formed 6% of the UK's imports in 1992, whereas the EU was the source of 52% of Britain's imports.

It is true that wage costs in the UK are more than double those in the NIAs. In 1993, hourly wage costs in manufacturing were the equivalent of $12 in the UK, compared with $5.6 in Hong Kong, $4.8 in Taiwan and $4.7 in South Korea. However, compared with other major industrialised economies the UK has low wage costs. In Germany in 1993, hourly manufacturing wage costs were $23.8, in France they amounted to $18.2, in Japan $16.5 and in the US $15.5. This should mean that the UK is, in fact, more competitive than these other industrial nations, although competitiveness depends on more than just relative labour costs. (The inclusion of non-wage items such as employers' social security contributions and other payroll taxes comprising the overall cost of labour probably improves the UK's position still further.) A country's competitiveness also depends on relative levels of productivity and the value of the currency compared with other currencies, or the exchange rate.

Table 12 *Market Shares of UK Trade(%)*

	Export market share		Annual export growth	Import market share		Annual import growth
	1983	1992	1983–92	1983	1992	1983–92
NIAᵃ	3	5	12	4	6	15
US	14	11	6	11	11	8
Japan	1	2	14	5	6	11
EU	46	56	10	49	52	10

ᵃNIAs comprise Hong Kong, Taiwan, Singapore, Malaysia, Thailand.

Source: *Lloyds Bank Economic Bulletin*, No. 182, Feb. 1994.

The comparatively small scale of the UK's trade with the NIAs suggests that it has not been an important factor in causing structural change. The fact that this trade is growing faster than trade with any other major area (imports from NIAs have been growing 5% p.a. faster during 1982–92 than those from the EU) indicates that it may have a significant impact in the future, especially where the competition benefits from widespread state subsidies. For example, since the early 1970s the domestic and the export growth of the South Korean conglomerates, Samsung and Hyundai, have been dependent on the availability of large-scale and heavily-subsidised credit facilities.

Structural weaknesses of the UK economy

The proposition that there are major structural or supply-side problems in the UK economy, which have manifested themselves in relatively low levels of productivity and which have been the root cause of any decline in the UK's industrial fortunes, is not a new one (Cambridge Economic Policy Group, 1976; Singh, 1977). The supply-side problems that have been most commonly cited are the UK's *industrial relations* structure, the overall level and type of *education and training* and its *investment* and *innovation* performance. Problems in these areas mean that British products, and especially manufactured goods, are not competitive in either price or non-price terms, like product design, reliability, quality, delivery and after-sales service. Such non-price factors, it is said, produce adverse income elasticities of demand for British products *vis-à-vis* those of the rest of the world. The argument runs that there is a lower world income elasticity of demand for UK goods than the British income elasticity for imports. This is particularly true in the case of manufactured goods. If world income levels and UK income levels both increase by, say, 10% and the income elasticity of demand for imports is equal to two, whereas the income elasticity of demand for exports is equal to one, then UK imports will increase by 20% and exports by only 10%. The result is a 'vicious circle' leading to industrial decline, the supply problems producing the adverse income elasticities. They result in an increasingly large excess in the value of imports of goods relative to the value of exports of goods. In other words, they lead to a mounting trade deficit.

In order to reduce the deficit, governments may pursue deflationary fiscal and monetary policies, which dampen aggregate demand and raise unem-ployment. Such policies provide even less incentive to invest in new products or processes and this exac-erbates the original supply-side problems. This type of argument also underpins the definition of dein-dustrialisation based on the foreign trade perfor-mance of the UK manufacturing sector. Deindus-trialisation occurs if manufacturing is unable to generate a sufficient surplus of manufactured exports over imports to keep the overall balance of payments[2] in balance, taking into account any net export of services, and at an acceptable level of employment and exchange rate.

The external macroeconomic problems of the UK have been given rather less significance by policy-makers in the 1980s and 1990s than previously, as the control of inflation has become the major objective of government macroeconomic strategy. However, particular macroeconomic policies and objectives are still likely to be constrained by large-scale and persistent balance-of-payments deficits. Figure 7, page 38, shows that the scale of any poten-tial problem for the UK and the US is larger than elsewhere. Since the mid-1970s, both have suffered larger and more persistent current-account deficits as a percentage of GDP than either Germany or Japan, although the recessionary effects of the early 1990s have led to a severe decline in Germany's relative position.

Furthermore, the debate concerning the structural problems of the British economy remains. It is argued that both the industrial relations structure of the UK and its education and training performance have contributed to low productivity and to a lack of flex-ibility in the economy. Skill shortages may mean that it is difficult to shift production sufficiently quickly from products that the world no longer wants towards those that are currently in high demand.

There have been major legislative changes in the field of industrial relations in the UK since 1979, mainly designed to reduce what was perceived by the government as excessive bargaining power on the part of the trade unions, but also with the intended effect of making the labour market more flexible. These were part of the so-called Thatcher reforms intended to reduce government intervention and to promote competition in the economy (and see Chapter 15). If there are fewer restrictive practices in existence that prevent workers from undertaking several tasks in a plant, then in principle, labour can be moved more easily from one task to the next and skill shortages will diminish. Labour market flexibility is discussed in more detail later in this chapter and

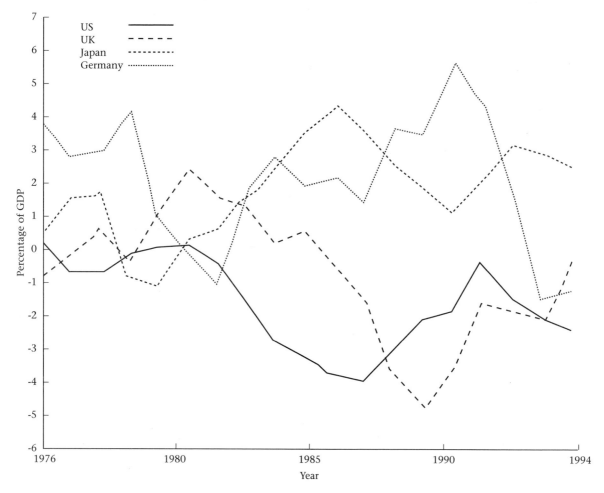

Figure 7 *Current account balances as a percentage of GDP 1976–94, selected countries. (Adapted from OECD Economic Outlook, June 1994.)*

in Chapter 14. There is a great deal of argument about precisely what greater labour market flexibility entails and quite how it may solve any underlying structural problems in the UK economy.

From the available evidence, Britain's expenditure on education, as a percentage of GDP, is at least as good as in most other industrial countries. The UK spends 5.2% of its public funds on education. This is a higher figure than Japan and Germany, but lower than the US, France and most other Western European countries. One area, however, where the UK performs poorly in comparison with the others is staying-on or participation rates for those aged 16 and over. A number of policy initiatives in recent years have concentrated on the need for improved vocational qualifications for the 16-plus age-group.

Despite the large increases in the numbers entering higher education since the mid-1980s, the proportion of 16–19-year-olds in education and training in the UK is still lower than in most other industrial countries. In 1991, 56% of those aged 16–19 in the UK were in full-time education or part-time education and training. This compares with a figure of 76% for France, 79% for Germany and 94% (of 15–18-year-olds) for Japan (Green and Steedman, 1993).

In fact, and perhaps rather surprisingly, there is not a great deal of evidence that greater levels of educational expenditure cause improved levels of productivity and economic growth. There is a good correlation between relative levels of per capita GDP and levels of basic education, as indicated in Figure

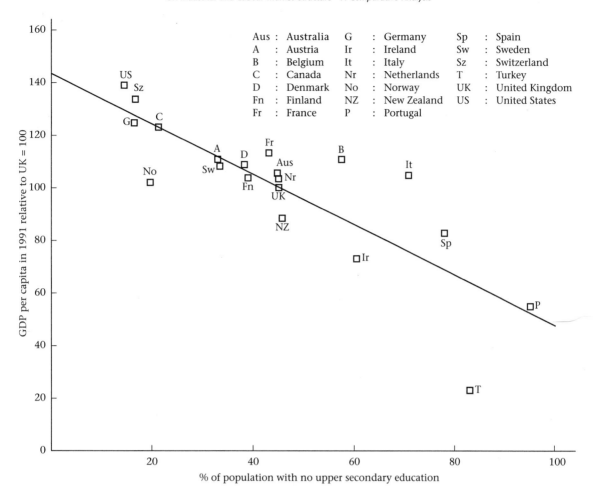

Figure 8 *Living standards and basic educational attainment in 1991, various countries. (Source: Robinson (1995), taken from OECD data.)*

8, although correlation does not imply causation; there may also be a two-way relationship between per capita GDP and educational standards. Higher GDP may require higher levels of education, but higher standards of living make it easier to afford better education (in which case education would be regarded as a consumption good with a high income elasticity of demand rather than as an investment good). There is a strong correlation between levels of basic educational attainment and labour force participation (Robinson, 1995) and it may be that one process by which better education leads to higher growth rates and improved standards of living is by having a larger proportion of the population at work. Once again, however, correlation does not imply causation.

Work undertaken by the National Institute of Economic and Social Research (NIESR) has compared similar plants in selected industries (biscuit manufacture, chemicals, clothing, engineering, furniture, metal working and textiles) in Britain, France and Germany. The studies concluded that, in general, productivity differences were due to the greater efficiency of operation in the German plants in particular caused by the higher skill level of the workforce, although the use of less technically advanced machinery and equipment was also found to be a significant contributory factor in a number of cases. The British skill shortage was found to be most pronounced at the middle-ranking and supervisory skill levels.

These studies provide some supportive evidence of a positive relationship between levels of education and productivity, although the differences in skills did not affect relative performance in every case, most notably in the chemical industry. O'Mahoney (1992) found a positive and significant causal link between skill differences and relative productivity levels (in this case within UK and German manufacturing), although the explanatory power of the relationship was quite small. The National Vocational Qualification (NVQ) scheme, set up in 1986, is designed to increase the overall amount of vocational training in the UK, although certainly in its early stages it was criticised for concentrating too much on the lower level awards rather than on the more advanced skills reckoned to be in short supply. Mason and Wagner (1994) provide confirmatory evidence of the relative shortage of those with intermediate qualifications (i.e. at craft or supervisory levels) in the UK compared with Germany. In Britain, 35% of the manufacturing workforce held such qualifications in 1990; in Germany, the equivalent figure (for 1989) was 68%.

At the senior managerial level a lower percentage of the top managers in the UK are graduates compared with other countries, and far fewer are graduate engineers. For example, in the UK about 40% of those in senior management posts are graduates, whereas the figure for Germany is nearer 70%. Most of the German managers have some kind of engineering background. They are presumably more likely to possess the requisite technical ability needed to make the best use of the resources available, although it could be argued that industry will benefit by employing the most highly qualified people whatever their field of study.

The total value of investment in capital goods in the UK as a share of GDP is lower than in its main competitors.[3] Lack of investment in modern equip-

Table 13 *Investment intensity in manufacturing industry, selected countries[a]*

	1980	1988
UK	3.7	3.8
US	4.0	3.6
Germany	4.5	4.8
France	5.2	6.2
Italy	7.4	6.0
Japan	3.0	4.2
Canada	5.5	5.6

[a]GFCF as a percentage of production in current prices.

Source: Adapted from OECD (1993).

Table 14 *Rates of return on capital in the business sector, selected countries*

	1970–76 (average % p.a.)	1977–93 (average % p.a.)
UK	10.3	9.9
US	15.8	15.6
Germany	13.7	12.5
France	13.3	12.3
Italy	11.4	12.7
Japan	19.4	14.3
Canada	13.9	16.6

Source: Adapted from *OECD Economic Outlook*, June 1994.

ment and up-to-date techniques of production will make a country's products less competitive and is likely to hasten its industrial decline. The annual increase of real gross fixed capital formation (GFCF, including residential) in the UK during 1979–94 averaged almost 2%, which was slightly above the average for Germany, France and Italy over the period, suggesting that some kind of catch-up process has been taking place, but below the US and Japanese figures of 3.2% and 3.6% respectively. On the other hand, on a more disaggregated basis, investment intensity in UK manufacturing has lagged behind that in most other industrial economies, as Table 13 reveals.

Table 14 shows that British industry has lower rates of return on capital than elsewhere, which may help to explain the relatively low investment intensity in UK manufacturing. However, the US has a similarly low investment intensity, but much higher rate-of-return figures. An alternative explanation of the low rates of return may be that an inefficient use of factor inputs, especially labour, leads to low labour productivity and this is responsible for both low investment and the poor rates of return. Another factor to consider in this context is the claim that, compared to firms in the UK and the US, German and Japanese companies benefit from a closer and more long-term commitment shown to them by their banks, which may be conducive to a greater level of investment, and more selective investment, by firms.

British industry suffers from a low rate of innovation in new products and processes compared with other countries, although not exceptionally so, as Table 15 shows. Most innovation is the result of R&D. Coe and Helpman (1994) estimate that a 1% increase

Table 15 *Gross Expenditure on R&D: International Comparisons*[a]

	1987	1992
UK	2.22	2.12
US	2.84	2.68
Germany	2.88	2.53
France	2.27	2.36
Italy	1.19	1.38
Japan	2.63	2.80

[a]As percentages of GDP.

Source: *Economic Trends* (CSO) Nos 490, August 1994, and 502, August, 1995.

in a G7 country's R&D stock raises its total factor productivity by 0.23%. Increased R&D spending by one country raises productivity in other countries, though by a smaller amount, through the diffusive effects of international trade.

Further evidence on relative levels of innovation can be gleaned from information on patents. Comparing levels of patent activity between countries can be misleading due to differing 'propensities to patent'. However, figures on patent applications in the US reveal the relative decline in UK activity. In the mid-1960s the UK was awarded 44.4 patents in the US per million of its population. By the mid-1980s this had fallen to 40.5. In the same period, Germany increased its patent activity in the US from 55.3 to 97.0 per million population and Japan raised its levels from 10.4 to 79.0 respectively (NEDC, 1991).

It is of interest to note that the 'new' endogenous growth theories (Romer, 1986; Scott, 1989), emphasise a greater understanding of the role of technical progress in economic growth. The common strand of these theories has been to provide a broader view of what constitutes capital and to stress the importance of knowledge. Knowledge (of, for example, how best to produce things) can increase the return on investment. Therefore, according to this argument it is important to invest in knowledge, which in turn can stimulate a country's rate of investment. In other words, a 'virtuous circle' between investment and knowledge can ensue. There are four areas that have so far been identified as crucial to a greater understanding of the process whereby capital, and hence knowledge, contribute towards growth: learning-by-doing, human capital, R&D and public infrastructure. The theories also stress the potential for international spillovers in these areas.

Evidence on the manufacturing trade performance of the UK in general suggests that it fulfils the criteria for deindustrialisation that were outlined previously. The manufacturing sector of the UK has not been able to meet the country's overall import requirements; it would also seem unlikely that it could do this at acceptable levels of employment. In the early 1960s, the value of the UK's exports of manufactures was twice as great as the value of its manufactured imports. In 1983, the first deficit was recorded; the value of manufactured imports exceeded the value of manufactured exports. The manufacturing trade balance has remained in deficit ever since.

There have been two reasons for the turnaround in the manufacturing trade performance of the UK. Firstly, *import penetration* in UK manufacturing increased from 14.6% in 1970 to 30.0% in 1990. In other words, imports of manufactured goods into the UK more than doubled as a proportion of domestic demand between 1970 and 1990. The growth of international trade has meant that import penetration in manufacturing has risen in most industrial economies during this period. The experience of the UK is broadly similar to what has happened in France, Italy and Germany. On the other hand, the UK's *export performance* of manufactured goods has not compared well with a number of its main competitors. In 1950 the UK's share of world exports of manufactured goods was 26%, but by 1970 it had fallen to 11% and by 1992 to 5.2%. Japan's share of world exports of manufactured goods increased from 9.7% to 12.8% between 1970 and 1990, Germany's from 16.6% to 17.5% and that of France from 8.2% to 8.8%. The UK's share of the total manufacturing exports of the main manufacturing countries has risen slightly, both in value and volume terms, since the mid-1980s. The UK may have benefited from an overall fall in world trade relative to output and from the existence of bilateral trade barriers between the US and Japan (Bank of England, 1994a). Between 1992–96 the UK's overall trading performance was boosted by an appreciable fall in the effective exchange rate and in relative unit labour costs (see next section). However, the current account surplus of £500 million in the second quarter of 1996, the largest and only the second quarterly surplus since 1987, was due principally to income from overseas investments of £3.7 billion and a trading surplus on services of £1.7 billion; there was a £3.6 billion deficit on traded goods during the period as higher consumer spending in the UK and overseas investments sucked in imports.

The individual firm as the instigator of structural change

An alternative analysis of structural change within industrial economies, and one which has particular relevance for the purposes of this book, centres on the firm as the main initiator of any change. The same industry or group of industries may experience similar levels of performance across countries. As has been noted, in most industrial economies during the last 15–20 years there has been a movement of resources away from relatively low-technology to higher-technology industries. However, there may also be international differences in the performance of individual industries, and an important reason for these differences may be distinct developments, whether organisational or strategic, at the level of the firm.

For example, for much of the 1970s and 1980s the motor vehicle industry performed relatively poorly (whether measured in terms of employment or output growth) in the UK, while it flourished in Japan. The prime instigating factor in the dramatic growth of the Japanese motor vehicle industry from the 1950s onwards has been the development and implementation by Toyota of the so-called 'lean manufacturing' techniques, which the other Japanese vehicle manufacturers also quickly adopted (although not necessarily with the same degree of success, as Case Study Two in Chapter 6 points out). It would appear that some companies seem better able to initiate and propel developments within their industries. Collins and Porras (1991) refer to them as 'visionary' companies, while Baden-Fuller and Stopford (1992) label them 'dynamic' or 'entrepreneurial' businesses. It is argued that such firms tend to have distinctive characteristics that separate them from other firms in their industries and these characteristics enable them to survive and to grow even when the market conditions are poor; once ahead they often remain ahead. The key to their success may lie in a clear and imaginative corporate image that is fostered by management and with which the employees can identify. This image is exploited by innovative strategic decision-making, which leads to the development and successful implementation of new products and new production or marketing techniques. As a result, these firms are in a position to deliver variety and/or quality at relatively low cost.

Companies that can be said to have led developments in their home (and in some cases international) markets through a combination of innovative production, organisational and marketing techniques are Body Shop and Marks and Spencer in UK retailing, Sony in Japanese electronic hardware, Benetton in Italian fashion retailing, Merck in US pharmaceuticals and McDonald's in US fast-food retailing. These companies have not always pursued effective policies. In the early 1990s, the performance of Body Shop suffered from ethical claims about the content of some of its products and the takeover in 1989 of Columbia Pictures in the US by Sony resulted in a large-scale financial loss on the venture. However, they have usually been at the forefront of developments in their respective industries.

It may also be possible for once-successful firms to re-exert themselves. In the US sports-shoe market, Nike's performance suffered after having gained a larger market share than Adidas, its main rival. Nike's performance revived when its own market share was exceeded by Reebok. In the late 1970s and the early 1980s, Harley-Davidson suffered severely from competition from Japanese motorcycle producers, but has since re-established itself via a process of internal reorganisation.[4] In worldwide terms the identity of the innovating company may change. In the motor vehicle industry, Ford initially pioneered the idea of mass producing cars at low cost. Mass-produced variety was introduced by Sloan, the founder of General Motors (GM), in the 1920s. Later Toyota was responsible for the introduction of lean manufacturing techniques. Wherever these innovations prove to be the catalyst for similar developments and improvements by the firm's major domestic competitors, the performance of whole industries may be substantially improved.

There is some evidence to support the notion that the firm may be more important than the industry as the source of structural change within countries and as the basis for the varying performance of the same industries between countries. In Section 2.2 it was noted that, in general, the evidence linking profitability to the level of industry concentration is fairly weak. Other evidence has confirmed that the industry is a poor indicator of firm-level profitability. In a study of over 4500 business units during 1974–77, Rumelt (1991) discovered that the choice of industry accounted for at most 8.3% of a firm's profitability, whereas strategy accounted for over 46%. Cubbin and Geroski (1987) examined 217 large British firms for 1951–77 and found that in most cases there were no significant industry effects on profits. Geroski and Jacquemin (1988) found that profit differences among 51 UK, 55 French and 28 German firms were more persistent than among industries, particularly in the case of the British companies. There is also evidence that profitability increases with the market share of firms (see Scherer 1980, for a summary of the earlier results, and also Ravenscraft, 1983). This evidence could be accounted for by the fact that firms with a strategic advantage grow rapidly and maintain their position of leadership in the industry. Of course, it could be that the evidence on the relationship between the market shares of firms and profitability is picking up Gibrat-type chance factors, although as Scherer states:

Appreciable market share and concentration increases are not merely the result of random Gibrat-like processes. The firms experiencing rapid market share gains are frequently found to have been doing something different with their products, services, promotional or distribution methods, price strategies, production processes, or the like. It is not a difficult leap to infer that if they were successful they must have been exhibiting superiority of some sort (Scherer, 1980:290).

It is impossible to say precisely how important individual corporate strategy is as a major determinant of structural change, and the evidence is still fairly limited in its scope. However, if, say, a substantial number of manufacturing firms are beset by sterile management teams, inappropriate internal structures and vague and limited strategic outlooks, then these factors together might provide a reasonable explanation for the relative decline of at least part of a country's manufacturing sector. Other examples of firms whose strategies can be said to have had a direct impact on industry performance by influencing the outlook and policies of rival firms are given in the case study at the end of the chapter.

3.3 INTERNATIONAL COMPETITIVENESS

Having examined the reasons for structural change it is worthwhile exploring in greater detail the ways in which the performance of countries, or their levels of competitiveness, can be ascertained. This will give greater insight into the usefulness of the various hypotheses advanced in the previous section. It will also allow a better assessment of the value to a country of particular industrial sectors, and especially manufacturing. Competitiveness can be measured in both price and non-price terms. The first subsection examines the various ways in which price competi-

tiveness can be calculated. It is followed by a discussion of non-price indicators, such as product quality, reliability, delivery and after-sales service.

Measures of price competitiveness

Reference was made in the previous section to the relatively low levels of productivity in the UK (and see Box 3.1, page 44). Table 16 shows that in most major sectors the UK scores fairly poorly in terms of the average *growth* of labour productivity over time. In industry (and manufacturing separately) and services only the US has fared worse. However, these figures span 30 years and mask periodic fluctuations in a country's fortunes. For example, during 1973–79 the real value added in manufacturing per person in the UK increased by just 0.6% p.a., whereas the average increase in the other major economies shown in the table during this period was 2.6%. Since then there seems to have been some kind of a catch-up process occurring, with the UK having higher productivity levels than in many other industrial economies. From 1979 to 1993, labour productivity in the UK business sector averaged 2.2% p.a., compared with an average figure of 1.6% for the OECD as a whole during the period.

Labour productivity can increase as a result of a fall in the number of jobs or because of a rise in output, or some combination of the two, and it is worth investigating which of these effects is more prominent. Figure 9, page 44, compares these two components of productivity in manufacturing in various countries for the periods 1970–80 and 1980–89. From 1970 to 1980, the productivity gains in Japan were due to value added growth rather than to the shedding of jobs. In Finland, the US and Canada the gains were due to a faster rate of

Table 16 *Real value added per person employed, major sectors 1960–90, selected countries (average % p.a.)*

	Agriculture	Industry	Manufacturing	Services
UK	4.9	2.8	3.1	1.6
US	3.1	1.6	2.7	0.9
Germany	6.3	n/a	n/a	2.0
France	5.5	4.1	4.5	1.6
Italy	5.4	4.3	5.6	2.0
Japan	4.0	6.2	7.6	3.8

Source: Adapted from OECD Historical Statistics, 1960–90.

Box 3.1 *Indicators of price competitiveness*

Productivity is the ratio of some measure of output (calculated either in physical terms by gross output or in financial terms by net output or value added, usually deflated by an index of producer prices to give the real value added) to a measure of one or more of the inputs (either labour or capital, or both) involved in the production of the output. If all inputs are used (i.e. labour and capital) total factor productivity can be obtained. If a single input is employed, partial factor productivity will be provided. Labour productivity is the most commonly used measure since labour is the most ubiquitous and often the most important input in production. Labour productivity is also the most easily measurable. It can be measured in terms of output per person or output per person-hour. Productivity increases can lead to lower costs of production and therefore lower prices of good and services. The lower prices may cause demand (by home and overseas customers) to rise. The higher output may create additional jobs. The *effective exchange rate*, calculated as an index number, is the value of a currency measured against a weighted (usually in terms of trade shares) average of other currencies. The *relative unit labour costs* are an index of unit labour costs for a particular country divided by an index of unit labour costs in other countries. *Relative export prices* of the UK are the price of UK exports divided by the price of exports of other countries. *Export performance* is defined as the ratio of export volumes to export markets for goods (where the export market for total goods for any country is the weighted sum of the individual export markets for food, raw materials, energy and manufactures).

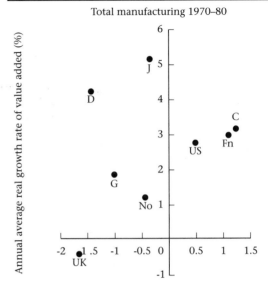

C	: Canada	G	: Germany	J	: Japan
D	: Denmark	It	: Italy	UK	: United Kingdom
Fn	: Finland	No	: Norway	US	: United States
Fr	: France				

(a) Annual average real growth rate of unemployment (%)

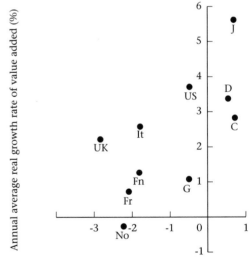

(b) Annual average real growth rate of unemployment (%)

Figure 9 *Employment growth and value-added growth in manufacturing 1970–89, various countries. (Source: OECD, 1993.)*

increase in output than in employment. In Denmark, Germany and Norway the rate of growth of output was positive, but the rate of growth of employment was negative (i.e. employment fell). However, in the UK productivity increases were due to the fall in the rate of employment exceeding the fall in the rate of value added. In the 1980s the rate of manufacturing employment growth was actually negative in many countries. Since the rate of growth of value added was about the same as before, in most places productivity rates were generally higher. The UK had the greatest fall in employment, just as in the 1970s, but its value-added growth rate was much higher, resulting in a much stronger labour productivity growth rate.

A drawback of the figures in Table 16, page 43, that compare growth rates in productivity is that there is no *base level* with which to make comparisons. Productivity may have been lower in the UK than in most other major industrial economies in the last 20–30 years, but the data would be of more use if it were possible to compare the initial productivity levels. The problem here is to convert the output figures to a common currency unit. Table 17 shows such a comparison using both current exchange rates and a purchasing power parity (PPP) series; the latter adjusts for exchange rate fluctuations.[5] These figures reveal that in general productivity levels were converging during 1970–90. In 1970 the US had a productivity level 50% above the OECD average (in purchasing power parity terms), but by 1990 this had fallen to a level 20% above the average. France and Germany were near the OECD average in 1970 and since then they have increased their relative level. The same can be said for Italy, although it started from a lower base. Japan had a productivity level 30% below the OECD average in 1970, but has since moved much closer to that average. The relative position of Canada has fallen, although it remains above the average. On the basis of these figures the relative productivity level of the UK would not appear to have changed much in the period, despite its recent faster rate of growth of productivity.

The productivity data given here are in terms of output per person. If productivity levels are compared on an output per person-hour basis the relative position of Japan is lower while the relative positions of most European countries are higher because of the

longer hours worked in the former.

When comparing relative UK labour productivity in marketable (i.e private sector) services with France, Germany and the US between 1973–93, O'Mahoney et al. (1996) found a different pattern from that experienced in manufacturing. The deterioration in Britain's position in total market services relative to France and Germany in the 1970s was less marked than in manufacturing. Compared with the US productivity in the UK improved in the 1970s. In the 1980s, productivity in Britain improved relative to the US and France but deteriorated relative to Germany. 1989–93 saw a further weakening of Britain's position compared to Germany and, to a lesser extent, the US. The growth rates of UK output and employment in market services were lower than in the other countries, except during 1979–89, when Britain's average growth rate of output exceeded all the other countries and there was higher employment growth in the UK relative to France and Germany.

A country's price competitiveness depends not just on its productivity levels, but also on other factors such as relative real wages and the value of the exchange rate. A fall in the value of a country's currency in terms of others (i.e. a depreciation) reduces the relative price of its goods, thereby improving its competitive position, although the price of imported goods rises. A country's competitive position will be improved still further if its real wage levels are relatively low. Unit or average labour costs (i.e. labour costs per unit of output) are dependent upon both wages and labour productivity.

Indices giving the effective exchange rate, relative unit labour costs, and relative export prices of the UK, expressed in terms of other OECD economies, are shown in Table 18, page 46 (see also Box 3.1, page 44). As can be seen from the figures in the first column of the table, sterling appreciated sharply between 1977 and 1981, due to the effects of North Sea oil. This led to a rise in relative export prices. The appreciation of sterling coincided with a period of rapidly rising labour costs and relatively low productivity, causing an equally sharp rise in relative unit labour costs.

The overall loss of competitiveness during the period amounted to over 50%, which was, according to the International Monetary Fund (the IMF), the largest loss ever recorded. The impact of North Sea oil on the UK economy is often referred to as an example of 'Dutch disease', a term coined to describe events in Holland following the discovery of natural gas there

Table 17 *Relative labour productivity in the business sector, 1970–90, Selected Countries[a]*

	1970	1975	1980	1985	1990
Based on purchasing power parities					
UK	87	88	89	90	90
US	151	141	130	126	120
Germany	96	98	101	102	105
France	101	104	106	108	115
Italy	94	99	105	100	102
Japan	70	74	79	83	89
Canada	115	118	113	114	108
Based on current exchange rates					
UK	69	72	91	73	85
US	178	139	118	146	105
Germany	94	114	123	88	119
France	95	118	126	93	123
Italy	74	80	90	74	107
Japan	57	72	81	88	106
Canada	150	140	109	124	106

[a]Labour productivity expressed as output per employee. OECD average equals 100 in each year.

Source: Adapted from OECD (1993).

Table 18 *Measures of price competitiveness for the UK, 1976–94[a]*

	Relative export prices	Relative unit labour costs	Effective exchange rate	Export performance[b] (%)
1976	84	73	n/a	–3.7
1977	88	72	n/a	2.6
1978	94	80	n/a	–2.7
1979	101	94	n/a	–3.6
1980	112	115	n/a	–3.1
1981	111	119	122.7	–4.1
1982	104	113	117.9	2.0
1983	101	103	110.4	0.5
1984	102	99	105.8	1.0
1985	100	101	106.2	2.4
1986	95	93	99.7	–1.1
1987	97	93	95.7	0.2
1988	102	98	101.7	–3.7
1989	99	100	99.1	–1.3
1990	100	97	97.9	1.1
1991	100	100	100	–2.3
1992	97	96	96.5	–1.4
1993	96	86	87.7	–0.4
1994	101	91	88.8	1.7

[a]The figures refer to manufacturing. Index 1991 = 100, expressed in a common currency. A fall in any of the indices in the first three columns denotes an improvement in competitiveness.
[b]These figures refer to all goods. They show the percentage change from the previous period.

Source: Adapted from *OECD Economic Outlook*, December 1995.

in the late 1950s. The appreciation of the pound was undoubtedly an important contributory factor in the decline of manufacturing at the time; other factors also played a part. The high interest rate policy adopted by the government from 1979 as part of its strict monetarist strategy to reduce inflation militated against a lowering of the exchange rate and exacerbated manufacturing's problems. Between 1979 and 1981, real manufacturing output and manufacturing employment both fell by 14.2%. The effect that the loss of price competitiveness has on manufacturing output and jobs may well be compounded by the behaviour of multinational firms, which may move a greater share of their activities to their overseas subsidiaries rather than face the prospect of having to raise prices or suffer reduced profits at home.

The fall in competitiveness was followed by an upward trend as the effective exchange rate and rela-

tive unit labour costs both fell. (It should come as no great surprise that these two indices often seem to move in the same direction, since a depreciation in the value of sterling against other currencies means that UK relative unit labour costs, measured in a common currency, must fall.) It is estimated that by 1985/6 the fall in the exchange rate was sufficient for competitiveness to have returned to 1977 levels. However, the trend was then reversed and the effective exchange rate rose, firms again suffering from the effects of an overvalued exchange rate. Their problems were increased by the high interest rates that also existed at this time due to the underlying weakness of sterling and the desire to combat inflation. In 1990, the UK entered the Exchange Rate Mechanism (ERM) of the EU at £1 = DM2.95, a level which was considered by many to be a high one and which would harm competitiveness. These considerations were confirmed when the UK was forced to abandon the ERM in September 1992, since when there has been a sharp fall in both the effective exchange rate and in relative unit labour costs; in the second half of 1996 the slide was halted as the effective exchange rate rose by 14%.

It would seem from the above analysis that the main indicator of a country's competitiveness is its exchange rate. The other measures of competitiveness are influenced by it and tend to be correlated with it. A fall in the effective exchange rate will almost certainly improve competitiveness. Exports will become relatively cheaper (although at the same time imports will become relatively more expensive). The effect on the volume of exports sold depends on the relative price elasticity of demand for exports and on how firms react to any changes in the comparative profitability of exporting (i.e. the prices of exports compared with domestic prices). The price elasticity of demand is a measure of the responsiveness of the demand for a product to a change in its price (in this case measured in terms of the exchange rate) *cet. par.* (see also Section 7.5).

The effect of changes in the exchange rate on exports can be seen more clearly by referring to the fourth column of figures in Table 18. The movements in export performance tend to follow the changes in the effective exchange rate: as the exchange rate falls so export performance improves. In fact, there is often quite a long time lag between the initial price, or exchange rate, change and the effect on the volume of goods sold abroad. In other words, the price elasticity of demand for exports is relatively low in the short term and higher, or more elastic, over a longer period. If export prices fall by, say, 5% the volume of exports does not respond in similar fashion and immediately rise by 5%. Initially, export volume may not rise by much at all and so the value of exports declines. Eventually, after a period of one to two years, consumers respond to the new prices, the volume of exports may rise by more than 5% and the value of exports increases. Any change in the value of a currency will also have an effect on import prices and on the volume of imports, although there may be a similarly delayed response. The net effect on the visible balance or on the balance of trade (the balance of the value of all goods imported and exported) depends, in good part, on the relative elasticities of demand for exports and imports. It is reckoned that UK exports are more responsive in the long term to price changes than are UK imports, although manufactured imports tend to be more responsive to price changes than are other types of imports. A fall in the value of the currency should cause a significant increase in the volume of exports sold. Therefore, it should lead to an eventual increase in the total value of exports. However, there will be a much smaller negative impact on the volume of imports, producing an eventual drop in the total value of imports. In other words, there should be a positive long-term net effect on the balance of trade following a fall in the value of the currency.[6]

Non-price measures

Data on differences in, and the importance of, non-price factors are quite rare because they are very difficult to quantify. Factors such as product reliability, quality, design and service are all likely to be heavily dependent on the levels of investment, innovation and skills in an economy. The importance of product design is indicated by the fact that for manufactured products, half the life-cycle cost, on average, is fixed or committed by the original design; as much as 80% of a particular product's final costs may be set by the time that production actually begins.[7] As has been pointed out, the UK's relative performance in the crucial areas of investment, innovation and so on has been quite poor.

Institutional factors may also have a part to play in this context. In German companies the role of the *Meister*, a supervisor with responsibility for both technical and training functions, is considered vital in maintaining production and quality. Japanese firms usually have close relationships with their main sup-

pliers. These relationships often mean that the supplying firms are heavily dependent on, or more specifically subcontracted to, a single customer (although recent trends suggest a gradual move away from such a system). The suppliers are obliged to meet stringent quality and delivery standards, although this may have the effect of raising costs of production. Institutional factors such as these mean that German and Japanese firms are geared to a system of continuous product improvement throughout the company (NEDC, 1991). Product innovation in the UK, on the other hand, is more a step-by-step process that takes place within specialised departments. A recent DTI (1995) study of the British and Japanese car parts industry found a large gap in quality levels between the two countries, a situation that was put down mainly to poor management in the UK plants.

The fact that the income elasticity of demand for UK imports is higher than that for UK exports, and that for manufactures the difference between the two is particularly large, provides some supportive evidence of a quality gap between Britain and elsewhere. This means that as incomes rise, better quality goods from abroad may replace those that are produced in the UK. However, there is some evidence that the income elasticity of demand for UK manufactured exports has been rising since the early 1980s as more efficient exporting firms replace the inefficient ones (Griffiths and Wall, 1995).

One way of assessing the relative importance of non-price factors is to compare the value per unit weight of exports between countries. This figure is determined by the division of the total value of exports in a particular industry by the total weight of those exports. In 1987, the value per ton of German exports in agricultural machinery was 3.6 times the UK level, in machine tools it was 5.6 times the UK level and in electrical pumps 4.6 times the British figure. The equivalent figures for the value per ton of Japanese exports were much closer to the UK levels, but nonetheless the Japanese figures were still higher. In agricultural machinery the Japanese figure was 1.2 times the UK figure, in machine tools 4.5 times the UK level and in pumps 1.3 times the British level (NEDC, 1991). These differences are unlikely to be explained in price terms, since if British goods were that much cheaper they would presumably account for a rising share of world markets, which they do not. It may be that UK firms are gearing their products more to the lower quality, and presumably lower technology, ends of the various markets. Evidence to this effect has been provided by the series of NIESR studies on particular industries mentioned in Section 3.2. The main conclusion of these studies was that the British firms either had lower rates of investment and consequently used less advanced equipment or employed a less qualified and less skilled workforce, or both were true.

On the other hand, there is no evidence that in general the UK is moving away from the production of high-technology manufacturing products. In fact, as was pointed out earlier, employment has fallen less in the relatively high-technology manufacturing industries of the UK than it has within its other manufacturing industries. The UK and Germany are the only two OECD countries where high-technology jobs represent more than 6% of total business sector employment. However, in particular industries there is evidence of lower quality British goods. The British products may also be relatively poorly marketed, although comparative research in this area is very limited. A comprehensive study of UK manufacturing firms concluded that, of the firms investigated, most performed badly on a wide range of marketing measures, covering overall marketing strategy, quality control, awareness of customer needs, branding, distribution policy and the development of new markets.[8]

It is impossible to say whether price or non-price factors are more important determinants of the competitiveness of the UK's products. In truth, it is likely to be a combination of the two, although in practice it may be difficult to disentangle the effects of each. Low investment may lead to relatively low productivity levels and high unit labour costs. It may also produce low quality products. Alternatively, rigid quality and delivery standards and checks may raise overall costs of production. An overvalued exchange rate may cause British companies to move down-market in order to maintain market shares. In order to compensate for the high foreign exchange values of their goods abroad firms may cut their prices. This may trim their profit margins, in which case they will have less profit to plough back into their businesses and less available for investment, and so on. However, whatever the relationship between price and non-price factors, the industrial sector, and especially manufacturing, is more prone to suffer from the effects of international competition because manufactured goods are more likely to be traded than, say, services. The question remains whether this really matters, or if instead in a 'deindustrialised' society other industries and industrial sectors can simply replace a depleted manufacturing base.

3.4 IS MANUFACTURING IMPORTANT?

Whatever definition of deindustrialisation is chosen, the UK economy seems to fit the bill. This is particularly true with respect to its manufacturing industry, where in the last 20–25 years the overall number of jobs lost in the UK has been greater, the growth of real output has been smaller and the export performance has been worse than elsewhere. On the other hand, manufacturing is in decline in virtually all the major industrial economies, and other industries and sectors, notably services, are replacing it.

A factor that is often overlooked amidst the changes that are taking place within industrial structures is that there is an increasing blurring of the lines between manufacturing and services (OECD, 1993). Services like design, marketing, distribution and advertising account for an important share of the inputs of manufacturing firms. General Motors (GM), one of the largest manufacturing companies in the world, has as one of its biggest suppliers a healthcare provider, Blue Cross-Blue Shield. In terms of output, one of GM's largest products is financial services, which along with EDS, its computing-services section (which was made an independent unit in 1995), accounts for 20% of total revenue. Twenty percent of Sony's revenue is derived from films and music. If marketing, finance, design and after-sales facilities are included, service activities account for about 50% of its business.

If the interrelationships between manufacturing and services are analysed in greater depth, it would appear that services are much more likely to be dependent on manufacturing firms than the other way about. This has important implications for employment:

The rate of purchase of service output by manufacturing firms is a much larger proportion per unit of gross output than is the reverse, namely, the purchase of manufactured goods for use as inputs by services. Thus manufacturing sustains a far higher proportion of jobs at any time than it appears to do from standard measures of sectoral employment shares (Greenhalgh, 1994:13).

It is also the case that a number of services, like transport, distribution and financial services such as banking and insurance, are complementary to manufactured goods. An increase in demand for manufactures would also lead to a rise in demand for such services. Therefore, despite the greater labour intensity of most services, a large number of jobs in the service sector are probably dependent on the general prosperity of manufacturing.

There is evidence of a faster rate of productivity growth in manufacturing compared with the rest of the economy for the UK (Leslie, 1993) and for other OECD economies (Oulton, 1994). A country with a large and thriving manufacturing sector may therefore have greater potential for rapid economic growth. A major reason why productivity levels are higher in manufacturing than elsewhere is that there tends to be a greater propensity to innovate in manufacturing industries. Despite the rapid rate of technical progress in some service industries, such as telecomunications and financial services, in general there is a greater intensity of innovation in new products and processes in UK manufacturing than in the economy as a whole, whether measured by numbers of patents or by survey records (Greenhalgh, 1994). A higher level of technical progress, especially in cost-reducing new processes, lowers the relative price of manufactured goods and improves the standard of living of consumers. Furthermore, if new manufacturing products are not being developed in the UK then they will have to be imported and this will add to any pre-existing balance-of-payments problems.

A declining manufacturing sector means that something should take its place in order to earn the foreign currency to pay for the UK's imports. Oil, however, has been diminishing in importance for some years as an export earner. Some services can be traded internationally, for example finance, tourism and telecommunication activities, but others like hotels, meals in restaurants or hairdressing cannot be transported across space. Therefore, they cannot earn the foreign currency required for imports. Besides, it is estimated that, in general, a fall of 1% in manufactured exports needs a compensatory 3% rise in the export of services (House of Lords, 1985). This is because the value added of manufactured goods is reckoned to be three times as great as that of service products. A period of rapid economic growth promotes imports, especially of manufactured goods, but insufficient foreign exchange may be earned to pay for them.

Despite the closer links between manufacturing and services, and the fact that many large manufacturing firms are also large-scale providers of services, manufacturing remains vital to a country's economic well-being. It has important implications for employment and not just within its own industries. Service firms are more likely to be dependent on manufacturers than are manufacturers on service firms. It can also

have a significant effect on economic growth. There is evidence that manufacturing possesses higher rates of innovation and higher levels of productivity than other parts of the economy. Finally, manufactured goods are tradeable. No other part of the economy is capable of entirely replacing its capacity as a foreign exchange earner.

3.5 THE STRUCTURE OF THE UK LABOUR MARKET

Employment characteristics and comparisons

It has been noted that there has been a major shift in the industrial pattern of the workforce in most OECD countries. In virtually every industrialised economy the service sector now accounts for a majority of the jobs. This is one change amongst many significant alterations that have taken place in employment patterns. Some of these changes have occurred over long periods, while others have taken place more recently.

The *working population* or *labour force* of the UK is about 27.5 million. This is just under half the total population, a proportion which is roughly the norm in an industrial society. The workforce consists of those people of working age (currently 16–64 for men and 16–59 for women; a state retirement age of 65 for women is to be gradually phased in) who are available for work. They are said to be *economically active*. It excludes students, housewives, the sick, those in prison, those taking early retirement and others; these groups are referred to as the *economically inactive*. The *workforce* comprises both the employed and the unemployed. The *activity* or *participation rate* is the ratio of the working (employed and unemployed) to the total population, or to any section of it whether by age, sex or race.

In the UK the total number of people in employment (including HM forces and work-related government training programmes) has varied depending on the state of overall economic activity, although there has been a small rise in total employment during 1984–94, as Table 19, page 50, confirms. The slow rise in employment has been a feature in most Western European economies. This is particularly apparent when contrasted with the US or Japan. Since 1960, employment has increased by 84% in the US and by 46% in Japan. In the same period employment within the EU has risen by just 6% in total.

Table 19 *Composition of the workforce in the UK, 1984–94 (000s)*

| | Employees in employment | | | | | | | |
| | Male | | Female | | | | | |
	Full-time	Part-time	Full-time	Part-time	Self-employed	Total employed[a]	Unemployed	Workforce
1984	10 829	790	5234	3889	2618	23 854	2910	26 764
1985	10 811	821	5312	3976	2714	24 128	3057	27 185
1986	10 625	852	5328	4081	2726	24 152	3103	27 255
1987	10 544	887	5481	4169	2996	24 699	2778	27 477
1988	10 766	932	5754	4288	3142	25 533	2225	27 758
1989	10 795	923	5922	4494	3425	26 319	1639	27 958
1990	10 752	1016	5912	4700	3471	26 564	1461	28 025
1991	10 204	1049	5738	4703	3316	25 640	2168	27 808
1992	9884	1070	5680	4725	3136	25 092	2627	27 719
1993	9618	1084	5618	4738	3098	24 722	2812	27 534
1994	9501	1134	5532	4826	3206	24 731	2545	27 276

[a]Includes HM forces and training schemes.   Source: *Economic Review Data Supplement,* September 1995.

Table 19 shows that any growth in employment in the UK in recent years has come entirely from increases in part-time employment, particularly among women, and in self-employment. During 1984–94 the number of full-time employees fell by 1 030 000 against a rise in part-time employment of 1 281 000 and an increase in self-employment of 588 000. In 1973, 16% of those in work in the UK were in *part-time jobs*. This figure had risen to 24.1% in 1994.[9] It is a higher percentage than in the US, where 18% of the workforce are part-timers, and Japan, where the figure is 21%, and only Denmark in the EU has a larger proportion of its workforce in part-time employment.

A rising female participation rate has occurred in all industrialised countries. The *male participation rate* in the UK has been falling for over 20 years, as it has in all major economies save Japan. This has been due to the combined effects of greater numbers staying on in higher education and more people opting for early retirement. In 1973 the figure stood at 93%; by 1993 it had fallen to 83.3%. The *female participation rate,* however, rose from 53.2% in 1973 to 64.3% in 1993. This is lower than in the US, where the equivalent figure is 69.1%, but it is higher than Japan and higher than in any other country in the EU, bar Denmark. Nearly half of working women in the UK work part-time. Much of the increase in demand for female labour has come from the expansion of the service sector, since certain service-sector jobs are particularly

suited to part-time employment. While most part-time jobs are considered to be permanent, staff in retailing and hotels and restaurants can be taken on during the busiest parts of the day, week or year. The public sector services like healthcare, education and administration have always employed large numbers of women, many on a part-time basis.

These trends have implications for profit-maximising firms. In the UK part-timers have traditionally been cheaper to employ than full-timers; they have had lower sick pay, holiday pay, redundancy and pension entitlements. In other EU countries, part-timers have usually had similar employment rights to full-time employees; in addition, social security taxes are normally only payable up to an earnings ceiling in these countries, in which case it can be more expensive to employ two part-timers than one full-timer. However, in March 1994, a House of Lords ruling announced that part-time workers in the UK should have the same employment rights as full-timers, thus overturning the principles enshrined in the Employment Protection Act of 1978 which gave weaker rights to those working less than 16 hours per week and no rights at all to those working less than eight hours per week. In September 1994, the European Court of Justice ruled that part-time workers should have the same rights as full-timers to join company pension schemes.

The growth in part-time employment is part of what is thought to be a trend in most industrial societies, and especially the UK and the US, towards more *flexible* patterns of work. It is claimed that, in an increasingly competitive industrial environment and with a more rapid pace of technological change, greater emphasis is placed on the need to adjust labour inputs to changes in demand as rapidly and as cheaply as possible; improved labour flexibility can achieve this. Flexibility can take a variety of forms (see Box 3.2).

Box 3.2 *Flexible work patterns*

Flexibility can refer to *numbers of jobs*: part-time, temporary or short-term and fractional appointments (i.e. a permanent post but at a fraction of a full-time one, such as a 0.5) create a greater number of individual jobs. Part-time employment is certainly growing, although data on how many people are actually employed on a short-term or fractional basis are in short supply. Gregg and Wadsworth (1995) point to increased job insecurity in the UK labour market in the sense that, between 1975 and 1993, the percentage of the working population of the UK who could be classified as full-time employees with tenure (i.e. having worked long enough to secure statutory minimum employment rights, such as protection from unfair dismissal) fell from 55.5% to 35.9%, while the share classified as having no tenure rose from 3.6% to 12.8%. Much of the increase in those without tenure has been due to changes in the qualification period for employment rights from six months in 1975 to one year in 1985 and to two years in 1993. The incidence of temporary work for entry jobs is relatively high. It is estimated that 43% of jobs that people are leaving are full-time permanent compared with 27% of re-entry jobs.[10] Part-time and temporary posts are both cheaper for firms to fill and often easier for them to do without should they need to reduce their number of staff. On the other hand, part-time and fractional jobs may fit the employment needs of some workers, especially the growing numbers of working mothers. Most people on part-time contracts claim that they are not seeking full-time positions.

Flexibility can also mean *flexibility of function*, i.e. workers who possess a variety of skills or who are able to undertake a range of tasks within a firm. This aspect of flexibility is the one which has, at least until fairly recently, probably been the least developed within British firms. It has always been quite common in service industries like hotel and catering and distribution and in the construction industry for workers to perform a number of different tasks. The introduction of lean production techniques, traditionally associated with Japanese firms and that rely on an increased level of automation, has hastened a greater flexibility of job function in British industry, especially in highly segmented product markets (see Chapter 6). Evidence of the flexibility of function within large Japanese companies is provided by the degree of job-changing: in some Japanese firms it is estimated that production-line workers change jobs every three to five months; managers change theirs every three to five years.[11]

A third aspect of flexibility refers to *time*. Firms have introduced greater flexibility in working hours for their staff.

Arrangements vary and so the evidence is fairly anecdotal; more companies are introducing contracts whereby staff are employed on the basis that a person is available for work when needed. As regards the numbers of hours worked, the average working week in the UK, including overtime, for all full-time workers was about 43 hours in 1994. The figure for male manual workers in manufacturing, including overtime, was over 45 hours per week. This is the highest figure in the EU. The length of the average working week in the UK has actually risen in the last decade, contrary to its downward trend in most other EU economies. There is also a wider distribution of hours worked in the UK than elsewhere in the EU. This may be explained by the fact that there is a higher proportion of part-time workers in the UK; there is also lower statutory regulation of working time. However, in November 1996, the European Court of Justice ruled that the EU Working Time Directive should apply to the UK, despite the objections of the UK government. This provides for a 48-hour average maximum working week on health and safety grounds, although there are exemptions such as transport workers and doctors in training. Workers in the EU as a whole work fewer hours than in the US or Japan, at least when the position is viewed over the complete year. It is estimated that people in the EU work, on average, 10% fewer hours each year than in the US and 20% fewer than in Japan. In the last 20 years, the total yearly number of hours worked has fallen in all industrial economies, but it has fallen most quickly within the EU, due to the greater statutory controls on working time. It may also be the result of the lower inequality of earnings in EU countries in general. Employees continue to put in relatively long hours where the perceived rewards for doing so are large, even though there may be a negative effect on productivity after a certain number of hours' work have been completed.

Flexibility of time can also be defined in terms of the extent of *labour mobility and tenure* in the labour market. In the UK in 1992, about 18% of workers had been with their current employer for under one year and 56% for less than five years. This compares with figures of 29% and 62% respectively for the US, but only 10% and 37% respectively in the case of Japan. In 1992 the average number of years that people had been with their present employer ranged from a low of 6.7 years in the US to a high of 10.9 years in Japan. In the UK the figure was 7.9 years, compared with 9.8 in Spain, 10.1 in France and 10.4 in Germany. In all countries, women have a shorter average job tenure, usually about two-thirds the average male duration. These figures exaggerate the extent of labour turnover, since they do not measure completed spells of employment but only how long someone has been employed in their current job.

Average job tenure has fallen in the UK and the US in the last two decades, although there has been a marked difference in the experiences of males and females. According to Gregg and Wadsworth (1995), median tenure for men has fallen by 20% in the UK since 1975, whereas median tenure for women has risen slightly. One person in five now stays in a job for less than a year, compared with 15% in 1975; only one person in ten has been in a job for more than 20 years, compared with 15% in 1975. Part-time work lasts, on average, about half as long as a full-time job. Temporary jobs typically last only one-tenth as long. Short-term job 'churning' has also increased. However, well-educated prime-age males seem to remain largely immune to these trends: there is little evidence of greater job instability or insecurity for this group of workers. In Japan, on the other hand, average job tenure has increased over this period. Japanese firms have always been

more likely than companies in Western Europe and North America to adopt a system of 'lifetime employment' for their employees, although this has mainly been confined to adult males who work full-time for large organisations; there are some signs that Japanese work practices are changing, albeit slowly, and that workers at all levels are having to accept the fact that their job may not be for life.

A final aspect of work practice flexibility that can be considered is *wage flexibility*, whereby pay is more closely related to the performance of a firm. In recent years, profit-sharing and productivity-bargaining schemes, usually involving tax concessions, have become increasingly popular forms of remuneration in many countries, including the UK, the US, Canada and France. However, the schemes have mainly been confined to the largest firms and in general bonuses have been found not to be strongly linked to corporate performance. In the UK the 1996 Budget began the process of phasing out tax relief on profit-related pay schemes.

Firms may achieve lower costs through greater flexibility in work practices, at least in the short term. They may also be able to take on, or offload, some forms of labour more quickly when necessary. On the other hand, a degree of job security may enable both the firm and the employee to take a longer-term view of their respective positions. Employees may be more willing to invest their time acquainting themselves with a firm's products and customers if they know their jobs are reasonably secure. Firms may be more willing to invest in training their workforce if they know that the workers are likely to remain with the company and not take the benefits of the training elsewhere, particularly to a competitor. These issues are discussed in more detail in Chapter 14.

Given the fact that the concentration of production is higher in the UK than in most other industrialised countries, it is not surprising to find that it has a larger proportion of workers employed in medium- and large-sized firms than elsewhere. The UK also has a sizeable self-employed sector, as has been mentioned. The self-employed in the UK account for about 11.7% of the total workforce, compared with 7.6% in the US, 7.7% in Germany, 11.5% in Japan, but 22.3% in Italy. During 1979–90 the UK had the fastest rate of growth of self-employment, nearly 6% in total, of any OECD country. However, this may have been due to the success of policies to encourage the unemployed to become self-employed rather than to any growth of the

entrepreneurial spirit. Furthermore, as and when firms adopt more flexible work practices so their demand increases for self-employed outsiders to do jobs, for example in finance, insurance and business services, that were previously undertaken by full-timers (a process known as 'outsourcing').

Unemployment characteristics and comparisons

The workforce comprises the unemployed as well as the employed. During the last 15 years in the UK there have been the sharpest changes in unemployment in any post-war period; between 1979 and 1982, unemployment rose from about 5% of the workforce to almost 11%. It remained at about this level until 1987 and then fell quickly to 5.5% in 1990. Since then, unemployment again jumped sharply to more than 10% of the workforce by mid-1993, falling back to 8% by 1996. (Precise comparisons are difficult due to the 32 definitional changes in unemployment that have taken place in the UK from 1979 onwards.) Table 20 shows that in the 1970s and early 1980s, unemployment rates in the EU were, on average, lower than in the US. Japan's system of lifetime employment has always helped it to achieve a much lower rate of unemployment than in other industrialised economies. From the mid-1980s onwards, however, unemployment levels have been higher in the EU than in the US; in 1995, unemployment

Table 20 *Average rates of unemployment,[a] selected countries (%)*

	Average Rate p.a.	
	1974–83	1984–94
UK	7.0	9.5
US	7.3	6.6
Germany	4.0	6.0
France	5.7	10.3
Italy	7.2	10.4
Japan	2.2	2.5

[a] Figures are standardised rates (showing the percentages of the total labour force) and are based on ILO/OECD guidelines.

Source: Adapted from *OECD Economic Outlook*, December 1995.

in the EU stood at an average of a little over 11.0%.

Changes in unemployment depend on the difference between the growth of the labour force and variations in the number of jobs. If the labour force increases, the number of jobs must grow simply to hold unemployment steady. In the 1980s the labour force of the EU grew at a faster rate than previously, as the population of working age increased and more women entered the labour market. However, the same changes also occurred in the US. In fact, the labour force grew more quickly in the US (and in Japan) than in the EU. The difference has been that, in the US, the growth in employment has outstripped the growth of the labour force, whereas the reverse has been true for the EU as a whole. In the UK, unemployment has been falling since mid-1993. It remains to be seen how many of the newly employed stay so on a permanent basis.

Institutional patterns and comparisons

About one-third of the UK labour force belong to trade unions, a fall from 1980 when union density formed 52% of the workforce. The proportion has fallen as employment has shifted from manufacturing to services, in which it has usually been more difficult to organise workers, as the proportion of part-time workers has grown and as a result of the industrial relations legislation in the 1980s that reduced union powers. A similar decline in trade union membership has occurred in many other industrialised economies. In Germany the percentage of the workforce in trade unions has fallen from 40% in 1980 to 34% in 1992, in France from 20% in 1980 to only 10% in 1992, in the US from 25% to 15% and in Japan from 33% in 1980 to 28% in 1992. Union membership in the UK is very concentrated, with about 80% of trade unionists belonging to the largest 20 unions. The current trend is for the largest unions to merge; the concentration of membership is likely to increase. On the other hand, collective bargaining on behalf of members in the UK tends to be relatively decentralised, taking place at the individual plant or single employer level. This is similar to the situation in the US, although it is in contrast to the more centralised and industry- or economy-wide bargaining that still predominates in many other Western European economies. Evidence on the impact of unions on relative wages in the UK and the US suggests that they are able to raise wages above the non-union level, but there are wide variations between industries; studies suffer from the difficulties of trying to compare the wage levels of similar unionised and non-unionised workers (see also Section 14.6).

Wage-fixing by institutions is virtually non-existent in the UK. Most of the remaining Wage Councils, set up originally to protect the pay of various groups of low-paid workers by establishing minimum rates, were abolished in 1993. Agriculture is the only industry now covered by any form of minimum wage legislation, the Agricultural Wages Boards setting minimum wages for various grades of workers. Most other countries in the EU operate some kind of minimum wage policy, although they vary widely in their level and coverage. In Ireland only a small minority of workers are covered. The Belgian system is nationwide and the legal minimum is set at 66% of average earnings. Germany and Italy do not possess a minimum wage policy *per se*, but national collective agreements have established wage floors in many industries. The US, Canada and Japan also have statutory minimum wage policies, although in the former two countries minimum wages are set quite low, at only about one-third of average male earnings. The US minimum wage of $4.25 per hour was raised to $4.75 in October 1996 and is due to increase to $5.15 in September 1997. The arguments about whether minimum wages protect the living standards of workers in low-paid jobs or instead cause greater unemployment among the workers they are supposed to help are taken further in Section 14.5.

3.6 CONCLUSIONS

Industrial structure refers to the relative importance of different industries in an economy and to the patterns of transactions between them. Industries can be divided into three broad sectors, primary, secondary (or industrial) and tertiary. Structural change can be explained by changes in demand and supply conditions, combined with the effects of foreign competition and the impact of the activities of multinational firms. In all industrial economies there has been a significant secular shift of resources from the primary to the secondary sector and subsequently from the secondary into the tertiary sector; the process began sooner in the UK than elsewhere because of its earlier industrialisation.

The main constituent of the secondary sector is manufacturing. There has been a relative decline in the importance of manufacturing in both output and employment terms in most industrial economies, a process known as deindustrialisation; the decline has been particularly marked in the UK. Deindustrialisation can also refer to an absolute decline in manufacturing output and employment or to the trade performance of the manufacturing sector. Within manufacturing there has been a shift from low-tech to high-tech industries in OECD countries.

Various hypotheses of structural change in the UK are considered: the stages of development hypothesis and the crowding out argument both lack empirical support, while competition from newly industrialised Asian economies is too small-scale to offer an effective account. Structural weaknesses in the British economy, such as the industrial relations system, the level and nature of education and training and the investment and innovation record, may have been important determinants of the decline in its industrial fortunes; they have resulted in relatively low levels of productivity and, it is argued, have made the UK's products less competitive abroad. However, since the late 1970s the UK has benefitted from higher productivity growth than in many other industrial economies; evidence on relative productivity growth using a common base indicates convergence.

A country's effective exchange rate would appear to be the most important indicator of its price competitiveness; other indicators, such as relative export prices and relative unit labour costs are influenced by it and tend to be correlated with it. There is evidence to suggest that in the past the UK has suffered at times from a lack of competitiveness caused by an overvalued exchange rate and the result of poor quality products. More recently, a fall in the effective exchange rate and in relative unit labour costs has led to an improvement in price competitiveness; as more efficient firms have replaced less efficent ones, so non-price competitiveness may also have benefited.

The strategies and vision of individual firms, by propelling developments in their respective industries, may stimulate improvements in performance in their respective industries; there is evidence that the firm may well be an important source of structural change.

The significance of the manufacturing sector for a trading nation like the UK is considered. The growing interrelationships between manufacturing and services are noted, although it is argued that services are more dependent on manufacturing than the other way about. There is evidence of a faster rate of productivity growth in manufacturing than in other parts of the economy, a function of the higher propensity to innovate in manufacturing. Manufacturing is also an important foreign exchange earner.

The main growth in employment in the UK in recent times has come from increases in part-time jobs, especially among women, and in self-employment. The growth in part-time employment may be regarded as one element in the trend towards a more flexible labour market, although such flexibility can be characterised in a number of ways: numerical and functional, and in terms of time, mobility and wages. Trade union density has fallen quite significantly in most industrialised economies in the last 15–20 years as labour has shifted from manufacturing to services and as the proportion of part-time workers has grown. Unlike most industrial economies the UK has virtually no minimum wage-setting policy; only agriculture has a Wages Board. However, the level and coverage of agreements varies widely between other countries.

Case Study One: Examples of 'entrepreneurial' firms[12]

William Cook manufactures steel castings in the UK. In 1978, demand for the product was declining, there was excess capacity in the industry and most British steel-casting businesses were operating at a loss. Cook had a small 2% market share, but in the early 1980s it undertook an investment programme with the objectives of improving efficiency, quality and capacity. However, it chose to remain in the lowest price part of the market, rather than opt for a high-value differentiated niche. Its emphasis on service to customers and quality of product led to increased market share and profits. Further market share gains resulted from an aggressive takeover policy, so that by 1988 it had become the largest firm in the industry, with a 30% market share. The Cook strategy of concentrating on reliability and quality may have stimulated other firms in the industry to follow suit; market demand and industry profitability have both risen in the 1990s, although to what extent these changes have been due to improved economic conditions rather than individual firm strategy is open to question.

In the US banking industry, Banc One has helped to stimulate both its own and market demand through a series of innovative policies. In the late 1980s and early 1990s, the industry suffered from excess capacity and falling profitability. Banc One, a small regional bank from Ohio, went against industry trends by concentrating on the retail and small commercial customer segments of the market. It developed an efficient data processing facility, which enabled it to take on work from other banks, and it placed much greater emphasis on customer service. Having established a good local reputation, it grew rapidly through a process of internal expansion accompanied by an active merger policy, in which strict financial targets were set for the acquirees. It also adopted a rule that it would not acquire an institution that is more than one-third its own size.[13] Banc One's growth strategy has been amply aided by the dismantling of the legal barriers in the late 1980s that had hindered the development of interstate banking in the US and which led to substantial entry by banks into other regional markets.

In the early 1980s, the EU domestic appliance market was also characterised by chronic excess capacity. The profits of the leading firms in the industry at the time, Indesit and Zanussi, were falling sharply. Plants had little resale value, which meant high sunk costs. Barriers to exit were compounded by government subsidies to inefficient domestic producers. Hotpoint, owned by General Electric of the US and GEC of the UK, was relatively small firm, with a 5% market share. In the early 1980s, against general market trends and projections, it invested in new plants, but on a smaller scale than had previously been regarded as optimal. For example, in 1982, it rebuilt its washing machine factory at Kinmel at half the optimum industry size. It concentrated on supplying a flexible product, tailored to the variable tastes of the individual national markets, in a mature market. This was accompanied by a distribution policy that concentrated more on the independent retailers than on the large retail chains. These strategies may have stimulated similar responses from rival firms, although the main structural change in the 1980s was the dramatic rise in market concentration due to a series of mergers and takeovers following the arrival of Electrolux into the industry (Bianchi and Forlai, 1993).

There are other cases of firms whose policies may have have had a significant influence on market performance by instigating structural change in the industry. The successful development and sale of the Swatch watch helped to revitalise the fortunes of the Swiss watch industry in the 1980s. However, in all these examples, changes in the external business environment also had an important impact on both individual firm and market profitability. Furthermore, the example of William Cook reveals that such firms may not always be successful. It expanded into the US in the late 1980s, but with some lack of foresight, and has since suffered a downturn in its fortunes.

Case Study Two: The impact of the exchange rate on international competitiveness and corporate strategies: the case of Toyota—a yen for better times?

The value of the Japanese yen has risen steadily during the last 15–20 years against most foreign currencies and especially against the dollar, although it depreciated quite sharply since 1995. In 1982, the yen dollar exchange rate was approximately Y235 to $1, by early 1995 the value of the yen had risen (and/or the value of the dollar had fallen) to around Y86 and by early 1997 it had fallen to around Y120. A progressive rise in the value of a currency relative to others means that the countries' exporters will need to adapt their policies continuously in order to remain competitive (although, as has been mentioned, a country's competitive position does not depend solely on its exchange rate). This is because an increase in value of a currency raises the price of goods sold in that currency. As a result, firms either have to try to sell at the higher price or try to lower their costs in order to maintain their profit margins. If the products that are sold abroad are manufactured goods, produced by multinational firms in highly competitive global markets, then the latter strategy may be the only viable option. Such a view was the one taken by Mr Hiroshi Okuda, Toyota's president, in 1995:

If Toyota raised export prices to adjust for the latest shift in the dollar it would price itself out of world markets (*The Financial Times*, 11 May 1995).

Toyota estimated that, at constant export prices, every Y1 shift in the value of the dollar, if sustained over a year, reduced Toyota's operating profit by Y10 billion. A rise in the value of a currency reduces the average value of that currency in terms of others at which firms expect to break even or cover their costs. In 1986, the breakeven value of the yen was reckoned to be over Y200 to $1; in 1995, it was estimated to be around Y90, although this has since been revised upwards to around Y100. Since about 35% of its annual domestic production of roughly four million units is exported, Toyota reacted to the latest rise in the value of the yen by instigating a two-year cost-reducing programme from 1993 to 1995. This lowered costs by $1.5 billion, or 1.8% of total costs. However, the Japanese commitment to lifetime employment meant that cuts in labour costs were mainly achieved by reducing working hours rather than by firing workers. Other cost savings were achieved by minimising the number of parts in new models and by using as many parts as possible from previous models.

The other main effect for Toyota of the rise in the value of the yen has been to increase its overseas production facilities. In 1995, Toyota produced about 1.2 million units abroad, mainly in the US. Between 1995 and 2000 (and despite the recent fall in the yen's value) it plans to increase its total output to six million units p.a., with virtually all the growth coming from expansion of its overseas facilities. Such overseas investment strategies have not been confined to car producers like Toyota. Overall, it is estimated that the proportion of Japan's manufacturing output overseas doubled in the decade to the mid-1990s to 10%. It now imports 90% of its pocket calculators and 66% of its colour TVs, mainly from Japanese 'offshore' plants in cheaper locations in South-east Asia. There are other effects of exchange rate fluctuations on corporate strategies to consider. The overseas plants tend to be mainly assembly operations (hence the term 'transplants' is frequently adopted), which means that a high-value yen raises the cost of imported Japanese parts. On the other hand, Toyota, like the other Japanese car producers, plans to use the overseas plants as bases from which to export to other countries in a particular region, and even back to Japan. In this way they can take advantage of a strong yen, although in the case of car production this reverse trade is only a small proportion of the total market. In 1995, Japan imported only about 7% of its total car sales, of which a third were made by Japanese-owned factories situated overseas. Where sales in Japan consist mainly of imports from Japanese subsidiaries abroad, however, as in calculators and TVs, the recent decline in the value of the yen can cause companies to revert to domestic production.

FURTHER READING

Blackaby, F. (ed.) (1978) *Deindustrialisation* (London, Heinemann/NIESR).

Kuznets, S. (1959) *Six Lectures on Economic Growth* (Toronto, Ontario, Free Press).

OECD, *Industrial Policy in OECD Countries, Annual Review*, 1994; *Employment Outlook*, July 1994; *Jobs Study*, 1995 (Paris, OECD).

NOTES

1. See *The Economist*, 11 January 1992, 'Innovation'.
2. The balance of payments records all the monetary transactions between the residents of a country and the rest of the world in a given period. The current account records the monetary transactions resulting from the import and export of goods (visibles) and services (invisibles). The capital account records all capital movements into and out of a country.
3. During 1980–90 the share of gross domestic fixed capital formation (GFCF) in GDP averaged 17.4% in the UK, 17.7% in the US, 20.5% in Germany and France, 21.5% in Italy and 29.5% in Japan (OECD Historical Statistics, 1960–90).
4. Television programme 'The Business', BBC, 17 August 1995.
5. The purchasing power parity (PPP) of a country's currency is the ratio of the price of a basket of goods in country A to the price of those goods in country B. If a basket of goods costs £5 in the UK and the same basket costs $10 in the US,

the PPP equals $10/£5. A PPP series represents a measure of the equilibrium exchange rate whereby the purchasing power of income is equalised across countries. In other words, the price of any product in the UK in sterling would be equal to the price of the product in US dollars multiplied by the relevant exchange rate, i.e. the sterling price of dollars, and so on across all countries. PPP figures should be treated with some caution. They are usually measured in gross output terms and so intermediate goods are ignored. If expenditure figures are used to calculate the respective GDPs, imports will be included and exports excluded. Finally, the choice of the base year may severely affect the figures.
6. The delayed response of consumers, at home and abroad, to the new set of relative prices following a devaluation or depreciation of a currency is known as the J-curve effect. The visible balance may deteriorate for one to two years before any improvement shows.
7. See *The Economist* 5 March 1994, 'Manufacturing Technology'.
8. See *The Financial Times* 4 May 1995, 'What's the Score?'
9. Definitons of what constitutes part-time employment vary from country to country. In the UK it is usually taken to refer to people working up to 16 hours per week.
10. See *The Guardian*, 11 November 1996, page 16, John Philpott and Nick Isles.
11. See *The Economist* 11 January 1992, *op. cit.*
12. These examples are taken from Baden-Fuller and Stopford (1992), although some of the conclusions are my own.
13. See *The Economist* 5 January 1991, 'How America's Banks Must Merge'.

Questions □ □ □

3.1 In the twentieth century services have accounted for an increasingly larger share of employment and output in all industrial societies. What reasons can you suggest for this trend? Can it lead to any problems for an economy?

3.2 The UK is the oldest industrial economy. Its private sector industry has also been starved of resources because of the growth of other parts of the economy. These two factors together can adequately account for the relative decline of the industrial sector of the UK since the Second World War. Critically evaluate these statements.

3.3 'Whatever definition of deindustrialisation is adopted the UK economy fulfils the particular criteria. Then again, the same can be said for most industrial economies.' Explain and discuss.

3.4 In the 1980s, output growth in most industrial economies was about the same as in the 1970s. Why, then, were productivity rates generally higher?

3.5 Discuss the relationship between the exchange rate and a country's competitive position, with particular reference to changes in the relative value of sterling in the last 20 years.

3.6 'A significant and rising part of the value added by manufacturers now consists of services' (*The Economist*, 19 March 1994). What sort of services? Discuss the problems that this may present for assessing structural change in an economy.

3.7 Explain what is meant by the female participation ratio. Why has it increased so rapidly in most industrial economies in the last 25 years?

3.8 Outline the different forms that flexible work patterns can take. Discuss their relative popularity in the UK.

3.9 Discuss the relative merits for firms of reducing average job tenure through the use of short-term contracts for employees.

3.10 In the US, employment grew by an average of 1.7% p.a. between 1977 and 1993, while at the same time the labour force increased by 1.4% p.a. In the major EU economies the reverse was true and the labour force tended to grow faster than employment during the same period. What do these different experiences imply about changes in unemployment in the two areas during this period?

CHAPTER 4

▶ *The Firm in Theory and Practice*

Chapter 1 briefly considered the essence of the firm in theory and in practice, with particular reference to the role and characteristics of the modern, large corporation. This chapter examines the nature of the firm in more detail, beginning by tracing the developments in the theory of the firm: it explores the relationships between traditional economic theory and the firm, discusses the *managerial* and *behavioural* theories of the firm and assesses more recent theoretical developments, such as *transaction cost* and *principal–agent* analyses. The internal organisation of the firm is examined at some length, the *U-form*, *M-form* and *matrix* forms of organisation all being critically evaluated. The nature of *entrepreneurship* is debated and its relationship with the firm is considered. The final section of the chapter details corporate institutional characteristics, such as *legal status*, *size distribution* and *multinational operations*. Since the book is mainly concerned with analysing the strategies of large firms, the nature and characteristics of multinational firms are examined in depth. At the end of the chapter there are two *case studies*. The first assesses the latest evidence on the capital structure and the performance of M-form organisations. The second examines the relative merits of Ford's matrix structure.

4.1 NEOCLASSICAL THEORY AND THE NATURE OF THE FIRM

In a perfectly competitive market the firm exerts no real power over its immediate environment. The major objective of neoclassical microeconomic theory was to analyse how market prices direct or allocate resources; firms simply play a bit-part within the overall scheme. In the Marshallian partial equilibrium approach, only a part of the system, such as an individual market, is examined; all other parts of the system are assumed to be unchanged. Firms and households represent the two groups of decision-makers. It is assumed that there are many buyers and many sellers in each market; individual participants therefore have little power to determine the price of any product or resource. Households aim to maximise their utility, or level of satisfaction from the combination of products that they purchase, subject to an income constraint. It is assumed that the owners/controllers of firms also have a single objective, namely to maximise profits. They sell a single and homogenous product, they produce it in a single plant and they have perfect knowledge of their costs of production and their revenues at different output levels. The assumption of the freedom of entry and exit of firms ensures that abnormal profit is purely a temporary phenomenon. In these circumstances each firm is seen purely as an abstract unit or *black box* whose sole function is to convert factors of production into output. The basis of neoclassical theory is the market and the interrelationship between market demand and market supply. Neoclassical theory as it relates to the firm is more a theory of supply, i.e. an explanation of how much is to be produced at a range of different prices, than a theory of the firm.

Such an analysis increasingly lacked empirical support, for even in the nineteenth century, firms were growing in size to the extent that they could dominate their markets. Such firms possessed the power or the discretion to make their own price and output decisions. They were engaged in strategic decision-making, for example in activities such as advertising and mergers. The fundamental problem of traditional theory was that it completely ignored the internal workings of the firm. Therefore, it provided no analysis of the decision-making process and no explanation of the factors that determine business success or failure.

The first person to tackle the intractabilities of the internal organisation of the firm was Coase (1937). His main concern was to determine why some types of economic activity were better co-ordinated by an enterpreneur than by the price mechanism. He concluded that firms exist because the price mechanism can be costly:

Table 21 *Developments in the theory of the firm*

Date	Theory/author	Premise/assumptions
Late nineteenth/ early twentieth centuries	Neoclassical	Firm viewed as 'black box' or abstract unit
1932	Berle and Means	Evidence of separation of ownership and control
1933	Robinson; Chamberlin	Theory of monopolistic competition
1937	Coase	Firm exists to minimise transaction costs
1939	Hall and Hitch	Evidence of markup pricing
Late 1950s/early 1960s	Managerial theories	Divorce of ownership and control; managerial objectives
Late 1950s/early 1960s	Behavioural theory	Bounded rationality; 'satisficing' behaviour
1972	Alchian and Demsetz	Team production as basis of the firm
1970s	Principal–agent analysis	Principal–agent relationships within the firm
Late 1970s/early 1980s	Williamson	Transaction cost theory of the firm

The main reason why it is profitable to establish a firm would seem to be that there is a cost of using the price mechanism (Coase, 1937:336).

The costs of using the price mechanism are various. There are problems of discovering the relevant prices. Secondly, there are costs involved in the negotiation of separate contracts for each market transaction. Thirdly, there are costs for buyers of of goods and services of negotiating long-term contracts in conditions of uncertainty. In other words, there are *transaction costs* involved in the price mechanism which necessitate the establishment of some alternative form of authority to the market, i.e. the firm, which can also allocate resources. The firm can internalise and minimise these costs.

Coase felt that the transaction costs mainly emanate from feelings of uncertainty about the future:

It seems improbable that a firm would emerge without the existence of uncertainty (Coase, 1937:338).

Why, then, do firms and markets co-exist, or, perhaps more pertinently, why do markets exist at all? Coase suggests that the main reason for this is the existence of managerial diseconomies of scale:

... as firms get larger there may be decreasing returns to the entrepreneur function, that is the costs of organising additional transactions within the firm may rise (Coase, 1937:340).

The increased costs of the managerial function place a kind of self-imposed limit on the size of the firm. It continues to increase in size only until the costs of arranging an additional transaction within the organisation is equal to the costs of organising the same transaction in a market or in another firm. Beyond that point other firms exist and market transactions between firms take place.

4.2 DEVELOPMENTS IN THE ANALYSIS OF THE FIRM

The increase in the size and power of the firm and the need to analyse markets that were not perfectly competitive led to a number of developments in the theory of the firm (see Table 21). In 1933, Robinson and Chamberlin both published works which underscored an alternative model of market behaviour known as monopolistic competition (see Section 8.4). This incorporated the notion of monopoly power, albeit temporary, into the theory of the firm. It employed a static partial equilibrium approach (whereby one equilibrium position, from which there is no need for further change, is compared with another) in which a profit-maximising firm, under conditions of certainty, operates in a given environment. In fact, this approach is the so-called *traditional theory* of the firm. It was developed in order to study monopolistic competition, although it was portrayed in its most complete form in the analysis of perfectly competitive markets. The static equilibrium traditional approach was also used to analyse monopoly situations. In addition, Sweezy (1939) employed the techniques of traditional theory to study oligopolistic behaviour.

In 1932, Berle and Means published evidence which questioned the assumption of profit maximisation as the key objective of firms. Their evidence suggested that there may be a separation or divorce of ownership and control within large organisations. They noted that the share ownership of large US companies was widely dispersed, a vast number of shareholders each owning a small proportion of a company's shares. The control of the organisation was left in the hands of the professional director/managerial group, who themselves each had very small shareholdings. This situation gave the managers the discretion to pursue objectives, other than profit maximisation, which suited their own ends. The relationship between ownership, control and objectives is discussed in more detail in Chapter 9.

A further large question-mark was placed against the basic assumptions of the traditional theory following the findings of Hall and Hitch (1939). They interviewed a number of British businessmen and found that business decisions, and especially pricing decisions, apparently took no account of the so-called 'marginal' rules of traditional theory. Instead they followed some kind of rule-of-thumb approach to setting prices. Corporate pricing decisions are discussed in Chapter 10.

These findings meant that the theory of the firm needed to come to terms with both the need for a greater awareness of the different objectives of firms and the need for a more realistic approach to business decision-making.

4.3 MANAGERIAL AND BEHAVIOURAL THEORIES OF THE FIRM

The question of firms having different, and sometimes competing, objectives was confronted in the *managerial theories* of the firm. These take as their basic assumption the existence of a divorce of ownership from control in large organisations, although their analysis lies within the traditional SCP paradigm in the sense that decision-makers have sufficient information to pursue optimising objectives. Each of the theories suggests that the controlling management group would pursue their own interests, although they are subject to some kind of profit constraint. Management is interested in seeking those objectives from which they obtain prestige, power and greater personal monetary reward. In so doing, costs may not be minimised and a level of organisational slack would be inbuilt into the system.

Baumol (1959) assumed that the prime objective of management would be to maximise sales revenue. Williamson (1964) put forward a more general utility-maximising model in which managerial interests are met by the optimisation of a function that includes a range of factors such as salaries, relative seniority as measured by the number and quality of subordinates, the level of fringe benefits and the amount of control that is exercised over the direction of a firm's resources. Marris (1964) was the first to introduce a more dynamic element into the theory of the firm by assuming that the managerial objective would be achieved by the maximisation of the firm's growth rate over time. In each case the firm is expected to achieve a certain level of profit in order to provide the shareholders with an acceptable return on their investment in the firm. This reduces the risk of them selling their shares and therefore lessens the possibility of takeover. The profit also helps to provide the required level of funds for capital investment purposes.

The case for a more realistic approach to business decision-making was taken up in the *behavioural approach* to the firm. Simon (1957) laid the foundations of this approach and the basic ideas were later developed by Cyert and March (1963). Simon introduced the notion of *bounded rationality*. This concept was adopted later by Williamson as part of his transaction cost approach to the theory of the firm (see Section 4.4). It is also implicit in the views of the Austrian revival mentioned in Section 2.2. People want to act rationally, but they are unable to do so because they possess cognitive limitations in formulating and solving complex problems and in processing information. If decisions are taken with incomplete information or in complex and uncertain situations, bounded rationality is likely to exist. As a result, individuals and groups will 'satisfice', or try to achieve certain goals, rather than having a maximising objective.

The importance attached to an understanding of the process by which knowledge is harnessed and exploited, at least from a macroeconomic perspective, was outlined in the endogenous growth theories in Section 3.2. The role of knowledge, and how best to benefit from it by ensuring a free flow of information and ideas, is equally important for the individual firm. One estimate calculates that, even in manufacturing companies, three-quarters of value added stems from knowledge of what sorts of products to produce and how best to produce them.[1]

Cyert and March put their ideas into a kind of formal framework, although it was still more a descriptive account of the behaviour of firms than an actual theory with predictive powers. They viewed the firm as a collection of interest groups with conflicting goals. Each goal has an aspiration level, or some kind of attainable or desirable objective. The firm is seen as an evolving and adaptable organisation that operates in an uncertain and changing environment. A knowledge of the behaviour of the main groups within the firm is vital in order to understand how the major decisions are made. Managerial and behavioural theories are discussed in greater depth in Chapter 9.

4.4 RECENT DEVELOPMENTS IN THE THEORY OF THE FIRM

Firms or markets?

In the 1970s and early 1980s there were several attempts to build on Coase's work on the nature of the firm. Alchian and Demsetz (1972) argued that it was *team production* that created the need for firms. Team production occurs when it is difficult, or impossible, to identify the contribution (in terms of individual productivities) of each input in the process of production. In other words individual outputs cannot be separately identified. For example, two people may have to work together in order to move a heavy cargo. If such an activity was left to the market it would face the free-rider problem. There would be an incentive for each member to shirk (and thereby enjoy more leisure time) because it would be impossible to tell who was doing the shirking. All members of the team would suffer equally from any reduction in total income and therefore the shirker would only bear the cost of a relatively small part of his shirking. Market rewards are directly related to the value of total output and so it is difficult for the market mechanism to provide individual incentives in these circumstances. If any member of the group puts in an additional effort, this person will not receive the full benefit of his or her efforts.

The solution to the problem, according to Alchian and Demsetz, is the need to *monitor* the behaviour of the inputs. A person should be appointed who will assess individual productivities and make rewards to resource owners on the basis of their individual contributions. The monitor should also possess the authority to hire and fire. The shirkers should be fired and they should be replaced by alternative workers or substituted by other inputs. The monitor's incentive to shirk is prevented by the receipt of any residual or net income or profit that is earned by the group. In other words, team production is best organised in the form of the 'classical capitalist' firm. The monitor is the authority figure who exercises the power to hire, fire and negotiate individual contracts and who receives any residual income from the teams' efforts.

Williamson (1975, 1981) took issue with the basic premise of Alchian and Demsetz, that working in teams provided the foundation for the organisation of economic activity into firms. Team production, as Williamson notes, normally only takes place within very small groups. In larger groupings, from single-plant firms upwards, technologies and outputs are separable. Therefore, the non-separability of individual outputs cannot be the main reason for the groupings of workers into firms, as Alchian and Demsetz claim.

Williamson maintains, like Coase, that the rationale for the existence of firms is the need to economise on transaction costs. His analysis of transaction costs is based on a model of human behaviour, the two main behavioural assumptions on which it relies being bounded rationality and *opportunism*. The concept of bounded rationality, first introduced by Simon, has been discussed previously. Opportunism refers to a kind of cunning, self-interested behaviour. Some people may behave in this way by only offering selective pieces of information or by actually being dishonest about the information that they provide, if they can do so without it being discovered and if such behaviour promotes their own interests. Opportunism is difficult to detect, although it is assumed that only some people behave in such a manner. However, transactions between prospective buyers and sellers may not occur unless some kind of arrangements can be found to overcome the problem. The most commonly quoted example of this sort of behaviour is in the second-hand car trade (e.g. Akerlof, 1970). The seller of a second-hand car may have much more knowledge of the true condition of the vehicle than the buyer. If this is so then the seller may select and even distort the information he or she provides about the car, as long as it is felt this type of behaviour will not be detected. The situation will continue and the second-hand car trade will decline unless guarantees, or some other means, can be provided that protect the interests of the buyer. There is a greater tendency for opportunism to occur the smaller the number of sellers in a market. Competition ensures that deceitful behaviour is quickly detected and the seller will go out of business. Thus, where there is, say, a single supplier of an input or where it is difficult to obtain information about alternative sources of supply, then it may be preferable to take on the activity oneself, i.e. to absorb it within the firm.

The kind of institutional arrangements that actually evolve from opportunistic behaviour depend on the nature of the particular transaction that is taking place. For Williamson the major factor that dictates whether the institutional arrangements will constitute a firm is *asset specificity* in production. The owner of a resource that exhibits asset specificity will have a strong incentive in maintaining the transaction for as long as possible in order to take advantage of the resource's relatively high value in its specialised use. By the same token, the buyer of the resource will also want to continue with the transaction, since there would be a much greater cost involved in obtaining unspecialised resources that are not particularly suitable for the task in hand from elsewhere. Both the buyer and the seller of the resource are effectively 'locked into' the transaction to a large degree. Transaction-specific investments are likely to be durable, or long lasting, so both sellers and buyers can take advantage of their respective investments over many periods.

Asset specificity can occur in three ways. Site specificity exists when separate stages in the production process, such as manufacture and retailing, are located in close proximity in order to economise on transport and inventory costs. Physical asset specificity arises where equipment is capable of producing a single product or input, such as specialised dyes used to produce a component. Human asset specificity results from on-the-job training or learning-by-doing that creates a specialised knowledge, for example an administrator's detailed grasp of the intricacies of the firm's wages system. Subcontracting may involve significant physical and human asset specificity, where suppliers are tied to meeting the needs of a single client. A subcontractor may supply an ignition system that requires the use of specialised knowledge and equipment to a single car producer.

Bargaining over transactions that include specific assets should involve relatively few people. However, if a highly specific asset has to be redeployed then productivity, and consequently the return to the asset, will be reduced. Since both the buyer and the seller of the asset would wish to avoid this situation, safeguards have to be written into the contract and this increases the costs of writing and negotiating it. If the transaction recurs, the costs of bargaining are likely to be large. The more specific the asset, the less likely the transaction will take place at the level of the market:

The normal presumption that recurring transactions for technologically separable goods and services will be efficiently mediated by autonomous market contracting is progressively weakened as asset specificity increases (Williamson, 1981:1548).

The advantage of having such transactions take place within a firm are various. Disputes can be settled more easily because firms have better access to the necessary information. Secondly, bargaining at the firm level reduces the risk of opportunistic wrangling over terms. Thirdly, where there is uncertainty about the future, firms have the advantage that they are better able to adapt to changing conditions. Finally, the more frequent the transaction the greater the need for a governance structure which internalises the bargaining procedure and which produces significant cost savings.

Principals and agents

At the same time that the transaction cost approach to the theory of the firm was being reformulated by Williamson, a second avenue was being explored. This analysis of the firm stemmed from two main sources. It developed from the work of Spence and Zeckhauser (1971) and Ross (1973) concerning the problems of arranging contracts in conditions of asymmetric information. It also arose from the writings of Jensen and Meckling (1976) on agency cost.

A *principal–agent relationship* occurs when one person, the principal, employs another, the agent, to act on his or her behalf, often in conditions of uncertainty. It is assumed that each wants to maximise his or her utility, but that each is subject to constraints. Information asymmetries, accompanied by self-interested behaviour, mean that the principal needs to design a payment system so that the agent will optimise his or her effort and share any risks. A number of these relationships exist within firms, for example between managers and shareholders or managers and workers. It is also possible to use principal–agent analysis to investigate the monitoring of, and incentives offered to, employees or to examine the relationship between a firm and its other stakeholders, such as its suppliers or creditors. For example, a principal–agent relationship exists between a firm, the principal, and its subcontractor, the agent.

The first of these relationships, between managers and shareholders, has the most effect on shaping the behaviour of the firm. Principal–agent analysis elaborates on the relationship between shareholders and managers that were initially examined in the managerial theories of the firm. It explores in greater detail the constraints imposed on each group's actions by the other. In these circumstances the shareholders are regarded as acting as the principals in a contract. They employ managers as agents who are responsible for controlling the firm. In principal–agent terminology the relationship between these two groups is one of '*hidden action*' or '*moral hazard*'. Management can take actions of which shareholders can only observe the outcomes. This is particularly true where shareholders employ, or have access to, limited or inadequate information.[2] In an uncertain world it is difficult for them to discover how managers are behaving; a serious '*adverse selection*' problem is said to exist. Shareholders cannot monitor the behaviour of managers without incurring additional costs, i.e. the costs involved in obtaining improved information. This means that managers have a certain amount of discretion to pursue their own interests, whatever these may be. Shareholders will then try to influence managerial behaviour through their compensation package, for example by giving management share ownership in the firm, or by offering them a share option scheme whereby they can buy shares at a certain price at some point in the future. By making management share in the risks of the firm, uncertainty is incorporated more fully into its analysis. However, there is no guarantee that composite reward schemes will necessarily force management to change from their own narrow objectives (see also Chapter 9).

Principal–agent analysis incorporates a number of the features of transaction cost theory into its framework of corporate behaviour. The principal is unable to observe the actions of the agent due to the existence of imperfect information and uncertainty. The self-interested behaviour of the agent is synonymous with opportunism; however, it also assumes that maximising behaviour is possible. The principal is presumed to have sufficient knowledge of the agent's utility function to be able to design a payment system to get the agent to behave as he or she, the principal, wishes. Transaction cost analysis probably provides a fuller explanation of the *raison d'etre* of firms, although its basic hypothesis, that firms exist to reduce costs, and the fact that it is also essentially a static analysis means that it may not yield a comprehensive and dynamic framework for analysing strategic decision-making.

4.5 DECISION-MAKING WITHIN THE FIRM

Whatever analytical viewpoint of the firm is taken, there is no disagreement about the fact that the firm is a decision-making unit. Decisions are taken in order to achieve its objectives. The crux of the decision-making problem for a firm is how to direct the conversion of its resources into marketable goods and services and to do so in such a way as to fulfil its objectives. Innumerable decisions are involved in this process. Therefore, it simplifies matters to divide them into three broad categories: *operating*, *strategic* and *administrative* (see Ansoff, 1965).

Operating decisions take up the bulk of the firm's time. They comprise the day-to-day decisions of the firm, usually with the aim of allocating its given resources as efficiently as possible (and hence minimising its production and transaction costs). The firm needs to decide what resources to allocate to its different products and functional areas (such as personnel, marketing and finance), what production levels should be and what stock levels to carry. It also has to make decisions about performance criteria and supervision. Major decisions have to be taken on what prices to charge and how the products should be marketed, although usually these are more likely to be considered part of the firm's strategic behaviour.

Strategic or planning decisions are specifically concerned with the selection of the firm's products (its product-mix) and its markets. For example, it needs to decide whether to develop its existing product lines and what policies to pursue in order to do so, or whether to diversity into other product areas, in which case it may wish to engage in some kind of takeover strategy.

Administrative decisions involve questions of how the organisation is to be structured to meet its objectives and how resources are to be acquired and developed. Decisions about the structure of theorganisation cover a variety of matters: the structure of authority, information flows, distribution channels and the location of facilities. Decisions concerning the acquisition and development of resources involve a number of other issues: staff training and development, financing, the securing of raw material sources and the acquisition of plant and equipment.

While the different types of decisions appear to be distinct, they are, in fact, interdependent. Strategic decisions impose operating requirements. If a new market has been identified and targeted, which is a strategic issue, a firm will need to adapt its operations, possibly by an extension of its facilities, so that its output can be timed to meet the demand for the product. Furthermore, the administrative or internal structure must be adequate for dealing with the strategic functions of the firm. A diversified firm may require a very different internal structure from a single-product firm. As the next section reveals, different internal structures have evolved, each of which is closely allied to a particular strategic stance.

4.6 THE INTERNAL ORGANISATION OF THE FIRM

Economic activity will be organised within firms if, compared to markets, they can economise on trans-action costs. However, production can be arranged within firms in a variety of different ways. Firms vary in size and in purpose. Their legal definitions are covered in Section 4.8. Almost all large firms are public limited companies, but their internal organisation varies. There are two broad types: the unitary or *U-form structure* and the multidivisional or *M-form structure*. More recently, a third form of internal organisation within large firms, the *matrix* structure, has been developed.

Chandler (1962, 1977) was the first to trace the historical development of the internal structure of firms. He concentrated on changes in the internal organisation of large firms in the US in the nineteenth and twentieth centuries, taking as his example the US railway system. The railways influenced the nature of the modern organisation by providing low-cost transportation; they also possessed distinctive organisational characteristics.

Chandler argued that the development of the modern organisation goes through a number of stages, described below.

4.6.1 Small, single-product organisations

Initially the small size of markets, poor and costly communication and the lack of large-scale power sources limited firms to small, single product organ-

isations that served local markets. The first 'natural' railways in the US in the mid-nineteenth century were lines of about 50 miles in length, each employing about 50 workers and being administered by a superintendent.

The U-form structure

Developments in transport and communication in the late nineteenth and early twentieth centuries, especially in the railways, led to the growth of mass markets and to the arrival of the large-scale organisation. The improvements in communications meant that firms could develop national distribution networks. This led to forward vertical integration on a wide scale as firms reduced their costs by integrating manufacture with distribution. The internal structure best suited to supplying a single, vertically integrated product on a large scale at low cost was reckoned to be the functional and centralised U-form organisation. In this structure the key operations of the firm are divided by major function. It has a single production division, a single marketing division, a single finance division and so on. Each department is run by a middle manager, who is directly responsible to the central authority, the chief executive office. This senior managerial group has responsibility for both strategic planning and everyday operating decisions within the firm. A typical U-form structure is shown in Figure 10.

In the railways, the volume of traffic and the size of the capital requirements meant that long hauls could only be achieved through common ownership of the individual units. Safety considerations quickly led to the development of a large-scale, hierarchical internal structure. Salaried managers emerged, each with specialised functional responsibilities, such as upkeep of the track, passenger traffic, freight traffic, the provision of fuel for the trains and accounting.

The U-form organisation has the advantage of allowing the chief executive office to stay in touch with every aspect of the firm's operations. It reduces

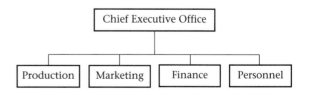

Figure 10 *The U-form organisation.*

problems of management control because information flows vertically and lines of communication are short. It also enables workers and managers to specialise in particular functional areas. However, according to Chandler, as firms grew in size the U-form firm faced a number of problems. The senior managerial team found it increasingly difficult to handle the number and range of tasks imposed upon them:

This situation arose when the operation of the enterprise became too complex and the problems of co-ordination, appraisal and policy formulation too intricate for a small number of top officers to handle both long-run, entrepreneurial, and short-run, operational administrative activities (Chandler, 1962: 382–3).

In transaction cost terms the bounds of rationality had been reached for the senior managerial group. They were forced to spend too much time on routine issues and insufficient attention was paid to strategic matters. This was a particular problem where firms wished to diversify their activities and produce a range of (relatively) unrelated products.

There are other drawbacks of U-form organisations. Co-ordination between the different functional departments may be difficult. As an example, if a new product is being developed, this may involve co-operation between the production, finance and marketing departments, which may be difficult to achieve. In other words, the U-form structure is likely to lead to increased *control* or *management costs* involved in co-ordinating the activities of the firm and in communicating with its other members. These costs rise when the management lacks the necessary information about, or skills to deal with, a particular activity. Furthermore, since the departments tend to be assessed according to criteria specific to each department, rather than on the basis of how they contribute to the overall performance of the company, this leaves the way open for middle management to pursue opportunistic goals to suit their own ends. For instance, heads of department may derive added status, and even monetary reward, by increasing the size of their departments. This may increase the costs and reduce the profits of the firm.

The M-form structure

In order to overcome these problems the M-form structure evolved. According to Chandler this form of organisation developed gradually and independently in several large US firms in the 1920s. Foremost amongst them were Du Pont and General Motors.

The M-form organisation is characterised by a decentralised structure, in which semi-autonomous divisions are organised along brand, product or geographic lines. It is an operating rather than a functional arrangement, although each division is organised along functional lines acting as a quasi-firm by having responsibility for the operations of a particular part of the organisation. It is assessed on the basis of how it has fared, in terms of say profit or sales, in its particular brand, product or geographic market. In other words, each division acts more or less as an independent profit centre. The M-form structure also has a 'general office' or corporate headquarters. This comprises a group of senior management whose tasks are to set the strategic goals of the company, to monitor the performance of the divisions and to allocate resources among the divisions. An 'elite staff' of specialists audits the divisions and may also inform and consult with the general office.

The M-form structure is shown in Figure 11. It differs from a holding company, an *H-form* structure, in that the latter tends to be multidivisional but without the central strategic control. Current examples of the M-form corporation include the chemical firms Ciba and ICI and the computer companies Microsoft and IBM. In 1994 the latter reorganised its operations into 14 customer-focused divisions. In the same year Air France reorganised its activities into an M-form structure by dividing its operations into 11 profit centres.

In the case of the US railway system the increase in the volume of traffic led to a slow change in its internal structure. It eventually evolved into what Chandler called the 'decentralised line-and-staff concept of organisation'. Geographic divisions were set up. Functional managers within each division reported to division superintendents, who in turn reported to the general superintendent and ultimately to the president.

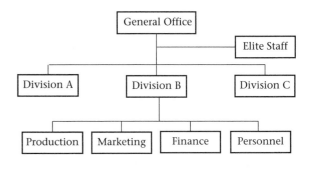

Figure 11 *The M-form organisation.*

For Williamson (1975, 1981) the main advantage of the M-form structure compared with the U-form organisation is that it can economise on transaction costs. The M-form structure has the ability to reduce the scope for both bounded rationality and opportunism. Bounded rationality is reduced by the division of the managerial function; operating decisions are taken at the divisional level, whereas strategic decisions are taken within the general office. Opportunism is reduced because divisions are assessed on the basis of performance criteria, such as profit or sales growth, that are more closely in line with the goals of the firm as a whole; the likelihood of diverse subgoals intruding into the system are reduced. These advantages mean that, compared with the other internal structures, the M-form organisation is more likely to behave like a neoclassical profit-maximising firm. The divisional structure can lead to improved information flows within the firm. Since each division has responsibility for a single product or geographic area it is better able to control and assess all the necessary information for a successful operation. The monitoring activities of the general office allow for improved resource allocation within the firm. The performance of individual products or product lines can be monitored and assessed and resources can be quickly reallocated to more productive uses. In other words, according to Williamson, the M-form organisation actually behaves like a miniature capital market. It is also suggested that the M-form organisation can lead to higher levels of growth than the U-form corporation. This is because the central office staff are freer to pursue strategic objectives like growth in an M-form environment. Growth through diversification of the product base may be particularly likely.

It is widely claimed that the M-form structure is particularly suited to meeting the organisational needs of conglomerate corporations that have diversified product-bases. Firms had begun to diversify their activities before the Second World War, albeit on a fairly small scale. However, it was not until after the War, and in particular from the mid-1950s onwards, that diversification developed as a major corporate strategy. Williamson (1981) notes that the merits of the M-form organisation in managing separable but related activities within its semi-autonomous divisional structure could be extended to managing more unrelated activities. By the same token the M-form structure could also be usefully applied to the management of the affairs of multinational corporations. The growth in the activities of these firms, each having production facilities in several countries, was also largely a post-Second World War phenomenon. Williamson argues that:

> ... the conglomerate uses the M-form structure to extend asset management from specialised to diversified lines of commerce. The MNE (multinational) counterpart is the use of the M-form structure to extend asset management from a domestic base to include foreign operations. Thus the domestic M-form strategy for decomposing complex business structures into semi-autonomous operating units was subsequently applied to the management of foreign subsidiaries (Williamson, 1981 : 1560–61).

However, the M-form should not be regarded as a panacea for every type of firm or for every situation. It may not be suitable where there are strong interrelationships, whether in terms of technology or demand, between the divisions. In these cases a more appropriate form of organisation may be required, such as the matrix structure. In practice, M-form firms may not be as decentralised as has been suggested. The functions and objectives of the central office staff and divisional managers may become rather blurred. Senior management from the general office can become involved in the operating decisions of individual divisions if particular problems need to be solved. Divisional managers may wish to concentrate on more strategic matters, such as new product development or takeover policies, especially if they prefer growth-oriented objectives. Furthermore, there is no reason to assume that central office staff will automatically regard profit as their key objective. They may be more interested in pursuing the managerial goals of growth or sales maximisation. In addition, it is not entirely clear on what basis resources should be allocated to the divisions. They can be assigned on profit criteria alone, or alternatively, growth prospects can also be included. The different criteria may conflict. Finally, it has been claimed that M-form structures may be more costly than other types because certain functions, such as design and marketing, are duplicated within the different divisions. However, any such overlap and wastage costs need to be weighed against the costs involved in adopting an alternative, and possibly inappropriate, internal structure.

Empirical evidence on the presence and performance of the U-form and M-form structures

The M-form structure was not widely adopted until after the Second World War. Between the late 1940s and the mid-1960s many large US companies turned to the M-form organisation. In many cases this was a response to the desire to diversify. In other words, the growth of diversification as a strategy led to the profusion of M-form firms in the US. Administrative structure followed strategy. A similar trend occurred in Europe, although rather later, for there too, diversified strategies preceded the growth of M-form firms, although often with a time-lag of anything up to 20 years. Firms would diversify their activities and only then consider changing their internal structure to an M-form of organisation. Between 1950 and 1970, many large European companies adopted the M-form structure (Caves, 1980); in 1960, only one-third of major British manufacturing companies were divisionalised, but by 1970 the figure had risen to two-thirds. As in other countries, the trend towards the M-form structure was reckoned to be in response to diversification (Channon, 1973).

Since, in principle, M-form organisations are more likely to behave like a traditional profit maximiser than an equivalent U-form firm, it would be expected that M-form firms would have higher levels of profitabilty. Most, although not all, studies tend to support this hypothesis. Steer and Cable (1978) investigated the effect internal structure had on the profitability of 83 large UK firms between 1967 and 1971. They found that the average price–cost margin was 6% and that the rate of profit for M-form firms was 2.33% higher than for U-form equivalents. Teece (1981) studied the profitability of the first and second firms to adopt the M-form structure in 20 industries in the US. He discovered that the difference in profitability between the two was reduced after the second firm had employed the M-form structure, a finding that supports the hypothesis that M-form firms are more profitable. On the other hand, Grinyer *et al.* (1980) found a negative association between both profit growth and rate of return and the degree of divisionalisation in 48 large UK companies. Cable and Dirrheimer (1983) reported no conclusive evidence that the adoption of the M-form structure leads to any significant increase in profitability among 48 West German firms in the early 1970s. They suggest the reason for this is that West German firms are more likely to be owner-controlled and will also have a greater degree of bank involvement in their affairs than would equivalent firms in the UK and the US. These factors reduce the scope for managerial discretion and increase the likelihood of profit-maximising behaviour in the German companies, whatever their internal structure. Reid (1987) points to the significance of bank interests in German firms and the lower

significance attached to profit in Japanese companies for the possible lower preponderance of the M-form in these countries than in the UK or the US. In general, it would seem that the evidence regarding the M-form hypothesis is not entirely conclusive (and see Case Study One, page 80).

The matrix structure

A relatively recent development in the internal organisation of the firm is the *matrix* structure. Like all formats it originated as a response to the changing nature of transactions. As new markets and technologies develop, the internal structure of the firm adapts accordingly. The existence of the matrix structure, which may adopt elements of both the U-form and M-form organisations, has been noted on several occasions (Knight, 1976; Caves, 1980), although it has not been subject to much analysis or empirical testing. The matrices that firms employ can take a variety of forms, but the usual combinations are either product and geographic divisions or functional and divisional structures.

The matrix structure is most likely to be employed when firms have to process a great deal of information. This may be due to excessive uncertainty about the future, the great complexity of the firm's tasks, or the strong interrelationships that exist between the firm's divisions. For example, some multinational companies simultaneously develop their regional and product bases; the complexity of the managerial task means that functions have to be subdivided. Marketing functions may be organised on a localised, regional basis within the geographic divisions, whereas product development, production and distribution may be arranged on a worldwide scale within the individual product divisions. The matrix structure has been identified in industries like aeronautics and car production, where there can be widespread economies of scale in production coupled with a segmented product market. Here technological interrelationships may mean that production is organised on a functional basis to take full advantage of the economies of scale, whereas marketing and distribution is arranged along divisional, product lines. An example of the matrix structure is shown in Figure 12. The structure was particularly popular among US multinational firms in the 1960s and 1970s, although more recently, many large multinationals have reverted to a divisionalised structure in order to simplify their operations. In 1995, Royal Dutch Shell proposed to abandon its 35-year-old matrix structure and return to a more divisionalised arrangement based along geographic lines. However, some large firms have recently adopted the matrix format. These include the white-goods producers Electrolux and Whirlpool, ABB, the large engineering multinational, and Deutsche Bank. In 1994/5 Ford reorganised its global activities into a matrix format (see Case Study Two, page 80).

It is said that the matrix structure has the advantage of improved and speedier information flows because formal channels are replaced by more informal, but direct exchanges; debate is encouraged. This may be of particular advantage in a large, multinational firm where communication between different regions and functional areas may be difficult due to the large scale of operations. Furthermore, it is claimed that the matrix structure benefits from having all levels of management involved in a greater variety of activities. However, there are also problems associated with matrix organisations; roles and responsibilities may not be clearly defined. For example, in a multinational corporation organised into regional and product divisions there is the problem of who has the final responsibility for new product development for a particular region. There may be added complications because most middle managers (e.g. plant managers) in a matrix structure will have to report to more than one senior. Conflict can easily arise and decision-making can be delayed as geographic, divisional and functional managers all debate particular issues.

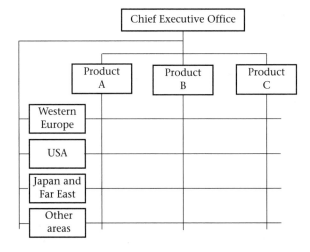

Figure 12 *The matrix organisation.*

4.7 ENTREPRENEURSHIP AND THE FIRM

In Section 3.2 it was noted that changes in industry performance may be instigated by the activities of individual firms. Examples of such 'visionary' or 'entrepreneurial' companies were also given in the case study at the end of Chapter 3. The term entrepreneurial in this context is no accident, since these firms were credited with discovering and developing opportunities for strategic and organisational change within their respective markets.

This does not necessarily mean that entrepreneurs and firms are one and the same, although the one may well beget the other. In fact, there has been a great deal of discussion about what the term 'entrepreneur' actually entails. It was originally coined by the French economist J.B. Say in the early nineteenth century. For Say, the function of the entrepreneur was to reallocate resources so as to secure a yield or profit. However, since both classical and neoclassical economists were largely concerned with the notion of the static equilibrium, the dynamic process of change towards that equilibrium, which inevitably involved some kind of entrepreneurship, was mainly ignored. It was not until the early twentieth century that the debate about the precise meaning and importance of the term became more intense. According to Knight (1921) the entrepreneur is a bearer of uncertainty, which in this sense is when the relative probability of different outcomes to any event cannot be predicted (see also Section 5.5). Such uncertainty is uninsurable, but entrepreneurs are willing to bear this uninsurable risk. Profit, the residual income after all other contractual payments have been met, is the reward for the uncertainty-bearing. Schumpeter (1943) regards the entrepreneur as having some kind of exceptional talent, which, through its innovative creativity, has disruptive effects. Opportunities for new products, processes, markets, sources of raw materials or organisational forms are grasped and exploited, but their introduction creates disequilibrium in the economy. Andrews (1949) and Penrose (1959) ally the entrepreneur more closely to the theory of the firm. For example, Penrose regards the qualities of the entrepreneur, such as versatility, imagination, fund-raising ability and ambition, as being important influences on the growth of the firm.

Kirzner (1979), linked with the Austrian school, sees the entrepreneur as any person who is alert to new profit possibilities. The profit results from knowledge: the knowledge to take advantage of hitherto untapped opportunities. The entrepreneur also acts as a co-ordinator of resources in order to secure the available opportunities. He or she persuades others to supply the necessary capital by offering a sufficiently high reward or interest payment. Thus, capital suppliers do not necessarily have to be entrepreneurs, or *vice versa*. The entrepreneur's reward is seen as a residual income rather than a contractual one. Like Schumpeter, entrepreneurship is associated with disequilibrium, but, unlike Schumpeter, it is also associated with the process by which the economy moves towards equilibrium. Shackle (1979) allies the entrepreneur closely with creative imagination; the entrepreneur imagines the opportunities available rather than anticipates them and chooses from a range of possible situations. In this sense, the ability to make choices, Shackle regards the entrepreneurial function as much more widespread in society than, say, Schumpeter, who sees it much more as a scarce commodity.

Casson (1982) has tried to bring together a number of the main strands from the different views. He defines an entrepreneur:

as someone who specialises in taking judgemental decisions about the coordination of scarce resources (Casson, 1982:23).

The entrepreneur is regarded as a specialist, who reallocates resources to meet his or her ends, with profit, the residual income, being the entrepreneur's reward for the successful judgements of situations. The entrepreneur will wish to keep the information on which the superior judgement is based as secret as possible, for increased information about profitable opportunities leads to imitation and competition and, unless barriers to entry exist, a lower return. Casson analyses the market for the entrepreneurial resource within a traditional demand and supply framework. Such an analysis suffers from the usual criticism of lack of realism, although it provides a useful synthesis and elaboration of the views expressed elsewhere and a suitable basis for further enquiry. It is assumed that in the short run there is an element of pure profit in the entrepreneurial reward, as a result of the monopolistic access to information. In the long run, increased competition reduces the reward, which is simply regarded as compensation for the time and effort involved. The level of the equilibrium reward depends on the relative demand for and supply of entrepreneurs. The demand for entrepreneurs is a function of the pace of change in the economy; the faster the pace of change, the higher the demand and the greater the reward. Their supply depends on social and institutional factors, which determine the

potential for entrepreneurship in a society, the ease with which it can be detected and the availability of funds for suitable projects (which is also a function of the distribution of income).

Entrepreneurs usually (although not necessarily) work within firms. As has been seen in this chapter, the firm can be regarded as a collection of contracts among individuals working as a team; transaction costs are thus reduced compared with exchange in the market. The person who first sees profitable opportunities for mutual co-operation, who puts the contracts together with team members and who then monitors behaviour and assesses performance and receives the residual income is the entrepreneur. Thus, the entrepreneur is often responsible for starting up new firms, although not all new firms should be regarded as entrepreneurial. Many simply copy the ideas of others. In other words, the owner-manager is not necessarily an entrepreneur. Entrepreneurship, at least in terms of alertness to opportunities, can also pervade a firm. The entrepreneurs, whoever they may be, may then seek to transfer as much as possible of the surplus profit of the firm into their own personal gain through promotion and the commensurate financial reward.

4.8 CLASSIFICATIONS OF THE FIRM

It is worthwhile examining the alternative ways in which firms, and in particular privately-owned firms, can be classified. In so doing, both the characteristics and the relative significance of large companies can be emphasised. It is clear from Section 3.1 that firms can be classified by industrial *sector*, i.e. whether they belong to the primary, secondary or tertiary sector. Firms can also be classified according to their *legal status* and by their *absolute size*. The latter categorisation also provides the basis for a detailed discussion of the concept of the *multinational enterprise*.

Legal definitions

In the UK firms can take a variety of legal forms:

(1) *The sole trader.* This was the original form of business enterprise. As the name implies, it is a business owned and run by a single person who is self-employed but who may employ others on a full-time or part-time basis. The sole trader usually uses personal funds to start the business and takes all the major decisions in running it. Numerically,

sole traders are by far the most common type of business enterprise. They are particularly popular in service sector industries like hotel and catering and distribution, and in construction. They also have the highest rate of turnover.

(2) *The partnership.* The need for greater capital than the sole tradership could provide led to the development of the partnership, which occurs when two or more people jointly finance and run a business. In other words, it is an unincorporated enterprise consisting of more than one person. Usually the number of partners is restricted to 20, but partnerships in some businesses, particularly the professions such as accountancy or law, are often allowed to exceed this limit. All partners are liable for any debts of the business without limit, although a rare form of this type of enterprise is the limited partnership in which 'sleeping' partners, who take no share in the management of the firm, are limited in their liability in the case of any debts that may arise to the amount of capital that they have invested.

(3) *Limited companies.* In the UK, The Joint Stock Companies Act of 1825 first allowed incorporation. This was a response to the increasing scale of production, especially in manufacturing, and the need for a greater level of funds to finance it. A company has its own legal identity. It is entirely separate, except in one or two instances, from those who own it. This means that the owner's or shareholder's liability is limited to the amount of the capital invested in the business. In other words, the limited company allows for the possibility of a separation of ownership from control. As has been noted, this has very important implications for corporate behaviour. Every company files a Memorandum and Articles of Association that details its objectives and constitution. In the UK, all companies must have at least two shareholders, although a distinction is drawn between *private* and *public* limited companies. Unlike public limited companies, private companies are unable to offer their shares for sale to the general public. This tends to restrict the size of such firms, although exceptions do occur such as Virgin (or IKEA, the Swedish furniture and household goods retail chain). It is quite common for the shareholders of small private companies to personally guarantee any loans that the company has taken out, in which case they would become liable for far more than the value of their original investment in the firm should the need arise.

Similar legal forms of enterprise exist in other industrialised countries. There are also other types of business enterprise in existence; in the UK these comprise the *public corporations*, which administered state-owned industries, and *consumer and worker cooperatives*. However, as has previously been pointed out and as the next subsection confirms, a very high proportion of employment and output in British industry is in the hands of a very small number of absolutely large firms, almost all of which are public limited companies. A similar concentration of economic activity in a relatively few hands, although probably not to quite the same degree as in the UK, occurs in other industrial economies. The precise ownership and control structure of large firms may differ between countries and this may have implications for business behaviour. Where such differences occur they are discussed at the appropriate point in the text.

The size distribution of firms

In this subsection the basis of the classification is the business *enterprise*. This is a business unit which is not a subsidiary of another company. Therefore, an enterprise may consist of a single establishment located on one site, or it may comprise a number of establishments as well as several subsidiary companies that it owns through having a controlling interest in their voting shares.

It is estimated that there are approximately three million enterprises in the UK, of which just over 93% employ less than 10 people. The vast majority of such organisations are sole traders and are referred to here as *very small firms*. They account for 26% of total

Table 22 *The share of very small firms (each employing less than 10 people) in the total number of firms and employment in selected Western European economies[a]*

Country	Share of total number of firms (%)	Share of total employment (%)
UK	93.2	26.2
Germany	87.3	17.1
France	93.2	28.2
Italy	92.0	47.5
Spain	94.4	24.1

[a]1990 figures for the UK, 1989 elsewhere.

Source: Adapted from *Enterprises in Europe*, European Commission, 1992.

Table 23 *The share of firms (with 10 or more employees) in the number of firms and employment, by size band in selected countries[a]*

Country	Share of number of firms (%)			Share of employment (%)		
	10–99[b]	100–499	500+	10–99	100–499	500+
UK	89.9	8.4	1.7	20.0	26.8	53.2
Germany	92.5	6.3	1.2	34.7	21.8	43.5
France	91.4	7.1	1.5	34.3	19.9	45.8
Italy	94.9	4.4	0.7	45.4	18.9	35.7
US	91.6	7.3	1.0	35.5	24.4	41.1
Japan	92.1	7.9[c]	–	n/a	n/a	n/a

[a]1990 figures for the UK, 1989 for other EU countries, 1986 for the US and Japan.
[b]Size band (number of employees).
[c]Japanese data only available for 100+ employees.

Source: Adapted from *Enterprises in Europe*, European Commission, 1992.

employment and 13% of total sales revenue or turnover, the employment percentage figure being higher because small firms in general tend to be more labour-intensive. A similar situation occurs in other Western European countries, where very small concerns dominate in terms of the number of firms but account for a fairly small proportion of total employment in each case. This is shown in Table 22, page 71.

It is only in Italy, where traditionally there has always been a large number of them, that very small firms account for a fairly substantial share of total employment. In the EU as a whole very small enterprises are responsible for the highest shares of employment in construction, distribution and hotel and catering.

Table 23 shows that *small firms* (i.e. those employing 10–99 people) account for a very high proportion of the total number of businesses which have 10 or more employees in all industrialised countries, but they account for a much lower percentage of total employment. Small firms form between 90% and 95% of all such enterprises, but they are responsible for only 20% (in the UK) to 45% (in Italy) of all employees. *Medium-sized companies* (employing 100–499 people) form a much smaller proportion of the total number of firms, about 7% on average, but account for between 20–25% of total employment. What is particularly striking about Table 23 is the concentration of employment within the *large firms*, each employing over 500 people. Most of these are public limited companies. These firms provide a very small proportion of the total number of companies in each country, but in most countries they employ over 40%, and in the case of the UK over 50%, of all workers. There is an even more marked concentration of production because large firms tend to be more capital-intensive than smaller ones. In the UK, firms that employ more than 500 people make

Table 24 *The number of firms, employment and net output (value added) shares, by size band in UK manufacturing, 1991[a]*

Employment size band	Number of firms	Share of total		
		Firms	Employment	Net output (%)
1–99	123,208	96.2	25.7	19.9
100–999	4138	3.2	24.6	22.7
1000–4999	462	0.36	20.5	23.0
5000+	95	0.07	29.2	34.3

[a]The percentage figures may not sum to 100% due to rounding.

Source: Adapted from Census of Production, Business Monitor PA 1002, 1992.

up less than 0.1% of all businesses (including very small firms), although they account for 34% of total employment and 41% of the total value of turnover.

The data in Table 24 confirm the data on aggregate concentration given in Table 6 (page 18), showing that the largest few manufacturing firms in the UK account for a high proportion of total employment and output. Only 95 manufacturing firms each employ more than 5000 people, but together these are responsible for nearly 30% of employment and over 34% of total net output.

Multinational corporations

The size of firms and the economic power that they may wield is taken to its most extreme form when considering *multinational corporations* (MNCs). A multinational firm may operate in many different countries; it transcends national boundaries, therefore it is capable of transcending national rules and laws. The ability to adopt an international perspective is at its peak within the largest group of MNCs, each of which takes a 'global' approach to its production decisions. In this subsection the multinational firm is defined and its historical development is briefly discussed. The theoretical basis for the overseas investment decision is covered in Chapter 13.

Any definition of 'multinationality' faces problems. Different measures of a company's size may yield very different interpretations of the extent of its foreign operations. A distinction also has to be made between absolute and relative indicators of such activities. The firms in Table 25, page 74, have been ranked according to the absolute size of their foreign assets. If such assets are shown in relative terms, as a share of their total, a different set of rankings would emerge. The order would change yet again if the ranking were by either the absolute or relative size of their foreign sales. Furthermore, when MNCs undertake *foreign direct investment* (FDI) abroad there is no precise definition of the extent of ownership that is required for control to take place. (Portfolio investment refers to loans to overseas firms or to the purchase of shares without a controlling interest.) Hood and Young (1979) have suggested that the parent firm should own at least 25% of the share capital of the foreign affiliate or subsidiary for control to occur, although this is very much an arbitrary definition.

The fact that multinationals transfer a package of resources or assets abroad, comprising capital, technical knowledge, managerial and organisational skills and ability and access to supplies and to markets, means that they may exercise effective control whatever their level of ownership. An additional problem of defining multinational operations is that data on FDI often understate the extent of multinational activity because foreign currency borrowings in overseas markets are ignored; also finance from locally-raised funds is ignored.

It is because of these difficulties that a fairly broad definition of the multinational organisation is usually adopted:

A multinational enterprise is a corporation which owns (in whole or in part), controls and manages income-generating assets in more than one country. In so doing it engages in international production, namely production across national boundaries, financed by foreign direct investment, (Hood and Young, 1979:3).

Using a broad definition of multinational activity, it is estimated that there are roughly 35 000 MNCs in total. Together they control, in some form or another, 170 000 foreign subsidiaries. Each MNC is likely to be large both absolutely and relative to its domestic market: in other words, most MNCs operate in oligopolistic markets at home. Investment in foreign subsidiaries can either take place by the building of new plant (on a 'greenfield' site) or by the takeover of existing facilities from other companies. There is a very high degree of concentration within multinational operations. The largest 100 MNCs probably account for 40–50% of the stock[3] of cross-border assets owned by all multinational firms. On this basis they own about 16% of the world's productive assets and the largest 300 MNCs own roughly 25%.

MNCs have gradually become more international in origin, although there is still a tendency for international firms to originate from one of just a few *home countries*, in which the *parent company* or head office is based. Originally, MNCs engaged in backward vertical integration in resource-based industries such as oil, lead, zinc, copper and aluminium in order to control the source of raw material supply. The *host country*, in which the foreign investment took place, was usually in the less developed areas of the world such as South-east Asia, Latin America or some parts of Africa, since these were where the raw materials were located. Initially, firms from the US and the UK dominated multinational operations in many of these extractive industries. US-based firms were keen to

Table 25 *The largest non-financial MNCs 1990, ranked by foreign asset value[a]*

Rank	Industry	Home country	Foreign assets ($bn)	% of total assets	Foreign sales ($bn)	% of total sales
1 Shell	Oil	UK/Holland	n/a	—	56.0[b]	49
2 Ford	Cars	US	55.2	32	47.3	48
3 General Motors	Cars	US	52.6	29	37.3	31
4 Exxon	Oil	US	51.6	59	90.5	86
5 IBM	Computers	US	45.7	52	41.9	61
6 BP	Oil	UK	39.7	66	46.6	79
7 Nestlé	Food	Switzerland	n/a	–	33.0	98
8 Unilever	Food	UK/Holland	n/a	–	16.7[b]	42
9 ABA	Electrical	Switzerland/Sweden	n/a	–	22.7[c]	85
10 Philips	Electronics	Holland	n/a	–	28.6[c]	93
11 Alcatel Alsthom	Telecommunications	France	n/a	–	17.7	67
12 Mobil	Oil	US	22.3	53	44.3	77
13 Fiat	Cars	Italy	19.5	29	15.8	33
14 Siemens	Electrical	Germany	n/a	–	15.1[c]	40
15 Hanson	Diversified	UK	n/a	–	5.6	46
16 Volkswagen	Cars	Germany	n/a	–	27.5[c]	65
17 Elf Aquitaine	Oil	France	17.0	40	12.2	38
18 Mitsubishi	Trading	Japan	16.7	23	41.2	32
19 General Electric	Diversified	US	16.5	11	8.3	14
20 Mitsui	Trading	Japan	15.0	25	43.6	32

[a]Where unavailable, foreign assets have been estimated for ranking purposes.
[b]Outside Europe.
[c]Including export sales.

Source: Adapted from *The Economist*, 27 March 1993, 'Multinationals'.

protect their own export markets, which they did by acquiring production facilities abroad, and British firms were able to develop their overseas facilities by taking advantage of the UK's colonial links. British and American MNCs were soon followed by firms from other Western European countries, such as France, Germany and the Netherlands, that were also keen to protect their markets and which could exploit their colonial connections.

Prior to the Second World War, American firms dominated multinational activities in manufacturing. They were able to take advantage of their greater size and so plan on a larger scale. They were also able to exploit their technological advantages in the high-technology products of the day such as cars, electrical goods and telephones. In manufacturing the host nation was virtually always where the market for the product was found; in other words, in a devel-

oped country. The concentration of multinational activity in the richest parts of the world is a trend that has continued to this day. Europe was usually the main recipient of the early FDI by US manufacturing firms.

After the Second World War, American FDI in manufacturing in Europe increased dramatically. This was a response to the need for foreign funds by a capital-starved Europe; it was also the result of improved transport and communication facilities. Outward FDI from Europe on a large scale did not really begin until the late 1950s. Initially, there was a certain amount of retaliatory FDI by European firms into the US, but a good deal of European overseas investment was into other European countries. As trade barriers fell within Europe, non-trade barriers, such as subsidies to domestic suppliers, increased. FDI was one way of overcoming these barriers. In some industries, such as chemicals, MNCs replaced international cartels. The tendency for European FDI to be concentrated in other European countries, and especially those with strong geographical and cultural links to the home country firm, has continued ever since. Japanese FDI was initially mainly in low-technology products like textiles, lumber, paper and steel. This was either to overcome tariff barriers or to take advantage of low-cost sites in other parts of South-east Asia.

The global strategies of the giant MNCs, originally based in the US and Europe but also more recently in Japan, developed from about the mid-1960s onwards. Investment decisions by the largest multi-nationals became based increasingly on the firm as a global entity with the subsidiaries under strong central control, i.e. from the parent firm in the home country. In manufacturing, MNCs tended to predom-inate in relatively high-technology products that were also characterised by a high degree of product differ-entiation, such as chemicals, pharmaceuticals, vehicle production, electrical goods and electronics. MNCs were able to exploit their superior technical, organi-sational and marketing knowledge through overseas production.

In some manufacturing industries like vehicles, electronics, and machine tools, different parts of the production process could be easily isolated and trans-ferred to different countries, a process known as *vertical disintegration.* Cost factors became increasingly important. The labour-intensive part of the produc-tion process could be undertaken where labour costs were lowest, while the final stages could be situated nearer to the intended market. The global strategy of

the multinational giants has been aided by other factors, such as the development of the Eurodollar market in the 1960s and the deregulation of the worldwide financial markets in the 1980s, which meant that the largest international corporations could obtain their finance from the cheapest source anywhere in the world. The demise of the planned economy in Eastern Europe and the adoption by China of more market-based principles has opened up other parts of the world to MNCs. In addition, developments in information technology have reduced the risk of long-distance management and facilitated the growth of global marketing strategies. Well-known brand names, like Coca-Cola and McDonalds, could be marketed using a single world-wide campaign. The flexibility to locate different parts of their production processes in different parts of the world has been accompanied by the growth of intrafirm trade. In the early 1970s intrafirm trade accounted for about 20% of world trade; by 1990 it was responsible for one-third and has also been accompanied by a profusion of joint ventures and alliances. More recently, as the trend for large firms subdividing into smaller units has quickened pace (see also Section 6.10), many of the largest MNCs have been shifting power within their organisations more to the regional level, especially in Europe.

In the 1980s, total FDI increased rapidly, especially during the second half of the decade. Table 26 shows that the total FDI outflows of $1005.4 billion from OECD countries during 1981–90 were over three times as great as in the previous decade when total outflows amounted to $302.3 billion. (The OECD

Table 26 *Outward and inward FDI flows, 1971–93, selected countries*

	Cumulative outward FDI (billions current $)			Cumulative inward FDI (billions current $)		
	1971–80	1981–90	1991–93	1971–80	1981–90	1991–93
UK	55.1	185.7	57.4	40.5	130.5	48.6
US	134.3	171.6	119.4	56.3	368.3	60.4
Germany	24.8	86.6	52.2	13.9	18.1	6.3
France	13.9	85.6	51.7	16.9	43.2	39.1
Italy	3.6	28.7	19.9	5.7	24.9	9.2
Canada	11.3	39.6	16.3	5.5	11.5	14.0
Japan	18.0	185.8	61.5	1.4	3.3	4.2
Switzerland	n/a	31.9	11.4[a]	n/a	12.4	3.1[a]
Total OECD	302.3	1005.4	483.7	188.3	821.1	319.3

[a]1991–92 data.

Source: Adapted from *UN Yearbook on Foreign Direct Investment,* 1993.

region is the origin of 90% of worldwide FDI outflows and 80% of all inflows.) The value of total outflows fell annually from 1990 to 1993 as the effects of the worldwide recession produced a fall in demand and in overseas investment plans.

The sharpest falls in inward investment have been into the US. During the 1980s the US was the only major OECD country that was a net FDI debitor, inward investment, at $368.3 billion, vastly exceeding outward investment, which totalled $171.6 billion. The US was the target of about 45% of all OECD outward direct investment during this period. In the early 1990s the reverse was time and total outflows from the US exceeded total inflows. There was also widespread evidence of disinvestment as overseas companies either sold their American assets or did not replace their ageing capital stock within the US.

There have been other changes in the origins and destinations of multinational operations in the last 20 years. From 1971–80 the UK and the US together accounted for almost 63% of total outward FDI by OECD countries, but during 1981–91 this share fell to barely a third. At the same time there have been large increases in outward FDI flows from Japan, Germany, France and Switzerland. In the early 1970s, over half of MNCs originated from the US and the UK, whereas by the early 1990s, just under 50% of MNCs were based in four countries: the US, Japan, Germany and Switzerland. The UK now stands seventh in the home country list, despite its continued large FDI total outflow. These changes can be partly explained by increases in the sizes of Japanese and continental European firms, both absolutely and relative to their domestic markets. As they grew they adopted more of an international outlook. Overseas investment by Japanese and German firms was aided by vast balance of payments surpluses and the traditionally high values of the yen and the mark respectively on the international markets. The surpluses provided a ready supply of capital. The high exchange values of the currencies meant that their exports were less competitively priced and hence overseas investment became a more attractive proposition.

The total stock of FDI has become more concentrated in the richest parts of the world. However, recently there has been a change in the relative position of developing countries as recipients of FDI flows. In the early 1970s, about 25% of FDI flows were to developing countries. In the mid-1980s this figure had fallen to below 20%, but by 1993 it had risen again

to nearly 40%. Much of this flow of investment had originally been concentrated in the newly industrialising countries of South-east Asia and, to a lesser extent, those in Latin America like Brazil and Mexico. The main reason for the dramatic turnaround in flows to the developing world has been the increase in importance of China as a host nation. By 1995 it was second only to the US as a recipient of FDI.

European overseas investment tends to have more of a localised regional bias than FDI by Japanese and American firms, as revealed in Table 27. In 1989, 44% of the stock of FDI from the EU was located in other EU countries. On the other hand, Japanese firms have invested predominantly in the US, while FDI by American companies has been more concentrated in Europe.

In 1991, over 40% of the stock of Japanese FDI was located in the US and a similar proportion of the stock of overseas investment by US-based firms was located in EU countries. Since a large proportion of multinational activity automatically takes place between the three large trading blocs of Western Europe, North America and Japan and the Pacific Basin, the percentage of total overseas investment that each has in the other two areas is bound to be quite high, as the table makes clear. For example, in 1991, 57% of the stock of inward FDI into the US originated from the EU and 21% came from Japan, and the latter's share is increasing quickly. Between 1989 and 1991 the value of the stock of Japanese FDI in the US rose by 32%, whereas the value of the stock of direct investment in the US originating from the EU increased by only 9.5%. In 1989, 28% of the stock

Table 27 *The main origins of the stock of FDI in the EU, the US and Japan*

Geographical source	Inward FDI (% of total stock)[a]		
	EU[b]	US[c]	Japan[c]
US	28	–	43
EU	44	57	28[d]
Japan	3	21	–

[a]Figures rounded to nearest whole.
[b]1989 figures.
[c]1991 figures.
[d]Figure for Europe as a whole.

Source: Adapted from OECD (1993).

of overseas investment in the EU came from the US and about 3% originated from Japan, a share which again has risen quite sharply since then. The EU has attracted an ever-growing share of world international investment flows in recent years. The share of worldwide FDI flows entering the EU rose from 29% in 1985 to 43% in 1991. Historically, the protectionist nature of Japan has meant that there has been a much lower level of inward FDI into Japan than into the other two areas, although most of the foreign investment that does take place there stems from either the US or the EU.

The extent of FDI in service industries has always lagged behind overseas direct investment in manufacturing. This may seem surprising given the fact that most service products cannot be traded across borders. If firms in the service sector want to sell their products in other countries, they usually have to engage in direct investment. There has been some multinational activity of activities in banking, the hotel industry, finance, car-hire firms and airlines since the 1960s, but it was not until the 1980s that there was a huge surge in FDI in services in general. By 1988–91, over half of the world flows in FDI were reckoned to be in services. This rapid increase in FDI in service products has been due mainly to the deregulation of the financial services industry

on a worldwide basis. A number of the largest MNCs operate their own financial service affiliates. In addition, the privatisation of state-owned services, such as electricity, water, airlines and telecommunications, in various countries has led to large increases in FDI in these activities.

Historically, the UK has always been very active as both a contributor to, and a recipient of, direct investment flows. It has usually been a net creditor, the value of investment abroad by British companies generally exceeding the value of direct investment into the UK, as can be seen in Figure 13. Outward investment has outstripped inward investment in all but one of the 10 years indicated.

The cyclical nature of direct investment flows can be witnessed when FDI is compared with changes in GDP. The ratio of both inward and outward direct investment to GDP was low in the 1960s in the UK. Both ratios rose rapidly in the early 1970s as a response to the entry of the UK into the EU. The ratios fell following the oil crisis of the 1970s. However, they rose sharply during the 1980s, as is clear from Figure 14, page 78, with firms becoming more global in their outlook. In the mid- to late 1980s the outward ratio exceeded the inward as British firms continued to expand their activities abroad. In the early 1990s the situation was reversed as British firms

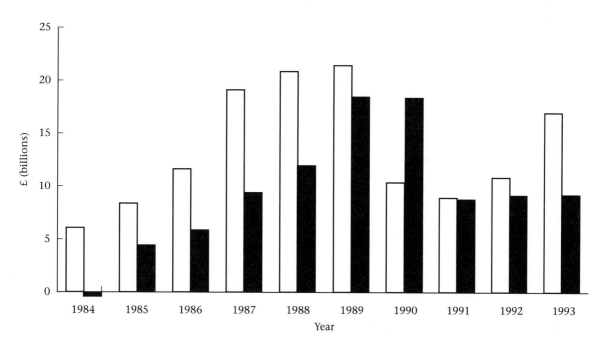

Figure 13   *Outward (□) and inward (■) flows of FDI for the UK, 1984–93. (Source: Economic Trends, No. 491, September 1994.)*

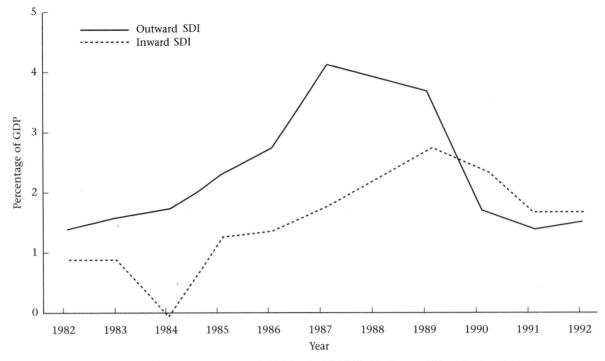

Figure 14 *Outward and inward FDI as a percentage of GDP for the UK 1982–92. (Source: UN yearbook on Direct Foreign Investment, 1993.)*

were badly affected by the recession and as foreign firms invested in the UK in preparation for the EU Single Market in 1993.

Table 28 shows that the share of the stock of total European FDI in the UK, at 41%, exceeds that of the US, although the latter, with 40.1% of the value of the total stock of direct investment in the UK, possesses by far the largest share of any individual country.

However, the US's share of the stock of FDI in the UK is falling (from 50.1% in 1984), while the share from within the EU (29.6% in 1984) is rising. Japan (less than 0.1% of the total share in 1984) shows the fastest rate of growth of inward FDI into the UK. In 1992, only about a third of the stock of inward FDI in the UK was in manufacturing, a decline from over 40% of the share in 1984. Services formed nearly 40% of the stock in 1992, of which the financial services industry made up almost a half. Oil accounted for most of the remainder.

Outward direct investment by British firms has always tended to have a more North American outlook than FDI from other European countries. At the end of 1992, North America accounted for 42% of the stock of overseas investment by British compa-

nies, the highest proportion from any EU country. The EU accounted for another 26% of the total stock of outward British investment, although this share has risen from 15.8% in 1984.

Table 28 *The origins of the stock of FDI in the UK at book value at end 1992*

	Percentage of total[a]	
EU	30.8	
Other Europe	10.2	
Total Europe		41.0
US	40.1	
Other North America	3.8	
Total North America		43.9
Japan	7.0	
Other developed	5.0	
Total other developed		12.0
Rest of world		3.2

[a]Figures do not sum to 100 due to rounding.

Source: Adapted from *UN Yearbook on Foreign Direct Investment,* 1993.

4.9 CONCLUSIONS

In a neoclassical, perfectly competitive world, the firm has no power over its immediate environment; it is regarded as an abstract unit whose sole function is to convert inputs into output. An analysis of the internal structure of the firm was largely ignored until, in 1937, Coase argued that the basis of the existence of the firm were the transaction costs inherent in the price mechanism. Another theoretical development in the 1930s, the monopolistically competitive model, incorporated monopoly power into the analysis of the firm, while empirical evidence at the time questioned the assumption of the traditional profit-maximising objective and the use of marginal rules in pricing decisions. There were further developments in the theory of the firm in the 1950s and 1960s: managerial theories examined alternative corporate objectives, although within an optimising framework, while the behavioural model analysed corporate behaviour based on the firm as a collection of interest groups while assuming bounded rationality.

In the 1970s and 1980s there were various attempts to build on the work of Coase. Alchian and Demsetz argued that team production and the concomitant monitoring function created the need for the firm. Williamson adopted the Coase principle that the basis of the firm was the need to economise on transaction costs: the existence of bounded rationality and opportunism in conjunction with asset specificity and small numbers bargaining combined to create advantages of having transactions occur within a firm. In principal–agent terms, the firm is viewed as a collection of contracts between individuals; the contracts are designed to reconcile opposing interests and to reduce agency costs. While these modern theories of the firm shed new light on the reasons for the firm's existence and offer interesting insights into the importance of its internal structure for corporate behaviour, the analysis is essentially static.

The decisions of the firm can be broadly divided into three main categories: operating, strategic and administrative. However, the different groups of decisions are actually interdependent; for example, strategic decisions may impose administrative or structural requirements on a firm. This interdependence is further explored in an investigation of the changing significance of the different forms of internal structure. Chandler, using US railways as an example, traced the development of the internal structure of the firm, from small, single product organisations to the functional U-form structure and on to the divisionalised M-form organisation. The latter, according to Williamson, is eminently suited to a strategy of diversification; by economising on transaction costs it can achieve higher profit rates than can other organisational forms, although this prediction is not entirely borne out by empirical evidence. The matrix structure became popular in the 1960s and 1970s among large MNCs, although some have since reverted to the M-form type.

The entrepreneur usually, although not necessarily, works within the firm. The entrepreneur is variously regarded as the bearer of uncertainty; as having exceptional talent, although with disruptive effects; as being alert to, and having the knowledge to take advantage of, new profit opportunities; as having creative imagination; and finally as a specialist decision-maker concerned with the co-ordination of resources and with profit as the ultimate reward.

Legally, the most common forms of classification of the firm are the sole trader, the partnership and the private or public limited company, although other types, such as the co-operative, also exist. In most industrial economies numerically the very small firm predominates, while output and employment is usually concentrated in the hands of a relatively small number of large organisations (and especially so in the UK).

A multinational corporation owns and controls production facilities in more than one country. In the first instance, MNCs engaged in backward vertical integration in extractive industries. Multinational activity in manufacturing was initially dominated by US-based firms and was often confined to relatively high-technology products; later, European firms and more recently, companies from Japan and other parts of South-east Asia have became more prominent in such manufacturing FDI. From the early 1960s a global corporate strategy was increasingly adopted by the largest MNCs. In the 1980s there was a huge increase in FDI in services, which now forms over half the total flows. The UK has always been very active as both a contributor to, and as a recipient of, FDI, usually operating as a net creditor.

Case Study One: The financial structure and performance of M-form firms

Recent studies have investigated (a) the effect of implementation of M-form on the firm's capital structure and (b) the impact of internal structure on profitability. Riahi-Belkaoui and Bannister (1994) examined the agency costs involved in the setting up M-form organisation, which, they hypothesised, would increase a firm's debt/equity ratio. The establishment of the M-form structure necessitates additional finance for two reasons: size and asset growth increases after adoption of M-form and costly co-ordination functions may be needed to realise the potential benefits. The capital market will impose an increased amount of debt because, by lowering potential agency costs, it will reduce the scope for opportunism by top management in the use of 'free cash flow' or discretionary investment expenditures.

They further hypothesised that a firm that diversifies into areas that are relatively unrelated to its existing product base will have a higher debt/equity ratio than a firm that diversifies into related product areas. Management prefer debt financing because it requires less dilution of their voting power than equity finance, but debt financing incurs mandatory interest payments. Hence, projects are preferred which have redeployable assets (i.e. which involve less sunk costs) and these tend to be in unrelated product areas. Riahi-Belkaoui and Bannister studied 62 very large, mainly American, firms that adopted the M-form between 1950 and 1978. They found that its implementation increased a firm's relative level of debt and hence concluded that this acted as a control mechanism on the discretionary powers of management. They also discovered that unrelated diversified firms have much higher debt/equity ratios than other diversified firms, which provided confirmation of their second hypothesis; however, the increased debt may also be the result of more general concerns about the problems that a change of internal structure may cause for a firm's performance (in which case equity finance may be harder to obtain).

Weir (1995) investigated the performance of the M-form by comparing profitability among different internal structures; from a transactional cost perspective the M-form firm would be more likely to exhibit profit-maximising behaviour and hence achieve higher profit levels than other types of organisation. Weir examined the internal structure and profit performance of 84 British medium and large firms (with turnover ranging from £2 million to £500 million, thus excluding the very largest firms). He found that there was an upper limit for the U-form structure of just over £30 million turnover, at which point presumably the bounds of rationality had been reached. This would support the transaction cost hypothesis of the need for structural change beyond a certain size of organisation. The M-form, or at least a corrupted or transitional form of it, predominated. In general, U-form firms performed poorly, their profits being lower than the industry average (measured over a three-year period) in most cases. However, there was no evidence that M-form organisations exhibited superior profitability, less than half performing better than their industry average. This may be because of ineffective monitoring of divisional heads, a lack of commitment by divisional managers to profit maximisation, partly driven by an inadequate reward structure, or poor appraisal of investment projects so that those expected to achieve the highest returns did not in fact do so. Thus, this evidence supports the idea that there may be an upper limit on the scale of activities undertaken by the existing management team, although it does not provide backing for the supposed superior profit performance of the M-form firms. Of course, it may be that the M-form firms perform better in terms of growth or some other criterion, or that only very large firms can benefit fully from the adoption of the M-form structure, and it is these firms that exhibit superior performance, although there is no conclusive evidence from elsewhere supporting either of these hypotheses.

Case Study Two: Ford's matrix structure

On 1 January 1995, after many months planning, Ford switched its internal organisation from a divisionalised format to a matrix structure. Previously, Ford's activities had been divided into five main regional groupings: North America Operations, Ford of Europe, Ford Asia-Pacific, the Latin America Group and Ford Mid-East and Africa. Each group operated, more or less, as an independent and separate business. The new structure relates specifically to its North American and European operations, the other area groupings remaining separate from the matrix organisation for the time being.

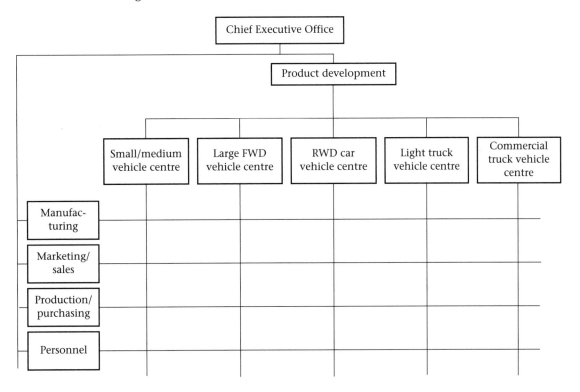

Figure 15 *A simplified version of the Ford matrix structure.*

It is claimed that the old system suffered from an excess of waste and duplication. These problems were brought into sharper focus by the development of Ford's so-called 'world' car. The European version of this, the Mondeo, was launched in 1993, the North American model, the Contour, being introduced a year later. It was felt that duplication could be avoided and the design, development and production costs of global models could be substantially reduced by combining the European and North American arms of the business. These now comprise five product divisions or 'vehicle centres'. Four of them, for large front-wheel drive (FWD) cars, rear-wheel drive (RWD) cars, light pick-up trucks and larger commercial trucks, are located in the US. The fifth, for small- and medium-sized cars is split between the UK and Germany. The five vehicle centres will act as fairly autonomous product divisions; they will design, develop and manufacture new models in their particular ranges for North America and Europe and they will also have responsibility for product marketing, cash flow and profitability. At the same time, a functional structure co-exists. Strategic co-ordination in manufacturing, marketing/sales, purchasing and personnel relations is to be undertaken by senior managerial staff, who are mainly located in the head office of the company in the US. They are able to contribute their expertise and advice at any stage of the production process in each of the vehicle centres. A simplified version of the structure is shown in Figure 15, page 81.

It is far too early to say whether the new structure will succeed in its aims of reducing overlap in Ford's operations, improving communication within the organisation and speeding up the decision-making process. One of the major problems that it may face, a drawback common to most matrix structures, is that middle managers will have responsibilities to two different groups within the organisation, the vehicle centres on the one hand and the functional departments on the other. This point has been made elsewhere:

... the new structure consists of a matrix in which most managers – an estimated 10 000 of them – will find their lives complicated ... by having more than one boss (*Financial Times*, 16 December 1994, 'Ford's Global Matrix Gamble').

Such a set-up could increase the risk of conflict and slow down important decision-making processes. The use of modern technology, such as video conferences and computer nets, aims to improve communication links between different decision-makers, like engineers and designers, in the organisation. This will, it is hoped, reduce the chances of time-consuming disputes.

Another possible problem is that, since the new vehicle centres will be developing and manufacturing products for the global market, they may create fairly standardised models in order to try to suit all regional tastes. In principle, although most new models are to be geared towards the global market, brands need to be sufficiently differentiated to meet different regional demands. However, this issue is at the heart of the problem that any vehicle producer faces, irrespective of its internal organisation: the need to produce models on a very large scale because of the very high minimum efficient scales of production for different operations, while at the same time tailoring them to meet the demands of individual and fragmented markets.

FURTHER READING

Clarke, R. and McGuiness, M. (eds) (1987) *The Economics of the Firm* (Oxford, Basil Blackwell), Chapters 1–3.

Jones, G. (1996) *The Evolution of International Business* (London, Routledge), Chapter 2.

Ricketts, M. (1987) *The Economics of Business Enterprise* (London, Harvester Wheatsheaf), Chapters 2, 3, 5.

Williamson, O.E. (1975) *Markets and Hierarchies: Analysis and Antitrust Implications* (New York, Free Press).

NOTES

1. See *The Economist*, 11 November 1995, Management Focus, 'Knowledge'.
2. The quality of information that shareholders in the UK have access to, mainly in company reports, has long been called into question. The Cadbury Committee's proposals (1992) on corporate governance concluded that interim statements, in particular, should have more comprehensive information. The Committee also suggested that all firms should possess audit and remuneration committees.
3. The stock of any variable is its accumulated quantity; the flow is the quantity of the variable measured over a period of time.

Questions ☐ ☐ ☐

4.1 'The operation of a market costs something and by forming an organisation and allowing some authority (an "entrepreneur") to direct the resources, certain marketing costs are saved' (Coase, 1937:338). What sort of marketing costs?

4.2 Explain why, according to Williamson, the greater the 'asset specificity' in production the more likely that a particular institutional arrangement will constitute a firm.

4.3 Give examples of how, and why, the principals in a contract in a firm might try to influence the agents' behaviour.

4.4 'Operating, strategic and administrative decisions are distinct, but they are also interdependent and complementary.' Explain and discuss.

4.5 'In the language of transaction cost economics, bounds on rationality were reached as the U-form structure laboured under a communication overload while the pursuit of subgoals by the functional parts ... was partly a manifestation of opportunism' (Williamson, 1981 : 1555). Explain and discuss.

4.6 Explain why it is hypothesised that, compared with the U-form enterprise, the M-form organisation is more likely to behave like a neoclassical profit-maximising firm. To what extent does empirical evidence support such a hypothesis?

4.7 'Empirical evidence on the internal structures and strategic plans of large firms suggest that it is more a case of structure following strategy than the other way about.' Comment on this statement.

4.8 In 1994, Air France switched from a hierarchical and centralised structure to a decentralised organisation based on eleven so-called profit centres. Outline the problems that may have been inherent in the original structure and discuss the difficulties that might arise within the new type of organisation.

4.9 'In a quest to increase competitive speed, and cut complexity and costs, most companies are streamlining their organisations by shifting the internal balance of responsibility and power sharply towards their international product divisions or "lines of business". This is being done at the expense of the other dimensions of the complex "matrix" organisations which these companies used to operate.'

'In moving so strongly to divisional structures ... companies are running a twofold risk of swinging the pendulum too far towards divisional management: loss of touch with national market differences; and demoralisation of the very managers on whom that responsiveness depends' (*Financial Times*, 25 November 1994).

Discuss the implications of these statements for companies like Electrolux and Ford, both of which have recently set up matrix structures.

4.10 Comment on the view that entrepreneurship is, by its very nature, bound to be an extremely scarce resource. Discuss the factors that might influence its quantity and quality within a country.

4.11 Discuss the problems involved in adequately defining the extent of multinational operations in a company. Outline the main changes that have taken place in the origins and destinations of FDI in the last 40 years.

CHAPTER 5

▶ Fundamental Concepts in Microeconomics and Business Decision-Making

In the previous chapter, the nature of the firm was discussed in some detail; the major decisions that firms are expected to undertake were also outlined. In this chapter, a number of different concepts are examined that have important implications for firms' decision-making; initially they are considered from essentially a traditional perspective under conditions of *certainty*. The chapter begins by discussing the significance of *time* in corporate decision-making and how decisions change during different time periods. This is followed by a discussion of the different *cost concepts* employed by accountants and economists, and their applicability to business decision-making. There are explanations of *incrementalism, marginalism* and *contribution analysis*. The techniques of *optimisation* are also discussed. Finally, the problems of incorporating *risk* and *uncertainty* into decision-making are examined. A *case study* of contribution analysis in a British Coal colliery completes the chapter.

5.1 DECISION-MAKING IN DIFFERENT TIME PERIODS

The short run and the long run

Every economic decision, whatever its content and whoever makes it, should take time into account. We live in a complex and ever-changing world. All economic (as well as social and political) factors vary over time, both in quantitative and in qualitative terms, although obviously some things take longer to change than others. For example, peoples' tastes may change virtually overnight, yet a large-scale advertising campaign can take years from initial idea to commercial implementation. A dynamic rather than a static approach should be taken in order to reach a correct decision on any issue, although for the sake of simplicity economic theory often takes a comparative static approach to problem-solving. In so doing, traditional analysis makes a distinction between the *short run* and the *long run*, and sometimes the *very long run*. It is important to note that these terms do not actually denote distinct periods of time.

The short run is defined as a situation in which at least one factor of production is *fixed* in supply. An example is prior capital expenditure in fixed assets such as plant and equipment. Firms can increase or decrease output only by adding or subtracting *variable* quantities of other inputs, such as labour or raw materials, to their fixed factors of production. The actual length of the short run can vary greatly from industry to industry. In a small retail outlet that is renting office space, the short run can be a very brief period defined, say, by the length of the lease. For a nuclear power plant that has made a huge investment in capital equipment, the short run may extend for many years until the equipment needs to be replaced. However, in principle the firm is faced mainly with operating decisions in the short run that take place in the *current period*. It will try to allocate its existing resources within the firm as efficiently as it can. Planning or strategic decisions are likely to be limited by the pre-existing size of its plant.

In the long run, all factors of production are variable. This means that a firm is concerned not just with operating decisions but also with with planning or strategic decisions about a possible extension or closure of its capacity or plant size. Any such decision may have implications in both *current and future* time periods. If a firm wishes to invest in an extension to the size of its existing facilities or in the building of a larger plant it will have to take into account estimates of costs and revenues both now and in the future before deciding whether the project is economically viable. Any such increase in the size of a firm's facilities also incorporates decisions about the direction of its expansion. This involves decisions about the possible development of its existing product lines or, alternatively, diversification into other product areas.

In the long run, it is still assumed that the *level of technology* is fixed. Technology here refers to the level of scientific knowledge that exists at any time. It is assumed that it is only possible to vary the level of technology in the very long run. The result of the introduction of new technology is that not just the quantity but also the quality of factors of production can be varied. An increase in quality can raise factor productivity, which can be achieved, for example, through a training programme that increases labour productivity or an R&D project that leads to an increase in the productivity of capital equipment. (The effects of training programmes are discussed in Chapter 14; decisions about investment in new capital projects are examined in Chapter 12.)

The relationship between the terms the short run and the long run and precise periods of time needs to be made completely clear. The long run may actually be a very short period of time. Since, at any time, a business is almost bound to have some fixed factors of production, then it is almost permanently in a short-run position. When a firm makes the long-run decision to invest in a new plant (or to extend the size of its existing plant) it will actually be in a short-run situation; it remains in that position until the new plant is up and running, at which time it will be in a new short-run situation.

Decisions involving more than one time period

Many decisions that are taken by firms need to take account of time and the effects of time. Given the specific meanings accorded to the terms 'the short run' and 'the long run', any decision that incorporates only a brief period will be referred to as *short-term* and one that involves a more prolonged period of time will be referred to as a *long-term* decision.

When faced with decisions that involve choices between having something today and having it tomorrow, most people would opt for the something today; thus, if offered the choice of having nothing now and £100 next year as opposed to £100 now and nothing next year, then naturally the latter option will be chosen. A positive *rate of time preference* places higher values on units of current consumption or income than on those accruing in the future. However, if the £100 is able to accrue interest over time the alternatives would be different. Assume that the £100 can earn a rate of interest of 10% per annum by being placed in a building society account. Then the choice becomes one of receiving nothing now and £110 (the original £100 + the 10%

rate of return) next year as opposed to £100 now and nothing next year. An incentive has been created to delay the immediate reward in favour of some future benefit; this incentive is a function of the passage of time and an acknowledgement that money can earn interest over time.

Since money can earn interest through time, it is said to have a time value. Therefore, all costs and revenues that accrue in the future have to be *discounted* backwards to the present time at an appropriate rate of interest; only then can they be compared with expenses incurred or with revenues received today. £100 now will be worth £110 in a year's time and £121 in two years' time assuming a rate of interest of 10%. Stating this in a more general form, after one time period £V the current or present value of a sum of money, at r% compound becomes

$$rV + V = V(1 + r)$$
$$\text{e.g. } 100(1 + 0.1) = 110$$

After two time periods the yield, Y, therefore is

$$Y = V(1 + r)^x (1 + r)$$
$$= V(1 + r)^2$$
$$\text{e.g. } 100(1 + 0.1)^2 = 121$$

After n time periods or years the yield becomes

$$Y = V(1 + r)^n \tag{5.1}$$
$$\text{e.g. } 100(1 + 0.1)^n$$

Given that V represents the sum of money due now and that Y represents the sum of money due in the future, then

$$V = \frac{Y}{(1 + r)^n} \tag{5.2}$$

Here $1/(1 + r)$ is the *discount factor* and r is the *rate of discount* or the *opportunity cost of capital*, since it is the rate of interest that could have been earned from the sum of money in its next best alternative use, i.e by placing it in a building society account. The discount factor needs to be applied to all sums due in the future in order to reduce them to their current or present values, V.

Any decision a firm takes that is likely to involve the generation of a *cash flow* of *net revenues* or *profits* (i.e. revenues minus current costs or costs per period) over a number of time periods should adopt discounting techniques. The investment in a capital project, like the building of a new plant, is the most obvious example of such a decision. Another is the development and commercial implementation of a new product. In each case the projected or estimated present values of the future cash flows should be compared with the current sacrifice that is being made in order to achieve them. The calculations in the case of a new plant may need to include the scrap or re-sale value of the old plant as well as the scrap value of the new plant when it has reached the end of its useful life. The current sacrifice is usually an estimate of the capital cost of the project. However, discounting methods can be used in other decisions. If a firm is trying to decide whether or not to lower the price of its product, the current sacrifice is the likely reduction in the cash flow in the current period before consumers have had time to adjust their buying behaviour. This can then be compared with estimates of the present values of future cash flows as consumers change their spending decisions in favour of the new product.

Discounting techniques can also be applied to the *profit-maximising procedure*. A profit-maximising firm will automatically *maximise its value*, since this is defined as the present value of the flow of profits over the time horizon of the firm. A short-run profit maximiser will maximise profits in the current period only. If the firm's time horizon covers a number of periods, it will want to maximise the present value of the flow of profits that accrue to it both now and in the future.

It is conventional when using discounting techniques to assume that all cash flows are received or are incurred at the end of each year. The present value of current and future flows of net revenues can be stated as

$$V = \frac{Y_1}{(1+r)} + \frac{Y_2}{(1+r)^2} + \frac{Y_3}{(1+r)^3} + \ldots + \frac{Y_n}{(1+r)^n}$$

where Y_1, Y_2, are the cash flows in years 1, 2 etc. This can be summarised as

$$V = \sum_{t=1}^{n} \frac{Y_t}{(1+r)^t}$$

and

$$NPV = \sum_{t=1}^{n} \frac{Y_t}{(1+r)^t} - C_0 \qquad (5.3)$$

where NPV is the *net present value* of a particular project and C_0 represents its current cost or sacrifice.

If this figure is positive (NPV>0) then the project is worthwhile undertaking, at least from a profit-maximisation standpoint. If projects are being compared, the higher the NPV the higher the ranking of the project. An alternative method of investment appraisal is the so-called *internal rate-of-return* (IRR) technique. The IRR is the rate of interest that equates the present value of the future returns to the initial cash outlay. In other words, it solves the equation for the discount rate that makes the NPV equal to zero:

$$\sum_{t=1}^{n} \frac{Y_t}{(1+i)^t} - C_0 = O \qquad (5.4)$$

In this equation, i is the IRR. If it is greater than the opportunity rate of interest, then it can be assumed that the project is feasible.

In practice, firms may be very uncertain about projected revenues and costs. Future levels of inflation and rates of interest and projected changes in taxation are all likely to complicate the issue. As a result, managers may delay making an immediate decision about a project, at least until they feel they have more worthwhile information. It also appears from this analysis that there is some unique 'market' rate of interest, r, whereas no such rate exists; borrowing and lending rates differ and the different sources of funds usually required for investment purposes have separate market rates. The problems of dealing risk and uncertainty are examined in more detail in Section 5.5, while investment appraisal techniques and the determination of the cost of capital for the firm are discussed more fully in Chapter 12.

5.2 COST CONCEPTS

When it comes to costs of production, uncertainty about the future is not the only problem faced by decision-makers. There is also the fact that much of the information on costs upon which businesses make their decisions is supplied by accountants. In some situations these data may not tally with the economist's view of costs; distinctions have to be drawn between the concepts used by accountants and those employed by economists before they can be correctly applied by firms. A number of examples are discussed below (see also Box 5.1, page 88).

Box 5.1 *Cost concepts*

The *opportunity cost* of a decision is the benefit sacrificed by not choosing the next best alternative course of action; it is the cost of an activity measured in terms of the opportunities or alternatives forgone. The opportunity cost may differ from the original price paid for resources or their *historical cost*. It is the current or future cost of resources that is important in decision making, not their past cost.

Explicit costs are the expenses paid to factors of production not owned by a firm for the use of their services. They are incurred in the current time period and are explicit because they are paid directly to the resource owners. *Implicit costs* are the opportunity costs of resources already owned by a firm, such as plant and equipment; they are what they could have earned in some alternative use.

The opportunity cost of supplying capital to a business is the minimum return expected for the risks involved. This minimum return is referred to as *normal profit*. It is that level of profit which will keep a firm in a particular line of business and which pays the financial suppliers a sufficient return to cover any risks involved. If the owners of capital earn a return above the normal level, or, to put it another way, if revenues exceed the value of the opportunity costs of all the resources tied up in a firm, this is known as *abnormal*, *supernormal*, *pure* or *economic profit*.

Fixed costs are current period costs that do not vary with output; they are incurred even if nothing is produced. *Variable costs* vary directly with output; if nothing is being produced they are zero. If a cost can be directly ascribed to the production of an individual unit it is called a *direct* or a *running* cost. If a cost cannot be separated it is known as an *indirect* or an *overhead* cost. Since overheads cannot be assigned to individual units of a product they are also referred to as *joint* costs.

Opportunity and historical costs

In the previous section the rate of discount was defined as the opportunity cost of capital. In more general terms, should a firm wish to employ a factor of production, it knows that the input may well have alternative uses. In order to obtain the use of its services, a firm will have to pay at least as much for an input as in its next best alternative use. For factors of production that a firm buys or hires, the opportunity cost is the price that is paid for them. If new employees are hired at a weekly rate of £400 per person, then that is the opportunity cost of acquiring this particular type of labour. The same is true for raw materials that the firm may purchase; the opportunity cost is the current market price paid for them. However, in the case of resources that a firm purchased some time ago and has since stored or held as inventories, the opportunity cost may differ from the historical cost.

For example, an electricity generating plant may have paid £25 a tonne for its coal supplies, most of which remains unused. The price of coal then rises to £30 per tonne on the international markets. For any current orders that the electricity generating plant has to meet, the opportunity cost of coal is £30 per tonne, not the £25 per tonne originally paid. The opportunity cost differs from the historical cost. In fact, technological change has contributed to a significant fall in the price of coal on the international markets during the 1980s and early 1990s, although usually the prices of resources rise over time due to inflation. For example, the current cost of salt sold by the two largest British producers, ICI and British Salt, exceeded its historical cost during 1979–84, as shown in Table 29.

Table 29 *A comparison of total costs of salt (in historical and current cost terms) sold by ICI and British Salt, 1979–84*

	Cost (£ per tonne)					
	1979	1980	1981	1982	1983	1984
Historical						
ICI	12.93	15.91	19.49	23.78	27.46	27.87
British Salt	12.42	15.58	16.74	19.72	21.53	22.89
Current						
ICI	15.19	18.42	24.05	28.46	32.78	32.59
British Salt	15.94	19.91	20.93	24.72	26.44	27.16

Source: MMC (1986:56)

Explicit and implicit costs

Accountants are mainly concerned with explicit costs. They include wages and salaries, raw material expenses, heating and lighting payments and rent on buildings. Their opportunity costs are simply the prices the firm has to pay for the use of them. Accountants impute an annual charge against revenue, known as depreciation, to determine the cost of assets like plant and equipment that were purchased in previous time periods. This annual charge, which represents the implicit cost of the firm's assets, is made throughout their productive life. However, economists are interested in the principle of efficient resource allocation and in the opportunity cost of any resource, whether purchased in the current period or in the past. For example, if a firm owns some land and buildings, the opportunity cost is the rent it could have received by letting them out to someone else. Alternatively, it is the interest that the capital tied up in the ownership of these assets could have earned if it was instead placed in, say, a building society. These are implicit costs; the implicit cost of the time of the owner of a firm is what might have been earned in the next best alternative employment.

Normal profit and costs

The concepts of explicit and implicit costs are useful in helping to distinguish between the meaning of profit as used by accountants and the way in which economists employ the term. By definition, profit equals total revenue minus total costs. For accountants the costs of any item are the monetary values involved in its production; these are the sum of the firm's explicit costs plus the depreciation cost of the firm's assets. However, economists are interested in a broader interpretation of the costs of a firm. Since decisions are based on choices between alternatives, the value of all resources, whether they represent explicit or implicit costs, is measured in terms of their opportunity costs to the firm. This is significant when considering the implicit costs of ownership of the firm. If the owners of capital do not earn normal profit, they will transfer their money elsewhere. On the assumption that all resources are paid according to their opportunity costs, then normal profit is counted as a cost to the firm.

For example, if a person puts £200 000 into setting up a travel business, the opportunity cost consists of what else could have been achieved with those funds, plus the alternative use that could have made of the time involved, both of which are implicit costs in this instance. The money could have been put into a high-interest building society account where, at a rate of 10% p.a., it would have made £20 000 in a year. Instead of running his or her own business, the person could have been working for somebody else, earning perhaps another £20 000 in the year. The normal profit in this instance is £40 000, £20 000 of which is the implicit cost of capital, or what the capital would have earned in its next best alternative use, and £20 000 as the implicit cost of labour, or the opportunity cost of the owner's time. The travel firm would have to yield at least the £40 000 before any abnormal or pure profit is to be made.

Different investments, or different lines of business, have different degrees of risk. Usually comparisons are made between investments with similar degrees of risk. Whether people undertake more risky investments depends on their attitude towards risk; if they do they will expect a higher return, or risk premium. There is very little risk involved in buying government bonds and securities, such as National Savings certificates. There is not much chance of purchasers of government stock losing their money, and returns are regular and secure. The expected return of investors is therefore quite low. Shareholders in a company that has a secure position in an established market are likely to be content with a lower, but more certain, overall return on their investments (in terms of both the share price and the flow of dividends over time) than are the suppliers of capital to a business that is introducing a new product into a relatively volatile market, such as fashion, in which demand fluctuates from month to month.

Fixed and variable versus direct and indirect costs

Fixed factors of production give rise to fixed costs of production. Examples are property taxes, the rental costs of hiring plant and equipment, the interest on loans or borrowed capital, some heating and lighting costs, the insurance costs involved in running a business, depreciation charges that are dependent on the ageing of fixed assets, marketing costs that are unrelated to a firm's output such as an advertising campaign that runs for a set period, and that part of managerial salaries that are unaffected by swings in a firm's production levels. Variable factors of production, in their turn, produce variable costs of production. Variable costs include raw material expenses, wage costs, those parts of depreciation charges and fuel costs associated with the use of the capital equipment, and sales commissions.

Sometimes variable costs are referred to as direct costs and fixed costs as indirect. However, direct and indirect costs are accountants' terms and they may not exactly match the fixed and variable categories used by economists. The rule used by accountants to distinguish between direct and indirect costs is the extent to which the cost can be separately attributed to the production of an individual unit of a product. Examples of direct or running costs, which can be separately attributed, are raw material charges, most labour costs and the machine time of individual units of output. Indirect costs or overheads comprise most heating and lighting expenditures, depreciation charges, administrative and managerial costs and rent and rates. These costs are inseparable in terms of the production of individual units of a product, although part of them may vary with output, in which case they are divided into fixed overheads and variable overheads.

5.3 INCREMENTALISM AND MARGINALISM

Besides the various cost concepts outlined above, for sound decision-making purposes a firm needs to be aware of the importance of, and the difference between, the incremental change and the marginal change of any decision.

Incremental changes

Whenever a decision is taken, a manager of a firm will want to know the effects of the decision and whether there is a better alternative. A knowledge of incremental changes is vital in these circumstances if the correct choices are to be made between alternative courses of action. For example, a firm may need to discover the effects on its costs of production, revenue and profit of a 25% increase in output levels. Alternatively, it may be interested in analysing the effects on revenue and profit of a 10% rise in the price of one of its products; it may wish to take account of the effects of the introduction of a new product. A firm needs to know which factors remain unchanged whatever way a decision goes and which factors are sensitive to, and affected by, the decision.

The *incremental change* is defined as the total change resulting from any decision. The incremental change associated with a new order would be the differences in costs, revenue and profit with the order and without it. For example, assume that a new order generates estimated extra revenue of £500 000 and that the additional costs of production are estimated to be £600 000. The latter comprise raw materials, extra labour costs, a charge made for overheads plus administrative and selling costs involved with the new order. They are shown on the left-hand side of Table 30. The firm rejects the order because it is unprofitable; projected costs exceed projected revenues and there is an overall loss of £100 000. However, the actual increase in costs may be less than those specified in the left-hand column, especially if the firm has been operating with spare or excess capacity in its use of labour or machinery and equipment:

Table 30 *The additional costs and revenues of a new order*

Additional revenue	£500 000	Additional revenue	£500 000
Additional costs		Incremental costs	
Labour	£150 000	Direct labour	£100 000
Raw materials	£100 000	Raw materials	£100 000
Fixed overheads (at 120% of labour and raw material costs)	£300 000	Variable overheads	£100 000
Admin. and selling costs (at 20% of labour and raw material costs)	£50 000		
Total additional costs	£600 000	Total incremental costs	£300 000
Profit/(loss)	(£100 000)	Contribution	£200 000

workers' time may not be fully utilised and machinery may not be used to its fullest capacity. Most firms operate with some spare capacity, especially in their use of machinery and equipment, to enable speedy reaction to any changes in demand for their products. When the economy is depressed and demand is low, there is an even greater likelihood of the existence of excess capacity. The incremental increase in costs may actually only be £300 000 because the existing workforce and plant are able to take on more work to cope with the new order. The direct part of labour costs is lower than the original estimate because some of the workforce can be more fully employed at their existing level of wages. There may not be so much need to employ new workers or to pay overtime rates to current workers. Overheads are lower because the spare capacity in machinery means that the only additional expenses are the extra heating, lighting and wear and tear resulting from the increased use of the existing equipment. These form the variable overheads. The fixed overheads that are allocated on the basis of a certain percentage of labour and raw material costs can be ignored. The same applies to administrative and selling expenses.

A decision is profitable if the additional or *incremental revenues* are greater than the additional or *incremental costs* of that decision. In this case the incremental revenues are £500 000 and the incremental costs are £300 000. The new order contributes £200 000 towards overheads and to profit and is therefore worthwhile undertaking. The *contribution* of any decision is equal to the incremental revenues minus the incremental costs involved. A decision should only be undertaken if it makes a positive contribution to overheads and to profit.

The only factors that are relevant in incremental reasoning are those that are sensitive to, or vary with, the decision. In the above example, those costs that are affected by the new order are the *relevant* or *avoidable* costs. They are the incremental costs, which can be incurred both now and in the future. In this example, they are the raw material, the direct labour and the variable overhead costs. The remainder of the labour cost would have been incurred anyway. Wages would have been paid to the workforce whether they were working at full capacity or not and the same applies to managerial salaries. The fixed overheads and the administrative costs would have had to be met irrespective of which way the decision went, since both were allocated according to a prescribed formula. These costs are therefore *irrelevant* or *unavoidable*. Some irrelevant costs are referred to as *committed* costs because the firm is committed to paying them now and in the future. In this example, they include the wage contracts that the firm would have had to honour, managerial salaries, plus any other costs that are independent of the decision. Interest payments on debt and rent and rate costs are other examples of committed costs. Other irrelevant costs are *sunk* costs which have been incurred previously. They are past costs and therefore cannot constitute incremental costs. These various cost concepts and their relationship with incremental reasoning are summarised in Table 31.

If a decision involves an extension of capacity most, if not all, costs and revenues are relevant to the decision. In fact, where decisions involve costs and revenues that are generated in future time periods, it is not the present value of the net revenue that is the important calculation in each period, but the present value of the contribution towards overheads and profit. The present values of the various contributions need to be summed (including any potential scrap values) and compared with the initial capital outlay on the project (which represents a negative contribution) in order to determine whether the venture is worthwhile.

Any long-term decision may involve additional costs and revenues. A new order may be for a product that has recently been introduced to a firm's product

Table 31 *Cost concepts and incremental reasoning*

Type of cost	Description	Applicability to incremental reasoning
Relevant or avoidable	Sensitive to the decision	Yes
Irrelevant or unavoidable:	Not sensitive to the decision	No
(a) Committed	Have to be paid now and in future	No
(b) Sunk	Previously incurred; past costs	No

line. Incremental revenue would then include not only the extra revenue from the sales of the new product, but also the effects of these sales on the demand for the rest of the firm's products. Sales of one of the other products in the firm's range may fall as a result of the new business. If a decision involves taking on extra labour, the new workers may be on relatively short-term contracts and consequently less likely to belong to the relevant trade union. This may cause some friction with the existing workforce leading to a lowering of efficiency and higher unit labour costs. All such changes need to be taken into account in incremental analysis.

Marginal changes

Marginal changes are an extreme example of incrementalism because they involve unit-by-unit adjustments. They also only apply to variations in output, whereas incremental analysis can be applied to changes in a range of variables, such as price, product range, techniques of production, product quality or output. Nevertheless, marginal changes are important to economists because they determine optimal or maximising conditions.

Marginal cost (MC) is the change in total costs (TC) from producing one extra unit of output Q:

$$MC = \frac{\Delta(TC)}{\Delta Q} \qquad (5.5)$$

where Δ stands for 'the change in'. In this case ΔQ is equal to one. TC is the sum of all the costs of producing a certain level of output. The first *derivative* of any function shows the change in the value of the dependent variable, total costs, for very small changes in the independent variable, output. The derivative gives a more precise definition of the marginal concept. In mathematical terms marginal cost can be expressed as the derivative of total cost with respect to output:

$$MC = \frac{d(TC)}{dQ} \qquad (5.6)$$

Marginal revenue is the change in total revenue (TR) from producing one extra unit of output:

$$MR = \frac{\Delta(TR)}{\Delta Q} \qquad (5.7)$$

where ΔQ is equal to one and TR equals price P times the units of output sold:

$$TR = PQ \qquad (5.8)$$

Table 32 *Hypothetical cost, revenue and profit schedules*

Price per unit (£)	Output (units)	TR (£)	TC (£)	Total profit π (TR –TC) (£)	MR (£)	MC (£)
	0	0	100	–100		
					100	25
100	1	100	125	–25		
					80	15
90	2	180	140	40		
					60	8
80	3	240	148	92		
					40	13
70	4	280	161	119		
					20	20
60	5	300	181	119		
					0	30
50	6	300	211	89		
					–20	40
40	7	280	251	29		
					–40	50
30	8	240	301	–61		

Marginal revenue can also be stated as the derivative of total revenue with respect to output:

$$MR = \frac{d(TR)}{dQ} \qquad (5.9)$$

The relationship between incremental and marginal concepts can be shown by examining the information in Table 32, page 92. Assume that a firm decides to reduce the price of its product from £100 to £80 per unit. The estimated revenue increases by £140 (£240–£100) and estimated costs rise by £25 (£150–£125). Such a decision would be a profitable option since the incremental revenue exceeds the incremental costs. However, there is no reason to suppose that £80 is the profit-maximising price. This will have to be determined by marginal reasoning.

Total profit, the difference between total revenue and total costs, is at its maximum where MC = MR, or where the fifth unit of output is produced. (In fact, the exact level of output where MC = MR lies between four and five units, but as output in this example rises by single whole units the fifth unit can be regarded as the profit-maximising position.) In order to understand exactly why profit is maximised when MC = MR, it is necessary to examine the optimisation process in more detail.

5.4 OPTIMISATION

The importance of profit

It was pointed out in the previous chapter that, while traditional economic theory assumes that firms are profit maximisers, other theories have suggested the possibility of different maximising objectives. They have also postulated that firms may not actually attempt to maximise anything at all. However, whatever the main objective of a business, profit remains a vital ingredient in its plans. Profit is needed in order to survive in business. Losses cannot be tolerated for very long, even by the largest company. A firm will either cease to exist and go out of business or become a target for takeover by another firm, especially if it stopped paying shareholders a dividend on their shareholdings. Profits also enable a firm to grow in size. By far the largest sources of finance for investment purposes are undistributed profits. Since profit plays such an important role in the decision-making processes of any firm it should have a particular

interest in discovering as much as it can about its profit-maximising position.

The profit-maximising position

Table 32 shows that when MR exceeds MC (MR > MC) the total profit (π) of the firm increases, and when MR is less than MC (MR < MC) π declines. By deduction, therefore, profit must be at its greatest, or maximised, at that level of output where MC = MR. This is logical, since if MR > MC, then by producing an extra unit of output a firm's profit must rise because the marginal unit adds more to revenue than it does to costs; similarly, when MR < MC, π must fall when an extra unit is produced. Table 32 also reveals that when MR = 0, total revenue (TR) is maximised. When MR is positive TR increases and when MR is negative TR declines. It follows that at the output where MR = 0, TR must be at its maximum. In mathematical terms the profit-maximising position can be demonstrated as follows, profit being the difference between total costs and total revenue:

$$\pi = TR - TC \qquad (5.10)$$

Marginal profit is the derivative of the total profit function. The first-order condition for the maximisation of a function is where the first derivative equals zero:

$$M\pi = \frac{d\pi}{dQ} = 0 \qquad (5.11)$$

$$\frac{d\pi}{dQ} = \frac{d(TR)}{dQ} - \frac{d(TC)}{dQ} \qquad (5.12)$$

Since d(TR)/d(TQ) equals marginal revenue and d(TC)/dQ represents marginal cost,

$$M\pi = MR - MC = 0 \qquad (5.13)$$

Thus, profit maximisation occurs where MR = MC. These relationships can also be shown diagrammatically. In Figure 16 (a), page 94, the MC curve is revealed as the traditional U-shape and the MR curve is indicated by a downward-sloping straight line, typical of an imperfectly competitive market (see sections 6.3 and 7.5 respectively). The profit-maximising level of output is shown as Q*.

Figure 16 (b), page 94, shows the relationships between the MC and MR curves and the TC, TR and π curves. The slope of a curve is found by drawing a line tangent to the curve at a particular point and

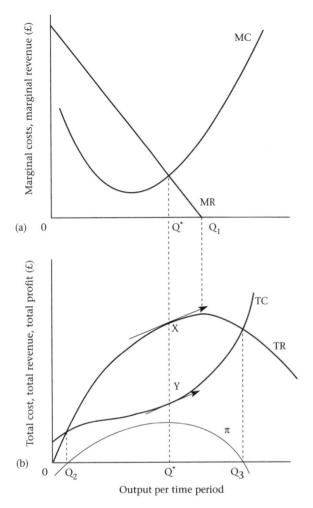

(a)

(b)

Output per time period

Figure 16 *The relationships between marginal cost and marginal revenue and total cost, total revenue and total profit curves.*

declines until output Q_3 where it again becomes zero as TR and TC intersect for the second time. Thereafter, TC > TR and the curve is negative. At output Q_1, where MR = 0, the TR curve is at its maximum; its slope therefore must be zero at this point.

It should be noted that, in principle, it may be possible for the marginal cost curve to cut the MR curve at two different points; the profit-maximising position can then be restated as being that level of output where at lower levels MR > MC and at higher levels MC > MR. Thus, in Figure 17 profit maximisation is achieved at Q_2, not at Q_1.

It is also worthwhile outlining the relationships that exist between marginal and average variables at this juncture, since this will simplify the exposition in later chapters. Any average value is found by dividing the total value by the number of relevant units. If a firm's total wage-bill is £4000 per week and it employs 10 workers, the average wage is £4000 divided by 10 or £400 per person per week. If it then employs one more person (the marginal person) but pays him or her a lower wage, say of £300 per week, the average wage is £4300 (£4000 plus £300) divided by 11, which is approximately £391 per person per week. In other words, when the marginal is less than the average, then the average value must fall. If, on the other hand, the marginal employee had been paid £500 per week the average wage would have risen. When the marginal value is greater than the average, the average must rise. It follows that if the average value is declining, the marginal must be less

calculating the slope of the tangent. (This is true only for very small changes in the independent variable.) At output Q^*, where MC = MR, the slopes of the TC curve, at point X, and the TR curve, at point Y, are equal. The tangency lines are parallel. This is as it should be, since d(TC)/dQ (MC) and d(TR)/dQ (MR) indicate the slope of the TC curve and the TR curve respectively at any point.

Logically, points X and Y are located where there is the greatest distance between TC and TR, since this is the profit-maximising output level. This can be confirmed by referring to the π curve, which peaks at Q^*. The π curve is negative until output Q_2 because TC > TR; it reaches its highest level at Q^*. It then

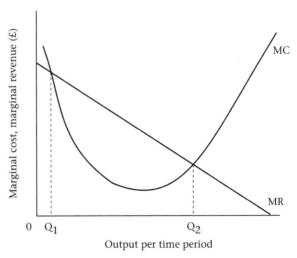

Output per time period

Figure 17 *Profit maximisation in a situation where MC = MR at two levels of output.*

than the average and if the average value is rising the marginal must be more than the average. If the marginal employee had been paid £400 per week, then the average wage would not have changed; when the marginal value equals the average, the average value remains the same. If this relationship were to be shown geometrically and the average curve were U-shaped, the marginal would cut it at its lowest point, i.e. where the average is neither falling nor rising. This is precisely the relationship that exists between marginal and average costs of production. It will be discussed further in Section 6.3.

5.5 DEALING WITH RISK AND UNCERTAINTY

Uncertainty pervades every economic decision, not just investment strategies. Because decision-makers do not have complete information, and in particular when they are uncertain about the future, they have to make estimates of crucial variables based on their expected values. In the absence of complete and perfect information there are likely to be several potential *outcomes* to any decision, the probability of each outcome varying. Any situation that has one or more possible outcomes is known as an *event*. For example, when throwing a dice, if the event is to gain an even score there are three possible outcomes. Alternatively, when tossing a coin there is only one possible outcome to the event of obtaining a 'head'. *Uncertainty* is said to occur when the relative probabilities of the different outcomes to any event are not known in advance. *Risk* is that situation when the relative probabilities are known in advance, like throwing a dice or tossing a coin. Uncertainty can be transformed into risk by estimating the relative probability of chance events.

The probability of any event, E_i, occurring is defined as

$$p(E_i) = \frac{n_i}{N} \tag{5.14}$$

n_i are the outcomes that correspond to E_i and N equals the total number of possible outcomes, where the probability of any outcome occurring must lie between zero and one, $0 < p(E_i) < 1$, and the sum of the various probabilities must equal one, $p(E_1) + p(E_2) + \ldots + p(E_n) = 1$. The probability of each outcome can either be assigned *a priori* (before the fact) or *a posteriori* (after the fact). In the former case each

probability is based on known mathematical properties, whereas in the latter case it is based on past experience under similar circumstances to the situation in question.

Any decision that a firm has to make under conditions of risk and uncertainty possesses a *probability distribution* of outcomes, i.e. a series of outcomes, each having a particular probability. The decision-maker may then have to compare this probability distribution with others based on alternative solutions to the particular decision under consideration. For example, a firm may need to decide between investing in a plant suitable for the UK market alone or investing in a larger plant geared more towards serving the whole EU market. A, the smaller UK plant, costs less than B, the EU plant (£5 million as opposed to £20 million), but the former generates lower present value cash flows throughout its life.

The present values are dependent on general economic conditions, here referred to as high, medium and low levels of demand. The probabilities of each level of demand occurring are assumed to be known and are the same for the UK and the EU. These probabilities sum to one. The situation is shown in Table 33, page 96, the information being displayed in the form of a simple *decision tree*. This is a diagrammatic portrayal of the decision-making process and facilitates the analysis of a series of decisions step by step through to a logical outcome.

The *expected value* of any outcome is equal to the value of that outcome multiplied by the probability of the outcome occurring. For each project, at each projected level of demand the expected present value of contributions is equal to the estimate of the present value multiplied by the probability of that particular level of demand occurring. Thus, in the case of A, the UK plant, if demand is assumed to be high the present value of contributions over the life of the plant is estimated at £10.5 million (assuming, say, a discount rate of 10%) and the probability of that level of demand occurring is thought to be 0.3. Therefore, the expected present value of cash flows equals £10.5 million times 0.3, or £3.15 million, and so on. Since most decisions involve several possible outcomes, the expected value of a decision equals the sum of the expected values of all the outcomes. In general terms the expected value, E, of X equals

$$E(X) = \sum_{i=1}^{n} p(X_i)X_i \tag{5.15}$$

Table 33 *A decision tree illustrating the expected values of a decision to invest in one of two plant sizes*

		State of demand	Probability	Present value of contributions (millions £)	Expected present value of contributions (millions £)
Small Plant (A)		High	0.3	10.5	3.15
		Medium	0.5	4.5	2.25
		Low	0.2	2.4	0.48
				Expected present value	5.88
Decision				Capital cost	5.00
				Expected net present value	0.88
Large Plant (B)		High	0.3	42.0	12.6
		Medium	0.5	20.0	10.0
		Low	0.2	3.0	0.6
				Expected present value	23.2
				Capital cost	20.0
				Expected net present value	3.2

where $p(X_i)$ is the probability of outcome X_i, which is multiplied by the value of the corresponding outcome and summed for all outcomes. In other words, the expected value is the average value for a probability distribution, where each outcome is weighted according to the probability of its occurrence. For each of the two plant sizes in Table 33 the expected present value of the decision to invest is the sum of the expected values for each level of demand. The capital cost is subtracted to give the expected net present value figure in each case: for plant A the expected present value is equal to £5.88 million, the capital cost is £5 million and hence the expected net present value comes to £0.88 million. Since the equivalent figure for plant B equals £3.2 million, then in these terms B would be preferred to A.

However, the dispersion of the possible outcomes has so far been ignored. If one of the plants has a greater range of possible outcomes than the other, then it may be considered more risky and not be pursued. Such considerations also need to be taken into account in the decision-making process. Casual inspection of Table 33 confirms that, while plant B has a higher expected net present value figure, its range of expected outcomes is much greater than for plant A.

This can be verified by calculating the *standard deviation* of each probability distribution, which indicates the average actual deviation of all possible outcomes (each of which is weighted by the probability of its occurrence) from the expected outcome. More formally, it is the square root of the sum of the squared and weighted deviations:

$$\sigma = \sqrt{\sum_{i=1}^{n} \left(X_i - E(X) \right)^2 p(X_i)} \qquad (5.16)$$

The standard deviations for the two plants are shown in Table 34, page 97. The *variance*, σ^2, is the sum of the squared, weighted deviations; hence, the standard deviation is the square root of the variance. The standard deviation of the expected present value of profits for A, the smaller, UK-based scheme, is £3.1269 million, whereas in the case of B, the larger EU plant, it is £13.8838 million. In other words, B, which yields the highest net present value figure, also has by far the highest dispersion of expected outcomes and must be considered a more risky venture. However, this may in part be due to the fact that, as the more expensive project, it is bound to have larger and more variable cash flows. A better indicator of relative risk (i.e. dispersion of outcomes relative to size) is the *coefficient of variation*. This is defined as the ratio of the standard deviation to the expected net present value $E(NPV)$:

Table 34 *Standard deviations of Plants A and B (millions £)*

Plant	X_i	$E(X)$	$(X_i - E(X))$	$(X_i - E(X))^2$	$(X_i - E(X))^2 \, p(X_i)$
A	10.5	5.88	4.62	21.3444	6.40332
	4.5	5.88	−1.38	1.9044	0.95220
	2.4	5.88	−3.48	12.1104	2.42208
				$\sigma^2 =$	9.77760
				$\sigma =$	3.12690
B	42.0	23.2	18.8	353.44	106.032
	20.0	23.2	−3.2	10.24	5.12
	3.0	23.2	−20.2	408.04	81.608
				$\sigma^2 =$	192.76
				$\sigma =$	13.8838

$$v = \frac{\sigma}{E(\text{NPV})} \qquad (5.17)$$

In the example shown in Tables 33 and 34, v for plant A is equal to 3.1269/0.88, or 3.55, whereas v for plant B equals 13.8838/3.2, or 4.34. On the basis of this criterion, A is less risky; whether project A or project B is chosen depends on the decision-maker's attitude to risk.

Attitudes to risk

In principle, attitudes towards risk can be divided into three broad categories:

(1) *Risk aversion* is the preference for risk avoidance. Risk averters prefer low-risk projects with certain, but perhaps moderate, returns.
(2) *Risk seeking* is the preference for risk and risky ventures. Risk seekers prefer high-risk projects with less certain, but with the possibility of high, returns.
(3) *Risk neutrality* refers to risk indifference. Those who are characterised by risk-neutral behaviour are indifferent between the low-risk project with lower but more certain returns and the high-risk project with higher but more variable returns.

Investors, speculators and gamblers generally show risk-seeking behaviour, but most business decision-makers are risk averters; they prefer less risky ventures to more risky ones. In order to understand how the various attitudes to risk impinge on the decision-making process, it is necessary to employ the notion of the utility obtained from different outcomes. Suppose two people find £500. Most people would split the money evenly between the two of them, but on this occasion person A offers person B the choice of a £300/£200 split in A's favour against tossing a coin for the whole amount. If B accepts the £200, she is then showing a preference for the certain £200 against the 50% possibility of gaining the £500. The certain £200 yields a greater level of utility than the disutility from the possibility of not gaining the £500. Alternatively, a firm may be toying with the choice of either investing in a totally risk-free venture, which has a 100% chance of success and which would yield an expected net present value of £20 000, or in a much more risky project which has only a 0.33 chance of success but if it succeeds would produce an expected net present value of £150 000. On the other hand, if it fails it yields no return at all. The certain value of the low-risk project is obviously equal to £20 000; the expected net present value value of the high-risk project is $(0.33 \times £150\,000) + (0.7 \times £0)$, or £50 000. Which project the firm decides to pursue depends on its attitude towards risk.

Attitudes towards risk can be incorporated into the decision-making process in various ways.

(A) THE CERTAINTY EQUIVALENT METHOD

The certainty equivalent of any decision is the certain sum of money that the decision-maker is indifferent about when compared with the expected net present value of a risky alternative. In the previous example about the choice facing individual B, if B was indifferent between the certain £200 and the chance of gaining £500, then the £200 is the certainty equivalent of taking the gamble of gaining £500. In the case of the firm, if it is indifferent between the two projects, then £20 000 is the certainty equivalent of the much more risky £50 000. In each instance, the fact that the certainty equivalent is less than the expected net present value of the risky alternative is indicative of risk-averse behaviour. A certainty equivalent greater than the expected net present value indicates risk-seeking behaviour. The size of the gap between the two values, whether lower or higher, indicates the extent of risk-averting or risk-seeking behaviour respectively.

The *certainty equivalent factor*, α, expresses the ratio of a certain sum to the expected value of a risky sum, where both yield the same levels of utility:

$$\alpha = \frac{\text{Equivalent certain sum}}{\text{Expected net present value of the risky sum}} \quad (5.18)$$

α can be used as a summary measure towards risk. In both the previous examples, the first concerning the choice facing the individual and the second the choice facing the firm, α is equal to 0.4. A value for α of less than one indicates risk aversion, a value for α of greater than one is indicative of risk-seeking behaviour and a value for α of one denotes risk neutrality. From equation (5.17) it can be seen that the certainty equivalent of an expected risky sum must be equal to α times the expected net present value. Obviously, for any decision the precise value of α depends on the perceived riskiness of the project and the attitude towards risk of the decision-maker.

(B) THE USE OF VARYING DISCOUNT RATES

An alternative method of incorporating risk into the decision-making process is to employ differential discount rates. The more risky the project, the higher the discount rate that is used. The rate of return that a project could be expected to earn in a completely riskless investment is known as the *pure return*. A *risk premium*, k, could be added to reflect the riskiness of the venture, where k indicates the difference between the expected rate of return achieved in a risky venture and the pure return. The problem of employing this method is what criterion to use in order to determine the degree of risk of, and hence the appropriate discount rate for, a particular project. In the previous example concerning the two plant sizes, A and B, in Tables 33 (page 96) and 34 (page 97), B has a higher coefficient of variation and should be assigned a higher discount rate than A, although it still may be

difficult to decide exactly what discount rate to adopt. The expected net present value of project B at the higher discount rate should then be compared with the expected net present value of project A at the original discount rate, 10%, in order to make the correct investment decision.

(C) GAME THEORY

The problems of accounting for risk and uncertainty can be tackled by the use of game theory, a mathematical technique that was first applied to aspects of economic behaviour by von Neumann and Morgenstern (1944). Various attitudes towards risk can be assumed using this technique. The one that applies specifically to risk-averse behaviour is the so-called *minimax* criterion, whereby the decision-maker should accept the 'best of the worst' outcomes. Again using the example of the two projects, A and B, it can be seen from Table 33 that the lowest present value of contributions for project A is £2.4 million, whereas the lowest present value of contributions for project B is £3.0 million. On this basis, project B should be accepted. Risk-seeking behaviour is characterised by a *maximax* strategy, in which the 'best of the best' outcomes is the favoured option. In Table 33 the highest present value of contributions figure for project A is £10.5 million; for project B it is £42.0 million. Project B is preferred according to this criterion. If the *Bayes–Laplace* criterion is adopted, each outcome is assumed to have equal probability, in which case project B, with the highest outcome, would again be accepted. While game theory is able to explore different attitudes towards risk, it takes no account of the dispersion of the outcomes. As a result, its solutions for preferred options may conflict with the solutions suggested by the other criteria for incorporating risk.

5.6 CONCLUSIONS

In traditional theory a distinction is made between the short run, in which at least one factor of production is fixed in supply, and the long run, where all factors of production are variable. While long-run decisions are essentially strategic and can have implications for both current and future time periods, the long run itself may actually only be a short period of time; usually the firm is in a short-run situation in the sense that it has some fixed inputs. Thus, the terms 'short term' and 'long term' are used to denote actual periods of time. Since money has a time value, costs and revenues that occur in the future need to be discounted to yield their present values. Any business decision that involves the generation of a flow of net revenues over a number of time periods should employ discounting procedures; the net present value and internal rate of return methods can be used to ascertain the viability of particular projects and to help choose between alternative projects.

From an economic perspective, it is the opportunity cost of resources, whether purchased in the current period or in the past and whether they represent explicit or implicit costs costs to the firm, that is the key to efficient decision-making. Normal profit, or the opportunity cost of supplying capital to the firm given the risks involved, is considered to be a cost by economists; any return above the normal is referred to as abnormal or pure profit. It is important for decision-making purposes to note the differences between the concepts of fixed and variable costs as employed by economists and direct and indirect costs, which are accountants' terms.

Sound decision-making should also distinguish between incremental and marginal changes. The latter refer to unit-by-unit adjustments in output, whereas the incremental change of any decision is the total change involved; it can be applied to changes in a range of variables, not just output. Only those factors that are relevant to, or vary with, a decision should be considered in incremental reasoning; sunk costs, incurred in the past, are irrelevant. Marginal changes are important for economists because they determine optimal or maximising conditions: the profit-maximising level of output occurs where marginal cost equals marginal revenue.

Uncertainty pervades virtually all economic decisions; uncertainty regarding the future means that the expected values of variables have to be estimated. Some projects will be more risky than others in the sense that they have a greater range of potential outcomes. Most business decision-makers are risk averse; they prefer to avoid risk. Attitudes towards risk can be incoporated into the decision-making process in a number of ways: through the certainty equivalent method, by the use of varying discount rates and via game theory.

Case Study: Contribution analysis of a National Coal Board colliery[12]

In justifying some pit closures in the early to mid-1980s, the arguments employed by then National Coal Board (the NCB) were sometimes based on the information obtained in document F23, a profit-and-loss account. The problem with this document was that it was a historical account, and as such, valued resources in terms of the actual or historical costs paid for their services. In addition, some of the costs, like early retirement costs and Area and HQ overheads that were included in the calculations were fixed overhead expenses. These costs were unavoidable and were therefore mainly irrelevant to a decision about whether or not to close a pit.

The relevant costs for decision-making purposes are the current and future costs of resources at the time the decision is made. If this sort of analysis was applied to the suggested closure of Cortonwood Colliery, which precipitated the miner's strike of 1984/85, a very different financial picture would have emerged compared with the NCB's own figures. In 1981/82 the NCB stated that its receipts were £44.3 per tonne and its operating costs were £50.5 per tonne, leading to a loss of £6.2 per tonne, or £1.7 million in total.

However, on the assumption that fixed costs (listed in F23 simply as other operating costs, overheads and services and depreciation) formed the same proportion of total costs in 1981/82 as in 1983/84, then between 17.2% and 23.1% of the unit costs were the unavoidable result of any decision to close Cortonwood. (Exact figures on some of the items were impossible to obtain from the available information, which is why the fixed cost element was given as a percentage range.)

A short-run contribution analysis of Cortonwood is shown in Table 35, page 100. Assumption one was based on an assessment of average costs for 1983/84, while assumptions two and three were derived from assessments of unit costs for 1981/82. In each case different assumptions were made about the precise nature of the particular cost items. The information in Table 35 provides a

Table 35 *Short-run Contribution Analysis of Cortonwood Colliery*

	Assumptions (based on average costs)		
	One 1983/84[a] (£)	Two 1981/82[b] (£)	Three 1981/82[c] (£)
Net proceeds	44.30	44.30	44.30
(Operating costs)	(50.50)	(50.50)	(50.50)
Profit/loss	(6.20)	(6.20)	(6.20)
Minus unavoidable costs:			
Surface damage	2.73	2.44	zero
VERS[d]	1.14	0.83	0.36
Depreciation	3.99	2.78	2.78
Overheads and services	3.79	3.94	3.94
Total unavoidable costs	11.65	9.99	7.08
Contribution	+5.45	+3.79	+0.88

[a]Assumes depreciation of 7.9% of annual average and overhead and service costs of 7.5% of unit costs
[b]Assumes depreciation of 5.5% and overheads and services of 7.8% of unit costs.
[c]Assumes perfect knowledge for surface damage, making it totally avoidable; VERS figure assumes cost remaining to NCB after government subsidies.
[d]Voluntary early retirement scheme.

Source: Berry *et al.* (1985).

snapshot picture of the financial position of the colliery based on a number of varying assumptions. In each case, and whatever the assumptions, it was estimated that the colliery would have made a positive contribution to overheads and to profit. Some of the assumptions may be questioned, such as that of fixed costs being a constant proportion of total costs in the two relevant years. In addition, no assumptions were made about expected future costs and revenues, which can alter markedly due to changing markets for different grades of coal and because of geological factors. However, the analysis indicates the dangers of making economic decisions on data based too much on accounting conventions.

FURTHER READING

Crowson, P.C.S. and Richards, B.A. (1975) *Economics for Managers* (London, Edward Arnold), Chapter 2.
Hill, S. (1989) *Managerial Economics: the Analysis of Business Decisions* (London, Macmillan), Chapters 1,2,4.

NOTES

1. This case is based on the article by Berry *et al.* (1985). The National Coal Board became British Coal in 1986.

Questions □ □ □

5.1 State whether you consider the following costs to be either fixed or variable:

(a) The rent of a shop premises
(b) Wages based on a piece-rate system
(c) Most administrative expenses
(d) The depreciation of an asset due to its ageing

(e) The depreciation of an asset due to its use
(f) Commissions paid to sales people
(g) The telephone bill of a company selling advertising space
(h) Interest payments on borrowed capital

5.2 A person is deliberating about setting up in business on her own. She confidently expects that the business will generate net revenues of £30 000 p.a. over the next three years. Beyond that the financial position is more uncertain. She would have to give up her job which pays £15 000 p.a. She would put £30 000 of her own funds into the business; alternatively, the £30 000 could earn a 15% rate of return in a high-interest savings account. Calculate the present value of the decision to set up in business and state whether it would be worthwhile. What other factors might be relevant to the decision?

5.3 A firm has a new order for one of its products which should yield additional revenues of £200 000. The additional costs of producing the requisite output are estimated to be as follows:

Raw material costs	£80 000
Labour costs	£60 000
Fixed overheads (at 100% labour costs)	£60 000
Variable overheads	£25 000
Fixed selling and marketing expenses	£28 000

However, spare capacity of labour means that the relevant labour costs are actually only £40 000. Based on this information should the firm accept or reject the new order? Explain your reasoning.

The order is for a product that has only just been introduced to the firm's product range. It is estimated that the increase in demand for the new product will cause a fall in sales of £75 000 for another product produced by the firm. Armed with this extra information should the firm now accept or reject the order?

5.4 Explain, with the aid of a diagram, why a sales-revenue-maximising firm would produce a higher output than a profit maximiser, *cet. par.*

5.5 Complete the following table (assuming constant marginal costs) and state the profit-maximising level of output:

Price per unit (£)	Output (units)	TR (£)	TC (£)	Total profit(£)	MR (£)	MC (£)
	0	0	50	−50		
					50	10
50	1	?	60	?		
					40	10
45	2	?	?	20		
					?	?
40	?	120	80	40		
					?	?
?	4	140	90	?		
					?	10
?	5	150	100	?		
					0	10
25	6	?	?	40		
					?	10
?	7	140	?	?		
					−20	−10
15	?	120	130	−10		
					−30	?
10	?	90	140	?		

5.6 A firm is debating whether or not to invest in a new plant costing £10 million. The plant would begin production one year after installation; it would have a life of five years, after which it could be sold for £500 000. The existing plant and equipment could be sold for scrap for £400 000 at the end of the first year's operations. It is estimated that the new plant would yield profits of £2.75 million during each of the five years of operation. The rate of discount is estimated to be 10%. Calculate the net present value of the project and state whether you think the firm should undertake the investment.

5.7 A computer software manufacturer has a choice between developing its facilities for either the domestic or the business market. Each would cost an estimated £10 million to develop, comprising mainly new plant and equipment. The present value of profits for each market depend on general economic conditions. If boom conditions prevailed, the estimated present value of profits over the lifetime of the business programme would be £40.5 million; if normal economic conditions existed, the present value figure would be £17.6 million; and if a recession occurred, the figure would come to £4.2 million. The equivalent figures for the domestic programme are estimated as £26.5 million, £15.5 million and £9.0 million respectively. The probability of boom conditions is 0.2, normal conditions 0.4 and a recession 0.4. Calculate the expected net present value for each market and state which of the two markets the firm should serve. Assess which is the more risky market and comment on whether this assessment affects the original decision.

5.8 A manufacturer of a component for precision instruments sells to a single purchaser at £120 per unit on sales of 500 000 p.a. Its unit costs are as follows:

Direct labour	£30
Raw materials	£20
Variable overheads	£20

Fixed overheads are estimated at 100% of direct labour costs. Another firm is willing to pay £170 per unit for the same number of component p.a., although some small adaptations would be needed in its manufacture. The new purchaser would also expect to be the sole buyer. The component manufacturer would not have to invest in an extension of its production facilities, but additional unit costs would comprise:

Direct labour	£10
Raw materials	£8
Variable overheads	£4

Fixed overheads would continue to be estimated at 100% of direct labour costs. By calculating the contribution per unit and the yearly incremental profit or loss, state whether the component manufacturer should take on the new order.

CHAPTER 6

▶ Production and Costs Analysis

In Chapter 5 it was pointed out that economists refer primarily to two decision-making periods, the *short run* and the *long run*. In the short run it is assumed that at least one factor of production or input is fixed in supply. As a result, the firm is preoccupied by operating decisions about how best to use its existing fixed assets, such as its plant and capital equipment. These decisions occur in the current period. If the firm wants to increase output in this period, it could do so fairly easily by taking on more employees and purchasing more raw materials, but decisions about varying the size of its plant or adding to its capital equipment take longer to resolve. In the long run, it is assumed that a firm is able to vary the scale of all its factors of production. This means that it can undertake planning decisions, such as investing in a bigger plant, that have implications both in the current and future periods. However, given the fact that the firm usually has some fixed inputs, it will often be in a short-run situation; once a new plant is installed, a new short-run position commences.

Production is the process of turning inputs into outputs. As a firm increases or decreases its *level of production*, whether by varying its number of employees or by changing the size of the plant, its *costs of production* rise and fall. The firm's costs of production are an important determinant of how much a firm produces. Furthermore, the relative costs of production of different inputs (i.e. the 'price' of labour compared with the 'price' of capital goods)

dictate the particular method or technique of production that a firm employs, for example whether labour-intensive or capital-intensive.

Decisions about how much to produce and by what methods to effect it are crucial to a firm's survival and prosperity in an uncertain and competitive environment. Assuming that profit is the key objective for any firm, ideally a firm will want to produce that level of output that maximises its profit, or yields the greatest difference between its total revenue and its total costs. In this chapter, the costs side of the equation is dealt with. Revenue decisions are discussed in the next chapter. It should be noted that when a firm maximises its profit, it automatically minimises costs for that particular level of output. However, the relationship does not necessarily run in the opposite direction: cost minimisation need not imply profit maximisation. If a firm actually wanted to minimise its costs it would produce absolutely nothing.

Since much of a product's costs is dictated by its design, especially in manufacturing, it is at this stage that the possibilities for *cost reduction* are most pronounced. Furthermore, as design and development are often extremely expensive processes, a firm will want to *recover these costs* as quickly as it can. These issues are pursued during the course of the chapter.

The chapter begins with a traditional explanation of production decisions based on the assumptions of a single-plant, single-product firm. The effects of these decisions on costs and cost curves are examined. *Economies of scale* at the level of the plant and the firm are explained and *economies of scope* are considered. *Learning effects* are discussed. The implications of the importance of a knowledge of *breakeven analysis* for business decision-making are also examined. The impact of changing technology on the optimum size of the firm is assessed. The ideas featured here are based on an understanding of, and form the theoretical foundation for, the practical cost concepts that were considered in the previous chapter. Several of the key concepts and issues developed in the chapter are analysed in two *cases*; the first examines evidence of economies of scale and scope in building societies and savings and loan organisations, and the second investigates the impact of modern production systems in car manufacture. *Isoquant and isocost* analysis provides a more sophisticated, yet traditional, treatment of the production decision of the firm; this is discussed in the appendix at the end of the chapter.

6.1 PRODUCTION FUNCTIONS AND PRODUCTION TECHNIQUES

A *Production function* examines the relationship between production or output and the inputs involved therein:

$$Q = f(X_1, X_2, X_3, \ldots X_n) \qquad (6.1)$$

In general terms, this formula states that output, Q, is a function of, or depends on, the inputs X_1, X_2, up to input X_n. The *production technique*, which is alternatively referred to as the *production method* or *production process*, describes the different ways of transforming the inputs into output. There may be a number of different techniques of production available for a certain level of output at any time. It is assumed that the firm will want to choose a *technically efficient* method of production. Any technique of production is technically efficient if it is impossible to reduce the amount of each input without reducing the level of output, *cet. par.* Different firms may choose different techniques to produce a similar good, but it is assumed that the current state of technology is given and is incorporated into the particular production function. The level of technology determines the productivity of, or return to, an individual input, with all other inputs held constant.

If it is assumed that there are just two inputs, labour, L, and capital, K, the general form of the production function becomes

$$Q = f(L,K) \qquad (6.2)$$

The exact mathematical form of the function is determined by empirical research.[1] In specific terms, values can be assigned to the inputs. In Table 36, L represents units of labour and K refers to the numbers of machines. They could quite easily refer to labour hours and machine time, or, conceivably, to other inputs. Computer-controlled machines, common-place not just in manufacturing, but throughout industry, still need people to operate them. Thus, L and K can be combined in various ways to produce different levels of output for a particular firm. For example, four units of labour and six units of capital together produce 134 units of output per time period. This level of output can also be produced if eight units of labour are added to three units of capital. In other words, labour has been substituted for capital, giving a more labour-intensive technique of production. Similarly, 69 units of output can either be produced by combining four units of labour with one unit of capital, or by a much more capital-intensive production process whereby a single unit of labour is added to four units of capital. (For the purposes of this example it is assumed that it is possible to produce single, physical levels of output. This is often implausible in service industries; it may also be impossible to isolate single units of individual products in the case of multiproduct firms.)

6.2 THE LAW OF DIMINISHING RETURNS AND RETURNS TO SCALE

The law of diminishing returns

Returns to a factor or input refers to changes in the level of output by varying just that input. In the short run, a firm's production decision is constrained by the fact that one input, for example the size of the plant, is fixed at a certain level. The production function is written as

$$Q = f(L, \bar{K}) \qquad (6.3)$$

where $\bar{K}$ means that the capital input is fixed. Short-run production decisions are dictated by the *law of diminishing returns*, which is alternatively known as

Table 36 *A specific production function*

K =	Output (units per week) for L =									
	1	2	3	4	5	6	7	8	9	10
6	91	106	120	134	146	158	164	168	171	173
5	80	96	110	124	136	146	154	158	161	163
4	69	85	100	113	124	134	143	148	151	152
3	50	71	86	100	112	122	131	134	133	131
2	20	44	69	87	100	106	107	106	103	98
1	5	16	50	69	82	80	77	73	67	58

the *law of variable proportions*. This law holds that as more units of a single, variable factor are added to a fixed factor, eventually each unit of the variable factor produces less extra output than the previous unit. In economic jargon, there comes a point where the diminishing returns to the variable factor causes its *marginal productivity to decline* and this, in turn, causes a fall in the average level of productivity (the relationship between marginal and average values was noted in Section 5.4). In more general terms, the incremental return to each additional unit of the variable factor at first increases, then decreases and eventually may become negative. In a car plant, for example, an increase in demand may be met by employing more workers. Initially, marginal productivity may rise as the capital equipment, i.e. the assembly line, is worked more fully. However, if more labour continues to be hired there will come a point where there are simply too many people to operate the machinery, and productivity falls.

In Table 36 if capital is fixed at two units and labour, the variable factor, is added to the fixed factor in single units, then *total output* or *total product* (TP), the complete output resulting from the employment of a certain amount of inputs in a particular production process, rises steeply at first but then increases at a slower rate; eventually it may even fall. This situation is shown in Table 37. The average product (AP) and the marginal product (MP) are defined as follows. *Average product* is equal to the total product divided by the units of the variable factor, labour (*L*):

$$AP = \frac{TP}{L} \qquad (6.4)$$

Marginal product is the addition to total product from employing one more unit of the variable factor:

$$MP = \frac{\Delta(TP)}{\Delta L} \qquad (6.5)$$

where ΔL is equal to one.

In mathematical terms, marginal product is the derivative of total product with respect to labour:

$$MP = \frac{d(TP)}{dL} \qquad (6.6)$$

Figure 18 shows the relationships between the TP, AP and MP curves. Initially, the TP curve is convex from below, reflecting increasing returns to the variable factor. Beyond point *X*, the point of inflection (where the slope of the curve is maximised), it becomes concave from below, denoting decreasing

Table 37 *Total Product (TP), Average Product (AP) and Marginal Product (MP) Schedules (assuming K constant at two units)*

L	TP	AP	MP[a]
0	0	–	
			20
1	20	20	
			24
2	44	22	
			25
3	69	23	
			18
4	87	21.75	
			13
5	100	20	
			6
6	106	17.67	
			1
7	107	15.28	
			–1
8	106	13.25	
			–3
9	103	11.44	
			–5
10	98	9.8	

[a]Equal to the incremental output.

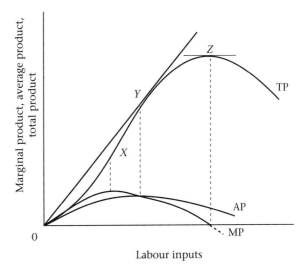

Figure 18 *Total product, average product and marginal product curves.*

returns to the variable input. Eventually it declines, an indication of negative returns. The typical S-shape indicates that total output is a cubic function of the variable inputs. At point *X*, where the TP curve is at its steepest, the MP curve is at its maximum; this is because MP measures the slope of the TP curve at any point. At point *Y*, MP equals AP. Since an increasing marginal product must pull up the average product and decreasing marginal product must push down the average product, the MP curve must cut the AP curve at its highest point, *Y*, on the diagram. The slope of a line from the origin to any point on the TP curve measures the AP at that point. MP equals the slope of the TP curve at any point, so AP must be equal to MP at point *Y*. At point *Z*, the TP curve is at its maximum. Its slope is zero and so this is also the point where MP is zero. Beyond this point TP declines and MP is negative.

In those cases where the fixed inputs are indivisible and cannot be broken down into smaller units, such as a typical manufacturing assembly line, it may be possible to employ too few or too many units of the variable input in relation to the fixed input. The TP curve will exhibit its typical S-shape. Alternatively, where a particular piece of equipment requires the use of, say, a single operative, a firm may be able to maintain the optimal capital/labour ratio over a wide range of output levels. The employment of inputs in fairly fixed proportions may well be the norm in most industries, at least in the short term, in which case the TP curve may be better approximated by a linear function of the variable input or inputs, as shown in Figure 19.

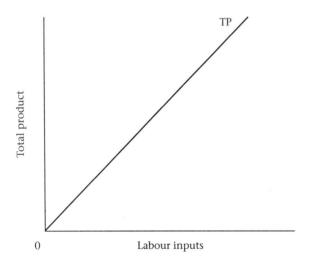

Figure 19 *A linear total product curve.*

Returns to scale

Returns to scale refers to the effect on output of a proportional increase in all inputs. If a production function exhibits *constant returns to scale*, it means that the proportional increase in the inputs is exactly equal to the proportional increase in output; doubling the inputs leads to a doubling of output. If there are *increasing returns to scale*, the proportional increase in output is larger than the proportional increase in inputs. By doubling the inputs, output increases by more than twice its original level; economies of scale exist.[2] In the case of *decreasing returns to scale*, the proportional increase in output is less than the proportional input rise. A doubling of the inputs leads to a less than twofold increase in output, indicating that there are *diseconomies of scale* in the production process. The main sources of economies and diseconomies of scale are discussed later in the chapter.

There are two other points worth noting at this juncture. It may be possible for a production function that exhibits increasing returns to scale to offset the decreasing returns to the single, variable factor if one factor is held fixed. However, this is unlikely; usually the incremental returns to a single, variable factor will decline. Secondly, returns to scale can vary over different levels of output. It is possible for a production function to exhibit increasing returns followed by decreasing returns to scale. In practice many production systems exhibit constant returns over large ranges of output.

6.3 COST FUNCTIONS AND COST CURVES

Traditional cost curves are derived from the short-run and the long-run production functions. In the short run, costs are based on the relationships between inputs and output with a given plant size. Short-run costs are instrumental in determining a firm's operating decisions. In the long run, costs reflect the relationships between inputs and output, assuming an optimally-sized plant for any level of output. Long-run costs form the foundations for a firm's strategic or planning decisions. Cost curves are drawn on the basis that costs are a function of output, *cet. par.*, i.e. assuming that other factors that might affect costs, such as a new technique that raises the relative productivity of capital, an improvement in managerial efficiency or a change in the wage rate, are held constant:

$$C = f(Q) \tag{6.7}$$

The effects of changes in output are shown by *movements along* the respective cost curves. If the *ceteris paribus* assumption is dropped and any of the other factors change their effect is shown by a *shift* of the whole cost curve.

6.4 COSTS OF PRODUCTION IN THE SHORT RUN

In the short run, costs can be divided into fixed costs and variable costs (see Box 6.1, page 108, for an explanation of short-run cost curves).

The breakdown of the costs (including capital equipment) of a typical mid-range model of a car is shown in Table 38.

The variable costs consist primarily of the raw materials and the labour costs involved in assembly and tooling. In other words, there is a high degree of 'cost-fixity' in the manufacture of a car, which reduces the scope for short-term cost competitiveness, at least once the design stage has occurred. (The design cost as a percentage of the total is quite small, but design commits most of the rest of the costs.) The significance of this point has been noted elsewhere:

... competition for market share is driven by the economics of manufacture – high investment costs, high break-even point and low incremental costs thereafter (Monopolies and Mergers Commission, 1992:3).

Rather than simply observe the nature of fixed and variable costs in total, it is of much more interest from the point of view of the firm's operating decisions to investigate what happens to costs as the level of production changes. The importance of average costs for decision-making can be noted in the deregulated US airline market, where the unit operating costs of the smaller, cut-price carriers like Southwest and America West remain lower than their larger rivals. In the third quarter of 1994, for example, the operating cost per available seat mile for Southwest was 7.03 cents and for America West 7.09 cents. This compares with figures of 8.08 cents for American Airlines, 8.32 cents for United and 8.66 cents for TWA in the same period. Despite the limited competition between the regional, short-haul carriers and the larger, long-haul firms, there has been significant cost-cutting by the larger firms, especially in terms of reducing their numbers of flights per destination; this has led to a lowering of the cost differences.[3]

The level of output at which the MC curve cuts the ATC curve is known as the *full or optimum capacity* of a plant. A firm may wish to produce at rather less than full capacity in order to give it some degree of flexibility in its operations. If it does, the difference between the firm's current output level and the level of full capacity output is known as its *spare or excess capacity*. Output levels beyond full capacity, where marginal costs usually rise steeply, are known as *over-full capacity*, although it may still be possible to produce profitably at these levels. A prime reason why a firm may wish to build a plant that has a capacity larger than the expected level of demand is that the demand for many products is variable. The demand for some products like ice-cream or holidays may be seasonal and fluctuate during the year. The UK car market has a yearly surge in demand at the beginning of August in order to secure the new registration. The capacity level of output therefore needs to be able to cope with this level of demand, thus creating extra pressure to stimulate demand during

Table 38 *The breakdown of the selling price to a dealer of a mid-range model of a car*

Cost category	Percentage of total
Raw materials	7.5
Manufacturing (mainly labour):	
Body assembly	7.9
Painting & assembly	6.8
Tooling for fitting	4.8
	19.5
Capital equipment:	
Exterior equipment	3.4
Electrical equipment	7.7
Internal equipment	9.8
Chassis equipment	13.0
Engine & transmission	13.8
	47.7
Design	3.6
Marketing	10.1
Manufacturer's profit	9.3
Guarantee	2.3
	21.7
	100.0

Source: Salvadori (1991:64).

Box 6.1 *Short-run cost curves*

In Figure 20 (a) the *total fixed cost* (TFC) curve, representing the addition of all the fixed costs, is shown as a horizontal straight line. It is fixed at a certain point on the vertical axis, point *V*, which is the amount of the fixed costs. The total *variable cost* (TVC) curve, showing the summation of all the variable costs, begins at the origin. When output is zero, total variable costs equal zero; as output increases, total variable costs increase. The shape of the TVC curve is determined by the law of diminishing returns. The TVC curve first rises quite slowly (corresponding to the section of the TP curve that rises quite rapidly) but then, from the point of inflection at *X*, ever more steeply as marginal productivity falls. This is because the additional units of output produced cost increasingly more in terms of wages. If each additional worker adds less and less to total output, their cost to the firm must gradually rise. The curve is convex when viewed from above until *X*, from whence it becomes concave. Such a curve denotes that total variable costs are a cubic function of output. *Total costs* are the sum of total fixed costs and total variable costs at any level of output. The total cost (TC) curve is exactly the same shape as the TVC curve, and hence it is also represented by a cubic function, but it begins at the level of total fixed costs. Its point of inflection is shown by point *W* in Figure 20(a).

Total fixed costs are by definition a fixed value. Increased production spreads the fixed costs over an ever greater level of output. Therefore, the *average fixed costs* (AFC) decline continuously:

$$AFC = \frac{TFC}{Q} \qquad (6.8)$$

The AFC curve is shown in Figure 20 (b) by a dashed line. It is asymptotic to the horizontal axis. Assuming that there is only one variable factor, labour, and that the return to labour (the wage rate) is constant, then the *average variable cost* curve, AVC, is inversely related to the AP curve. As the AP curve rises the AVC curve falls; as the AP curve falls the AVC curve rises. The shape of the AVC curve can also be found from the TVC curve, as shown in Figure 20 (b). When the TVC curve rises at a diminishing rate, then the AVC curve falls. When the TVC curve begins to increase more rapidly, the AVC curve rises. According to traditional economic theory the AVC curve is U-shaped, as Figure 20 (b) indicates.

$$AVC = \frac{TVC}{Q} \qquad (6.9)$$

The TC curve is the addition of the TFC and TVC curves. Therefore, the *average total cost* (ATC) curve is the vertical summation of the AFC and AVC curves. It is also U-shaped. Initially it declines and then it rises as the increase in average variable costs outweighs the fall in average fixed

costs. As average fixed costs get progressively smaller, the distance between the AVC and ATC curves narrows. Average total costs are often referred to simply as *average costs* or *unit costs*.

$$ATC = \frac{TC}{Q} \qquad (6.10)$$

The other curve shown in Figure 20 (b) is the *marginal cost* curve, MC, which is also U-shaped. It is inversely related to the MP curve. It declines at first as marginal productivity increases, but diminishing returns mean that the MC curve will eventually rise (beyond the inflection points *W* and *X*) as the MP curve starts to fall. Marginal costs measure the change in total costs from producing additional units: they depend solely on variable costs. Marginal cost is equal to the slope of the TC and TVC curves at each output level. The MC curve cuts the ATC and AVC curves at their lowest points in Figure 20 (b) (which correspond to points *Y* and *Z* where rays from the origin are tangent to the TC and TVC curves respectively).

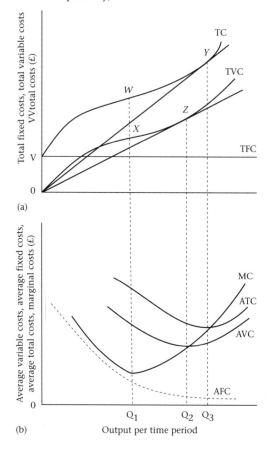

(a)

(b)

Output per time period

Figure 20 *The relationships between short-run cost curves.*

the rest of the year. The same is true in the hotel and catering and tourism industries in their off-peak seasons. The demand for many products may be cyclical and vary every few years by following the ups and downs in general economic activity. Fads or fashion may mean that the demand for a product increases fairly suddenly or more rapidly than was originally estimated. Prozac, the anti-depressant 'wonder drug' is a case in point.

By allowing for excess capacity a firm may be able to produce some expected, average level of output per period. It can then increase output quickly in response to a sudden and temporary rise in demand, although some of the increase in sales may be met by a run-down of its stocks of finished goods. However, these can be added to when demand falls back, while repeated and costly price changes can also be avoided. Of course, if any increase in demand is considered permanent, the firm may well decide to build a new plant, should the rise in sales be sufficiently large to warrant such a decision. Hotpoint was able to combat any fluctuations in demand for household appliances by responding quickly to market changes. When it introduced the washer-drier, sales were forecast at only 10% of capacity output. Actual demand was much higher and its production was easily adjusted so that 50% of its output was devoted to the new product (Baden-Fuller and Stopford, 1992). Excess capacity also gives a firm greater flexibility, should breakdowns of machinery and equipment occur, and can allow for indivisibilities in the production process.

In these situations the marginal productivity of the variable input is likely to remain constant (as, therefore, is the average productivity) over a fairly wide range of output. A plant with built-in spare capacity is more likely to be characterised by a linear total product function, as identified in Figure 19, page 106, and hence a linear TVC curve. It will exhibit widespread constant marginal and average variable costs, which facilitate the firm's pricing and other operating decisions. A linear TVC curve is of the form

$$TVC = a + bQ \qquad (6.11)$$

where estimation of the coefficient b indicates marginal cost, since this is equal to the derivative of total variable cost with respect to output. The TVC curve and associated MC and AVC curves are shown in Figure 21. In (b) the MC and AVC curves are constant until output Q_1 is reached, reflecting the

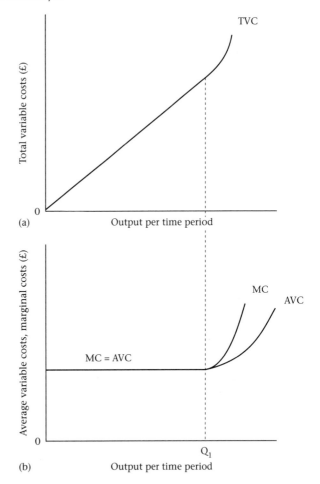

Figure 21 *A linear total variable cost curve and constant marginal cost and average variable cost curves.*

planned spare capacity of the plant. At output levels beyond Q_1, diminishing returns to the variable factor occur and costs begin to increase. The rise in marginal costs causes an increase in average variable costs. It is estimated that most plants in the UK and the US operate, on average, at some kind of *normal capacity*, which is between 75% and 85% of their full capacity at any time (although the average degree of capacity utilisation is higher in Japan). Most evidence also suggests that, for the firms studied, marginal costs are constant over a fairly wide range of output, implying that firms tend to operate with constant input ratios wherever possible. Since marginal costs are constant, so are average variable costs. A linear total variable cost function (and by definition a linear total cost function) is also confirmed by most empirical studies.

6.5 COSTS OF PRODUCTION IN THE LONG RUN

The *long-run average cost* (LRAC) curve shows the least-cost method of production for any level of output. It represents the locus of points of various short-run average total cost (SRAC) curves. Every plant size, or level of fixed input, is represented by a SRAC curve. Therefore, each point on the LRAC curve is a point of tangency with a corresponding SRAC curve. The LRAC curve is often referred to as an *envelope curve* of all the SRAC curves. It is a planning curve in the sense that it guides firms in their decisions to plan for expected output changes. From the LRAC curve the firm is able to determine what size of plant to establish in order to produce its expected level of output at minimum cost.

For example, if plant-level technical economies of scale exist (see next section), giving increasing returns to plant size, each successive SRAC curve will be positioned lower and to the right of the previous one. This can be seen in Figure 22. $SRAC_2$ lies lower and to the right of $SRAC_1$, $SRAC_3$ lies lower and to the right of $SRAC_2$, and so on. Beyond the MES level of output the LRAC curve becomes constant. Successive SRAC curves would lie to the right of $SRAC_4$, but they would be at the same level of unit costs as each other.

In this situation, if the firm decides to produce output level Q_1 it has the choice of three plant sizes: $SRAC_1$, $SRAC_2$ and $SRAC_3$. It will choose the plant size that yields the lowest average costs for that particular level of output, $SRAC_2$, giving average costs of

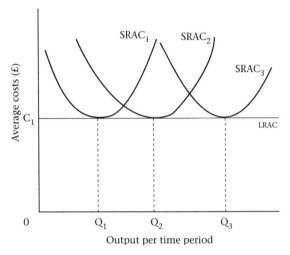

Figure 23 *The relationship between short-run average costs and long-run average costs assuming constant returns to scale.*

C_1. Note that this level of output can be produced by operating a smaller plant, $SRAC_1$, at full capacity. However, it is better that the firm underutilises (since the tangency point is to the left of its minimum point) a larger plant, $SRAC_2$, rather than operates the smaller plant at the lowest point on its particular curve. In fact, this situation occurs until the MES level of output. Lower unit costs are achieved by underutilising successively larger plants rather than by operating smaller plants at their full or designed capacity. On the other hand, a plant larger than $SRAC_2$, such as $SRAC_3$, would give the firm greater flexibility regarding future increases in demand, but, since it is not tangent to the LRAC curve at Q_1, yields higher unit costs.

Where there are constant long-run average costs, each SRAC curve's tangency point is at its minimum point. This can be seen more clearly in Figure 23, which shows the relationship between the LRAC curve and various SRAC curves, assuming that constant returns to scale exist. Larger output levels can be produced by building successively larger plants, each of which is designed to produce that particular level of output, Q_1, Q_2, Q_3 and so on.

Finally, if plant-level diseconomies of scale exist, yielding decreasing returns to plant size, successive SRAC curves will lie higher and to the right. The various tangency points on the LRAC curve must be to the right of the minimum points of each SRAC curve. The least-cost level of output will be better achieved in each case by overutilising a smaller plant than by utilising a larger plant at full capacity.

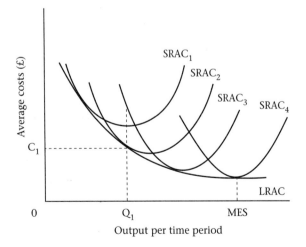

Figure 22 *The relationship between short-run average costs and long-run average costs assuming increasing returns to scale up to the MES level of output.*

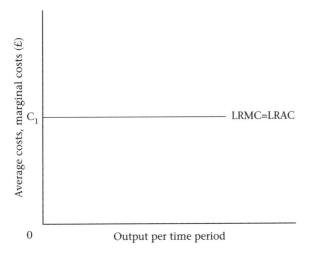

Figure 24 *Constant long-run marginal costs and long-run average costs.*

Long-run marginal costs (LRMC) have the same relationship with long-run average costs as exists between marginal costs and average costs in the short run. If the LRAC curve is declining the LRMC curve must lie below it because long-run marginal costs are pulling down the long-run average costs. Conversely, if the LRAC curve is rising the LRMC curve must lie above it, since the long-run marginal costs are pushing up the long-run average costs. If long-run average costs are constant long-run marginal costs must also be constant and equal to them, as shown in Figure 24.

It is worth noting (see Bailey and Friedlander, 1982) that the relationship between average cost and marginal cost indicates the degree of returns to scale. If total costs are defined as $C = C(Q)$, then $AC = C(Q)/Q$ and $MC = dC/dQ$. Therefore, scale economies, S, are measured by

$$S = AC/MC = \frac{C(Q)}{QdC/dQ} \qquad (6.12)$$

which is the reciprocal of the elasticity of cost with respect to output Thus, $S \gtrless 1$ represents increasing, constant or decreasing returns to scale.

6.6 SOURCES OF ECONOMIES AND DISECONOMIES OF SCALE

Single-plant economies and diseconomies of scale

There are several sources of technical economies of scale at the single-plant level. As output increases, both labour and machinery can be put to more specialised tasks, hence raising input productivity and reducing unit costs. Some inputs, for example the optimal size of plants in industries like nuclear power or electricity generation, cannot be broken down into smaller units; they are indivisible. They are likely to achieve higher levels of efficiency at larger rather than lower output levels. The same sort of reasoning can apply to the managerial function: the greater the number of workers that can be supervised by a manager the more the cost of the managerial function can be spread and the lower its unit cost. The technical relationship between the surface area of a container and its volume, whereby the former increases at a slower rate than the latter, means that the unit cost of storage in industries like petrol refining and cement production falls with increased size. Finally, the levels of stocks of raw materials, components and finished goods, plus the size of the workforce required to repair breakdowns of machinery and equipment, are all likely to increase less than proportionately with volume, causing a fall in their cost per unit of output.

There is also the likelihood of *diseconomies of scale* at the single-plant level: the larger the plant the greater the chance of labour specialisation. However, the work may become repetitive and offer little stimulation; as a result, productivity may suffer, forcing unit costs upwards. There is also the proba-

---

Box 6.2 *Classifications of economies of scale*

When discussing economies of scale, distinctions should be made between *technical* and *pecuniary* sources and between economies at the level of the *single plant* and at the *firm* level, especially if it operates a number of plants, i.e. is *multiplant*. Technical economies are the result of the actual organisation of the production process: they reduce the physical quantity of inputs per unit of output. They represent the genuine social gains from economies of scale because they result in fewer resources being required per unit of output. Pecuniary economies, which usually occur at the firm level, are achieved by a firm paying lower input prices. They arise because of the market power of the firm and benefit the firm alone. Diseconomies of scale can occur at either level. Firms may also be *multiproduct*, in which case it is necessary to distinguish between *ray* or *overall* scale economies that arise when the outputs of all products are increased by the same proportion simultaneously and *product-specific* economies that occur when there is an increase in output of one product alone.

bility of managerial diseconomies in large plants as the bounds of rationality are reached. An increase in size adds to bureaucracy: any decision passed down is likely to become distorted if it has to go through various administrative layers. By the same token information moving in the opposite direction may become equally twisted. A reduction in the quality of messages, in whichever direction they move, raises average costs of production.

Multiplant economies and diseconomies of scale

The existence of economies or diseconomies at the firm level also causes a fall or a rise in average costs. Pecuniary economies are the result of the bargaining power that a large firm can exert in the market. It may be able to negotiate a loan at a lower rate of interest than a smaller firm. Transport costs may be less because a large firm can secure preferential rates. Similarly, advertising may be cheaper to purchase. A large firm will probably be able to buy its raw materials in bulk from its suppliers at a reduced unit cost. The large supermarket chains, Sainsbury, Tesco and Argyll (the owners of the Safeway group) are able to obtain cheaper produce in this way because of their dominant (monopsonistic) buying power. However, the same advantages may arise because of technical economies of scale. If a large firm can secure a cheaper loan, it may be because of the perception that its greater size makes it less risky, as there is more chance of it being able to repay the loan. Bulk buying, resulting in lower unit costs, may be the result of lower transaction costs from a few, big orders on the part of both the supplier and the large buyer.

Technical economies of scale can also arise because a firm operates a number of plants. Duplication can be avoided in services like accountancy, market research, personnel and maintenance. Multiplant firms may be more capable of financing and sustaining an R&D programme, which ultimately can lead to the development of new processes that reduce average costs. However, this reduction may be counterbalanced by the possibility of excessive bureaucracy in large-scale R&D departments, with the result that there may be similar problems regarding the dissemination of information as in the case of the single-plant organisation, leading to higher unit costs. Technical and pecuniary economies often occur simultaneously and it is extremely difficult to separate their effects, although both will lead to a reduc-

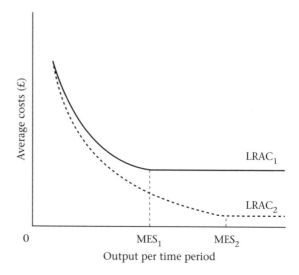

Figure 25 *The effect of multiplant economies of scale on long-run average costs.*

tion in unit costs. Eventually, as is the case at the single-plant level, managerial diseconomies of scale may cause unit costs to rise.

Firm economies of scale can have a profound effect on a firm's unit costs. In Figure 25, MES_1, on $LRAC_1$, indicates the level of output at which all single-plant technical economies of scale have been exhausted. If firm-level economies of scale exist, long-run average costs fall more rapidly, as shown by $LRAC_2$. The minimum efficient *firm* size is MES_2, at which point all firm economies of scale have been tapped. However, for multiproduct firms, it is not clear whether the cost reductions are the result of overall or product-specific economies of scale. Empirical research has made some progress in distinguishing between the two, as can be seen in Case Study One on page 119.

6.7 EVIDENCE OF ECONOMIES OF SCALE

Evidence of the existence of economies of scale in various industries has usually sought technical rather than pecuniary explanations. A summary of the main evidence for the UK and the EU is given in Table 39.

At the single-plant level, the first two columns in the table show that the MES as a percentage of output varies considerably between industries. Naturally, the MES is always a much lower

Table 39 *Evidence of single-plant economies of scale in selected manufacturing industries in the UK and the EU*

Industry	MES as % of output		% rise in costs at one-third MES
	UK	EU	
Beer	12	3	5
Cigarettes	24	6	2.2
Oil Refining	14	2.6	4
Integrated steel	72	9.8	10
Cement	10	1	26
Petro-chemicals	23	2.8	19
Paint	7	2	4.4
Ball-bearings	20	2	8–10
Televisions	40	9	15
Refrigerators	85	11	6.5
Glass bottles	5	0.5	11
Washing machines	57	10	7.5
Bricks	1	0.2	25[a]
Nylon and acrylic	4	1	9.5–12[a]
Cylinder blocks	3	0.3	10[a]
Tyres	17	3	5[a]

[a]The percentage increase in costs for bricks, nylon, cylinder blocks and tyres is at 50% MES.

Source: Pratten (1989).

percentage of EU output than for UK output, although there are considerable variations across industries at both the national and international levels. In the majority of the investigations the MES scale of output is less than 5% of total EU output. This figure suggests that, in most industries, the EU market can support at least 20 plants. For the UK alone, MES is above 10% in most cases, and often substantially so, suggesting that only a very small number of plants would be able to survive in each industry.

Another method of assessing the effects of economies of scale on an industry, as shown in the third column of Table 34, page 97, is to see by how much unit costs increase at a certain percentage of MES output. In the majority of instances the cost disadvantage for plants at a third (or a half) MES is only around 10%; smaller plants do not incur a large cost penalty. In other words, the evidence seems to give rather contradictory signals about the extent and impact of economies of scale in the industries studied. Lyons (1989) has summarised other evidence, mainly for the UK and the US, on the pervasiveness of plant scale economies in manufacturing and has concluded that while they occur in most industries, they do not generally preclude single-plant small firms. The fact

that plant economies of scale have been discovered in many manufacturing industries, accompanied by constant returns beyond MES, whereas diseconomies of scale have not (at least not over the range of plant sizes that have been investigated), leads to a general presumption that the LRAC curve is actually more L-shaped than U-shaped. However, the drawbacks of the empirical methods mean that this is still a rather grey area. Evidence of firm economies of scale is complicated by having to deal with the problems of multiplant and multiproduct firms. A study of firm scale economies from the same source as in Table 39 has found that, for the six manufacturing trades for which estimates are available, the average MES at the firm level as a proportion of the EU market is 34% and for the UK 55%. The average increase in costs at half the MES output is 9%. These figures, although based on a very small sample of industries, confirm the presence of firm-level economies of scale.

The data in Table 39 are obtained from engineering studies of long-run costs, in which production engineers and technicians estimate the expected costs of producing certain output levels, usually on the basis of the existing production function. This method has the advantage that it is based on the current level of technology and on current input prices, but the problem with it is that, when applied to much larger output levels, it tends to underestimate costs, especially the additional administrative expenses involved in operating larger plants.

Some other studies have used the survivor technique, developed by Stigler (1958). The basic premise of this method of cost estimation is that the most efficient firms will survive and grow through time. The firms or plants in an industry are classified by size and the output or employment share of each group is calculated over time. If the share of a group falls, then it is assumed that this class size has relatively high average costs, and vice versa. The survivor technique is relatively simple to apply, but suffers from serious limitations. It assumes that firms operate in competitive markets, in which there are no barriers to entry or collusive price agreements allowing less efficient firms to survive. It is also assumed that firms must have the same objectives and that technology and input prices are unchanged, since any of these can have an impact on market shares. The estimation of long-run costs by the use of statistical techniques, whereby costs are regressed against output, usually employs cross-sectional data, since it is easier to compare the costs of different plant sizes at a particular point in time rather than examining changes in the scale of a single firm over time. In brief, the data assume that all the observed plants are operating at their optimal levels, at the respective tangency points on the LRAC curve, that they are all using the latest technology and that interplant input prices and managerial ability do not significantly differ. Since factors such as these can affect the interplant cost–output observations the estimated function may not prove very reliable.

A number of more recent studies have used econometric methods to estimate multiproduct economies of scale and economies of scope at the firm level; they have tended to concentrate on the deregulated British and American financial services sectors, covering banking, life insurance companies and building societies or savings and loan associations (see Case Study One on page 119).

6.8 ECONOMIES OF SCOPE

Economies of scope arise from multiproduct operations, but specifically they occur where two or more products are produced jointly (Panzar and Willig, 1981). They exist if the total cost of producing two products is less than if produced separately. This can be stated more formally as follows:

$$C(Q_1 + Q_2) < C(Q_1, 0) + C(0, Q_2) \qquad (6.13)$$

where C equals total cost and Q_1 and Q_2 are the outputs of goods 1 and 2 respectively.

The existence of *sharable* or *quasi-public* inputs provide the platform for economies of scope. An input is sharable or quasi-public if its use can be shared between several outputs without congestion. This particular characteristic creates various possibilities for economies of scope. In the first instance, for joint products like mutton and wool (see Section 10.3), interdependencies in the production process mean that an increase in the production of one automatically leads to an increase in the production of the other. Secondly, a firm may utilise the spare capacity arising from indivisibilities in the production process to produce or to market other products for which the joint cost is less than if they were produced individually. Thirdly, the skills and knowledge gained from developing, producing or marketing one product can then usefully be applied to other products. In the 1970s, consumer electronic companies in Japan successfully used the same materials and processes that they had employed in the production of transistor radios to the manufacture of televisions and video recorders. Economies of scope may yield significant increases in revenue for a firm, but with much smaller cost increases, thereby raising profits substantially.

6.9 IS BIGGER NECESSARILY BETTER?

The evidence on long-run costs strongly suggests that there are definite benefits of large size in particular industries, at least at the single-plant level. On the other hand, size does not always imply competitive success. Very large companies can suffer from excessive bureaucracy and an inflexibility to adapting to change. In transaction cost terminology, the problems of bounded rationality and opportunistic behaviour lead to growing control loss. General Motors, IBM and Philips all faced problems from competition by smaller rivals in their respective home markets during the late 1980s. These difficulties led to changes in the internal structures of IBM and GM, both of which tried to reduce transaction costs by moves towards greater decentralisation. Philips attempted to reduce inflexibility by adopting a more international perspective through the hiring of a larger number of senior executives from outside the firm.

The issue of the relative advantages of size is again clouded by the reference to both plants and firms, yet some relevant points can be raised and some conclusions can be drawn. In some highly capital-intensive and high-technology industries increased automation and the use of computers may increase MES, enhance economies of scale and make even longer production runs more efficient. In other sectors, modern technology may reduce MES and make it possible to reap economies of scale at lower output levels, thereby increasing the efficiency of smaller-sized plants. Transportation costs may play a part in determining optimum size. In the case of high-weight, low-value products like cement and sand, average transportation costs rise quickly with increased output; hence the inclusion of transport costs reduces the MES level of output quite substantially. For relatively low-weight, high-value goods such as machine tools and semi-conductors, on the other hand, unit transportation costs increase much more slowly as output increases; the effect of including transport costs is to lower MES output by much less. However, improvements in transport technology have tended to reduce the relative importance of transport costs in most sectors; they are unlikely to be nearly as significant a factor as they once were in influencing the optimum size of plant or the location decision. Finally, there is the nature of the product market to consider. Where the market is highly segmented firms may wish to produce a larger range of products, in which case so-called 'mass customisation' and the pursuit of multiproduct economies of scale and economies of scope may be ranged against the traditional advantages of mass production techniques.

Evidence from Sections 2.3 and 4.8 confirms that in all industrial economies, small firms dominate numerically, while most economic activity is concentrated within large organisations. This is especially true in manufacturing industries. However, as noted in Section 2.3, there is no evidence that average levels of market concentration or levels of aggregate concentration are rising. In fact, they may even be falling. There is also evidence that the average size of plant is decreasing, providing further support for the idea that large firms may be 'downsizing', or splitting their activities into smaller, autonomous units in order to compete more successfully. If this is the case, firm or multiplant economies of scale and economies of scope may be more eagerly sought than those at the single-plant level.

In a number of manufacturing industries, such as motor vehicles, clothing, textiles, mechanical engineering, metal goods and steel, small firms survive alongside much larger organisations by meeting the needs of a segmented market and providing specialised products. This is also true in the case of services such as airlines and travel and tourism. For many other service industries in which the consumer travels to the firm to consume the product, the most efficient scale of production is inevitably small. Figure 26 shows the average cost curves for two differently-sized plants in an industry. The smaller plant, shown by $SRAC_1$, is at a cost advantage for shorter production runs, until output Q_1. Beyond Q_1, the larger plant, indicated by $SRAC_2$, has lower unit costs. For example, in Europe smaller electric arc steel-making plants survive alongside the much larger integrated basic oxygen plants by concentrating on small production runs and specialised products, like high-value stainless steel (Aylen, 1990).

In many manufacturing industries the optimum scale of activities probably remains quite large, at both the plant and the firm levels. This is especially true where long production runs are necessary in order to recover high design and development costs as quickly and as efficiently as possible. In pharmaceuticals, the only manufacturing industry in the UK that has seen a significant increase in employment in the last 20 years, the cost and riskiness of research into new drugs is such that only very large firms can survive in the industry. It was the desire to achieve greater economies of scale in R&D that led to Glaxo

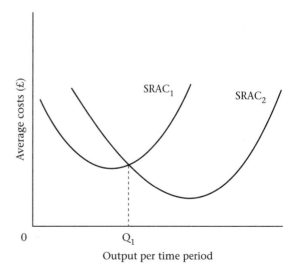

Figure 26 *Cost comparisons of two differently-sized plants.*

acquiring Wellcome in 1995. On the other hand, where the transaction costs of buying in certain activities from the market are lower than if firms were to supply them themselves, then firms will contract-out for such services. This may even be true in the case of R&D activities in the pharmaceutical industry. In 1994, US pharmaceutical companies entered into 117 joint ventures with small biotechnology firms to buy in the results of their research. Presumably, this is felt to be a cheaper method of conducting research than if the large firms were to perform it all themselves.

In conclusion, the impact of scale on costs is likely to vary from industry to industry, but in a number of cases the combined effects of modern technology and segmented markets may enhance the relative efficiency of smaller and medium-sized enterprises. In others, large-scale operations remain the optimum size.

6.10 THE EFFECTS OF EXPERIENCE

In principle, the latest technologies are only able to be introduced in the very long run. Of course, the results of these technical advances, new products and processes, can actually be introduced at any time and once they are introduced a learning process begins. People, both managers and operatives, learn from experience how to use the new equipment or how to produce and market the new product. The more experience they gain, the more adept they become and so their productivity rises and average costs fall. Engineers and technicians may also become more aware of the most suitable techniques of production. As a result, economies of scale can be more fully exploited and both short-run and long-run average cost curves will fall.

The *learning curve* shows the relationship between the unit costs of output and the cumulative output of a product, at constant input prices. Obviously, learning effects are greater in the case of new products or production processes compared with those products or processes that have been in existence for some time. In theory, therefore, firms have an incentive to be the first-mover in developing a new product or investing in the latest technology, although in practice, imitators often secure the greatest cost advantages.[4]

In Figure 27 (a), output Q_1 is produced with plant size $SRAC_1$ on $LRAC_1$. Over time, as experience is gained, there is a rise in productivity of the variable inputs, leading to a fall in the short-run marginal cost, average variable cost and average total cost curves. Also, as plant-level economies of scale become easier to achieve, increasing returns to scale are more obviously revealed in the shape of the LRAC curve. Output Q_2 is produced by plant size $SRAC_2$ on $LRAC_2$. Figure 27 (b) shows the learning curve. CQ_1 is the level of cumulative output where the learning process has been exhausted.

It is estimated that the combined effect of the three factors – technology, learning and scale – results, on average, in a decline in unit production costs of about 20% each time accumulated output is doubled. If a firm develops a range of products and exploits any

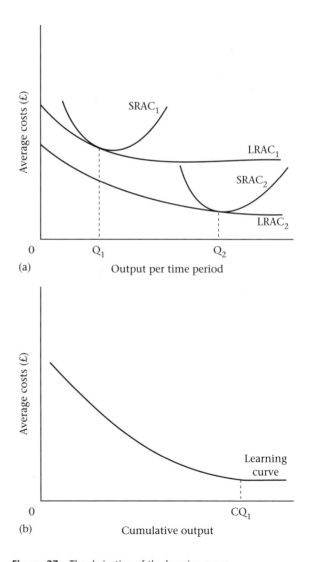

Figure 27 *The derivation of the learning curve.*

economies of scope in addition to the other advantages, the benefits can be even greater. It could then move from one learning curve to another, each with falling unit costs. For example, in the manufacture of aircraft there is widespread agreement that aircraft production has a labour 'learning elasticity' of roughly 0.2, i.e. a doubling of cumulative output produces a 20% reduction in labour costs of production; a labour learning curve of 80% exists. Unit production costs in total in the industry fall by 10% as cumulative output is doubled (Klepper, 1991). Bowen (1991a) found that in the semiconductor industry, learning effects reduce production costs by 20–30% when cumulative output is doubled. This is mainly due to a reduction in the number of defective chips per production run as experience of operating in the industry increases.

6.11 BREAKEVEN ANALYSIS

Breakeven analysis has important implications for business decision-making. The breakeven output is that level of output where total revenue equals total cost. At outputs less than the breakeven point, a firm will make a loss, and at outputs beyond the breakeven point, it will achieve a profit. (As a result, it is sometimes referred to as *cost–volume–profit analysis*.)

It should be noted that, when using traditional total cost (TC) and total revenue (TR) curves as in Figure 28(a), there are two breakeven levels of output, Q_1 and Q_2, at points X and Y respectively. Hence, in order to simplify the analysis, linear TC and TR functions are often used in breakeven analysis, as indicated in Figure 28(b). This results in a single breakeven level of output, at point X. The linear TR function assumes constant prices and the linear TC function assumes constant marginal costs. These may be reasonable assumptions to make over a limited range of output, but eventually price may have to drop in order to increase sales. Furthermore, the reduced efficiency of the variable input beyond the capacity level of output will eventually cause variable, and total, costs to rise.

In algebraic terms the breakeven output level can be found as follows:

TR = $P \times Q$
TC = TFC + (AVC $\times Q$)

where P is the price per unit, Q the quantity, TFC the total fixed cost and AVC the average variable cost.

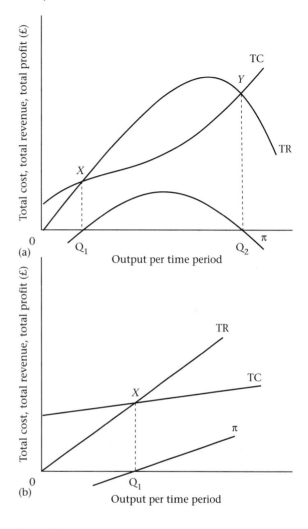

Figure 28 *Breakeven levels of output.*

The breakeven output is found where TR is equal to TC:

$P \times Q$ = TFC + (AVC $\times Q$)

Therefore

$Q(P - AVC)$ = TFC

and

$$Q_B = \frac{TFC}{P - AVC} \qquad (6.14)$$

where P minus AVC is equal to the contribution to profits per unit of output or the average profit contribution. The breakeven output is found by simply dividing the total fixed costs by the per unit profit contribution, although this is only true in the case of linear total revenue and total cost functions. Where either or both of these functions are not linear the average profit contribution varies with output.

Breakeven analysis is not only important because it tells a firm beyond what level of sales it will begin to make a profit. If it is felt that a certain breakeven level of sales cannot be achieved, a firm may wish to assess what effect an increase in price will have on the breakeven output. Obviously, the rise in price will reduce sales and lower the breakeven quantity. If it is estimated that the new breakeven quantity can be attained, the firm may decide to go ahead and charge the higher price.

Breakeven analysis is also useful in assessing the feasibility of different methods of production. If a firm is comparing alternative methods of production against a given total revenue function, then the more highly automated or capital-intensive the proposed production system, the greater the fixed costs as a proportion of total costs and the higher the breakeven level of output, or the longer the time taken to achieve it. This can be confirmed by reference to equation (6.14). The higher are total fixed costs the greater is Q_B, the breakeven level of output. However, once the breakeven quantity has been achieved profits tend to rise faster in an automated system compared with a more labour-intensive system that has a lower proportion of fixed costs. In general terms, with other things being equal, the more capital-intensive an industry's production methods the greater its likely breakeven level of output. In the aircraft production industry, which is highly capital-intensive, it is estimated that the breakeven point for a typical aircraft project is reached about 12 years after the original investment in the project has occurred (Klepper, 1991).

For any level of output, the greater the fixed costs as a percentage of the total, or the more automated the production system, the higher the *operating leverage* that a firm has. This is an elasticity indicator in the sense that it measures the responsiveness of the total profit of a firm to changes in output. The degree of operating leverage is equal to[5]

$$\frac{\text{Percentage change in profit}}{\text{Percentage change in output}} \qquad (6.15)$$

In the case of linear cost and revenue functions operating leverage is highest around the breakeven level of output. Profit is at or near zero at this point

and therefore any percentage change in profit is likely to be large in response to a relatively small change in output.

Breakeven analysis is an extremely useful decision-making weapon for a firm. It facilitates sound decision-making in a number of important areas such as pricing, sales and the choice of production techniques. However, the problems surrounding the assumption of linear total cost and total revenue functions have been mentioned. Both may only hold over a limited range of output.

6.12 CONCLUSIONS

A production function examines the relationship between production and the relevant inputs. It is assumed that a firm will opt for technically efficient methods of production. In the short run the production decision is constrained by the fact that at least one input is fixed in supply. Production decisions are dictated by the law of diminishing returns. The declining marginal productivity of the variable input underlies the traditional S-shaped total product curve. However, it may be that, where a firm employs inputs in relatively fixed proportions, a linear total product curve is the more likely outcome. A proportional increase in all inputs results in increasing, constant or decreasing returns to scale, depending on whether the proportional increase in output is more (due to economies of scale), the same as or less than (because of diseconomies of scale) the proportional input rise.

Cost curves are derived from specific production functions: the traditional short-run U-shaped marginal cost, average variable cost and average total cost curves emerge from the law of diminishing returns. In practice, plants are likely to be operated with some built-in flexibility in order to cope better with temporary demand fluctuations and breakdowns in machinery and equipment; in these circumstances marginal and average costs may remain constant over fairly large output ranges.

The key long-run decision for a firm is to decide the size of plant suitable for a certain level of output; assuming economies of scale (diseconomies of scale) exist it is preferable to underutilise (overutilise) a larger (smaller) plant than to operate a smaller (larger) plant at optimum capacity. Technical and pecuniary economies of scale and those at the level of the plant and the firm are considered. There is evidence of plant-level economies of scale in many manufacturing industries; they are accompanied by constant costs beyond MES, producing L-shaped LRAC curves. However, the deficiencies of the empirical techniques used mean that such conclusions should be treated with some caution. More recent studies have concentrated on estimating multiproduct economies of scale and economies of scope, specifically in the deregulated financial service industries of the UK and the US. In a multiproduct setting, a distinction needs to be made between ray and product-specific economies of scale. The former arise when the outputs of all products are increased by the same proportion simultaneously; product-specific economies of scale occur when there is an increase in the output of just one of the products; economies of scope exist if the total cost of producing two products is less than if produced separately.

Greater experience in using new techniques or in marketing new products causes productivity to increase and unit costs to fall; economies of scale can be more fully exploited. The learning curve shows the relationship between average costs and cumulative output for a product. It is estimated that the combined effect of technology, learning and scale results in a 20% fall in unit costs each time accumulated output is doubled.

Finally, breakeven analysis is discussed. The breakeven level of output is where total revenue equals total cost. Algebraically it can be shown that breakeven output is found by dividing total fixed costs by the per unit profit contribution. Breakeven analysis has important implications for pricing and sales policies and in the choice of production technique.

Case Study One: Economies of scale and scope in financial services

A large number of studies have been undertaken of the financial services industries of the UK and the US since the early 1980s, in order to assess the impact on costs of reduced regulatory controls and technological changes. In particular, they have concentrated on the possibilities for the achievement of firm-level economies of scale and economies of scope. The general consensus (although a good deal of individual variation persists) seems to be that economies of scale exist for banks, life insurance companies and building societies (or savings and loan associations), although only up to a certain size of company. Economies of scope also exist, although there is not universal agreement on this point.

Two of the studies (McKillop and Glass, 1994; Gropper, 1995) have undertaken econometric investigations of the cost structures of, respectively, building societies in the UK and their equivalent institutions in the US, savings and loans (S&L) associations. In both countries, legislative changes enable them to offer a larger range of products rather than just mortgages, such as consumer and commercial lending, stockbroking facilities and other investments, although S&Ls in the US are still required to hold at least 70% of their assets in housing-related investments.

Before examining the results of the studies it is worthwhile explaining some of the concepts in more detail. *Ray* (sometimes referred to as overall) *economies of scale* occur when total costs increase less than proportionately for a composite change in output. They can be measured by the ratio of the relevant average and marginal costs. Ray average costs are defined as $RAC(Q) = C(tQ)/t$ where t is the number of units of a composite commodity consisting, say, of two outputs. Therefore, ray scale economies can be measured by

$$S = \sum \frac{C(Q)}{Q_i MC_i} \tag{6.16}$$

where the denominator denotes the sum of the marginal costs of the individual products weighted by each output. $S \gtrless 1$ indicates increasing, constant or decreasing returns to scale. As in the single-product case, ray scale economies are defined as the reciprocal of the elasticity of cost with respect to output.

Product-specific economies of scale occur when total costs increase less than proportionately to a change in the output of one product only. In order to measure *product-specific economies* it is necessary to introduce another concept, the *average incremental cost*, AIC, or the average cost of producing only good 1 (of two goods). This is given by

$$\text{AIC}_1 = \frac{C(Q_1,Q_2) - (0,Q_2)}{Q_1} \tag{6.17}$$

The average incremental cost is defined as the addition to total cost of producing a certain output of a particular product compared with not producing it at all, divided by the output of that product. Product-specific returns to scale for any product can then be defined as the ratio of the average incremental cost to the marginal cost:

$$S_i = \frac{\text{AIC}_i}{\text{MC}_i} \tag{6.18}$$

As before, $S \gtrless 1$ indicated increasing, constant or decreasing returns to scale.

Economies of scope, S_c, are measured by the proportion of total costs saved by producing jointly two products:

$$S_c = \frac{C(Q_1,0) + C(0,Q_2) - C(Q_1,Q_2)}{C(Q_1,Q_2)} \tag{6.19}$$

Thus, $S \gtrless 0$ determines whether or not economies of scope exist.

Conflicting results have been reported. McKillop and Glass (1994) examined the accounts of 89 British building societies for 1991 using a two-output, three-input model; the products were divided into two groups: mortgage products and other commercial assets, comprising other advances and investments. The main results of the study for different classifications of institution are shown in Table 40.

Table 40 *Estimates of economies of scale and scope for UK building societies*

Building society grouping	Overall scale economies[a]	Product-specific economies		Economies of scope
		Mortgage products	Other commercial assets	
National	0.937*	1.113*	6.538	−0.734
Regional	1.011	1.072*	8.007	−0.571
Local	0.956*	1.156*	7.992	−0.459
All	0.974*	1.121*	7.835	−0.522

[a]Measured by the sum of cost elasticities with respect to outputs. A value less (greater) than 1 indicates economies (diseconomies) of scale.
*Significantly different from 1 at the 5% level.

Source: McKillop and Glass (1994).

There is evidence of significant economies of scale for national and local societies but not for regional institutions, a fact put down to the relatively small customer base within which they tried to sell their new products. The nominal values for product-specific economies reveal increasing returns to scale for both mortgages and other commercial assets, although in the latter case the results are not significantly different from one. In other words, product-specific economies only exist for mortgage products. The values in the final column show only diseconomies of scope, although other evidence revealed no significant cost disadvantages for national societies in producing the two products jointly. They would appear to be the only institutions sufficiently large to exploit the opportunities for diversification following deregulation.

Gropper (1995) undertook a similar regression analysis (based on a five-output, three-input model), of 1589 S&Ls in the US using 1988 data. Ray economies were measured using the formula in equation (6.16). Very different results were obtained throughout: moderate but significant overall economies of scale were reported for institutions up through the mean output size, but beyond this level, constant returns to scale seemed to predominate. Product-specific scale economies existed only for non-mortgage activities, like commercial loans and direct investments. Economies of scope were significant over a large range of outputs; they were highest for the smallest institutions. These results merely serve to confirm the general conclusions about economies of scale and scope in financial service institutions stated in the introduction: economies of scale seem to exist for building societies and S&Ls, at least up to an average size of institution; there is also some evidence of economies of scope, although what size of institution is most conducive to their capture is impossible to say.

Case Study Two: Modern production systems in car manufacture

The car market is a mature one, where worldwide production of vehicles (including trucks and buses) has levelled off at about 48 million units a year. A mature market is usually characterised by high degree of competition and segmentation. In order to gain access to as many of the segments as possible firms may wish to produce a relatively small number of each of a large variety of models.

The changes in the market mean that firms have had to adapt by introducing more flexibility into their production systems, although precisely what form the flexibility takes varies between firms and between countries. In general terms, a *flexible manufacturing system* is said to be one that uses a high level of automation and computer technology in order to enable production to react more quickly to changing demand, thus giving firms greater flexibility to produce a larger range of products and at lower average costs than more traditional techniques of production.

Japanese car producers have been quoted as the archetypal flexible manufacturers; this view has been based on the sort of evidence shown in Table 41, page 122, which reveals that, compared with Western producers, Japanese methods have been characterised by a high degree of automation, teamwork, machine and job flexibility and quality control. Collectively these methods have been referred to as *lean manufacturing* (a term coined originally by Womack *et al.*, 1990). Since the cost of designing and developing a new model for the world market has been variously estimated at £1.5–2 billion, there is significant emphasis on the avoidance of waste at any stage of the production process in order to recover these costs as quickly and as efficiently as possible. Reducing the number of defective parts can achieve this aim; so can the process of keeping stocks to a minimum and only supplying parts when required, or, in other words, 'just-in-time'.

In fact, the flexibility that car firms have sought has mainly been to match the same components to different models. This is because the MES level of output for some operations, like the casting of engine blocks or the pressing of body panels, is much higher than for others, such as assembly operations.

Table 41 *Car production methods in Japan, the US and Western Europe[a]*

	Japan	US	Western Europe
Layout			
Factory space (per sq. ft per car p.a.)	5.7	7.8	7.8
Size of repair area (% of assembly space)	4.1	12.9	14.4
Stocks (for 8 sample parts)	0.2	2.9	2
Employees			
Workforce in teams (%)	69.3	17.3	0.6
No. of job classifications	12	67	15
Training new workers (hours per worker)	380	46	173
Quality (defects per 100 cars)	60	82	97
Automation			
(% of process automated)			
Welding	86	76	77
Painting	55	34	38
Assembly	2	1	3

[a]The figures are the average for car plants in 1989.

Source: *The Economist*, 17 October 1992.

Components may be purchased from other manufacturers or, as is more likely in the case of the Japanese companies, from component suppliers with whom they have a one-to-one relationship. They can then be fitted to the relatively few models that most car firms produce. For example, Nissan, Ford and General Motors/Vauxhall each produce only two models in the UK. However, within each model there are likely to be innumerable variants on the basic theme.

The instigator of lean manufacturing was Toyota, which gained from the benefits of learning-by-doing. The other major Japanese car companies followed suit, although not always entirely successfully. The same can be said for the Western European and North American firms when they introduced greater flexibility into their production systems. There is certainly evidence of higher productivity levels (measured in terms of hours taken to assemble a car) in Japanese car plants compared with elsewhere (Womack *et al.*, 1990). However, when allowance has been made for differences in the degree of capacity utilisation and vertical integration between the Japanese plants and those in other countries, the productivity variations are significantly smaller. Japanese car plants tend to operate at a much higher level of capacity utilisation and with a lower degree of vertical integration than the plants in other major car-producing countries. (Wherever they are located, because of their close relationships with their suppliers, the Japanese plants operate essentially as assembler/manufacturers rather than as complete manufacturers of units. This fact explains why the Japanese car transplants in the US and Europe are, by and large, 'screwdriver' or low-value-added assembly operations with relatively little local content.) If performance is measured in terms of value added per worker for a given year, in US dollars, so allowing for differences in degrees of vertical integration, significant differences in the performance of car plants within countries as well as between countries have been discovered. Toyota outperforms everybody, including the other Japanese car firms, but the latter are also outperformed by Ford US (Williams *et al.*, 1992). In other words, Toyota would appear to stand out as more the exception than the rule in the Japanese car industry.

FURTHER READING

Bailey, E. and Friedlander, A.F. (1982) Market structure and multi-product industries. *Journal of Economic Literature*, **20** (September), 1024–48.

Koutsoyiannis, A. (1979) *Modern Microeconomics*, 2nd edn (London, Macmillan), Chapters 3,4.

Neale, A. and Haslam, C. (1994) *Economics in a Business Context*, 2nd edn (London, Chapman and Hall), Chapter 2.

NOTES

1. A linear production function takes the form

    $$Q = a + bK + cL$$

    where *a*, *b* and *c* are the coefficients or the parameters of the equation.

    A power function, such as the Cobb–Douglas function (Cobb and Douglas, 1928), indicates a multiplicative relationship between the inputs and output. This is expressed as

    $$Q = aK^b L^c$$

    The power function can be transformed into a linear function by logarithms and then estimated.

    A cubic production function is of the form

    $$Q = a + bKL + cK^2L + dKL^2 - eK^3L - fKL^3$$

    This exhibits first increasing and then decreasing returns to scale.

2. Returns to scale refer only to technical economies of scale.

3. See *The Economist*, 5 November 1994, 'Come Fly the Unfriendly Skies'.

4. Edwin Mansfield has found that over a 30-year period, and on average, imitators can make a new product for two-thirds the cost and time it takes the innovating firm (*The Economist*, 11 January 1992, 'Innovation').

5. At any output this can also be shown to be equal to:

    $$Q\ CP - AVC$$
    $$Q\ CP - AVC - TFC$$

Questions ☐ ☐ ☐

The Appendix should be read before some of these questions are attempted.

6.1 Units of the variable factor, *X*, are added in single units to the fixed factor, *Y*. Total product figures are as given. Complete the average product (AP) and marginal product (MP) figures.

State the number of units of the variable factor that should be employed to obtain optimum efficiency:

(a) in terms of its incremental return.
(b) in terms of its output per unit.
(c) in terms of the utilisation of the fixed input.

Units of variable factor	Total product (TP)	Average product (AP)	Marginal product (MP)
0	0	—	
1	12		
2	30		
3	50		
4	67		
5	81		
6	93		
7	101		
8	106		
9	108		
10	106		

6.2 The isoquant diagram shows the optimal combinations, of labour at L_1 and capital at K_1 for producing output level Q_1 of a particular product.

(a) Show the effect of a fall in the relative cost of labour on the optimal input combination.

(b) Show the effect of a simultaneous and proportionate increase in the cost of both inputs.

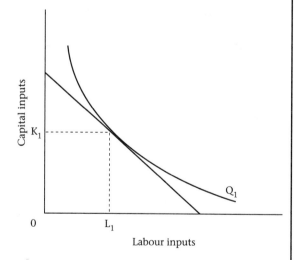

6.3 A manufacturer of hand-painted pots and other handicrafts faces the following production function. Machine time costs £12 per hour and labour costs are £10 per hour. The monthly budget is £6000.

Machine hours (hundreds per month)	Output (hundreds of units per month) for labour hours per month of					
	100	200	300	400	500	600
5	123	200	235	265	290	302
4	125	190	228	258	280	290
3	112	176	212	245	265	274
2	88	154	182	205	224	226
1	40	122	168	182	190	186

(a) If machine time is initially fixed at 100 hours per month, calculate the incremental and average hourly return to labour.

(b) Assuming both inputs can be varied, estimate the maximum level of output that the company can produce within its budget constraint and the optimal input combination for this output.

6.4 A cost function is of the form TC = 550 + 0.75Q, where TC are expressed in £, and Q, the rate of output, equals 5000 units.

(a) What are the total fixed costs?
(b) What are the total variable costs?
(c) What are the total costs?
(d) What are the average fixed costs?
(e) What are the average variable costs?
(f) What are the average total costs?
(g) What are the marginal costs?
(h) Calculate the incremental costs of an increase in output to 6000 units.

6.5 A bed manufacturer has fixed costs of £50 000 per week. Variable costs amount to a constant £40 per unit per week until capacity output of 1500 beds. Beyond that level they rise steeply: at an output level of 1600 beds weekly, total variable costs amount to £96 000, and at 1800 beds weekly they come to £144 000.

(a) Calculate the manufacturer's average variable costs and average total costs at output levels of 1000, 1500, 1600 and 1800 units per week.
(b) Plot the AVC and ATC curves facing the bed producer. Sketch in the MC curve.

6.6 Given the cost structure of the car industry, comment on the relative merits for UK manufacturers of the new registration scheme on 1 August each year.

6.7 A firm produces a single product in a single plant using two inputs, labour and capital. Input prices are fixed. Show diagrammatically:

(a) a series of isoquants exhibiting first increasing, then constant and finally decreasing returns to scale;
(b) an LRAC curve consistent with the isoquant series in (a).

6.8 Six plants in an industry are observed at a particular point in time. Their estimated output levels and associated total costs are shown below:

Plant size	Optimum output (units)	Total costs (£)
1	1000	20 500
2	2750	48 125
3	5200	65 000
4	8250	80 850
5	10 700	104 860
6	12 300	120 540

(a) Assuming that the observations all indicate tangency points on the LRAC curve, what do they suggest about the estimated shape of the LRAC curve in the industry?
(b) What does the shape of the LRAC curve imply about the probable degree of capacity utilisation of each plant?

6.9 'The methodological problems involved in estimating economies of scale are such that any results should be treated with the utmost caution.' Explain and discuss.

6.10 'Recent evidence on the size of businesses suggests that many may be seeking the benefits of firm-level economies of scale and economies of scope rather than single-plant economies of scale.' Explain and discuss.

6.11   A pub sells its speciality lunches at £4 per head. Total fixed costs amount to £50 000 and variable costs average out to £2 per lunch.

(a) Calculate the annual breakeven number of lunches for the pub.

(b) The pub currently sells 50 000 meals p.a. Calculate the operating leverage at this level of output. (Choose any small percentage change in output.)

(c) The pub is planning an extension of its activities, wishing to sell 75 000 lunches p.a. In order to do this it estimates that its fixed costs will rise to £75 000, but its variable costs will fall to £1.60 per unit sold. Calculate the breakeven level of output and the operating leverage in these circumstances.

APPENDIX. ISOQUANT AND ISOCOST ANALYSIS OF PRODUCTION DECISIONS

Isoquant and isocost analysis assumes the variability of all inputs. In other words, it provides an analytical basis for long-run decision-making, in which the firm can expand or contract its capacity at the single or multiplant levels or can switch between capital-intensive and labour-intensive production techniques. However, the analysis can equally be applied to short-run production choices. The explanation that follows is based on the assumption of expansion or contraction at the level of the single plant for a single-product firm.

According to the data in Table 36, page 104, the firm in question could increase the scale of its production by employing more of both inputs. Alternatively, it could produce the same level of output by substituting labour for capital, or vice versa. The various production methods can be shown graphically by means of *isoquants*. An isoquant (which literally means 'of equal quantity') is a curve that shows the various combinations of inputs that generate the same level of output. It was pointed out previously that, from the production function data shown in Table 36, an output of 134 units could be achieved in a number of different ways. The isoquant corresponding to this output is shown in Figure 29. More isoquants can be drawn, giving an *isoquant map*. In Figure 30, page 126, each isoquant shows the different combinations of inputs that are capable of producing other output levels.

Isoquants that lie above and to the right of Q_2, such as Q_3, portray higher levels of output and those below and to the left of Q_2, like Q_1, indicate lower levels of output. Isoquants are drawn on the assumption that firms make rational and consistent choices; they have the following characteristics:

(1) Higher isoquants are always preferred to lower ones.

(2) They cannot intersect. If they did, it would imply that two maximum levels of output were attainable from a given combination of resources.

(3) They are convex to the origin, or when viewed from below.

This is best explained in terms of the *marginal rate of technical substitution (MRTS)* between the inputs. The MRTS measures the rate at which one factor of production is substituted for another when output is held constant. It is equal to the slope of the isoquant at any point. In Figure 29, at point A six units of capital and four units of labour are employed, at point B four units of capital and six units of labour and at point C three units of capital and eight units of labour. The MRTS of the move from A to B, as labour is substituted for capital, equals AD/DB or 2/2:

$$\text{MRTS} = \Delta K/\Delta L = 2/2 = 1 \qquad (6A.1)$$

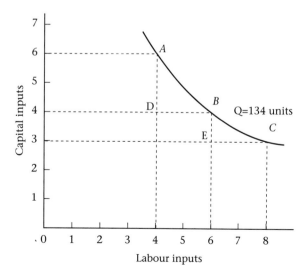

Figure 29   *An isoquant.*

125

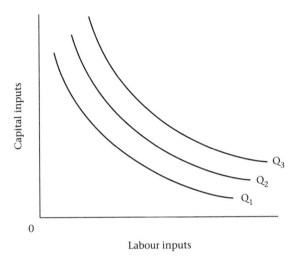

Figure 30 *An isoquant map.*

Moving along an isoquant, the loss in output due to a decrease in use of one input must be exactly matched by the additional output from the increase in use of the other input (for output to remain the same). In other words, the respective changes in output are negatively related. In practice, it is more likely that firms would make incremental rather than marginal changes in their use of inputs, but assuming marginal changes are possible the following condition must hold:

$$- MP_L \times \Delta L = MP_K \times \Delta K \qquad (6A.2)$$

This can be rearranged as

$$- MP_L/MP_K = \Delta K/\Delta L = MRTS \qquad (6A.3)$$

The MRTS is equal to the negative ratio of the marginal products of the inputs, and this is equal to the slope of the isoquant. Moving along an isoquant from left to right, the MRTS (and hence the slope) diminishes; the move from B to C in Figure 29, page 125, is indicated by BE/EC, or 1/2. Thus, as labour is substituted for capital larger incremental exchanges of labour for capital are required; the notion of diminishing marginal productivity means that the ratio MP_L/MP_K falls.[1]

The precise nature of returns to scale can be indicated on an isoquant map by examining the distance between successive isoquants (along a ray out of the origin) that represent multiples of some original level of output (i.e. Q, $2Q$, $3Q$ etc.). If constant returns to scale exist, the isoquants are equally spaced, as indicated in Figure 31(a). Where the distance between successive isoquants increases, decreasing returns to

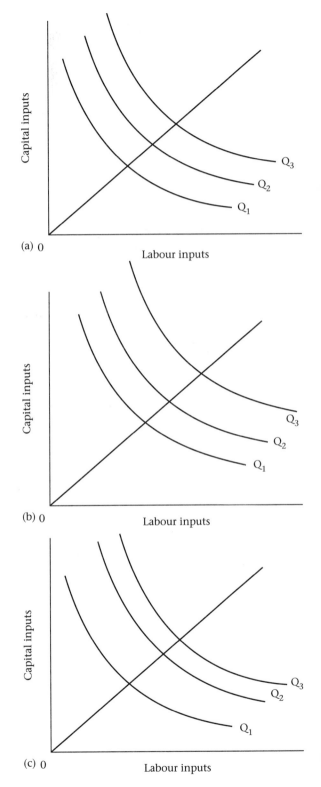

Figure 31 *Returns to scale.*

scale are evident, as shown in Figure 31(b). Finally, should the distance between consecutive isoquants decrease, increasing returns to scale is indicated as portrayed in Figure 31(c).

Economically efficient methods of production

Where at least some degree of substitution between inputs occurs, a firm may be able to choose between numerous technically efficient methods of production. For a firm to decide how much to produce and what method of production it should employ, it will need to take into account the relative prices of, or returns to, the factors of production. Only then will it be able to determine the *economically efficient* technique, which will be the one with the lowest costs for a certain level of output.

For example, if the rental price of capital is assumed to be fixed at £500 per week and the price of labour is set at £250 per week then, for an outlay or total cost of £2500, the firm could purchase either five units (£2500/£500) of capital or 10 units (£2500/£250) of labour. Alternatively, it could purchase other combinations of labour and capital, given their relative prices, for this same level of expenditure. If these points are plotted on a graph, the budget line joining them is called an *isocost* (literally, 'of equal cost'). This is shown in Figure 32. An isocost shows the various combinations of inputs that can be purchased by a firm for a certain outlay or at a certain cost.

More generally, if P_L is the unit price of labour and P_K is the unit price of capital, then the total cost, C, of a particular level of output using the inputs labour and capital is given by

$$C = P_K K + P_L L \qquad (6A.4)$$

This can be rearranged as

$$K = \frac{C}{P_K} - \frac{P_L}{P_K} L \qquad (6A.5)$$

This is a straightforward linear equation for K. The first term in the equation gives the intercept for capital inputs on the Y-axis of the graph. It is the total cost divided by the unit price of capital, where $L = 0$. The slope of the isocost is given by the negative ratio of the relative prices of the inputs:

$$\text{Slope} = -\frac{P_L}{P_K} \qquad (6A.6)$$

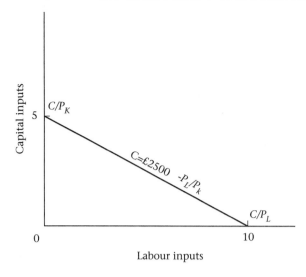

Figure 32 *An isocost.*

The effect of a change in total costs

A change in the firm's total outlay or total costs, given no change in the relative prices of the inputs, is shown by parallel shifts in the budget line. In other words, other isocosts can be drawn for different levels of expenditure. Each isocost represents a different level of costs. Isocosts to the left of the £2500 budget line represent lower total cost levels and those to the right indicate higher total cost levels. Such an *isocost map* is shown in Figure 33.

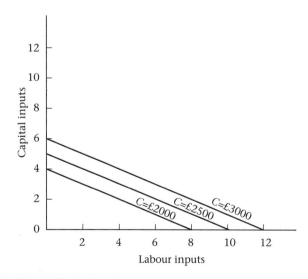

Figure 33 *An isocost map.*

The optimal input combination

If isoquants and isocosts are plotted on the same graph, the least-cost method of producing a certain level of output can be determined. It is also possible to ascertain the highest level of output that can be achieved from a given outlay. This can be seen in Figure 34. Three output levels are indicated by the isoquants Q_1, Q_2 and Q_3. In each case the optimal or least-cost input combination occurs at the point of tangency between the isoquant and the lowest possible isocost curve, i.e. at points X, Y and Z respectively. At each of these points the slopes of the isoquant and the relevant isocost must be equal. The slope of the isoquant is equal to the MRTS. This is the same as the negative ratio of the marginal products of capital and labour.

The slope of the isocost is equal to the negative of its input price ratio, Or in other words, at X, Y and Z the following condition holds:

$$\text{MRTS} = \frac{\text{MP}_L}{\text{MP}_K} = \frac{P_L}{P_K} \tag{6A.7}$$

If these terms are rearranged:

$$\frac{\text{MP}_L}{P_L} = \frac{\text{MP}_K}{P_K} \tag{6A.8}$$

The firm should employ inputs such that the ratios of the marginal products to the prices of all inputs are equalised. Put differently, the least-cost method of producing any level of output is where the marginal product per pound spent is the same for each input.

Expansion paths

The line that connects the various tangency points between isocosts and isoquants is known as an *expansion path*, since it shows the least-cost input combinations a firm chooses as it expands its scale of production.[2] The long-run expansion path in Figure 34 is shown by the connection of the points X, Y and Z. The short-run expansion path, with the capital input constant, is shown by the horizontal straight line at $\bar{K}$. However, it is still assumed that input prices are held constant.

The effect of a change in relative input prices

Suppose the price of labour rises (i.e. there is an increase in the wage-rate) while the price of capital remains the same and all other relevant factors are unchanged. The relative price of the inputs has altered, which will cause a change in the economically efficient method of production. Less labour can now be employed for any given outlay.

For instance, in the previous example, with a budget of £2500 a firm could employ 10 units of labour at a price of £250 per person per week, if the

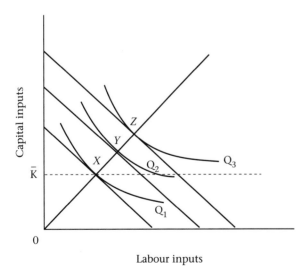

Figure 34 *The relationship between isocosts and isoquants showing short-run and long-run expansion paths.*

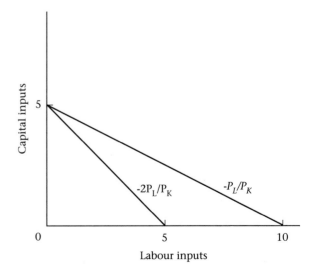

Figure 35 *The effect of an increase in the wage-rate on the slope of the isoquant.*

whole budget was allocated to labour. If the weekly price of labour doubled to £500 per person, the firm could only afford to purchase five units of labour. The effect of the increase in the price of labour is to make the slope of the isocost twice as steep, as indicated in Figure 35. This is because the intercept term in equation (6A.5) has not changed, whereas the slope coefficient, P_L/P_K, has doubled. All other isocosts reflecting the new set of relative prices will be parallel to the new isocost.

A change in relative input prices will also have an impact on the firm's optimal expansion path. This can be seen in Figure 36. The original expansion path is assumed to be $0A$, which passes through point X, at which point a L_2K_1 input combination is employed. A doubling of the relative price of labour, *cet. par.*, would steepen the slope of the isocost, from $-P_L/P_K$ to $-2P_L/P_K$. The expansion path shifts to $0B$, passing through point Y. At this point a lower level of output is produced using a more capital-intensive input combination, L_1K_2. Further increases in the firm's outlay are shown by parallel shifts in the new isocost (shown by the dashed line) along expansion path $0B$.

Variations in the relative prices of inputs can help to explain changes in production techniques through time. Over time capital has become cheaper relative to labour, especially as new production methods have become more diffused throughout the economy. Capital has been substituted for labour in all industrialised economies, as witnessed by the widespread use of computers and robots in industry. In other

words, there has been a shift from an expansion path like $0A$ to one such as $0B$ in Figure 36. However, an increase in capital intensity may also have a 'knock-on' effect for labour costs. Bowen (1991a) notes that labour costs have fallen in the EU semiconductor industry following increased automation.

If firms are able to locate in different countries, they can vary their production techniques according to the available supply, and relative cost, of the factors of production. This has significant implications for cost-reducing policies, especially given the fact that labour costs often account for a high proportion of total costs. Multinational companies have an incentive to site their most labour-intensive processes, such as assembly operations, in those areas where labour is most plentiful and comparatively cheap, like the newly industrialising countries of the Far East and Latin America, or in the lower-wage countries of the EU, like Spain and Portugal. Their capital-intensive techniques are more likely to be situated in, say, the US or in other parts of Western Europe. For example, Nike maintains all its product development in Oregon in the US, its home base, but subcontracts production to 40 different locations, mostly in South and South-east Asia. If wages in one host country rise, it shifts production to another. Bowen (1991b) stresses the importance of labour costs in determining the location of consumer electronic assembly plants in Europe:

What can be deduced ... is the ease with which the assembly stage for most consumer electronics can be separated from the main production activity. This implies that labour costs are the critical factor determining the location of assembly (Bowen, 1991b: 264).

NOTES

1. Isoquants need not be negatively sloped over their whole range; they can exhibit a positive slope. This can occur if the marginal product of either input becomes negative when too much of it is used in relation to the other. If either marginal product is negative, the ratio of the marginal products must be positive, and so will be the slope of the isoquant. The positive sections of an isoquant indicate technically inefficient combinations of inputs because more of one input and not less of the other is used to produce the same output level compared with the negatively sloped section of the curve.

2. The expansion path will only be a straight line if the production function is homogenous (such as the Cobb–Douglas function). A production function is homogeneous of degree n if the multiplication of all inputs by the same constant λ results in the multiplication of output by λ^n. If $n = 1$ the function is said to be linearly homogenous, in which case it exhibits constant returns to scale.

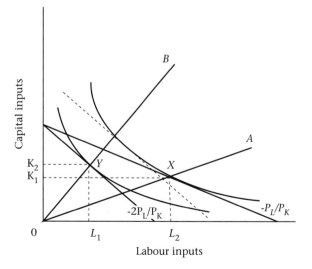

Figure 36 *The effect of an increase in the wage–rate on the optimum expansion path.*

CHAPTER 7

▶ *Demand and Revenue Analysis*

Successful decision-making by a firm depends crucially on a good knowledge of demand and the revenues so generated. *Demand* refers to the amount of a product that consumers are willing to buy at a given price and during a specified period of time. It is an *effective demand* in the sense that consumers must not only want a particular product, but they must also be able to pay for it. Most people may want to own a Rolls-Royce or a Picasso, but very few of us actually have the ability to pay for either. Demand becomes effective only when a want or need is supported by the means to pay for it.

A firm needs to be aware of both the nature and level of demand for its products for efficient decision-making; the more knowledge that it has of its demand and of the factors that determine it, the more effective its decision-making. Successful short-run operating decisions depend on a sound understanding of demand. A firm is then better able to determine how much to produce and what production techniques to employ, what price to charge and what stock levels to hold. Reasonable estimates of expected future demand also form a vital part of a firm's long-term planning decisions. If demand is expected to grow strongly over a number of years, a firm can invest confidently in an extension of capacity. If demand is forecast to grow only slowly, it may decide instead to invest in a large-scale advertising campaign in order to try and boost demand. A projected fall in demand, on the other hand, may lead to the closure of some or all of its facilities.

The level and type of market demand is also an important determinant of the characteristics of the market structure in which a firm operates. The different types of market structure are discussed fully in the next chapter.

In this chapter the traditional approach to individual consumer behaviour is discussed, with particular emphasis on *indifference curve analysis*; the individual's *demand curve* is derived. This is followed by an account of a more recent explanation of what determines individual consumer choice between products, or the *attributes or characteristics* approach to consumer behaviour. Since firms are mainly interested in understanding those factors that influence the total or market demand for a product and the sales revenue that stems from it, the *demand function* and major determinants of market demand are examined. *Movements along* a demand curve are distinguished from *shifts* in the demand curve. A summary measure of the responsiveness of market demand to changes in the value of each independent variable is provided by the *elasticity of demand*. Various elasticity measures are examined and their significance for corporate decision-making is considered; the recent evidence of estimates of elasticities of demand is summarised. A *case study* of the demand for beer in the UK is given at the end of the chapter.

7.1 INDIFFERENCE CURVE ANALYSIS AND CONSUMER BEHAVIOUR

Consumers, usually grouped into households, purchase goods and services. Therefore, an analysis of demand is an analysis of consumer behaviour. Various theories that analyse how consumers behave have been employed by economists; in all of them consumers are assumed to act *rationally*. In traditional economic theory it is assumed that the objective of consumers is to buy that collection of goods and services that maximises their *utility*, subject to a budget constraint. In other words, consumers rationally allocate their limited incomes to purchase the particular bundle of products that gives them the greatest level of satisfaction.

The assumption that consumers always act rationally may seem rather extreme, but it does not necessarily deviate that much from general consumer behaviour. Occasionally people act in an irrational way when buying products; they may buy something, an item of clothing for example, on a whim and afterwards wonder why they purchased it. They may also buy things out of habit without discovering whether an alternative product or brand would give them greater satisfaction. Of course, rational thoughts may not be immediately obvious when deciding to have the third or fourth pint of beer, or gin and tonic. In general, however, the majority of people behave in a fairly rational manner when buying most items. They buy those products from which they expect to obtain the greatest value, and they probably behave in this way most of the time.

The first approach to explaining consumer behaviour, the *marginal utility* model, was developed in the mid- to late-nineteenth century.[1] In this approach it is assumed that the utility gained from consuming each unit of a product is directly measurable. As a result, it is possible to predict exactly how much of each good should be purchased to maximise a person's utility. It is based on the assumption of *diminishing marginal utility*, where marginal utility is equal to the change in total utility from consuming an extra unit of a product. The utility gained from each successive unit falls as additional units of a product are acquired. The second theory of consumer behaviour, *indifference curve* analysis, was developed in the 1930s,[2] specifically to take account of the main limitation of marginal utility theory, i.e. that, in practice, utility is not directly measurable. The indifference curve model assumes that it is possible to rank goods, or bundles of goods, in order of preference, but only according to their relative amounts of utility rather than their absolute amounts. Indifference curve analysis proceeds on the basis that a person would prefer to buy one selection of books compared to another, or is indifferent between the two selections, but it cannot state exactly by how much the first selection is preferred to the second. The indifference curve model is a somewhat less restrictive approach to analysing consumer behaviour than marginal utility theory, although it is still based on a number of qualifying assumptions. It is analogous to isoquant analysis that was explained in the Appendix to Chapter 6.

In general terms, the *utility function* relates total utility (TU) to the quantities and qualities of the individual products consumed, here represented by X_1 to X_n:

$$TU = f(X_1, X_2, X_3, \ldots X_n) \qquad (7.1)$$

In more specific terms, a consumer's demand for just two items can be considered. Assume that a consumer likes to wear jeans and trainers and therefore possesses several pairs of each. The person is asked how many pairs of each he would like to have in a particular time period and whether he is indifferent between various combinations of them; the consumer

expresses indifference between having, say, eight pairs of jeans and one pair of trainers, or five pairs of jeans and two pairs of trainers or three pairs of jeans and four pairs of trainers, and so on. Of course, there may be combinations of the two products that the consumer likes less, such as two pairs of jeans and four pairs of trainers. There may also be combinations he prefers to any of the above, like eight pairs of jeans and two pairs of trainers.

An *indifference curve* can be constructed showing the combinations of the two goods that give the consumer the same level of satisfaction. This is shown in Figure 37. The curve represents all combinations of the two goods (or all 'market baskets') that give the same level of total utility to a consumer and about which the consumer is indifferent. Each combination of jeans and trainers that yields the same level of satisfaction or utility describes a particular point on the indifference curve. For example, the possession of eight pairs of jeans and one pair of trainers is indicated by point *A* on the graph, five pairs of jeans and two pairs of trainers by point *B* and three pairs of jeans and four pairs of trainers by point *C*.

An *indifference map* shows various indifference curves, each of which indicates different levels of utility for a consumer. Each indifference curve in Figure 38 portrays those combinations of two goods (here referred to simply as good *X* and good *Y*) that yield a particular level of utility for a consumer. Indifference curves have similar (although not identical) characteristics to isoquants:

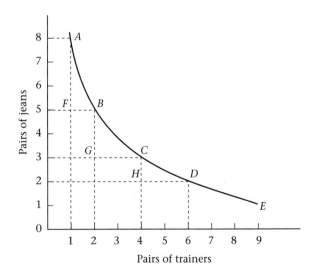

Figure 37 *An indifference curve.*

Figure 38 *An indifference map.*

(1) Consumer choices are assumed to be consistent in that more is always preferred to less. Combinations of goods on higher indifference curves are always preferred to those combinations represented on lower curves. Thus, in Figure 38, indifference curves to the right of I_2, like I_3, show combinations of goods that yield higher levels of utility for a consumer; indifference curves to the left of I_3, like I_1, show combinations that give lower levels of utility.

(2) An indifference curve has a negative slope throughout its range (unlike an isoquant which can have a positive slope). This is due to the fact that for consumers to remain at the same level of utility, then should the quantity of one product fall, the quantity of the other product must increase, *cet. par.*

(3) Indifference curves cannot intersect because the point of intersection would imply two different levels of utility from the same combination of goods.

(4) They are convex to the origin, or when viewed from below. Thus, the slope of each indifference curve decreases when moving from left to right along the curve.

The last characteristic can be better explained in terms of the *marginal rate of substitution* (MRS) between the products. The MRS measures the amount of one good, Y, that has to be substituted for a one-unit increment of another good, X, in order that total utility remain constant:

$$MRS = \underline{\Delta Y / \overline{\Delta X}} \qquad (7.2)$$

The MRS is equal to the slope of the indifference curve at any point. Since the slope of the indifference curve falls when moving down the curve, then the MRS must diminish as more of one product is exchanged for the other. Thus, as Y is substituted for X, the number of units of Y necessary to compensate for a given unit of X will fall. In Figure 37 the MRS between A and B is AF/FB, or 3/1; between B and C it equals BG/GC, or 2/2; between C and D the MRS equals CH/HD, or 1/2: the MRS of jeans for trainers falls as jeans are substituted for trainers.

In fact, the assumption of diminishing MRS is closely allied to the notion of diminishing marginal utility which is the cornerstone of marginal utility theory. Indifference curve analysis is simply substituting one stringent assumption for another fairly restrictive assumption. For utility to remain the same along the length of an indifference curve, the loss of utility from a decrease in the consumption of one product must be exactly matched by the extra utility from consuming an additional unit of the other product:

$$- (MU_y \times \Delta Y) = MU_x \times \Delta X \qquad (7.3)$$

MU refers to marginal utility. Equation (7.3) can be rearranged as

$$- MU_x/MU_y = \Delta Y/\Delta X = MRS \qquad (7.4)$$

The concept of diminishing marginal utility for individual products is implicit in the notion of diminishing MRS and in the shape of an indifference curve. The MRS diminishes, or the slope of the indifference curve (given by $\Delta Y/\Delta X$) falls, when moving from left to right along the curve. As more X is consumed so less Y is consumed. The MU of X decreases and the MU of Y increases as the relative consumption of X increases. Therefore, MU_x/MU_y falls and the MRS falls.

The budget constraint of the consumer

Consumers' spending decisions are constrained by how much of each product they can afford to purchase. The quantity of each product that any consumer actually purchases is determined not just by individual tastes and preferences, but also by the prices of the products and by how much is available to be spent on them; available income is a function of current income and accumulated wealth. A *budget line* can be constructed that enables a consumer to decide exactly how much of each product he or she will purchase. It takes into account both the relative prices of the products and available income.

Assuming that just two products are available to be purchased, the budget constraint can be written as

$$B = P_Y Y + P_X X \qquad (7.5)$$

B is the total income or budget available to be spent, P_Y and P_X are the unit prices of goods Y and X respectively and Y and X are the number of units purchased of each product. Solving equation (7.5) for Y to obtain a linear function, it becomes

$$Y = \frac{B}{P_Y} - \frac{P_X}{P_Y} X \qquad (7.6)$$

B/P_Y is the intercept of the budget line on the Y-axis of a graph. It indicates how much of product Y can be purchased if all of a consumer's budget is spent on it and none on product X. $-P_X/P_Y$ indicates the slope of the budget line.

Returning to the original example and the consumer's choice between jeans and trainers and assuming that the price of jeans (shown on the Y-axis) is £50 each and the price of trainers (shown on the X-axis) is £100 per pair, then the budget equation can be written as

$$B = £50Y + £100X$$

Solving for Y this becomes

$$Y = \frac{B}{£50} - \frac{£100}{£50} X$$

If the person has, say, a budget of £500 per time period to spend on the two goods, then, if all the budget is spent on jeans, 10 pairs can be purchased (i.e. B/P_Y or £500/£50). On the other hand, if the total budget is spent on trainers, only five pairs can be bought (i.e. B/P_X or £500/£100). This yields the two endpoints of the budget line, as shown in Figure 39. It intercepts the Y-axis at 10 units or pairs of jeans (i.e. at $0X,10Y$) and the X-axis at five units or pairs of trainers (i.e. at $5X,0Y$).

Utility maximisation

If various indifference curves are superimposed onto the budget line shown in Figure 39, it is possible to discover the utility maximising position of the consumer. This is where the budget line is tangent to the highest possible indifference curve. The optimal combination of goods is at point J in Figure 40, where indifference curve I_2 is tangent to the budget line. At this point Y_1 of good Y, or approximately five pairs of jeans, and X_1 of good X, or approximately two pairs of trainers, can be purchased. No other combination of the two products can provide as much satisfaction for the consumer, given

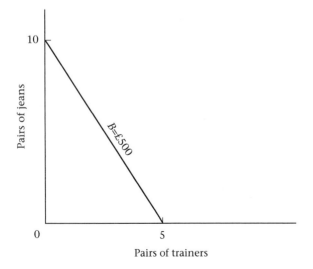

Figure 39 *A budget curve.*

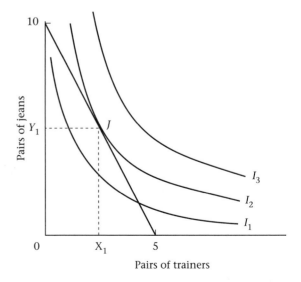

Figure 40 *The utility maximisation position for a consumer.*

the budget constraint. To put the previous statement another way, this particular combination of jeans and trainers is the lowest-cost method of achieving the level of utility provided by indifference curve I_2.

The slope of the budget line is given by the ratio of the product prices, $-P_X/P_Y$. Equation (7.4) stipulated that the MRS, which indicates the slope of an indifference curve, is equal to $-MU_X/MU_Y$. At any tangency point such as J in Figure 40 the slopes of the budget line and the relevant indifference curve must be equal. Therefore, at J:

$$-\frac{P_x}{P_y} = -\frac{MU_x}{MU_y} \tag{7.7}$$

Hence

$$\frac{MU_x}{P_X} = \frac{MU_y}{P_Y} \tag{7.8}$$

In other words, a rational consumer would maximise his or her utility at the point where the marginal utility per pound spent is the same for each product. This is analogous to the conclusion in the Appendix of Chapter 6 where it was stated that the least-cost method of production for a firm is where the marginal product per pound spent is the same for each input.

The effect of a change in income

If a person's *money* or *nominal income* increases, then it would be expected that the demand for most commodities would rise. Assuming that there also is no change in prices, then *real income*, or the purchasing power of money income, will also rise. The more a person has to spend, the further from the origin the budget line. This can be seen in Figure 41. An increase in income causes a parallel outward shift of the budget line; a consumer is able to buy more of both available products. Initially, utility is maximised at point J, at the tangency of budget line AB and indifference curve I_2. Following the income rise, utility is maximised at K, the tangency point of the new budget line, CD, and the highest possible indifference curve, in this case I_3. The line joining the utility-maximising points is known as the *income–consumption curve.*

In Figure 41 both products are assumed to be *normal goods*; their demand increases as income rises. In other words, since income and demand both move

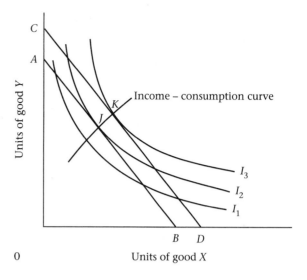

Figure 41 *The effect of a change in income.*

in the same direction, the income effect is positive. The income effect for some goods is negative (and the income–consumption curve will have a negative slope) because, as income rises and consumers switch to more desirable substitutes, the demand for them falls. They are termed *inferior goods*. Examples include basic foodstuffs, like potatoes or cheap cuts of meat, or inexpensive forms of travel, such as bus journeys. The demand for these sorts of products may rise in a recession if people lose their jobs and their incomes fall.

The effect of a change in relative prices

If the price of one of the products changes relative to the other, then the budget line will pivot. Thus, if the price of good X rises relative to good Y, the budget line will swing inwards. (The intercept term in equation (7.6) is unchanged, while the slope coefficient has increased.) This is shown in Figure 42, page 136 by a movement of the budget line from AC to AB. Initially utility is maximised at K, the tangency point of AC and indifference curve I_2; following the price rise the new optimal consumption point is given by J at the tangency point of AB and indifference curve I_1. The line connecting these utility-maximising points is known as the *price–consumption curve.*

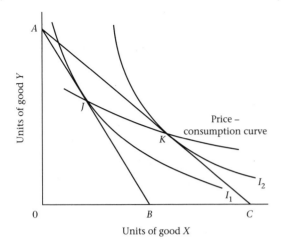

Figure 42   *The effect of a change in the price of good X.*

The Derivation of the Individual Demand Curve

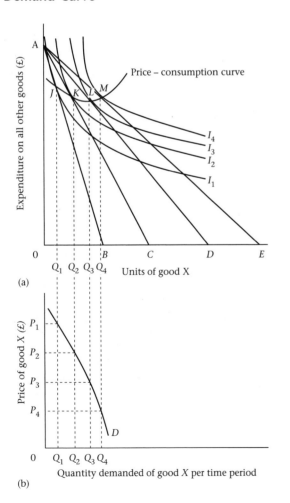

(a)

(b)

Quantity demanded of good X per time period

In Figure 43 (a) the vertical axis is redefined as expenditure on all goods other than good X. Changes in the price of good X are shown by pivoting the budget line from A, where it intersects the vertical axis; thus, a swing inwards from AC to AB indicates a rise in the price of X, while a swing outwards from AC to AD indicates a fall in the price of X. J, K, L and M show the optimal consumption points at various prices of X. The quantities demanded at the different prices can be transferred to the demand curve in Figure 43 (b), which portrays a negative relationship between price and quantity demanded for good X, *cet. par.*

The income and substitution effects of a price change

If the price of one of two products rises, a consumer will be affected in two ways:

(1) The *income effect* means that the consumer cannot afford to purchase as much as before because real income has fallen.
(2) The *substitution effect* means that the consumer will substitute the good which has become relatively less expensive for the one which has become relatively more expensive, assuming that real income is held constant.

As noted above, should the price of X rise relative to good Y, then the budget line swings inwards. In Figure 44 the original optimum combination of X and Y is at F on budget line AC and indifference curve I_2. The rise in price of X shifts the budget line to AB. The consumer's new equilibrium is at H on indifference curve I_1. The move from F to H can be split into two parts. Since AB does not touch the indifference curve I_2, a new budget line is shown, DE, that is parallel to AB and is tangent to I_2 at point G. As DE is parallel to AB, it reflects the new price ratio. DE is drawn on the assumption that the consumer's income has increased sufficiently so that it is possible to remain on the same indifference curve and at the same level of utility (i.e. there has been no change in real income). Therefore, the income effect has been

Figure 43   *The derivation of the demand curve from the price–consumption curve.*

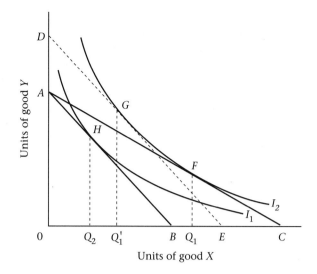

Figure 44 *The income and substitution effects of a change in the price of a normal good.*

excluded from the analysis and the move from *F* to *G* is purely the substitution effect, due solely to the change in relative prices and which is always negative. In this case the quantity demanded of good *X* falls from Q_1 to Q_1'.

The move from *G* to *H* is the income effect of the price change, the rise in price of *X* meaning that the consumer's real income has fallen. The price increase produces a lower level of utility from the same outlay as before. This is indicated by the lower indifference curve, I_1. Since the price ratio is the same on *AB* as on *DE*, the move from *G* to *H* must be the income effect of the price change. The fall in real income leads to a fall in quantity demanded, from Q_1' to Q_2. Thus, the overall effect of the price rise is to cause a movement from *F* to *H* in Figure 44 and a fall in quantity demanded from Q_1 to Q_2. This change can be divided into two parts, the substitution effect, from *F* to *G*, and the income effect, from *G* to *H*. In the case of normal goods, the income and substitution effects on quantity demanded reinforce each other. They are both negative and lead to a fall in quantity demanded following a rise in the price of a product, and vice versa.

In the case of inferior goods, the income and substitution effects do not have a reinforcing effect on quantity demanded. They work in opposite directions. If the price of an inferior good rises, the substitution effect will be the same as for a normal good, i.e. quantity demanded will move in the opposite

direction to the price change. However, the income effect will be positive in this instance, as shown in Figure 45.

The rise in price of *X*, an inferior good, has the same effect on the budget line as in the case of the normal good in Figure 44. The budget line shifts from *AC* to *AB* and the original equilibrium is at *F*. The substitution effect causes a movement along the indifference curve, I_2, to *G*, as before. Demand falls from Q_1 to Q_1'. The income effect in this case is different; the increase in the price of *X* means that the consumer's real income has fallen and therefore, because *X* is an inferior good, more of it is purchased. The income effect is shown by the move from *G* to *H*. Quantity demanded increases as a result of the fall in real income, from Q_1' to Q_2. The net effect is to cause a fall in quantity demanded from Q_1 to Q_2, the negative substitution effect outweighing the positive income effect.

A special type of inferior good is a Giffen good, so-called after Sir Robert Giffen who studied the Irish famine in the 1840s. He claimed that potato consumption rose following price increases. This was because the price rise meant that the Irish people could not afford to buy as much meat and so they had to eat more potatoes in order to survive. No other cases of Giffen goods have been discovered, although this may be due more to the problems of empirical investigation than to the fact that they do not exist. For Giffen goods the income effect

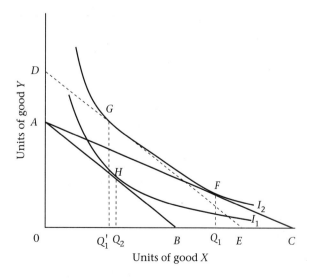

Figure 45 *The income and substitution effects of a change in the price of an inferior good.*

outweighs the substitution effect. Overall, there is a positive relationship between price and quantity demanded. As price rises so quantity demand rises, and vice versa. This is because the product, in this case potatoes, accounts for a large proportion of consumers' expenditure. A rise in its price will cause a substantial drop in real income; the income effect is therefore very large.

Indifference curves may lack practical relevance, but indifference curve analysis can still yield useful insights into present-day consumer behaviour. Consumers are likely to have some idea of the sorts of goods that usually give them the greatest levels of satisfaction and of the relative importance of these goods in their spending plans. Thus, the theory helps to explain how consumers behave and analyses the types of decisions with which they are faced. More pertinently, the analysis underlies the shape of the demand curve.

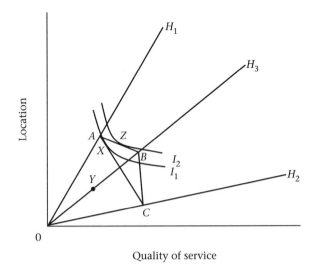

Figure 46   *The characteristics approach to consumer behaviour.*

7.2 THE CHARACTERISTICS APPROACH TO CONSUMER BEHAVIOUR

The *characteristics* or *attributes* approach to consumer behaviour was devised by Lancaster (1971). Like the traditional theories of consumer behaviour, it is based on the assumption of utility maximisation. It also employs indifference curve analysis. However, it differs in its basic premise, which is that consumers buy products not because of a desire for the products themselves but because of the characteristics they possess. It is these characteristics from which consumers derive utility. For example, a car is bought not just because of its make, but also because of its comfort, its power, its safety, its efficiency and so on. The demand for hotel accommodation may be a function of a number of factors: location, ambience, quality of service and the range of facilities offered. In those markets where products are differentiated, such as most consumer goods, new products tend to have the same or at least very similar characteristics as the old ones, but in different proportions.

Since consumers are assumed to gain utility from the attributes that products possess, this means that those products with closely related attributes are related in the mind's eye of the consumer. Therefore, given a whole range of products, each with different characteristics, it should be possible to obtain a certain collection of characteristics by purchasing various combinations of products. A consumer will

need to choose the most efficient way of achieving the goal of utility maximisation.

For example, suppose a particular product, hotel accommodation, can be classified according to the two main characteristics that are important to a particular consumer or group of consumers; these are assumed to be location and quality of service. Assuming that these attributes are both measurable, they can be plotted on a graph. Assume also that different hotels supply these two characteristics in different ratios and offer them at different prices. This situation is shown in Figure 46.

Initially, it is assumed there are just two hotels, indicated by the rays H_1 and H_2. Hotel H_1 offers a higher location/service ratio than H_2, whereas the latter has the opposite combination of characteristics. A consumer needs to decide how to allocate his expenditure in order to maximise utility, given a certain budget constraint. If all the person's income is spent on staying in hotel H_1, then a certain number of nights' stay could be purchased; the two attributes would be consumed in the relevant proportion. This is indicated by point A; similarly for hotel H_2, giving point C. The line connecting A and C is the *efficiency frontier* of the consumer. The particular combination of characteristics offered by each hotel is divided by the respective price charged in order to ascertain the quantity of characteristics per pound spent. Just as in indifference curve analysis, an increase in the budget would move the efficiency frontier outwards parallel to itself. If the relative prices of the goods were to change, its slope would alter. The consumer's utility is maximised at that point where an indifference curve between collections of characteristics is tangent to the efficiency frontier. This is indicated by point X in Figure 46, where indifference curve I_1 is tangent to the efficiency frontier between H_1 and H_2. Since X lies between H_1 and H_2 the consumer's utility is maximised by purchasing a mixture of the two products, i.e. by dividing his time between the two hotels.

If a new hotel is built with the same two characteristics but in different proportions, the consumer's optimum position may change, depending on the price charged by the new hotel. Assume that all the consumer's income is now spent on staying in the new hotel, shown by the ray H_3. However, it charges a price such that only the number of nights indicated by point Y could be purchased. Since Y lies below AC it would be inefficient to consume that particular combination of characteristics at that price. There would be no demand. Suppose that the price charged by hotel H_3 is reduced and that point B now indicates the number of nights that could be purchased if the entire budget of the consumer were spent on staying at the hotel. The curve ABC represents the new efficiency frontier. The consumer's utility is now maximised at a point such as Z, which lies on a higher indifference curve, I_2, than before. Thus, the price of a new product must be set at such a level that it can induce consumers to switch from combinations of H_1 and H_2 to combinations including H_3.

The Lancaster approach is designed to deal with aspects of consumer behaviour, such as quality variations and the introduction of new products, which traditional theory ignores. These considerations are particularly significant in industrialised economies in which there are a huge variety of products, many of which are highly differentiated and which have closely related but not identical characteristics. The approach also has important implications for firms' decision-making. It is useful in that it indicates to firms the types of product attributes upon which consumers base their spending decisions. Firms have an incentive to gear their products to particular segments of the market within which a particular group of consumers have similar tastes and who desire product characteristics in similar ratios. However, such a strategy must be based on a knowledge of the bundles of characteristics that these groups of consumers desire. The measurement of many product characteristics, like comfort, excite-ment, prestige, ambience and so on, are based on the subjective assessments of consumers. This creates difficulties in their precise identification.

Bajic (1993) attempted to overcome this problem in the identification of car characteristics by using proxy indicators, which may not be intrinsically valued in themselves, such as wheelbase, width, weight and axle length, for some of these characteristics. Weight can serve as a proxy for space, luxury and quality of ride, wheelbase and length help to determine the stylishness of the car and legroom space and width indicate roominess. Despite the existence of multicollinearity[3] between some of the pairs of proxy variables, Bajic found evidence of implicit markets for car characteristics, each of which has significant own-price elasticities; there are also positive cross-price elasticities between the characteristics, although not exclusively so (see Section 7.5 for definitions). Of course, subjectivity remains a problem, in this case on the part of the researcher. A choice still has to be made about which proxy variable best describes each particular characteristic.

7.3 THE DEMAND FUNCTION

The previous two sections have analysed the behaviour of the individual consumer, whereas firms are faced with the *total* or *market demand* for a product at any time. However, since market demand is simply the aggregate of individual demand, it is possible to understand a great deal about the nature of market demand by an examination of individual demand.

The most important factor affecting demand is the price of the product. In the previous section it was pointed out that, for all normal goods and for non-Giffen inferior goods, there is a negative or inverse relationship between the price of a product and its demand. As the price of a product rises (falls) relative to other goods, the quantity demanded falls (rises), *cet. par.* This is the so-called *law of demand*. The price of the product is always given as the first independent variable in the market demand function, although other factors can also affect demand. These comprise advertising expenditures on the product, the product quality, the price of substitute goods, the price of complementary goods, incomes, tastes and so on. The *market demand function* for any product, X, shows the relationship between the total demand for the product (for an individual firm or for an industry) and all the factors that might affect it per time period. It can be expressed as

$$Q_X = f(P_X, A_X, N_X, P_Z, Y, T) \qquad (7.9)$$

In equation (7.9), Q_X denotes the quantity demanded of product X per period of time; P_X refers to the price of the product; A_X stands for advertising and other marketing expenditures. A positive relationship between total advertising spending and the demand for any product will be expected. The quantity demanded will increase as advertising expenditure increases. (Of course, higher advertising by the producers of competing products may reduce the demand for the product, just as increased advertising by the producers of complements can have the opposite effect, an increase in demand for X.) N_X refers to the nature of product X. This encompasses the product quality, design and style and includes the standard of service and after-sales service, the nature of the product guarantee and so on. The better quality a product or the better the quality as perceived by consumers (since perceived product quality can be influenced by advertising) the greater the quantity demanded. If the quality of a product declines compared with competing products, its quantity demanded may fall for the individual firm. The first three items in the demand function, P_X, A_X and N_X, are particularly important for an individual firm because they are *endogenous variables* over which it has direct control. The other variables, which are generally outside the control of the firm, are known as *exogenous variables* although tastes can be influenced by advertising.

P_Z denotes the price of substitute and complementary goods. There is a positive relationship between the price of substitutes and the demand for a particular product. If the price of a substitute rises (falls) the demand for competing products rise (fall). For example, if the price of audio cassettes rises there will be an increase in demand for CDs. Often such a relationship is more marked between different brands of the same product. If the price of Nike trainers rises, for example, consumers may well switch to the competing Avia or Adidas brands because they now offer better value for money. There is a negative relationship between the price of complements, which are goods which are demanded in conjunction with a particular product, and the demand for the good itself. If the price of a complementary product rises (falls) there will be a fall (rise) in its quantity demanded and therefore a fall (rise) in the quantity demanded of the complement. If the price of CD players rises, people will buy fewer of them and, as a result, there will be a fall in demand for CDs. If there is a general rise in the price of trainers, the resulting fall in demand may well also cause a fall in demand for sports socks.

Y stands for income. To be strictly accurate it stands for average per capita disposable income, i.e. average income per head after direct taxes have been deducted. As incomes rise, the demand for most things increases: there is a positive relationship between income and market demand. However, as has already been noted, this is not the case with inferior goods; there is a negative relationship between income and the demand for inferior goods. T refers to tastes and preferences by consumers. The more that people prefer a product the more of it they will purchase. Tastes are influenced by among other things advertising, fashion and what others buy.

Other factors may need to be included in the function, such as the size and the age distribution of the population and, in the case of products like ice-creams, soft drinks and sports goods, the weather. Government policies can also have an important effect on the quantity demanded of many products. Changes in direct taxation will affect disposable incomes; if the government is instrumental in changing the exchange value of the pound, this will have a significant effect on the demand for British goods sold abroad. Government policies can also have a more direct impact on the demand for certain goods: a decision to spend more on defence will have a positive effect on the demand for defence goods.

The actual form of the demand function depends on empirical investigation. However, if, for the sake of simplicity's sake, it is assumed that the relationship between quantity demanded and its determinants is linear, the function may take the following form:

$$Q_X = a + bP_X + cA_X + dN_X + eP_Z + fY + gT \qquad (7.10)$$

In equation (7.10) the term a represents the quantity demanded of good X that is independent of the other variables in the equation. b,c,d etc. are the coefficients that indicate the marginal effect of each independent variable on the quantity demanded.

For example, a demand function may have been estimated as follows:

$$Q_X = 10000 - 2400P_X + 0.15A_X - 1250P_Z + 0.25Y \qquad (7.11)$$

If P_X is equal to £5, A_X equals £250 000, P_Z equals £4 and Y is equal to £18 000, and these values are substituted into equation (7.11), then

$$Q_X = 10000 - 12000 + 37500 - 5000$$
$$+ 4500 = 35000$$

The quantity demanded of product X is equal to 35 000 units per time period.

7.4 THE DEMAND CURVE

The *demand curve* portrays the relationship between the price of a product and the quantity demanded, *cet. par.* In other words, the quantity demanded of product X is expressed solely as a function of the price of X. In the previous example, if all the other factors are held constant, then quantity demanded can be given as a function of price:

$$Q_X = 10000 - 2400P_X + 37500 - 5000 + 4500$$

Hence

$$Q_X = 47000 - 2400P \qquad (7.12)$$

It should be noted that when plotting demand curves, economists follow the convention set by Marshall (1890) and place price, the independent variable in equation (7.12), on the vertical axis of a graph and quantity demanded, the dependent variable, on the horizontal axis. In fact, the independent variable should be shown on the horizontal axis and the dependent variable on the vertical axis. Therefore, for the purposes of the demand curve, price needs to be expressed as a function of quantity demanded, even though the price of the product is actually the independent variable. Dividing both sides of equation (7.12) by a thousand for convenience, then subtracting 47 from each side and dividing through by 2.4, gives

$$P_X = 19.5833 - 0.4167Q_X \qquad (7.13)$$

In general terms, the relationship between price and quantity demanded, with price as the dependent variable, can be expressed as

$$P_X = a - bQ_X \qquad (7.14)$$

where a is the intercept term on the vertical axis of a graph (i.e. the value of P_X where $Q_X = 0$) and b is the value of the slope. b has a negative sign to reflect the inverse relationship between price and quantity demanded. The demand curve representing equation (7.13) is shown in Figure 47. The intercept value on the horizontal axis indicates the value of Q_X at zero price.

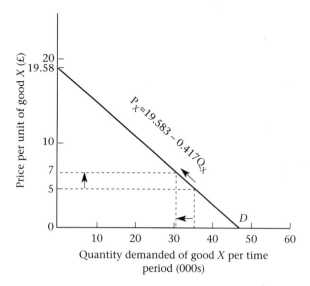

Figure 47   *A linear market demand curve.*

From an analytical perspective, it is important to distinguish between *shifts* in the demand curve and *movements along* the demand curve; it is also then possible to appreciate the precise cause of any change in demand for the product. A movement along a particular demand curve is caused by a change in the price of the product itself, while holding constant all the other determinants of demand. In the previous example, if P_X increases to £7 per unit, the quantity demanded, Q_X, in equation (7.11) falls to 30 200 units. This is shown as a movement along the demand curve in Figure 47. On the other hand, if there is a change in one or more of the other factors that affects demand there will be a shift of the whole demand curve, either to the right for an increase in demand or to the left for a decrease in demand.

If Y increases to £25000, Q_X increases to 36750; more is now demanded at the original price. Quantity demanded as a function of price would now be expressed as $Q_X = 48750 - 2400\,P_X$, and the new demand curve function would given as $P_X = 20.3125 - 0.41670\,Q_X$ (having divided through by a thousand). The effect of the increase in Y is shown in Figure 48, page 142 by the shift in the whole demand curve from D_2, the original level of demand, to D_3. However, if P_z increases to £6 per unit, the value of Q_X would fall to 32500, and less is now demanded at the original price. The new functions (again having divided through by a thousand) are $Q_X = 44.5 - 2.4P_X$ and $P_X = 18.5417 - 0.4167Q_X$. The demand curve

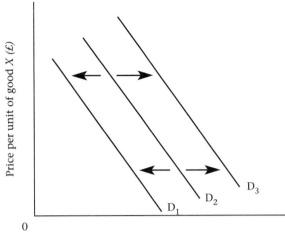

Figure 48 *Shifts in the demand curve.*

shifts to the left in Figure 48 from D_2 to D_1. If price is held constant, an increase in the value of a variable with a positive coefficient or a decrease in the value of a variable with a negative coefficient in equation (7.11) will lead to a shift in the demand curve to the right. Obviously, any change or changes in the opposite direction will shift the demand curve to the left.

In order to distinguish more fully between the effects of a change in price, which causes a movement along a demand curve, compared with a change in any of the other factors that affects demand, which result in a shift of the whole curve, the convention is to refer to the former as a *change in quantity demanded* and the latter as a *change in demand*.

7.5 ELASTICITY OF DEMAND

It is not enough for a firm to know that demand changes as a result of a change in one or other of its determinants. What is needed is by how much demand changes or, to put it another way, the responsiveness of demand to a change in any one of the independent variables. This is particularly important in the case of factors such as price and advertising that the firm can control. A firm can only pursue an effective price or advertising policy if it has a good idea how demand will react to a change in either of them. It is also important for a firm to

be aware of the effects on the demand for its products of changes in exogenous variables, such as incomes and the prices of other products; it can then respond effectively. A knowledge of the concept of *elasticity of demand*, first developed by Marshall (1890), is vital in this regard.

In general terms, elasticity is defined as the percentage change in a dependent variable as a result of a percentage change in an independent variable. Assuming that Y is the dependent variable and X is the independent variable, this can be stated as

$$\text{Elasticity} = \frac{\text{Percentage change in } Y}{\text{Percentage change in } X} \quad (7.15)$$

or

$$\text{Elasticity} = \frac{\Delta Y/Y}{\Delta X/X}$$

$$= \frac{\Delta Y}{\Delta X} \times \frac{X}{Y} \quad (7.16)$$

In more specific terms, various types of demand elasticity can be indicated, each depending on the identity of the independent variable. The main categories are own-price, cross-price, income and advertising elasticities of demand. They are examined in turn.

Own-price elasticity of demand

In equation (7.18) the value of $\Delta Q_X/\Delta P_X$ is negative, reflecting the inverse relationship between price and demand; the values of price elasticities are usually

---

Box 7.1 *Own-price elasticity of demand*

Own-price elasticity of demand (usually referred to simply as price elasticity of demand) is defined as the responsiveness of demand for a product to a relatively small change in its price (The effects of comparatively small changes in price can be more accurately gauged than larger changes). It can be expressed algebraically as

$$e_p = \frac{\text{Percentage change in } Q_X}{\text{Percentage change in } P_X} \quad (7.17)$$

Equation (7.17) can be written as

$$e_p = \frac{\Delta Q_X}{\Delta P_X} \times \frac{P_X}{Q_X} \quad (7.18)$$

shown as negative, but it is the absolute value of the figure rather than the sign itself which is significant. Thus, if the value is greater than one (i.e. $e_p > 1$) demand is said to be *elastic*. In this case a small percentage fall (rise) in price causes a larger percentage rise (fall) in demand. Demand is sensitive to the price change. If the value is less than one (e_p <1) demand is *inelastic*. A percentage fall (rise) in price produces a smaller percentage rise (fall) in demand, which is not particularly sensitive to the price change. If the value is equal to one ($e_p = 1$) demand is said to be of *unitary elasticity*. A percentage fall (rise) in price leads to an equal percentage rise (fall) in demand.

In principle, the value for price elasticity can vary from zero to infinity. If the value is zero ($e_p = 0$) demand is said to be *totally inelastic*: whatever the price the quantity demanded remains unchanged. The demand curve in such a situation would be a vertical straight line at the level of the quantity demanded, Q_1, as shown in Figure 49(a). If the value is infinity ($e_p = \infty$) demand is said to be *perfectly elastic*. There is an infinite demand at a certain price, but if the price is raised only slightly demand will disappear completely. The demand curve is a horizontal straight line set at the particular price level, P_1, as shown in Figure 49(b). The different values and definitions of price elasticity of demand are summarised in Table 42, page 144.

In fact, it is possible to measure elasticity by two different methods, depending on the amount of information a firm has at its disposal and how large a change in the independent variable is under consideration. If a firm has sufficient knowledge of its demand function, the *point* elasticity of demand formula can be used. Not surprisingly, this gives a measure of elasticity at a particular point on a demand curve. (This was the definition of elasticity of demand adopted originally by Marshall.) Since elasticity is being measured at a single point only very small changes in price are considered relevant.

The formula to measure point elasticity is

$$e_p = \frac{dQ_X}{dP_X} \times \frac{P_X}{Q_X} \qquad (7.19)$$

The term dQ/dP, the derivative of Q with respect to P, measures the rate of change of quantity demanded with respect to a change in price at a single point (i.e. it is valid for very small changes in P and Q). dQ/dP is also the reciprocal of the slope of a straight line, or $1/b$ in equation (7.14). In equation (7.11) it is denoted by the coefficient for the price variable,

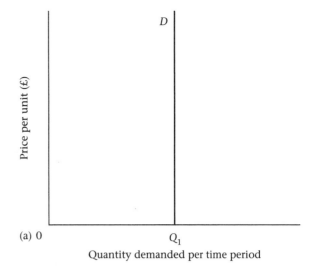

(a)

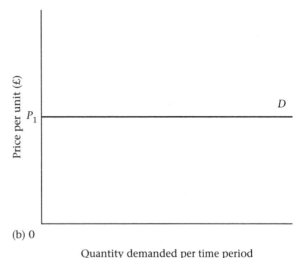

(b)

Figure 49 *Totally inelastic and perfectly elastic demand curves.*

–2400, since this indicates the marginal effect of price on quantity demanded. In this equation if P_X equals £5, Q_X is equal to 35 000. Slotting this information into equation (7.19) it becomes

$$e_p = -2400 \times \frac{5}{35000} = -0.3428$$

Since the value of the figure is less than one, demand is inelastic at this point on the demand curve. However, at other points on a linear demand curve the value of elasticity of demand varies along the curve: the slope of a straight line is constant and hence the reciprocal of the slope, or the term dQ/dP

Table 42 *Price elasticity values and definitions*

Value	Elasticity	Definition
$e_p = 0$	Totally inelastic	Q_X independent of change in P_X
$0 < e_p < 1$	Inelastic	Lower percentage change Q_X than in P_X
$e_p = 1$	Unitary elasticity	Same percentage changes in Q_X and P_X
$1 < e_p < \infty$	Elastic	Greater percentage change in Q_X than in P_X
$e_p = \infty$	Perfectly elastic	Q_X infinite at a certain price

must be constant. However, P_X and Q_X obviously vary along the line. At the point where P_X is at its maximum the value of Q_X is zero. Therefore, price elasticity is equal to infinity at this point because Q_X is the denominator in equation (7.19). Where Q_X is at its maximum, P_X is zero; price elasticity is zero at this point. The value of e_p changes along the demand curve, as Figure 50 makes clear. It falls from infinity, where it intersects with the vertical axis, to zero, where it coincides with the horizontal axis. At the mid-point it is equal to one, or unitary elasticity.

A firm may not have adequate information about its demand function to be able to calculate price elasticity at a particular point. The firm may also be interested in discovering how demand responds to larger, incremental changes in price than can be accommodated by the point elasticity formula. In these circumstances it may employ a different formula to calculate price elasticity, the *arc* formula. This measures elasticity between two points on the demand curve (i.e. along the arc that connects them). In the previous example, where P_X is £5 the point elasticity is –0.3428. However, where P_X is £7, Q_X equals 30 200 and the point elasticity is equal to $-2400 \times (7/30\,200)$, or –0.5563. At higher prices, as consumers become more price sensitive, the value of e_p rises. The arc or averages method measures the average value of elasticity between the two prices. It is given by the formula

$$e_p = \frac{\Delta Q_X}{\Delta P_X} \times \frac{(P_1 + P_2)/2}{(Q_1 + Q_2)/2} \qquad (7.20)$$

If this formula is adopted, the value of price elasticity is the same at either price level:

$$\frac{4800}{2} \times \frac{6}{32600} = -0.4417$$

This value lies between the two values calculated using the point elasticity formula. As such, it summarises the values of the elasticities at the various points between the two prices.

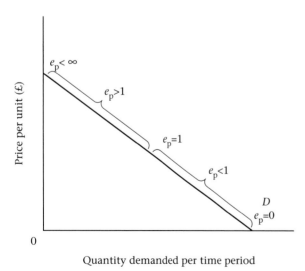

Figure 50 *Varying values of elasticity along a linear demand curve.*

Factors that determine price elasticity of demand

(A) THE POSSIBILITY OF SUBSTITUTION

It was noted in Section 7.1 that the substitution effect of a price change is always negative: should the price of a product rise (fall) relative to other goods, consumers will switch to purchasing substitute products and the demand for the product will fall (rise). In general, the more substitutes that exist for a product (and the more easily substitutable that it is), then the greater the change in the demand for it in response to a price change: the greater the possibility of substitution for a product the greater its elasticity of demand. In part, the extent of possible substitution for a product depends on how it is defined: the more general the definition the less likely that substitutes will exist and the more inelastic the demand for the product. For example, if the price of mobile phones rises, the demand for them probably will not fall very much. People will still want to buy them, especially if they are considered to be a fashion accessory. However, if the price of one make or brand of mobile phones increases relative to the others, then demand for it will probably fall quite significantly as consumers switch to buying the competing brands. The demand for mobile phones in general is much more inelastic than the demand for the individual brands.

(B) THE PROPORTION OF INCOME SPENT ON A PRODUCT
Generally speaking, the lower the share of one's income spent on a product, the lower will be its elasticity of demand. An increase in the price of any normal product will lead to a fall in real income and to a fall in demand. If the product accounts for a comparatively small share of a consumer's income, like newspapers or soft drinks, a rise in price will cause a negligible fall in real income. Demand is not likely to be greatly affected by the price rise. It will be relatively inelastic. On the other hand, if the price of new cars rises creating a much larger drop in real income, their demand is likely to be significantly reduced. Demand is much more elastic.

(C) LONG-TERM EFFECTS
It is worth noting that, although *time* is not a determinant of elasticity of demand *per se*, the demand for most products is much more elastic in the long term than in the short term. This is because it takes time for consumers to react to changes in price, or indeed to changes in any other variables that might affect their spending decisions. For example, if the price of oil increases substantially, there will probably be an initial moderate reduction in demand as consumers cut down on the use of their cars (or central heating if it is oil-fired), wherever this is possible. Demand is relatively inelastic in the short term. However, over time, consumers may switch to buying more fuel–efficient cars or to using other forms of central heating. They may use their cars less and start using public transport more; eventually, they may even stop owning cars altogether. Demand is much more elastic in the long term. The same point was made in Section 3.3. The price elasticity of demand for UK exports is reckoned to be more

elastic in the long term than in the short term as overseas buyers gradually react to changes in the foreign exchange values of British goods.

The relationship between elasticity of demand and revenue

There is a very important relationship between price elasticity of demand and the total revenue (TR) of a firm. Total revenue, remember, is calculated by multiplying the price of the product by the number of units sold. It may be mistakenly thought that all any firm has to do to increase its total revenue is to reduce its price. More consumers will then buy the product and total revenue will rise. Of course, armed with a knowledge of price elasticity of demand, anybody could destroy this argument very quickly. A price reduction will only increase total revenue if the increase in demand is proportionately larger than the fall in price, i.e. if demand is elastic.

Table 43 *The relationships between price elasticity of demand and revenue*

Price per unit (£)	Output (Units)	TR (£)	MR (£)	Price elasticity value[a]
100	0	0		
			90	
90	1	90		−19
			70	
80	2	160		−6.33
			50	
70	3	210		−3
			30	
60	4	240		−1.86
			10	
50	5	250		−1.22
			−10	
40	6	240		−0.82
			−30	
30	7	210		−0.54
			−50	
20	8	160		−0.33
			−70	
10	9	90		−0.18
			−90	
0	10	0		−0.05

[a]Arc elasticities calculated.

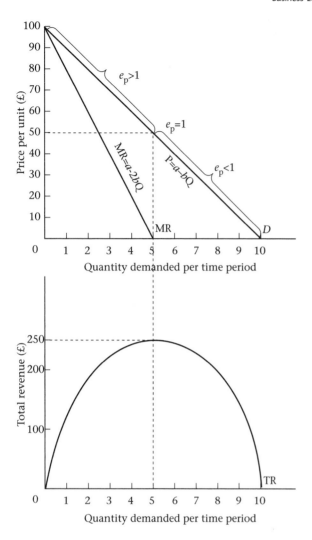

Figure 51 *The relationships between price elasticity of demand, marginal revenue and total revenue.*

The relationship between price elasticity and revenue can be analysed more clearly by reference to Table 43, page 145, the data from which are summarised in Figure 51. Before examining the relationship between price elasticity and total revenue, it is worthwhile analysing the relationships between marginal revenue and the demand curve and between marginal revenue and price elasticity.

Firstly, the MR curve is twice as steep as the demand curve. (The demand curve is also the average revenue curve, AR, since AR = TR/Q, where Q is the price per unit; the demand curve indicates the price that can be charged for each unit sold.)

The proof of this is quite straightforward:

$$TR = P \times Q$$

Substituting the linear demand curve function, $P = a - bQ$, from equation (7.14) into the above:

$$TR = (a - bQ) \times Q$$

$$TR = aQ - bQ^2 \qquad (7.21)$$

Marginal revenue is the derivative of total revenue with respect to output, or $d(TR)/dQ$. Therefore

$$MR = a - 2bQ \qquad (7.22)$$

In other words, the MR curve has the same intercept term, a, as the demand curve; it starts from the same point on the vertical axis. However, it has a slope of $2b$, twice that of the demand curve.

A second important relationship that can be deduced from the information in Table 43, page 145, and Figure 51 is the one between price elasticity and marginal revenue. Marginal revenue is positive in the range where demand is price elastic; it is zero where demand is equal to unitary elasticity; it is negative in the range where demand is price inelastic. Marginal revenue is positive and demand is price elastic ($e_p > 1$) from £100 to £50 per unit. Marginal revenue is negative and demand is price inelastic ($e_p < 1$) for prices below that level. This relationship can be summarised by the formula

$$MR = P\left(1 + \frac{1}{e_p}\right) \qquad (7.23)$$

A proof of this equation is given at the end of the chapter.[4] It was noted in Section 5.5 that a firm's profit-maximising position is where marginal cost is equal to marginal revenue. Substituting MC for MR in equation (7.23) and rearranging:

$$P^* = MC\left(\frac{e_p}{e_p + 1}\right) \qquad (7.24)$$

P^* refers to the profit-maximising price. Equation (7.24) is a very useful aid for firms when calculating their optimal pricing strategies. For example, if a firm's marginal cost is a constant £5 and its price elasticity is estimated at −1.5, then its profit-maximising price is equal to

$$P = £5\left(\frac{-1.5}{-1.5 + 1}\right) = £15$$

Having examined the relationships between marginal revenue, demand and price elasticity, the relationship between price elasticity and total revenue can now be specified more exactly. As price is reduced in the range of output where demand is price elastic (and MR > 0), then total revenue increases. Of course the reverse also holds: an increase in price in the same range will reduce total revenue. This is because the percentage change in demand outweighs the percentage change in price. At unitary elasticity (where MR = 0) total revenue peaks; the percentage change in demand equals the percentage change in price. Price reductions (increases) in the range where demand is price inelastic (and MR < 0) lead to falls (rises) in total revenue because the percentage change in demand is less than the percentage change in price.

These points can be summarised as follows:

(1) If demand equals unitary elasticity, marginal revenue is zero and total revenue is unaffected by a change in price.
(2) If demand is price elastic, marginal revenue is positive and a change in price leads to a greater proportional change in demand. Total revenue will move in the opposite direction to the price change.
(3) If demand is price inelastic, marginal revenue is negative and a change in price leads to a smaller percentage change in demand. Total revenue will move in the same direction as the price change.

Cross-price elasticity of demand

If the products are substitutes they will have a positive cross elasticity of demand; if the price of good Z increases, people will buy less of it and more of the substitute, good X. If the products are complements they will exhibit a negative cross elasticity of demand; if the price of good Z increases, consumers will buy less of it and also less of the complement, good X. The closer the relationship between the products, whether substitutes or complements, the larger will be the effect of a change in the price of one product on the demand for the other product and the higher the cross elasticity figure, whether posi-

---

Box 7.2 *Cross-price elasticity of demand*

Cross-price elasticity of demand (or just cross elasticity of demand) is defined as the responsiveness of the demand for one product, X, to a change in the price of another product, Z. It is measured by the formula

$$e_c = \frac{\text{Percentage Change in } Q_X}{\text{Percentage Change in } P_Z} \quad (7.25)$$

The point cross elasticity formula can be expressed as

$$e_c = \frac{dQ_X}{dP_Z} \times \frac{P_Z}{Q_X} \quad (7.26)$$

The are formula for cross elasticity is

$$e_c = \frac{\Delta Q_X}{\Delta P_Z} \times \frac{(P_{Z1} + P_{Z2})/2}{(Q_{X1} + Q_{X2})/2} \quad (7.27)$$

---

tive or negative. If the products are unrelated, the cross elasticity will have a value of zero, or very nearly zero, in which case a change in the price of one good has no effect, or a negligible effect, on the demand for the other good. These values are summarised in Table 44.

Assume a demand function takes the following form:

$$Q_X = 250 - 24P_X + 0.002A_X = 36P_{Z1}$$
$$- 27.2P_Z^2 + 0.01Y \quad (7.28)$$

If P_X is equal to £3, A_X equals £100 000, P_{Z1}>, the substitute, equals £3.5, P_{Z2}>, the complement, equals £2.5 and Y is £15 000, and these values are slotted into equation (7.28), then

$$Q_X = 250 - 72 + 200 + 126 - 68 + 150 = 586$$

The value of the coefficient for the substitute, P_{Z1}, is 36 (or dQ_X/dP_{Z1}). P_{Z1}, is given as £3.5 and Q_X is calculated as 586. If these values are slottted into equation (7.26), the point cross elasticity for the substitute good equals

$$e_c = 36 \times \frac{3.5}{586} = -0.2150$$

Table 44 *Cross elasticity values and definitions*

Value	Type of product	Definition
$0 < e_c < \infty$	Substitute	Q_X change in same direction as P_Z change
0	No relationship	Q_X unchanged as P_Z changes
$-\infty < e_c < 0$	Complement	Q_X change in opposite direction to P_Z change

The coefficient value of the complement, P_{Z1}, is 27.2 (or dQ_X/dP_{Z1}). P_{Z1} equals £2.5 and Q_X is 586. Hence, the point cross elasticity of the complement is

$$e_c = 27.2 \times \frac{2.5}{586} = -0.1160$$

The substitute has a positive cross elasticity and the complement a negative elasticity, which is as it should be. The relatively low values of the cross elasticity figures indicate the probability of only a moderate relationship in either case.

The fact that a higher cross elasticity figure indicates a closer relationship between the products has important implications for the determination of a firm's market, as was pointed out in Section 2.1. Markets are often defined in terms of the extent to which products can be referred to as close substitutes. However, the problem with using cross elasticity to determine the closeness of substitution is that the figure itself gives no indication of the precise relationship between the two products. The higher the figure the closer the relationship, but what should be the critical level? Naturally the cross elasticity figure should be positive, but it is impossible to say whether it should be two or three or higher before products can be considered close enough substitutes to belong to the same market. As a result, the concept of cross elasticity of demand is, at best, a partial solution to the problem of how best to define a market.

Income elasticity of demand

The value of income elasticity of demand can either be positive or negative. It is positive for all normal goods. As incomes rise, so does the demand for most products, although the extent of the response depends on the nature of the good. Some goods may be income elastic. The percentage change in demand exceeds the percentage change in income, in which case they have an income elasticity greater than one. They are commonly referred to as *luxuries*, although

---

Box 7.3 *Income elasticity of demand*

Income elasticity of demand is defined as the responsiveness of demand to changes in income. It is measured by the formula

$$e_y = \frac{\text{Percentage change in } Q_X}{\text{Percentage change in income}} \qquad (7.29)$$

Once again, the elasticity measure can be expressed in one of two ways. The point income elasticity formula is

$$e_y = \frac{dQ_X \times Y}{dY \times Q_X} \qquad (7.30)$$

The arc income elasticity formula can be expressed as

$$e_y = \frac{\Delta Q_X}{\Delta Y} \times \frac{(Y_1 + Y_2)/2}{(Q_1 + Q_2)/2} \qquad (7.31)$$

---

only in the sense that they respond strongly to changes in income. Housing, consumer durables and holidays are likely to fall into this category. As incomes increase (for example, during an economic upturn) the demand for such goods will increase quite significantly. On the other hand, some products may exhibit income inelasticity: the percentage change in demand is less than the percentage change in income which brought it about. Their income elasticity value is less than one. These products are called *necessities*, although, again, only in the sense that they are fairly unresponsive to income changes. Examples of such products are certain basic foodstuffs, some clothing items and most toiletries. Income elasticities are negative in the case of inferior goods. As incomes rise, the demand for these products falls as consumers switch to superior, or what are considered to be superior, substitutes. The values and definitions of income elasticities are summarised in Table 45.

In equation (7.28) the coefficient for income is given as 0.01Y, which is the value of dQ_X/dY in

---

Table 45 *Income elasticity values and definitions*

Value	Type of product	Definition
$-\infty < e_y < 0$	Inferior goods	Q_X change in opposite direction to Y change
$0 < e_y < 1$	Necessities	Q_X change in same direction but smaller percentage change in Q_X than in Y
$1 < e_y < \infty$	Luxuries	Q_X change in same direction and greater percentage change in Q_X than in Y

equation (7.30). Y is given as £15 000 and Q_X is equal to 586. Putting these values into equation (7.30), the point income elasticity can be obtained:

$$e_y = 0.01 \times \frac{15000}{586} = 0.2560$$

The relatively low, but positive value for the income elasticity indicates that the product comes into the 'necessity' category of goods. When incomes are increasing, producers of 'luxury' products with relatively high income elasticitites should face better sales prospects than the producers of 'necessities' which have lower income elasticities. For example, the demand for a good with an income elasticity of two will increase by 2% for every 1% rise in incomes. A product with an income elasticity of 0.5 will only experience a 0.5% increase in demand; on the other hand, the latter may be less affected by a downturn in economic activity. Forecasts of growth prospects for the economy will have important implications for the planning decisions of the producers of both types of goods.

Advertising elasticity of demand

Since, other than price, advertising is probably the main item in the demand function of a firm over which it has most control, it is important that the firm has some idea about how demand responds to changes in its advertising budget. There is usually a positive relationship between the demand for a product and the amount spent on advertising it, although demand is likely to become less responsive as the scale of advertising rises. In other words, the value of the advertising elasticity will probably decline the greater the advertising budget.

As before, the point advertising elasticity can be calculated by slotting the relevant values from equation (7.28) into the relevant formula, in this case equation (7.34). The advertising coefficient (dQ_X/dA_X) is 0.002, A_X is given as £100 000 and, with Q_X equal to 586, the point advertising elasticity becomes:

$$e_a = 0.002 \times \frac{100000}{586} = 0.3413 \qquad (7.35)$$

The figure indicates that sales of this product are not particularly responsive to increases in advertising. For every 1% increase in advertising sales increase by about 0.34%

Box 7.4 *Advertising elasticity of demand*

Advertising elasticity of demand is defined as the responsiveness of the demand for a product to a change in its advertising budget. Advertising elasticity can be measured by the formula

$$e_a = \frac{\text{Percentage change in } Q_X}{\text{Percentage change in advertising budget}} \qquad (7.32)$$

As is the case with the other elasticities, the advertising elasticity can be measured by either the point or the arc method. The point advertising elasticity formula is represented by

$$e_a = \frac{dQ_X \times A_X}{dA_X \times Q_X} \qquad (7.33)$$

The arc formula for advertising elasticity can be expressed as

$$e_a = \frac{\Delta Q_X}{\Delta A_X} \times \frac{(A_1 + A_2)/2}{(Q_1 + Q_2)/2} \qquad (7.34)$$

7.6 ESTIMATES OF ELASTICITIES

Estimates of price, income and cross elasticities for various products from different studies are given in Table 46, pages 150–2. The price elasticity estimates are all negative, as would be expected, but they vary in their scale. There is some evidence that the more broadly defined the product, the lower its substitutability and hence the more inelastic the demand. For example, in the Household Food Consumption and Expenditure Survey, HFCES (1989), meat and meat products in general have a price elasticity of –0.49, whereas individual meats have higher elasticity figures. The availability of substitutes also plays a large part in the size of the various tourism figures in the Syriopoulos and Sinclair (1993) study. The estimates of the price elasticities for tourism in the Mediterranean from other European countries are usually quite high because the host countries act as substitute destinations for each other, whereas the figure for US demand in Spain is relatively low, presumably because the product in this case is perceived as Europe as a whole rather than individual countries. The HFCES survey also shows that most staple foods, like milk, potatoes and bread, for which there are usually no close substitutes and which are often quite cheap, have very low price elasticities.

There is also confirmatory evidence that time affects the price elasticity of demand. The Dahl (1986) survey of the demand for petrol reveals a lower

Table 46 *Various estimates of price, income and cross elasticities*

Data period	Study	Product	Value of elasticity	Country
Price elasticities				
1970–83	Atkinson *et al.* (1990)	Alcohol	–1.12	UK
1960–87	Syriopoulos and Sinclair (1993)	Tourism, e.g:		Mediterranean
		British in Greece	–2.54	
		British in Spain	–0.72	
		W. Germans in Spain	–1.66	
		Americans in Spain	–0.28	
		French in Portugal	–1.88	
		Swedish in Italy	–1.34	
1980–87	Alexander *et al.* (1994)	Ethical pharmaceutical drugs, e.g:		Various
		UK	–2.80	
		France	–0.63	
		Germany	–2.07	
1987	Chang and Hsing (1991)	Residential electricity	–1.19	US
1984–89	Household Food Consumption and Expenditure Survey (HFCES, 1989)	Foodstuffs, e.g:		UK
		Milk	–0.19	
		Cheese	–1.20	
		Carcase meat	–1.37	
		Other meat and meat products	–0.49	
		Potatoes	–0.21	
		Frozen peas	–1.12	
		Fruit juices	–0.80	
		Bread	–0.09	
1987/88	Yen (1994)	Alcohol	–0.34	US
1990	Greening (1995)	Petrol	–0.00 to –0.66	US
1960–92	Uri (1995)	Sugar, 1960–77	–0.47 to	US
		1978–84	–0.86	
		1985–92	–1.02	
Survey	Dahl (1986)	Petrol	–0.48 to –1.61 (short run) –0.13 to –0.60 (long run)	Various
Income elasticities				
1970–83	Atkinson *et al.* (1990)	Alcohol	1.00 to 1.50	UK
1984	Sawtelle (1993)	Various, e.g: Food at home	–0.11	US
		Alcohol	0.04	
		Utilities	0.29	
		Transport	0.25	
		Healthcare	0.81	
		Entertainment	0.58	
		Tobacco	0.03	
		Clothing	0.30	

Table 46 *continued*

Data period	Study	Product	Value of elasticity	Country
1960–87	Syriopoulos and Sinclair (1993)	Tourism, e.g:		Mediterranean
		British in Greece	1.05	
		British in Spain	0.90	
		W.Germans in Spain	0.81	
		Americans in Spain	0.72	
		French in Portugal	1.45	
		Swedish in Italy	0.91	
1980–87	Alexander *et al.* (1994)	Ethical pharmaceutical drugs, e.g:		Various
		UK	1.03	
		France	1.31	
		Germany	1.55	
1987/88	Yen (1994)	Alcohol	0.40	US
1989	HFCES (1989)	Foodstuffs:		UK
		Milk	−0.02	
		Cheese	0.19	
		Carcase meat	−0.01	
		Sugar	−0.54	
		Potatoes	−0.48	
		Fresh fruit	0.48	
		Fruit juices	0.94	
		Bread	−0.25	
		Instant coffee	0.23	
Survey	Dahl (1986)	Petrol	0.66 to 1.94	Various
Cross elasticities				
1960–87	Syriopoulos and Sinclair (1993)	Tourism, e.g UK demand:		Mediterranean
		Greece with respect to Spain	0.20	
		Greece w.r.t. Portugal	0.53	
		Greece w.r.t. Italy	−0.04	
		Spain w.r.t Portugal	4.08	
		Spain w.r.t. Turkey	−7.73	
		Italy w.r.t. Portugal	−4.40	
1985	Chang and Hsing (1991)	Electricity w.r.t. gas	0.30	US
1982–89	HFCES (1989)	Beef and veal w.r.t. mutton and lamb	0.13	UK
		Beef and veal	0.03	

Table 46 *continued*

Data period	Study	Product	Value of elasticity	Country
		w.r.t. pork		
		Tea w.r.t. instant coffee	–0.10	
		Instant coffee w.r.t. tea	–0.11	
1960–92	Uri (1995)	Sugar w.r.t. sugar substitutes:		US
		1960–77	0.21	
		1978–84	0.27	
		1985–92	0.96	

long-run price elasticity figure than the equivalent short-run estimate. However, Uri (1995) estimates that the demand for sugar has become more elastic over time, although this is probably due to the recent increased availability of sugar substitutes.

The income elasticity of demand figures confirm that the so-called luxury products like tourism (and, it would seem, pharmaceutical drugs) tend to have higher elasticities than other products. Staple foods are inferior goods in the sense that they have negative income elasticities; the demand for them rises as incomes fall.

The cross elasticity estimates reveal a number of low, positive figures between combinations of products, for example between the demand for electricity and the price of gas and the demand for beef and veal and the price of mutton and lamb and pork. These products are weak substitutes for each other. By the same token, some of the holiday destinations are also shown to be fairly weak substitutes from the point of view of British tourists. However, those that have a negative relationship are revealed as complements. (Such a result may be expected for Greece and Italy, but not for Spain and Turkey or Italy and Portugal which, given the size of the parameter estimates, calls into question the reliability of the relevant data.) Tea and coffee are also shown, rather surprisingly, to be complements, albeit weak ones.

7.7 CONCLUSIONS

Demand analysis is concerned with effective demand: the demand for a product must be accompanied by the ability to pay for it. A firm needs to be aware of both the level and type of effective demand for its products for sound decision-making. Economic analysis emphasises the behaviour of the individual consumer, whereas the firm is concerned with the total or market demand; however, since market demand is the aggregate of individual demand, then it may be possible to understand a good deal about market demand from a study of individual demand.

In traditional theory the consumer's objective is to maximise utility, subject to a budget constraint. According to indifference curve analysis, it is possible to rank bundles of goods according to their relative amounts of utility. It can be shown that the rational consumer maximises utility where the marginal utility of each pound spent is the same for each product. Indifference curve analysis may lack practical relevance, but it underlies the shape of the individual's demand curve, which reveals a negative relationship between price and quantity demanded, *cet. par.*

The effect of a change in price on quantity demanded can be divided into two parts: the income effect and the substitution effect. In the case of normal goods the income effect reinforces the negative substitution effect; for inferior goods the two effects work in opposite directions, but the negative substitution outweighs the positive income effect, although in the case of Giffen goods the reverse is true. Thus, for normal goods and non-Giffen inferior goods, the law of demand dictates that as the price of a product rises (falls), the quantity demanded falls (rises), *cet. par.*

In the characteristics approach to consumer behaviour, the consumer is still concerned with utility maximisation, but utility is derived from the attributes that products possess rather than from the products themselves. Collections of characteristics can be obtained by buying various combinations of goods. Armed with a knowledge of groups of consumers who desire product characteristics in particular ratios, a firm can then gear its products towards certain market segments, although, since some characterstics are based on subjectivity, they may be difficult to identify and measure.

The market demand function indicates the relationship between the total demand for a product and the factors that may affect it per time period. A firm is likely to be particularly interested in the impact of endogenous independent variables, such as price, advertising and product quality, over which it has direct control. The market demand curve portrays the relationship between the price of a product and the quantity demanded, *cet. par.* It is important to distinguish between movements along a demand curve, caused by a change in the price of a product and resulting in a change in quantity demanded, and a shift of the whole demand curve, caused by a change in one or more of the other factors affecting demand and leading to a change in demand.

It is particularly important for a firm to know by how much demand changes in response to a change in any of the independent variables, or, in other words, to have a knowledge of elasticity of demand. Various elasticity measures are considered: own-price elasticity, cross-price elasticity, income elasticity and advertising elasticity. The relationship between total revenue and price elasticity is noted: if demand is price elastic (inelastic), total revenue will move in the opposite (same) direction as any price change. The most recent elasticity estimates are examined.

Case Study: Empirical investigations of the demand for beer in the UK– a round up of the usual suspects?

Studies of the demand for beer have rounded up the usual suspects: the price of beer, the price of substitutes, such as wine and spirits, the level of real income and advertising expenditures. Notice that taste, a rather nebulous but nonetheless important term covering all social and cultural factors, is not included because of the difficulties of measurement, although advertising could influence it and therefore might be regarded as a proxy indicator. Walsh (1982) estimated the demand function for beer as follows:

$$ABN = -0.004 - 0.13RPB + 0.06RPS - 0.03RPW + 0.13RYN + 0.61PUBSN + 0.10BRAN \quad (7.36)$$
$$(1.4) \quad\quad (1.2) \quad\quad (0.9) \quad\quad (0.5) \quad\quad (2.8) \quad\quad (0.9)$$

In equation (7.36), ABN refers to alcohol consumed in beer per time period, RPB, RPS and RPW are the real price indices for beer, spirits and wine respectively, RYN is real income per adult, PUBSN stands for the number of licenses (per 1000 adults) and BRAN is real beer advertising expenditure. The study has a moderate explanatory power (the coefficient of determination, R^2 = 0.44). Estimates of the coefficients (which are estimated in logarithmic form and therefore indicate the elasticities of the different variables) do not vary greatly from subsequent studies that have been undertaken, and which employ fewer independent variables (see for example Duffy, 1987; Jones, 1989; Selvanathan, 1991). Their results are summarised in Table 47.

Table 47 *Estimates of the elasticity of demand for beer*

| Study | Data period | Elasticity values | | | | |
| | | Own price | Cross price | | Income | Advertising |
			WRS	WRW[a]		
Walsh	1956–75	–0.13	0.06	–0.03	0.13	0.10
Duffy	1963–83	–0.36	n/a	n/a	0.71	0.05
Jones	1964–83	–0.39	–0.17	0.10	0.31	n/a
Selvanathan	1955–85	–0.13	0.08	0.05	0.52	n/a

[a] WRS stands for 'with respect to spirits'; WRW stands for 'with respect to wine'.

The studies show that beer tends to have a very low price elasticity (–0.13 to –0.39). This helps to explain the constancy of real beer expenditure in the UK despite the fairly steady fall in consumption per head since the late 1970s, implying an increase in the relative price of beer. The cross elasticities of demand for beer are also very low: the demand for beer is not affected much by changes in the price of spirits or wine. The income elasticity of demand for beer is positive but low (estimates range from 0.13 to 0.71), indicating that beer is classified as a necessity and also that the demand for it may not be greatly affected by fluctuations in economic activity. The downward trend in consumption since the late 1970s may have more to do with changing habits and lifestyles than with changing economic conditions. Beer also seems to have a low advertising elasticity (0.05 to 0.10); advertising has an affect on demand, but not a strong one. Interestingly, the strongest influence on beer consumption in the Walsh study seems to stem from the number of outlets (0.61), although this could quite easily be regarded as a supply variable, in which case the above function could actually be tracing the supply curve rather than the demand curve for beer. The other studies may also suffer from similar identification problems (Glen, 1990). All in all, the studies of beer demand do not seem to have had significant explanatory power. This may be because the fairly radical changes in the nature of the product, and in particular the growth of lager consumption which now forms over 50% of sales in volume terms, need to be addressed. The various market segments (traditional beer versus lager consumption and home versus outside consumption) may require separate analysis.

FURTHER READING

Koutsoyiannis, A. (1979) *Modern Microeconomics*, 2nd edn (London, Macmillan), Chapter 2

Lancaster, K. (1971) *Consumer Demand: A New Approach* (New York, Columbia University Press)

Mansfield, E. (1979) *Microeconomics: Theory and Applications*, 3rd edn (New York, W.W. Norton and Company), Chapters 2–5.

NOTES

1. Marginal utility theory was developed in the 1870s by several economists working independently of each other: William Stanley Jevons, 1835–82, in England, Karl Menger, 1840–1921, in Austria and Léon Walras, 1834–1910, in Switzerland.
2. Indifference curve analysis is associated mainly with Eugen Slutsky, 1880–1948, of the USSR, Vilfredo Pareto, 1848–1923, of Italy and Sir John Hicks, 1904–92, of England.
3. Where it is difficult to disentangle the respective effects of two or more of the independent variables on the dependent variable, then they will be statistically correlated.
4. The proof is as follows:

$$\text{TR} = P \times Q$$

$$\text{MR} = \frac{d(\text{TR})}{dQ} = \frac{d(P \times Q)}{dQ} = P \times \frac{dQ}{dQ} + Q \times \frac{dP}{dQ}$$

$$= P + Q\,\frac{dP}{dQ}$$

Factoring out P:

$$= P\left(1 + \frac{Q}{P} \times \frac{dP}{dQ}\right)$$

Where $(Q/P) \times (dP/dQ)$ is the reciprocal of the term for price elasticity of demand. Thus

$$\text{MR} = P\left(1 + 1/e_p\right)$$

Questions □ □ □

7.1 If people prefer holidaying in the Seychelles to holidaying in Majorca, why do more people holiday in Majorca?

7.2 The diagram shows a consumer's budget line and relevant indifference curve. The consumer's equilibrium position is at *Z*. The budget equation contains the following information: $£600 = 40P_Y + £40X$.

(a) What is the maximum number of units of good *X* that could be purchased?
(b) What is the unit price of good *Y*?
(c) Calculate the slope of the budget line.

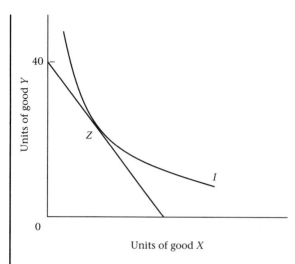

Figure Q.7.2 *Units of good X*

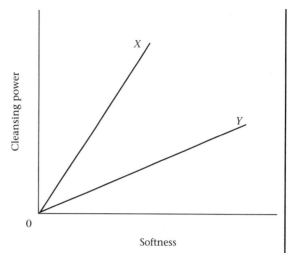

Figure Q.7.4

(d) A new budget equation is given as: £600 = 40P_Y + £50X. What is the maximum number of units of good X that could now be purchased?

(e) Assuming that good X is a normal good, show diagrammatically how the new budget equation might affect the equilibrium position of the consumer.

7.3 Show, with the aid of diagrams, how each of the following affects the demand for tickets (per week) at the Screen One cinema, assuming *ceteris paribus* in each case:

(a) A fall in the average price of a ticket.

(b) A fall in the price of video recorders.

(c) A successful promotional campaign by the management to attract more custom.

(d) Both (b) and (c).

7.4 In a particular area, two brands of washing powder, X and Y, account for most of the market. It has been discovered that the two main characteristics from which consumers derive utility are cleansing power and softness. Brand X has a higher cleansing power to softness, and brand Y has a higher softness to cleansing power. The two brands are indicated by the two rays, X and Y, in the diagram.

(a) Show an efficiency frontier and a possible equilibrium position for a consumer.

(b) A new washing powder, brand Z, is introduced onto the market which has the same two characteristics but in proportions that place it between

X and Y. Show the ray for brand Z. Indicate on your diagram two different prices for brand Z, such that (i) the consumer is faced with an inefficient choice of characteristics and (ii) the consumer is faced with an efficient choice of characteristics. Show a new possible equilibrium position for the consumer when given the latter choice.

7.5 The most popular route of a bus company is the round trip to and from a neighbouring town. However, the route is fiercely competitive. The company decides to employ a firm of business consultants, who estimate the demand function for the number of trips over a period of time as follows:

$$Q_X = 30000 - 1750P_X + 1425P_Z + 245.2A_X + 0.1Y$$

where Q_X is the number of trips taken on the route, P_X is the price of the product, P_Z is the price charged by a rival, A_X is the advertising budget of the company on the route and Y refers to average per capita disposable income. Current values of the independent variables are $P_X = £4.50$, $P_Z = £4.75$, $A_X = £145$ (in hundreds of £) and $Y = £16\,000$.

(a) Calculate the market demand, Q_X.

(b) Express P_X as a linear function of the quantity demanded, Q_X.

(c) The firm wishes to know the effects of changes in the various independent variables on demand. Calculate the point price elasticity of demand, the point cross elasticity of demand, the point income elasticity of demand and the point advertising elasticity of demand for the product.

7.6 'Evidence from around the world suggests that smoking is highly price elastic: when the price of cigarettes goes up, smoking declines' (*The Guardian*, 28 October 1993). Critically evaluate this statement.

7.7 The weekly demand function for Supremo coffee is estimated as

$Q_X = 19.75 - 3.25P_X$

where Q_X = thousands of 300 g jars and P_X = £4.75 per jar.

(a) Calculate the point price elasticity of demand for jars of coffee.
(b) Assuming a constant marginal cost of £3, calculate the profit-maximising price.

7.8 A minicab firm is considering setting up business. Estimates from other firms in the area suggest that the demand function per period takes the following form:

$Q_X = 3000 - 400P_X$

where Q_X is the number of weekly trips and P_X is the price charged per mile.

(a) Calculate the number of weekly trips it could sell if it charged a price of £1.50 per mile.
(b) What price should it charge if it wanted to sell 2600 trips per week?
(c) Calculate the point price elasticity of demand at a rate of £2 per mile. What will be the probable effect on revenue of an increase in the rate charged per mile?

7.9 A hairdresser plans to increase her average price from £12.50 to £15. She estimates that this will increase annual revenue from £225 000 to £247 500 (based on a working year of 300 days).

(a) Calculate the average number of daily cuts at the original price and at the new price.
(b) Would you estimate the demand elasticity to be price elastic or inelastic?
(c) Calculate the arc price elasticity of demand.
(d) The hairdresser then decides to increase her annual promotional budget, mainly by advertising in the local papers, from £5000 to £6000. It is estimated that this will raise total revenue at the new price from £247 500 to £292 500. Calculate the arc advertising elasticity of demand.

7.10 In August 1993, News International reduced the price of *The Times* from 45 to 30p. Prices of the other 'quality' dailies remained unchanged until August 1994. The daily circulation of *The Times* increased from 354280 in August 1993 to 442106 in September 1993 and to 599358 in July 1994.

(a) Calculate the arc price elasticities of demand for *The Times* during each of the two periods August 1993 to September 1993 and August 1993 to July 1994. Why do you think there is a difference in the price elasticities in the two periods?
(b) Discuss the implications for total revenue of your answers in part (a). (Note: your answers can be verified from the above figures.)
(c) If a long-term incremental analysis was being undertaken of the possible impact on the revenue of News International of the decision to lower the price of *The Times,* what other factors would need to be considered?

7.11 The table below shows the estimated elasticities for alcoholic beverages in Australia. They were estimated using a fairly sophisticated model in which the various elasticities were allowed to vary over time.

(a) On the basis of the figures discuss the likely effect of increases in the prices of alcoholic drinks on the revenue of the producers.
(b) Discuss the likely impact of an increase in the price of beer, wine or spirits on the demand for each of the other two products.
(c) Discuss the effect of rising real incomes over time on the demand for these alcoholic drinks.

Elasticities for beer, wine and spirits in Australia

Product	Price elasticities			Income
	Beer	Wine	Spirits	elasticities
1956–7				
Beer	−0.10	0.03	0.07	0.71
Wine	0.26	−0.57	0.31	1.11
Spirits	0.34	0.17	−0.52	2.34
1976–7				
Beer	−0.12	0.03	0.08	0.82
Wine	0.12	−0.27	0.15	0.51
Spirits	0.35	0.17	−0.52	2.34

Source: Clements and Johnson (1983).

CHAPTER 8

▶ Corporate Decision-making within Alternative Market Structures

It is now possible to bring together the concepts that have been developed in the last two chapters to show how cost and demand conditions together determine the market structure in which firms operate; it is also possible to show how the competitive environment influences corporate decision-making. Economists have developed numerous models or theories which analyse the decision-making processes of the firm. In most circumstances it is assumed that a firm will pursue those policies that enable it to satisfy its objectives and to gain an advantage over its competitors.

Generally, the models have concentrated on explanations of price and output strategies. They assume different demand and cost conditions and these, in particular the nature of elasticity of demand for the product and the extent of economies of scale, help to determine the *market structure*. Most of the theories of the firm assume that the structure of the market influences the policies or *behaviour* of firms and ultimately their level of *performance*. However, as was pointed out in Section 2.2, a process of 'reverse causation' may be equally likely. The chapter begins by outlining the main structural characteristics of the different market models. Traditionally, economists have identified four major market structures or forms. These are *pure* or *perfect competition, monopoly, monopolistic competition* and *oligopoly*. The three latter types are examples of *imperfectly competitive* market structures. Perfect competition and monopoly represent the two extreme forms of competition and are examined first. Next the theory of monopolistic competition is discussed. Since most large firms operate in

an oligopolistic environment the analysis of this market form is examined in some detail: the *interdependence* and *uncertainty* that characterise oligopoly are outlined; the *game theory* approach to oligopolistic behaviour is explained; the *kinked demand curve* model is examined; *collusive models*, such as *cartels* and *price leadership*, are also discussed. The final section in the chapter features a *case study* of price leadership in the UK car and salt markets. The arguments surrounding the welfare implications of monopoly power are discussed in Chapter 15.

8.1 THE MAIN TYPES OF MARKET STRUCTURE

It is assumed, at least for the time being, that firms have the same objective whatever the market structure in which they operate: the objective is to maximise profits and in particular short-run profits; it is also assumed that there are many buyers in each type of market environment.

In a *perfectly competitive* market, many firms sell identical or homogenous products, i.e. the products are perfect substitutes. There is a very low degree of market concentration. Both consumers and producers possess perfect knowledge of market conditions. Consumers have complete information about where to obtain the best bargains, and producers have perfect information about the prices of factors of production and about the level of demand at different prices. In fact, firms in perfect competition are *price takers* in the sense that the price of the product is predetermined via the interaction of market demand and market supply. Firms, which are assumed to operate a single plant, sell all they can at the market price; therefore, each firm faces a perfectly elastic demand curve for its product. There is also complete freedom of entry to, and exit from, the industry. Since there are a very large number of relatively small firms plant economies of scale are non-existent.

In *imperfectly competitive* markets, firms are *price makers*. They can determine their own prices. Prices in these markets are often referred to as *administered* because they are determined by a single decision-making body, the firm. The extent to which a firm can set its own prices is mainly influenced by the degree of product differentiation that exists in each market. The fact that each firm's product is not a perfect substitute for that of its competitors gives it a degree of monopoly or market power over its pricing strategy. It knows that it can raise its price and not lose all its customers; in other words, each firm is faced with a downward-sloping demand curve for its product. Imperfectly competitive markets are also characterised by imperfect information. Consumers simply do not possess the information to distinguish adequately between the products produced by each firm in the market. Furthermore, it is unlikely that there will be complete freedom of entry and exit in imperfectly competitive markets.

Monopoly lies at the opposite end of the competitive 'spectrum' to perfect competition. In theory, a monopoly occurs where there is a single seller of a product that has no close substitutes. Significant barriers to entry are likely. A *natural monopoly* exists, at least in the single-product case, where falling long-run average costs occur up to and beyond the level of market demand, so that only one firm can benefit from economies of scale. Other examples of monopolies are referred to, at least in theory, as *pure monopolies*. In practice, a dominant firm can exert significant market or monopoly power with far less than 100% control of the market. The legal definition of a monopoly in the UK is where any firm has more than a 25% market share.

A *monopolistically competitive* market exhibits far lower seller concentration than a monopolist. There are many firms whose products are differentiated to some extent: in other words, the products are close substitutes. It is quite easy to enter such a market, i.e. barriers to entry are minimal. An *oligopolistic* market usually has a high degree of seller concentration: it is dominated by a few large producers, although a fringe of smaller firms may also exist. The products of the dominant firms are considered to be substitutes, but are highly differentiated. It is likely to be difficult to enter such a market; however, some oligopolistic markets may be considered contestable, at least temporarily (see Chapter 2).

Most oligopolies are characterised by differentiated products, in which case they are known as imperfect oligopolies. However, there are some oligopolies with homogenous products, such as in the production of cement, steel or aluminium. They are referred to as perfect oligopolies. For present purposes it will be assumed that all oligopolies are imperfect. No distinction will be drawn between the behaviour of firms in either type of oligopolistic market. The main structural features of the four major market forms are summarised in Table 48.

8.2 PERFECT COMPETITION

In a perfectly competitive market the equilibrium price is determined by the interaction of the forces of demand and supply. In Section 7.4 it was shown that that the market demand curve is downward-sloping from left to right. The market supply curve is upward-sloping from left to right, again assuming *cet. par.* Firms will supply or offer for sale more of the product the higher the price; they will do this in the hope that they will make a larger profit. The attraction of making higher profits at higher prices will also lure new firms into the industry, which also has the effect of increasing supply.

Market price determination in perfect competition

In Figure 52 the market price always tends towards the equilibrium, P^*, where market demand equals market supply. This is the *market clearing price*. If the price was P_1 there would be *excess supply* for supply exceeds demand at that price. Firms are likely to lower their prices in order to rid themselves of excess stocks of goods. The result is that the market price will tend to fall towards the equilibrium level. As it does so, there is an increase in the quantity demanded while, at the same time, firms offer less for sale; eventually demand equals supply at the equilibrium price. On the other hand, at a price of P_2 there is *excess demand*. Since firms are able to sell all they can at higher prices, the market price will tend to rise towards the

Table 48 *The major structural characteristics of markets*

Market	No. of firms	Nature of product	Barriers to entry
Perfectly competitive	Many	Homogenous	None
Monopolistically competitive	Many	Differentiated	Very low/absent
Oligopoly	Few dominant	Highly differentiated	Likely
Monopoly	One	Sole product	Very likely

equilibrium level, creating a fall in the quantity demanded and a rise in the quantity supplied as firms offer more for sale. Once again, demand and supply are equated at the equilibrium price.

Algebraically, the market demand and market supply curves may be given by the following equations:

$$P_D = 16.7 - 0.002Q \qquad (8.1)$$

$$P_S = 0.25 - 0.005Q \qquad (8.2)$$

where equation (8.1) denotes the demand curve and equation (8.2) denotes the supply curve. Note that the supply equation shows a positive relationship between price and output, reflecting the upward-sloping nature of the curve. In equilibrium demand equals supply, hence

$$16.7 - 0.002Q \quad = \quad 0.25 + 0.005Q$$

$$0.007Q = \quad 16.45$$

$$Q^\star = \quad 2350$$

and

$$P = \quad 16.7 - 0.002(2350)$$

$$P = \quad 16.7 - 4.7$$

$$P^\star = \quad £12$$

Thus, the equilibrium market quantity, $Q^\star$ is equal to 2350 units and the equilibrium market price, $P^\star$, is equal to £12.

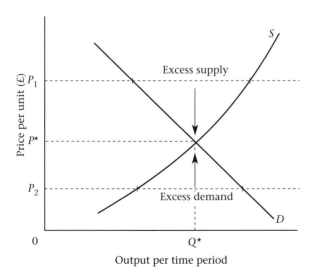

Figure 52 *The tendency towards equilibrium in perfect competition.*

Market and firm equilibrium in perfect competition in the short run

Since perfectly competitive firms take the market price as given, their only real decision would appear to be what level of output to produce. However, the assumptions of the model mean that this decision is also virtually automatic. The individual firm faces a perfectly elastic demand curve for its product. It is able to sell all that it can at the prevailing market price. Therefore the firm's marginal revenue is equal to its price: the revenue it obtains from selling incremental units is given by the price of the product, the marginal revenue curve and the demand curve being one and the same. At the same time, any firm can maximise its profits by equating marginal revenue and marginal cost, as proved in Section 5.5.

In Figure 53(a), page 160, the equilibrium market price is indicated by $P^\star$, which is also the profit-maximising price for the individual firm, as shown in Figure 53(b). If the traditional short-run U-shaped marginal cost and average cost curves from Section 6.5 are added to the graph of the individual firm the profit-maximising level of output will be at $Q^\star$, where marginal cost equals marginal revenue. In other words, since price is equal to marginal revenue for a perfectly competitive firm and, in order to maximise profits it equates marginal revenue with marginal cost, therefore it must equate price and marginal cost. This rule, that price equals marginal cost ($P = MC$), applies to all perfectly competitive firms.

The total profit of the perfectly competitive firm portrayed in Figure 53(b) is given by the rectangle $P^\star$ ABC. This is simply the difference between total revenue and total costs. Total revenue is the price per unit, $0P^\star$, multiplied by the output, $0Q^\star$, or the rectangle $0P^\star$ $AQ^\star$. Total costs are calculated by multiplying the unit costs, $0C$, by the number of units sold, $0Q^\star$, or the rectangle $0CBQ^\star$. The difference between them is the rectangle $P^\star ABC$.

The situation described in Figure 53(b) depicts a short-run equilibrium position of the perfectly competitive firm. There are numerous other equilibrium situations that could have been shown, each a function of the market price and the particular firm's cost conditions. In all cases the firm's equilibrium position would be found by equating its marginal cost and marginal revenue, which in perfect competition (and only in perfect competition) is equal to the price. The firm's equilibrium output level would automatically follow. In the example shown in Figure 53, the firm is making *abnormal* or *supernormal* profits; these are

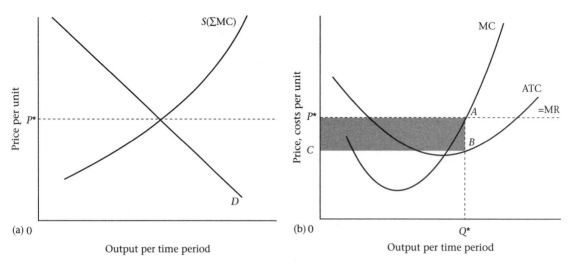

Figure 53 *(a) Market and (b) firm equilibrium in perfect competition in the short run.*

are profits above the normal return to capital, or the normal level of profit, as explained in Section 5.2.

The effects of an increase in supply in perfect competition

The existence of supernormal profits acts as an entry signal to firms outside the industry. In addition, existing firms may expand their operations. The effect is to cause an increase in market supply and a fall in price. This process continues until all the supernormal profit has been eroded away (i.e. as long as $P > ATC$). This is illustrated in Figure 54. In Figure 54(a) the market supply increases from S_1 to S_2 and, as a result, the market price falls from P_1^* to P_2^*.

The firm's situation is shown in Figure 54(b). When the price is P_2^* it produces Q_2^*; at this price no supernormal profits remain. This position (i.e. when all supernormal profits have been eliminated and each firm is achieving normal profits) also represents the long-run equilibrium position of the firm. Output Q_2^*

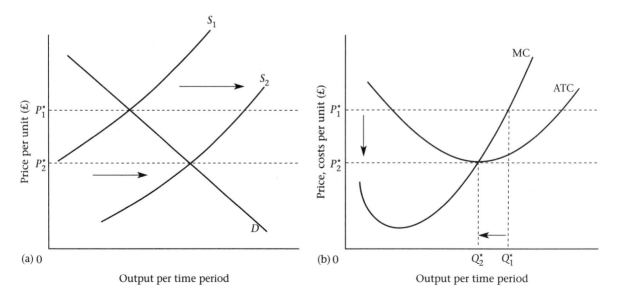

Figure 54 *The effects of an increase in supply on (a) market and (b) firm equilibrium in perfect competition.*

is inevitably at the minimum point on the average cost curve. Each firm equates price (and hence marginal revenue) with marginal cost in order to maximise profits. Since the marginal cost curve cuts the average cost curve at its lowest point, the normal profit position must be at the lowest point on the average cost curve; in Section 6.5 it was noted that each point on the LRAC curve is a point of tangency with a SRAC curve. Thus, the long-run equilibrium position is where

$$P^* = MR = SRMC = LRMC = SRAC = LRAC$$

The supply curve in perfect competition

The short-run market supply curve is the horizontal summation of the supply curves of the individual firms that make up the market. In fact, each firm's short-run supply curve is actually represented by its marginal cost curve. This can be seen more clearly by reference to Figure 55, which shows the effects of different prices on the quantity supplied by a competitive firm. Since price equals marginal cost, it follows that the perfectly competitive firm's marginal cost curve must trace out its supply curve. At a price of P_3 the firm will offer an output of Q_3 for sale. At P_2 it offers Q_2 and at P_1 it offers Q_1.

It should be noted that P_1 is below the firm's average total cost curve. At this price the firm is actually making a loss. However, since it is still equating marginal revenue and marginal cost, it is minimising its losses. In the short run the firm will continue to produce (and this is a generally applicable rule) as long as its price is at least as great as its average variable cost, even though the price may be below average total cost, i.e. when $AVC < P < ATC$. At any price above average variable cost, the firm will be making some contribution to fixed costs and to profit for each unit sold. If the price is below the firm's average variable cost, it is better that the firm cease production and incur a loss equal to its total fixed costs. If it continued in production at such a price, it would not even be covering its total variable costs; it would be making a greater loss than if it stopped producing. That is why P_1, the minimum point on the average variable cost curve, is referred to as the *cut-off* or *shut-down* price. It also represents the lowest point on the firm's short-run supply curve. The firm's supply curve is the marginal cost curve above the average variable cost curve (the solid section in Figure 55). Thus, the market supply curve in the short run in perfect competition is actually the horizontal summation of each firm's marginal cost curve above its average variable cost curve.

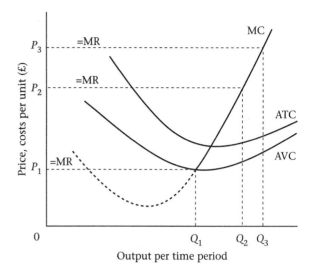

Figure 55 *The short-run supply curve of the firm in perfect competition.*

In the long run, the shape of the industry supply curve depends on the effects of expansion or contraction of the industry on firms' costs. For example, suppose that following an increase in demand and a rise in price, supernormal profits are created and new firms are attracted into the industry; the supply curve shifts to the right and price falls. If the price falls back to its original level (assuming no change in costs), then the long-run supply curve will be horizontal at the original price. It is a constant cost industry. However, the increase in industry supply may have an effect on costs. The arrival of new firms may create a shortage of inputs or add to pollution and congestion, pushing up factor prices and raising costs. The price is unable to fall to its original level and the industry supply curve is upward-sloping; it is an increasing cost industry, the subject of *external diseconomies of scale*. If, on the other hand, the entry of new firms causes costs to fall (due, say, to the establishment of specialist suppliers or the result of improved communications), the long-run supply curve is downward-sloping. This is an example of a decreasing cost industry, the result of *external economies of scale*.

It is debatable whether perfectly competitive markets actually exist in reality. The nearest examples are probably the stock market and the foreign exchange market. In each case there are many buyers and many sellers and the units of the product that is being traded, a company's shares or a country's currency respectively, are regarded as identical by the various parties. Even in these instances, however, there may be some doubt about whether all concerned have access to exactly the same information at all times. It is probably better to regard the theory of perfect competition as a basis from which to develop some of the other theories of the firm that may be more easily applied to practical situations.

Despite its lack of realism, the perfectly competitive model retains an important place in economic theory because of its implications for economic welfare. Assuming that perfect competition (and hence $P = $ MC) exists throughout the economy and that prices fully reflect the true opportunity costs of production, including externalities, and with a given income distribution, then there will be a Pareto-efficient allocation of resources. This is because prices reflect the true values that consumers attach to purchasing products and marginal costs reflect the true opportunity costs of producing those products. In other words, a perfectly competitive economy automatically yields an optimum allocation of resources. In addition, since in the long run, firms in a perfectly competitive industry operate at the lowest point of the LRAC curve (where MC = AC), then they are all also producing at the least-cost output, for any given level of technology. The efficiency aspects of perfect competition have important policy implications, which are discussed further in Chapter 15.

8.3 MONOPOLY

Firms in all the other market forms – monopoly, monopolistic competition and oligopoly – are price makers. They are able to set their own prices, although there is no guarantee that consumers will necessarily buy at these prices.

A *monopolist* is the sole supplier of a product, for which there are no close substitutes. (The word monopoly, from the Greek, literally means single seller.) The monopolist's supply is the same as the market supply and its demand is the same as the market demand. Monopoly is the polar opposite of perfect competition; they represent the two extreme market models. Monopolies persist due to barriers to entry. As discussed in Section 2.4, these are obstacles to potential entrants that lie on the boundaries of markets. They make it more costly or more difficult for new firms to enter a particular market.

As mentioned above, a single-product natural monopoly exists when only one firm is able to take advantage of plant-level economies of scale; more specifically, it occurs when a firm can produce a given level of output cheaper than can any combination of two or more firms, in which case the cost function is said to be subadditive (Baumol *et al.*, 1982). Thus, a market is a natural monopoly where

$$C(Q) < \sum C(Q_i) \qquad (8.3)$$

The single firm can produce the given level of output Q (where $Q = \sum Q_i$) for less than any other combination of firms. A multiproduct natural monopolist exists (and cost subadditivity occurs) when there are decreasing average incremental costs of each product plus economies of scope. The utilities, such as gas, electricity, the railways and telecommunications, are multiproduct in the sense that they are subject to varying demands throughout the day which are best treated as separate products with different costs of production. The fact that these industries have been regarded as natural monopolies was an important justification for their original state ownership and operation as single businesses.

The monopolist's equilibrium position

A profit-maximising monopolist, like any profit maximiser, will produce at the point where its marginal revenue is equal to its marginal cost. It is faced with a downward-sloping demand curve which is also the market demand curve. In Figure 56 the associated marginal revenue curve and the traditional short-run cost curves are added. The equilibrium level of output is Q_M and the equilibrium price is P_M. Note that, since the monopolist is faced with a downward-sloping demand curve, price exceeds marginal revenue. As a profit maximiser it equates marginal revenue and marginal cost. Hence, its price must exceed its marginal cost, i.e. $P > $ MC. This rule applies in all forms of imperfect competition because firms that operate in any of these market conditions face downward-sloping demand curves.

The abnormal profit, which is referred to in this case as *monopoly profit*, is shown in Figure 56 by the rectangle P_M *ABC*. The presence of barriers to entry means that any monopoly profit is likely to persist. It will not be eaten away by an invasion of new firms attracted by the prospect of obtaining some of the profit for themselves.

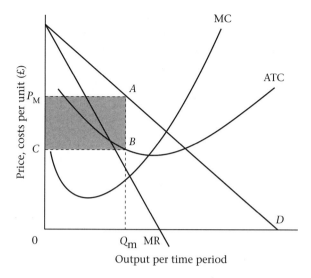

Figure 56 *The equilibrium position of a monopolist.*

Algebraically, the equilibrium position of the monopolist can be calculated as follows. Assuming that the industry demand curve is given as

$$P = 114 - 0.01Q \qquad (8.4)$$

The marginal revenue curve has the same intercept and twice the slope:

$$MR = 114 - 0.02Q$$

Assume also the total cost function is given by the quadratic equation

$$TC = 2550 + 24Q + 0.02Q^2$$

Then marginal cost equals

$$MC = 24 + 0.04Q$$

Equating the expressions for marginal revenue and marginal cost:

$$
\begin{aligned}
MR &= MC \\
114 - 0.02Q &= 24 + 0.04Q \\
0.06Q &= 90 \\
Q &= 1500
\end{aligned}
$$

Substituting for P:

$$
\begin{aligned}
P &= 114 - 0.01(1500) \\
P &= 99
\end{aligned}
$$

The profit-maximising output is 1500 units and the profit-maximising price is £99. The monopoly profit is equal to total revenue minus total cost:

$$
\begin{aligned}
TR - TC &= P \times Q - (2550 + 24Q + 0.02Q^2) \\
&= 1500 \times 99 - (2550 + 24(1500) + 0.02(1500^2)) \\
&= 148500 - (2550 + 36000 + 45000) \\
&= 143500 - 83550 \\
&= 64{,}950
\end{aligned}
$$

The monopoly profit equals £64950.

In theory, a monopolist's product has no close substitutes, although in practice a certain amount of competition usually exists between it and other similar products. The railways compete with other forms of transportation such as travel by road, air and even sea. (Witness the price war that has arisen between the Eurostar rail services and the cross-channel ferries and airlines since the Channel Tunnel opened.) The UK Post Office is in competition with firms like DHL, Federal Express and TNT for some of the services that it provides, such as parcel delivery. Telephone companies are now in competition in many countries with cable TV companies for the right to supply telephone services. Gas and electricity services compete both within and between households. It is very unlikely that a product has absolutely no close substitutes of any kind, even if the extent of competition is actually quite small.

It is also important to note that the monopoly power of a firm may be dictated by the extent of the regional market which it serves; this is especially true in the case of services. If a small town has, say, a single restaurant, then it will have a monopoly of the area, since consumers will not want to travel far to eat out. The spatial limits of markets have to be taken into account before they can be correctly identified as belonging to one market form or another.

Multiplant monopolies

So far it has been assumed that the monopolist is operating a single plant. However, it is more likely to have a number of plants, i.e. to be *multiplant*. If this is the case the firm will have to decide not just its profit-maximising price and output, but also how to allocate its total output between its plants. (The same sort of analysis could apply equally to firms in other forms of imperfect competition.) If, as may be quite likely, the different plants have different cost structures, the firm will want to produce each incremental unit in the lowest-cost plant.

For example, assume that the firm operates just two plants, A and B, and that plant A has lower average costs than plant B. This situation is shown

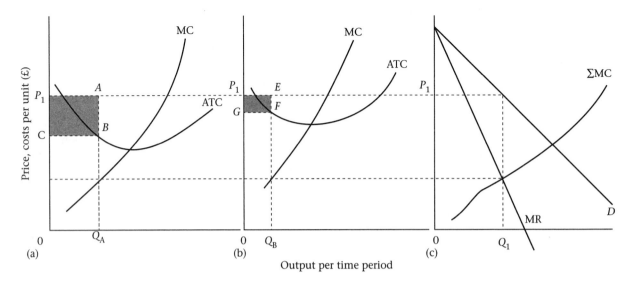

Figure 57 *The equilibrium position of a multiplant monopolist. (a) plant A; (b) plant B; (c) the firm.*

in Figure 57. In order to maximise profits the firm will need to ascertain its overall marginal cost curve and equate this with its marginal revenue curve. It does this by summing the marginal cost curve of each plant horizontally, so yielding the 'total' marginal cost curve of the firm ΣMC. (The kink at the lower end of this curve reflects the cost differences between the plants. At the lowest cost levels, the marginal costs of plant A only are relevant.) The firm's profit-maximising output is given by Q_1, where $\Sigma MC = MR$, and its profit-maximising price is P_1. The marginal cost in each plant is equal (shown by the dashed line), since each incremental unit is produced in the plant with the lowest marginal cost. If this were not the case the firm could reduce its marginal costs and increase its profits by moving production from the higher-cost to the lower-cost plant for each unit of output produced. If $MC_A < MC_B$ the firm would reduce output in plant B and increase output in plant A. Therefore, output Q_A is produced in plant A and output Q_B is produced in plant B, where the respective marginal costs are equalised. Q_A and Q_B sum to Q_1. The firm's total profit is the addition of rectangle $P_1 ABC$ from plant A and rectangle $P_1 EFG$ from plant B.

Algebraically, the equilibrium position of the profit-maximising, multiplant monopolist can be found as follows. Assume that the industry output is produced in two plants, A and B. If the industry demand curve is given by

$$P = 200 - 0.1Q \qquad (8.5)$$

Therefore, the marginal revenue function will be

$$MR = 200 - 0.2Q$$

The output of each plant, Q_A and Q_B, sum to Q. Hence

$$MR = 200 - 0.2(Q_A + Q_B)$$

The total cost curves of each plant are denoted by the functions

$$TC_A = 60 + 20Q_A$$
$$TC_B = 30 + 0.05Q_B^2$$

Therefore

$$MC_A = 20$$
$$MC_B = 0.1Q_B$$

If each marginal cost is equated with the common marginal revenue:

$$200 - 0.2Q_A - 0.2Q_B = 20$$
$$200 - 0.2Q_A - 0.2Q_B = 0.1Q_B$$

Hence

$$180 - 0.2Q_A = 0.2Q_B$$
$$200 - 0.2Q_A = 0.3Q_B$$

Solving for Q_A and Q_B, $Q_A = 700$ and $Q_B = 200$. Total output, Q, is thus $Q_A + Q_B = 900$. Substituting for P:

$$P = 200 - 0.1(900)$$
$$P = £110$$

Total profit, π, is equal to TR − TC, where TR = $P \times Q$:

TR = $900 \times 110 = 99000$

TC = $[60 + 20(700)] + [30 + 0.05(200)^2]$

   = $14060 + 2030 = 16090$

π = $99000 - 16090 = £82910$

8.4 MONOPOLISTIC COMPETITION

It was pointed out in Section 4.2 that Chamberlin (1933) and Robinson (1933) separately developed the theory of *monopolistic competition*. It is a model that incorporates features from both the previously-outlined theories, perfect competition and monopoly. When the theory of monopolistic competition was developed it was an attempt to make the theory of the firm more realistic. At the time a growing number of firms possessed some degree of monopoly power, while remaining in strong competition with their major competitors.

Accordingly, in this model it is assumed that there are many firms, each selling a product that is slightly differentiated from the product of its rivals. This gives each firm in the market a certain amount of power over its pricing policy, although the extent of the discretion that it possesses is limited by the existence of close substitutes. This means that the demand curve that each firm faces is likely to be fairly elastic. If it raises its price, the firm will lose some customers, although not all of them; if it lowers its price, it will gain some customers from its competitors. (The more differentiated a firm's product, the lower its degree of substitution and the more inelastic is its demand.) The assumption of unrestricted entry means that the presence of abnormal profits will attract new firms into the industry in the long run until the entire profit has been acquired and there is no incentive for further entry, just as in a perfectly competitive market.

Like a monopolist, the individual firm in monopolistic competition is able to set its own price in order to maximise its profits. It will produce at an output and sell at a price where marginal cost equals marginal revenue. The equilibrium position of a typical firm is shown in Figure 58. It produces an output of Q_1 and sells at a price of P_1, the profit being given by the rectangle P_1ABC. Note that the firm's demand curve is relatively elastic.

Examples of monopolistically competitive markets are more likely to be found in the service sector. In

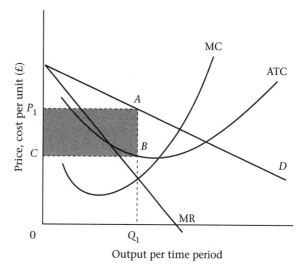

Figure 58   *The equilibrium position of a monopolistically competitive firm.*

many service markets a large number of sellers exist, each producing a product that is slightly differentiated. Examples include estate agents, retailing, hairdressers, dry cleaners, hotels and restaurants. These activities can quite legitimately be labelled as monopolistically competitive in a large town or city, in which there are usually plenty of sellers in close proximity in each market that produce similar products. However, in one small town there may only be a single restaurant, estate agent or whatever; in another there may be just two or three firms competing against each other. In these cases it becomes more difficult to classify the market structure as monopolistically competitive. The designation of the correct market form depends on a reasoned assessment of the geographic limitations of the market.

8.5 OLIGOPOLY

An *oligopoly* is a market structure in which there are only a few firms (the word oligopoly, from the Greek, literally means few sellers). The products of these firms are usually highly differentiated. The word 'few' is never really strictly defined, but it probably means anything from two to ten dominant firms. Where two firms dominate a market it is known as a *duopoly* and regarded as a special case. Since there are only a few sellers in the market, each firm's actions are bound to have a direct effect on the demand of the other firms, which in turn may respond with actions of their own. For example, if one firm lowers its price, this will affect the sales of the other oligopolists. They may retaliate by lowering their prices, in which case the increase in sales experienced by the original firm may not turn out to be as much as it expected. In other words, there is a great deal of *interdependence* and *uncertainty* in an oligopolistic market: the firm's actions are mutually dependent, yet they are uncertain about how their rivals will react to any policy change that each of them may make. Barriers to the entry of new firms are common in oligopolies. For example, firms in an oligopolistic market may experience increasing returns to scale up to a potentially large level of output relative to total demand. A few firms only would be able to survive at the optimum size. However, as was noted in Section 6.9, the impact of modern technology on the optimum scale of production means that, in some industries, the position of the dominant firms may be increasingly threatened by their smaller rivals.

Many industries are oligopolies. A large number of manufacturing industries in the UK exhibit quite high, or even very high, levels of concentration and hence are classified as oligopolistic. Some are duopolies with just two firms producing a large proportion of the output. This is the case in the tobacco and the soap powder and detergent industries in the UK. In the majority of instances, oligopolistic firms are of large absolute size. They need to be if a few of them are responsible for producing most of the output of a national, or even international, market. However, at a more local level the firms can actually be quite small, but they may still be able to exercise some degree of control over a particular market. In those service markets where just two or three small firms compete, the actions of each may affect the sales of the others. If one dry cleaners reduces its prices, this may have a dramatic effect on the sales of its main rival located a few hundred yards away. On the other hand, a localised market may be dominated by a few sellers, each of which appears quite small-scale, but which in fact is part of a national chain. Individual petrol retail outlets are fairly small and the policies of one such retailer may have a significant impact on the sales of its near neighbours. However, the retail outlets are mainly owned by one of the large petrol distributors. The petroleum industry is an example of a national (and international) oligopoly at the refining and distribution stage and a local oligopoly at the retail stage.

8.6 THEORIES OF OLIGOPOLISTIC BEHAVIOUR

Game theory

The techniques of game theory, introduced in Section 5.5, can be usefully applied to oligopolistic markets in which uncertainty and the interdependence of actions are rife. An example of the game that has special relevance to oligopolistic behaviour is the *Prisoner's Dilemma*. Two prisoners are held in custody, accused of committing a serious crime. The prisoners, who are held separately, know that for the case against them to stand any chance of success at least one of them needs to confess and plead guilty. They also know that, if both confess, they will receive a much lighter sentence than if found guilty at a later date. The choices facing the two prisoners, Smith and Jones, are shown in the matrix of Table 49.

The actual choices made by the prisoners determine the respective *payoffs* that each may expect from the respective strategies. The payoffs are measured in terms of years of imprisonment. In the table the first figure in each element of the matrix is the payoff to prisoner Smith and the second figure is the payoff to prisoner Jones. Assuming that the prisoners behave *non-co-operatively*, the dilemma that each faces is which strategy to choose. Looking at the situation from Smith's point of view, if he does not confess to the crime the case against him will collapse due to lack of evidence and he will receive no sentence; but this outcome will only happen if Jones also does not confess. On the other hand, if Smith does not confess and Jones does, the evidence against Smith will be such that he will receive the maximum sentence of 12 years. Alternatively, if Smith confesses he will be sentenced to 10 years imprisonment assuming that Jones also confesses, but only five years if Jones does not confess and Smith's evidence can be used against Jones.

Jones is confronted with the same dilemma. This is a *symmetrical* game in that each prisoner is faced with exactly the same respective payoffs. It is also a

Table 49 *The Prisoner's Dilemma*

Smith's choices	Jones's choices	
	Confess	Do not confess
Confess	10,10	5,12
Do not confess	12,5	0,0

non-zero sum game; the outcomes do not add up to zero. In these circumstances the interests of the two 'players' (i.e. the two prisoners) are not mutually exclusive and it may be possible for them both to benefit from some form of co-operation. In a *co-operative* game the players are able to *collude* and make formal, binding agreements with each other in order to pursue some joint objective. (In a zero sum game, under certain assumptions, one player's gain will be the other's loss, no matter what the outcome.)

The Prisoner's Dilemma game has direct applicability to oligopolistic behaviour. Assume that the two players are duopolists; they are the two firms that dominate a market. They each have a range of prices that they can set for their product. The most commonly-set prices are shown in the matrix in Table 50. The two firms, A and B, usually charge between £7 and £10 for the product. The effects of setting different prices on their respective profits are shown in the matrix. In each case A's profits are indicated first. Thus, if A sets a price of £8 and B charges £7, then A would expect to make a profit of £20 million and B would expect a profit of £36 million.

The advantage of applying this type of analysis to oligopolistic behaviour is that it can show a variety of strategies that may be adopted by the two firms. For example, if each firm wanted to employ a fairly safe or risk-averse policy it would set a price of £7. This is known as the *minimax* or 'best of the worst' strategy. At this price, whatever the other firm does, the worst outcome would yield a profit of £25 million for each firm. At all other prices the worst profit outcome is lower than this figure. A price of £7 gives the least worst outcome, hence the term minimax strategy.

Alternatively, if either of the firms were to adopt the most risky policy, in other words it were a risk seeker, it would set a price of £8. This is called the

maximax or 'best of the best' strategy. The objective in this case is to make the highest level of profit possible, irrespective of what the other firm does. By setting a price of £8, each firm hopes to make a profit of £47 million, but this will only be achieved if the other firm sets a price of £10. Of course there is no guarantee that it will do this, especially if it too is pursuing a maximax strategy. If one of the firms sets a price of £8 and the other sets a price of £7, the profits of the former will fall to £20 million. That is why this is such a high-risk strategy.

Both the above strategies are examples of non-co-operative policies. If the firms colluded and wished to *maximise their joint profits* they would each set a price of £9. At this price the combined profits of the firms would amount to £80 million (£40 million plus £40 million), a total not exceeded anywhere else on the matrix. In this way the two firms combine to act as a single firm, in other words as a monopolist. They would be setting the same price as a profit-maximising monopolist. Formal arrangements to fix prices and/or output by a group of firms, usually via some central organising agency, is known as a *cartel*. Such procedures are deemed to be illegal in most countries. In the UK any such agreement between two or more firms is likely to be sent for investigation by the Director-General of Fair Trading (DGFT) to the Monopolies and Mergers Commission (MMC). Most collusion between firms is informal and takes the form of *tacit understandings*.

In fact, the joint profit-maximising equilibrium position is *unstable*. It could only arise by mutual and formal agreement, and even then firms may have an incentive to cheat on the arrangements. The joint profit-maximising position would not arise through the independent actions of the two firms because if either firm raised its price to move towards that position it would make less profit and the other firm would make more. Neither firm has an incentive to increase its price in the first place. Furthermore, even if the joint profit-maximising position is attained it may not last. Each firm can increase its profits by cutting its price, as long as the other firm does not follow suit. For example, if firm A lowered its price from £9 to £8 and firm B maintained a price of £9, A's profits would rise from £40 million to £44 million. However, since B's profits would then fall to £26 million, it too would have an incentive to cut its price. B may decide to lower its price to £7 on the assumption that A keeps its price at £8. B would then expect its profits to rise to £36 million. Since A's profits will fall to £20 million in these circumstances,

Table 50 A payoff matrix for two firms[a]

	B's prices			
A's prices	£7	£8	£9	£10
£7	25,25	36,20	42,18	45,14
£8	20,36	32,32	44,26	47,15
£9	18,42	26,44	40,40	43,35
£10	14,45	15,47	35,43	34,34

[a]Each element gives the expected profits of the two firms in £ million. In each case A's profit figure is given first.

it has a further incentive to lower its price again, and so on. A price 'war' has broken out, from which ultimately neither firm will benefit. Individual and combined profits are likely to be lower than they otherwise would have been. This explains why prices in oligopolistic markets tend to be fairly stable or *sticky*, especially if firms are risk averse. No firm would want to change its pricing policy if there was a risk of making less profit or of starting a price war. (See the case study at the end of Chapter 10 for confirmation of this.)

That is not to say that price wars do not occur in oligopolies; they are more likely to happen in certain situations. For example, one firm may have a larger market share than its rivals and it may hope to drive them out of the market by pursuing an aggressive pricing strategy. Price wars are also likely to take place where the market demand for a product is falling and individual firms are concerned about maintaining their market shares, or where new entry has recently taken place, especially if on a relatively large scale. During 1993–95, News International used its dominant position in the UK national daily newspaper market (where its titles have approximately 37% of the overall market) to try to increase its market share by significantly lowering its prices. News Corporation, the Australian-based controlling group, hoped to absorb any reduction in profits, or even losses, from such a strategy within its overall operations. In 1993, it cut the price of its main title in each of the two market segments, the 'tabloid' and the 'quality' sectors. It was only in the quality market that other firms retaliated with price cuts of their own, due to the facts that the price reduction was more substantial and that the competition was fiercer in this sector. News International gained some increase in market share in the quality sector during the period, although no rival firm was forced to leave the industry. Eventually, prices were returned to their original levels (although this was in good part due to the large increase in newsprint costs that had occurred and which affected all firms in the industry).

A price war developed in the US tobacco industry in the 1980s and 1990s as a result of falling market demand. As in many other countries, increased awareness of health issues had meant that cigarette consumption had been falling in the US for many years. In the early 1980s, the dominant brand of cigarette in the US was Marlboro, manufactured by Philip Morris, which had roughly one-third of the market. In the late 1980s, RJR Nabisco, the main rival

of Philip Morris, began to produce cut-price, and lower quality, cigarettes. The market share of Marlboro fell sharply. By 1992, it had reached 22%, very much a case of a 'brand on the run'. In April 1993, Philip Morris eventually retaliated by reducing the price of Marlboro from $2.15 to $1.75 per packet.

Finally, the opening of the Channel Tunnel in 1994 inevitably led to price wars with both the cross-channel ferries and the airlines. Fares on Eurotunnel's car transporter service were competitively set to undercut the ferries, with the result that the latter have been forced to lower their prices. It is estimated that the introduction of the Eurostar passenger service, operated by European Passenger Services, through the tunnel has forced down average airline economy fares between London and Paris or Brussels by 25–30%.[1]

Models of oligopolistic behaviour

(A) THE KINKED DEMAND CURVE

Numerous models of oligopolistic behaviour have been proposed; some have remained, others have been discarded. One that has maintained its place of prominence in the economic literature is the *kinked demand curve* model. This was introduced more or less simultaneously by Hall and Hitch (1939) in the UK and by Sweezy (1939) in the US. The basic premise of the theory is that all the firms in the industry assume that rivals will match price reductions but they will not react to price increases. These different reactions to price cuts and price rises will mean that the typical firm will face a kinked demand curve, as shown in Figure 59.

Assume that the original price is P_1 and the original output is Q_1. At prices above P_1 the demand curve is fairly elastic, since rivals are not expected to follow price rises. Customers simply switch to buying the rival's product; the demand for the firm's product falls quite substantially. This part of the demand curve is shown by dX in Figure 59. At prices below P_1 the demand curve is quite inelastic. Rivals match price cuts and so there will not be much change in the firm's demand. This section of the demand curve is indicated by XD in Figure 59. Therefore, the actual demand curve that the firm faces is dXD. The associated marginal revenue curve comprises two sections. The first section, shown by dY, relates to the elastic part of the demand curve, dX; dY is twice the slope

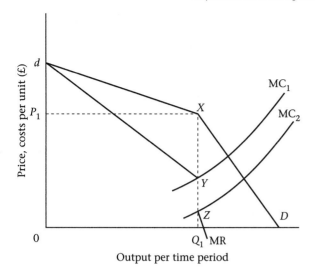

Figure 59 *The kinked demand curve model.*

of *dX*. The second section, *ZMR*, corresponds to the inelastic part of the demand curve; *ZMR* has double the slope of *XD*. The marginal revenue curve has a discontinuous section in the middle. Assuming that the marginal cost curve, MC, passes through *Y* or *Z*, or any point between them, the profit maximising price and output will remain at P_1 and Q_1 respectively.

The kinked demand curve model is not a tool for analysing the pricing decisions of oligopolistic firms. It does not explain the level of the price or output at which the kink in the demand curve occurs. It is not a theory of pricing behaviour, although it does help to explain why prices in oligopolies are often fairly rigid or sticky. Costs can rise or fall, but as long as the MC curve lies within the vertical section of the MR curve (i.e. between points *Y* and *Z*, as indicated by curves MC_1 and MC_2 respectively) a profit-maximising firm will not alter its price or output. Similarly, demand can also alter without there being a corresponding change in the profit-maximising price. If demand in the industry increases, the demand curve facing the firm will shift to the right. The firm will increase its output in order to meet the rise in demand, but as long as the MC curve remains within the vertical section of the new MR curve, the price will not change.

(B) COLLUSIVE MODELS

The inherent uncertainty within oligopolies means that there is a strong incentive for the main protag-

onists to collude. This behaviour can be one of two types: *formal,* which usually takes the form of some kind of cartel arrangement, or *informal* or *tacit,* where most firms in an industry tend to follow a particular firm's lead in price-setting, even though no rigid rules of behaviour exist.

FORMAL ARRANGEMENTS

Price- and output-fixing cartels are illegal in all major industrialised countries; they still exist, although they are often quite short-lived. International cartels usually transcend national laws and so are more likely to persist. The two main ones are IATA, the International Air Transport Association, which determines prices and various other facets of the behaviour of the world's scheduled airlines, and OPEC, the Organisation of Petroleum Exporting Countries, which dictates the prices of petroleum products. However, the power of both these organisations was reduced dramatically in the 1980s due to excess capacity in their respective industries, in the former case this being the result of the growing deregulation of the world's airline markets and in the latter due to the increase in non-OPEC supplies. The influence of the international telephone cartel, operated by the world's main telephone companies in the 1980s and early 1990s and governing the prices of international calls, has steadily diminished as a result of the actions of the various legislative bodies that exist in most countries and in the EU as a whole to counter the activities of cartels (see also Section 15.3). Nevertheless, despite the existence of these bodies, there are numerous examples of other cartels operating not only at the international level, but also at national and local levels. Since the early 1980s, cartels have been discovered in the UK in betting shops, black-top road surfacing, buses, concrete, cross-channel ferries, fuel oil, glass, insurance, milk, roofing and sugar. Such a list is not confined solely to the UK. Similar examples could be quoted from within most industrial economies. In February 1994, the European Commission fined 16 major European steel firms a total of 104 million Ecus (about £75 million) for operating a cartel in the supply of steel beams to the construction industry. Other large fines were levied by the Commission in 1994 on firms operating cartels in the European cartonboard, PVC and cement industries (CEC, 1994).

The popularity of cartels obviously suggests that, despite the legal constraints, there are often significant potential benefits for members. In fact, a *profit-maximising cartel* operates in exactly the same way as

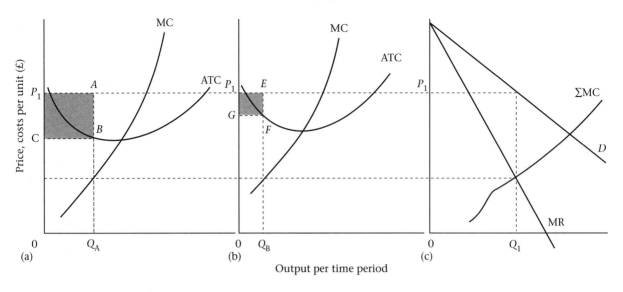

Figure 60 *The equilibrium position of a cartel. (a) firm A; (b) firm B; (c) the cartel.*

a multiplant monopolist, the difference being that the monopolist owns its individual plants, whereas the cartel simply controls the activities of its constituent firms.

Assume that the cartel operates just two firms, A and B, and that A has the lower costs. The situation is shown in Figure 60. The cartel finds its aggregate marginal cost curve by horizontally summing the marginal cost curve of each firm to give Σ MC. (The kink at the lower end reflects the cost differences of the two firms.) The cartel's profit-maximising output is Q_1, where Σ MC = MR, and its profit-maximising price is P_1 in part (c) of the figure. At this point the marginal cost of each firm is equal (as shown by the dashed line), since each incremental unit has to be produced in the firm with the lower marginal cost. If this were not so, then the cartel could reduce its marginal cost and increase its profit by moving production from the higher-cost to the lower-cost firm. For example, if $MC_A < MC_B$, the cartel would reduce output in firm B and increase output in firm A until the marginal costs were equalised. Therefore, output Q_A is produced in firm A and output Q_B is produced in firm B; Q_A plus Q_B equals Q_1. The total profit of the cartel is given by the addition of the rectangle P_1ABC and the rectangle P_1EFG.

In the case described above, the outputs of the individual firms are decided on the basis of their respective costs, given the profit-maximising price. Cartels may adopt other criteria in order to divide up the market, for example by geographic means, in terms

of the output capacities of the member firms or simply on the basis of their bargaining skills. However, whatever criteria are employed, most cartels are inherently unstable and consequently many do not last very long. The member firms often have difficulty on agreeing how the market should be divided, especially if they are of different sizes or have different costs. The greater the number of firms that belong to the cartel the more difficult that agreement becomes. (These factors explain why cartel and other collusive agreements are far easier to arrange and to maintain in *tight* oligopolies, characterised by high levels of concentration and high entry barriers, than in looser oligopolistic structures where levels of concentration and entry barriers are relatively lower). Such problems are compounded by the possibility of the entry of new firms into the industry or where the industry is subject to stable or falling demand. Furthermore, even where agreement has been reached, individual members have a strong incentive to cheat on the arrangement by undercutting the agreed price.

For example, if one of the cartel members reduces its price below the agreed cartel price it is likely to gain a large increase in sales, *cet. par.* In other words, it is subject to a relatively elastic demand curve for its product. This can be seen in Figure 61. Initially, the firm sells at the cartel price, P_{cartel}, and produces output Q_{cartel}. By undercutting the cartel price, its demand increases substantially. It produces an output of Q_1, where its MC curve meets the relevant MR

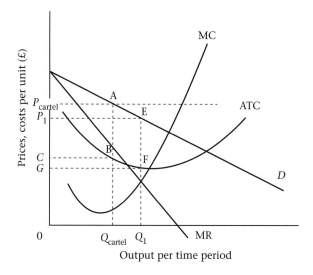

Figure 61 *Undercutting the cartel price.*

curve, and sells at a price of P_1; profits increase from $P_{cartel}ABC$ to P_1EFG. However, the *ceteris paribus* assumption is not likely to hold. Other firms in the cartel will experience a fall in their sales and reduce their prices. A price war will develop and the cartel will collapse or, at the very least, become far less powerful.

The price of crude oil fell dramatically in 1985 because many of the OPEC members had previously failed to adhere to their output quotas. This had put pressure on the agreed price for some time as supply increasingly outstripped demand. Once Saudi Arabia, the largest producer, also decided to raise production above its quota limit, the price of oil was bound to fall. Since then, the price of crude oil has remained at around £10 per barrel, rather than the £22–24 that it was before 1985. OPEC's problems were compounded by the fact that it was no longer responsible for producing the majority of the world output of oil. By the late-1980s, over half the consumption of the West came from non-OPEC sources. OPEC's internal wrangles, coupled with the fact that it now controls under 50% of global output, have led to a significant reduction of its power.

TACIT AGREEMENTS
Price leadership models implicitly incorporate the likelihood of tacit or informal collusion by oligopolists. As the name suggests, these models assume that one firm sets the prevailing price in the market

and the others follow suit (a procedure alternatively referred to as *parallel pricing*). Where product differentiation exists, prices may not be exactly matched, but they will certainly move in the same direction, usually upwards. There are two main forms of price leadership, *dominant-firm* and *barometric*.

Dominant-firm price leadership. This explanation of oligopolistic behaviour assumes the existence of a dominant firm with a large market share, together with a number of smaller rivals. The dominant firm, which may also be the lowest-cost producer, sets the price of the product and the smaller firms simply follow suit by setting the same price; in other words, they act as price takers.

The model assumes that all the firms in the industry are profit maximisers. It is also assumed that the dominant firm has knowledge of the market demand and of the marginal costs of the smaller firms. Since the smaller firms are price takers, they act like perfectly competitive firms and regard their marginal cost curves as their supply curves. Therefore the dominant firm knows the market demand curve and the total supply curve of the smaller firms. It obtains the latter by the horizontal addition of the marginal cost curves of the other firms. The price leader can then find its own demand curve by taking the difference between the market demand and the total supply of the smaller firms at any price. This can be seen in Figure 62, page 172. Figure 62 (a) shows the market demand curve and the aggregate supply curve of the smaller firms; from this information the dominant firm can construct its own demand curve. At P_1 the smaller firms supply all that the market requires. The demand facing the price leader is zero. This gives the intercept of the price leader's demand curve with the vertical axis in Figure 62 (b). At P_2 the residual demand facing the dominant firm is equal to the distance CE. This provides a second point on its demand curve (given by P_2H in Figure 62 (b)). At P_3 the entire market demand, equivalent to the distance P_3F, is met by the price leader. At prices below this level, the market demand curve and the leader's demand curve are identical. That explains the kink (at J) in the dominant firm's demand curve, D_L, in Figure 62 (b). The associated marginal revenue curve, MR_L, and the dominant firm's marginal cost curve, MC, are also shown. Its profit-maximising output and price are Q_L and P_L respectively. This means that the smaller firms supply the amount P_LA in Figure 62 (a) and the dominant firm supplies the amount AB (which is equal to the distance P_LG or $0Q_L$ in Figure 62 (b)). Each of the

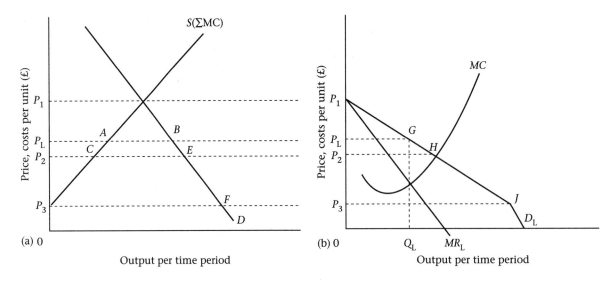

Figure 62 *Dominant-firm price leadership. (a) other firms; (b) dominant firm.*

smaller firms is also maximising its profits, since it takes the price P_L (which is equal to its marginal revenue) and produces the level of output where this price equals its marginal costs.

Algebraically, the equilibrium position of the dominant-firm price leader can be found as follows. Assume that the market demand function, where quantity is in thousands of units, is given as

$$Q = 50 - 0.25P \qquad (8.6)$$

and that the supply function of the fringe of small firms is given by

$$Q_{small} = 0.15 \qquad (8.7)$$

The demand facing the dominant firm price leader, given by Q_L, is therefore

$$Q_L = 50 - 0.25P - 0.15P$$
$$Q_L = 50 - 0.4P_L$$

Hence

$$P_L = 125 - 2.5Q_L$$
$$MR_L = 125 - 5Q_L$$

The total cost function of the dominant firm is given by

$$TC_L = 200 + 10Q + 0.5Q^2_L$$
$$MC_L = 10 + Q_L$$

The profit-maximising position of the dominant firm is where $MC_L = MR_L$. Equating the two:

$$125 - 5Q_L = 10 + Q_L$$

Hence

$$115 = 6Q_L$$
$$Q_L = 19.17$$
$$P_L = 125 - 2.5(19.17)$$
$$= 77.075$$

The dominant firm sells 19 170 units at a price of £77.075 each.

The total output of the industry is therefore

$$Q = 50 - 0.25(77.075)$$
$$Q = 30.73 \text{ or } 30730 \text{ units}$$

The small firms supply

$$Q_{small} = 0.15(77.075)$$
$$Q_{small} = 11.56 \text{ or } 11560 \text{ units}$$

In the UK, Thomsons usually acts as the dominant firm price leader in the tour operating market. The prices that it sets for its holidays are matched by others in the industry for similar destinations and resorts. Ford often acts as price leader in the UK new car market, although other firms sometimes take the lead in setting prices (see the case study on page 173).

Barometric price leadership. In cases of barometric price leadership, the price leader, the identity of which may shift from firm to firm, has the ability to decide when the time is right for prices in the industry to change. This is usually in response to a change in one or more of the market conditions, such as an increase in demand or in costs, that affects the industry as a whole. The price leader is not necessarily the largest firm in the industry. The other firms in the industry will follow suit with similar price adjustments as long as they agree that the time is right to do so. If they do not follow the price leader, then the latter will have to adapt or even scrap its price change, in which case the leadership role may shift to another firm. In the UK duopolistic salt market, ICI has generally acted as price leader and British Salt has followed its lead in price-setting, despite the latter possessing a slightly higher market share (see the case study below).

8.7 CONCLUSIONS

This chapter considers how corporate decision-making differs between market structures. Traditionally, economists have concentrated on the examination of price and output strategies within four main market models: perfect competition, monopoly, monopolistic competition and oligopoly. In a perfectly competitive environment comprising many sellers and a homogeneous product, firms act as price takers and, in so doing, equate price with marginal cost ($P = MC$); in the other market forms, in which firms have some degree of market power to determine their own pricing policies, price exceeds marginal cost ($P > MC$). A monopoly, characterised by a single seller of a product which has no substitutes, lies at the opposite end of the competitive spectrum to perfect competition.

A perfectly competitive economy, where prices fully reflect the true opportunity costs of production and with a given income distribution, automatically yields an optimum allocation of resources. Since the assumption of freedom of entry and exit means that all firms operate at the minimum of the LRAC curve, then they will also produce at the least-cost output for a given level of technology.

A natural monopoly (at the single product level) occurs where there are falling long-run average costs up to and beyond the level of market demand. A multiproduct natural monopolist exists when there are falling average incremental costs of each product plus economies of scope. Other monopolies are known, in principle, as pure monopolies. Any monopoly profits are likely to persist due to barriers to entry. A multiplant monopolist equates the horizontal summation of the respective marginal cost curves with its marginal revenue curve in order to maximise profits. Output is allocated between the plants (and total cost is minimised) by equating the marginal costs in each plant.

The theory of monopolistic competition combines elements of both the perfectly competitive and the monopoly models. It is assumed that there are many firms, each selling a product that is slightly differentiated from its competitors and thus providing some discretion over pricing policy. The presence of abnormal profit attracts new firms into the industry until the profit has been acquired and there is no incentive for further entry.

An oligopolistic market comprises a few dominant sellers (often with a fringe of smaller firms) that usually sell differentiated products. Such markets are characterised by the interdependence of firms' actions and uncertainty over the reactions of rivals to specific policy changes. Given these features and the concomitant problems of predicting corporate behaviour, a number of models have been developed to explain oligopolistic conduct. Game theory can be usefully applied to a study of oligopoly; a variety of strategies can be considered and the incentive to collude is revealed. The kinked demand curve model is discussed: this does not analyse pricing behaviour *per se*, although it can help to explain the stickiness of prices. Collusive models are also examined: a distinction is drawn between formal agreements, such as cartels, and informal or tacit arrangements, as exemplified by price leadership models. It is noted that the analytical techniques that feature in the profit-maximising cartel parallel those of a multiplant monopoly.

Case Study: Two examples of price leadership

The Monopolies and Mergers Commission (MMC) investigated the UK new car market in 1992 (MMC, 1992). This was with a view to ascertaining whether a monopoly situation existed and, if so, whether any of the facts operated against the public interest. In so doing, price leadership in the industry was examined.

In the UK car market, Ford, the dominant firm with a 25% market share, is generally recognised as the price leader. For example, in the period from 1986 to the end of July 1991, the three largest suppliers of new cars in the UK, Ford, Rover and Vauxhall, usually increased their prices in the same month with Ford often in the lead (see Table 51). Ford moved before the other two on seven of the 14 occasions it raised its prices. It also moved first in conjunction with Rover on two other occasions. In July 1991, Ford took the lead in reducing prices in response to weak demand and large stocks of unsold vehicles. The report found evidence of two monopoly situations in the industry (a scale monopoly in favour of Ford and a complex monopoly arising from the distribution of new cars by all producers).

No comment was made regarding any lack of price competition, possibly because other firms occasionally led the price round (Rover was the first to move on five of the 16 times it raised prices).

Table 51 *The dates of general price increases by the largest three suppliers in the UK car market, 1986 to mid-1991*

| Year | Date (day/month) of price increase by | | |
	Ford	Rover	Vauxhall
1986	1/1	15/2	14/1
	17/8	18/8	10/9
1987	4/1	12/1	5/1
	11/5	4/5	11/5
	17/8	1/9	24/8
1988	4/1	11/1	7/1
	16/5	16/5	16/5
	15/8	15/8	22/8
1989	3/1	1/1	3/1
	n/a	15/5	n/a
	14/8	14/8	21/8
1990	2/1	1/1	2/1
	1/5	26/6	8/5
	13/8	18/9	4/9
1991	21/1[a]	11/2	14/1
	n/a	1/7	n/a

[a]Except Granada/Scorpio models, where the date was 4/2.
Source: MMC (1992:90).

The MMC examined the white salt market in 1986 in order to assess the extent of the monopoly situation that existed in the industry (MMC, 1986). It discovered that the industry was dominated by two firms that between them supplied virtually the entire market. British Salt produced 50% of total output and ICI had a 45% market share. Significant barriers to entry were found to exist. These took the form of the substantial capital costs involved in investing in and developing brinefields, the planning rules for their development that favoured the existing firms, the long-term relationships that the established firms had built up with their major customers and the excess capacity that existed in the industry.

It would be expected that, in the case of a homogenous product like salt, prices would be broadly similar. However, it was discovered that the price similarities were not due to competition between the two firms, but were the result of a complicated system of price leadership rules:

The evidence shows that price notifications are so interwoven that the price follower knows in advance what the price leader's increase will be, and before the price leader actually implements his price increase he knows that his lead is being followed (MMC, 1986:81).

From 1981–86, ICI took the lead in setting prices, notifying British Salt in November of each year of its intentions. At the same time, ICI also gave informal notifications to its major customers. The price increases faced by a number of the major customers of each firm and the dates that they were implemented are shown in Table 52. Generally, ICI was the first to establish the new price.

The Commission concluded that price competition in the industry was extremely limited. This was particularly surprising given the fact that British Salt had much lower costs (£22.89 per tonne in 1984) than ICI (£27.87 per tonne). As a result, British Salt was able to achieve a 56% return on capital employed, compared with ICI's 24%. The Commission recommended that price controls be imposed upon British Salt, given the fact that it followed the lead of the higher-cost producer in setting prices and was able to achieve an excessive level of profitability.

Table 52 *Price Increases[a] of salt and dates of implementation by major customers*

Customer	British Salt		ICI	
	Month in which increase implemented	Increase (£/tonne)	Month in which increase implemented	Increase (£/tonne)
A	Feb. 81	2.15	Jan. 81	2.18
	Feb. 82	3.69	Jan. 82	3.90
	Feb. 83	2.63	Feb. 83	2.45
	Jan. 84	1.60	Feb. 84	1.63
B	Jan. 81	2.15	Jan. 81	2.14
	Jan. 82	3.69	Jan. 82	3.70
	Jan. 83	2.61	Jan. 83	2.72
	Jan. 84	1.60	Jan. 84	1.63
C	Jan. 81	1.43	Jan. 81	1.42
	Jan. 82	2.87	Jan. 82	2.85
	Jan. 83	1.87	Jan. 83	1.86
	Jan. 84	1.13	Jan. 84	1.25
D	Jan. 81	2.12	Jan. 81	2.49
	Jan. 82	4.93	Jan. 82	5.19
	Jan. 83	3.20	Jan. 83	1.65
	Jan. 84	2.20	Jan. 84	2.19
E	Jan. 82	5.25	Jan. 82	5.28
	Jan. 83	3.99	Jan. 83	4.03
	Jan. 84	n/a	Jan. 84	n/a
F	Jan. 83	–	Jan. 83	2.55
	Jan. 84	1.60	Jan. 84	1.63
G	Jan. 83	3.71	Jan. 83	3.30
	Jan. 84	2.30	Jan. 84	2.27
H	Jan. 83	2.40	Jan. 83	2.41
	Jan. 84	n/a	Jan. 84	1.63
I	Jan. 83	3.57	Jan. 83	3.61
	Jan. 84	2.50	Jan. 84	2.19
J	Jan. 83	3.41	Jan. 83	3.21
	Jan. 84	2.20	Jan. 84	2.20
K	Jan. 84	1.60	Jan. 84	1.60

[a]Prices include all delivery charges and are net of any discounts.

Source: MMC (1986:42).

FURTHER READING

Baumol, W.J, Panzar, C. and Willig, D. (1982) *Contestable Markets and the Theory of Industry Structure* (San Diego, CA, Harcourt Brace Jovanovich).

Hay, D.A. and Morris, D.J. (1979) *Industrial Economics: Theory and Evidence* (Oxford, Oxford University Press), Chapters 4,5.

Mansfield, E. (1979) *Microeconomics: Theory and Applications*, 3rd edn (New York, W.W. Norton and Co.), Chapters 9–12.

NOTES

1. See *The Economist*, 7 October 1995, 'An Oncoming Train'.

8.1   Market structures can be divided into four main types: perfect competition, monopoly, monopolistic competition and oligopoly (including duopoly). State which of the following features belong to which type of market structure (some may belong to more than one type).

(a) Firms are price takers.
(b) Firms are price makers.
(c) Barriers to entry exist.
(d) There are many sellers, each selling a differentiated product.
(e) A few large firms supply most of the market.
(f) Two firms dominate a localised market.
(g) Plant economies of scale occur beyond the level of market demand.
(h) The market exhibits a high degree of seller concentration.
(i) Firms sell homogenous products.
(j) It is relatively easy to enter, and leave, the industry.

8.2   The market for pork is assumed to be perfectly competitive. Show diagrammatically the effects on the market price and output of the following (assume *ceteris paribus* in each case):

(a) An increase in demand.
(b) An increase in the wage-level in the industry.
(c) (a) and (b) together.

8.3   Demand and supply equations in the perfectly competitve market for wheat are as follows:

$$P_D = 20 - 0.02Q$$
$$P_S = 0.2 + 0.04Q$$

where Q equals thousands of bushels and P equals the price per bushel.

(a) Calculate the equilibrium price and output in the industry.
(b) A single producer has the total cost function:

$$TC = 5Q + 0.2Q^2$$

How much would this firm produce at the market price?

(c) How much profit would it make?

8.4   A hotelier in a holiday resort has to decide whether to remain open in the off-peak season, which runs from the beginning of October to the end of March. The hotel has 50 rooms and achieves an average daily occupancy rate of 50%. The average price of a room in the off-peak is £25 per day. Fixed costs are £100 000. The total variable cost function for a typical 30-day period in the off-peak is

$$TVC = 100 + 10Q + 0.02Q^2$$

Should the hotel remain open?

8.5   A monopolist supplier of electronic components is faced with the following demand and total cost functions:

$$P = 250 - 0.002Q$$
$$TC = 30000 + 10Q + 0.004Q^2$$

(a) Calculate the profit-maximising price and output.
(b) Calculate the monopoly profit.

8.6   Two ferry companies, Atlantis Ferries (A) and Ballyline (B), operate as a cartel on the North Sea route. Demand is estimated as

$$Q = 1200 - 5P$$

where Q equals hundreds of passengers.

The total cost function of each firm is identified as

$$TC_A = 40 + 25Q_A$$
$$TC_B = 0.1Q_B^2$$

(a) Calculate the profit-maximising cartel price and the level of output of each firm.
(b) Calculate the total profit achieved by the cartel. Atlantis decides to cheat on the cartel by reducing its price. By so doing, it estimates its new demand and total cost functions to be

$$Q_A = 2800 - 20P_A$$
$$TC_A = 60 + 30Q_A$$

(c) Calculate the new profit-maximising price and output for Atlantis.
(d) What is the effect on Atlantis's profits?

8.7   Critically assess the theoretical justification for, and the practical application of, the theory of monopolistic competition.

8.8   The following matrix shows the expected profits in millions of pounds of two duopolists, A and B, at various prices. A's profits are shown first in each case.

A's prices	B's prices			
	£6	£8	£10	£12
£6	30,30	40,24	50,20	55,16
£8	24,40	35,35	53,32	60,18
£10	20,50	32,53	46,46	51,39
£12	16,55	18,60	39,51	38,38

(a) What is the minimax price?
(b) What is the maximax price?
(c) What is the joint profit-maximising price?
(d) Explain why joint profit-maximising can only be achieved by some kind of formal arrangement. Why is such an agreement inherently unstable?

8.9 'The kinked demand curve model does not explain how oligopolistic firms determine their prices. In fact, it does not really explain their behaviour at all. Therefore, its continued presence as a keystone of oligopolistic theory is difficult to defend.' Explain and discuss.

8.10 A supplier of ready-mixed concrete acts as a price leader for the industry. Its total revenue and total cost functions are as follows:

$$TR_L = 100 - Q^2_L$$
$$TC_L = 400 + 15Q + 0.2Q^2_L$$

where Q_L is equal to thousands of hundredweights.

(a) Calculate the price and output, in hundredweights, of the price leader.

There are 10 smaller firms in the industry, each with identical total cost functions:

$$TC_{small} = 20 + 40Q + 6Q^2$$

(b) Calculate the combined output of the smaller firms.
(c) What is the profit of the price leader?
(d) What is the profit of each small firm?

8.11 In the late 1980s and early 1990s, OPEC operated a policy of maintaining low crude oil prices. Discuss the possible reasons for, and dangers to OPEC members of, such a policy.

CHAPTER 9

▶ *Ownership, Control and Corporate Objectives*

The possibility of a separation or divorce of ownership from control in large organisations was discussed briefly in Section 4.2. There it was noted that the wide dispersion of share ownership in large US companies, coupled with small shareholdings by managers, can give rise to a divergence of interests between shareholders and managers. The meaning of the terms *ownership* and *control* are discussed in greater depth. The empirical evidence on the *separation of ownership and control* in large UK and US organisations is investigated in more detail. Reference is also made to the system of corporate governance in Germany and Japan. The effect of the divorce of ownership and control on *business objectives* is considered. The *behavioural* model of corporate behaviour is examined. The *managerial* theories of the firm of Baumol, Williamson and Marris, which are based on the assumption of a divorce between ownership and control, are discussed in some detail. The divergence of interests between managers and shareholders as a *principal–agent* problem is explored. Finally, the various *constraints on managerial decision-making* are explored. The *case study* at the end of the chapter investigates the relationship between managerial pay schemes and corporate performance.

9.1 OWNERSHIP, CONTROL AND ITS SEPARATION

The fact that there may be a separation between ownership and control in large organisations begs the question of what precisely the terms *ownership* and *control* mean. In Section 4.4 it was pointed out that firms exist in order to economise on the costs of transactions between various resource owners, particularly where resources exhibit asset specificity. However, by definition, resource owners own their own resources. The resources are not owned by the firm, although, of course they will be contracted to it. Contracts establish property rights, in this case between the members of the firm. In order to minimise on transaction costs some kind of monitoring role within the firm is necessary. The role of the monitor is to appraise and direct the resources within the firm (including the right to hire and fire) and to claim the firm's residual income. In essence, these are the two functions that define corporate ownership and control. Traditionally, they are identified with share ownership in a joint-stock company. Shareholders take the risks by supplying the equity capital and they manipulate the firm's resources in order to maximise their residual income flow.

In the joint-stock company the right to claim the residual income of the firm is distinct from the right to monitor the firm's resources. Such a divergence of property rights gives rise to the possibility of a complete separation of the two functions and hence to a system of corporate governance in which there is the separation of ownership from control. Shareholders provide the equity capital, but the major operating and strategic decisions are taken by a group of professional managers, who may well have only a very small shareholding interest in the firm. As a result, there may be a definite divergence of interests between managers and shareholders.

The more recent evidence seems to cast some doubt on the extent of managerial control in large firms, first identified by Berle and Means (see Box 9.1, page 180). Both British and American companies appear to be subject to various kinds of ownership control, at least in principle. Of particular importance in this respect appear to be the fairly sizeable shareholdings of a small number of large financial institutions. These may give them the power to influence corporate behaviour, although whether they actually exercise this power is another matter. However, compared with their German and Japanese counterparts, shareholdings in large corporations (especially in the US) can be quite fragmented. For example, the largest shareholder in General Motors of the US is Wells Fargo Nikko Investment with 2.3% of the total equity value, followed by Alliance Capital Management with 2.0% and Bankers Trust with 1.8%. The largest individual holdings in Japan's Mitsubishi Corporation are

Box 9.1 *Evidence of a divorce between ownership and control*

Berle and Means (1932) were the first to employ empirical evidence to question whether a separation of ownership from control and a corresponding divergence of interests between shareholders and managers may exist in large firms. They investigated the 200 largest non-financial US firms and found that in 1929, 44% were classified as 'management-controlled'. This they defined as a situation where no one person or group of people owned 20% or more of the voting equity. In only 11% of cases did any individual or group own more than 50% of the voting strength. Control was defined more specifically as the power to select the board of directors. In other words, a widespread dispersion of share ownership existed. Larner (1966) redefined management control as a situation where no individual or group held 10% or more of the voting capital on the basis that effective control could, in fact, be exercised with a lower voting capability. According to this criterion, 84.5% of the 200 largest non-financial US corporations were defined as management-controlled in 1963.

In the UK the trend towards a wide dispersion of shareholding was probably slower than in the US (possibly due to the greater relative importance of private limited companies in Britain), but for 1951, Florence (1961) found that only 7% of the largest firms (each with a share capital of over £3 million) had a single majority shareholding and that, in only 5.5% of the remainder did the largest 20 shareholders together have a majority position. For firms with a share capital of between £0.2 and £3 million each, the corresponding figures were under 1% and approximately 10% respectively.

Thus, it would appear that, in both the US and the UK, the share ownership patterns imply widespread managerial control in large organisations. However, the question remains: precisely what proportion of share ownership is required in order to exercise effective control? Nyman and Silberston (1978) argued that a number of different factors should be considered when assessing the control of a firm and not simply share dispersion: ownership control was reckoned to exist when an individual, institution or cohesive group, or the board of directors and their families, had a shareholding of more than 5%, although some kind of relationship between the Chairman and the Managing Director and the firm's founder and family could also produce ownership control, even without a 5% shareholding. On this basis the study concluded that 56.25% of 224 of the largest UK organisations showed some kind of ownership control according to one or more of the relevant criteria. The growing predominance of financial institutions as industrial shareholders (whose power may be understated due to features like interlocking directorships) was also noted, despite there being very few cases of an institution holding more than 5% of one company's shares. Cubbin and Leach (1983) developed a measure of 'degree of shareholder control'. For a coalition of the largest shareholders, control was said to depend positively on the proportion of shares held by the group and negatively on the extent of dispersion of the remaining shares. The degree of control was regarded as a function of the controlling group being able to win a contested vote. They also noted that any application of their results to aspects of corporate behaviour and performance needed to take into account the location of the control (within the board or not) and the precise nature of the shareholdings (whether by executive and non-executive directors or by non-board individuals, other firms or financial institutions).

Cosh and Hughes (1987) compared the ownership patterns of 27 large UK companies with 27 equivalent US firms for 1981. They found that the mean percentage of shares held by board members was 0.19% in the UK and 5.7% in the US. Financial institutions were infrequent holders of over 5% of equity, but they were by far the most significant group of shareholders. For example, in the US sample the median company had about eight shareholdings by financial institutions each of over 1%, amounting to about 15% of the shares in aggregate. The equivalent figures for the UK sample were about seven shareholdings totalling about 11% of the shares. As with earlier studies it was noted that the prevalence of interlocking directorships may underestimate the power of the institutions. In the US sample, for instance, 41 institutions held 21% of the total stock and accounted for 75% of share-based interlocks.

---

taken by Meiji Life Insurance and Tokio Marine and Fire Insurance, each with 6.1% of total equity, followed by Mitsubishi Trust which has 5.2%. In Germany, Mercedes AG has 25% of the total equity value of Daimler-Benz, with Deutsche Bank and the Kuwait Investment Office having 24% and 14% respectively.[1] The shareholdings may also be more transitory in the British and American companies. In addition, despite recent signs of a more active role by a few institutional investors, most seem to prefer inactivity to co-ordinating intervention.

The UK/US system of corporate governance, in which shareholdings can be relatively dispersed and shareholders may play little part in monitoring management, is sometimes referred to as 'market-based' or 'equity-based', to distinguish it from the so-called 'bank-based' system that is said to characterise the financial structures of Japan, Germany and a number of other Western European economies. Two factors differentiate the German/Japanese model[2] of corporate governance from the Anglo-American variety: banks own sizeable proportions of equity in firms, besides being significant lenders to them, and cross-shareholdings between companies are common. Thus, a significant proportion of a company's shares may be held long-term in relatively friendly hands. In Japan a *keiretsu* firm usually owns less than 2% of any other member firm, but it has a similar stake in every firm in the group, so that 30–90% of a firm is owned by other group members. In the horizontal bank-centred *keiretsu*, banks are represented on the board of companies, with one bank acting as the main bank with direct monitoring possibilities.[3] German companies own over 40% of total equities and often may hold a dominant shareholding, although there is no equivalent of the *keiretsu* system. Banks in Germany can wield apparent significant power, not just through their shareholdings but by casting proxy votes for customers who keep their shares with the bank. German public companies (of which there are actually relatively few) have a two-tier board structure. Banks are prominent on their supervisory boards, whose membership is divided equally between shareholders and employees. The supervisory boards appoint the management boards.[4] In both countries, banks can play an important role in helping firms that face problems, especially in Japan where banks become closely involved in what Mayer (1987) calls 'direct managerial control' by organising the response of other financiers and by possibly offering additional finance.

The potential for greater control and monitoring of managerial behaviour may well exist within the bank-based system of corporate governance. However, this does not mean that shareholder interests predominate: the objectives of other stakeholders in a firm, such as management, employees and lenders, are often accorded at least as much weight. Furthermore, the extent of the control exercised by the banks may not be as strong as it appears. In Germany, supervisory boards usually act more in an advisory capacity with the management boards exercising effective day-to-day control over company policy. The monitoring role of banks has been called into question following the financial problems of several large companies, such as Daimler-Benz and Klockner-Humboldt-Deutz, the engineering conglomerate. The banks have reacted by reducing their shareholdings in some instances (for example, in 1994

Deutsche Bank lowered its equity stake in Daimler-Benz from 28.1% to the current 24%). The power of Japanese banks in corporate affairs has diminished because they have had to contend with their own financial problems; in addition, other sources of finance have been made available through the deregulation of the financial markets. As a result, in Japan, bank lending to firms has fallen significantly (see also Section 12.7).

9.2 THE IMPLICATIONS OF THE SEPARATION OF OWNERSHIP AND CONTROL FOR BUSINESS OBJECTIVES

Assuming that a divorce between ownership and control exists, its implications for business objectives is analysed most extensively in the managerial theories of the firm, although behaviouralists like Cyert and March (1963) also developed a framework of corporate behaviour in which alternative objectives were considered (see also Section 4.3). According to the *behavioural model* the firm is viewed as a coalition of interest groups, including managers, shareholders, employees, customers and suppliers. Each of these groups has goals which result from interaction and bargaining and which may conflict. In a situation of uncertainty and with incomplete information, bounded rationality leads to the satisficing of these goals rather than to their maximisation. The desired goals may include the following: costs to be kept as low as possible through long production runs; a certain level of sales or market share to be achieved; stockholding costs to be reduced; personnel problems to be avoided by offering continuity of employment; a particular level of profit or rate of return to be sought, and so on. Each goal takes the form of an 'aspiration level', which may change if targets are not met or if there is a change of emphasis by coalition members. The firm is viewed as an 'adaptive organism' more concerned with solving immediate problems than with having the time or the capability to gear its strategies towards the maximisation of particular variables.

The behavioural model was the first to incorporate the idea of 'organisational slack'. These are payments to the various groups of the coalition over and above those required for the continued maintenance of the organisation.[5] Slack can accrue to the members of any group, but senior managers are reckoned to be in the best position to receive such payments, which arise mainly in growth periods. Managerial slack can take the form of higher salaries and fringe benefits or reduced effort. Slack acts as a built-in stabiliser; when demand is low, slack can be cut and other aspiration levels need not be changed; in boom periods, slack payments increase, thus reducing both profits and the need for upward revisions in other aspiration targets.

In the managerial theories of the firm, slack payments accrue more or less entirely to managers, although it is assumed that decision-makers have sufficient knowledge to be able to maximise their desired objectives. Managers are interested in maximising their own utility, whether expressed in terms of income and other financial rewards or in terms of status, power and security. It is argued that these variables are more closely allied to the size of the firm rather than to its profitability. Size enhances status and, in all probability, gives managers greater power to control the resources of the firm. It increases managerial job security by making it more difficult for the firm to be taken over. There is also some evidence that managerial remuneration is more closely tied to size rather than to profits (see Devine *et al.* (1985) and George *et al.* (1992) for a summary of the evidence). However, profit remains an important ingredient in the firm's plans: to avoid the risk of takeover, as a source of finance and to survive in competitive markets. Managers may also have a more direct interest in the profitability of a firm through share ownership and option schemes. Thus, in all the managerial models, profit forms an important constraint on the firm's plans.

9.3 MANAGERIAL THEORIES OF THE FIRM

Various *managerial models* have been advanced. The three most popular theories are considered, with particular reference to their implications for corporate behaviour.

Baumol's sales maximisation model

Baumol (1959) suggested that managers wish to maximise sales revenue rather than profits, although they would be subject to some kind of profit constraint (which is not clearly defined) in order to satisfy shareholders and to avoid a fall in the price of shares. Figure 63 shows the traditional total revenue (TR), total cost (TC) and total profit (π) curves

for a firm. (It should be noted that the model only investigates the equilibrium position of the individual firm: the relationship between the firm and the industry is not dealt with.) It is assumed that the firm is a sales-maximising monopolist operating in a single period. A profit maximiser would produce output Q_M, whereas the unconstrained sales maximiser produces output Q_S. The latter is also the level of output if the profit constraint is at or below π_1. Any profit constraint below this level would therefore not be operative. If the profit constraint were higher, at for example π_2, then output would be reduced to Q'_S. Assuming that the profit constraint is below the level of maximum profits the sales maximiser will always produce a larger output than the profit maximiser and, given a downward-sloping demand curve, it will charge a lower price.

If advertising is introduced into the model, then the profit constraint will always be operative (assuming that sales revenue increases with advertising), since the firm will utilise any profits above the minimum to advertise and hence raise sales. Advertising expenditure by a sales maximiser will be at least as much as, and usually more than, a profit maximiser.

Baumol also examined the position of the sales maximiser in a dynamic, multiperiod setting, in which profits are endogenously rather than exogenously determined as in the single period case (see also George *et al.*, 1992). In this instance the managerial objective is to maximise the rate of growth of sales. It is assumed that sales growth can be financed

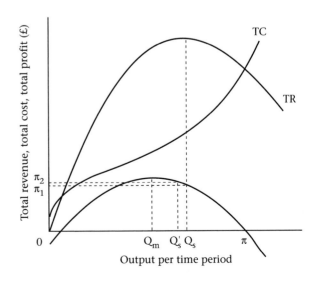

Figure 63 *Sales revenue maximisation.*

entirely from retained profits. Therefore, current sales revenue, R, will grow at an annual growth rate of $g\%$. The future revenue stream is given by

$$R, R(1 + g), R(1 + g)^2 \ldots R(1 + g)^n \qquad (9.1)$$

The present value of this stream, S, is estimated by

$$S = \sum_{t=0}^{n} R \left(\frac{1 + g}{1 + r} \right)^t \qquad (9.2)$$

where r is the rate of discount. The firm chooses values of R and g so as to maximise the present value, S. The growth function of the firm, derived from the profits function, is shown in Figure 64. The highest growth rate, g_{max}, is where profits are maximised. Thus, both R and g increase until this point, but beyond it R continues to increase whereas g falls. In other words, beyond output R_1 there is a choice between higher current sales revenue and a higher rate of growth of sales.

The firm chooses the combination of R and g that maximises the present value of sales revenue, S. The iso-present value curves, $V_0, V_1 \cdots V_n$, in Figure 65 show those combinations of R and g that yield the same present values. The firm chooses the highest possible iso-present value curve; it is in equilibrium where the growth curve is tangent to the highest curve, i.e. at point X in Figure 65. At X, R^* and g^* are the respective level of current sales and the growth rate that maximise the present value of sales.

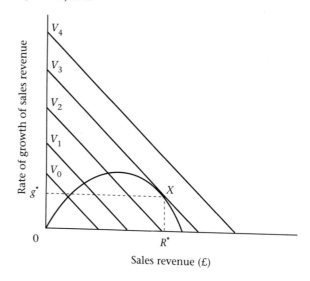

Figure 65 *The equilibrium values of current sales revenue and the rate of growth of sales revenue.*

Figure 66 shows that R^* determines the current equilibrium level of output, Q^*, which is derived from the TR curve. Given the profit function, the firm requires a level of profits π^* in order to finance the optimal growth rate g^*. Thus, the profit constraint is now endogenously determined. The multiperiod sales maximiser produces a higher output (and charges a lower price) than a profit-maximising firm: given the negatively-sloped iso-present value curves, the equilibrium position must occur on the downward-sloping section of the growth curve (in Figure 65).

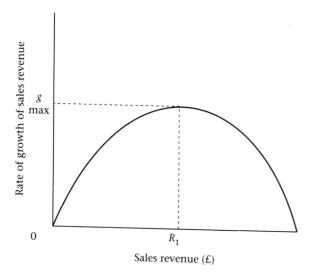

Figure 64 *The relationship between current sales revenue and the rate of growth of sales revenue.*

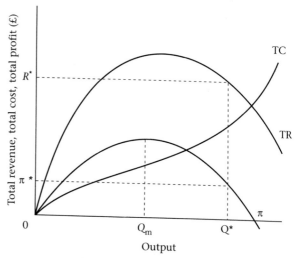

Figure 66 *Multiperiod sales revenue.*

Williamson's utility maximisation model

Williamson (1964) put forward a more general model of managerial utility maximisation, which examined in detail the discretionary behaviour of managers. Managerial utility is assumed to be a function of a range of influences, such as salary, status, prestige, security and power. Of these variables only salary is measurable, hence utility is actually expressed in terms of three main factors:

$$U = f(S,M,I_D) \qquad (9.3)$$

where S stands for staff expenditure, including managerial salaries, M refers to emoluments or slack in the form of spending on company cars, lavish offices and expense accounts and I_D denotes discretionary investment expenditures, which are expenditures on projects undertaken beyond those necessary for the normal operation of the firm, i.e. beyond the profit-maximising level. The profit constraint enables a sufficient dividend to be paid so as not to threaten managerial job security. In this case (and contrary to Baumol's model) reported profits are often higher than the minimum necessary and the excess is used to finance discretionary investments.

Assuming that emoluments are zero ($M = 0$), then utility is a function of S and I_D. The function can be shown diagrammatically by the construction of a managerial indifference map. In Figure 67 each curve, M_1, M_2 etc. shows combinations of staff expenditures, S, and discretionary profit (i.e. profit above the minimum necessary to meet the constraint), π_D, yielding identical levels of utility for managers.

Profit is a function of output and staff expenditures, S. Initially, as output increases both profits and staff expenditures rise. The latter is assumed to be positively related to demand, thus allowing a higher price to be charged for the same output. Beyond the maximum profit point, however, profits decline (due to rising production costs and the necessity of having to charge a lower price in order to sell more), while staff expenditures continue to increase. The profit–staff curve (which excludes the profit constraint) is also shown in Figure 67. The equilibrium position of the firm is given by point X, where the profit–staff curve is tangent to the highest possible managerial indifference curve, M_3. According to this model, a firm will spend more on staff expenditures than a profit maximiser (S_1 as opposed to S_M): given that the indifference curves are convex to the origin, then the equilibrium position must occur on the downward-

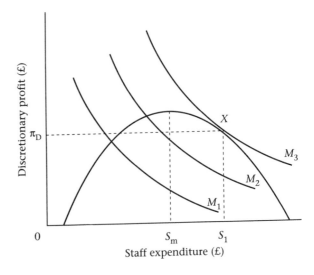

Figure 67 *Managerial utility maximisation.*

sloping section of the profit–staff curve. A firm with this managerial utility function will also have a higher output, lower price and lower profits than a profit-maximising firm.

Williamson provided some empirical support for his model, although he also admitted that it mainly applied to U-form firms, since M-form organisations would be more likely to exhibit profit-maximising behaviour (see Section 4.6). In other words, for Williamson, organisational form is a more important influence on managerial behaviour than the possibility of a divorce between ownership and control.

Marris's growth maximisation model

Marris (1964) assumes that managers aim to maximise the rate of growth (i.e. the rate of change in the size) of a firm, subject to a security constraint. The objective of the shareholders is to maximise their wealth or the return on their investment in the firm, comprising both dividends and capital gains. This is determined by the discounted stream of future earnings of the firm's current shares and is equivalent to its market value (see Section 12.6). The crux of growth models of the firm is the assumption of a two-way relationship between growth and profits (see Downie, 1958). The means for growth comprise productive capacity and customers. To expand the capacity of the firm, finance is required and this depends crucially on profits. However, to attract additional customers in existing and new product markets, it is necessary to reduce prices and to increase demand-inducing expenditures, such as advertising and R&D, which will eventually be at the expense of profits. Thus, in order to avoid either growing excess capacity or growing excess demand, Marris assumes that a firm will attempt to maximise its balanced rate of growth. In other words, the rate of growth of product demand should equal the rate of growth of capital supply. Marris confines his analysis to 'steady state growth' situations, in which all the main variables are assumed to grow at a constant exponential rate over time.

The rate of growth of a firm is constrained by two main factors, the managerial constraint and a financial constraint, the latter set by the desire of managers to achieve maximum job security. Marris adopts the Penrose (1959) concept of a limit on the rate of managerial expansion because the training of new personnel takes time and inexperienced staff should be restricted in the tasks that they undertake. The R&D department, the source of new products and processes, is similarly constrained in its absorption of new personnel. Thus, the firm's 'productive opportunity' (the set of activities that it can undertake at a profit) in any period is finite, placing an upper limit on the rate of growth. However, the productive opportunity is continually enlarged through time; managerial services are released as projects are realised, and the managerial services available to the firm change as existing members benefit from their experiences and as new members are taken on.

The financial constraint is characterised by a limit to the funds that can be raised for expansion purposes. Given the rate of profit, in order to finance increased growth it is possible to increase debt or profit retention or to reduce liquidity. The higher the debt or leverage ratio (the ratio of the value of debt to total assets) the greater the risk of bankruptcy. The lower the liquidity ratio (the ratio of liquid to total assets) the similar the effect. The higher the liquidity ratio, on the other hand, the greater the takeover threat. Similarly, the higher the retention ratio (the ratio of retained to total profits) the lower the profits available for distribution to shareholders and the increased chance of them selling their shares resulting in a fall in the share price, thus also causing an increased risk of takeover. These three ratios are combined (quite how is not made clear) into a financial security constraint which is positively related to the debt and retention ratios and negatively related

to the liquidity ratio. It is determined by the attitude to risk of the management.

Assuming a given financial security constraint, the maximum balanced rate of growth of the firm depends on two factors: the rate of diversification, d, and the average rate of profit, m. It is assumed that the firm grows by diversification. d is positively related to demand-inducing advertising and R&D expenditures, but the latter are negatively related to m, the profit margin, because a higher profit rate implies less expenditure on advertising and R&D (prices are assumed to be given). A lower expenditure on advertising and R&D also suggests a lower rate of success of product innovation and hence a lower rate of d. However, the success rate of new product development is also a function of d. The higher is d, the more likely that the new products are not researched or marketed sufficiently thoroughly as managements' bounds of rationality are reached.

Thus, the rate of growth of demand, g_d, increases with d as unused resources are tapped and new opportunities are tackled by management; m increases. However, g_d increases at a decreasing rate as the firm comes up against the managerial constraint and the rate of successful new products falls. Since the main method of increasing d, higher advertising and R&D expenditures, are negatively related to m, the average profit rate, then a higher d implies a lower m. m also falls as the efficiency with which management can cope with additional new products declines; as g_d increases, m falls. There is a negative relationship between profitability and growth. This is shown by the demand growth curve, g_d, in Figure 68, page 186. The profit-maximising growth rate is given by g_m.

Assuming that the main source of funds is retained profit, then the higher is m, the higher the rate of growth of capital supply, g_c. With a given retention ratio the relationship between m and the rate of growth of capacity is linear, as shown by the supply of capital curve, g_c, in Figure 68. The slope of this curve is given by a, the security constraint. An increase in a (implying a less risk-averse attitude on the part of management) indicates a rise in available finance, for example via an increase in the retention ratio; the curve pivots to the right. In equilibrium:

$$g_d = g_c = g^* \qquad (9.4)$$

Where g^* is the optimal growth rate and

$$g_d = f_1(m,d)$$
$$g_c = f_2\bar{a}(m,d)$$

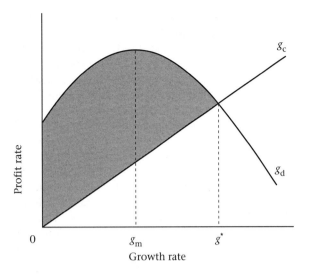

Figure 68 *Demand growth and supply of capital curves.*

subjective value on it, increasing the prospects for takeover. The security constraint is therefore expressed in terms of the minimum valuation ratio or the maximum takeover threat that managers are prepared to accept. Managerial utility is a function of growth and security, the latter expressed in terms of the valuation ratio. The greater the propensity that managers have for risk-seeking behaviour the lower the valuation ratio that they are prepared to accept. Hence there is a trade-off between growth and job security.

The trade-off relationships for both shareholders and managers are shown in Figure 69 (see Radice, 1971). In Figure 69 (a) shareholder utility is maximised at X, where the demand growth curve, g_d, is tangent to the highest possible shareholder indifference curve, I_2. This yields a growth rate of g_v.

where $\bar{a}$ is the given security constraint. The shaded area indicates the profit-growth rate combinations available to the firm. Shareholders' wealth is determined by the current market value of the firm, comprising both dividends and capital gains, the latter derived from share price appreciation. Therefore, shareholder utility depends on both profits (dividends) and growth (capital gains). Managers may wish to increase the rate of growth of the firm by retaining more profit for reinvestment purposes, thus reducing the amount currently available for shareholders in the form of dividends. However, there is a trade-off for shareholders between current dividends and retentions. If the expected present value of earnings from future projects are at least equal to the value of the current dividends not distributed, then shareholders will be satisfied. Otherwise, they will dismiss the management or, more probably, sell their shares, causing a dilution of their value and making the firm ripe for a takeover bid, thereby increasing the job insecurity of the existing management team.

The perceived riskiness of a firm also depends on its size. Firms of larger absolute size are generally less prone to takeover. Marris introduced the notion of the *valuation ratio* ((stock market value)/(book value of a firm's assets)) to take account of this. Given the inverse relationship between growth and profits, a fall in the stock market value of the firm will cause a fall in its valuation ratio; the firm may become undervalued in the sense that another firm places a higher

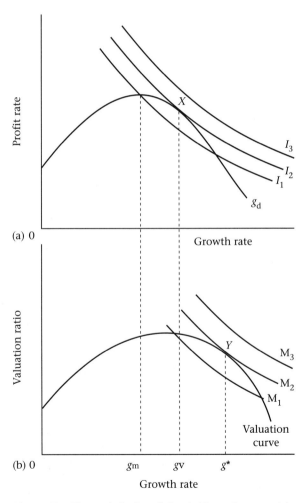

Figure 69 *The maximisation of shareholder and managerial utility.*

At this point the current share price and hence the current market valuation of the firm are maximised. Assuming a given book value, X is also the peak of the valuation curve shown in Figure 69(b). Managerial utility is maximised at Y, the point of tangency of the valuation curve and the highest possible managerial indifference curve, M_2. The optimum growth rate so determined, g^*, is the same as that derived in Figure 68 from the intersection of the demand growth and capital supply curves.

In comparison with a profit maximiser a growth-maximising firm will have a higher growth rate, lower profits and higher advertising and R&D expenditures. The main attraction of the Marris model is that it formalises a number of important behavioural features of large firms, such as growth, diversification and financial strategies, within a dynamic framework. It also shows that growth and profits can be competing goals. However, the major drawback of the model lies in the assumption of steady-state growth; a particular rate of current demand-inducing advertising and R&D expenditure will inevitably produce a particular rate of demand growth in the future. In other words, that part of the external environment of the firm concerning factors such as consumer susceptibility to advertising, brand loyalty and lack of information, referred to by Marris as the 'superenvironment', is assumed to be constant. The firm is assumed only to be able to influence its immediate environment. The problem with this assumption is that it ignores the crucial features of oligopolistic interdependence and uncertainty (a problem common to all managerial theories). For example, a particular level of advertising or R&D expenditure by one firm may be taken up by other firms, leading to a more rapid rate of growth of demand than had originally been envisaged.

There is very little evidence that managerially-controlled firms actually behave very differently from profit maximisers. Radice (1971) investigated 86 British firms, each with assets of over £5 million, in three industries, food, electrical engineering and textiles, and found that those which were owner-controlled had higher profit and growth rates than those which were managerially-controlled. There is no evidence from the US of markedly different levels of profit and growth-rate performance between the two types of firm (see Devine *et al.* (1985) for a summary of the evidence). The relationship between the valuation ratio and the probability of being taken has been investigated on a number of occasions, most notably by Singh (1975) in a large-scale study of the characteristics of acquired and non-acquired firms in the UK covering the periods 1955–60 and 1967–70. In the first period it was established that the non-acquired firms on average had higher valuation ratios, growth and profit rates; they were also larger and had lower retention ratios. However, there was considerable overlap between the two groups of firms and in the second period the differences between them were even weaker. Kuehn (1975) reported an inverse relationship, although weak, between the valuation ratio relative to the industry average and the probability of being taken over in 1554 UK acquisitions during 1957–69. Buckley (1972) claimed a similar result for 65 non-financial mergers in the UK in 1971. Newbould (1970), on the other hand, studied 64 mergers in the UK during 1967–68 and found that only 41% of the acquired firms had a valuation ratio lower than the industry average. Levine and Aaronovitch (1981) reported that acquired companies had lower valuation ratios than acquiring companies, although they were not compared with the industry average. In general, it appears that acquired companies are less highly valued than companies on average, but that the inverse relationship between stock market valuation and the likelihood of takeover is rather weak.

9.4 DIVERGENCE OF INTERESTS AS A PRINCIPAL–AGENT PROBLEM

In Section 4.4 it was argued that the relationship between managers and shareholders can be defined in principal–agent terms. Shareholders act as principals in a contract and they employ managers as their agents. However, informational asymmetries may well exist. Shareholders are only able to observe the outcomes of the actions of managers rather than observing the behaviour leading to the outcome. On principal–agent terms, a situation of moral hazard arises. Managers may prefer to pursue their own interests rather than take actions (involving additional effort) that coincides with the objectives of shareholders. Information asymmetries between the two groups may also mean that shareholders do not have the same information that is relevent to a particular action taken by managers. Therefore, shareholders may have little idea whether the action is optimal. A serious adverse selection problem is also said to exist. In these circumstances, any divergence of interests between shareholders and managers may be articulated in opportunistic agent or managerial behaviour. The shareholders as principals will then try to reduce these opportunistic tendencies and influence agent behaviour by establishing an optimal contract in which the interests of the two, principals and agents, coincide. The form of the contract depends on the available information and on the attitudes to risk of both parties.

The principal–agent problem can be expressed in game theory terms as a two-person, non-co-operative and non-constant sum game. For example, Table 53 shows three mutually exclusive states of the world, indicating an uncertain environment. The agent is able to exert two levels of effort, or actions; the outcomes are represented by cash-flows and are dependent upon the relevant state of the world. (This explanation is based on Strong and Waterson, 1987.) Initially, it is assumed that only moral hazard results from any informational asymmetry.

E_1, the greater effort, leads to a larger expected cash flow, although the respective outcomes are not solely dependent on effort; they also vary with chance. The respective utility-maximising functions of the principal and the agent are as follows (assuming that the principal is risk-neutral and the agent is both risk- and effort-averse):

$$U_p = X - Z \tag{9.5}$$
$$U_a = \sqrt{Z} - E^2 \tag{9.6}$$

where $X = f(S,E)$ and Z gives the monetary compensation for the agent. $\sqrt{Z}$ indicates a diminishing marginal utility of money, a characteristic of a risk averter. The negative sign for E indicates that the agent is risk-averse. The principal's utility function is linear with respect to income. Utility maximisation implies that each individual attaches utilities to the respective outcomes, weights them by their probabilities of occurring, or 1/3, and sums the results.

Assuming that the agent's action is jointly observed (i.e. there are no informational asymmetries), then

the optimal contract comprises a fixed sum and is dependent solely on the effort involved. Assume also that the agent must receive an opportunity wage giving a minimum level of expected utility, otherwise the person would transfer his/her services elsewhere. Given that the minimum expected utility of the agent is equal to, say, 106, and an effort level of E_1 is employed, the principal would offer a compensation package of 28 900, where $106 = \sqrt{28900} - 8^2$. The principal derives an expected utility of 41 000, or 70 000 – 28 900. The agent, by receiving a fixed remuneration, bears no risks; the risk is borne entirely by the principal. The optimal contract to ensure that the agent provides the lower effort, E_2, would be for the principal to offer a fixed sum of 20 164 ($106 = \sqrt{20164} - 6^2$). The principal would then derive an expected utility of 29 836 (50 000 – 20 164).

Once moral hazard is introduced into the analysis, the principal would only be able to observe the outcome of the agent's efforts, not the effort itself. The agent would simply put in the lower effort, E_2, giving a greater likelihood of a lower potential cash-flow outcome. The principal's task in these circumstances is to design a remuneration scheme such that the agent operates in accordance with the principal's interests. The principal needs to ensure that the agent undertakes the greater effort, E_1, by designing a package in which the agent secures remuneration equivalent to the minimum expected utility of 106 and also that the expected utility from choosing E_1 is no less than that from choosing E_2. Such a remuneration package can be calculated by solving the two simultaneous equations

$$\tfrac{2}{3}\sqrt{Z}_{90} + \tfrac{1}{3}\sqrt{Z}_{30} - 64 = 106$$
$$\tfrac{2}{3}\sqrt{Z}_{90} + \tfrac{1}{3}\sqrt{Z}_{30} - 64 = \tfrac{2}{3}\sqrt{Z}_{30} + \tfrac{1}{3}\sqrt{Z}_{90} - 36$$

Solving these equations yields a remuneration of 12 996 when an outcome of 30 000 is observed and one of 39 204 when 90 000 is observed. Assuming that 12 996 represents the basic remuneration, the agent receives an incentive bonus of 26 208 (39 204 – 12 996) if 90 000 is the observed outcome. The principal is left with an expected utility of $\tfrac{2}{3}$ (90 000 – 39 204) + $\tfrac{1}{3}$(30 000 – 12 996) or 39 532. This solution is the best that can be obtained in the circumstances, but it is inferior to the original fixed contract, which is Pareto optimal, since the agent is no better off and the principal is worse off. In the previous case the risk-averse agent bears no risk, but in this instance some of the risk is transferred to the agent in the form of the incentive payment.

Table 53 *Cash-flow outcomes assuming different states of the world and effort levels*

	State of the world		
Effort	S_1	S_2	S_3
$E_1 = 8$	30 000	90 000	90 000
$E_2 = 6$	30 000	90 000	30 000

The example can take into account the problem of adverse selection by assuming that the agent possesses perfect information regarding the state of the world before either effort level is selected. If the principal is also party to this information the agent would be offered a fixed remuneration. However, with a fixed income the agent's utility is maximised by always choosing effort level E_2, whereas the utility-maximising rule for the principal is to choose E_2 if either S_1 or S_2 occurs but E_1 if S_3 occurs (thus maximising the probability of the 90 000 outcome). In the presence of informational asymmetries (assuming that only the outcome is jointly observed) the agent would have an incentive to convey to the principal that S_3 had occurred even when it had not. Therefore, the agent needs to be paid a sufficient bonus, payable on an outcome of 90 000, in order to ensure the selection of E_1 when S_3 occurs. The size of any incentive payment necessary to induce selection of the higher level of effort will depend on the agent's attitude to risk given that the greater effort may only result in the lower outcome and hence in a relatively small income.

9.5 THE CONTROL OF MANAGERIAL BEHAVIOUR

The principal–agent relationship examined in the previous section involved the contract between a single principal and a single agent. However, since a firm constitutes a variety of interest groups (management, shareholders, banks and other creditors, employees and suppliers) it can be viewed as a nexus of both implicit and explicit contracts involving many agents and many principals. In this sense, managers may be constrained in their actions in a number of different ways: through the direct actions of shareholders, via the takeover mechanism, by the activities of banks and other lenders, as a result of the disciplines of the product market and by the market for managers. Thus, a series of principal–agent relationships may exist within a firm: for example, senior managers act as agents in their relationship with shareholders, but as principals in their relationship with lower-level managers. In each case, the principals in the relationship may try to ensure that the agents operate in the formers' interests by designing a suitable remuneration package. In this section the various constraints on managerial behaviour are examined. In so doing, the extent to which agents in a contract can be persuaded by principals to act in their (the principals') interests is also discussed.

Shareholder control

In theory, shareholders have the right to dismiss the incumbent management if it is felt that they are not operating in the shareholders' interests. The shareholders can group together and vote out the incumbent management at the annual general meeting (AGM). Of course, a wide dispersal of shareholdings makes such a task difficult, but the use of proxy votes may make it a feasible possibility. However, while invitations to AGMs include proxy forms, shareholders are typically requested to place proxy votes with current board members. Given the limited information to which shareholders are privy, the cost of obtaining and employing the additional information to oust the existing management team may appear excessive; it certainly may be more than any prospective increase in share value thought likely to result. In addition, any such action on the part of an individual shareholder or group of shareholders faces the free-rider problem (see Note 2, Chapter 4).

There has been some evidence of greater involvement in the affairs of companies by institutional shareholders in recent years in the UK and the US. This may be a function of the increase in relative importance of single institutional shareholdings in particular companies, hence reducing the problems of free riding. Most interventions by British institutions, however, have occurred either to aid a firm suffering severe financial problems or to prevent management plans for issuing new equity. Some American institutions have become more active investors. Calpers, the California Public Employees Retirement Scheme, actively targets poorly performing companies and has had considerable success in improving shareholders' returns. Another fund manager, Fidelity, which owns around 2% of American shares, lobbied for change at Kodak in 1993 and succeeded in pressurising the board to oust the chief executive, although such active campaigning by institutional shareholders remains the exception rather than the rule.[6]

Prowse (1992) has noted that, compared with the US, the more concentrated share ownership pattern in Japan, in which almost 50% of total stock is held by banks and insurance companies and another 25% by other companies, has facilitated a closer monitoring of managerial behaviour. Gilson and Roe (1993) have emphasised the importance of the role played by cross-shareholdings in Japan in reducing managerial opportunism, especially when the related parties are making large 'relation-specific' investments. In the

UK and the US, shareholders are more likely to try to influence managerial behaviour by designing a compensation package to enable the interests of the two groups to coincide more closely, as agency theory implies. This can be done by incorporating some kind of incentive scheme, involving direct shareholdings, share options or profit-related bonuses, into the managerial reward structure. Such composite pay packages can take a variety of forms, but evidence of their impact is not conclusive. Cosh and Hughes (1987) reported that the large absolute level of financial involvement in their firms by senior managers suggests that their interests might be quite closely related to those of shareholders. Jensen and Murphy (1990), on the other hand, found that managerial compensation packages gave them little incentive to side with shareholder objectives. In fact, the evidence in general only reports a weak relationship between executive pay and measures of corporate performance, such as profitability and share-price value, suggesting that principals do not have sufficient knowledge of the utility functions of agents to persuade them to alter their behaviour (see also the case study on page 193).

The takeover constraint

An alternative form of action available to shareholders is to sell their shares if it is felt that the incumbent management are inefficient. If this is done on a sufficiently large scale, the share value of the company will fall and it may become ripe for takeover. The potential acquirer will hope to utilise the assets of the undervalued firm more efficiently by replacing the existing management team. Since it would do this by buying the shares relatively cheaply, this would appear to be a more efficient method of management control than the replacement of managers by the existing shareholders. However, there are obvious informational asymmetries in the takeover process. In principal–agent terms a situation of adverse selection exists between the two (or more) firms involved. The principal, in this case the bidding firm, may not be privy to all the relevant information about its potential victim. Alternatively the agent, or the target firm, can use various informational signals to portray itself in the best possible light, for example by cutting back on investment spending to improve its current profit position or by raising dividend payouts as a sign of future earnings' prospects. (The concentration on such short-term

criteria can also have harmful consequences for the long-term welfare of the firm.) A bidder may not be able to distinguish between inefficient firms and those that are being run efficiently and whose poor performance is the result of prevailing market conditions.

Another problem inherent in the takeover mechanism is that both potential acquiring firms and the shareholders of the target face the free-rider problem. There are considerable search costs involved in assessing firms for possible acquisition and a takeover bid signals to other firms the identity of a potential target; thus their search costs are reduced. If all firms behave similarly and wish to save on search costs, there will be suboptimal resources devoted to monitoring potential targets. In addition, existing shareholders may well interpret a takeover bid as a sign of an inefficient management team. If they then reject the bid they can free-ride as minority shareholders on the assumption that the prospects for the firm will improve following any managerial reorganisation. If all shareholders behave in the same way, the bid must fail. In the UK, the City Code on Takeovers and Mergers, administered by the Takeover Panel, offers guidance on the compulsory purchase of shares by acquirers once a proportion of the equity has been obtained. Management are also not able to contest or to preempt a bid by acting strategically until an offer is imminent or has been made. The City Code is not statutory, however.

Most evidence on the effects of mergers does not support the view that they act as an effective constraint on the actions of managers. A large-scale survey of the evidence on the effects of British mergers by Hughes (1993) found that targets are generally less profitable than on average; their profitability and share price may fall one year or less prior to takeover. The main distinguishing characteristic between acquirees, acquirers and others, however, is the size of the firm, the largest in particular being much less likely to be taken over. Hence, a managerial strategy to increase size via takeover may well enhance their job security. The facts that shareholders of acquiring firms do not usually gain from takeovers, while target shareholders do, and that merging firms' profit performance is generally disappointing, together provide further evidence in support of managers pursuing their own self-interests. The smallest quoted companies are also thought to be relatively safe from takeover, a function of their concentrated and family-dominated shareholdings. The evidence does not provide a great deal of support, except perhaps among some medium-sized quoted firms, of an efficient market for corporate control where the best-run and presumably most profitable companies naturally acquire the least profitable ones. In Germany and Japan there is a far lower rate of takeover activity compared with the situation in the UK and the US. In particular, the hostile takeover is noticeable by its virtual absence in Germany and Japan.

Banks and other lenders

A principal–agent relationship between lenders and firms can also be suggested, since the former will only lend under certain conditions. Informational asymmetries may result from the arms' length relationships that exist between firms and the main institutional lenders, banks, in the UK and US. Banks are mainly concerned about the risk of default. Debt payments have to be made no matter how well or badly a firm is performing; the greater the debt the greater the risk of default. The main constraint on management, therefore, is likely to be the threat of bankruptcy or liquidation, since lenders are more concerned about poor rather than good levels of performance; thus, they wish to ensure that managers avoid investment projects with high downside risk. The bankruptcy threat can act as a strong constraining influence on managerial behaviour: bankruptcy is usually taken by providers of finance, either shareholders or prospective lenders, as a sign of managerial inefficiency, whether such a view is justified or not. As a result, managerial reputations and future job prospects may be severely damaged (although whether bankruptcy is a realistic scenario for many large firms is a moot point).

Managers may still wish to take on a certain amount of borrowing as an attempt to signal to the financial markets that their interests are closely allied or 'bonded' to the firm and its performance. In any case, and has previously been pointed out, some level of borrowing is usually necessary given that all sources of finance, including retained profit and new share issues, are finite. The fact that bankruptcy can act as an important constraint on managers means that lenders may exert a stronger form of control than, say, shareholders.

As noted in Sections 2.3 and 9.1, banks in both Germany and Japan have closer relationships with companies than is the case in either the UK or the US. They are also major shareholders. As a result,

banks may perform important monitoring functions in Germany and Japan; consequently, the scope for managerial discretion may be reduced. Prowse (1992) investigated 85 Japanese *keiretsus* and found that in 55 cases the largest shareholder is also the largest creditor. Managerial discipline is exercised through a complex web of suppliers, customers and financiers that may be both creditors and shareholders. Lenders are also more risk-averse than shareholders and this means that the former are more likely to be interested in securing some reasonable return on assets rather than the higher average rate of return that satisfies the interests of shareholders. The increased significance of bank interests and of loan finance in Germany and Japan is implicit in the greater weight that is given to objectives such as the security and size of a business, its long-run continuance as a separate entity and its financial autonomy, rather than to current levels of profitability. However, this does not mean that managers do not put their own interests first. The recent problems encountered by Daimler-Benz in Germany suggests that the control exercised by banks in large firms there may not have been particularly effective. The rapid expansion policy undertaken by Daimler-Benz in the late 1980s resulted in the largest loss in German corporate history; it is now placing much greater emphasis on shareholder value as a key motive.

The product market

Product market competition may also act as a constraint on managerial behaviour. In perfect competition, any firm must pursue a profit-maximising objective, since if it did not it would be eliminated from the market. Once market power is introduced into the equation, however, the need to profit maximise becomes less pressing and managers have the discretion to implement their own objectives. Gilson and Roe (1993) have suggested that the existence of product market competition is one of the key monitoring variables for Japanese companies. It may also be seen as an important contributory factor towards superior Japanese industrial performance.

Leibenstein (1966) introduced the idea of *X-inefficiency* to describe the situation whereby a firm with market power and protected by barriers to entry lacks the competitive stimulus to employ its resources efficiently and minimise costs. In a later work, Leibenstein (1979) applied this concept to an analysis

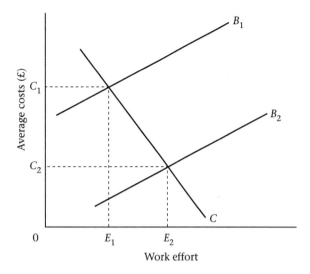

Figure 70 *Leibenstein's X-efficiency theory of costs.*

of the nature of the product market and its impact on managerial behaviour. Leibenstein argued that there is a two-way relationship between work effort and average production costs. As the effort of workers increases, specifically with the help of efficient monitoring, average costs fall. This is shown by the curve C in Figure 70. However, as costs rise and the very survival of the firm is threatened, monitoring is intensified and work effort increases. This relationship is identified by curve B_1.

The intersection of these two curves determines the equilibrium level of effort, E_1, and costs, C_1. The position of the B curve is a function of the competitive environment. The more competitive the market conditions (or, according to Leibenstein, the greater the 'environmental tightness') the more the pressure generated from both peer workers and managers to increase effort for a given level of costs. The B curve shifts from B_1 to B_2; the new equilibrium level of effort is E_2, with average costs of C_2. The firm has become more X-efficient.

An increase in competition will not necessarily eliminate managerial discretion. The agency costs of monitoring, for example, persist. Hart (1983) argued that managerial discretion will also be influenced by the ownership structure of firms in a market. If a market comprises profit-maximising firms (termed 'entrepreneurial' firms by Hart) and managerial firms, then the former are capable of lowering price to increase market share; the managerial firms will have to reduce managerial slack in order to meet their minimum profit constraints. Managerial firms may be more able to increase demand through non-price means, however, which may help to maintain their degree of managerial discretion.

The managerial labour market

The internal and external markets for managers can provide other means for disciplining their behaviour. Managers compete with both their fellow (inside) work colleagues and outside rivals. Fama (1980) argued that managerial reputations and levels of remuneration depend on the performance of the firm. If managers are associated with poor performance, such as bankruptcy or takeover, their employment and earnings potential will be adversely affected. An *ex post* settling up process is assumed to occur, whereby failure results in future reductions in income equivalent to the decline in performance. Thus, managers have a strong incentive to avoid shirking, to establish a good reputation and hence to maintain or enhance their value on the external managerial labour market. This they do by being associated with successful performance, which may involve a greater alignment of their interests with those of the shareholders. At the same time, a two-way monitoring process occurs in the internal labour market; this encourages long-term commitment by rewarding seniority. Senior managers naturally monitor their subordinates and it is claimed that an upward monitoring process also takes place. By so doing, junior managers can take advantage by overstepping incompetent or shirking managers. In addition, the marginal products and the monetary rewards of the lower-level managers are perceived as being inexorably linked to those of the upper-level management team. Thus, the former will wish to see the top managers choose those policies that send the correct signals to the managerial labour market.

These arguments assume that managerial labour markets operate efficiently and in the absence of informational asymmetries. If managers do not change companies very often (and most evidence suggests that they do not) their services cannot be valued by the external market. The development of incentive systems within internal labour markets can help to overcome the problem, but there remains the question of to whom the person at the very top is answerable. If the other constraints do not operate efficiently (and for large firms in the UK and the US they may not) the answer is effectively nobody. A final point to note is that where ownership is dispersed (and even when it is not), managers at all levels are mainly appointed by other managers. A good external candidate for a senior position, for example, may expose the shortcomings of the existing management team and hence not be appointed. Thus, there may be no obvious reason for assuming that managerial labour markets will operate any more efficiently in disciplining managerial behaviour than the other forms of restraint that have been discussed previously.

9.6 CONCLUSIONS

In the joint-stock company the potential exists for a separation of ownership from control, given the fact that the right to claim the residual income of the firm is distinct from the right to monitor the firm's resources. There is a wide dispersion of share ownership among large firms in the UK and the US, although the proportion of ownership necessary to exercise effective control is keenly debated; the sizeable shareholdings of a small number of large financial institutions in both countries are noteworthy in this regard. However, the more market-based governance systems of the UK and the US are often distinguished from the so-called bank-based systems of Germany and Japan, where banks act as significant shareholders as well as being the main creditors and in which shareholdings tend to be more concentrated.

A divorce between ownership and control has important implications for corporate decision-making and objectives. Alternative objectives were initially considered within the behavioural model of the firm, which was also the first to incorporate organisational slack into its analysis. Slack payments over and above those necessary for the continued survival of the organisation accrue most readily to senior management, and this hypothesis provides the basis for the managerial theories of the firm. These theories assume that managers wish to maximise their own utility, whether expressed in terms of financial remuneration or through status, power and job security, although they are subject to some kind of profit constraint. Three managerial models are discussed: Baumol's single and multiperiod sales revenue maximising theory, the more general Williamson utility maximising analysis and Marris's growth maximising model. The latter also incorporates a theory of takeover behaviour. Given the two-way relationship between growth and profitability, a too-rapid rate of expansion may cause a fall in the stock market value of the firm and in its valuation ratio, which increases the likelihood of takeover and threatens job security; empirical evidence reports only a weak negative association between stock market value and takeover.

The divergence of interests as a principal–agent problem is considered. Informational asymmetries between shareholders and managers create situations of moral hazard and adverse selection problems, leading to opportunistic agent (managerial) behaviour. Shareholders as principals will try to reduce this behaviour by setting up contracts in which the interests of the two groups coincide more closely.

A variety of principal–agent relationships can exist within a firm. Thus, a number of different constraints on managerial behaviour are examined, although their effectiveness in reducing agency costs and managerial discretion is questioned: there is only a fairly weak empirical relationship between composite managerial reward schemes and measures of corporate performance (see the case study below); the takeover mechanism does not seem to provide a particularly powerful constraint; banks as the principal lenders may have the potential to exert stronger control, although this potential may have been exercised more capably in the bank-based regimes, at least until recently. In principle the actions of managers are open to a number of constraints, although the extent to which they operate as effective deterrents remains questionable.

Case Study: Managerial pay schemes and corporate performance

There is plenty of evidence that the reward packages for senior executives have become more diverse. In 1979, only 8% of large UK firms had an annual bonus scheme for their top executives, whereas by 1995, well over 75% employed additional bonus incentives. In the US the equity involved in management pay plans accounted for almost 10% of outstanding shares in the 200 largest firms in 1995, up from less than 7% in 1988[7]. However, most evidence also suggests that the relationship between these pay schemes and measures of corporate performance is fairly weak, which runs counter to the predictions of principal–agent analysis, whereby remuneration schemes are designed to provide a closer alignment between the interests of the top management and the shareholders.

Cosh and Hughes (1987) reported that corporate executives in Britain and America held relatively small percentages of shares in their respective companies, especially in the UK. In absolute terms, on the other hand, such holdings represented substantial individual wealth. Hence it was thought that they could be considered important from a motivational point of view. In the US, 17.5% of executive directors and 15.5% of all directors were sterling millionaires through holdings of their own companies' stock. These figures rose to 33% and 21% respectively when stock options (allowing managers to buy shares at a certain fixed price at some point in the future) were included. Directors in the US had much larger average shareholdings than directors in the UK, but even in Britain there were some sizeable holdings. However, Jensen and Murphy (1990) studied the salaries and bonuses of 2505 Chief Executive Officers (CEOs) in 1400 large US companies from 1974 to 1988 and found that a $1000 change in corporate value corresponded to a change in median CEO compensation of just $2.59 over a two-year period, suggesting that the compensation packages do not give senior executives a sufficient incentive to align more readily with shareholder interests. Conyon *et al.* (1995) noted that executive remuneration grew by 336% in real terms in the FTSE-100 firms in the UK between 1980 and 1993. By surveying the latest evidence from the UK and the US, they concluded that the link between pay (defined as base salary plus bonus) and share-price performance is weak and is actually becoming weaker. The relationship between wider measures of compensation (including share incentives and stock options) and performance, although not widely investigated, also does not appear to be very strong.

As Conyon *et al.* noted, the majority of the studies (which mainly apply to the UK and the US) that have estimated the relationship between pay and performance have undertaken a simple regression for person i in year t of the following form:

$$\Delta\log(\text{remuneration}_{it}) = a + b(\text{performance}_{it}) + e_{it} \tag{9.7}$$

where b is regarded as the an estimate of the sensitivity of pay to performance (and e is an error term that captures any changes in the dependent variable that the equation cannot explain). There are two basic drawbacks of such an analysis. In the first place, it is often difficult to identify the top director or to obtain adequate data on total compensation, especially stock options. Secondly, there may be problems in correctly specifying and measuring performance. It may be unclear whether b is identifed from most principal–agent models which specify simple linear incentive contracts. Furthermore, performance may be measured either in accounting terms, such as rate of return or earnings per share or by using a market-based indicator like shareholder wealth.

Notwithstanding these problems, there are a number of reasons why the monetary incentives offered to managers may not tie their interests more specifically to those of shareholders. Bonuses are usually based on the annual growth in profits, dividends or earnings per share, all factors which can be subject to manipulation in the short term by management. Managers may become more risk-averse if all components of their remuneration package are geared to the interests of a single firm. They may wish to avoid investing in risky (and possibly longer-term) projects with high expected returns which might add to the wealth of shareholders who usually possess much more diversified portfolios. Share-option schemes are designed to overcome such problems, since any downside risk can be avoided by managers by opting not to buy the shares if their price is below the exercise price. However, these schemes often pay out even if a firm's share price has risen by no more than the stock market as a whole, irrespective of the company's individual performance.

A number of recent corporate compensation schemes have been based less on standard measures of performance and geared more towards the individual needs of companies. In principle, they are designed to tackle more effectively the various aspects of the constraints that shareholders wish to impose on managers. Thus, 3M, the American conglomerate, has included the contribution to product innovation in its remuneration package and The John Lewis Partnership, the British retailer, has introduced open performance reports that emphasise the personal qualities of senior staff. However, while the evidence may need to take greater account of the motivational impact of the absolute levels of wealth that accrue to executives through their compensation packages, in general there would still seem to be ample scope for large discretionary payments. In the UK and the US these may well be a function of the system of corporate governance, whereby the person at the very top of the tree may not, in effect, be directly answerable to anybody and hence have a great deal of freedom in determining his or her own contract.[8]

Composite executive compensation packages for executives have also become more popular in other industrialised economies. Salary differentials between managers at similar stages in their careers in performance-paying firms in Japan, such as Tokyo Gas and Fujitsu, have increased from 2–3% to 10–20% in recent years. In Germany, a number of organisations, including Daimler-Benz and the recently privatised Post Office, have introduced executive performance-related pay schemes. However, Prowse (1992) has noted that managerial shareholdings are far less significant in large Japanese firms than in their American equivalents. Only 12.2% of Japanese presidents held more than 0.5% of their company's stock in 1981, compared with 22.6% of US CEOs. There is also evidence that executive income in Germany and Japan is even less closely linked to the performance of their companies (especially in the short term) than in the UK and the US (Mullins and Wadhani, 1989). This may be due to the fact that objectives other than profitability have been given greater relative prominence within Japanese and German firms, at least until recently.

FURTHER READING

Devine, P.J., Lee, N., Jones, R.M. and Tyson, W.J. (1985) *An Introduction to Industrial Economics*, 4th edn. (London, George, Allen and Unwin), Chapter 4.

Koutsoyiannis, A. (1979) *Modern Microeconomics*, 2nd edn (London, Macmillan), Chapters 15–18.

Strong, N. and Waterson, M. (1987) Principals, agents and information, in R. Clarke and T. McGuiness, (eds) *The Economics of the Firm* (Oxford, Basil Blackwell).

NOTES

1. See *The Economist*, 8 October 1994, Economic Focus: 'The Smack of Firm Government'.
2. In fact, the German and Japanese systems differ in many important respects, but they are often placed together for comparative purposes.
3. *Keiretsu* can be divided into bank-based horizontal *keiretsu* and manufacturing-based vertical *keiretsu*, consisting of a chain of dealers and suppliers. The top six horizontal *keiretsu* employ 5% of the Japanese workforce and are responsible for 16% of corporate sales (*The Financial Times*, 30 November 1994). Equity stakes by banks are limited to 5% of any one company's shares.
4. Commercial banks own 9% of all quoted stock in Germany. The three largest commercial banks hold 76 seats on the boards of the largest 100 companies (DTI, 1989).
5. Organisational slack is related to, but not identical with, the concept of X-inefficiency referred to in Section 9.5. Organisational slack is regarded as the difference between maximum and acceptable levels of performance, whereas X-inefficiency is the difference between maximum and actual levels of performance. However, since they are both measures of 'reserve resources' they tend to increase or decrease together and lead to non-profit-maximising behaviour (Hay and Morris, 1979).
6. See *The Economist*, 29 January 1994, 'Corporate Governance'.
7. See *The Economist*, 3 June 1995, 'Executive Pay Around the World'.
8. Conyon (1994) reported that, in response to the recommendations of the Cadbury Committee (see Note 2, Chapter 4), more companies are reporting the existence of remuneration committees. In 1988, 54% of 286 companies from *The Times* 1000 indicated their existence; by 1993 the proportion so doing had risen to 94%. Non-executive directors account for, on average, about 40% of the main board (compared with over 66% in the US). They also make up the larger proportion of directors on remuneration committees. However, in 40% of listed companies it was found that the Chief Executive or the chairman actually sits on the remuneration committee.

Questions □ □ □

9.1 Examine the view that recent evidence has cast doubt on the extent of managerial control in large firms in the UK and the US. Discuss the implications for corporate objectives.

9.2 Compare the so-called 'market-based' system of corporate governance in the UK and the US with the 'bank-based' system found in Germany and Japan, with particular reference to the potential for the control of managerial behaviour.

9.3 Discuss the role, and significance of, slack payments in behavioural and managerial theories of the firm.

9.4 'Profit plays a relatively insignificant role in managerial plans and this is reflected in the lack of importance attached to explanations of the profit constraint in managerial theories of the firm.' Explain and discuss.

9.5 In a managerially-controlled firm, given a sufficiently risk-seeking attitude on the part of management, there is no limit to its rate of growth. Explain and discuss.

9.6 'The firm can be regarded as a nexus of contracts involving many agents and many principals. In such a situation informational asymmetries and opportunistic behaviour abound; hence divergent interests persist.' Explain and discuss.

9.7 Discuss the theoretical justification for, and empirical relationships between, composite managerial reward schemes and corporate performance.

9.8 'Managers are constrained in exercising their discretion in a variety of ways. Mainly, however, the constraints are ineffective and managerial objectives predominate.' Explain and discuss.

CHAPTER 10

◗ *Pricing Decisions*

Pricing decisions within different market models were discussed in Chapter 8; pricing in a multiplant firm and the pricing policies of cartels were also examined. This chapter takes the analysis further by reviewing a number of other key pricing strategies that the large firm is likely to pursue. It begins with an analysis of pricing procedures that retain the assumption of *certainty*, i.e. when the firm has certain and complete knowledge of its demand and cost functions. The price strategies covered are *limit pricing*, by which the firm prices to deter the entry of new firms (non-price strategies are also briefly assessed); *price discrimination*, whereby the firm subdivides its market into various segments and prices accordingly; *predatory pricing*, where a firm prices with the express intent of eliminating competition; *joint-product pricing*, whereby the firm prices in a multiproduct setting; *peak-load pricing*, in which pricing policy is influenced by changing demand conditions in different time periods; and *transfer pricing*, or the pricing of products transferred between the various divisions of a firm. It then examines pricing procedures under conditions of *uncertainty*, i.e. when the firm does not have complete and certain knowledge of either or both of its demand or cost functions. In these conditions the firm is likely to employ *markup* or *cost-plus pricing* techniques. The importance of the need to incorporate an *estimation of demand* into the pricing formula is examined and the relationship between the markup procedure and profit-maximising behaviour is discussed. Finally, *new product pricing strategies*, such as *skimming* and *penetration pricing* are considered. The *case study* outlines the latest evidence on

the pricing decision, with particular reference to the reasons for price stickiness in oligopolies.

10.1 LIMIT PRICING

The traditional theory of the firm is only concerned with the actual entry of new firms into an industry. However, incumbent or established firms need also to take into account the threat of *potential entry*, which can have a significant influence on their strategic decision-making. Bain (1956) argued that assuming sufficiently high barriers to entry (i.e. if there is effectively impeded entry), then incumbent firms will not necessarily price at the short-run profit-maximising level. They will instead take a longer-term view (he assumed firms to be long-run profit maximisers) and set a *limit price*, which is the highest price that they can charge without inducing entry. In other words, profits in the current period are sacrificed for higher profitability and market share in the future (see also Section 2.4).

Bain's ideas were later developed by others, such as Sylos-Labini (1957) and Modigliani (1958), into a model of entry-forestalling oligopolistic behaviour in which new entry depends on the anticipated profitability of breaking into a market. In summary, the model assumes that all firms, incumbents and potential entrants alike, face the same L-shaped LRAC curve. Demand is known and price is set by the price leader. Specifically the model is based on what is referred to as the *Sylos postulate*. This is governed by two assumptions, one concerning the behaviour of the incumbent firms and the other the behaviour of the new entrant. The incumbent firms do not expect entry into the market at less than the MES level of output. The potential entrant expects the established firms to maintain their pre-entry output levels.

In Figure 71, page 198, LRAC is the long-run average cost curve for both established firms and new entrants and D is the market demand. Given the Sylos postulate, the new entrant expects to be faced with the level of demand (on the market demand curve) to the right of the output of the established firms. Therefore, the incumbent firms will establish a limit price at that output level so that, if new entry occurred at MES, the price would fall below the competitive price (i.e. the price that would be charged if the market were perfectly competitive) and entry would be unprofitable. In the figure, X is the MES level of output, Q_C is the competitive output, P_C is

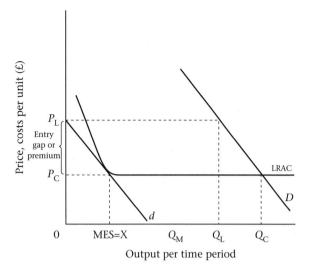

Figure 71 *Limit pricing and the Sylos postulate.*

the competitive price, Q_L (which equals $Q_C - X$), is the relevant limit output and P_L is the limit price. Demand curve d indicates the potential entrants' demand curve at the limit price. The distance between P_L and P_C, the maximum amount by which price can exceed average costs without inducing entry, is known as the *entry gap* or *premium*. The entry gap and the limit price are determined by the following factors:

(1) The MES level of production. As X increases, so will the entry gap and the limit price, *cet. par.*
(2) The size of the market at the competitive price. As Q_C decreases, the entry gap and the limit price rise, *cet. par.*
(3) The price elasticity of market demand. As price elasticity falls, the entry gap and the limit price rise, *cet. par.*
(4) The level of technology and the prices of the inputs, which determine the shape of the LRAC and the competitive price, P_C. As P_C increases, so do the entry gap and the limit price, *cet. par.*

The formula for the limit price was summarised by Modigliani as

$$P_L = P_C \left(1 + \frac{X}{Q_C \times e_p}\right)^1 \tag{10.1}$$

The prevention of entry by the incumbents at MES or above is, in fact, a special case. In more general terms,

[1] (i.e. note one at the end of the chapter.)

where entry at below MES is possible, the incumbents need to set a limit price such that entry at any level of output would not be considered worthwhile. The level of output that prevents entry would be greater and the limit price lower than in the special case.

The limit pricing model based on the Sylos postulate has been criticised on a number of grounds, the main one being that the basic premise of the postulate, that established firms maintain their pre-entry output, is an unrealistic and entirely defensive strategy. It also implies that the market price is determined by how much the new entrant sells. It may be preferable for the incumbents to pursue other strategies, like increasing their pre-entry output and allowing the price to fall or increasing their post-entry output and initiating a price war with the new entrant. These strategies are likely to be more successful when the incumbents are financially strong, as in UK food retailing. Faced with the entry of discount stores in the early 1990s, the main supermarket chains cut the prices of many of their major-selling items, a policy which so far has reduced the growth of the discounters' market shares. An alternative strategy, a mixture of partly reducing output and partly allowing the price to fall, has also been successfully employed in some industries.

The second major criticism of the limit pricing model is that it implicitly assumes that the potential entrants are relatively small. However, the entrant may be a large-scale diversifier already established in another industry and engaged in a process of cross-entry. In this case the scale economy barrier, or for that matter any other type of barrier, may not be considered a major obstacle to entry. The diversifier may be able to enter at below MES output and indulge in short-term losses, especially if encouraged by the incumbents' level of profits, in order to gain a foothold in the market. The entry of Virgin into the airlines and soft drinks markets is a case in point.

The model also ignores dynamic considerations. It assumes that firms may trade short-term profits for long-term profitability and market share within a static environment. In fact, incumbents may employ a policy of allowing entry gradually. Besides, in a growing market the incumbents may be less concerned about limit pricing and the threat of entry.

Two other qualifications of the model should be mentioned. It makes the assumption that the established firms successfully collude over price (and possess the knowledge of cost and demand conditions in order to do so). It also ignores strategies other than price, such as investment in productive capacity, that established firms can use to deter entry. For example, Spence (1977) related investment in capacity to limit pricing. In Figure 71, it is claimed that if a firm has a capacity output of Q_L then it will then be able to produce a pre-entry output, Q_M (and price accordingly), that maximises short-run profits and uses the extra capacity, $Q_M Q_L$, as an entry-fore-stalling tactic. Sunk costs play an important role in this strategy for both the incumbent and the entrant. Sunk costs commit the incumbent to a particular course of action and so issue a credible threat to intruders. Sunk costs also provide a disincentive to entry for potential newcomers. However, Spence does not explain why potential entrants expect the incumbent to increase its output to the full capacity level post-entry. According to Dixit (1980), if the incumbent is expected to reduce its output post-entry, then there is no point in investing in excess capacity. However, by making irreversible investments pre-entry the incumbent is able to sink some of its marginal costs and lower its post-entry marginal costs relative to an entrant's; this should then deter entry.

These models suffer from the same problem as the traditional limit pricing model, namely the assumption of certainty about rivals' costs and about demand conditions. Empirical evidence on the significance of excess capacity as a barrier to entry is sparse. Lieberman (1987) found evidence of significant excess capacity in the US chemicals sector, but this was mainly held to accommodate demand variability and investment lumpiness. In only three out of 38 products studied was there any evidence of incumbents holding excess capacity for entry deterrence purposes. Firms can use other non-price strategies to hinder new entry, such as advertising and R&D (discussed in the Chapter 11) and also policies towards vertical integration and diversification (considered in Chapter 13).

10.2 PRICE DISCRIMINATION

Price discrimination (see Box 10.1) enables a firm to achieve a higher revenue from a given level of sales (and thereby to obtain higher profits). Various conditions must hold in a market for successful price discrimination to occur:

(1) The seller needs to have a significant amount of monopoly power in order not just to identify the various market segments but more importantly to control the supply of the product and the prices in the different parts of the market. In other words, the firm needs either to be a monopolist, or instead an oligopolist working in close harmony with the other firms in the market.

(2) The different market segments must be entirely distinct, so that it is impossible for a customer belonging to one group to re-sell the product to a customer in another group.

(3) The different market segments must exhibit differing price elasticities of demand.

(4) It must be profitable to discriminate, i.e. the transaction costs involved must be less than the extra revenue so generated.

Box 10.1 *Price discrimination*

Price discrimination occurs when different buyers or groups of buyers, in separate market segments, are charged different prices for the same product for reasons not associated with differences in costs. Thus, price discrimination exists when price differences fail to reflect cost differences or when customers are charged the same price despite cost differences. There are three main categories of price discrimination. *First-degree price discrimination* occurs when each customer is forced to pay the highest price that he or she is willing to forgo for the product. In practice, first-degree price discrimination is rare because it assumes that a firm has exactly the right information to charge the maximum amount that each customer is willing to pay for the product. A possible example is provided by a street vendor who is prepared to haggle with individual customers over the price of his wares. *Second-degree price discrimination* occurs when consumers are charged a flat rate for the first block of units consumed, a lower rate for the next block of units and so on; this policy, sometimes carried out by the utilities, is also known as *block tariff pricing*. *Third-degree price discrimination*, the most popular form of price discrimination, occurs when different groups of buyers, such as domestic versus business customers or adults as opposed to children, are charged different prices for a product. Examples of third-degree price discrimination abound. The utilities often charge differential rates for business customers compared with domestic users. Children are charged lower prices than adults in cinemas and on aeroplanes, buses and trains. Students can often obtain lower prices in restaurants or hairdressers and they may also be able to secure journals and magazines at preferential rates. Shops may charge higher prices in a city-centre store than in an out-of-town branch, irrespective of transport cost differences. In all these cases, firms are taking advantage of the differing elasticities of demand between the various market segments of their products.

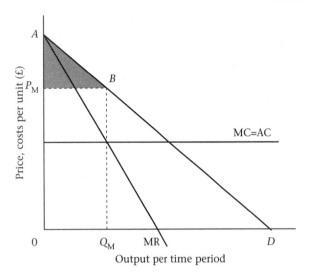

Figure 72   Consumer surplus of a monopolist.

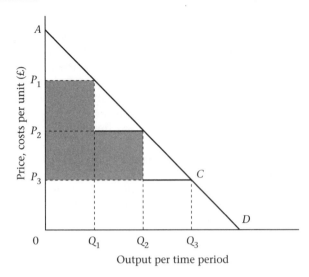

Figure 73   *The effects of second-degree price discrimination on consumer surplus.*

In first-degree price discrimination the seller extracts all the *consumer surplus* from the buyers, where this is defined as the value to consumers of purchasing a certain quantity of a product over and above the outlay involved in acquiring that quantity. In Figure 72 a monopolist facing constant costs maximises profits at a price of P_M and at an output of Q_M. The total value to consumers from purchasing the quantity Q_M is the area beneath the demand curve, $0ABQ_M$. The total outlay (or total revenue for the seller) incurred in purchasing Q_M is the rectangle $0P_M BQ_M$. Therefore, the total consumer surplus is the shaded triangle $P_M AB$. By expropriating the consumer surplus the total outlay of consumers and the total revenue of the firm increases, in this case to comprise the entire area $0ABQ_M$. This is because the demand curve becomes the firm's MR curve.

The effects of second-degree price discrimination can be seen in Figure 73, where it is assumed that the uniform price of P_3 is set at the level of constant costs, in which case the consumer surplus is indicated by the triangle P_3AC. If the firm charges a price of P_1 for the first block of output, Q_1, a lower rate, P_2, for the next block of units consumed, Q_1Q_2, and a third rate, P_3, for the final block of output, Q_2Q_3, it will extract the extra consumer surplus and gain the additional revenue shown by the shaded area in the diagram. This mode assumes that consumers have identical demand curves, which they do not, and that the firm has the requisite information to be able to expropriate the consumer surplus as shown, which

is unlikely. British Gas charges lower rates to domestic customers for successive blocks of units consumed, as indicated in Table 54.

In the case of third-degree price discrimination the firm has to decide how much to produce in total, how much to sell in each market and at what price in order to maximise profits. The analysis of third-degree price discrimination is very similar to that of the multiplant firm or of the profit-maximising cartel that were examined in Chapter 8. In this instance it is assumed that the firm divides the market into two distinct segments, A and B; segment A has a more inelastic demand than segment B. The firm maximises profits by equating the marginal cost of the total output with the marginal revenue of each

Table 54   *Prices charged to domestic customers by British Gas, 1995*

	Price (Pence)
Standing charge	10.390[a]
Gas consumption per year (kWh)	
0–73 200	1.520[b]
73 201–146 536	1.420[b]
146 537–293 071	1.380[b]
293 072–732 678	1.340[b]

[a]Per day.
[b]Per kilowatt hour.

market segment. This is because each incremental unit should be produced in the submarket which contributes most to the firm's revenue, i.e. the one that has the highest marginal revenue. If this were not so, the firm could increase its revenue, and its profit, by producing more in the higher-revenue market segment and less in the lower-revenue market segment. Thus, if $MR_A > MR_B$ the firm would increase its output in segment A and reduce output in segment B until the marginal revenues were equalised. The firm finds its total MR curve by horizontally summing the MR curves in markets A and B.

The aggregate marginal revenue curve is shown in Figure 74(c) by ΣMR (the kink in the curve is due to the fact that the demand curve in market A intercepts the price axis at a higher level). The firm's profit-maximising output is Q, where $\Sigma MR = MC$. At this point the marginal revenues in markets A and B are equal, which can be seen by tracing a line back from the firm's profit-maximising position. The firm produces Q_A in segment A and Q_B in segment B; $Q_A + Q_B = Q$. It sells at a price of P_A in segment A and P_B in segment B. In so doing, it taps some of the consumer surplus in market A that would exist if only one price were charged. The total profit of the firm is given by the addition of the shaded area in each market segment in the figure, i.e. $P_A ABC + P_B DEF$.

Algebraically, the equilibrium position of a firm engaging in third-degree price discrimination can be

found as follows. Assume that the firm, a monopolist, can divide its market into two distinct segments, A and B. The demand in each segment and the firm's total cost function are estimated as

$$P_A = 100 - 0.02Q_A$$
$$P_B = 50 - 0.01Q_B$$
$$TC = 1000 + 20Q$$

where $Q = Q_A + Q_B$. Therefore

$$MR_A = 100 - 0.04Q_A$$
$$MR_B = 50 - 0.02Q_B$$
$$MC = 20$$

Equating marginal cost with marginal revenue in each segment:

$$100 - 0.04Q_A = 20$$

Therefore $Q_A = 2000$ and

$$P_A = 100 - 0.02(2000) = £60$$
$$50 - 0.02Q_B = 20$$

Therefore $Q_B = 1500$ and

$$P_B = 50 - 0.01(1500) = £35$$

The total profit of the firm is equal to total revenue minus total cost:

$$TR_A = 2000 \times £60 = £120000 \text{ and}$$
$$TR_B = 1500 \times £35 = £52500$$

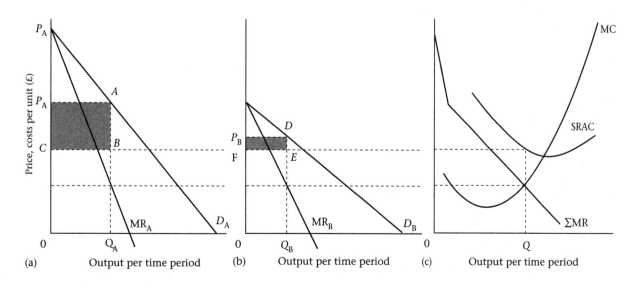

Figure 74 *Third-degree price discrimination. (a) Segment A; (b) segment B; (c) the firm.*

$$TR_A + TR_B = £172500$$
$$TC = 1000 + 20(Q_A + Q_B) =$$
$$= 1000 + 20(3500) = £71000$$
$$\pi = £172500 - £71000 = £101500$$

Predatory pricing

Sometimes a firm may practice price discrimination with the express intent of removing competition from a particular market. *Predatory pricing* refers to the situation where a large and financially powerful firm prices one or more of its products below costs and, by covering any losses from the funds generated from within other parts of its organisation, intends to secure the demise or the takeover of a smaller rival or rivals. (It can also be used to prevent entry.) Such a tactic is more likely and more advantageous to a dominant firm when a market is segmented, because price cuts can be imposed in one part of a market while other segments are left untouched. It is also more likely to occur when capital markets are imperfect. Predatory pricing, it is argued, lowers rivals' equity and by so doing raises their interest rate charges because bankruptcy risk is greater. They may then be forced to leave the industry. A firm may also gain a reputation for predation, which can be used to deter the growth or new entry of a rival, although the dominant firm may have to act on its reputation in order for it be effective.

The main problem with predatory pricing is how to define it. Areeda and Turner (1975) suggested that the appropriate test should be based on a price–cost criterion: if a firm prices below marginal cost (for which a proxy is average variable cost), then this is evidence of predation. The marginal cost pricing rule also has the advantage for policy-makers that pricing below marginal cost is indicative of resource misallocation. The problem then becomes one of distinguishing between fixed and variable costs, or, more pertinently, in determining which costs are avoidable in a particular instance. Areeda and Hovenkamp (1992) have noted that a predatory pricing rule should be based on those costs which are variable in the relevant time period only.

The problems of defining predatory pricing mean that any examples have to treated with some caution. In the US in 1993 Wal-Mart, reputed to be the world's largest retailer (1992 sales $55 billion) was found guilty by an Arkansas court of predation by deliber-

ately aiming to oust three small pharmacy businesses (combined 1992 sales about $16 million) by selling prescription drugs at below cost. As soon as the competition vanished, Wal-Mart raised its prices on the goods.[2] In 1995 the UK bus company Stagecoach was found guilty of predatory behaviour by the Monopolies and Mergers Commission (MMC, 1995). Between September 1994 and February 1995, Busways, a Stagecoach subsidiary, cut prices and introduced new services in South Shields in the North-east of England with the express intent of the takeover of a rival, Hylton, or at the very least its removal from the busiest routes in the area. Despite the fact that Busways covered its variable and semi-variable costs during the relevant period, its actions were considered predatory and against the public interest because of their adverse effects on competition. The fact that predatory policies occur in what is considered to be a relatively contestable market should not be thought surprising: predation in markets with high entry barriers (and high sunk costs) is not likely to be necessary either to deter entry or to induce exit. However, even in markets characterised by relatively low entry barriers, new firms may become increasingly deterred from trying to gain entry if incumbents have established a reputation for predatory tactics in order to oust possible competitors; as in the later case, predation can create entry barriers where few previously existed.

10.3 JOINT-PRODUCT PRICING

Many large firms produce a variety of products, a number of which are technologically related in the sense that it is not possible to produce a certain quantity of one product without producing a quantity of another product. Such products are referred to as *joint products*; joint costs of production, usually overheads, are incurred in their production. There are two types of these products, those that are produced in fixed proportions and those that can be produced in variable proportions. The classic example of the former is beef and hides from a cow, although there are other examples like milk and butter or wool and mutton. Examples of the latter include gas and coke and petrol and heavier oils, like heating oil and diesel fuel. Where the production of one product is the direct result of a change in the output of another product it is known as a *by-product*.

The particular characteristic of joint products of significance to a firm is that an incremental change in the output or the price of one of the products must have an effect on the output and the price of the other product. In other words, a firm has to decide on the optimal output and pricing strategy of joint products, given the fact that there will be simultaneous variations in a number of its key decision variables. A firm has to take account of the effects of a change in output or price on the marginal revenue and marginal cost of the product in question plus the effects of the change on the marginal revenue and marginal costs of all related products. In such a case the condition for profit maximisation is as follows (Needham, 1978):

$$\sum MR_i = \sum MC_i$$

or

$$\sum (MR_i - MC_i) = 0 \qquad (10.2)$$

MR and MC show the respective changes in the *i*th decision variable, say the output of the *i*th product, on the firm's total revenue and total cost. For optimality to occur, the sum of the effects of the change in this decision variable on total revenue must equal the sum of the effects of its change on total costs; alternatively, the net effect of an incremental change in the decision variable on profits must be zero. Equation (10.2) can be rewritten as

$$\sum MR_i = \sum MC - \left(\sum MR - MR_i \right) \qquad (10.3)$$

The optimal condition is defined as one in which the effect of a change in a decision variable on a firm's total revenue equals the effects of a simultaneous change in all decision variables on the firm's total costs minus the effects of a simultaneous change in all other decision variables on the firm's total revenue. The term indicated on the right-hand side of equation (10.3) is known as the *marginal opportunity cost*. In other words, the profit-maximising level of output for each joint product is where its marginal revenue equals the marginal opportunity cost, where the latter is defined as the joint marginal cost minus the sum of the marginal revenues associated with the other joint products.

Where the joint products are produced in variable proportions, and assuming that the demand for the individual products is independent, the diagrammatic analysis is identical to that of the price-discriminating

monopolist that was shown in Figure 74, page 201. In that instance the firm's problem was to allocate its output between different markets. In this case the firm's decision is how to allocate its output between its various joint products. Some of the costs of the individual products can be separately determined; not all the costs are joint costs. The solution is the same: the marginal revenue curve of each product is summed horizontally to discover the aggregate marginal revenue curve. Marginal revenue for each product is then equated with the marginal cost.

In the case of joint products that are produced in fixed proportions, the diagrammatic explanation is based on the vertical summation of the marginal revenue curves of the various products. This is shown in Figure 75 for two such products, A and B. In this case the costs of the individual products cannot be separately determined; all the costs are joint costs. The two products form a 'bundle' of output.

Figure 75 indicates the demand curve for each joint product, D_A and D_B, plus the associated marginal revenue curves, MR_A and MR_B. It also shows the overall marginal cost curve, MC. The two marginal revenue curves are summed vertically to yield the marginal revenue curve, ΣMR: any level of output indicates revenues received from the sale of both products. The 'kink' in MR indicates the output level

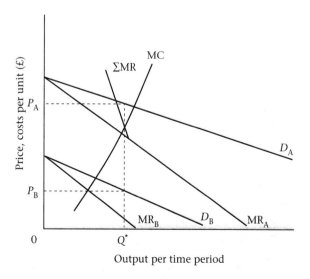

Figure 75 *The equilibrium position of a firm producing joint costs in fixed proportions.*

at which MR_B becomes negative. Beyond that point, ΣMR coincides with MR_A. The profit-maximising level of output, Q^*, is where ΣMR is equal to the firm's marginal cost curve, MC. The profit-maximising price for each joint product is determined by the intersection of the vertical dashed line at the profit-maximising output level with each product's demand curve. The respective prices are P_A and P_B.

Algebraically, the equilibrium position of a profit-maximising firm producing two joint products, A and B, in fixed proportions can be found as follows. Assume that the firm produces a bundle of output, every unit of which comprises a single unit of product A and a single unit of product B. The demand curves for the two products and the total cost function are estimated as

$$P_A = 200 - 0.1Q_A$$
$$P_B = 180 - 0.15Q_B$$

and

$$TC = 50000 + 20Q + 0.2Q^2$$

Therefore

$$MR_A = 200 - 0.2Q_A$$
$$MR_B = 180 - 0.3Q_B$$

and

$$MC = 20 + 0.4Q$$

Since the products are produced in fixed proportions the MR functions are added vertically to give the combined MR function, ΣMR, i.e. $\Sigma MR = MR_A + MR_B$:

$$(200 - 0.2Q_A) + (180 - 0.3Q_B) = 380 - 0.5Q$$

The combined marginal revenue function is equated with marginal cost to find the profit-maximising level of output:

$$380 - 0.5Q = 20 + 0.4Q$$
$$Q = 400$$

The price of each product can be found by substituting for Q:

$$P_A = 200 - 0.1(400) = £160$$
$$P_B = 180 - 0.15(400) = £120$$

At the profit-maximising level of output marginal cost is given by

$$MC = 20 + 0.4(400) = £180$$

Since one unit of output consists of one unit of A plus one unit of B, $Q = Q_A = Q_B$. Hence

$$MR_A = 200 - 0.2(400) = £120$$
$$MR_B = 150 - 0.3(400) = £60$$

Thus

$$MC = \sum MR \text{ or } MR_A + MR_B$$

The profit of the firm is equal to total revenue minus total cost:

$$TR = (P_A Q) + (P_B Q) = (£160 \times 400) +$$
$$(£120 \times 400) = £64000 + £48000 = £112000$$
$$TC = 50000 + (20 \times 400) + (0.2 \times 400^2) =$$
$$£90000$$
$$\pi = £112000 - £90000 = £22000$$

10.4 PEAK-LOAD PRICING

Peak-load pricing refers to those situations where products are consumed in different time periods, and pricing strategy is a reflection of this. Higher prices are charged in the periods of peak demand due to the higher costs involved in supplying the product at these times. For example, telephone companies usually charge higher prices for calls made at peak times (see Table 55) and some electricity companies charge business customers higher rates during the day than during the night. Both are examples of peak-load pricing. Peak-load pricing can be viewed as a special case of a joint product produced in fixed

Table 55 *Peak-time pricing by BT and Mercury, 1995*

	Pence per minute for a UK call		
	Local	Regional	National
BT			
Daytime (Mon.–Fri. 8am–6pm)	4.0	8.3	9.8
Evenings and night (Mon.–Fri. before 8am and after 6pm)	1.7	4.0	5.8
Weekend (midnight Fri–midnight Sun.)	1.0	3.3	3.3
Mercury			
Standard (Mon.–Fri. 8am–6pm)	7.4	N/A	6.4
Economy (all other times)	2.45	N/A	2.5

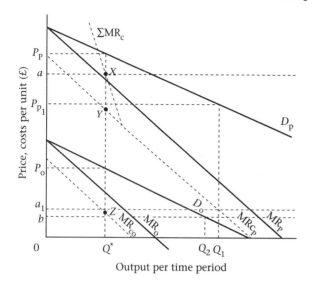

Figure 76 *Peak-load pricing.*

proportions. The output consumed in each time period is supplied by the same capacity output, which differs in its utilisation in the different periods. Peak-load pricing is essentially a problem of the allocation of the joint costs involved in supplying a product in different time periods.

The situation can be shown diagrammatically. In Figure 76, D_p and D_o represent two different time periods, peak and off-peak demand respectively, that are of equal length and are independent of each other. Both capacity and operating costs are assumed to be proportional to output in each period. Marginal and average capacity costs per unit of output are equal to a and marginal and average operating costs are equal to b in both periods. The relevant marginal revenue curves are denoted by MR_p, for the peak period, and MR_o, for the off-peak. If the operating cost curve is subtracted from the MR curve in each period the net marginal revenue of capacity curve for each period can be ascertained. They are shown by the dashed lines, MR_{cp} and MR_{co}, respectively. They are summed vertically to give ΣMR_c. The intersection of this curve with the marginal cost of capacity curve, at X, gives the profit-maximising level of capacity, Q^*. The marginal opportunity cost of capacity in each period equals the difference between the joint marginal cost of capacity, a, and the sum of the net marginal revenue of capacity in all other periods, or in this case the one other period. Thus, in the peak period the marginal opportunity cost of capacity equals $Q^* Y$ and in the off-peak it equals $Q^* Z$. The

output level in each period is found by equating the relevant marginal revenue curve to the sum of the marginal opportunity cost of capacity for each period and the marginal operating cost. In this case both periods produce output Q^*; demand is fully utilised in both periods. The optimal price in each period is determined by the intersection of this output line with the relevant demand curve, yielding P_p and P_o respectively. A higher price is charged in the peak period.

If the marginal capacity cost were much lower, say a_1, the optimal capacity is Q_1. In the off-peak period the price would not cover operating costs at this capacity output. The price in the off-peak period has to be set equal to the marginal operating cost, or the marginal opportunity cost in the off-peak, at which point an output of Q_2 is produced. Since capacity is not fully utilised in the off-peak, the marginal capacity cost is borne by the peak-time users, who pay a price of P_{P1}.

Such a profit-maximising solution to the peak-load pricing problem involves a degree of price discrimination because marginal revenue is equated with the joint marginal cost in each period. Since the price–marginal revenue relationship depends on the elasticity of demand in each time period or, submarket, the different prices charged will only fully reflect the cost differences between the markets if elasticities are the same in all submarkets. (In a welfare maximising solution, prices will be set equal to marginal costs, in which case no element of price discrimination would exist.)

10.5 TRANSFER PRICING

Transfer pricing refers to the pricing of products, specifically a component or an intermediate product, that are exchanged between one division of a firm and another. The problem for the firm is to price the product in order to maximise profits in the organisation as a whole. In the case of a multidivisional M-form enterprise that is organised into independent profit centres, optimal transfer pricing can facilitate profit maximisation by the individual units as well as by the complete firm, although any possible divergence of interests between the divisions and the head office (i.e. the maximisation of divisional profits versus the maximisation of profits in the organisation as a whole) have to be satisfactorily resolved. Where no external market for the transferred product exists, cost-based transfer prices, based on the internal costs of the firm, are usually adopted. Market-based transfer prices (which can also be based on the prices of competing products) will be used otherwise. Initially in this section, transfer pricing assuming no external market for the product is discussed. This is followed by an examination of transfer pricing assuming either a perfectly competitive or an imperfectly competitive external market for the transferred product. In each case it is assumed that the firm involved is a profit maximiser and that there is complete independence of costs and demand functions between its divisions.

Transfer pricing assuming no external market

Assume a firm has two divisions, A and B. For example, these might be the manufacturing and distribution divisions respectively of a vertically integrated multidivisional firm, in which case division A transfers its product to division B for distribution. In these circumstances the firm's costs are divided between the two divisions. This situation is shown in Figure 77.

D_F, MR_F and MC_F are the demand, marginal revenue and marginal cost curves for the firm as a whole. MC_A is the marginal cost curve of division A, found by subtracting the marginal cost of division B from the marginal cost of the firm as a whole. NMR_B is the net marginal revenue curve of division B, which

is the marginal revenue of the firm minus the marginal cost of division B. The firm maximises its profits at P^* and Q^*.

At Q^*, $NMR_B = MC_A$. This is because $NMR_B = MR_F - MC_B$ and $MC_A = MC_F - MC_B$. Since $MR_F = MC_F$ at Q^* and MC_B is common to both equations, $NMR_B = MC_A$ at Q^*. In other words, the transfer price, P_T, is set equal to the marginal cost of division A, the transferring division. It is only at this transfer price that each division maximises its profits. Hence, so does the firm. Division A can sell all that it likes at P_T, which therefore represents its MR curve. $MC_A = MR_A$ at Q^*. For division B, P_T represents its effective marginal cost curve, which it equates with its NMR. $MC_B = MR_B$ at Q^*.

Transfer pricing assuming a perfectly competitive external market

In this instance it is assumed that the firm's product can also be purchased from other firms which operate in a perfectly competitive environment. An example might be a multinational rubber producer (Hood and Young, 1979). It is assumed once again that a firm comprises a manufacturing and a distribution division, labelled A and B. Division A's product is also available from outside firms. The situation is shown in Figure 78. The curves are labelled as in Figure 77. The firm maximises its profits at P^* and Q^*, as before.

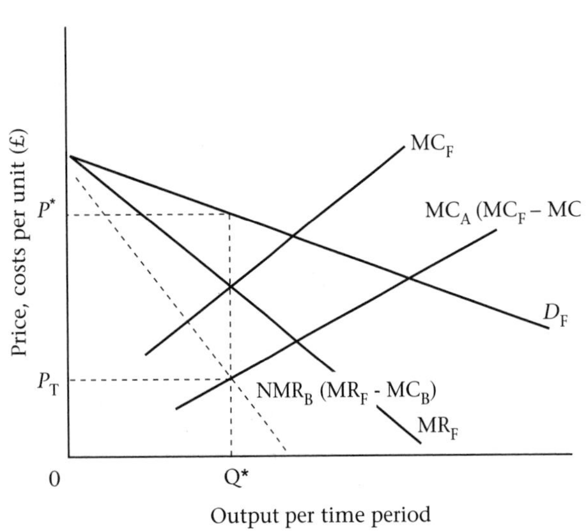

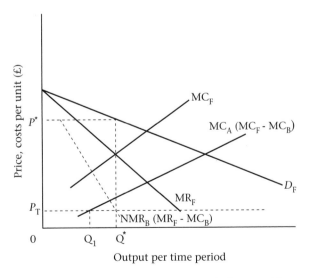

Figure 77 *Transfer pricing assuming no external market.*

Figure 78 *Transfer pricing assuming a perfectly competitive external market*

The transfer price, P_T is set equal to the external market price. At this price, division A only wishes to sell Q_1 units, where $MC_A = MR_A$ (since $P_T = MR_A$). Division B wants to buy Q^* units, where $NMR_B = MC_B$ (since $P_T = MC_B$). Therefore, it has to buy the difference, $Q_1 Q^*$ in the open market.

Transfer pricing assuming an imperfectly competitive external market

In this case the firm's product can also be purchased in an external imperfectly competitive market. For example, an electronics company or an electrical manufacturing firm might sell components produced by one of its divisions to its competitors. The situation is shown in Figure 79. The demand and marginal revenue curves of the external market are shown in part (a) and the net marginal revenue curve of division B, the distribution division, is shown in part (b).

Figure 79(c) shows the total market facing division A, the manufacturing division. ΣMR is the horizontal summation of MR_E and NMR_B. The firm behaves exactly like a third-degree price discriminator, since elasticity of demand varies in the two markets. It equates ΣMR with MC_A and produces a total output

of Q^*. Q_1 is sold in the external market and Q_2 in the internal market, at which points the marginal revenues in each market (or, to be precise, the marginal revenue in the external market and the net marginal revenue in the internal market) are equalised. P_1 is the price charged in the external market and P_T is the internal transfer price.

Firms probably apply the above procedures in determining their transfer prices, or some variant of them, although it is doubtful if the demand functions of rival firms for inputs or for final products can be considered completely independent, since they are competing in the same markets. The correct transfer price may also be difficult to calculate, especially where no external market for the product exists. Evidence suggests that firms use both cost-based and market-based prices and, at times, prices that are negotiated between the divisions and the head office. Prior to 1988 the transfer price used by the plasterboard manufacturer, British Gypsum (BG), in the purchase of liner paper, for which there is no UK market, was set by the most similar product in the product range of its parent company, BPB. The arrival of other plasterboard manufacturers requiring liner paper led BG to pay liner paper prices similar to those paid by its competitors on deliveries from mainland Europe (MMC, 1990).

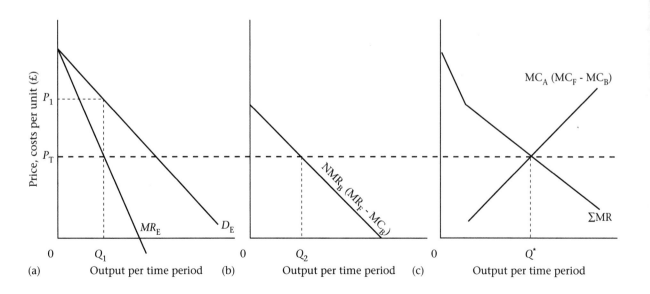

Figure 79 *Transfer pricing assuming an imperfectly competitive external market. (a) External market; (b) internal market; (c) total market.*

The transfer pricing policies of MNCs are affected not just by the state of competition for intermediate products but also by a range of additional factors, such as having to deal in different currencies and with varying tax and inflation rates. Low transfer prices might be used to reduce import duties payable by an overseas subsidiary. Alternatively, high transfer charges may be made on transfers to a subsidiary in a relatively high tax country in order to 'shift' profits to a subsidiary in a low tax country. Evidence of the extent of transfer pricing by MNCs is difficult to obtain because the firms themselves often have a vested interest in shielding these types of activities from the investigative eyes of external bodies. The US probably has the most sophisticated system for detecting transfer price manipulations. In April 1992 there were allegations in Congress of losses of billions of dollars from the tax avoidance tactics of foreign, and especially Japanese, affiliates. In 1989, for example, overseas MNCs in the US reportedly earned an average 0.51% net return on assets, while US-owned companies earned 1.97% (Cleeve, 1994).

10.6 PRICING UNDER CONDITIONS OF UNCERTAINTY

The market models that were discussed in Chapter 8 and the various other pricing models and techniques that have been examined so far in this chapter are based on the common assumption that firms have full and certain knowledge of their demand and cost functions and can price their products according to traditional, profit-maximising rules by equating marginal revenue with marginal cost. In fact, in practice, firms may be very *uncertain* about their demand and cost functions because they do not possess the necessary information. This is not to suggest that firms are unable to pursue the pricing strategies outlined thus far, simply that they may have to implement them with incomplete information.

Empirical evidence (summarised in Hay and Morris, 1979; Scherer, 1980; Devine *et al.*, 1985; see also Section 4.2) has for long suggested that many firms do not use marginalist principles for pricing, rather they employ some kind of rule-of-thumb *markup* or *cost-plus* procedure, whereby price is determined by the addition of a percentage, markup, sometimes refered to as the gross profit margin (GPM), to average

variable costs (see also the case study on page 212. Thus

$$P = AVC + GPM \qquad (10.4)$$

or, in other words, the markup is equivalent to the per unit profit contribution towards overheads and profit, or $P - AVC$. It is thought that most firms that engage in markup pricing first establish their normal level of capacity utilisation in order to determine the desired level of output. They then add on the markup to their known average variable costs, which are assumed to be constant over a wide range of output (and which are hence equivalent to marginal costs). This situation is shown in Figure 80, where Q_1 is the desired level of output and P_1 is the price charged after the addition of the relevant markup. In other words, according to this procedure the main preoccupation of firms is not output determination as in traditional theory but the setting of price.

In principle, the scale of the markup can be determined by a number of factors and in particular by the extent of actual competition and the threat of potential competition. An oligopoly characterised by a very few sellers and high barriers to entry and featuring a tight collusive agreement (i.e. where demand is relatively inelastic) would be able to charge a higher price than an industry consisting of a larger number of firms, lower entry barriers and with a much looser arrangement, *cet. par.* An increased threat of entry may also cause incumbents to lower their markup and perhaps follow a limit pricing

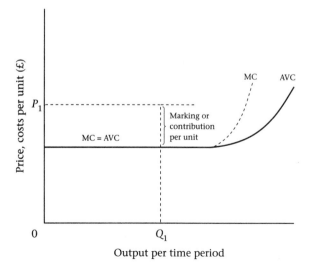

Figure 80 *Markup pricing.*

strategy. Corporate objectives can also affect the size of the markup; a sales maximiser will set a lower markup than a profit maximiser, *cet. par.* (See also Box 10.2.)

An alternative explanation of the determination of the markup, and one which implicitly assumes that firms make some estimate of future demand, is the suggestion that the size of the markup is directly related to the need for investment funds (Eichner, 1973). According to this view (which is based on the fact that most investment is financed through internal sources), firms set their prices so that they have sufficient profits to plough back into the business in order to finance their investment plans. It is assumed that firms base their investment decisions on the need to keep their capacity in line with the expected growth of demand. In other words, excess

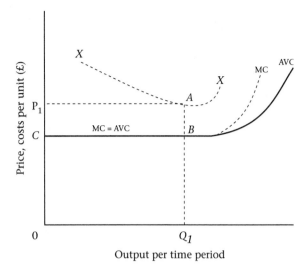

Figure 81 *Average full cost pricing.*

Box 10.2 *The markup and market conditions*

It might be expected that markup pricing is specifically cost-influenced, but the markup can also be sensitive to demand conditions. The fact that firms employ their normal level of output in their pricing decisions suggests that they must make some estimate of demand. In other words, the desired level of capacity utilisation is likely to be related in some way to the expectation of the future level of demand. The studies of markup pricing suggest that, while firms do not adjust their prices immediately a change in demand or costs occurs, as strict adherence to marginal behaviour would dictate, they do vary the markup according to market conditions. Thus, if a firm incorrectly estimates the level of demand, then it may adjust its markup, although in what direction, and by how much, would also depend on the actions of its competitors. If, say, market conditions are depressed and a firm overestimates demand, it may wish to raise its price in order to take account of the higher unit costs of a lower output, but it will be reluctant to do so alone. If the lower demand was considered to be permanent the firm may consider lowering the markup, but it may fear initiating a price war. Boom conditions are usually associated with higher markups, although, once again, a firm will be reluctant to act independently, unless it is the price leader and it is sure that others in the industry will follow suit. In the case of a persistent increase in demand, firms are likely to increase their capacity by investing in new plant and equipment. Thus, firms may act as if they adhere to marginalist rules, even if they do not have the full information to apply them strictly (see also the case study on page 212).

capacity is planned to remain at a more or less constant level. Hence, markup decisions are directly related to expectations of demand.

In Figure 81, Q_1 is the desired level of capacity utilisation and P_1 is the price after the inclusion of the desired markup. The curve *XX* is a *constant rate of profit curve* for all levels of capacity utilisation.

This would show the prices that would have to be charged at different levels of capacity utilisation to yield a constant amount of profit and thus rate-of-return on capital employed (Kregel, 1976:139).

At output Q_1 and price P_1 the total profit comprises the rectangle P_1ABC. Since, by definition, the constant rate of profit curve must include an estimate of average fixed costs, it is also referred to as the *average full cost curve* and the pricing technique under these conditions as *average full cost pricing*. An increase in expected future market growth would produce a higher *XX* curve. However, firms using this procedure still base it on a normal or desired level of capacity utilisation that is closely related to their estimate of demand.

In fact, it can be proved quite easily that there is an inverse relationship between the markup and the estimate of elasticity of demand, assuming profit-maximising behaviour. It was shown in Chapter 7 (see Note 4) that

$$MR = P\left(1 + \frac{1}{e_p}\right)$$

If AVC is constant it must be equal to MC. The profit-maximising condition is MC = MR. Therefore

$$AVC = MR$$

$$= P\left(1 + \frac{1}{e_p}\right) = P\left(\frac{e_p + 1}{e_p}\right)$$

Thus

$$P = AVC\left(\frac{e_p}{e_p + 1}\right)^3 \qquad (10.5)$$

[3] (i.e. note three at the end of the chapter)

For example, if elasticity of demand is estimated to be equal to –3, then substituting this value for e_p into equation (10.5) gives a value for P of AVC × 1.5. In other words, the markup is equal to 0.5 or 50%. If elasticity of demand were estimated at –4, the equivalent markup would be equal to 0.33 or 33.3%, if it were estimated at –5 the markup would equal 0.25 or 25% and so on. Thus, the higher the elasticity of demand the lower the profit-maximising markup, *cet. par.* Multiproduct firms often set higher markups on products with few substitutes and hence lower elasticities of demand compared with those that have a larger number of substitutes. In supermarkets, basic items like bread, milk and potatoes are often marked up higher than those products such as beer, chocolate and coffee for which a large number of brands, and hence a greater degree of substitutability, exists. Price controls on the deregulated UK utilities are imposed in order to take account of the lack of substitutes and the potential for high markups. Thus, markup pricing implicitly takes account of the extent of competition in the industry and the nature of elasticity of demand for the product.

10.7 NEW PRODUCT PRICING

So far the pricing strategies discussed in this chapter have centred on established products. However, a range of other problems arise in the pricing of completely new products. It should be noted that products that are simply variants on an existing theme and which combine existing product characteristics in different ways, such as a new model of a car or a new 'improved' washing powder, are not considered new products. The main problem facing the firm introducing a completely new product, which is therefore in the introductory stage of its product life cycle, is that it has no idea of its poten-tial demand. It also has to estimate its probable cost function. Having made estimates of both demand and costs, the firm then has to decide upon its pricing strategy for the new product. The main choice is between an initial high skimming price or a low penetration price (Dean, 1950).

A *skimming* price policy involves a high initial price in order to 'skim' the cream off the market and make as much profit from the product as quickly as possible, followed by a series of price reductions over time in order to increase sales continuously. It is analogous to third-degree price discrimination over time. A price skimming strategy is often accompanied by high promotional spending, which also has the effect of maintaining the product's uniqueness. It is more likely to be used if some or all of the following conditions hold:

1   Demand for the product is relatively inelastic in the early stages of its life. This is especially important in the case of products that have a quality image, like calculators, personal computers and most white goods, which can then be priced accordingly when they are first introduced to the market. Demand inelasticity is also significant for products that have a relatively short life-span, like some fashion items.
2   The market can be easily segmented and the firm can take advantage of this in its pricing strategy.
3   Economies of scale are not considered especially significant and so there are no great cost disadvantages by restricting output in the early stages of the product's life.
4   The initial high price is not thought likely to attract new entrants in the short term; other barriers to entry, such as patents or high R&D costs, are likely to exist.

A *penetration* price policy involves a low initial price with the aim of achieving as large a market share as quickly as possible and extending it still further in the future. It is more likely to be used if some or all of these conditions apply:

1   Demand for the product is relatively elastic in the early stages of its life.
2   Economies of scale are significant, so there are substantial cost advantages for the pioneering firm of producing on a large scale.
3   The threat of entry may be considered likely, so the new firm wants to establish a large market share as quickly as possible.
4   The firm has a relatively long-term time horizon.

Penetration pricing is used mainly for food and other basic household items. Direct Line also used this strategy in its introduction of direct-sale insurance in the UK.

It should be noted that the two policies are not mutually exclusive. A firm may charge a high skimming price initially and later adopt a penetration pricing strategy if market conditions change, for example if barriers to entry fall over time and potential entry becomes more likely.

10.8 CONCLUSIONS

This chapter examines a number of the pricing strategies employed by large firms. Initially it is assumed that the firms possess complete knowledge of their demand and cost functions and aim to maximise profits; the pricing techniques are discussed on this basis.

Limit pricing deals with the threat of potential competition rather than with how to cope with actual competition. The traditional limit pricing model is based on the Sylos postulate and the key assumption that a potential entrant expects incumbents to maintain their pre-entry output levels; the entry gap or premium is positively related to MES and the competitive price and negatively related to the size of the market and price elasticity of demand. However, incumbent firms may adjust their pre-entry output levels and use other strategies to deter entry besides price, such as investing in spare capacity. Furthermore, it is implicitly assumed in the basic model that potential entrants are relatively small; a large-scale diversifier may more easily circumvent potential barriers to entry.

Price discrimination occurs when a firm varies its prices for the same product between market segments for reasons not associated with costs. Successful price discrimination requires that a firm has a significant degree of market power, that market segments are distinct and that they have different elasticities of demand. Three categories of price discrimination, first, second and third degree, are considered and examples of each type are provided. In each case the seller expropriates consumer surplus from the market and increases its revenue (and profits) from a given level of sales. Predatory pricing can be regarded as a form of price discrimination which has the express intent of removing competition from the market by pricing below costs; definitional problems arise from ascribing the particular costs involved in the relevant time period.

In those situations where a firm produces joint products that are technologically related and which involve joint costs of production, then a change in one decision variable, say the price or output of one product, will have an impact on the price and output of the other joint product(s). A profit maximiser will equate the sum of the marginal revenues of a change in any such decision variable with the sum of the concomitant marginal costs. Joint products can be produced in fixed or in variable proportions. Peak-load pricing is sometimes practised by the utilities; a product is produced in different time periods and pricing policies reflect this fact. It can be viewed as a special case of a joint product produced in fixed proportions; it is essentially a problem of allocating the joint costs that are involved in supplying a product in different time periods.

Should a firm exchange components between its divisions, it is likely to engage in transfer pricing. In an M-form organisation this technique can facilitate profit maximisation in its individual divisions as well as in the firm as a whole. If there is no external market for the transferred product the firm will employ cost-based transfer prices; market-based prices are used otherwise, although the pricing decision is influenced by whether the external market is perfectly or imperfectly competitive. Evidence suggests that firms employ both cost- and market-based transfer prices and also prices negotiated between the divisions and the respective head offices.

In practice, firms may be uncertain about their cost and demand functions; empirical evidence has highlighted the popularity of cost-based pricing practices, in which firms establish their normal level of capacity utilisation and add a markup to average variable costs. Alternatively, the average full cost pricing technique assumes that firms seek a constant rate of profit in order to have sufficient funds to plough back into the business and price accordingly. In this case the markup is directly related to some expectation of demand. The theoretical relationship between the size of the markup and price elasticity of demand is considered. Empirical evidence reveals that the markup is strongly influenced by market conditions and the state of competition.

Finally, skimming and penetration pricing strategies for new products are discussed and the conditions necessary for their sucessful implementation are outlined.

Case Study: The pricing decision in practice—let's stick together

Studies of the pricing decision at a disaggregated level using data on individual companies and plants are quite rare. In the UK, Hall and Hitch (1939) questioned 38 manufacturing companies about their pricing decisions, and more recently the Lloyds Bank Small Business Research Trust (1995) investigated price-setting procedures among 350 small firms; both surveys reported the extensive use of cost-based pricing practices. In the US, more studies have been performed, with the definitive recent work being that by Blinder (1992) of 72 firms. In the autumn of 1995 the Bank of England (1996) undertook a survey of the pricing behaviour of 654 British companies; the results form the basis of this case study.

Forty-two percent of the firms questioned in the Bank of England (BofE) study were classified as large, each having more than 500 employees, 39% were medium-sized, each with 101–500 employees, and the remainder were classified as small businesses. Sixty-eight percent of the sample were manufacturing firms and 64% could be regarded as oligopolistic in the sense that they each had between one and 10 major competitors. The survey applied the work of Blinder to the UK by comparing the relative popularity for firms of different 'theories' of price setting, with particular emphasis on the reasons for price stickiness. The two most popularly recognised theories in the British survey, with a 54% and a 47% recognition rate respectively, were constant marginal costs (and hence constant average variable costs) and cost-based pricing, the latter being more popular among smaller companies. The existence of implicit and explicit contracts between customers and firms and co-ordination failure, whereby no firm wishes to be the first to change price for fear of starting a price war, were also found to be important reasons for price rigidity. In the US, Blinder found that the most significant factor explaining price stickiness (at least among those companies that recognised it) was changes in non-price variables such as product quality, delivery times or after-sales service, implying variations in real underlying prices.

The median company in the BofE study reviewed its prices once a month, but confirmation of price stickiness was provided by the fact that prices were changed only twice a year (although previous surveys in the US had found that, on average, firms changed their prices just once a year). This suggests that the informational costs (of obtaining data to check if the current price is correct) are not the only significant transaction costs involved in changing prices; there are also other costs, like the expense involved in changing price lists (physical menu costs) and the fears of starting price wars or breaching customer contracts. Large firms reviewed prices most often, although firms (which need not be of large absolute size) in the most concentrated industries changed prices least frequently. The latter is consistent with some, although not all, previous American evidence and supports the notion of greater price collusion in more highly concentrated industries.

Despite the prevalence of cost-based pricing the main factor determining the actual price charged was found to be market conditions: 40% of companies stated that they set prices at the highest level the market could bear and an additional 25% said that they set prices in relation to their competitors. Cost-plus markups were more important for smaller firms and market conditions less so, especially in retailing. Market considerations were also found to be important in explaining price increases or decreases, although price setting was asymmetric in the sense that major differences were reported between those factors affecting price increases and those that led to price reductions. Cost increases were far more important in pushing prices up than were cost decreases in pulling prices down (although this may be due to the relative rarity of cost reductions); on the other hand, an increase in demand was less likely to lead to a price rise than would an decrease in demand produce a price cut. The main factor causing a price cut was a price reduction by a rival, presumably in order to maintain market shares. In boom conditions, firms were more likely to increase overtime working than to increase prices or capacity, although a combination of price, capacity and overtime would be considered if the increase in demand was thought permanent.

Thus, the survey confirms the significance of cost-based pricing procedures. However, the influence of market conditions and the degree of competition in price setting lends support to the idea that many firms may adopt marginalist principles, although lacking the necessary information to practise them fully.

FURTHER READING

Devine, P.J., Lee, N., Jones, R.M. and Tyson, W.J. (1985) *An Introduction to Industrial Economics*, 4th edn (London, George Allen and Unwin), Chapter 6.

Hirshleifer, J. (1956) On the economics of transfer pricing, *Journal of Business*, **29** (June), 172–84.

Koutsoyiannis, A. (1979) *Modern Microeconomics*, 2nd edn (London, Macmillan), Chapters 7, 11–14.

Kregel, J.A. (1975) *The Reconstruction of Political Economy: An Introduction to Post-Keynesian Economics*, 2nd edn (London, Macmillan).

NOTES

1. $e_p = (\Delta Q/\Delta P)/(P/Q)$. $P = P_C$, $Q = Q_C$, $\Delta Q = X$ and $\Delta P = P_L - P_C$. Therefore, $e_p = (X/(P_L - P_C))/(P_C/Q_C)$.

Rearrange to give the formula for P_L.

2. See *The Economist*, 23 October 1993, 'The Man Who Beat Wal-Mart'.

3. Equation (10.5) only applies where the value for price elasticity is more than one; this is where MR > 0, a condition that must hold in order to maximise profits at MC = MR, given that MC > 0.

It can also be noted that, since

$$AVC = P\,(1 + (1/e_p)),$$

therefore

$$MC = P\,(1 + (1/e_p)),$$

Rearranging this equation gives

$$(P - MC)/P = 1/e_p$$

which is the familiar condition (known as the Lerner Index) whereby the optimal markup on price is equal to the reciprocal of the price elasticity of demand.

Questions □ □ □

10.1 An established firm has lower unit costs at all output levels than potential entrants. Contrast short-run profit behaviour with limit pricing policy under these conditions, assuming that the Sylos postulate holds. Discuss the limitations of the limit pricing model based on the Sylos postulate.

10.2 Distinguish between the various types of price discrimination. Discuss the conditions necessary for each to take place and any possible welfare implications.

10.3 A book publisher with a significant amount of monopoly power decides to charge students a lower annual rate for a journal compared with the rate charged to the general public. The general public's demand is estimated as $Q_1 = 4000 - 20P$, whereas the students' demand is estimated as $Q_2 = 4000 - 40P$. The firm's total cost function is given by the formula,

$TC = 100\,000 + 10Q$.

(a) Calculate the profit maximising price and level of annual sales in each submarket.
(b) Calculate the total profit of the publisher under these circumstances.
(c) Compare the level of profit in (b) with the profit that the publisher would have made had it charged the same price to all its customers.

10.4 A mining company produces two minerals in fixed proportions, one to one. The demand curves for the two products are estimated as $P_A = 175 - 0.1Q_A$ and $P_B = 250 - 0.05Q_B$. The total cost function of the firm is estimated as $TC = 100\,000 + 20Q + 0.1Q^2$.

(a) Calculate the profit-maximising level of output (in kilos per week) and the price (per kilogram) of each product.
(b) Calculate the total profit of the firm.

10.5 Chillout PLC is a large M-form producer of an item of freeze-drying equipment for food manufacturers. It is divided into distinct profit-maximising manufacturing and distribution divisions. There is no external market for the firm's product. The monthly demand function is given as $P = 380 - 0.02Q$. The total cost function of the firm is estimated as $TC = 150\,000 + 20Q + 0.04Q^2$. The total cost function of the distribution division is estimated as $TC = 50\,000 + 10Q + 0.01Q^2$.

(a) Calculate the transfer price and the level of output of the firm. (Hint: remember that the marginal cost of the manufacturing division equals the marginal cost of the whole firm minus the marginal cost of the distribution division.)

(b) Show that at the appropriate transfer price the level of output supplied by the manufacturing division equals the level demanded by the distribution division.

(c) Calculate the total profit of the firm under these conditions.

Assume now that Chillout can purchase its product from other firms, which operate in a perfectly competitive market. The external market price is given as £100.

(d) Calculate the demand of the distribution division at this price. Assess how this demand is broken down between purchases from the firm's manufacturing division and purchases from the open market.

(e) Assess the effect of the existence of the external market on Chillout's profitability.

10.6 'Markup pricing procedures are based entirely on costs. Demand considerations are deemed superfluous to the pricing decision.' Explain and discuss.

10.7 A profit-maximising manufacturer of chili sauce estimates its weekly demand function as $Q = 30 - 10P$, where Q equals thousands of bottles. The price is set at £2 per bottle. Costs are a constant £0.80 per unit sold.

(a) Calculate the profit-maximising markup (hint: you will need to calculate the price elasticity of demand in order to do this). Show that the price charged is not optimal.

(b) Given the estimated elasticity of demand, calculate the optimal price and output.

10.8 Discuss the conditions necessary for the successful implementation of skimming and penetration pricing policies. Examine the reasons why a firm may change from using one policy to the other during the course of the product life-cycle.

CHAPTER 11

▶ *Advertising and Branding Decisions*

Advertising and other forms of promotional activity affect consumer preferences by enhancing brand loyalties. They act as important determinants of the degree of product differentiation, which in turn is instrumental in defining markets and market segments. By engaging in such *non-price competitive practices* a firm aims to influence the shape and position of its demand curve. Advertising and other marketing strategies also affect a firm's costs. By affecting both demand and costs these promotional activities can strongly influence the degree of competition in a market. The relative importance of advertising in the total marketing mix has diminished in recent years, but it still represents a significant outlay for most large firms. It also probably has a stronger effect on sales than other promotional weapons. Therefore, much of this chapter concentrates on an analysis of the nature and effects of the advertising decision.

We begin by discussing the nature of advertising and examining its relative significance across countries and between product groups; the marked differences in *advertising intensities* across product groups are noted. The *optimal level of advertising expenditure* of the firm is briefly examined; optimisation of the advertising budget alone is considered, followed by an explanation of the joint optimisation of advertising with price. The effect of the nature of the product on advertising expenditures is discussed; particular reference is made to *search* and *experience* characteristics. The two-way relationship between *advertising and the degree of competition* is assessed; the influence of the degree of seller concentration on

advertising intensity is examined; then the effects of advertising on the competitive process are discussed; the empirical evidence on the relationships between advertising and market concentration, prices and profits is outlined. *Advertising as an investment* is briefly considered. *Brand-name* strategies are examined, with particular emphasis on the relationships between advertising, branding and product quality. At the end of the chapter there is a *case study* investigating advertising and the importance of branding in the soluble coffee market of the UK.

11.1 THE NATURE AND EXTENT OF ADVERTISING

Advertising has been defined as

mass paid communication, the ultimate purpose of which is to impart information, develop attitudes and induce action beneficial to the advertiser (Colley, 1961: 51).

As pointed out in Section 7.3, advertising and price represent the two main strategies that a firm has at its disposal that can directly influence the demand for its product. A successful advertising campaign can boost sales by shifting the demand curve to the right; if advertising budgets are reduced, demand falls and the demand curve shifts to the left. According to Colley's definition the purpose of advertising is to *inform* on the one hand and to develop attitudes or to *persuade* on the other. As regards the former function, consumers would like to exercise rational choices, but imperfect information means they are bounded in their rationality; an asymmetry of information occurs between buyer and seller. Advertising improves the flow of information and helps consumers to make better-informed choices. It can also reduce transaction costs. This is the view of advertising that the Austrian school would be more likely to support. Alternatively, by developing attitudes, advertising attempts to direct and to cajole consumer preferences. In practice, it may be extremely difficult to disentangle the informative aspect of advertising from its persuasive function. However, the distinction between them is important in determining the overall effect of advertising on society as a whole. By improving the flow of information and enhancing the competitive process, advertising can have a beneficial effect on economic welfare. On the other hand, by directing consumer preferences, wasting resources and increasing market power it may have harmful welfare consequences.

Advertising is only one of the many forms of *promotional activity* a firm has at its disposal, the others including incentive promotions, free samples, shows, exhibitions and the employment of sales representatives. In fact, these other forms of promoting products, especially price promotions, have become increasingly popular: in 1980 in the UK, advertising formed two-thirds of total marketing spending by firms, whereas by the early 1990s the other forms of promotion accounted for well over a half of all marketing expenditures. The latter aim to increase market share quickly and hence boost short-term profitability, even though they may be used over an extended period. For example, British brewers have used the '13.5% extra free' promotion in the off-licence canned beer market for so long and to such an extent that the 500 ml size can has now come to represent consumer expectations. In the US, grocery-coupon redemption doubled between 1985 and 1992, to $4.6 billion. By the early 1990s, 60% of breakfast cereals were bought on promotions. In the sense that price promotions seek the 'quick fix' of rapid improvements in profitability, they may be symptomatic of a preference within large British and American companies for short-term strategies that may override longer-term aims.

However, since advertising still represents a large-scale item of expenditure for many large firms, especially among certain consumer goods, the advertising decision will be analysed in some detail. This is also due to the fact that advertising represents a more likely method of increasing sales than the other forms of promotional activity. Jones (1995) tracked the effect of advertising on the sales of 142 branded goods in the US during 1991–92 and found that 70% of the campaigns boosted sales immediately, even if in many cases the impact was fairly small. However, adverts had a much greater effect on sales and profits than money-off promotions, which were usually loss-making. The importance of advertising as a strategic weapon for the individual firm can be clearly shown by the success of Microsoft's huge marketing expenditure (reckoned to be close to $1 billion, a high proportion of which comprised its largest ever press and television advertising campaign) heralding the launch of the Windows 95 computer program. As a result, over seven million copies were sold in three months. On the other hand, sales of Virgin Cola, introduced in the UK in 1994 as a rival to the other cola brands, have been relatively poor: about half the expected one billion cans were sold in the first year of production, a fact

Table 56 *Changes in the relative significance of media outlets for advertising expenditures in UK, 1970–92, at current prices (%)*

Year	Press	TV	Outdoor and transport	Cinema	Radio
1970	72.2	22.6	4.0	1.1	0.2
1975	70.5	24.2	3.6	0.7	1.0
1980	66.6	26.6	4.1	0.7	2.1
1985	64.4	29.8	3.6	0.4	1.8
1990	64.4	29.5	3.6	0.5	2.1
1992	62.2	31.7	3.6	0.6	2.0

Source: Adapted from *Advertising Statistics Yearbook*, 1993.

directly attributed to the very low-key advertising campaign, only amounting to about £750 000 per quarter.

The relative significance of the various media outlets for advertising expenditures in the UK over the last 20 years or so is shown in Table 56. The major change, not surprisingly, has been the relative growth of TV advertising, mainly at the expense of the press.

Advertising intensity varies widely, both between countries (expressed as advertising relative to GDP) and within product groups (expressed as advertising relative to sales revenue). Table 57 shows the differences in advertising intensities within various industrial economies. The fact that the UK has a higher advertising intensity than, say, France suggests that the products which are advertised most heavily tend to be relatively more important in the UK than in France.

Table 57 *Advertising expenditure as a percentage of GDP, selected counties, 1982–94*

	1982	1986	1990	1994
UK	1.19	1.44	1.50	1.39
US	1.40	1.55	1.50	1.31
Canada	1.01	1.07	1.11	0.95
Germany	0.75	0.78	0.89	0.96
France	0.50	0.61	0.78	0.62
Italy	0.38	0.53	0.61	0.54
Netherlands	0.77	0.79	0.92	0.89
Spain	0.72	0.98	1.55	0.97
Japan	0.74	0.84	0.99	0.81

Source: Zenith Media Ltd., 1995.

Table 58 *Advertising/sales ratios for various product groups in the UK, 1991*

Product group	Advertising/sales ratio (%)
Cold treatments	20.27
Shampoos	14.75
Vitamins	12.43
Cereals	9.78
Motor insurance	9.61
Toothpaste	8.11
Coffee	6.42
Video games	4.84
Cat food, canned	3.77
Motor engine oil	3.71
Potato crisps	3.42
Watches	2.96
Newspapers	2.12
Cars, new	2.06
Condoms	1.79
DIY decorating	1.50
CD players	1.35
Lager	1.26
Beer	0.93
Carbonated soft drinks	0.86
Washing machines and dryers	0.68
Trainers	0.61
Jeans	0.58
Spectacles	0.15
Curtains	0.09
Hairdressing	0.01

Source: *Advertising Statistics Yearbook*, 1993.

The variations in advertising intensities among product groups in the UK are given in Table 58. Similar patterns emerge in other countries; products with high advertising intensities in the UK usually exhibit similarly high advertising intensities in other industrialised countries. Some goods, for example various pharmaceutical products and toiletries, have high advertising intensities, while others, like curtains and hairdressing, hardly seem to be advertised at all. It should be noted that certain products, such as new cars, are advertised very heavily in absolute terms, although compared with the value of sales their relative level of advertising appears quite small. For example, in 1991 the total advertising budget for new cars in the UK was well over £300 million, by far the largest sum for an individual product area. (In the US in the same year, the amount spent on advertising new cars exceeded $6 billion.)

Sections 11.3 and 11.4 examine some of the possible explanations for the differences in advertising intensities between products; they investigate the relationships between product characteristics and advertising and between the degree of market concentration and advertising. Initially, however, the optimal advertising decision of the firm is briefly discussed.

11.2 THE OPTIMAL LEVEL OF ADVERTISING

An advertising campaign by a firm will achieve a positive contribution as long as the incremental revenues derived from it exceed the incremental costs involved. The latter cover both the actual advertising expenditures themselves plus the additional production costs from any increase in sales. In profit-maximising terms a firm will purchase advertising up to the point where its marginal cost equals the marginal revenue derived from it. The marginal cost of advertising is given by the formula

$$MC_a = \frac{\partial(TC)}{\partial Q} \times \frac{\partial Q}{\partial A} + 1 \qquad (11.1)$$

where Q is output, TC represents production costs and A denotes advertising expenditure, which, it is assumed, can be purchased at a constant cost per unit. The marginal revenue associated with advertising (assuming firms behave atomistically) is given by

$$MR_a = P\,\frac{\partial Q}{\partial A} \qquad (11.2)$$

where P is price.[1]

Dorfman and Steiner (1954) developed a more elaborate analysis of advertising expenditures, in which advertising and price are determined together. This is usually referred to as the *elasticities approach*, since Dorfman and Steiner show that the optimal advertising intensity for a profit-maximising firm is a function of the ratio of the advertising elasticity of demand to price elasticity of demand:[2]

$$\frac{A}{PQ} = -\,\frac{\text{Advertising elasticity of demand}}{\text{Price elasticity of demand}} \qquad (11.3)$$

where A is advertising expenditure, P is price and Q is output. Their model has been adapted by Nerlove and Arrow (1962) to take into account the dynamic effects of advertising:

$$\frac{A}{PQ} = - \frac{\text{Advertising elasticity of demand}}{\text{Price elasticity of demand } (r + d)} \quad (11.4)$$

where r is the rate of discount of the firm and d is the depreciation rate of the effectiveness of the advertising expenditure over time.

There are a number of problems with the traditional, marginalist approach towards optimal advertising decisions by a firm. Most significantly, it assumes that the firm has complete knowledge of its cost, demand and advertising functions. In practice, this is very unlikely. It also assumes an absence of strategic responses, whether price or advertising, by rival firms. The model also takes no account of other forms of promotional and marketing expenditures, which can influence the effectiveness of advertising, although this defect is also true of most models and explanations of advertising behaviour. However, the notion that advertising intensity depends on the ratio of advertising elasticity of demand to price elasticity of demand is not entirely without foundation. In Section 2.1 it was pointed out that, in those segments of the new car market particularly associated with image or style, consumers tend to be influenced at least as much by advertising as by price. It may be that products which are in some way connected with image or style, like certain brands of lager, fashion accessories and cosmetics, have higher advertising intensities than other products because their demand is more responsive to advertising than to price (see also Clarke, 1985). In other words, the nature of the product can have a significant effect on advertising and price elasticities of demand and hence on advertising intensities.

11.3 ADVERTISING INTENSITY AND THE NATURE OF THE PRODUCT

Probably the most notable feature about relative advertising intensities is that consumer goods are much more heavily advertised than producer or industrial goods. There are various reasons for this. The markets for producer goods are generally quite small and hence not particularly suited to large-scale advertising campaigns. The buyers of producer goods, although often quite well informed about their products, usually require specific information and this can be better provided by sales representatives. Whatever advertising does exist for producer goods is likely to be of the informational variety.

There are also wide variations in advertising intensities between consumer goods, as can be seen from Table 58, page 217. Certain types of consumer goods may be more prone to particular types of advertising. If consumers are faced with imperfect information about products they will undertake *search* activities in order to improve their knowledge (Stigler, 1961). Search may consist of verbal contacts between consumers, reading publications and journals and visiting retail outlets. Firms can also help to provide the available information via advertising. According to Stigler the proportion of the market that receives the information from any advertising message is subject to diminishing returns. Customers also enter and leave the market continuously. Stigler surmised that the greater the 'turnover' in potential buyers the greater the level of advertising, *cet par*. However, as turnover increases relative to the number of potential customers receiving the information, eventually the optimal level of advertising will decline. The Stigler analysis relates specifically to informational advertising. Doyle (1968), on the other hand, put forward reasons for the prevalence of persuasive advertising. Goods that are relatively cheap are unlikely to lead to a great deal of search activity on the part of consumers and hence are more likely to be subject to persuasive advertising. The same can be said of goods which consumers find hard to appraise because of their complexity, like many consumer durables.

Nelson (1974) elaborated on these points by suggesting that consumer goods can be split into those with *search* and those with *experience qualities*. Goods with search qualities can be evaluated prior to purchase; hence, search qualities include style, size, weight and colour, search products comprising most items of clothing, curtains and jewellery. Goods with experience qualities can only be appraised after purchase. Experience qualities cover factors like taste or effectiveness; thus, experience goods include many food items, alcoholic drinks, shampoos, hair conditioners and the repair expenditures of consumer durables. In the former case, advertising is more likely to be informational, whereas for experience goods, advertising will be more likely to influence and persuade the consumer. Experience goods are advertised more intensively because consumers have no other source of information and firms are seeking to persuade. The fact that search qualities enable consumers to seek out the most appropriate purchases also means that the demand for search products is more responsive to price than is the demand for experience goods, which is more susceptible to persuasive advertising campaigns. In other words, search goods have a lower advertising to price elasticity ratio than experience goods and hence a lower advertising intensity. Nelson confirmed this hypothesis in an investigation into 40 products in the US in 1957. (Darby and Karni, 1973 introduced a third category, *credence goods,* whose qualities are not easily identifiable, even after repeated purchases, e.g. the services of doctors, lawyers and accountants.)

Davis *et al.* (1991) took the analysis further by dividing products into four categories: search, short-term experience, long-term experience and goods where experience is of little value. They then analysed the advertising intensities of over 300 products in the UK in 1989. They found that search products were advertised least intensively with an average advertising/sales ratio of 0.41. These were followed by goods where experience is of little value, such as new cars and other consumer durables, which are purchased only rarely. They had an average advertising intensity of 1.79. On the other hand, short-term experience goods, like instant coffee, facial tissues or lager, had an average advertising intensity of 3.56. Consumers are able to decide quite quickly whether it is worth purchasing them again. The most intensively advertised were long-term experience goods, such as hair conditioner, shampoo and cat food, with an average advertising/sales ratio of 5.04. Consumers can only glean the necessary information about these products if they buy them repeatedly over a long period. However, this sort of analysis still may not be able to explain satisfactorily the large absolute amounts spent on advertising some products. As has been mentioned, the advertising/sales ratio for new cars is relatively low because the absolute level of sales is so high. It may be that new cars actually represent some kind of long-term experience good about which consumers feel that they gain useful knowledge from their occasional repeat purchases. The fact that £100 million was spent on advertising various brands of lagers in the UK in 1991 could be more to do with perpetuating a particular product image than with anything else; the value of image may outweigh the value of experience of the good in the mind's eye of the consumer.

Davies *et al.* also analysed the relationship between advertising/sales ratios and the frequency of purchase. Goods purchased very frequently would be expected to have low advertising intensities; potential customer turnover would be low. Customers would also not be likely to forget information about the

product if it were purchased frequently. By the same token, goods purchased only once, or at least very seldom, would also probably have low advertising/sales ratios. The study found that the highest advertising ratios were for those products bought less than once a month and more than once every six months. It also found a positive relationship between advertising intensity and product quality in the case of long-term experience goods, whose attributes cannot easily be monitored. Consumers continue to purchase the product if it is perceived to be of good quality and a high advertising intensity may be regarded as indicative of good quality.

Finally, advertising intensity may vary with the degree of product innovation in a market. Markets that have a high level of product innovation may have a high advertising intensity in order to keep consumers well informed about the new products, models or brands that are available. Table 58, page 217, confirms that products with a high turnover of products and brands, such as pharmaceuticals, toiletries, some groceries and video games, all have relatively high advertising intensities.

11.4 THE EFFECT OF SELLER CONCENTRATION ON ADVERTISING INTENSITY

According to the Dorfman–Steiner analysis, the lower the price elasticity of demand for the product, the higher is its advertising intensity, *cet. par.* This implies that there should be a linear relationship between the degree of concentration in an industry and advertising/sales ratios. In perfectly competitive industries, characterised by very low seller concentration, the demand for each firm's product is perfectly elastic. Advertising is non-existent, perfectly competitive firms having no need to advertise because they sell a homogenous product. Each firm's product is a perfect substitute for the products of all the other firms in the market. In more concentrated markets there is a lower degree of substitutability between the products of rival firms. Product differentiation means that each firm's product is not a perfect substitute for the products of the other firms in the market. The demand for each firm's product tends to be more price inelastic; advertising intensity is greater, *cet. par.* If this argument is taken to its logical conclusion, the highest advertising intensity would be in the most highly concentrated markets of all, pure monopolies. Assuming no rivals, there is no product substitutability. However,

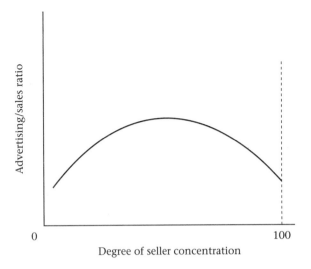

Figure 82 *The relationship between the degree of seller concentration and advertising intensity.*

the fact that the pure monopolist faces little or no competition reduces its incentive to advertise.

Such an analysis of the relationship between seller concentration and advertising intensity is far too simplistic. It takes no account of the impact on advertising intensity of the nature of the product or of rivals' reactions to one firm's advertising campaign. In fact most, although not all, evidence suggests that advertising intensity is highest in moderately concentrated industries. Advertising/sales ratios decline as high levels of concentration are reached. In other words, there is thought to be some kind of quadratic inverted U-shaped relationship between the degree of seller concentration and advertising intensity (see e.g. Clarke, 1985; Devine *et al.*, 1985; and Shepherd, 1990 for a summary of the evidence). The relationship is shown in Figure 82.

There are two other points that should be noted. Firstly, the relationship only applies to those products that are likely to be advertised, not to all products. Secondly, a number of the studies in this area have not made it completely clear in which direction the basic tenet runs, seller concentration determining advertising intensity or the other way about. Thus, any general conclusions about the relationship need to be treated with some caution.

Various reasons have been advanced for why advertising intensity should rise with the degree of seller concentration. The 'stickiness' of prices in oligopolistic markets means that firms are more likely to engage in various forms of non-price competition.

Obviously, firms with the greatest incentive to pursue rivalrous policies are those that have the most to gain by taking sales from their competitors. The competitiveness and uncertainty found among oligopolistic firms gives them this incentive. A price cut, should it occur, can be matched quickly by rival firms, whereas an advertising campaign takes a long time to mount and cannot be so easily followed by rivals, at least not without a long time lag. Any firm clearly has an incentive to undertake a campaign and so steal a march on its rivals.

The characteristic uncertainty and interdependence of oligopolistic markets and their effect on advertising budgets can be seen more clearly by the use of game theory (see also Sections 5.5 and 8.6). Assume that two duopolistic firms, A and B, dominate a market. Each one is aware that its advertising outlay will have a stong influence on not just its own, but also the other firm's sales and profit. There are various advertising strategies that each can pursue. These are summarised in Table 59, which shows a symmetrical, non-zero sum game, in which the outcomes do not add to zero. If both firms spend £2.0 million on advertising in a year, they each make an expected £6.0 million profit as a result of the campaign. If either firm increases its advertising budget to £3.0 million, while the other firm keeps its spending at £2.0 million, then the profit of the former rises to £8.5 million and the profit of the latter decreases to £5.0 million. As is the case with price strategy, there are various policies that each firm can follow. However, in this instance, there is a long time lag between the conception of the idea for an advertising campaign and actually putting that campaign into practice. This means that each firm has an additional incentive to mount some kind of campaign each year in order not to lose sales to its rival. The problem is

Table 59 *A payoff matrix for two firms, indicating advertising strategies*[a]

	B's advertising outlay p.a. (£ millions)		
A's advertising outlay p.a. (£ millions)	2	3	4
2	6.0, 6.0	5.0, 8.5	2.5, 9.0
3	8.5, 5.0	8.0, 8.0	7.0, 7.5
4	9.0, 2.5	7.5, 7.0	6.5, 6.5

[a]Each element gives the expected profits of the two firms in £ millions, A's profit figure being given first.

how much to spend, especially if the two firms do not co-operate in any way. If each firm is risk-averse it would spend £3 million. Then, no matter what the other firm does, the worst that could happen is that it would make £7.0 million profit. This is the *minimax* or 'best of the worst' strategy. On the other hand, the *maximax* or 'best of the best' tactic, suitable for a risk seeker, would be to spend £4 million on advertising in order to try to secure expected profits of £9 million. However, this would only be achieved if the other firm obligingly spends only £2 million. Of course, assuming that the two firms are not co-operating, there is no reason why this should occur. If each firm spends £4 million, profits are less than if each had only spent £3 million, new sales per advertising message perhaps becoming harder to attract. The effectiveness of additional messages may decline the more that is spent, a topic that is dealt with in more detail in the next section.

Another possible reason why advertising intensity may rise with the degree of seller concentration is the suggestion of a positive relationship between concentration and profitability; such a relationship is by no means proven (see Section 2.2), but assuming that it exists, then the higher price–cost margins provide firms with the necessary funds for large-scale advertising campaigns. In addition, high advertising expenditures may have the effect of raising entry barriers and reducing the scope for competition (see next section). The evidence on the relationship between profitability and advertising intensity is fairly mixed. It is also complicated by the possibility of a two-way relationship between the two variables, although profit margins appear to be a stronger determinant of advertising/sales ratios than the reverse process, advertising intensity determining profits (see Hay and Morris, 1979; Devine *et al.*, 1985; Ferguson and Ferguson, 1994).

Eventually, at relatively high concentration levels, advertising intensity may fall. In highly concentrated markets there is less scope to attact sales from rivals and so less incentive to engage in intensely competitive and expensive advertising campaigns. In a tight, highly concentrated oligopoly there is also likely to be a greater recognition among rival firms of the mutually beneficial effects of reducing their respective levels of advertising. In addition, highly concentrated oligopolistic markets are more likely to be fairly mature. In a mature market there is less scope to attract entirely new sales and hence less incentive to undertake large-scale advertising campaigns.

11.5 THE EFFECT OF ADVERTISING ON THE DEGREE OF SELLER CONCENTRATION

It was noted in the previous section that there may be a two-way relationship between advertising intensity and the competitiveness of a market, as indicated by its degree of market concentration. This section examines the arguments and the evidence regarding how advertising intensity might affect the degree of seller concentration and also prices.

Advertising can increase the degree of seller concentration in a market by acting as a barrier to entry. Product differentiation, particularly when associated with advertising, was given as one of the main exogenous barriers to entry in Section 2.4. Firms can also use advertising as a strategic weapon to hinder possible new entry. According to Comanor and Wilson (1967) there are two main ways in which advertising can represent a barrier to new entry. Firstly, established firms build up considerable brand loyalty towards their products through advertising. Therefore, prospective new entrants have to advertise at least as much and probably a lot more than existing firms in order to build up a similar stock of goodwill towards their own brands. Furthermore, the large initial outlay on advertising, which is in addition to the other capital requirements necessary to enter a particular market, may act as another obstacle to entry.

Secondly, there are economies of scale within advertising itself. Advertising costs per unit of output may fall because there are lower unit costs in purchasing larger amounts of advertising messages. Advertising economies may be either pecuniary or technical. Pecuniary economies are usually the result of large advertising campaigns that secure preferential rates; technical economies may stem from the more efficient organisation of advertising resources as more is spent. In addition, the advertising messages may become increasingly effective the more that they are repeated (rather than less effective as surmised in the previous section), in which case sales will rise proportionately more than the quantity of advertising. The positive relationship between the quantity of advertising and the effectiveness of the messages is more likely to occur after some threshold level of advertising is reached; this is needed to provide the initial stimulus to demand. The question of whether advertising messages become more or less effective the more that they are repeated is a controversial one.

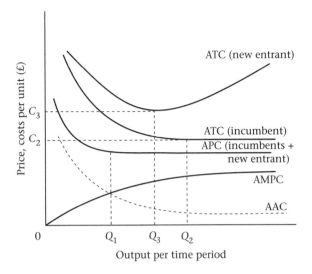

Figure 83 *Advertising as a barrier to entry. AAC = average advertising costs; AMPC = average market penetration costs; APC = average production costs; ATC = average total costs.*

According to Stigler (1961) there are diminishing rather than increasing returns to the frequency of advertising messages. Consumers become more aware of the product the more that the message is repeated. Therefore, fewer new customers can be tapped. Evidence is limited, but tends to support the hypothesis of the declining effectiveness of repeated advertising messages (Schmalensee, 1976; Jones, 1995).

The role of advertising as a barrier to entry is shown in Figure 83. Q_1 gives the MES for production for incumbents and Q_2 the MES in both production and advertising, providing a minimum average cost of C_2. The effects of the additional penetration costs for a new entrant are to restrict the MES level of output to Q_3 and to raise minimum average costs to C_3. C_2C_3 indicates the entry gap, given small-scale entry (i.e assuming that Q_3 is a relatively small fraction of the market).

Evidence on the extent to which advertising intensity acts as a barrier to entry is fairly mixed. Some studies conclude that advertising has little or no impact on barriers to entry, while others find evidence that it does act as an obstacle to prospective new firms (See Ferguson and Ferguson, 1994).

The strategic use of advertising may also have indirect consequences for seller concentration; in this way advertising can act as an endogenous entry barrier. The strategic role of advertising varies depending on the likelihood of entry (Lyons, 1987).

Assuming that advertising is necessary in order to inform possible customers of a firm's existence and that, once informed, some customers will continue to purchase the product from the incumbent and do not need to be further informed, then advertising has the direct effect of increasing the firm's market share and reducing the potential market for an entrant. The larger its market share the greater the cost to the incumbent of having to fight a price war. If entry is possible but not inevitable, it may adopt a 'lean and hungry look' and reduce advertising expenditure as a signal to the prospective entrant that the incumbent is prepared to engage in a price war on entry. In such circumstances, therefore, the established firm may underinvest in advertising as a strategic deterrent to entry, as long as the indirect effect of the possibility of a price war and reduced post-entry market share for the newcomer outweighs the direct effect of low advertising increasing the entrant's expected market share. On the other hand if entry is inevitable the incumbent may adopt a 'fat cat' pose, suggesting little desire to fight a price war. It increases its advertising in order to raise its market share and hence reduce the potential market of the entrant. In this case the incumbent strategically overinvests in advertising, which raises its market share, reduces the potential share of the entrant and indirectly acts as a counterbalance to a price war. Of course, if the prospective new entrant is a large-scale diversifier rather than a fairly small-scale rival, its incursion into a market is far less likely to be impeded by the prospect of either having to fight a price war or of having to undertake a sizeable advertising campaign.

Advertising can also reduce competitiveness in a market by increasing the extent of perceived product differentiation on the part of consumers, who are persuaded to purchase a product that they may not necessarily want. The effect is to lower both the price elasticity of demand and the cross elasticity of demand for the product, increase market power and raise prices. In addition, a successful advertising campaign may involve an element of luck. The success of some campaigns may set up, or reinforce, Gibrat-style influences on market concentration (see Section 2.3). Examples of firms that have succeeded in gaining rapid market shares by pursuing some kind of innovative marketing technique or advertising campaign were discussed in Section 3.2. On the other hand, the informational role of advertising raises both price and cross elasticities in a market by adding to the information that consumers have about the available products. The extra information has the effect

---

Box 11.1 *Evidence on the effects of advertising*

The evidence on the effects of advertising on market concentration is fairly inconclusive. Studies either report a positive relationship, a negative relationship or no relationship between the two variables (See Clark, 1985; and Ferguson and Ferguson, 1994; for a summary. More recently, Sass and Saurman, 1995, found a negative relationship in local malt beverage markets in the US.) The issue is clouded by the previously alluded-to possibility of a two-way relationship between advertising and market concentration.

The results of studies assessing the implications of advertising for prices are equally mixed. These studies investigate the effects of advertising on relative prices by comparing prices for advertised and unadvertised brands; they also examine the effect of advertising on the level of absolute prices in a market. In each case, in relative price terms or in absolute price terms, there is evidence of advertising having either a positive, a negative or no effect on prices. For example, Stephen (1994) found that there was no difference between the fees of solicitors who do advertise and who do not advertise. On the other hand, for lower-priced property some forms of advertising reduce the absolute level of prices, a conclusion which is consistent with the advertising-as-information view. Lal and Matutes (1994) also found a negative relationship between advertising and prices in certain retail markets, whereas Sibly (1995) reported a fairly neutral effect of advertising on absolute prices. (See Ferguson and Ferguson, 1994 for an excellent summary of the earlier evidence of the effects of advertising on prices.) The extent to which advertising determines concentration may also be deduced by examining its effect on the stability of market shares. If advertising enhances concentration it should stabilise market shares. If, on the other hand, it promotes competition market shares should be more unstable. Das *et al.* (1993) found a positive relationship between advertising intensity and market share instability, as did Berndt *et al.* (1995). Their conclusions supported most other evidence in this area. Caves and Porter (1978) and Meisel (1981) reported a positive relationship between the number of brands in a market, and consequently other forms of non-price competition such as advertising intensity and market share instability. In other words, this evidence suggests that the pro-competitive, and hence the informational, role for advertising is paramount.

---

of reducing market power and lowering prices. Furthermore, by increasing sales advertising can lead to lower costs and prices via the exploitation of production economies of scale.

11.6 ADVERTISING AS AN INVESTMENT

In Section 11.2 it was pointed out that the Dorfman–Steiner theory can be adapted to take into account the dynamic effects of advertising. Advertising may not just have an impact on sales in the current period; a particular campaign can have a lagged effect on sales in future periods. A firm may be able to take advantage of this fact by continuing its advertising campaign over several time periods. By capturing the delayed response on the part of consumers from each campaign, a cumulative effect on sales may be observed.

The fact that advertising can have an effect on sales revenue in several periods suggests that it can be thought of more as an investment project than as a current cost. It will then need to be compared with all the other investment projects that a firm is currently appraising. A higher relative net present value or rate-of-return figure signals its potential feasibility.

11.7 BRAND-NAME STRATEGIES

A *brand name* is a title or label that is given usually to a group of products (although it can be given to a single product) in order to identify it more closely in the mind's eye of the consumer. It is important to distinguish between products and brands, although the two terms are often used interchangeably. Jeans is the generic term, Levi Strauss, Wrangler, Lee, Joe Bloggs and so on are the brand names. Each of these brand names may also cover a variety of other types of clothing, such as shirts, jackets, T-shirts and sweaters.

Advertising is often vital for a firm in developing and perpetuating the image of a brand. Establishing and maintaining a desired product image and the reputation for quality that may go along with it is the main benefit to be derived from an effective branding policy. Once customers have become accustomed to purchasing a particular brand (and hence have been been captured) they often remain loyal and are willing to pay more for the branded items than for similar unbranded goods; increased sales and profits follow. Thus, brands are often associated with a particular level of quality, whether perceived or genuine. On the other hand, brand loyalty backed up by persuasive advertising may form an effective

---

Box 11.2 *The importance of branding*

Evidence of the importance for a firm in gaining and maintaining a successful brand name is shown by the fact that in a number of acquisitions the brand has been purchased at well above its current estimated value: Kohlberg Kravis Roberts paid $25 billion for RJR Nabisco, over double its book value; Philip Morris purchased Kraft for $12.9 billion, four times its book value; Nestlé bought Rowntree for £2.4 billion, five times its book value. Once established, brands often remain popular: in 19 out of 22 product categories in the US the main brand in the early 1990s had also been the brand leader in 1925. In fact, consumers ranked General Electric second in the food blender category, although the company had not manufactured the product for more than 20 years.[3] In Japan, where the number of new products has always been high, the preponderance of brands reached epidemic proportions during the 1980s: about 700 new soft drinks were launched each year in the late 1980s, 90% of which did not last longer than a year.[4]

barrier to entry. Brands also enhance and perpetuate the segmentation of markets. They enable firms to position their products correctly in order to secure maximum competitive advantage. In Section 2.1 it was noted that the European new car market can be divided into (at least) seven distinct segments. Within each segment each branded producer offers alternative versions of the same model in order to secure as great a share of the segment as possible; new models can also be more effectively introduced and marketed using the established brand name.

Successful branding is a function of a number of (usually interdependent) factors. Doyle (1989) identified four main areas that can determine brand performance: quality, innovation, superior service and differentiation. However, quality, embodying features like reputation, performance and durability, is itself a function of process and product innovation and pre- and after-sales service activity. Porter (1980) centred on product differentiation, based on the adoption of an identifiable brand image, as the key factor in determining a profitable branding strategy:

Differentiation provides insulation against competitive rivalry because of brand loyalty by customers and resulting lower sensitivity to price. It also increases margins, which avoids the need for a low-cost position (Porter, 1980: 38).

Differentiation can encompass the other factors identified by Doyle: product quality, the employment

of the latest techniques and features and superior customer service. Since experience (and credence) goods are more price inelastic and will more probably have higher advertising intensities than search products, they are also more likely to be based on a branding strategy that differentiates them in various ways from rival products. One way is to employ persuasive advertising techniques.

Branding also enables firms to engage in a *product proliferation* strategy, whereby the 'characteristics space' is filled by a number of different brands, with the result that the gaps left in the market are insufficient for potential new entrants to produce profitably at the MES level of output. Product proliferation offers greater choice to the consumer, but it also acts as another potential obstacle to new entrants. Such a strategy is popular in a number of industries, such as breakfast cereals, soaps and detergents, and beer and lager production. In each of these industries the incumbents produce a large variety of brand-name products designed to capture as much of the product space as possible. The worldwide cosmetics industry is the latest in which product proliferation strategy has prospered:

... the $66 billion cosmetics business is becoming just another consumer-goods industry dominated by three or four giants, each owning many brands, competing with a range of retailers' own-brands and products designed for niche markets. A combination of high margins and fragmented local markets made cosmetics an inevitable target for the consumer-goods giants (*The Economist*, 21 October 1995: 97).

The largest cosmetics companies and some of the brands that they supply are shown in Table 60. The competition between these manufacturers to capture and maintain market shares, coupled with competition from retailers selling their own brands, has led to an explosion of new product launches. In the first quarter of 1995, over 100 new scents were launched. In order to survive in such a competitive environment, some of the relatively smaller firms have had to develop niche markets. For example, Japan's Shiseido, although a mass-producer at home, sells its products as top of the range elsewhere.

While brand performance is a function of a number of different factors, it is managerial recognition and development of these factors that is the key to a successful branding strategy. This point has been made elsewhere:

... it is important to note that it is not brands per se which add value but, rather brand management skills ... Such skills

Table 60 *The world's largest cosmetics companies and selected brands, 1994*

Company	Turnover[a] ($bn)	Selected cosmetic and scent brands
L'Oreal Group	8.17	Lancôme, Plénitude, Ralph Lauren
Procter & Gamble	6.00[b]	Cover Girl, Max Factor, Oil of Olay
Unilever	5.62	Calvin Klein, Chesebrough-Pond's, Elizabeth Arden
Shiseido	4.80	Clé de Peau, Issey Miyake, Jean Paul Gaultier
Estée Lauder	2.94	Aramis, Clinique, Prescriptives
Avon Products	2.60	Anew, Avon Colour, Daily Revival
Johnson & Johnson	2.50	Neutrogena, Johnson's Baby Care, RoC
Sanofi	1.98	Nina Ricci (56.8%), Parfums Yves Saint Laurent, Yves Rocher (62.8%)
Wella Group	1.90	Charles Jourdan, Gucci, Parfums Rochas
Beiersdorf	1.86	Juvena, La Prairie, Nivea

[a]Includes scents and skin- and hair-care products.
[b]Estimated.

Source: *The Economist*, 21 October 1995, 'Brands and the Cosmetic Industry'.

are revealed in the marketing plans of companies, and are manifested in decisions regarding price, distribution and communications for the product or service in question. Clearly, a brand will only be as strong as the management processes which support its marketing position (Egan, 1994: 76).

However, the short-term corporate philosophy which may have been instrumental in bringing about a fall in the relative importance of advertising and the growth of price promotions may also have had an impact on branding strategies. Some firms have suffered from having brand managers remain in their jobs for only a couple of years. As a result, such brands may have been denied the necessary product development. This problem has been exacerbated by a policy of charging excessively high prices for some well-known brands. Procter & Gamble's Pampers was for long the acknowleged brand leader in the nappy market, but a price premium of almost 35% above its rivals has led to a steady decline in its market share. 'Brand-stretching', or the use of a brand name to cover an increasingly diverse range of items, created image problems for both Levi Strauss and Gucci. Cadillac suffered from taking its top-of-the-range brands downmarket.[5]

Other market developments have had implications for brand strategies. The growth of own-label retailing (in the UK, own-labels accounted for 36% of the grocery market in 1994, in Germany 23%, in France 20% and in the US 18%) has resulted in large consumer-goods conglomerates like Procter & Gamble and Unilever dispensing with lesser-known brand names and putting a greater effort into their more successful items. In Japan, the recession of the early 1990s and the declining levels of corporate profitability led to a sharp downturn in the number of new brands that were introduced. Ajinomoto, a large food company, launched an average of 31 new kinds of frozen foods each year in the late 1980s; in 1992 it introduced 19. In 1988, Matsushita had 5000 audio products available; in 1993, it had cut this to 1000.[6] A successful branding strategy needs to be based on an efficient managerial response to changes in market conditions.

11.8 CONCLUSIONS

Advertising both informs and persuades: the net effect on economic welfare of advertising (at least from a traditional perspective) has to balance improvements in information flows and enhanced competition against the direction of consumer preferences, increased market power and the possible waste of resources. Other forms of promotional expenditure, especially price promotions, have assumed increased significance in recent years. However, advertising expenditure remains a significant outlay for many large firms; it is also more likely to have a positive impact on sales than the other types of promotional spending. The growth in the relative importance of TV advertising is noted; the greater advertising intensity (advertising relative to respective GDPs) of the UK and the US compared with other industrial economies is highlighted; the variations in advertising intensities (advertising relative to sales) between product groups is commented upon.

The optimum level of advertising for a profit-maximising firm is where the marginal cost of advertising equals the marginal revenue derived from it. On a somewhat more sophisticated level, it can be shown that the optimum advertising intensity is a function of the ratio of the advertising elasticity of demand to price elasticity of demand.

Consumer goods are more highly advertised than producer goods. There are also wide differences in advertising intensities between consumer goods: search goods, for which advertising is more likely to perform an informational function, are less intensely advertised than experience goods, which are subject to both informational and persuasive forms of advertising. Empirical evidence confirms that short-term and long-term experience goods are most heavily advertised. Advertising intensity also varies with frequency of purchase and with the the degree of product innovation.

A two-way relationship exists between the degree of seller concentration and advertising intensity: on the one hand, higher seller concentration may lead to greater advertising intensity and on the other hand, advertising intensity, by acting as a barrier to entry, can enhance the degree of seller concentration. Empirical evidence suggests that advertising intensity is highest in moderately concentrated industries; evidence on the effect of advertising intensity on seller concentration, however, is fairly inconclusive.

Since advertising can affect sales in future periods as well as in the current period, it can be regarded as an investment by the firm, in which case the initial capital outlay is compared with the sum of the discounted net revenues associated with the campaign.

Branding strategies, of which advertising usually forms an integral part, are examined. The importance for a firm of establishing and maintaining a brand image and the reputation for quality associated with it, is discussed. Branding also enables a firm to engage in product proliferation, whereby the characteristics space is filled by offering for sale a number of different brands; this can reduce the scope for profitable entry. It is argued that the key to a successful branding strategy is management skills in determining those factors that influence brand performance and in responding effectively to changes in market conditions.

Case Study: Advertising and branding in the soluble coffee market-instant success?

The instant or soluble coffee market was investigated by the Monopolies and Mergers Commission (MMC, 1991) in order to assess whether the market for instant coffee manufacture constituted a monopoly and, if so, whether any aspect of it operated against the public interest. Since this market is dominated by a few firms, each of which is engaged in heavy advertising of its most popular brands, it also provides a useful example of a number of the issues raised in this chapter.

The major suppliers and brands

The instant coffee market in the UK is a highly concentrated oligopoly. As Table 61 indicates, it is dominated by a few large suppliers, of which by far the largest is Nestlé with a market share of 56% by value and almost 48% by volume. (The disparity between the value and volume figures reflects the higher realisation net of rebates and discounts achieved on Nestlé brands compared with other firms.) The second largest supplier is General Foods Ltd (GFL), a subsidiary of Philip Morris Companies Inc., which has just under a quarter of the market in both value and volume terms. GFL is followed by Lyons Tetley, a subsidiary of Allied Domecq PLC, with slightly more

Table 61 *Market shares of major suppliers and main brands for instant coffee in the UK in 1989*

Company	Market shares	
	Value (%)	Volume (%)
Nestlé	56.0	47.5
Nescafé	40.8	35.7
Nescafé decaffeinated	2.9	2.4
Gold Blend	7.1	5.3
Gold Blend decaffeinated	2.4	1.7
Blend 37	1.3	1.0
Others	1.5	1.3
GFL	24.7	24.9
including:		
Maxwell House	8.7	8.7
Maxwell House Decaff.	0.5	0.5
Kenco regular	2.3	1.8
Kenco Decaff.	1.1	0.8
Café Hag granules	3.4	2.9
Café Hag Freeze-Dried	0.6	0.4
Mellow Birds	2.4	2.4
Other	0.4	0.4
Brooke Bond	5.7	5.7
including:		
Red Mountain	4.6	4.6
Red Mountain Decaff.	0.7	0.7
Lyons-Tetley	8.3	12.8
Other suppliers	5.2	9.2
Brand analysis		
Nestlé	56.0	47.5
GFL	19.5	18.0
Brooke Bond	5.7	5.7
Other branded	3.5	4.7
Own label	15.2	24.1

Source: MMC (1991:13).

than 8% by value and almost 13% by volume. The fourth largest supplier is Brooke Bond, a subsidiary of Unilever PLC, with nearly 6% of the market. The other suppliers together have a little over 5% of the market in value terms and 9% in volume terms. In value terms the C_2 ratio is 80.7 and the C_4 ratio equals 94.7.

The table also shows that the best-selling brand (combing regular and decaffeinated types) is Nescafé, with a 38% volume share, followed by GFL's Maxwell House, with a 9% share and Nestlé's Gold Blend 7% by volume. The fourth-selling brand is Brooke Bond's Red Mountain with a market share of just over 5%. All Nestlé's coffees are sold under the Nestlé brand. GFL does not employ such umbrella branding, but instead uses a range of seemingly unconnected brand names.

Own-label brands (supplied by many of the major food retailers) account for about a quarter of the market by volume. Lyons-Tetley concentrates on supplying own-label coffees to the supermarket chains, which explains why its unit realisations are less than the market average. About

260 brands of instant coffee were available in the market at the time of the report. Most instant coffee is sold in the main supermarket chains in which there are 33–38 different brands usually available, including own-label. The market can also be subdivided according to the type of coffee, whether freeze-dried, granular, powdered or decaffeinated.

The branding of instant coffee

As was pointed out in Section 11.3, coffee is classified as a short-term experience good. Consumers can decide quite quickly, maybe after a single purchase, whether it is worth buying a particular brand again. Such a good is usually associated with a strong branding policy and heavy levels of advertising.

Many instant coffees are strongly branded and advertising plays an important role in the branding process. Nescafé has made a long-term investment in the brand's development. It has promoted the quality aspect of the instant coffee market through a combination of packaging, name, style, advertising and pricing strategies. All the major suppliers have adopted similar branding strategies, in which product quality plays a key role. As a repeat purchase experience good, product quality is considered an essential part of the branding strategy for instant coffee. There is also evidence of product proliferation. This is largely based on taste positioning strategies, in which taste is classified according to colour intensity, roastiness, bitterness, body, degree of Arabic flavour, juiciness and smoothness.

The suppliers undertake a variety of promotions in addition to their advertising activities. The promotions consist either of direct-to-the-consumer strategies (using the press or door-to-door leaflets), in-store promotions or 'on-label' promotions geared towards the current purchases of consumers. Such promotions aim to increase brand loyalty and encourage a greater frequency of purchase. Nestlé reported that it considers such promotions to be more short-term in their effects, whereas advertising campaigns are regarded mainly as long-term investments in the brand name.

Advertising strategies

Table 62 shows that there is a considerable amount of advertising and promotional activity within the industry, some of which may be considered symptomatic of excessive rivalry. Between 1985 and 1989, advertising and promotional outlays doubled for both Nestlé and GFL, although the real increase was rather less than this because of the 63% increase in television rates (which accounts for half the total expenditures) during the period. One reason for the high levels of advertising in the industry is the nature of the product. Experience goods are advertised heavily because consumers are not able to seek out other sources of information. In these circumstances, firms can use advertising to persuade consumers to purchase their particular brand or brands.

Instant coffee is the sort of product that is bought sufficiently frequently (i.e. less than once a month and more than once every six months) to benefit from high levels of advertising. Producers of soluble coffee also advertise heavily in order to exploit the quality, or the perceived quality, of the product. High advertising intensity is often associated with good quality, all the more so if the characteristics of the product cannot be assessed prior to purchase.

Nestlé's ratio of advertising and other promotional costs to sales is about 13%, which is lower than that of GFL and Brooke Bond. In fact, GFL spends almost as much as Nestlé on advertising and promotional activity, although it only has half Nestlé's market share, indicating that firms in the industry feel the need to match the scale of each other's campaigns. The higher advertising/sales ratios of GFL and Brooke Bond compared with Nestlé may be indicative of their desire not to lose market share. For example, the introduction of the Red Mountain brand by Brooke Bond in 1982 led to a significant surge of advertising spending by all the major producers. Nestlé's

Table 62 *Advertising and promotional expenditure by major instant coffee suppliers in the UK, 1985–89 (£ million)*

Company	Date launched	1985	1986	1987	1988	1989		1985–89
						TV	total	cumulative
Nestlé		14.7	19.3	25.0	30.3	15.3	30.8	120.1
Nescafé	1939	9.3	12.3	15.7	18.4	6.9	18.5	74.2
Blend 37	1955	0.7	1.0	1.3	1.3	1.4	1.8	6.2
Gold Blend	1965	4.2	5.1	6.4	8.3	6.6	8.4	32.2
Fine Blend	1973	0.3	0.5	0.6	0.6	—	0.4	2.5
Nescoré	1975	0.1	0.1	0.1	—	—	—	0.3
Elevenses	1977	0.1	0.1	0.1	0.1	—	—	0.4
Alta Rica/Cap Colombie	1985	—	0.2	0.3	0.6	0.4	0.8	1.9
Non-brand	—	—	0.4	0.9	—	0.9	2.2	
GFL		10.8	19.2	21.1	28.3	17.5	29.9	109.3
Maxwell House	1954	8.1	11.4	14.2	16.8	8.2	14.5	67.3
Café Hag	1979	1.5	1.9	2.2	4.7	4.1	5.9	16.2
Mellow Bird's	1972	1.0	1.8	1.8	1.8	0.5	1.3	7.8
Kenco	1988	—	—	—	2.7	4.7	5.6	8.3
Master Blend	1986	0.1	4.0	2.9	2.2	—	0.3	9.5
Brooke Bond		2.2	3.2	4.4	6.3	2.7	5.8	21.9
Red Mountain	1982	1.4	2.7	4.4	6.1	2.7	5.6	20.2
Other	—	0.7	0.5	0.1	0.2	—	0.2	1.7

Source: MMC (1991:22).

lower advertising intensity could also be explained by economies of scope; it may benefit from 'spillover' effects from one of its brands to another, given that all its brands share the same Nescafé name.

The large capital outlay required for an effective advertising campaign (estimated at £5 million for a national launch of a branded soluble coffee) suggests that such a cost might represent some kind of barrier to entry, although the sum is not out of line with advertising of other branded grocery products. The advertising costs involved in launching Kenco in 1988, amounting to over £8 million in under three years, are indicated in Table 62. On the other hand, advertising costs are probably far lower for entry into more limited local or regional markets or for certain specialised or 'niche' markets. In fact, between about 1988 and 1990, over a dozen new instant coffee brands were intoduced into the UK market. These included new brands by established firms like GFL and Brooke Bond as well as brands produced by new entrants such as Food Brands and Douwe Egberts. The latter have a premium price position and are geared towards the higher-quality market segment. There has also been a large growth in own-label brands, which do not require specific advertising.

Given the rate of new entry, the level of advertising spending does not represent an insurmountable obstacle for prospective new suppliers in the soluble coffee market. As such, advertising does not appear to hinder the competitive process, although, given the fact that not all the new brands can be regarded as direct competitors of those of the major sellers, this may not be true in all market segments. Persuasive advertising lowers competition by increasing perceived product differentiation. As a result, price and cross elasticities are reduced, and prices and profits in the industry are raised. There is evidence of low price and cross elasticities for instant coffee (see Section 7.5) However, there is little evidence, at least according to the report, that advertising, or monopolistic power within the industry *per se*, has resulted in higher prices and profits, despite the fact that Nestlé has a higher level of profitability than the rest of the industry. The report argues that competition remains sufficiently effective to bring a wide range of prices and quality, as well as improvements in quality and in perceived value for money.

Conclusions

Instant coffee manufacture is a highly concentrated market, dominated by Nestlé. All the major producers sell a variety of brands, except Lyons-Tetley, which concentrates on supplying own-label brands. As a short-term experience good, soluble coffee is strongly branded and highly advertised. An association with perceived product quality is a significant part of the branding process. Brand proliferation based on taste positioning is evident. Other promotional activities are also an important part of the overall marketing mix, although, compared with advertising, they tend to be regarded as relatively short-term strategies. The nature of the product, and in particular its experience characteristics, frequency of purchase and quality, all help to account for the high levels of advertising. There is also some suggestion of highly competitive advertising to maintain market shares. The cost of launching a new brand is high. However, while it would appear that advertising does not represent a major barrier to entry or has had any significant anti-competitive effects on prices or profits in the industry, it may be questioned whether this is the case in all market segments.

FURTHER READING

Clarke, R. (1985) *Industrial Economics* (Oxford, Basil Blackwell), Chapter 6.

Hay, D.A. and Morris, D.J. (1979) *Industrial Economics* (Oxford, Oxford University Press), Chapter 12.

Porter, M.E. (1980) *Competitive Strategy: Techniques for Analysing Industries and Competitors* (New York, Free Press).

NOTES

1. In imperfectly competitive conditions,

    $$MR_a = \frac{\partial(TR)}{\partial Q} \times \frac{\partial Q}{\partial A}$$

    where Q = output, A = advertising expenditures and TR = total revenue.

2. This can be derived as follows (see also Ferguson and Ferguson, 1994, Appendix 2). Assume $Q = f(P,A)$ and $C = f(Q,A)$, where Q = output, P = price, A = advertising expenditure, which can be purchased at a constant cost per unit, and C = total cost. Therefore $\pi = PQ - CQ - A$

    Partially differentiating to give the first-order conditions for profit maximisation:

    $$\frac{\partial \pi}{\partial P} = Q + P\left(\frac{\partial Q}{\partial P}\right) - \left(\frac{\partial C}{\partial Q}\right)\left(\frac{\partial Q}{\partial P}\right) = 0 \quad (1)$$

$$\frac{\partial \pi}{\partial A} = P\left(\frac{\partial Q}{\partial A}\right) - \left(\frac{\partial C}{\partial Q}\right)\left(\frac{\partial Q}{\partial A}\right) - 1 = 0 \quad (2)$$

Dividing equation (1) by $P(\partial Q/\partial P)$, rearranging and substituting the formula for price elasticity of demand gives

$$\frac{P - (\partial C/\partial Q)}{P} = -\frac{1}{e_p} \quad (3)$$

Rearranging equation (2), multiplying by P and substituting into equation (3) gives

$$\frac{P(\partial Q)}{\partial A} = -e_p \quad (4)$$

Multiplying equation (4) by A/Q and rearranging gives

$$P\left(\frac{\partial Q}{\partial A}\right)\left(\frac{A}{Q}\right) = -e_p \times \frac{A}{Q} \quad (5)$$

Substituting the formula for advertising elasticity of demand, equation (5) can be rewritten as

$$\frac{A}{PQ} = -\frac{e_a}{e_p} \quad (6)$$

3. See *The Economist*, 7th September 1991, 'Managing the Brands'.

4. See *The Economist*, 24 April 1993, 'Rethinking Japanese Marketing'.

5. See *The Economist*, 7 September 1991, *op. cit.*

6. See *The Economist*, 24 April 1993, *op. cit.*

11.1 'The prevailing view is that advertising does not direct or cajole consumer preferences, rather it helps them to make better-informed choices.' Explain and discuss. To what extent does empirical evidence support this statement?

11.2 A firm estimates its sales-advertising function as follows:

$$Q = 10000 + 500A - 0.5A^2$$

where A represents advertising expenditure in thousands of pounds. Current advertising expenditure is £50 000, the firm sells its product at £8 per unit, average variable costs are a constant £3.20 and fixed costs (excluding advertising) are £70 000 over the relevant time period.

(a) Calculate the expected level of sales and profits.
(b) Assess the effects on sales and profits of a projected increase in the advertising budget to £70 000.

11.3 'The move away from advertising and branding in favour of price promotions is symptomatic of a general trend towards the increased use of short-term strategies by large firms.' Explain and discuss.

11.4 In 1991 the advertising/sales ratio for cough remedies in the UK was 17.87, for books it was 1.81 and for gas cookers it was 0.13. Why should such large differences exist between product groups?

11.5 A producer of electric shavers faces a demand function of $Q = 500 - 10P$ and a total cost function

(excluding advertising) of $TC = 100 + 10Q + 0.1Q^2$, where Q refers to output (in thousands of units) and P denotes the price. Calculate the profit-maximising output and price and the level of profit, given an advertising budget of £500 000. It is estimated that the advertising elasticity of demand equals 2. Calculate the effect of a 25% increase in the advertising budget on the firm's profit position.

11.6 A pharmaceutical company is developing the vitamin pill side of its business. It is contemplating what marketing options to choose. Given that this is a growth market, but that it is also very competitive, what types of advertising and branding policies would you advise? Discuss the problems inherent in the strategies.

11.7 A profit-maximising firm wishes to achieve a target rate-of-return of 6% on its investments, of which advertising is one. The expected rate-of-return from spending £1 million on advertising is 10%, from spending £2 million it is 8% and from spending £3 million it is 6%. How much should the firm spend? What effect would an increase in the target rate-of-return have on advertising expenditure?

11.8 'The two-way relationship between market concentration and advertising means that it is impossible to say with any certainty which is the dominant variable, concentration or advertising; the empirical evidence reflects this uncertainty.' Explain and discuss.

CHAPTER 12

▶ *Investment and Finance Decisions*

Investment refers to any act that involves a current sacrifice in exchange for some kind of future gain or stream of benefits. Investment usually includes a commitment of funds on the part of the firm, as, say, in the purchase of plant and equipment. In this sense it can either refer to the replacement or to the expansion of existing plant and equipment. It can also involve the commitment of funds to other activities, like an advertising campaign of the development of a new product. Expansion investment projects enable a firm to grow *internally*. Internal expansion can take place at home or abroad and can encompass the horizontal growth of a firm's existing product market or it can apply to the development of new areas of interest through either vertical or conglomerate multimarket expansion. A firm can also grow *externally* via mergers and takeovers. Mergers and multimarket growth strategies are considered in Chapter 13.

The first part of this chapter deals specifically with the investment decision of the firm. Section 5.1 featured an examination of the importance of taking into account the time value of money in long-term decision-making. In this context the net present value and internal rate-of-return methods of investment appraisal and the problems of dealing with uncertainty and risk were discussed in Section 5.5, it was noted that in a situation of risk and uncertainty, a firm will need to calculate the expected values of projects. For reasons of simplicity, this chapter begins by assessing the various investment techniques assuming that the objective of the firm is to maximise its long-term value under conditions of *certainty*. The

rule-of-thumb investment appraisal techniques, the *payback* and the *book* or *average rate-of-return* methods, are analysed; the *net present value* and *internal rate-of-return* methods are discussed in more detail; the *profitability index* is also examined. *Uncertainty* is introduced into the analysis by discussing the effect that *inflation* can have on the investment decision; the *investment decision in practice* is examined.

The second half of the chapter discusses how the *cost of capital* is determined for use in the discounting approaches of investment appraisal. The determination of the cost of capital is closely bound up with the *financing decisions* of the firm. Hence, in order to appreciate the *optimal capital structure* of the firm it is necessary to understand what determines the relative costs of raising funds from a variety of sources. The *traditional* and *Modigliani–Miller* explanations of the cost of capital and optimal capital structure are examined, both of which assume the existence of a perfect capital market; this is followed by a discussion of the *principal–agent* approach that incorporates market imperfections. The *case study* at the end of the chapter examines the Channel Tunnel investment and financing decisions.

12.1 THE INVESTMENT DECISION

For current purposes it will be assumed that investment involves a commitment of funds by the firm, although, as originally noted in Section 5.1, this need not always be the case. For example, a decision to reduce the price of a product can be regarded as an investment in the sense that it involves a current sacrifice, an initial fall in cash flows before consumers have adjusted their spending patterns, followed by a stream of future benefits as they adapt their purchasing behaviour in favour of the relatively cheaper good; however, there is no initial capital outlay.

Since investment projects usually have ramifications for both the current and future periods they form the basis of the firm's long-term strategic decision-making. Sometimes an investment project will simply comprise *replacement investment*, which is necessary when outdated and worn-out equipment and machinery needs to be renewed. This is a fairly standard decision-making procedure and one that usually does not require a great deal of analysis by the firm. However, if the replacement investment also incorporates the latest technology, which has the effect of reducing production costs and/or increasing product quality, a more detailed appraisal of the project may be required. At other times the project may be an example of *expansion investment*, which is specifically geared towards the growth of the business, either through the extension of existing product markets or by the development of completely new products. In such cases a comprehensive review of the project should be undertaken in order to assess its potential for the firm. When making an investment decision, particularly one involving the potential growth of the business, it is likely that the firm will have to choose between competing projects, or more pertinently between competing uses of its funds.

A firm will only take on an investment project if it is expected to increase profitability and ultimately the value of the firm (although projects that comply with environmental and health and safety legislation usually offer no direct commercial return). Hence, the firm needs to assess whether a project will itself be profitable or, if it is comparing projects, which one is likely to be the most profitable. A number of investment appraisal techniques are available to the firm. Whatever the appraisal technique employed, a firm should compare the sum of the post-tax net revenues (or more exactly the sum of the various contributions) over the projected life of the project with the initial outlay or capital cost. Any possible scrap values of the project (and/or of the project that is being replaced) should also be taken into account.

12.2 THE PAYBACK AND BOOK RATE-OF-RETURN METHODS

These methods of investment appraisal are defined in Box 12.1, page 235. Assume that a project (A) involves an initial capital cost of £200 000 and that it has a projected life of five years. Its contributions after taxes are £65 000 in the first year, £80 000 in the second year and £60 000 in each of the other three years. It has a scrap value of £10 000 at the end of its life. These figures are shown in Table 63. The payback period for the non-discounted cash flow is just before the end of the third year, or 2.92 years to be exact. The main advantage of the payback method is its simplicity. However, there are two basic problems. Firstly, if the payback period is calculated on the basis of the non-discounted figures, the time value of money is ignored. This problem can be rectified by using present value figures. These are shown (given an assumed cost of capital of 10%) in the right-hand column of the table. On the basis of these

Table 63 *Assumed costs and revenues of a capital project (A)*

Year	Contributions (£)	Present values (£) (at 10% discount rate)
0	(200 000)	(200 000)
1	65 000	59 091.5
2	80 000	66 112
3	60 000	45 078
4	60 000	40 980
5	70 000[a]	43 463
		54 724.5

[a]Includes scrap value.

discounted figures the payback period is 3.72 years. The second problem with the payback method is that it takes no account of the income flows that accrue to the project after the expiration of the payback period. In other words, it favours short-term projects over those that have longer income streams or whose yearly contributions increase through time.

According to the figures in Table 63 the average of the non-discounted contributions is £67 000. Hence, the book rate of return (BRR) is equal to £67 000/£200 000, which is 0.335 or 33.5%. As with the payback method, the BRR is attractive in its simplicity, but if undertaken in a non-discounted form it fails to take into account the time value of money. In order to incorporate this feature into the investment decision the net present value and internal rate-of-return techniques need to be reconsidered; the profitability index can also be introduced.

12.3 THE NET PRESENT VALUE, INTERNAL RATE-OF-RETURN AND PROFITABILITY INDEX TECHNIQUES

In the example given in Table 63 the NPV is found by summing the present values of the various contributions and deducting the initial outlay from this figure. The present value of the contributions (at a discount rate of 10%) sum to £254 724.5. Subtracting the outlay of £200 000 from this yields an NPV figure of £54 724.5. Since this is positive (i.e. NPV > O) the project should be accepted, at least in principle (or, if projects are being compared, then the one with the highest NPV should be accepted). A firm may only actually accept a project if the NPV is sufficiently large to make allowances for uncertainties over projected income streams. In these circumstances the

Box 12.1 *Methods of investment appraisal*

The *payback period* is the amount of time it takes for a project to repay its initial capital cost: the shorter the payback period the more acceptable the project. The *book* or *average rate of return* is equal to the average annual net revenues (usually non-discounted) of a project divided by the initial capital outlay:

$$\text{BRR} = \frac{(\sum_{t=1}^{n} Y_t)/n}{C_0} \qquad (12.1)$$

where Y_t represents the sum of the net revenues over the number of years n of the project, and C_0 indicates its initial capital cost.

Equations (5.3) and (5.4) defined the *net present value* (NPV) and the *internal rate of return* (IRR) respectively as follows:

$$\text{NPV} = \sum_{t=1}^{n} \frac{Y_t}{(1+r)^t} - C_0 \qquad (12.2)$$

$$\text{IRR} = \sum_{t=1}^{n} \frac{Y_t}{(1+i)^t} - C_0 = 0 \qquad (12.3)$$

A third investment appraisal method that uses discounting procedures is the *profitability index* or the *benefit/cost ratio*. This is defined as the ratio of the present value of the net revenues of a project to its initial capital cost. In other words, it shows the present value of benefits per unit of expenditure or cost. The index is expressed as follows:

$$\text{PI} = \frac{\sum_{t=1}^{n} \frac{Y_t}{(1+r)^t}}{C_0} \qquad (12.4)$$

expected values of the future cash flows (based on probability distributions of projected outcomes) are the relevant figures to use.

In order to calculate the IRR (i.e. to solve for i in equation (12.3)) an iterative procedure is often used. Since a discount rate of 10% yields a positive net present value, the IRR must be greater than 10% in order to make the NPV equal to zero; various discount rates are used until the correct value is found. In fact, the IRR in this case is 20.34%.[1] If this figure exceeds the current cost of capital of the firm, the project should be accepted, given the previous proviso about the uncertainties over future income streams.

In the example shown in Table 63,

$$\text{PI} = \frac{£254724.5}{£200000} = 1.27$$

Thus, the PI measures the relative profitability of investment projects, as opposed to the net present value method which measures their absolute levels of profitability. The decision rule for the PI is that any project should be accepted as long as PI > 1.

The discounting investment appraisal techniques can be compared on the basis of two different decisions. The three methods yield the same response in the case of the accept or reject decision, at least when there is no capital constraint (i.e. assuming no restrictions on the supply of capital). When the IRR of a project is greater than the opportunity cost of capital, it must have a positive NPV. NPV > 0 is also indicative of a PI > 1. According to all three criteria the project should be accepted.

However, when it comes to the ranking of projects, differences may occur according to which method is employed. One of the main reasons why problems arise is that it is implicitly assumed in the NPV and PI methods that net revenues are reinvested at the relevant discount rate, whereas according to the IRR technique net revenues are reinvested at the IRR.

The differences between the techniques become particularly acute when two or more projects are being compared that could do the same function for a firm, even though they may not cost the same; in other words, the projects are mutually exclusive. This point can be clarified by examining the relationship between the NPV and IRR criteria more closely. For any investment project the discount rate where the NPV is zero is equal to the IRR; in the case of project A it is 20.34%. At a discount rate of 10%, the NPV for A equals £54 724.5. Where the contribution figures are not discounted, the discount rate must be zero. In this instance, when the contribution figures are summed and compared with the initial cost of capital, the difference is £135 000. These three points can be plotted on a graph. The relevant curve, labelled A, is shown in Figure 84, page 236. This graph also shows a curve for a second project, project B, which may be able to perform the same task for the firm as A, but has an initial capital cost of only £110 000. The relevant data for project B are shown in Table 64, page 236.

If the two projects are compared using the NPV and IRR techniques, conflicts arise. Project B has the higher IRR (24.98%) and would always be preferred to project A on the basis of the IRR method of investment appraisal. On the other hand, since the two curves intersect at approximately the 17% discount rate, at lower rates than this the NPV method would rank project A higher than project B; but at rates higher than 17% it would rank them the other way about. Thus, the problem with the NPV method is

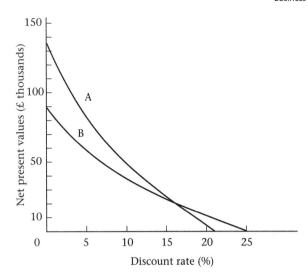

Figure 84 *The relationship between net present value and internal rate of return.*

Table 64 *Assumed costs and revenues of a capital project (B)*

Year	Contributions (£)	Present values (£) (at 10% discount rate)
0	(110 000)	(110 000)
1	30 000	27 273
2	50 000	33 056
3	40 000	30 052
4	40 000	27 320
5	40 000	<u>24 836</u>
		40 801

that it does not yield a unique result. The problem with the IRR technique is that at those costs of capital below 17% the IRR method would actually recommend the wrong project, the one with the lower NPV.

This does not necessarily mean that one method should automatically be preferred to the other. In fact, in many of the situations where investment projects are being compared it is unlikely that the relevant decision would take place at or near the point where the curves actually cross and so any potential conflict is reduced. In general terms the IRR suffers from the fact that in certain situations, for example when a project yields negative contributions in years other than the first one, no single solution may result. The NPV method necessitates calculations of present values for each discount rate, although it may be preferable to employ a technique such as this that gives a straightforward indication of whether a project is profitable, especially if it is assumed that the key objective of the firm is to maximise its long-term value.

Another area of conflict in the ranking of projects occurs when the NPV and PI methods are being compared. Since the NPV method is an absolute indicator, it tends to have an in-built bias towards larger projects with the potential for greater absolute profit flows. This can be a particular disadvantage where capital is 'rationed', in other words when only a certain amount can be raised, whether from internal or external sources. The PI method has the advantage in these circumstances of ranking projects according to their relative levels of profitability, so enabling the firm to make a more efficient assessment of its investment opportunities.

12.4 THE EFFECT OF INFLATION ON THE INVESTMENT DECISION

One of the main areas of uncertainty in investment decisions concerns projected rates of inflation, especially if variations in the general level of prices are expected to occur during different time periods. Costs and revenues are more difficult to predict in a period of high inflation and/or when the future level of inflation is likely to be different from that observed in the past. There are additional problems for investment appraisal if relative changes in the prices of particular outputs or inputs occur or are thought likely to occur. Furthermore, high and variable rates of interest rates that accompany high and variable periods of inflation make it much more difficult for firms to calculate the appropriate discount rate that needs to be applied to an investment project.

In principle, a firm should be mainly concerned with the expected *real* rate of return from any project. However, when projects are evaluated under inflationary conditions it is essential that like is compared with like; the expected future income flows and the discount rate must both be measured either in nominal or money terms or in real terms. Stated very simply the rule is as follows: if expected income flows are evaluated in nominal terms (i.e. they are calculated allowing for changes in the effects of inflation) or if relative changes in costs or prices are expected, then a nominal discount rate should be used. If, on the other hand, future cash flows are estimated at current prices, giving a real cash flow, then a real discount rate should be employed.

The following formula can be used to reduce the nominal discount rate to the real rate:

$$\frac{1+m}{1+p} = 1 + l \qquad (12.5)$$

where m is the money or nominal discount rate, l is the real rate and p is the rate of inflation (assuming that all costs and revenues increase by the same constant rate). For example, if the nominal discount rate is 10% and the inflation rate is 5%, then the real discount rate equals $(1.10/1.05) - 1$, which amounts to 0.0476 or 4.76%.

In the UK, both average inflation and inflation volatility were much higher in the 1970s and 1980s than in the 1950s and 1960s (they were also higher compared with their major competitors). Between 1945 and 1965 the average retail inflation rate was about 3.75% p.a., while from the mid-1960s until 1990 it ran at almost 9% p.a. Its variance was also four times as great in the latter than in the earlier period. Such an inflationary climate (and the government-induced stop–go policies that accompany it) can have an adverse effect on investment decisions taken by the individual firm as well as on the overall level of investment. Since 1991, annual average retail price inflation has been just over 3%, signalling both a lower cost of capital for firms as well as reduced uncertainty about its prospective value. However, there is evidence that firms are often still basing their investment decisons on the higher inflation climate of the past by applying relatively high discount rates to projects (see next section). If firms seek excessive (real) returns on their investments they may then miss out on a number of sound investment opportunities.

12.5 THE INVESTMENT DECISION IN PRACTICE

It was noted in Section 3.2 that the UK's comparative aggregate investment record has tended to lag behind that of its main competitors. There is also evidence of lower real rates of return on investments in the business sector in the UK than elsewhere. However, since there is no general agreement on the precise causes of investment, either at the aggregate or at the individual firm level, it is even more difficult to hypothesise on the reasons for differences in comparative international levels of investment. Surveys of investment intentions by British firms usually cite expectations of future levels of demand and the degree of capacity utilisation as prime instigating factors (see e.g. Bank of England, 1994b). The capital structure of firms has also been quoted as an important influence on investment in the UK in recent years, with the priority of many companies seen as the reduction of the high levels of debt incurred in the late 1980s rather than the adoption of new projects. Aggregate investment also appears to be inexorably linked with a country's rate of technical progress (see Box 12.2).

12.6 THE CAPITAL STRUCTURE OF THE FIRM

Investment in capital assets naturally requires finance. Since the method of finance that is employed defines the cost of capital for the firm, which, in turn, affects the amount of investment undertaken, it is obvious that the investment and finance decisions of the firm are inexorably linked. Finance can be raised from a variety of sources: the two major *external* sources are the issuing of shares and the issuing of bonds or debentures plus short-term loans, whereas retained profits represent the prime *internal* source of funds. The relative costs of these funds may vary. The finance decision centres on the determination of the most efficient mix of funds or, to put it another way, the *optimal capital structure* of the firm.

The cost of capital

The *cost of capital* or the discount rate is only equivalent to the market rate of interest assuming a perfect capital market, in which case all projects with a positive NPV at the market rate would be adopted (and the IRR would be equal to the market rate). However, the market is not perfect and, even if it were, lending and borrowing rates differ; they also often vary with the extent and duration of a loan. Besides, there is no one, simple market rate to use as a guide. Each source of finance has its own market rate. The decision regarding which source to use depends on a number of factors, such as the ownership structure of the firm and its attitude towards risk, as well as tax considerations (given that interest payments on loans are tax deductible for firms, whereas dividend payments are not). Thus, a key financial decision for a firm is to decide on its cost of capital.

Initially, the traditional and Modigliani–Miller approaches towards capital structure are examined,

---

Box 12.2 *Investment appraisal in practice*

Recent evidence on the use of investment appraisal techniques suggests that British firms use a wide variety of criteria (Sangster, 1993; Bank of England, 1994b; Peacock *et al.*, 1994). The Sangster survey of 94 medium- and large-sized Scottish firms found that firms often used more than one criterion to assess the feasibility of projects. The payback criterion was the most popular method employed, although it was hypothesised that, compared with the results of previous studies, the use of discounted cash flow techniques appeared to be increasing. In general, larger firms were more likely to use more sophisticted discounting techniques. The Bank of England (1994b) study of 250 large and medium-sized firms, mainly in the manufacturing sector, found that 70% made some use of discounted cash flow techniques, but again this was often in conjunction with other criteria: 40% of the firms, and especially the smaller ones, also reported employing payback methods. In a small-scale study of investment appraisal techniques in the hospitality industry, Peacock *et al.* found that the smaller establishments relied exclusively on the rule-of-thumb criteria, whereas discounting techniques were more likely to be employed by the larger chains.

There is no evidence that firms in other industrialised economies have employed more elaborate investment criteria than those used by British companies. In fact, the reverse may be true. Marsh (1990) concluded that discounted cash flow techniques are less popular in Japan than they are in the UK and the US, although there does seem to be a greater emphasis in Japan on linking investment plans to corporate growth objectives rather than to short-term profitability alone. There is also evidence that British firms adopt relatively short time horizons for investments (Cosh *et al.*, 1990) and may employ higher costs of capital than equivalent German and Japanese companies (McCauley and Zimmer, 1989). The fact that firms in the UK tend to use high factors to discount future cash flows was emphasised in the Bank of England study, which found that the average target post-tax real rate of return adopted by the surveyed companies was about 15% and the average nominal rate was around 20%. Seventy percent of the firms in the study had not adjusted their target costs of capital to take account of the lower inflation and interest rates typical of the 1990s, which may well have a detrimental effect on their investment plans. The use of high discount rates has been confirmed in other studies: a significant number of firms investigated have reportedly employed a nominal discount rate together with cash flows in current prices or in real terms, leading to an underestimation of the real profitability of projects and to a downward bias in investment planning (Coulthurst, 1986).

---

both of which assume the existence of a perfect capital market. This is followed by a discussion of the agency approach that takes into account informational asymmetries and objectives other than traditional value maximisation.

The traditional approach towards the cost of capital and optimal capital structure

It is assumed that the objective of the firm is to maximise the market value of the firm and that there is a perfect capital market; for simplification purposes it is also assumed that only two sources of finance, equity and debt, are employed. The total market value of the firm, V, is the sum of the market value of debt, B, and the market value of equity, S. Total expected earnings are defined as the sum of the earnings of debtholders or interest payments plus the net return to shareholders (all of which are distributed). The cost of capital or the capitalisation rate is the discount rate applied by a firm's capital suppliers to the present value of the stream of future total earnings. It has traditionally been defined as the weighted average of the costs of the different sources of finance. Given only two sources, equity and debt, the cost of capital comprises the weighted average of the cost of equity and the cost of debt.

The cost of equity is the minimum rate of return that a firm must make on its equity so as to leave unchanged the price of the shares. In other words, it is the rate of return that shareholders expect to earn, over the years, from holding the firm's shares. For current purposes it is assumed that the firm's stream of earnings is not expected to grow over time.[2] The cost of debt is taken as the rate of interest payable on fixed interest debt. It should also be adjusted for tax. More specifically, it is the discount rate that debtholders employ to ascertain the present value of their stream of earnings.

Denoting the cost of debt by k_d, the cost of equity by k_e and the overall, weighted cost by k_o then

$$k_0 = k_e \frac{S}{V} + k_d \frac{B}{V} \tag{12.6}$$

Thus, k_o is the weighted average of the equity and debt discount rates, with the weights given by the relative proportions of equity, S/V and debt, B/V, in

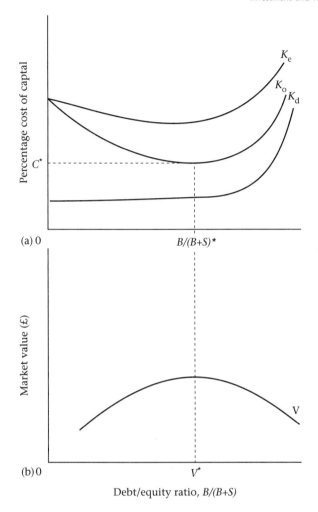

(a) 0 $B/(B+S)$*

(b) 0 V*

Debt/equity ratio, $B/(B+S)$

Figure 85 *The cost of capital, the value of the firm and capital structure.*

the firm's assets. Assuming that earnings are independent of the method of finance, then the value of the firm, V, is maximised when k_o is minimised.

The cost of each form of finance and the weighted cost are shown in Figure 85 (a) relative to the firm's gearing (debt/equity) ratio. k_d is lower than the cost-of-equity curve, k_e, because loan finance is considered less risky given that interest payments have to be paid before any returns are made to shareholders. Initially, the cost of debt is fairly constant, but it increases sharply as the gearing ratio continues to rise. Debtholders require a higher return to compensate them for their perceived increased risk, especially in the event of a downturn in the firm's fortunes and the possibility of bankruptcy.

Eventually the increased risk may outweigh the higher return demanded and the curve rises ever more steeply. This can be seen in Table 65. Two firms have the same value of capital assets, £1000 (given as book value). A 100% fall in earnings for firm B, financed through a combination of equity and debt, leaves a far lower surplus after payment of interest than for firm A, financed entirely by equity.

As noted, the equity cost curve, k_e, is higher than k_d because shareholders, as residual income earners, naturally incur greater risk than debtholders. The k_e curve also rises as the gearing ratio increases, signifying increased risk on the part of shareholders. Their residual level of earnings falls as more debt is taken on. There is also an increased variability of the earnings yield, as can be seen in Table 65. The fall in earnings causes a much greater decline in the rate of return on equity in firm B (from 20% to 5%) than in firm A (from 15% to 7.5%). As a result, shareholders will expect a higher return; the cost of equity capital rises.

The weighted average cost-of-capital curve k_o, starts at the same point as the k_e curve, where a company is 100% equity financed. As the debt/equity ratio increases, so k_o falls as additional, cheaper debt is taken on. Eventually k_o rises when both k_d and k_e increase as the gearing ratio continues to rise. Thus, k_o is U-shaped. The optimal capital structure, $(B/(B + S))$*, corresponds to the minimum cost of capital, C*, in Figure 85 (a). The minimum cost of capital is equivalent to the maximum value of the firm, V*, in Figure 85(b).

Table 65 *Corporate capital structure and the cost of capital*

	Firm A (£)	Firm B (£)
Total equity	1000	500
Total debt (at 10% interest)	0	500
Total value	1000	1000
Earnings	150	150
Less interest on debt	0	50
Total net equity returns	150	100
Rate of return on equity	15 %	20 %
Earnings (fall by 100%)	75	75
Less interest on debt	0	50
Total net equity returns	75	25
Rate of return on equity	7.5%	5 %

The Modigliani–Miller (MM) view

Modigliani and Miller (1958) argued that, assuming a perfect capital market and no taxes, both the value of the firm and the capital cost are constant; they are independent of the firm's capital structure. Thus, there is no optimal capital structure (for firms of similar size and risk).

For example, assume that two firms have the same expected earnings, say £5500, and are considered to have the same degree of risk. Both, therefore, are subject to the same capitalisation rate by investors, $k_e = 0.5$. However, the two firms are financed differently. The first firm, A, is financed entirely by equity, whereas firm B is financed partly by equity and partly by debt. Assume also that investors can lend and borrow at similar rates to firms and that the interest rate equals 10%. The situation is shown in Table 66.

The market value of B exceeds that of A, $V_B > V_A$. Assume an investor owns 10% (0.1) of the equity of B at a cost of 0.1 (£10 000), or £1000. The person's income is equal to 0.1 (£5000), or £500. By implication, the individual is confronted with the debt/equity ratio of the firm (0.5) imposed by managers. If the person sells the shares in B he or she will receive £1000.

In order to create the same ('home-made') leverage, he or she borrows £500 and buys £1500 of shares in firm A, thus securing 13.6% of the equity and 13.6% of its earnings. The investor's income is now 0.136 (£5500) minus the interest payable on the personal debt, or 0.1 (£500). This amounts to £750 – £50, or £700. The fact that firm B is overvalued causes investors to sell the shares in B, causing a fall in the price and to buy shares of A resulting in a price increase. These 'arbitrage operations' continue until

Table 66 *Corporate capital structure assuming a constant capitalisation rate*

	Firm A (£)	Firm B (£)
Total equity (market value)	11 000	10 000
Total debt	0	5000
Total market value	11 000	15 000
Earnings	5500	5500
Less interest on debt	0	500
Total net equity returns	5500	5000
Rate of return on equity	50%	50%

$V_A = V_B$. Thus, MM's first proposition is that the market value of a firm is independent of its capital structure and is given by capitalising its expected earnings at a discount rate appropriate to its risk class.

Their second proposition is that the rate of return on equity in a company with some debt is equal to the rate of return of a pure equity stream, k_o, plus a risk premium equal to the debt/equity ratio times the difference between k_o and k_d:

$$k_e = k_0 + \frac{(k_0 - k_d)\ B}{S} \tag{12.7}$$

This function is assumed to be linear. k_e increases at such a rate to offset exactly the use of the relatively cheaper debt (which is a more secure form of finance) in order that the overall cost of capital remains constant no matter what the debt/equity ratio. MM also postulated that the value of a firm is unaffected by its dividend policy. A change in dividend policy, in effect, changes the financial structure of the firm, which has already been shown to have no effect on the value of the firm. MM base their hypotheses on an analysis of firms of similar risk. By implication, if the degree of risk varies so will the value of the firm. Thus, according to this theory it is the riskiness of a firm's assets that determines its value and not its financial structure.

In a later paper, MM (1963) argued that, because interest payments on debt are tax-deductible in most industrialised countries, net returns to shareholders and the market value of the firm increase as gearing rises. This is due to the tax savings (or the tax shield) of the greater debt. To state this another way, the cost of capital declines continuously as the gearing ratio increases. The MM cost-of-capital curves with and without corporate tax are shown in Figure 86. Therefore, when taking tax into account the value of a firm is not independent of its capital structure. The optimum capital structure would be where a firm is completely debt-financed.

In practice, it has been argued, there is a limit to how much debt any firm would incur because of the fear of eventual bankruptcy. Miller, however, hypothesised that a more likely explanation as to why companies issue both debt and equity (and also why debt/equity ratios had not risen in line with corporate taxes in many countries in the decades prior to the 1980s) is that the financing decisions of firms depend on the difference between corporate and personal taxes and this difference had not changed very much. Companies will issue equity rather than debt if the tax saving to the investor exceeds the

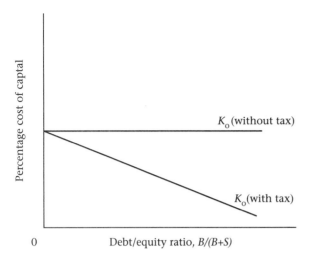

Figure 86 *Modigliani–Miller cost-of-capital curves with and without corporate tax.*

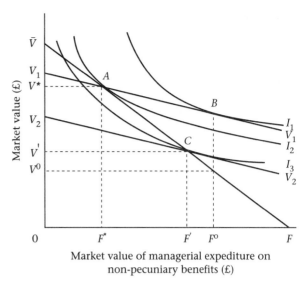

Figure 87 *Equity ownership, the value of the firm and the level of managerial non-pecuniary benefits.*

corporate tax bill. However, in the 1980s, tax rates fell. In the US, for example, the highest income tax rate was set at 28% (down from 50%) from 1986, while the corporate tax rate was lowered (from 46%) to 34%. In these circumstances (and contrary to the Miller hypothesis) companies would have a greater incentive to issue debt because the tax savings exceed those for investors in equity. Richard Brealey and Stewart Myers put forward a possible solution to this apparent contradiction by suggesting that if companies do not make a profit, then the expected tax shield may actually be less than 34%. The tax benefits from issuing debt may fall as debt increases because firms have no profit to set it against. Therefore, according to this line of reasoning, the optimal capital structure is determined by the expected corporate tax shield.[3]

The agency approach towards optimal capital structure

Whatever the nature of the relationship between capital structure and taxation, it cannot be assumed that financial markets operate efficiently and costlessly. In reality financial markets, like all others, are beset by informational asymmetries. Jensen and Meckling (JM) (1976) have put forward a theory of capital structure and market value based on the agency costs of financial decisions, in which asymmetric information and contractual incompleteness are important constituents.

Specifically, JM hypothesise that an entrepreneur or a manager of a firm will adopt a set of activities such that the value of the firm is less than if that person were the sole owner, given that the interests of the owner-manager deviate from those of outside financiers (an argument in accord with the managerial theories of the firm explained in Section 9.3). For example, suppose that a firm is of a given size, is financed solely by equity and is owned entirely by a single manager. The situation is shown in Figure 87, where the market value of the firm, V, is measured along the vertical axis and the market value of the stream of non-pecuniary or fringe benefits, F, is measured along the horizontal axis. According to JM the latter include factors such as luxurious and well-appointed offices, attractive secretarial staff, warm personal relationships with employees, charitable contributions and so on. Extra non-pecuniary benefits are assumed to be at the expense of pecuniary benefits. Therefore, the budget constraint under which the owner-manager operates (or the trade-off between V and F) is given by the line $\overline{VF}$. Since it is assumed that every £1 of current value of non-pecuniary benefits withdrawn from the firm reduces its market value by £1, then the slope of $\overline{VF}$ is −1. The utility of the owner-manager, which is a function of pecuniary and non-pecuniary returns, is indicated by a set of indifference curves, I_1, I_2 etc. Utility for the owner-manager is maximised at A, where indifference curve I_2 is tangent to $\overline{VF}$. The value of the firm is V^* and the value of non-pecuniary benefits will be F^*.

If the owner-manager sells part of the equity, then he or she (as manager) will not bear the full cost of any fringe benefits he or she consumes. Suppose he or she sells a proportion of the equity, $1 - \alpha$, to an outsider and keeps the remaining share, α. The cost to the owner-manager of consuming £1 of non-pecuniary benefits would now only be α times £1. Assuming that an outside investor pays $(1 - \alpha)V^*$ for the share of the equity, then the owner-manager would increase his or her consumption of non-pecuniary benefits.

The budget constraint shifts to V_1V_1 (which passes through A on the assumption that the same combination of pecuniary and non-pecuniary benefits could be consumed as before); this has a slope of $- \alpha$. The utility of the owner-manager is maximised at B where V_1V_1 is tangent to indifference curve I_1. The value of the firm falls to V^0 ($1 - \alpha$ of which is borne by the outsider) and the owner-manager's consumption of fringe benefits rises to F^0.

However, assuming that expectations are rational and that accurate forecasts of the future can be made based on current information, then the outside investor would be aware that the owner-manager is likely to increase non-pecuniary consumption following his or her reduction in share ownership. Therefore, the outside investor would only be willing to pay $1 - \alpha$ times the expected value of the firm for his or her equity stake, given the induced change in behaviour of the owner-manager. V_2V_2 (with a slope of $- \alpha$) represents the trade-off facing the owner-manager after the sale; utility is maximised at C (on $\overline{VF}$), giving a value for the firm of V' and leading to the consumption of non-pecuniary benefits of F'. This price, it is argued, is satisfactory to both the buyer and to the seller of shares; if the equilibrium point was to the left of C on $\overline{VF}$ the owner- manager would have sold the shares for less than the outside investor was willing to pay, whereas if the equilibrium point was to the right of C on $\overline{VF}$ the outside investor would have paid more for the shares than they were worth. The distance V^*V' is referred to by JM as the 'residual loss' and here represents the total agency cost engendered by the sale of outside equity. The reduction in the value of the firm is borne entirely by the owner-manager, who would only sell such an equity stake in the firm if the incremental gain in consumption of non-pecuniary benefits exceeded the incremental fall in value.

JM argue that, in practice, it is usually possible for outside shareholders to monitor the activities of managers in order to try to reduce their consumption of fringe benefits, the main weapon that shareholders have at their disposal being the design of composite remuneration schemes (although, as noted in Section 9.5, the effectiveness of such schemes in changing managerial behaviour remains in doubt); other means include auditing, formal control systems and budget restrictions. Since such monitoring activities reduce the value of the firm for shareholders, they will take this into account in deciding what price they are prepared to pay for any equity stake in the firm. The monitoring expenditures can also be undertaken by the managers themselves (in which case they are referred to as 'bonding costs') in order to convince the shareholders that non-pecuniary consumption would be limited. Such expenditures might include the use of outside auditing or contractual restrictions on managerial decision-making. Managers incur these bonding costs as long as the incremental increase in the value of the firm exceeds the value of the perquisites forgone.

Since outside equity leads to agency costs and a reduction in the value of the firm, a question might reasonably be posed as to why more firms are not mainly debt-financed. The answer, according to JM, is that there are also agency costs involved with debt. A highly-leveraged capital structure encourages the owner-manager to pursue projects with high downside risk. Lenders could, in principle, draw up contracts restricting managerial discretion, but they would need to be extremely detailed in order to do so effectively; hence they would be seen as prohibitively costly. Furthermore, the adjudication process associated with bankruptcy lowers any potential payoffs to lenders. However, debt is still incurred by companies because of the tax advantages previously mentioned and in order to take advantage of investment projects where the incremental wealth so created exceeds the incremental cost of debt (and this is lower than the incremental cost associated with new equity).

Finally, JM determine the optimal capital structure of the firm by analysing the changes in agency costs involved with both outside equity and debt as the debt/equity ratio varies. Figure 88 shows a firm of given size, where the horizontal axis measures the debt/equity ratio. The curve AS represents the agency cost of outside equity. As the proportion of outside equity increases (i.e. moving from right to left along the curve) the owner-manager's incentive to exploit the outside equity and hence equity agency costs both rise. Curve $0B$ shows the agency costs associated

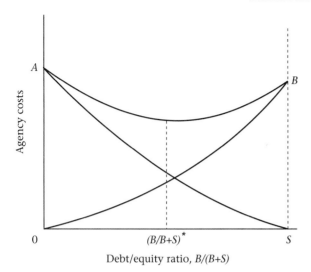

Figure 88 *Agency costs as a function of the debt/equity ratio.*

with debt: the greater the proportion of debt, the greater the incentive to undertake risky projects. The curve AB represents the sum of the agency costs from outside equity and debt finance. They are minimised at $(B/(B + S))^*$, which denotes the optimal capital structure of the firm. JM hypothesise that an increase in the scale of outside financing for a firm of given size increases the agency costs of finance (indicated by an upward shift of the cost curves). The agency costs also increase with the size of firm due to the more complex monitoring function.

The agency approach towards optimal capital structure benefits from taking into account asymmetric information between the firm and its financiers, although, while alternative objectives are considered, optimising behaviour is still presumed possible. There are agency costs involved in outside finance which vary as the debt/equity ratio varies; an optimal capital structure can result.

12.7 COMPARATIVE CAPITAL STRUCTURES

In Section 9.1 the equity-based financial systems of the UK and the US were compared with the bank-based systems of Germany and Japan. The two types of system offer contrasting pictures of corporate governance, although some of the differences between them may be diminishing as bank interests decline in importance in Germany and Japan and as profit-based pay schemes become more popular in both countries. When comparing capital structures, the bald figures suggest that a much greater difference exists between Japan and the UK and the US than between Germany and the Anglo-American model. In the UK the debt/equity ratio for non-financial enterprises fell from 1.13 in 1982 to 0.63 in 1993, whereas it moved in the opposite direction in the US, rising from 0.46 in 1981 to 1.03 in 1993. The debt/equity ratio in Japan fell from 5.04 in 1981 to 3.88 in 1993, although this was still a much higher ratio than in the UK or the US. In Germany the equivalent figure was much lower than in Japan and remained fairly constant, shifting from 1.78 in 1981 to 1.57 in 1993.[4]

Edwards and Fischer (1994) have produced other evidence portraying the apparent relative insignificance of debt in Germany. They found that between 1970 and 1989, bank borrowing accounted for just over 11% of German manufacturers' investment in physical assets. This was lower than in the UK during the same period and much lower than in Japan (the equivalent figures being 16.2% and 30.5% respectively), although the German figure may underestimate the importance of bank interests there for the reasons given in Section 9.1: they hold a significant proportion of shares, exercise proxy votes on behalf of other shareholders and are well represented on the boards of companies. In fact, bank lending accounted for most of the German companies' debt during the period in question and much of it was relatively long-term, whereas in the UK only a quarter of British corporate debt consisted of bank loans, nearly two-thirds of which was short-term. However, comparative data need to be treated with some caution. Differences in accounting techniques need to be considered: for example, historical-cost accounting techniques undervalue equity capital more in Germany than they do in the UK. German firms can reinvest pension contributions and if treated as debt they can inflate the debt/equity ratio. In Japan a significant proportion of debt consists of short-term loans and trade credits.

The use of dividend payouts as a signal to shareholders concerning the future prospects for a firm was mentioned in Section 9.5. It was also pointed out that high payouts may have a detrimental effect on a firm's long-term value by limiting the scope for investment and other long-term plans. In fact, dividend payout ratios (as a percentage of post-tax profits) have traditionally been higher in the UK and the US, especially in the former country compared with

Germany and Japan. In 1993, for example, the ratio for British firms stood at 74%, compared with 56% in the US, 40% in Japan and 35% in Germany.[5]

12.8 CONCLUSIONS

Investment refers to any activity that involves a current sacrifice in exchange for future gain or stream of benefits. It usually, although not necessarily, includes a commitment of funds on the part of the firm, for example in fixed assets like plant and equipment, which can comprise either replacement or expansion investment. A firm will often have to choose between competing projects or, in other words, between competing uses of its funds.

Investment projects are normally undertaken with the express intent of increasing profitability. Various methods of investment appraisal are considered on the basis of this criterion. The rule-of-thumb payback and book rate-of-return techniques are assessed, but neither specifically takes into account the time value of money and the need for discounting. The NPV and IRR methods both incorporate this feature into investment appraisal, as does the profitability index, which measures the relative profitability of projects. These three techniques are compared and contrasted.

The impact on the investment decision of the uncertainty engendered by inflation is considered: costs and revenues become more difficult to predict, especially when future levels of inflation are expected to differ from those encountered in the past. When projects are evaluated in inflationary conditions like must be compared with like: expected income flows and the discount rate must both be measured either in nominal terms or in real terms.

In practice, British firms use a variety of investment appraisal methods; larger firms are more likely to use the more sophisticated discounting procedures; this is in accord with evidence from elsewhere. However, there is also evidence that firms in the UK employ high discount rates; many have also been slow to adapt to the lower inflationary climate of the 1990s.

Investment and finance decisions are closely linked: investment in capital assets requires finance, the method of finance defines the cost of capital and this can affect the amount of investment undertaken. The overall cost of capital consists of the weighted average of the costs of the different sources of finance. The basis of the finance decision is the derivation of optimal mix of funds or the optimal capital structure of the firm. The traditional and Modigliani–Miller (MM) approaches are based on a long-term value maximising objective assuming a perfect capital market. In the traditional approach the weighted cost-of-capital curve is U-shaped: low gearing reduces the cost of capital, while higher gearing raises it; the minimum point of the curve identifies the maximum value of the firm. According to MM, assuming no taxes, the value of the firm and its capital cost are constant; hence there is no optimal capital structure. However, the inclusion of tax deductible interest payments leads to a lower cost of capital as gearing increases, in which case the optimal capital structure would be where a firm is completely debt-financed. However, it is argued that firms take on both equity and debt due to the fear of bankruptcy or where finance decisions depend on the difference between corporate and personal tax levels, although the lower tax rates of the 1980s reduced the relative advantage of equity over debt.

The agency approach towards optimal capital structure benefits from the inclusion of informational asymmetries and contractual incompleteness. It is argued that, assuming a separation of ownership from control and a consequent divergence of interests, there are agency costs involved in outside finance; since these vary as the debt/equity ratio varies, an optimal capital structure can result. Agency costs rise with outside financing for a firm of given size; they also increase with the size of firm.

Finally, alternative financial structures are compared. It is noted that debt/equity ratios are much higher in Japan than in the UK or the US. Debt finance in Germany appears to be far less significant than in Japan, although bank lending is generally longer-term than in the UK. Dividend payout ratios are higher in the UK and the US than in Germany and Japan.

Case Study: Eurotunnel's Profit Forecasts-Sunk Costs

The scale of the Channel Tunnel project and the risks and uncertainty involved has meant that it has been subject to large revisions, firstly in cost, and more recently, in revenue forecasts. This study summarises the profit projections of Eurotunnel, the firm overseeing the project, and examines some of the assumptions that underlie its financial forecasts; it also outlines the implications of its refinancing deals.

When it was started in 1987, Eurotunnel estimated the total capital costs at £4.8 billion spread over a six-year period. However, when completed in 1994, the eventual capital cost was more than double the original estimate, at almost £11 billion. It was because the tunnel opened a year late, plus the fact that from 1994 the project began to incur interest charges that previously had been rolled up in its debt, that Eurotunnel had to engage in a refinancing exercise in order to counteract its negative cash flow. This took place in 1994 and involved extra funds of £1.2 billion, largely in the form of additional borrowing from the 225 banks that act as its main creditors (and in the process increasing its gearing ratio to 4.66).

At the time of the refinancing announcement, Eurotunnel put forward new profit projections for the project for each year until 2013 and each tenth year thereafter until 2051, the last year of the so-called concession period when the tunnel's legal monopoly will expire. Some of these figures are shown in Table 67. On the basis of its 1994 forecasts, Eurotunnel expected to break even in 2002. However, there have already had to be a number of major revisions to these figures. Delays in starting the full service meant that revenues in 1994 were only 22% of their original target, while 1995 revenues were 56% of the target projection. This led to the suspension of interest payment on its £8.9 billion debt. The additional agency costs involved in any future refinancing deal have led the banks, as principals in the contract, to propose extra constraints on management. The proposed debt-for-equity swap (agreed with the banks in October 1996) is also regarded as a partial solution to the interest payment problem, although the monitoring costs involved in greater outside equity may be reflected in a lower price for the shares.

The 1994 forecasts were based on a number of key assumptions, some of which can be questioned and which, therefore, may have a significant impact on the profit forecasts and the projected breakeven time period. For example, in the past, Eurotunnel has tended to adopt a broad definition of the cross-channel market, covering travel over much of Western Europe. The actual market may be much narrower than Eurotunnel has projected; for example, passengers

Table 67 *Eurotunnel's profit projections, 1994–2051*

	£ million						
	1994	2000	2013	2023	2033	2043	2051
Revenue	137	1056	2261	3584	5285	7201	9300
Operating costs	(144)	(311)	(614)	(951)	(1390)	(1917)	(2478)
Depreciation and ammortisation	(87)	(170)	(205)	(294)	(421)	(622)	(1100)
Interest	(286)	(606)	(420)	(338)	(325)	(139)	138
Post-tax profit (loss)	(382)	(89)	569	1273	2006	2921	3786

Source: Eurotunnel Rights Issue, May 1994, selected figures.

travelling to the more distant destinations may prefer to fly. Eurotunnel has estimated that it will attract a third of the passenger traffic and almost a fifth of the freight traffic of this broad market by 2013, by which time it projects that the total market will have doubled in size. The latter is not an unreasonable estimate, given that it grew by a third between 1986 and 1993. Eurotunnel has also assumed that revenues and operating costs will rise in line with inflation and that inflation in both the UK and France will remain at their recent relatively low levels. In fact, over the last 10 years, ferry prices have risen by 2.5% below the rate of inflation and airline prices 4.5% below the rate of inflation.

There are also more positive aspects of current revenue trends to consider. The Dover/Folkstone–Calais ferries and the airlines (on the more local routes) have both suffered reductions in market shares. By mid-1996 the Le Shuttle car sevice had captured about 45% of this growing market. Furthermore, Eurotunnel has lower marginal and variable costs compared with its competitors; since its assets are non-transferable, any operating income is preferable to none. Thus, it should benefit in the long term from the price war started by the ferry operators.[6]

Any investment project necessarily involves estimates of future costs and revenues. There are enormous difficulties involved in making accurate forecasts for large and very long-term projects such as the Channel Tunnel, since the forecasts implicity involve massive uncertainty. The Eurotunnel revenue forecasts for next century can only be made on the basis of best guesstimates, especially given the number of variables involved. Their accuracy depends on the extent to which Eurotunnel's assumptions concerning the nature of the market and market trends are borne out by the facts. Some of these assumptions may have appeared questionable in the past, but financiers would presumably prefer to face the additional monitoring costs involved in any refinancing deal to the costs of bankruptcy.

FURTHER READING

Douglas, E.J. (1992) *Managerial Economics: Analysis and Strategy*, 4th edn (Englewood Cliffs, NJ, Prentice Hall), Chapter 15.
Koutsoyiannis, A. (1982) *Non-Price Decisions: The Firm in a Modern Context* (London, Macmillan), Chapters 4, 8–10.
Reekie, W.D. and Crook, J.N. (1995) *Managerial Economics: A European Text*, 4th edn (London, Prentice Hall), Chapter 14.

NOTES

1. The internal rate of return can easily be calculated by the use of a computer or a business calculator.
2. In a growing firm the cost of equity can be found by solving for the discount rate r (where the sum of the discounted present value of future dividends is equal to the market price of shares) in the equation

$$P_0 = \frac{D_0}{1+r} + \frac{D_0(1+g)}{(1+r)^2} + \frac{D_0(1+g)^2}{(1+r)^3} + \cdots + \frac{D_0(1+g)^n}{(1+r)^{n+1}}$$

This simplifies to

$$P_0 = \frac{D_0}{r-g}$$

or

$$r = \frac{D_0}{P_0} + g \; (= k_e)$$

where P_0 is the current market price, D_0 is the present level of dividend and g is the expected constant dividend growth rate. Thus, assuming an efficient and well-functioning capital market, any change in P is a function of changes in either r or g.

3. See *The Economist*, 8 December 1990, School's Brief: 'Unlocking Corporate Finance'.
4. See OECD Non-financial Enterprises Financial Statements, 1990 and 1994.
5. See *The Economist*, 29 January 1994, 'Corporate Governance'.
6. See *The Economist*, 30 April 1994, 'Eurotunnel's Incredible Forecasts'.

12.1 Compare and contrast the discounting methods of investment appraisal assuming that the objective of the firm is to maximise its long-run value. Given that discounting techniques are implicitly more accurate than the more traditional appraisal methods, why are they not more popular?

12.2 An investment project costs an initial £500 000. It has a life span of five years, at the end of which time its resale value equals £100 000. Its post-tax contributions are £120 000 in years one and two and £140 000 in each of the remaining three years. The assumed discount rate is 10%.

(a) Calculate the payback period for the non-discounted and the discounted contributions.
(b) Calculate the book rate of return on the basis of both the non-discounted and discounted figures.
(c) Assess whether the project should be accepted using the NPV, IRR and PI techniques of investment appraisal.

12.3 A multiproduct firm is deciding on the pricing strategy for one of its products, which has an estimated five more years of its life to run. Due to the threat of entry the firm has the choice of limit pricing or short-run profit-maximising strategies. The projected cash flows (net of all relevant costs) in money terms are as follows:

	Cash flow (£ million) for year				
	1	2	3	4	5
Limit price per time period	5.0	5.0	2.5	1.5	0.5
Short-run profit maximising per time period	8.0	3.0	2.0	0.5	0.0

The expected real rate of return from investment in new products is 5%. Inflation is expected to average 3% p.a. over the next five years. Which strategy best suits its goal of long-term profit maximisation?

12.4 A firm is debating whether to introduce a new product. The launch will involve an initial outlay of £10 million covering investment in new plant and machinery (which has a scrap value of £1 million at the end of the fifth year) plus marketing costs. The estimated contributions over five years (in real terms) are as follows:

Contribution (£ million) for year				
1	2	3	4	5
4.0	4.0	6.0	6.5	7.5

The new product is a replacement for an existing product, whose contributions (in nominal terms) are estimated as follows:

Contribution (£ million) for year				
1	2	3	4	5
4.0	3.5	3.0	2.5	1.5

The plant and equipment for the old product have a scrap value of £0.5 million at the end of year five. The real rate of return is 4% and the expected rate of inflation is 3% p.a. Advise the firm on its deliberations.

12.5 'Since both the cost of debt and the cost of equity rise as the gearing ratio increases, then the overall cost of capital curve must be upward-sloping.' Explain and discuss.

12.6 Corporate interest payments on debt are tax deductible in most industrialised countries. Hence, the optimal capital structure should be one in which a firm is completely debt-financed. Explain why, in fact, this is not the case.

12.7 'Monitoring activities reduce the value of the firm; hence, the greater the proportion of outside ownership the greater the agency costs and the lower the value of the firm.' Explain this statement and discuss its relevance for the firm's optimal capital structure.

CHAPTER 13

▶ Mergers and Multimarket Strategies

A firm often expands by moving into different markets. Such expansion may take the form of *vertical* growth into different stages of production or *conglomerate* growth into new product markets. It may also comprise some form of *multinational* expansion into new geographic markets overseas; this can either involve the horizontal expansion of the existing product base abroad or growth into new stages of production or into new product markets. As was pointed out in Chapter 12, a firm can grow either internally, by investing in new plant and equipment, or externally via mergers and takeovers.

The internal growth decision was examined in Chapter 12. The first part of the chapter investigates the prevalence of *merger activity* in the UK and elsewhere. In the following sections the main reasons for growth by vertical integration, diversification and multinationalisation are examined. In each case traditional explanations are compared with the transaction cost approach. The final section has a *case study* on tests of the transaction cost approach towards vertical integration.

13.1 THE NATURE AND EXTENT OF MERGER ACTIVITY

The terms *mergers* and *takeovers* (or acquisitions) are usually used interchangeably, as they will be here, although there are actually important distinctions between them. Legally, a merger occurs when two (or more) firms combine to form a new legal entity, whereas a takeover takes place when one company acquires a controlling interest in the voting equity of another company. In economic terms it is more useful to regard a merger as taking place with the mutual consent of the respective managements of the merging firms, while a takeover involves the raider firm bidding for the shares of the victim company, often without the support of the victim's management.

Mergers generally occur in *waves,* with booms followed by periods of less intense activity. For example, the UK has experienced three merger waves this century, in the 1920s, the late 1960s and early 1970s and in the mid- to late 1980s. In each case the wave has coincided with peaks in share prices. The 1980s wave featured a number of characteristics that distinguished it from the earlier peaks in activity. For the first time conglomerate deals predominated, representing over 50% of all acquisitions. Secondly, the 1980s wave witnessed the evolution of the market for corporate control, in which the management of companies is regarded as a commodity that, in principle, can be bought and sold like other commodities (although, as noted in Section 9.5, there is not a great deal of evidence to suggest that an efficient market exists). The third distinguishing characteristic of the latest merger wave was that large companies became more vulnerable to takeover. In most instances, however, the purchaser was an even larger firm, suggesting that immunity from takeover is moving up a notch in size to the very largest firms.

Table 68, page 250 reveals that there is a greater level of merger activity, both in volume and value terms, within the UK compared with its major European competitors. The volume of activity in Germany is also quite high, but the much lower total value of transactions implies that smaller and medium-sized companies (usually privately-owned) are more prone to acquisition there than are larger firms. Anglo-American firms have traditionally been regarded as the most merger active and continue to be so. The penchant that British firms have for merger activity is confirmed by the fact that, during the 1980s boom, the most common type of merger within the EU was one in which one British firm acquired another British firm. The UK is also the largest buyer of non-British European companies, followed by the US. British and American companies are the largest overseas buyers of firms in each other's country.

However, there is evidence of recent increases in levels of merger activity by firms from other countries. In the 1980s boom the second most common form of merger within the EU was one in which one French company acquired another. Japanese companies were

Table 68 *The number and value of mergers in selected Western European Economies, 1993–95*

	1993		1994		1995	
	Number	Value (£m)	Number	Value (£m)	Number	Value (£m)
UK	1248	17 360	1555	25 272	1694	67 747
Germany	1154	5594	1305	9511	460	2394 *a*
France	n/a	n/a	262	7459	54	418 *b*
Italy	131	2484	141	4571	113	4342 *c*

*a*Until end May.
*b*Until end March.
*c*Until end October.

Source: *Acquisitions Monthly*, various issues.

the second largest non-European acquirers (after the US) of European firms in 1995. However, an important distinguishing characteristic of Anglo-American merger activity compared with elsewhere is the presence in the UK and the US of the *hostile* or *contested* bid. The hostile takeover is very rare in the rest of Europe and unknown in Japan. This is largely because of the existence of practical devices (for example, the ability to issue shares to friendly third parties in Europe) and institutional features (there being far fewer companies whose shares are freely tradeable in Europe and the existence of the Japanese *keiretsu*) that together create barriers to acquisition activity and which help to make hostile bids relatively rare.

13.2 VERTICAL INTEGRATION

As noted in Section 2.2, vertical integration (VI) denotes the extent to which a firm operates in successive markets. Backward or upstream vertical integration (BVI) occurs when a firm moves into the preceding stage of production, such as the production of raw materials or other inputs. Thus, the exploration and transportation of oil by a petroleum firm is an example of backward vertical integration. Forward or downstream stream vertical integration (FVI) refers to a move into the subsequent market. A petroleum firm with its own retail outlets (i.e. petrol stations) would be an example.

Box 13.1 *The measurement of vertical integration*

The extent of VI is thought to vary between industries and also by firms within the same industry. The problem with estimating the degree of VI is that it is notoriously difficult to measure. It is also particularly important to identify the form if integration that is being measured, whether interindustry or intraindustry. A number of indicators have been employed:

(1) The ratio of value added to sales, the implication being the higher the ratio the more integrated the firm. However, the main problem with this measure is that it is affected by the stage at which the firm operates: the closer the firm to primary production, the higher the ratio, *cet. par.* The same problem arises in comparing industries: primary product industries have higher value added/sales ratios than other industries. Besides, integration by a firm between separately classified industries (such as by a canned food manufacturer into cans) has no effect on the recorded ratio

in either industry. In this sense the ratio only measures intrafirm VI.

(2) The ratio of 'auxiliary' activities of a firm (measured in terms of either employment or sales) to its total activity, where auxiliary activities are defined as those supplying inputs into the primary activity or which contribute to downstream processing or distribution of the latter. However, this measure often requires rather arbitrary definitions of the different activities and may also involve careful distinctions between VI and diversification.

(3) A measure of the scale of intrafirm flows of output relative to market transactions or external sales (Davies and Morris, 1995). Given the problems of obtaining data on intraindustry flows within the firm, measures of interindustry integration are relied upon; the scale of intrafirm flows of output across industries are imputed from input–output tables and

---

information on market shares of firms across industries. Thus, FVI in any industry is measured by the proportion of industry sales accounted for by the intrafirm flows of output sales from firms in the industry to their plants in other industries. Similarly, BVI in any industry is measured by the proportion of industry expenditures accounted for by intraindustry purchases by firms in the industry from their plants in other industries. Forward and backward vertical integration in industry j are defined respectively as

$$\text{FVI}_j = \frac{\sum\limits_{k \neq j}^{r} \sum\limits_{i = l}^{n} X_{jk}^{i}}{X_j} \qquad (13.1)$$

$$\text{BVI}_j = \frac{\sum\limits_{k \neq j}^{r} \sum\limits_{i = l}^{n} X_{kj}^{i}}{X_j} \qquad (13.2)$$

where n is the number of firms in any broad sector, such as manufacturing, r is the number of industries, X_{jk}^{i} is the flow of output within firm i from its plants in industry j to its plants in industry k and X_j represents the total sales of industry j (including intrafirm flows to other industries, but excluding sales within the industry).

In order to impute intrafirm flows between two industries it is assumed that input proportions are fixed (which may underestimate intrafirm flows because vertically integrated decisions are based on internal rather than market prices and an integrated firm is likely to employ more of an input when substitution between inputs is allowed). It is also assumed that internal transactions are always preferred to the market (which may overestimate flows where firm i sells from industry j to external customers in industry k, while at the same time buying in k from external suppliers in j). Given these qualifications, Davies and Morris (1995) estimated the extent of VI in 1986 for UK manufacturing in 79 three-digit industries. The most integrated industries were found to be grain milling, inorganic chemicals and paper and board (forwards) and man-made fibres and bread and biscuits (backwards). In general the degree of VI was fairly modest: among the leading integrated firms only 10–15% of total cross-industry transactions were internalised.

It should be noted that alternative strategies are open to a firm other than either dealing on the open market or vertically integrating. Two (or more) firms at successive stages in the production process may remain separate but operate some kind of vertical linkage or co-ordination strategy, such as agreements concerning supplies, sales or R&D; they could also operate a franchising arrangement (see Chapter 15). In the car industry, acknowledgement of the apparent advantages of the long-term relationships between producers and suppliers inherent in the Japanese *keiretsu* system led to the establishment of more informal producer/supplier arrangements among Western firms. In three years, Ford reduced the number of its suppliers by 45% and Motorola by 70%, but closer relationships were formed with the survivors. Similar partnership arrangements have spread to other areas, including retailing and healthcare services.[1] Like VI itself, vertical linkages may benefit from transaction cost savings (see below), but may suffer from the need to co-ordinate possibly conflicting managerial strategies between the different firms.

Motives for vertical integration

There are a number of motives for VI. In this subsection we concentrate on two of the most significant reasons for the strategy (which may equally apply to horizontal expansion): to improve efficiency and the pursuit of market power. The welfare implications of VI are also examined.

(A) EFFICIENCY-ENHANCING MOTIVES

Production or technical efficiencies arising from the technological interdependence of different production processes are often cited as a prime reason for VI. The classic example is the production of steel, for which a number of the processes have to be undertaken at high temperatures. By avoiding the need for the reheating of the product, substantial cost savings can be achieved if the various stages are located at a single site. Transport costs are also minimised. Similar fuel economies can be harnessed in other basic metal industries. Petroleum and petrochemicals, pulp and paper, and textiles are further examples of industries in which VI often yields technical efficiencies. Additional economies can be gained from expansion through VI if advertising and other promotional expenditures and levels of inventories can be reduced per unit of output. However, in a number of cases, plants are designed and built to cope with the requisite level of integration arising from technological interdependence; as a result enhanced production efficiencies are unlikely to arise from expansion through a strategy of VI. On the other hand, the discovery of new interdependencies may well provide a motive for integration, all the more so given the increasingly rapid pace of technological progress in many industries.

It has been argued that VI may well achieve greater savings in transaction costs than through efficiencies in production costs. Transaction costs arise due to the existence of the behavioural attributes of bounded rationality and opportunism, accompanied by the transactional characteristics of asset specificity, uncertainty and frequency (see Section 4.4). According to Williamson (1981) the higher the transaction costs, the greater the gains from integration. The problems of market co-ordination are likely to be at their most acute (and hence transaction costs will be at their highest) in conditions of technological interdependence between production processes and when transaction-specific assets are required. Thus, according to this argument, it is the savings in transaction costs arising from technological interdependence that act as the stimulus for vertical integration, not the production economies.

There are other ways in which transaction cost savings may provide a motive for VI. Non-integration may entail negative externalities in either production or distribution because of uncertainty regarding the quality of the raw materials offered by an upstream supplier or about the quality of the service provided by a downstream distributor of a final product. In addition, if a new product should require specialised inputs, uncertainty about the product's prospects may mean that the supplier of the inputs is reluctant to provide them for the innovating producer. VI may be the only viable solution in each case.

A high level of VI may also be likely in the initial or introductory stage of a product's life, irrespective of whether specific assets are required, simply because specialist suppliers or distributors do not yet exist. Then again, a VI strategy may be popular in a product's maturity when a reduction in the number of firms in a market forces suppliers into vertical arrangements with them (see Section 2.5).

There are difficulties in measuring transaction costs, especially those arising from uncertainty and small numbers. Various studies have revealed their significance as a motive for vertical integration, usually using proxy measures for estimation purposes (see the case study on page 266). However, it might be questioned why more cross-industry transactions are not internalised among the leading integrated firms if the perceived advantages of VI are so great. In addition, any cost savings that result from VI would need to be weighed against the possibility of increased management costs as a firm takes on additional activities. The M-form internal organisation can facilitate an increase in the range of activites that a firm

undertakes and at the same time reduce uncertainty and economise on transaction costs, at least in principle; hence, it may increase the scope for integration (see Section 4.6).

(B) MARKET POWER MOTIVES

It has been argued (notably by the Chicago school) that the pursuit of market power is not a likely basis for VI and that, even if it were, there would not be any socially harmful consequences. In fact, there may even be beneficial welfare effects associated with the strategy. However, as will be made clear, such an argument is based on rather restrictive assumptions. It depends on the nature of the market conditions existing in the different stages of production and, in particular, on the extent of input substitutability.

For example, if a perfectly competitive firm operating at one stage of production integrates with a similar firm at an adjacent stage there will be no effect on market power or on price and overall profitability. The same can be said for a monopolist integrating with a single perfectly competitive firm.

In fact, a similar conclusion can also apply should a monopolist acquire the entire perfectly competitive industry at an adjacent stage, but in this case only assuming that fixed input proportions exist for the product of the downstream industry. Such a situation is shown in Figure 89. It is assumed that there are two vertical stages in the production process, with a downstream perfectly competitive industry producing a final product, X, and buying an input, A, from an upstream monopolist. Further assumptions are that production costs are constant, they are not affected by integration and that a single unit of A is required for each unit of output of X.

In Figure 89 (a), D_X indicates the demand curve for the final product. AC_X shows the average costs of production excluding the costs of input A. Figure 89 (b) shows the demand curve for the input, D_A, which is derived from the difference between D_X and AC_X. MR_A is the associated marginal revenue curve. AC_A gives the average cost of producing input A. Thus, prior to integration, the monopolist supplier produces a profit-maximising output of Q_A and sells at a price of P_A. The equilibrium position of the competitive industry is where price equals the constant average (and hence marginal) costs, including P_A, giving a price of P_X and an output of Q_X. Post-integration the monopolist's demand curve becomes D_X; its costs are represented by AC_A plus AC_X. Since both demand and average costs have increased by AC_X, the relevant marginal revenue and marginal cost curves will also

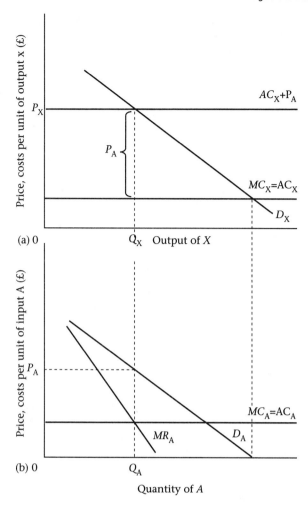

(a) 0 Q_X Output of X

(b) 0 Q_A

Quantity of A

Figure 89 *Vertical Integration between a monopolist and a perfectly competitive industry.*

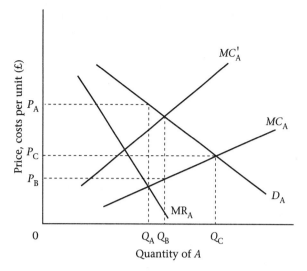

Quantity of A

Figure 90 *Vertical integration between a monopolist and a monopsonist.*

have increased by identical amounts and the profit-maximising level of output remains unaltered, as does the final product price. Profits in the industry are not affected.

Taking a second example, it is assumed that the supplier of the input is a monopolist as before, but on this occasion the producer of output X is the sole purchaser of input A; in other words it is a monopsonist. Since a single seller faces a single buyer, a bilateral monopoly exists. It is again assumed that fixed input proportions occur in the manufacture of the final product and, for ease of exposition, it is also assumed that the input is produced with increasing marginal costs. This is shown by the curve MC_A in Figure 90. The demand curve for the input, D_A, is derived from the demand curve for X; it is the

marginal revenue product of X. The associated marginal revenue curve is indicated by MR_A; the monopolist supplier maximises profits by producing Q_A and charging a price of P_A.

Assuming that the monopsonist could use its power to force the supplier to behave competitively, then MC_A would represent the supply curve of the industry or the buyer's average cost curve. The curve marginal to this, MC'_A, represents the buyer's marginal cost curve; the rising supply price of A indicated by MC_A means that MC'_A increases faster than MC_A. The buyer equates the marginal revenue of A (represented by D_A) with its marginal cost, MC'_A. It would therefore wish to purchase output Q_B at a price of P_B. The actual price and output lie between the two price/output combinations and depend on the relative bargaining strengths of the individual parties. If VI takes place it is probable that the price of the input would be determined by transfer pricing, in which case the price would be set at the competitive level equal to marginal cost, at P_C, giving an output of Q_C (assuming no external market for the product; see Section 10.5). Such a price might also be achieved through a process of negotiation, but it is more likely to be reached via VI, which also, it can be argued, reduces transaction costs and avoids opportunistic behaviour. Thus, in these circumstances VI enhances social welfare: allocative efficiency is improved and transaction costs are lowered. In support of this argument, Kerkvliet (1991) examined seven vertically integrated and 13 non-integrated mine-mouth, coal-fired, electric generating plants for 1979–87 in the US and found evidence of significant differences in the allocative efficiency of the integrated versus the non-integrated plants and of large increases in technical efficency with VI. Transaction-specific investments provided coal buyers with monopsony power, which is exercised by the non-integrated plants but not by the integrated ones.

However, the Chicago school view that the monopolistic implications of vertical integration are either benign (as in the first example above) or beneficial (as in the bilateral monopoly case) should not be implicitly accepted. If variable input proportions are used in the production of the final product, then less of input A will be used as its price increases. Therefore, a monopolist producer of A will not be able to extract the full monopoly profits from the final product industry. In these circumstances there is an incentive for VI, partly for reasons of efficiency enhancement, but also because of the possibility of increased market power.

In Figure 91, based on forward integration by a monopolist input supplier into a competitive industry, it is assumed that some degree of substitutability between inputs A and B in the production of X is possible. Isoquant X_1 shows the various combinations of A and B that can be used to produce the relevant output of the final product. Prior to integration and assuming a monopoly price for A, the isocost line is given as PP'. The optimal input combination is shown by point C. The isocost line MM'

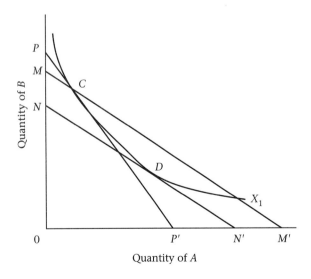

Figure 91 *Vertical integration assuming variable input proportions.* Source: Vernon and Graham, 1971.

(which by construction is drawn through point C) indicates the marginal cost of A. Hence, PM is the profit accruing to the monopolist supplier of A (in terms of B). Post-integration production, based on the marginal cost of A, occurs at D, on the lower cost curve NN'. A is substituted for B in production. The improvement in efficiency leads to an increase in profit (in terms of B) of MN. In fact, profits may increase by more than this because the integrated firm now has the power to change the price and output of X.

Thus, assuming variable input proportions, integration can be undertaken for market power motives and consequently economic welfare may be reduced. However, the policy implications of VI are still unclear because a reduction in welfare does not necessarily follow from the analysis: assuming no change in price and output, then increased profits could simply result from improved efficiency in resource use. In practice, downstream market conditions other than competitive ones may need to be taken into account.

There are also the entry-deterring effects of VI to consider. Should VI be efficiency-enhancing, then a non-integrated potential entrant would be at a relative cost disadvantage at its stage of production. Full integration would be necessary for entry. Furthermore, the monopolisation of upstream inputs or downstream distributive outlets by an integrated producer and the use of predatory tactics, such as refusal to supply or purchase and other non-competitive strategies may make non-integrated entry more problematic. However, fully integrated entry may face the capital requirements barrier (see Section 2.4).

Thus, public policy towards VI needs to consider both the possibility of production efficiencies and transaction cost savings as well as the potential for adverse market power consequences (and the associated possibility of discriminatory pricing) to determine the overall welfare implications. Such considerations form part of competition policy. This is discussed further in Chapter 15, where particular cases are cited.

13.3 CONGLOMERATE DIVERSIFICATION

A conglomerate firm produces a number of different products; it is multiproduct and ostensibly operates in different industries. Thus, diversification examines the extent to which a firm is multiproduct. A distinction can be made between *lateral diversification*, in which the products are related in terms of demand or supply, or *pure conglomerate diversification*, whereby the products have no obvious links. Lateral growth or *product extension diversification* can be subdivided into *marketing concentricity* if the products are demand-related and *technological concentricity* where there are production relationships.[2] Most diversification involves some kind of lateral growth into related product areas.

As has been noted, conglomerate mergers accounted for over 50% of all merger activity in the UK during the last merger wave. Diversification was also a contributory factor in the growth of aggregate concentration in the 1960s (see Section 2.3). In the US conglomerates have had even more of an impact. Conglomerate mergers accounted for almost a half of total mergers by the end of the 1970s. During the 1950s and 1960s, aggregate concentration rose substantially, while there were only slight increases in levels of market concentration (Scherer, 1980). The implication of this is that large firms grew by diversification rather than by increases in market shares. More recently the strategy among some large firms in a number of countries (for example, ITT and IBM in the US, British Aerospace and BP in the UK and Daimler-Benz in Germany) has been to hive off what are regarded as peripheral activities and to concentrate on core businesses, although it is too early to say whether this is part of a general trend away from diversification.

In the remainder of this section we discuss the main motives for diversification and consider its policy implications. Efficiency factors, managerial motives and risk-reducing reasons for diversification are discussed. The public policy ramifications of diversification are then examined.

Motives for diversification

(A) EFFICIENCY-ENHANCING MOTIVES

The efficiency motive for diversification centres on the employment of underutilised, specialised assets in alternative uses. Internal rather than market transactions will occur when transaction costs are high. The concept of economies of scope, introduced in Section 6.8, may be considered relevant in this regard. Economies of scope arise from joint production and exist specifically when the cost of producing two products jointly is less than the sum of their separate production. The basis for economies of scope is the existence of sharable or quasi-public inputs in the production of two or more goods. However, Teece (1980, 1982) has argued that economies of scope are

---

Box 13.2 *The measurement of diversification*

The extent of diversification varies between firms and industries; it is estimated that petroleum products, chemicals and textiles are among the most diversification-intensive manufacturing industries in the UK (in the sense that firms classified as belonging to these industries are the most diversified). Like VI the extent of diversification may depend on how particular industries are classified. Given this proviso, diversification can be measured in a number of ways:

(1) In terms of the number of industries in which a firm is active. However, this may be a misleading indicator when a high proportion of the activities are relatively small.

(2) As a ratio of the main activity of the firm (measured in terms of either sales or employment) to its total activity, although this measure may rely on a somewhat arbitrary definition of what constitutes the main activity; it also gives no indication of the range of activities undertaken by a firm.

(3) By the use of summary measures, such as the Utton index. Utton (1979) defines the W index of diversification as follows:

$$W = 2 \sum_{j=1}^{r} js_j - 1 \qquad (13.3)$$

where s_j denotes the percentage of the firm's activity in the jth industry and r refers to the number of industries in which the firm is active. The index varies between one for a completely specialised firm and r where a firm is equally active across all industries. Thus, if a firm operates in four industries with the proportions 0.4, 0.3, 0.2 and 0.1, the index is calculated as $W = 2(0.4(1) + 0.3(2) + 0.2(3) + 0.1(4)) - 1 = 3.0$. This index benefits from being a summary measure of diversification, although relatively unimportant activities may be allocated quite significant weights.

---

neither necessary nor sufficient for a strategy of diversification. If the sale or lease of the sharable inputs involves negligible transaction costs (i.e. should a ready and well-informed external market exist for their use), then there is no reason to presume that internal multiproduct operations will take place. If, on the other hand, there is an inefficient market for the sale or lease of these inputs, then high transaction costs will provide an incentive for multiproduct operations. Alternatively, high transaction costs may stimulate conglomerate activity (because of spare capacity in resource use) in the absence of economies of scope. In other words, according to this argument it is the presence of transaction costs that provides the basis for diversification, not the existence of economies of scope:

Diversification can represent a mechanism for capturing integration economies associated with the simultaneous supply of inputs common to a number of production processes geared to distinct final product firms (Teece, 1980: 224).

A firm may possess a number of specialised resources that are common to a range of activities, each of which may also exhibit spare capacity at any time. They include the following: indivisible capital assets, human capital which can be enhanced by know-how gained through learning-by-doing and managerial ability. Teece concentrates on specialised and indivisible capital assets and know-how as being particularly conducive to diversification, particularly the product extension variety. The more specialised the capital asset and the smaller the number of parties involved in any negotiations, the less the likelihood of market contracts taking place. By diversifying and keeping the asset within the firm, transaction costs can be reduced. The transfer of tacit or informal know-how or knowledge, whether organisational or technical, involves significant transaction costs. Buyers are uncertain precisely what they are purchasing and hence how to value it and sellers are unable to reveal the value of the know-how because they would then reveal the knowledge itself (a situation referred to by Arrow (1962) as the 'fundamental paradox' of information). Therefore, transactions involving know-how lead to costly haggling and the possibility of opportunism, all the more so the more frequent is the required exchange of information. In addition, a knowledge of organisational routines may necessitate the transfer of a team of people, rather than a single individual, in order to secure an effective transfer of knowledge by one firm to another. A firm may pursue diversification as a superior option to repeated contractual bargains.

Evidence in support of the transaction cost motive for diversification is relatively scarce; it is also usually based on proxy indicators of the main independent variables. Teece cites the diversification of oil firms into alternative fuel markets as consistent with a desire to share technical know-how across products. Ingham and Thompson (1994) linked 292 new entries into 13 product markets by 47 UK building societies during 1987–91 to the need to exploit specific and under-utilised assets or capabilities, measured as follows:

(1) branches/total assets (representing the availability of resources);

(2) headquarters staff/total assets (representing specific human capital);
(3) accumulated surplus/total assets (representing the availability of funds for investment);
(4) advertising/total assets (to indicate brand-name capital).

(B) MANAGERIAL MOTIVES

Section 4.6 examined the Williamson (1975, 1981) hypothesis that specific managerial resources can be more effectively utilised within an M-form structure than in other organisational forms and that such an internal structure is likely to be associated with a policy of diversification. According to Williamson the M-form structure takes on the properties of a miniature capital market. It is more able to allocate capital to high-yield uses than the external market because senior managers are better informed about internal investment opportunities and individual projects can be effectively controlled and monitored. On the other hand, risk-averse managers may avoid risky investments. They may also pursue policies at odds with the interests of shareholders, as discussed more fully in Chapter 9. Such policies include the growth maximisation strategy put forward by Marris.

Marris (1964) has argued that managerially-controlled firms seek growth mainly through a policy of diversification. It is assumed that the managerial objective is to maximise the rate of growth of the firm, subject to a job security constraint and the main means to growth is diversification. Mueller (1969) has also equated the managerial desire for growth with conglomerate activity. Mueller postulated that growth-maximising managers have a lower cost of capital than shareholders. The opportunity cost of funds for managers is the marginal cost of funds within the firm, whereas the equivalent for shareholders is the return on the highest-yielding investment in other firms. As a result, managers engage in a higher level of investment in productive activities than that which maximises shareholder welfare. This raises the optimal level of the firm's investment in horizontal, vertical and conglomerate activities; assuming that public policy constraints prevent horizontal and vertical growth, this will lead to increased investment in diversification. Conglomerate mergers will be pursued most actively, since they provide a quicker route to growth than a diversification strategy based on internal growth.

Another managerial motive for diversification is that being risk-averse and having all their financial (not to say employment) interests tied up in a single firm, they are more likely to opt for a risk-reducing diversification strategy (see below). There is some evidence that managerially-controlled firms are more prone to conglomerate acquisition activity than are equivalent owner-controlled organisations (see Clarke, 1987).

(C) RISK-REDUCING MOTIVES

The risk-reduction motive for diversification is analogous to the notion of 'not putting all one's eggs in one basket'. Good performance in one part of a firm's business can be offset against poor performance elsewhere, leading to a lower expected variation in overall performance (such as the rate of return) and a lower degree of risk. This idea is based on the simple statistical hypothesis that, when comparing the expected earnings of a diversified firm with the earnings of a group of independent firms producing the same product range, the variation in the combined expected earnings of the diversified firm is likely to be lower.

Such a situation would appear to have obvious attractions for suppliers of capital. However, shareholders can achieve a similar degree of diversification in their portfolios and a similar reduction in risk by diversifying their purchase of shares in various specialised companies. There may be high transaction costs involved in such a strategy, but these can be avoided by purchasing a unit trust. Debtholders, on the other hand, may be attracted by the reduced risk of default in a diversified company, since poor performance in one area of the firm can be covered elsewhere. As a result, diversified firms should be able to raise more debt finance than specialised firms (see Case Study One, page 80, for confirmatory evidence). The reduced risk of default may also make cheaper loan finance a possibility. The increased gearing will confer tax advantages on the diversified company, since interest payments on debt are tax-deductible. Diversified firms can also reduce their overall tax liability by offsetting losses in one area against profits in another. Shareholders will benefit from the resulting rise in the post-tax value of the firm.

The public policy implications of diversification

Diversification has a number of important public policy implications, specifically relating to the competitive process. However, views about its effects vary widely. The Chicago school argues that, since diversification by definition occurs in other markets, it cannot affect the degree of competition in a particular market. Diversification may also have efficiency-enhancing effects. On the other hand, it has been argued that the size of conglomerate firms and the dominance that they are able to exert in a number of different markets can have both efficiency-reducing and possible anti-competitive consequences, such as an enhanced ability to price discriminate.

The efficiency-enhancing potential of diversification has been noted: where a firm has spare capacity in resource-use, then there is significant scope for transaction cost savings through a diversification strategy, at least in principle. It could also be argued that the greater potential for career-enhancement within large, diversified organisations attracts better quality managerial and other staff compared with smaller, specialised firms. If this were true, although a somewhat contentious premise, then costs may be further reduced as a result of productivity gains. The supposed long-purse advantages of access to plentiful and relatively cheap finance (both internal and external) by conglomerate firms, plus the fact that they are better able to cope with temporary losses, gives them a greater chance of entering and remaining in new markets than specialised firms. Therefore, diversification may stimulate competition in a new market, at least in the short term. However, if a conglomerate then uses its financial muscle and power in different markets to exclude its rivals, possibly by various anti-competitive practices, competition may ultimately decline. The overall competitive constraint on a market will also fall should a potential entrant diversify into a market by acquiring an existing firm, in which case the number of potential and actual competitors declines by one; however, if the acquiree is small but is subsequently developed into a larger organisation by the diversifier, then competition may ultimately increase.

Once established in a market, a diversified firm may deliberately attempt to exclude rival firms by the use of predatory pricing tactics (see Section 10.2), especially since it has the capacity to cross-subsidise losses in one area of its activities against profits in another (although this policy presumes that the firm is sufficiently profitable elsewhere in its business to be able to do so). The long-purse argument may also enable the conglomerate firm to outstay rivals in a price war. Diversification may further encourage a predatory strategy because the reputation for predation in one market may spill over to other markets. Levy (1989) has argued that a conglomerate firm has the additional advantage of being able to transfer other specific assets, not just financial resources, between uses, thus reducing the cost of, and increasing the likelihood for, predation. On the other hand, if a rival is also diversified it can employ its assets in other uses during the predatory period and re-enter a market when price rises, hence reducing the effects of predation.

The fact that diversified firms operate in a number of different markets increases the prospects for some kind of reciprocal arrangement between two or more diversifying firms, whereby, say, a branch of firm A only agrees to buy firm B's output as long as B purchases an input supplied by another branch of firm A. In such circumstances any transaction cost savings would need to be weighed against enhanced market power effects, although the arrangement is only likely to have anti-competitive consequences where firm A has significant market power in its different markets in the first instance. A diversified firm is also well-suited to the imposition of a tied sales policy on other firms, by which the purchase of a product is tied, say, to the purchase of the machinery and equipment to make the product. Finally, very large diversified firms, each with activities in many markets whose operations necessarily impinge on the activities of the other conglomerates in a number of areas, may develop 'spheres of influence'. Competition is restricted because each firm has to weigh up the implications of actions in one market against retaliatory actions in that market and in other markets. The policy implications of these and other strategies are considered in more detail in Chapter 15.

13.4 MULTINATIONAL EXPANSION

The nature and extent of multinational activity was examined at length in Section 4.8. Here we discuss the reasons for overseas expansion by multinational corporations (MNCs) by examining the main theoretical approaches to foreign direct investment (FDI).

The original theoretical basis for FDI was founded in international economics. Firms were essentially regarded as arbitrageurs of capital. The profit-maximising MNC shifts capital from low-return countries to where it can obtain a higher rate of return. Thus, the home bases of MNCs should be those countries well endowed with capital, in which the marginal productivity of capital is relatively low, while host countries will have higher marginal productivities. However, Hymer (1960) questioned such an analysis on various empirical grounds:

(1) Traditionally the US had been a net exporter of FDI, but a net importer of portfolio foreign investment.
(2) Many industrialised economies were both home and host countries for MNCs.
(3) FDI tended to be concentrated in specific industries, rather than in specific countries.

The capital-arbitrage hypothesis also implicitly assumes that the rate of return on capital is the same in all industries in a country, in other words that long-run perfectly competitive conditions exist throughout the economy. However, FDI would not exist in perfect competition, since under such conditions no firm would gain a competitive advantage by investing abroad. Instead, Hymer postulated that MNCs possess *firm-specific* (alternatively referred to as *ownership* or *strategic*) advantages over local firms, mainly of a monopolistic nature, and they could exploit these through overseas investment. As Kindelberger (1969) has also pointed out:

For direct investment to thrive there must be some imperfection in markets for goods or factors, including among the latter technology, or some interference in competition by government or by firms, which separate markets (Kindelberger, 1969:13).

Kindelberger highlighted four main sources of transferable advantages: departures from perfect competition in goods markets, such as product differentiation, marketing skills and collusive pricing; departures from perfect competition in input markets, including access to patented or proprietary knowledge, differences in access to capital and managerial skill differences; internal and external economies of scale, particularly arising from vertical integration; and government policies in respect of taxes, tariffs and other factors that may restrict production or entry. For example, it has been suggested that a reason for the surge in Japanese FDI, both in terms of wholly-owned susidiaries and joint ventures, in the car and electronic industries in the US and Western Europe in the mid- to late 1980s onwards was the much improved ownership advantages of the Japanese firms relative to their Western counterparts (Dunning, 1993).

According to the Hymer–Kindelberger approach, FDI is preferred to exporting in order to avoid tariff and transport costs. Hymer also argued that FDI is preferred to some kind of overseas licensing arrangement because of imperfections in the market for knowledge (arising from the concentration of buyer and seller power and the Arrow paradox that was discussed in the previous section). Licensing involves heavy transfer or transaction costs to ensure that the contractual arrangements are adhered to correctly.[3] It is postulated that FDI takes place when the costs of setting up and running an overseas subsidiary are less than the transfer costs involved in a licensing arrangement with local producers.

An alternative analysis of multinational expansion, but one which is also based on imperfectly competitive market structures, is that by Knickerbocker (1973), who argued that the interdependence between oligopolists will instigate a 'follow-the-leader' type approach to FDI. Such a strategy is more likely to occur in fairly loose-knit oligopolies where firms do not have the necessary experience of operating in the industry to co-ordinate their plans. They adopt a defensive strategy by imitating the actions of the first firm to establish production facilities abroad in order to negate any competitive advantage that the initiating firm might gain. An analysis of multinational activity based on oligopolistic action and reaction can help to explain the 'bunching' of entry into some new overseas markets that occurs, although it does not account for overseas investment by the lead firm, nor does it explain FDI by established MNCs.

A dynamic explanation of overseas investment was proposed by Vernon (1966), who utilised the concept of the *product life cycle* (see Section 2.5) to analyse the production and locational decisions of MNCs. Vernon related the changes that a product undergoes during the various stages of its life to the move from export-servicing of a foreign market to foreign-affiliate production. Therefore, firm-specific advantages in the form of a new product or process are exploited by overseas production. Originally, Vernon applied the theory mainly to US-based innovation and production. Firms there, it was argued, have an incentive to develop products geared to the high-income consumer and directed to labour-saving devices.

In the introductory stage of a product's life there is an inherent tendency to locate at home; any foreign demand, which is likely to be small, will be met by exports. As demand increases in the next stage and production expands, so foreign demand increases. The overseas demand is mainly met by exports, although an analysis of the relative costs of exporting versus FDI may lead to some overseas

production in other advanced economies: assuming profit maximisation, as long as the marginal production costs of exports plus the transport and tariff costs are greater than the average production cost of locating abroad, the firm would undertake FDI. Western Europe would be the preferred location, since it has a similar level and nature of demand to the US but where (at the time of the original thesis) labour costs are lower. In the third stage, by which time a standardised product has emerged, price competition is all important. The priority is to minimise costs; labour-intensive production and assembly processes are located, through FDI, in developing countries with very low labour costs. In other words, overseas production shifts down the income scale, from the US, to Western Europe and finally to developing countries.

The original version of Vernon's model was designed to explain the post-war growth of US-based MNCs into Europe, mainly in manufacturing. It has subsequently been overtaken by events, although it may still have some applicability to firms investing abroad for the first time.[4] Product cycle explanations may also have some relevance to the FDI decision of service MNCs in areas like banking, insurance, advertising and hotels, which set up foreign facilities having first serviced the home market. However, locational factors are more important determinants of much such FDI, given the fact that many services cannot be traded across space. In addition, the model has far less relevance to the activities of global firms, that may segment the market according to local tastes and which may locate production processes abroad (such as component assembly) at the earliest stage in a product's life. In order to counter some of these these objections, Vernon (1974, 1979) modified the model to take account both of innovations originating outside the US and of the oligopolistic behaviour of MNCs. The three stages of the cycle were referred to as innovation-based oligopoly, mature oligopoly and senescent oligopoly. Vernon hypothesised that the US would have a comparative advantage in labour-saving innovations, Europe a comparative advantage in capital- and material-saving products and processes, while Japanese firms would have an incentive to conserve material, capital and space. Initially production would take place at home so as to co-ordinate production with R&D and marketing. In stage two, oligopolistic rivalry results in the setting up of production facilities in the markets of competitors in order to protect global market shares. Relative cost differentials assume increased significance in stage three as entry barriers decline.

There are a number of *locational factors* that are important in determining where and why firms may set up production facilities abroad. Natural resource endowments provide an incentive for BVI by MNCs engaged in their exploitation. The created resource endowments (for example, skills and informational infrastructure) within international financial centres may stimulate horizontal overseas expansion in services like banking and insurance (Jones, 1996). Relatively cheap labour creates 'offshore' production facilities; traditionally, Japanese manufacturing FDI was able to take advantage of the cheaper labour costs of nearby developing economies, a number of which are now themselves the newly industrialising economies of South-east Asia. The imposition, removal or change in the level of tariff and non-tariff barriers to trade can have a profound effect on FDI; witness the large increase in overseas investment flows into the EU prior to the establishment of the Single Market in January 1993. Other host country policies, whether supportive or hostile towards inward FDI, can have a major impact on FDI by influencing the overall investment climate in a country.

As mentioned above, Hymer argued that FDI would be preferred to an alternative arrangement like licensing due to informational asymmetries in the market for knowledge. This aspect of Hymer's theory was developed by, among others, Buckley and Casson (1976), Rugman (1981) and Hennart (1982) into a so-called *internalisation* view of the reasons for multinational expansion, with its emphasis on the relative costs of internalising economic activity. Its foundations, however, are firmly embedded in *transaction cost analysis* (Teece, 1986).

According to Teece, a firm will become multinational if:

(1) it possesses specialised assets that give it an advantage over indigenous firms (the strategic advantage factor);
(2) the assets can be better utilised in production units in foreign locations (the location factor);
(3) full value can be obtained from the assets by their transfer internally within the firm to another subsidiary.

In other words:

The multinational enterprise and foreign direct investment represent a response to high transaction costs by firms with unique assets/capabilities which have value when utilised

in production facilities located in foreign markets (Teece, 1986:27).

Thus, according to this argument, given any locational and strategic advantages, it is transaction costs that determine the overseas investment decision. In the case of the *horizontal* multinational enterprise, where the firm produces essentially the same product from each plant in a number of different overseas locations, the overseas investment decision is based on the fundamental paradox of information (given that the asset in question is the market for knowledge). This is especially pertinent when there are problems in patenting the know-how because property rights cannot be enforced. Since much technical know-how is tacit and cannot be codified (unlike, say, the formula for a chemical compound or the code of a computer software program) and may therefore require personal contact, enforceable contractual arrangements may prove to be an impossibility. Further contractual problems arise if it should be deemed necessary to send a whole team of people abroad for an effective transfer of information, especially when a succession of transfers is contemplated. The more complex the know-how to be transferred, the higher the prospective transaction costs and the greater the incentive for horizontal investment abroad. MNCs may also wish to utilise their marketing and managerial expertise and know-how to maintain product quality. For example, the horizontal expansion of multinational firms in low-technology services, such as hotels and fast-food, can be explained by the desire to avoid debasement of the quality of a branded good.

Casson (1987) argued that the importance of collusion can provide an alternative motive for horizontal international integration. Global profits in an industry may be increased by collusion between firms that operate in different localities. A merger between firms (and hence the establishment of a MNC) may be preferable to, say, a cartel because of the saving on monitoring costs. As has been noted, cartels have other inherent problems (see Section 8.5). In post-war Europe many MNCs replaced cartels, although government opposition to the foreign control of strategically-important industries, such as the mining of some raw materials, shipping and aviation, can still lead to their domination by international cartel arrangements.

Evidence supporting the transaction cost approach towards multinational activity suffers from the familiar measurement problems. Studies have mainly concentrated on the relationship between certain non-tradeable specific assets and the degree of multinational activity, but the intangibility of these assets makes them difficult to measure; proxy indicators are provided by estimates of the outlays that firms make in order to develop the assets, such as R&D and advertising expenditures. In other words, it is the outlays on specific assets that are being investigated, not the transaction costs that might arise from them. Caves (1982) and Teece (1986) both refer to a number of US studies confirming a positive and significant relationship between the proportion of foreign subsidiary assets in the total assets of US firms and the importance of R&D and advertising outlays to the industry.

The transaction cost analysis of the *vertical* multinational firm, in which the outputs of some plants serve as inputs for the plants in different countries, is based on the importance of the same concepts as those underlying the vertically integrated domestic business: asset specificity, uncertainty and frequency. The vertically integrated multinational internalises the market for an intermediate product in the same way that the horizontally based multinational internalises the market for specific assets like know-how. The more transaction-specific the assets (whether human or physical) involved in production, the higher the prospective transaction costs from market trading and the greater the incentive for integration. For example, assume that, in order to produce at lowest costs, a smelter in a home country needs to be designed to process a particular grade of ore. If the smelting operator undertakes the necessary specific investment, then recontracting hazards may arise if the ore is found in only one or two overseas locations. Specifically, the supplier may behave opportunistically and increase the price of the ore or reduce its quality. *Ex ante* BVI can reduce this risk. Uncertainty regarding the quality of either the raw materials supplied by an upstream overseas firm or the finished product offered for sale by a downstream foreign distributor provide further incentives for VI by MNCs.

Tests of the transaction cost theory of international vertical integration are fairly sparse, although Stuckey (1983) reported extensive vertical integration (as well as joint ventures) in the international aluminium industry. Aluminium refining facilities have to be sited near to bauxite mines to minimise transport costs and the investments involved are very large and highly specific. Integration therefore reduces the scope for haggling and opportunism. Similar considerations apply to the international copper and petroleum industries.

Transaction cost analysis, or internalisation theory which is based upon it, can help to provide a theoretical framework for multinational expansion, although it is more concerned with examining the reasons for the replacement of international markets with multinational organisations than with questioning why some firms are more successful than others at becoming global entities. It is also essentially a static analysis. *Eclectic* theories of multinational expansion have been developed (see e.g. Dunning, 1993) that incorporate the various theoretical approaches into a unifying, dynamic framework, in which international production is regarded as a function of ownership, internalisation and locational factors whose significance may vary from case to case. Political, legal and cultural considerations are also taken into account. The problem with such an approach, or paradigm as Dunning terms it, is that it lacks predictive power, although it is useful in revealing the diverse and complex nature of the overseas investment decision and the various factors that determine it.

13.5 INTERNATIONAL TECHNOLOGY-BASED STRATEGIC ALLIANCES

An alternative to complete ownership of overseas assets is some kind of strategic alliance (SA) or collaboration between two or more firms in different countries. The popularity of such deals is reckoned to be increasing at a rapid rate.[5] Since many of them involve the development, diffusion and commercialisation of technological knowledge, this section concentrates on the reasons for, and the impact of, technology- or R&D-based arrangements.

The term strategic alliance as used here encompasses any form of collaboration from informal agreements to deals involving an exchange of ownership; it includes licensing, distribution and supply agreements, collaborative research, technological exchanges, management contracts as well as equity ventures comprising either joint ownership of an enterprise or the partial acquisition of one firm by another. International alliances naturally imply cross-border deals.

Not surprisingly, R&D-based SAs are concentrated in high-technology industries, like microelectronics, aeronautics, defence, pharmaceuticals and biotechnology, and in those industries that have the greatest tendency to use high-technology techniques, such as vehicle production. They tend to be more popular among large firms, given the high costs and risks involved, although smaller companies are increasingly becoming involved in deals with their larger customers.

There are various motives for SAs, including the enhancement of market power, the overcoming of entry barriers into new markets, the transference of organisational and complementary knowledge and as a means of reducing hostile reactions from foreign governments. They offer the following potential advantages:

(1) The sharing of the high costs of specific investments in new product and process development. It is estimated that the cost of developing a new global car is about £2 billion, a price which even many large firms are reluctant to face alone. In semiconductor production, IBM of the US joined forces with Japan's Toshiba and Siemens of Germany in 1992 to develop the new DRAM memory chips, the design and manufacture of which exceeded £2 billion.

(2) The acceleration of the manufacture and commercialisation of innovations, especially given the widespread existence of shorter product cycles coupled with the more rapid diffusion of technology.

(3) The ability to take advantage of economies of scale and scope (technological development usually involves high fixed costs, which are predominantly sunk) and the spreading of risks. The increasing convergence of technologies, as between computing and telecommunications, heightens the risks of having to manage complementary technologies.

(4) The advantage of co-operating with rivals, thus reducing competition; this may also have the effect of the opening up of new markets. Reciprocal access to the Japanese market through SAs is a major incentive for many Western firms. Procter & Gamble and IBM have each built up large sales in Japan through a series of alliances.

(5) The enhancement of the ability to compete globally.

However, there are also potential problems involved with such arrangements. SAs may suffer from the incompatibility of mixing different corporate cultures, particularly in the case of international alliances. Another drawback is concern about rivals being able to gain a competitive edge through too easy access to information (given the public good characteristics of knowledge) and/or home markets, especially in the case of horizontal alliances. In addition, firms may be more concerned about running their core businesses than with investing sufficient time and effort in the efficient operation of the joint venture. Finally, as is the case in semiconductors, there is often a close link between basic research, corporate R&D activities and manufacturing and marketing resources. Thus, co-operation at various stages may be necessary to gain the full and speedy benefits of a particular project.

Game theory and transaction cost analysis can help to explain the reasons for opting for some kind of joint strategy as opposed to full-scale FDI or market transacting. As Dunning (1993) points out, there are two branches of game theory that analyse the determinants and likely outcomes of, respectively, non-co-operative, or forced, and co-operative, or voluntary, agreements. Non-co-operative game theory helps to analyse the conditions under which co-operative agreements can emerge between egotistical partners with no central authority. The theory of co-operative games, on the other hand, analyses the bargaining tactics of partners who have to decide on the partition of the payoff. The problem is that neither branch of the theory is able to cope adequately with the fact that, in SA situations, rivalrous and co-operative behaviour can occur together. *Almost non-co-operative* and *almost co-operative games* have been developed to analyse these situations; they conclude that a co-operative agreement is continually evolving and that its survival is best achieved by taking a long-term view.

From a transaction cost perspective, the rationale for SAs compared with full ownership of a subsidiary is that they occur when the transaction costs involved in their formation and implementation are less than the costs of full ownership, given the fact that the assets of one or both parties are specific to the transaction. Firms prefer R&D-based alliances to full ownership in order to avoid or reduce the control costs of rigid internal structures, high capital costs and the riskiness of investments. They are preferred to market contracts because, it is argued, they provide a superior monitoring mechanism and create a closer alignment of incentives to share information on technologies and guarantee performance (assuming, as before, specificity of assets by one or both parties). Transaction cost theory again provides a useful framework for analysis, although eclectic explanations may provide a better account of the various reasons for the many different types of SAs. In practice, political, legal and cultural factors also need to be considered.

Much is made of the apparent lack of success of SAs. It has been estimated that up to 80% of alliances end in a sale by one of the partners to the other.[6] Incompatibility and the problems of differing corporate cultures are the reasons usually cited for failure. However, in welfare terms a few potential advantages of R&D alliances can be suggested. Given a non-optimal supply of R&D by firms (see Section 15.5), joint ventures can lead to greater efficiency, both in terms of the quantity of research and the diffusion of knowledge flowing from it. They can reduce R&D duplication, help to raise productivity (and hence reduce prices) and improve the competitiveness of domestic MNCs. They may promote innovations that otherwise would not have occurred. R&D co-operations can also internalise the externalities created by significant R&D spillovers, a factor that may otherwise lead to underinvestment in R&D.

Against all this it is necessary to weigh their prospective social costs:

(1) the possible anti-competitive impact of horizontal agreements:
(2) the creation of additional entry barriers (for example, agreements between integrated firms could lead to entry barriers downstream);
(3) the stifling of entrepreneurial and innovative activity by the establishment of government-backed SAs and via the co-option of innovative rivals;
(4) the restriction of the diffusion of technology.

In addition, collusive activity in R&D may also lead to other forms of collusion, as in pricing. Finally, technological knowledge may be too easily lost. Many of the deals struck by US companies with Japanese firms in the 1960s and 1970s led to a large-scale outflow of know-how from the US with little chance of access to the Japanese market in return. As a result, American firms lost market share to Japanese companies in cars, consumer electronics, steel, semiconductors, machine tools and in many other industries.

In assessing the precise welfare implications of SAs it should be noted that it is difficult enough to measure the impact on output and profits of R&D *per se*, let alone the effects of international R&D-based alliances. The share of international joint ventures in total R&D activities would first have to be established and then their relative impact would have to be determined. Whatever their overall effects there is little doubt that R&D-based international alliances represent a growing share of global innovative activity. Their location and popularity may depend ultimately

on the relationship between multinational firms and governments, a subject to which we now turn.

13.6 THE RELATIONSHIPS BETWEEN HOST GOVERNMENTS AND MULTI-NATIONAL CORPORATIONS

Host country policies can have a significant influence on both the scale and nature of inward investment. A government may have an open policy towards FDI, in which case ownership structures are not usually specified and very few controls are imposed on foreign firms other than those that are placed on national firms. On the other hand, controls of varying severity may be imposed on inward FDI (culminating in the nationalisation of the foreign-owned assets); alternatively, they may be placed on ownership structures. For example, it may be that for both political and economic reasons a host government would prefer some kind of collaborative arrangement between the overseas company and a local firm or firms, in which case a joint alliance would be a more likely outcome than full-scale FDI.

In general, it would appear that attitudes by policy-makers towards MNCs have become much more supportive since the early 1980s. The increased glob-alisation of production, characterised by the growth of all forms of international transactions, especially by MNCs, coupled with technological advances, which have had the effect of widening the available options to firms in the location of their value-adding activities (witness the trend for establishing an R&D presence in each of the major economic regions of the world) have, it is argued, combined to raise the bargaining power of many MNCs *vis-à-vis* host governments. In game theoretical terms, the relationship between MNCs and host economies can be regarded as a bilateral monopoly bargaining model. The MNC has the package of resources needed by the host economy, whereas the latter possesses various factors required by the MNC, such as its market, cheap labour and natural and created resource endowments, which can be combined to produce a favourable investment opportunity for the overseas firm. Bargaining skills and the relative power of the two parties determine the outcome, defined in terms of the sharing of the return from the industry. Naturally, if the power of one of the parties increases, then it will expect to secure a greater share of the rewards.

Prior to 1930, most governments operated fairly open policies towards inward FDI. Between 1930 and the 1970s, however, there was a worldwide growth in restrictions (for example, tariff and non-tariff barriers such as exchange controls and the screening of particular projects) towards MNCs as the powers of national governments increased and their interests were perceived as divergent from those of international enterprises. Inward investment tended to be regarded more as a substitute for domestic investment than as a complement to it. For example, during the 1960s a policy of promoting national champions in Europe was combined with growing concern about the large outflows of capital in the form of interest, profits and management fees associated with foreign-based MNCs, their 'footloose' nature and the fact that they might deprive local firms of capital and skilled labour and managerial resources. French policy towards inward FDI at the time was mainly geared towards the avoidance of becoming over-reliant on American technology.

Despite the fact that there has been a general easing of policies by host governments towards foreign MNCs since the early 1980s following a long period of increased restrictions, there have been significant national differences within these overall trends. The UK and the US have traditionally had a relatively open policy towards MNCs, whereas Japan has had a much more restrictive policy. Similar policy differences can be observed within developing countries. Singapore has had a much more open policy compared with the restrictive stance taken by India. Since the early 1980s, these policy positions have converged as many governments have sought to encourage MNCs to invest in their countries through a series of financial inducements in order to gain access to the latest technologies and organisational skills and to markets. At the same time, federal US legislation (although not state legislation) has tended to become more restrictive by, for example, blocking takeovers of US firms by foreign investors. This has been largely in response to concern about the tax-avoiding policies of foreign MNCs (see Section 10.5). Such a policy stance has provided greater incentives for the establishment of joint ventures in the US. Nevertheless, FDI is now generally regarded as complementary to domestic investment rather than as a substitute for it. Governments increasingly view inward investment as a method of improving the efficiency of resource usage and as a means to raising living standards and enhancing national competitiveness in a global economy. Whether such a view is entirely justifiable is another matter. Reference has been made (see Case Study Two, Chapter 6) to the

fact that many of the Japanese car-producing plants in UK and the rest of Europe are essentially low-value-added assembly operations with relatively little local content. Initially, the inflow of funds has a positive impact on the capital account of the balance of payments and new jobs are created. However, there are future outflows of profits and management royalties to consider, on the current account any export earnings have to be weighed against the import of components and the net effect on employment depends on the extent to which sales by the foreign-based subsidiaries displace domestic production.

In transaction cost terms the essence of the FDI process is what Williamson (1981) has termed 'the fundamental transformation'. The outcome of any bargaining between the host economy and the MNC depends on the relative desire that each party has for the transaction to take place. If a multinational presence in a country involves the deployment of specific assets, then prior to the investment the firm can bargain for favourable terms with a host government. Once the deal has been signed and the investment sunk, the position of the MNC may become weaker. It may be vulnerable to opportunism by the host country, characterised by pressure for renegotiation of the contract. The bargaining position of the host country improves further as it gains access to the latest technologies and develops the skills to employ them. The fact that most post-war FDI ventures in developing countries, particularly those in resource-based industries, have involved some form of *ex post* recontracting (such as renegotiations and surtaxes) is testament to the existence of such opportunistic host country behaviour. However, in manufacturing there may be more obvious benefits for host countries in being the recipients of a continual inflow of FDI funds, given both the pace and the increasing complementarity of technological advances. The favourable stance that most countries now take towards inward FDI has also strengthened the relative bargaining position of MNCs. A host country would be reluctant to gain a reputation for opportunistic behaviour when it is keen to attract and maintain inward investment.

Despite a general acceptance by policy-makers of the advantages of attracting FDI, there is little evidence that governments have adopted a systematic strategy towards MNC-based activities. As Dunning (1993) has pointed out, the probable exception to this is Japan, which regards both inward and outward direct investment as an important part of its general microeconomic policy initiatives towards such areas as R&D, education and training, competition, environmental issues, transport and communication, and technology transfer and dissemination:

In turn, this strategy has been systematic in its objective of improving the long-term competitive advantage of the Japanese economy by reducing the transaction costs facing its firms in their attempts to improve their capabilities and restructure the activities of their firms to meet the challenges of the global marketplace (Dunning, 1993:349).

Such a policy stance might be usefully contrasted with that of the UK government, which has enthusiastically supported inward investment since the early 1980s, but has tended to isolate the strategy from its other industrial policy initiatives.

13.7 CONCLUSIONS

A firm can expand by moving into different markets. Various such multimarket strategies are considered – VI, diversification and multinational expansion. These strategies can take place through internal means, via investment in new plant and equipment, or externally, by mergers and takeovers.

The nature and extent of merger activity is considered. Mergers occur in waves, with periodic highs and lows of activity. During the last merger wave in the UK, during the mid- to late 1980s, conglomerate deals predominated. British and American firms are more merger-intensive than firms from elsewhere; the hostile takeover, in particular, is largely peculiar to these countries.

VI refers to the extent to which a firm operates in successive markets. BVI occurs when a firm moves into the preceding stage of production, whereas FVI refers to a move into the subsequent market. Measures of intraindustry and interindustry VI are critically assessed. In general, the extent of VI appears fairly modest. Other forms of vertical linkage between firms are outlined.

The two main motives for VI, efficiency enhancement and the pursuit of market power, are examined. Efficiency improvements are likely to result from the technological interdependences of production processes and can involve production efficiencies

and transaction cost savings, the latter usually being accompanied by the transactional characteristics of asset specificity, uncertainty and frequency. Tests of the transactional cost motive for VI are considered in the case study that follows this section. The Chicago view that, from a welfare perspective, the monopolistic effects of VI are at worst benign and at best beneficial can be challenged by assuming variable input proportions in the production of the final product.

A conglomerate firm produces a number of different products; thus, diversification examines the extent to which a firm is multiproduct. A distinction can be drawn between lateral diversification, in which there is some relationship between the products in either demand or supply terms or pure conglomerate diversification, whereby the products have no obvious links. The different methods of measuring diversification are appraised. The main motives for diversification are examined; these can be divided into efficiency enhancement, managerial reasons and risk-reducing factors. The competitive effects of diversification are also considered.

The main reasons for, and theoretical approaches to, multinational expansion are discussed: the argument that MNCs possess firm-specific advantages that can be exploited by overseas production is explored; the product cycle model of FDI and the locational factors underlying multinational growth are examined; the internalisation approach, with its analytical roots embedded in transaction cost analysis, is also discussed. The feasibility of taking an eclectic approach towards multinational expansion is considered.

The reasons for the increased popularity of international R&D-based strategic alliances (SAs) are discussed. It is argued that, despite their apparent lack of success, there may be a number of positive welfare implications.

Finally, it is noted that, in general, host government policies towards MNCs have become much more supportive in recent years, given the perceived advantages of attracting inward FDI in a world of rapidly changing and increasingly complementary technologies; however, most countries do not take a systematic policy stance towards MNC-based activities.

Case Study: Tests of the Transaction Cost Analysis of Vertical Integration

A number of studies have been undertaken in recent years to test the transaction cost hypotheses that a strategy of vertical integration would offer substantial advantages when transactions have the characteristics of asset specificity, frequency and uncertainty and in situations of small numbers bargaining. The studies have used a variety of measurement indicators as a proxy for these characteristics. Their results have generally supported the predictions of transaction cost analysis.

Lieberman (1991) examined asset specificity in the US chemicals industry and found a significant positive relationship between the extent of BVI in 203 firms in various sectors of the industry at the end of 1980 and asset specificity by the downstream firm. It was also suggested that firms in the industry vertically integrated in order to reduce uncertainty over variability in the input market. An equation of the following form was estimated:

$$BVI = 1.4CONC + 5.7SUNK + 2.1GAS + 6.2IMP - 2.1SHARE + 28.2UPVAR \tag{13.4}$$

BVI, the dependent variable, is a plant-level measure of the extent to which a firm produces the primary input and the downstream product at the same geographic site. CONC is a reciprocal of the number of upstream suppliers and as such is indicative of small-numbers bargaining problems. The importance of specific physical assets is shown by two measures: SUNK refers to the investment cost of the plant, whereas GAS indicates whether the upstream input is a gas, thus giving a potential need for interplant pipelines. IMP is the cost of the upstream input as a fraction of total production cost on the assumption that the larger the share the greater the likelihood of backward integration. SHARE refers to a firm's consumption of an input as a proportion of the total quantity produced by the upstream industry. Finally, UPVAR indicates uncertainty by measuring the propensity to integrate when other buyers of the input have high demand variability. The estimates of GAS, IMP and UPVAR were statistically significant at the 1% level, whereas SUNK was significant at the 5% level. The coefficients for CONC and SHARE were statistically insignificant. Thus, it was concluded that firms integrated in order to avoid bargaining problems associated with large sunk investments and *ex post* lock-in. The fact that input suppliers charged a higher price premium when the input was a substantial cost component (as shown by IMP) was regarded as further proof of the need for investment in fixed assets. Firms also integrated backwards in order to avoid variability in the input market that was independent of fluctuations in their downstream market (although other measures of demand variability, not shown here, were statistically insignificant).

Masten *et al.* (1989), in a study of 118 vehicle components used by Chrysler, Ford and General Motors in the US, stressed the importance of highly specific human capital (defined as engineering effort) as an incentive for vertical integration. They estimated the following equation:

$$VI = 10.47 + 4.45ENGINEERING + 0.92ASSET - 2.29SITE \qquad (R^2 = 0.36) \tag{13.5}$$

The dependent variable, VI, is the percentage of the component needs of the company produced within the firm. The independent variables are measured on a scale of 1 (low) to 10 (high). ENGINEERING measures the extent to which a transaction requires transaction-specific technical know-how or human capital, indicated by the degree of engineering effort; ASSET measures the importance of transaction-specific physical assets; and SITE measures the importance of locating upstream production close to subsequent manufacturing stages. The ENGINEERING coefficient was significant at the 1% level, although the other coefficients were found to be statistically insignificant. The R^2 figure, however, shows only a modest explanatory power. It was concluded that the key incentive for vertical integration was the need to invest in highly specific human capital, thus reducing opportunistic behaviour by bringing critical employees in-house.

Other studies have also found support for the transaction cost theory of vertical integration. Caves and Bradburd (1988) investigated 83 US four-digit producer goods industries for 1975 and discovered that the degree of FVI rose with supplying industry and buying industry concentration (consistent with problems regarding small-numbers bargaining), with indices of spending on R&D (a measure of investment in highly specific human capital) and with capital/labour ratios (an indicator of investment in specific physical capital). The higher costs of non-integrated producers compared with their integrated counterparts in a study of 74 firms in the US electricity generation and distribution industry in 1981 were attributed by Kaserman and Mayo (1991) to substantial market uncertainties, the problems of small-numbers bargaining and externalities, as well as to an inefficient combination of inputs (assuming a monopolistic supply of inputs and variable proportions in the use of inputs at the downstream stage).

Thus, the results of the studies are generally consistent with the transaction cost view of vertical integration, although the explanatory variables are often imperfect measures; omitted variables may also bias the results. In addition, it should be noted that, in all cases, any benefits of integration may be limited by the increasing costs of managerial oversight as firms take on more activities.

FURTHER READING

Clarke, R. and McGuiness, T. (eds) (1987) *The Economics of the Firm* (Oxford, Basil Blackwell), Chapters 5,6.

Dunning, J.H. (1993) *The Globalisation of Business* (London, Routledge).

Jones, G. (1996) *The Evolution of International Business* (London, Routledge).

Koutsoyiannis, A. (1982) *Non-Price Decisions: The Firm in a Modern Context* (London, Macmillan), Chapters 5–7.

NOTES

1. See *The Economist*, 14 May 1994, Management Focus 'Partnerships'.
2. This classification is based on that by the US Federal Trade Commission, which also refers to market extension diversification involving the sale of existing products in different geographic areas.
3. The Hymer analysis was based on imperfections in the market for knowledge that arose from market concentration rather than from the existence of transaction costs.
4. As Jones (1996) notes, there is considerable historical evidence linking FDI with technological leaders in particular countries.
5. See *The Financial Times* 2 October 1995, 'Today's Friend, Tomorrow's Foe'.
6. *The Financial Times, op. cit.*

Questions □ □ □

13.1 'The main managerial motive for merger, in whatever direction, is to increase the size of the firm; in that way immunity from takeover is increased and managerial job security is enhanced.' Explain and discuss.

13.2 Discuss the view that the more likely source of improved efficiency resulting from vertical integration is savings in transaction costs rather than production cost benefits. To what extent is this view supported by empirical evidence?

13.3 'The pursuit of market power is not a strong reason for vertical integration and, even if it were, there are not likely to be any significant detrimental welfare effects.' Explain and discuss.

13.4 'It is the existence of transaction costs that provides the key motive for diversification, not the presence of economies of scope.' Explain and discuss.

13.5 Comment on the view that, since shareholders can obtain a similar degree of diversification in their portfolios by investing in a unit trust as they can from investing in a diversified firm, there would appear to be little risk-reducing benefits of conglomeration for suppliers of capital.

13.6 'By definition, diversification occurs in different markets. Therefore, it cannot affect the degree of competition in a particular market.' Comment on this statement and discuss the policy ramifications.

13.7 Comment on the view that, given the complexity and diversity of FDI, a theory of mutinational expansion has to take an eclectic stance.

13.8 'The product cycle model of overseas investment was geared specifically towards explaining the reasons for the post-war growth of US-based manu-faturing MNCs. It has little relevance for an analysis of recent trends in FDI.' Explain and discuss.

13.9 'The fact that international joint ventures are usually short-lived and result in a sale by one of the parties to the other suggests that the drawbacks of these alliances greatly outweigh their potential benefits.' Discuss this statement and comment on the public policy implications.

13.10 Examine the reasons for the change in the policy stance taken by most host countries towards inward FDI since the early 1980s. Discuss any potential problems for host economies of this change in attitude.

CHAPTER 14

▶ *Labour Market Decisions and the Firm*

The key structural and institutional characteristics of the labour markets of the UK and its major competitors were described in Section 3.5. These characteristics can have important effects on the main employment and other labour market decisions undertaken by the individual firm, since all such decisions have to be made within the context of an external framework itself determined by legislation, custom and practice and the existence of employee groupings. This chapter examines the role of economic theory in explaining the main labour market decisions facing the firm: how much labour to hire and at what wage rate; how to organise production flexibly so as to maximise labour productivity; how to attract and retain skilled labour; and how to motivate employees to perform to the best of their abilities.

The chapter begins by examining the relevance of *neoclassical theory* for explaining the diversity and complexity of these decisions in modern labour markets; the neoclassical approach is contrasted with the *structural* view of the labour market; the so-called *new economics of personnel* is discussed, which incorporates transaction costs analysis and agency theory and which emphasises the efficient organisation of the workplace. The policy implications of the different theoretical approaches towards particular issues, such as *minimum wages, education and training* and the role and effects of *trade unions* are investigated. The final section reviews the main public policy weapons used to improve *labour market flexibility* and assesses their impact. The *case study* at the end of the chapter analyses the effects of flexible work agreements at the plant level.

14.1 THE NEOCLASSICAL APPROACH TO THE LABOUR MARKET

The basis of the traditional approach to the labour market is that labour is a factor of production and, like any good or factor of production, it behaves according to the 'laws' of supply and demand. In other words, the notion that labour actually comprises people with human attributes tends to be subsumed beneath the prime consideration of explaining the mechanism by which the factor of production, labour, is allocated within society. Thus, given a perfectly competitive environment comprising individual decision-makers who have no power to determine prices, in which both workers and jobs are assumed to be homogenous, where perfect mobility is assumed and where all economic agents possess perfect information, the price of labour (i.e. the wage rate) and the level of employment are determined via the interaction of the forces of market demand and market supply.

Labour demand is a derived demand; it is derived from the demand for the final product. At the individual firm level, assuming that labour is the only variable input and that it can be added to a fixed amount of physical capital (i.e. that the firm is operating in the short run), the law of diminishing returns holds and the marginal productivity of labour falls as the labour input rises; the output of the firm increases but at a decreasing rate. The addition to total revenue from employing an extra person is denoted by the *marginal revenue product of labour*, MRP_L, which is the marginal product of labour times marginal revenue ($MP_L \times MR$). Assuming a perfectly competitive product market, the price of the product, P, is equal to marginal revenue, MR. Therefore, the MRP_L is equal to the *value of the marginal product of labour*, VMP_L, defined as the marginal product of labour multiplied by the product price ($MP_L \times P$). The MRP_L (or VMP_L) curve has a similar shape to the MP_L curve, given that the former is multiplied by a constant figure, where $P = MR$. This can be seen in Figure 92, page 270.

The employment decision of the firm is dictated by its profit-maximising objective. It will hire new employees and its profits will rise as long as MRP_L exceeds the additional cost of hiring another person, or the marginal cost of labour (MC_L). Given a perfectly competitive labour market, then the individual firm faces a perfectly elastic supply curve of labour; hence the MC_L is equal to the wage rate, W. Thus, the firm employs more labour where

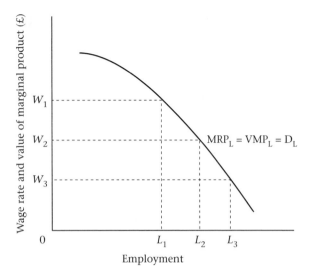

Figure 92 *The demand curve for labour of a firm assuming perfectly competitive product and labour markets.*

$MRP_L > W$. If, on the other hand, $MRP_L < W$ the firm can increase its profits by reducing its demand for labour.

The optimal or profit-maximising level of employment for the firm is where $W (= MC_L) = MRP_L$: at a wage of W_2 the firm employs L_2 people; at a higher wage, W_1, fewer employees, L_1, are demanded, while at the lower wage, W_3, the quantity of labour demanded increases to L_3. Thus, assuming perfectly competitive product and labour markets, the downward-sloping part of the VMP_L curve represents the firm's demand curve for labour; the higher the wage rate or the price of labour, the lower the quantity of labour demanded, *cet. par.* If, however, the product market is imperfect, the product demand curve will be downward-sloping. Therefore, the price of the product falls with increases in output; the marginal revenue from additional output is less than the price of that output and $MRP_L < VMP_L$; employment levels will be lower at each wage level under imperfectly competitive product market conditions, *cet. par.*

It should be noted that the short-run industry labour demand curve in a perfectly competitive environment is not simply the horizontal sum of the demand curves of the individual firms as they have been previously defined. This is because, as the wage rate falls, all firms respond by increasing employment and output, leading to a decline in the product price and shifting the MRP_L curve to the left. As a result, the individual firm's labour demand curve is steeper than where price is unchanged. The industry labour

demand curve is the horizontal sum of these curves and hence is less elastic than the individual MRP_L curve.

In the long run, it is assumed that the quantity of all factors of production can be varied. Given the fact that some degree of substitutability between them is possible, the firm has to decide how much of each factor to employ. The decision rule is the one referred to in the Appendix to Chapter 6. The firm employs inputs such that the ratios of the value of their marginal products is equal to the ratio of their prices.

The quantity of labour is a function of the number of workers and the hours worked per unit of labour. Thus, any analysis of labour supply needs to consider both participation rates of the population as a whole and average hours supplied per worker. It should also take account of the fact that the appropriate decision-making unit is the household, in which family utility maximisation is the relevant goal; therefore, the effect of a wage rise for one member of the household on the labour supply of other family members should be considered. It is assumed that labour market participants devote their time to market work and non-market activities called leisure. The net effect on market labour supply of a rise in the wage rate depends on the balance of the income and substitution effects (see Section 7.1). Traditional theory presumes that the market supply curve of labour is upward-sloping, implying that the substitution effect of an increase in the wage rate, which raises the opportunity cost of non-market activities, outweighs any reduction on the market labour supply due to the income effect.

In Figure 93 the market demand and supply for labour curves have been summed from the individual curves of firms and households. The wage rate and the level of employment are determined by the interaction of the market demand and market supply curves, D_L and S_L. The equilibrium level of wages and employment settle at W* and L* respectively. At a higher wage, W_1, there is an excess supply of labour. Workers not in employment offer themselves for jobs at lower wages; as wages fall, firms increase their demand for labour. Wages move downwards towards the equilibrium level; eventually labour demand equals labour supply. Where an excess demand for labour exists, as at W_2, wages will move upwards towards the equilibrium level. Firms bid up wages in their desire to hire more labour and consequently households offer a greater labour supply to the market; eventually market equilibrium is restored. Any unemployment is either voluntary or comprises those changing jobs.

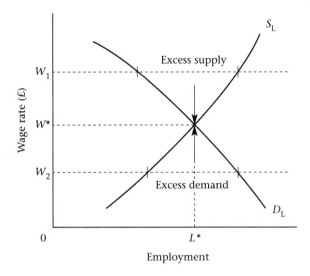

Figure 93 *The tendency towards equilibrium in a perfectly competitive labour market.*

The impact of labour market imperfections (monopsonistic buying power on the part of a firm or the monopolistic supply of labour by a trade union) on wages and employment within a neoclassical framework is examined in Sections 14.5 and 14.6. The existence of wage differentials can be assimilated into the neoclassical approach by relaxing the assumption of the homogenity of labour and jobs. Workers are assumed to have different preferences towards work and non-work activities; utility is derived from a combination of the pecuniary and non-pecuniary returns from employment; it is the 'net advantages' of employment that are equalised. In this environment, wage differentials are based on differences in skills and abilities that arise solely from investment in education, training and experience. Such an investment in 'human capital' improves a worker's skills, which raises marginal productivity and the value of the marginal product; the demand curve for labour shifts to the right and relative wages rise. The labour market can be regarded as a series of occupational submarkets in which productivity and therefore wages are regarded as worker- rather than job-determined. However, any employment or wage discriminatory practices of a sexual or racial origin are ignored.

The neoclassical model is capable of further adaptation. For example, in a situation of imperfect information regarding either the availability of labour or job opportunities, it is assumed that both firms and households undertake search strategies to improve the information available to them; the optimal strategy in each case is determined by the equalisation of the marginal costs and the marginal benefits of additional search. While traditional theory is capable of a good deal of flexibility and is able to offer an analysis of a number of the features of modern labour markets, there are also serious limitations. It ignores the problems involved in intrafirm decision-making, where information flows may be asymmetric between different groupings or among teams. It also assumes that marginal product is easily quantifiable. However, there are difficulties in defining the marginal product of certain occupations (as in many services) or where work takes place in teams (as is the case with a number of modern work practices). This problem is discussed further in the transaction cost approach to labour organisation, which is explained in Section 14.3. Traditional theory also fails to account for the barriers to labour mobility that divides labour markets into distinct segments and where wages are attached to jobs rather than to workers, a subject to which we now turn.

14.2 THE SEGMENTED LABOUR MARKET

The idea that the labour market can be split into different segments originates from Kerr (1954), who referred to the 'balkanisation' of the labour market. While there is little agreement among the different theories of labour market segmentation about which jobs belong to which sectors, there is agreement that there is little intersectoral mobility of labour. The 'structured' sector is usually taken to comprise two segments: *internal labour markets* (ILMs), which are governed by established rules and procedures, and *external labour markets* (ELMs), dictated by factors such as wage levels and the availability of workers. In 'structureless' markets, on the other hand, pricing and allocating decisions are determined mainly by competitive forces.

ILMs are largely immune from competitive pressures. They are said to have arisen as technological demands have increased the extent of job and human asset specificity; thus, many jobs require increasingly specific skills, to adopt Becker's (1964) terminology. These skills are determined by a firm's production function and are not transferable between firms, in which case productivity and wages become job- rather than worker-oriented. Other skills, such as those gained from an apprenticeship to be a plumber or an electrician, can be classified as more general in that they enhance individual productivity but the skills derived are not necessarily job-specific. Some ILMs are occupation-wide; examples are the medical and legal professions. Established procedures dictate both intra- and interfirm movements of labour; these occupations are characterised by the possession of relatively general skills.

In ILMs, jobs are filled mainly (although not exclusively) by internal promotion; relatively high wages, secure employment patterns, job ladders and seniority payments are designed to reduce labour turnover and the associated fixed labour costs of hiring and firing, including the firm's investment in job-specific training. Firms adopt comprehensive search and screening processes before hiring new recruits; frequent job-changers are less likely to be hired. Sets of institutional rules and procedures (dictated by custom and practice) delineate the boundaries of ILMs and determine their pay structures; specific internal wage structures accompany ILMs. A plant or firm may therefore pay higher wages at all skill levels than other establishments in a particular area for similar workers; there is evidence of quite substantial intraindustry and intraoccupational wage dispersion within a local labour market. There may be some movement between ILMs and ELMs at various 'ports of entry' to ILMs, although these can be quite restricted. Jobs in university teaching, for example have in the past been limited to entry at the lowest grades or at the full professor level. On the other hand, there is probably little movement between structureless markets and ILMs. Studies of the characteristics of particular industrial and occupational labour markets in the UK suggest that ILMs are more pronounced for technical, managerial and professional employees than in the case of manual workers, for whom internal promotion is not a strong feature.

It is claimed that the inherent features of Japanese work practices (lifetime employment, a seniority system based on tenure and enterprise unions) are similar to the characteristics of ILMs. However, while this may be true, the lifetime employment contract only applies to a relatively small proportion of the workforce, male employees working in large organisations. There is evidence of wide differences in wage and job security between the major manufacturers and the smaller subcontracting firms.

The notion of the segmentation of the labour market was taken to its extreme by Doeringer and Piore (1971), who divided it into two distinct sectors, the primary and the secondary, each with separate characteristics and behavioural rules. The concept of the *dual labour market* was developed to explain urban poverty and long-term unemployment in the US. In the UK it has been used to analyse the position of the low paid. Thus, the secondary sector can be equated with the structureless markets noted above; it is dominated by 'bad' jobs which exhibit the opposite characteristics (relatively low wages, insecurity of employment and a lack of firm-specific training) to the 'good' jobs found in ILMs. These jobs tend to be concentrated in certain low-technology industries, such as clothing, textiles, distribution and catering. According to the dual labour market hypothesis they are jobs that also tend to employ relatively high proportions of sexually and racially disadvantaged workers with poor prospects, a factor which serves to reinforce the innate characteristics of secondary sector employment.

The dual labour market approach implies that there is a natural trend for the dichotomy in job opportunities between the two sectors to increase over time. In the primary sector the higher wages and seniority rights characteristic of ILMs enhance job security, whereas in structureless markets lower wages and a lack of specific training add to employment instability. The basic distinction into 'haves' and 'have-nots' or 'good' jobs and 'bad' may be rather too simplistic a description of the complexities of modern labour markets. However, the employment prospects of secondary sector workers have certainly not been helped by the permanently higher levels of unemployment that now characterise many industrialised economies. In Section 3.5 it was noted that flexible work practices may have been accompanied by an increase in job instability and insecurity in the UK, although not among groups such as well-educated prime-age males. This has led Gregg and Wadsworth (1995) to conclude that:

The British labour market can increasingly be categorised as having primary and secondary sectors. The secondary sector is characterised by higher labour turnover among the least-skilled, young and old, and those in atypical employment. For those at the margins, employment in the 1990s has become far more unstable ... Hence the secondary labour market has become far riskier (Gregg and Wadsworth, 1995:89).

14.3 THE NEW ECONOMICS OF PERSONNEL

The so-called new economics of personnel is based on transaction cost and principal–agent analyses of labour markets, in which the characteristics of the appropriate organisational structure for labour and the specifics of the labour contract are examined in greater depth.

The *transaction cost* theory of the labour market investigates the nature of labour transactions and relates them to the particular features of an organisational structure: an organisational structure for labour needs to be closely allied to the attributes of the labour transactions in order to minimise transaction costs. In the case of continuous or long-term labour market transactions there are two important attributes that should be considered:

(1) the degree to which human assets are transaction-specific;
(2) the extent to which the productivity of individual workers can be evaluated.

Specific skills result in 'task idiosyncrasy' according to Williamson *et al.* (1975). In such circumstances, continuity of the employment relation is a source of value added and there are implications for organisational structure. Since it is costly for the employer to teach another worker the same skill, there is an inherent element of bilateral monopoly in the employment contract; the more specific the skill involved the greater the prospective cost to the employer and hence the more carefully drafted the employment contract.

As regards the second characteristic of continuous labour contracts, the extent to which marginal productivity can be measured, it may be difficult to assess the contribution to output of individuals when tasks are non-separable and production takes place in teams (see also Section 4.4). It may be possible to assess the intensity of work effort by individuals, although payment based on such an assessment may be difficult to enshrine in a contract. In these circumstances, when employee productivity or work effort can be monitored only imprecisely, there is scope for opportunistic behaviour by individuals in working less hard. This may apply equally to workers and to management, since all employees have their own interests which may conflict with other interests within the firm; employees are also capable of exercising some degree of control over work done after the employment contract has been signed.

The organisational structure should adapt to fit the particular characteristics of the labour transactions in order to enhance efficiency; thus, where human assets are highly specific to a firm and individual contribution to output is difficult to measure, an alternative

to spot market competitive contracting (where wages can be quite easily related to marginal productivity) is required. The characteristics of ILMs, by maintaining employment stability, are regarded as being capable of reducing bounded rationality and opportunistic bargaining and hence minimising transaction costs. In these circumstances, wages are attached to jobs, and hierarchical wage structures, job ladders, seniority payments and internal promotion become the norm. The ILM is regarded by Williamson (1975) as a co-operative solution to the problem of individual self-interest in organisations.

Principal–agent analysis applied to work contracts centres on the need to design payment or incentive schemes (whether implicit or explicit) so that self-interested employees avoid shirking. A worker caught shirking could be fired, but this may not be a sufficient sanction if other employers are either not aware of the person's past employment history or discount its significance, in which case the sacked worker may quite easily find alternative employment. In these circumstances, incentive systems may need to be introduced in order to lower monitoring costs and to ensure that employees make the desired amount of effort; any divergence of interests between the employee and the organisation as a whole can then be avoided. The incentive schemes can take various forms (see Box 14.1).

Thus, according to the new economics of personnel, ILMs are a response to the problems of opportunism and asymmetric information when skills are job-specific and in situations where individual productivity cannot be accurately deduced. However, even in situations where marginal productivity is indeterminate, a firm usually needs to make some assessment of individual performance, whether based on absolute or relative criteria, in its wage-setting; the criterion adopted may then be used as a proxy for productivity. In this sense, the overall value of the product of labour could be distributed and redistributed among the members of the firm according to changes in, say, assessments of their relative worth.

Box 14.1 *Payment incentive schemes*

THE 'EFFICIENCY WAGE' HYPOTHESIS

This originated from studies of developing countries where it was noticed that higher wages improved nutrition and health and thereby raised productivity. In the current context, if a firm pays above the going rate, then an employee will pay a penalty by shirking since, if fired, the person would not be able to gain such lucrative employment elsewhere. Thus, the need for monitoring is reduced; effort (and hence productivity) is not independent of the wage paid.

DEFERRED COMPENSATION OR 'BOND-POSTING'

Under such a scheme a person receives a low wage initially, which is likely to be less than the value of marginal product, and a higher wage, which may well exceed the value of marginal product, in later years. Obviously the individual has an incentive to remain with the firm and to avoid shirking in order to secure the higher wage (Lazear, 1981). In effect the employee is posting a bond with the firm which can be collected later in the form of the higher wages. The firm itself, of course, could renege on the scheme by firing the employee as soon as the wage reaches the level for the re-posting of the bond (and hence securing for itself the difference between the cumulative wages and the cumulative marginal products), but it may not wish to gain a reputation for defaulting. Furthermore, since the wage exceeds the value of marginal product in the later years of employment, then some kind of automatic retirement age may need to be incorporated into the work contracts (as is often the case in work contracts with large organisations). Kotlikoff and Gokhale (1992) estimated the age–productivity profiles of 300 000 employees of a Fortune 1000 firm during 1969–83. They found that, in each of the five occupation/sex groups considered, productivity fell with age, with productivity exceeding earnings when young and vice versa when old.

RANK-ORDER TOURNAMENT PAYMENT

This scheme may be particularly applicable when individual marginal products cannot be specified with any degree of accuracy. In fact, as Malcolmson (1984) has pointed out, it is precisely in these situations that some kind of incentive scheme is warranted:

Under such circumstances a payment scheme based directly on a measure of individual performance is unenforceable, and, unless some other kind of incentive scheme is available, the principal will be unable to enforce more than minimal compliance by the agent in the performance of his task (Malcolmson, 1984:487).

It is argued (see also Lazear and Rosen, 1981) that contracts with payments based on the ranking of employees' performance can be made enforceable as an incentive scheme even in a situation of asymmetric information in which employees are unable to verify the employer's observation of their performance. Since

a contract linking wages directly to an assessment of individual performance is unenforceable, then a certain proportion of the workforce can be offered higher wages based on their relative performance in the rank order of employees. According to Malcolmson the internal incentive structure of such contracts generates the features of employment arrangements often found in large organisations: hierarchical wage structures, a high degree of internal promotion, low ports of entry, seniority payments and wages attached to jobs rather than to workers. In other words, rank order contracts are associated closely with ILMs.

14.4 THE ECONOMICS OF EDUCATION AND TRAINING

According to neoclassical analysis, wage differentials are principally explained in terms of differences in education, training and experience. Education and training can also help workers to gain acceptance into ILMs. Therefore, it is important to understand the decision-making processes of labour market participants towards education and training and to assess the public policy implications.

Explanations of educational and training decision-making usually begin with *human capital analysis*. This approach is firmly rooted in neoclassical theory and in its most basic form (assuming perfectly competitive conditions, including perfect capital markets, and no differences in natural abilities) asserts that education or training is the sole source of income differences between individuals and between jobs. It is regarded as an investment by the student or worker which improves skills; this raises marginal productivity which causes an increase in the value of the marginal product and ultimately in earnings.

The decision-maker has to weigh up the relative costs and benefits of the investment. The costs comprise the current sacrifices in pursuing the course of study or training programme; they consist of the costs of the course itself, such as books and fees (the latter may be paid by the state, although higher education in the UK is increasingly becoming the concern of the individual, the replacement of grants by loans being the first step in the process), plus the opportunity costs of the income that could have been earned by working. The benefits or rewards are the prospective higher earnings (which in essence comprise the difference between actual earnings and earnings had the investment not been undertaken) achieved throughout life. It is assumed that, in order to decide whether the additional study is worthwhile, an individual applies normal investment appraisal procedures. Thus, if C_0 is the cost of an additional year's course of study and Y represents the present value of the expected returns over the length of the remaining working life, n years, discounted at rate r, then the net present value of the decision to invest is given by

$$\text{NPV} = \sum_{t=1}^{n} \frac{Y_t}{(1+r)^t} - C_0 \qquad (14.1)$$

If the resulting figure is positive, then the investment in education or training is considered to be worthwhile. Where C_0 is equal to the sum of the present value of the future returns (i.e. where NPV = 0) the rate of discount is also the internal rate of return of the investment decision, or the rate of interest from an investment in, say, government bonds that would yield an equivalent return to the additional net income following the period of further training.

As Figure 94 indicates, an individual age–earnings profile typically shows earnings increasing at first, reaching a peak or plateau and then flattening out or even declining due to a combination of the effects of physical decline in strength or health and the possession of outdated knowledge and skills.

Thus, it would appear that people benefit from other forms of human capital gained during working life and in particular from on-the-job training which may be provided by firms. It would also seem apposite for firms and/or the government to instigate some kind of training strategy throughout working life in order to maintain maximum employee effectiveness.

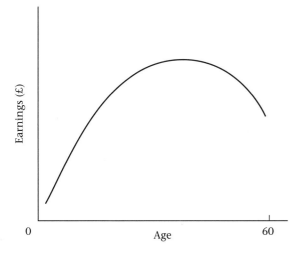

Figure 94 *A typical age–earnings profile.*

Mincer (1974) estimated that education combined with an estimate of work experience together account for about 30% of overall earnings' differentials. (The other important explanatory factors comprise innate ability, drive and dynamism and the environmental influences of family and socio-economic background.)

Becker (1964) analysed on-the-job training within a neoclassical framework. *General training*, such as an apprenticeship, raises a person's productivity in any firm and hence creates an increase in market value and potential earnings. Since the skills gained could in principle be used by any employer, it is argued that the trainee should bear all the costs and receive all the benefits of completely general training. *Specific training* increases a person's productivity only in the firm in which the training is given; the skills gained are specific to the firm and have no other value in the market. Since the firm receives the benefits of the higher productivity of the trainee, it should bear all the relevant costs of training.

In practice, most training probably falls between these two extremes, although it is useful to make comparisons on this basis in order to assess the allocation of the costs and benefits between employees and employers. The particular circumstances, assuming perfectly competitive conditions, are shown in Figure 95, page 276. Figure 95(a) indicates the situation when the training is general. W_0 gives some notion of the 'market wage' and equivalent value of marginal product. W_T shows the wage (and marginal product) of a person undergoing training. $W_T < W_0$ shows that earnings are forgone, this representing the trainee's investment. Post-training skills raise marginal product and wages to W_T'; $W_T' > W_0$, indicating the return on the investment. This assumes, of course, that prospective employers possess the necessary information to be able to determine whether skills are general. In fact, firms may be prepared to pay a substantial proportion of general training costs (by paying higher wages than W_T) because other employers undervalue the general training provided elsewhere.

The situation for specific training, shown in Figure 95(b), is more complex. W_0 indicates the market wage and equivalent value of marginal product of the untrained worker; by bearing the costs of the training the employee would have to accept a wage less than could be obtained if the training were not undertaken. There is no guarantee of receiving a higher wage after the training is completed and, since the training is specific, it cannot be used in alternative

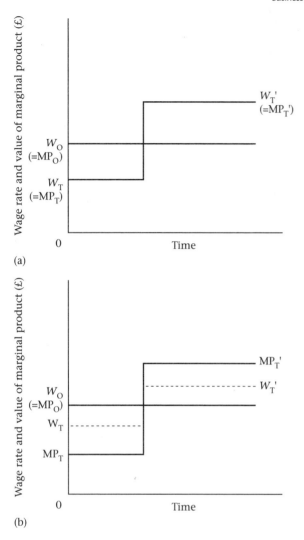

(a)

(b)

Figure 95 *The allocation of the costs and benefits of (a) general training and (b) specific training.*

employment. On the other hand, the employer may be reluctant to bear all the costs of such training because the trainee may impose an opportunistic threat to leave before the firm can gain the benefits of the person's higher productivity. Thus, the costs and benefits of specific human investments are likely to be shared between employees and employers; the dashed line represents such a cost/benefit-sharing pattern, with the individual paid more than the value of marginal product during training ($W_T > MP_T$), while the firm receives some of the benefits ($W_T' < MP_T'$) in the post-training period.

The sharing of training costs and benefit can also be couched in deferred compensation terms, given

that the employee receives a lower wage initially in anticipation of higher wages later. In this sense the employee is establishing a contract with the employer. As noted in the previous section, the firm may not wish to secure a reputation for reneging on such contracts (whether explicit or implicit); hence long-term employment relationships may result. There is evidence that a greater stability of employment is associated with more formal firm training. In the US it is estimated that only 10% of young recruits have any kind of formal company training, compared with around 70% in Japan and Germany. However, as tenure with a particular employer rises, so does the likelihood of training; in the US only 8% of those with a firm for less than one year had any kind of training, compared with 25% for those with the same employer for 15 years.[1] The move towards more flexible contracts may have been at least partly responsible for the demise of the apprenticeship system in the UK.

Studies in the UK and the US have reported individual or private rates of return of between 10% and 15% for particular levels of education (primary, secondary, higher) or for additional years of higher education. These rates of return (which ignore any consumption benefits of, say, meeting new friends) generally decline with additional schooling: the rate of return for primary schooling is higher than the rate of return for secondary schooling, which is greater than the rate of return for higher education. This is a reflection of the fact that higher costs and a shorter payoff period means that greater investment yields lower returns after some point; even so, education would appear to be a worthwhile investment on the basis of these figures. Rates-of-return figures for periods of on-the-job training are generally reckoned to be higher because they usually do not involve forgone earnings; hence, the costs are much lower. On the face of it, these figures would appear to support the human capital theory of the link between education, productivity-enhancing skills and earnings. However, lower reported rates of return for young people in the UK who invest in vocational training may be a reflection of the modest improvements in earnings that are expected to result.

Social rates-of-return figures are reckoned to be about 10–20% lower than private rates of return because of the public subsidy element of most education, but still appear quite high. From a human capital perspective it can be argued that the social returns to education and training are high because a better educated and trained workforce is not simply more productive but also contributes to higher national income via production externalities in the form of reduced skill blockages. These may be complemented by consumption externalities, such as better informed consumers and the likelihoods of a healthier population and a more crime-free society. However, as noted in Section 3.2, evidence of a causal relationship between such investment in human capital and higher levels of productivity and national income is only surprising in its relative scarcity. The problem with the oftquoted evidence from Mincer that uses a measure of experience to explain earnings' differentials is that the presumed link between experience and productivity is empirically contentious.

An alternative model of education and training, associated with Arrow (1973), views their social returns as being much lower. According to this approach, known as the *screening hypothesis*, education acts as a filter or screen to identify or signal pre-existing talents. Thus, a history graduate entering a career in, say, marketing is hired, not because he or she has been specifically trained for that particular form of employment (although it can be argued any educational attainment adds to a person's general skills), but because a degree signals to a prospective employer that a person has sufficient capabilities to undertake the particular job. In other words, qualifications indicate a person's 'trainability'. It is assumed that, since most skills are acquired through on-the-job training, an employer will prefer to hire someone of high ability and hence requiring relatively low training costs; good qualifications indicate the identity of such a person. The screening hypothesis argues that education has little, if any, effect on productivity, although it remains the basis of lifetime earnings. Someone with the best qualifications gets the most rewarding jobs with the highest pay. Thus, individuals act rationally in obtaining qualifications since the private returns are still high; firms are rational in using them to indicate how to reduce their hiring costs. The main difference between this model and human capital theory lies in the social returns to education. In the screening hypothesis, private and social returns are regarded as similar. The benefits of education are viewed solely in terms of how well it allocates labour between jobs; the better the allocation, the higher the level of output.

The problem in choosing between human capital and screening theories is that they both predict significantly higher earnings for the better qualified; thus, empirically it is difficult to distinguish between them. The lifetime employment ethos in Japan may imply the need for a strong emphasis on screening workers direct from school. Other support for the screening hypothesis comes from what is known about the recruitment policies of employers. Many employers emphasise a person's social skills in their hiring policies rather than particular qualifications, although actual academic performance is given greater weight for higher educational achievements.

Public policy implications

Neither theory offers much in the way of precise policy prescriptions. Acceptance of the human capital approach implies that educational and training markets are potentially efficient. For example, firms will offer the right amount of specific training for their needs; the poaching of workers by other firms is pointless because the skills gained are unique to the firm in question. Firms will respond to the demand for general training, which in any case is financed by employees. Informational asymmetries and imperfect capital markets may be compensated for by the provision of educational or training vouchers and manpower forecasts of potential labour demand. Alternatively, it may be argued that evidence of high social returns to education provides support for subsidies. There is a weaker case for subsidising education according to the screening hypothesis because private and social returns are regarded as similar, although, since it is assumed that most skill acquisition is gained on-the-job and should be decided by each firm, a stronger case can be made for subsidising training; precisely how such a policy should be implemented, however, is not apparent.

By the late 1970s, many countries had moved away from the relatively active approach towards industrial training policies of the 1960s and early 1970s that involved an increased level of government involvement, towards a more neutral policy stance that supports market forces rather than directing them. In the UK, more recent policy initiatives have been directed at the appropriateness of school education and the school-to-work transition; private sector bodies have also been given a greater role in formal training schemes. There is a widespread belief that both the quantity and quality of on-the-job training provided by firms is insufficient and inadequate to cope with the demands of international competition, although there is a lack of empirical evidence to support such a view.

There are two broad approaches towards post-16 educational needs: The US, Japan and France have a school/college-based system of full-time academic and vocational learning for post-16-year-olds. Germany (where it is referred to as the 'dual system') and Switzerland, on the other hand, follow a more apprentice-based and employer-led training system with a day-release component. It can be argued that the training provision for young people influences the amount and type of adult training by firms. Thus, Germany has a highly structured, although voluntary, system of adult on-the-job training, whereas in the US, despite serious misgivings, the educational system is still regarded by employers as the basis for the provision of general skills.

The UK government approach in recent years has tended to place greater emphasis on vocational and employer-led schemes than on school-based ones, although there is little evidence to suggest that one type of system is preferable to the other. The Youth Training (YT) programme, which replaced the Youth Training Scheme (YTS) in 1990 and which currently enrols about 200 000 per annum, is designed to give all 16- and 17-year-olds the chance to gain National Vocational Qualification (NVQ) awards, which are given parity with academic qualifications. Training and Enterprise Councils (TECs) (or Local Enterprise Councils in Scotland), also established in 1990, are private companies that contract with the government to equate the level and type of training with local needs. As such, they are responsible for the administration of much of the training apparatus, including YT and Employment Training (ET); the latter is geared towards aiding the adult long-term unemployed. These schemes generally have had poor success rates; for example, in 1996 it was reported that only 27% of adults in TEC courses had found employment.[2] As noted in Section 3.2, criticism has been levelled at the schemes for emphasising lower-level skills rather than the more advanced skills reckoned to be in short supply. As regards training provisions for those in work, voluntary Industrial Training Organisations (ITOs) had replaced the statutory Industrial Training Boards (ITBs) in 1981; the latter were designed to meet the training requirements of adults in work through a levy-grant system. There is evidence that ITOs have performed adequately in certain industries, although in others the voluntary nature of the system has meant that some training needs have not been been met satisfactorily (O'Connell, 1990).

Government-supported training schemes in other countries have often reported similarly poor results.

The German dual system, for example, has been criticised recently for producing insufficient numbers of lesser-skilled but supposedly more flexible workers.[3] The problem for policy-makers is that, while training and education are regarded as being of major economic and political concern in every industrialised country, both the predictions of economic analysis and the results of empirical evidence are only able to offer rather vague policy prescriptions. As a result, the questions of what are the correct policies to adopt, to what ends and who are the best providers of the various schemes, will remain largely unanswered.

14.5 THE MINIMUM WAGE CONUNDRUM

The increases in the US federal minimum wage in the late 1980s and again in 1996/97 and the prospect of the implementation of such a policy by the incoming Labour administration in the UK in 1997 have sparked a renewed interest in the economic effects of *minimum wages*, especially with regard to the employment of those people that they are specifically designed to protect, the low paid. In Section 3.5 it was pointed out that, while most industrial economies have some kind of minimum wage policy, the legislation differs significantly in content and coverage across countries. This relates in particular to differentiation across age groups (minimum wages are not graded by age in the US, Canada or France, whereas several countries have specific age minima); there is also different treatment according to sector, occupation and region. In the UK, following the abolition in the 1980s of most of the selective controls that existed under the auspices of the Wages Councils, the only group still covered by any form of minimum wage policy are agricultural workers.

The employment effects of minimum wages are shrouded in theoretical and empirical controversy. The imposition of a minimum wage above the equilibrium in a perfectly competitive labour market results in a decline in employment, as shown in Figure 96. The enforcement of a minimum wage at W_1 creates an excess supply of labour L_1L_2, L_1L^* of whom were previously employed and who can be regarded as unemployed as a result of the wage rise; the remainder, L^*L_2, were encouraged to enter the labour market by the introduction of the minimum wage and therefore it is not quite so obvious that they became unemployed following the imposition

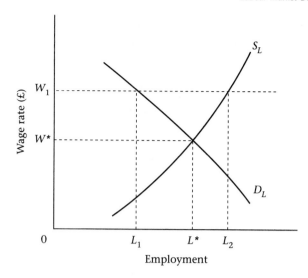

Figure 96 *The effect of the imposition of a minimum wage in a perfectly competitive labour market.*

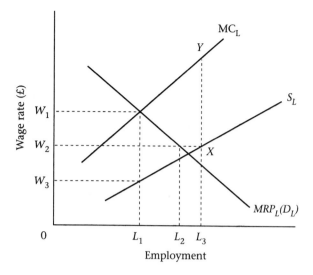

Figure 97 *The effect of the imposition of a minimum wage in a monopsonistic labour market.*

of the higher wage. In these circumstances the scale of job losses depends on the size of the minimum wage and the elasticity of demand for labour. The more elastic the demand for labour, the greater the job losses, *cet. par.* Since the demand for low-skilled workers is thought to be relatively wage elastic, the employment consequences of a minimum wage in a competitive environment may well be quite large.

A monopsonistic and profit-maximising firm employs labour such that the marginal cost of labour is equal to the marginal revenue product of labour, where the latter represents the firm's labour demand curve assuming imperfectly competitive product market conditions. The marginal cost of labour curve, MC_L, lies above the supply curve of labour, S_L; this is because when employment is expanded, higher wages are paid not just to the last person employed but also to all existing workers.

In Figure 97, the firm employs L_1 workers and pays a wage of W_3, which is less than the value of the marginal product. If a statutory minimum wage is imposed (and effectively enforced) at, say, W_2, then employment would increase. The firm's supply curve becomes W_2XS_L; below W_2 the firm cannot hire labour, whereas at W_2 it can employ any amount of labour until L_3. Since the marginal cost curve of labour is now represented by W_2XYMC_L, the firm employs L_2 workers, where this curve intersects with the MRP_L curve; employment has increased despite the imposition of the higher wage. In fact, in these

circumstances any minimum wage as high as W_1 will lead to an increase in employment. Of course, if labour is organised in trade unions, then the wage level may be higher than the agreed minimum anyway, in which case relatively few workers will be affected. We shall return to this point in the next section.

An alternative explanation of monopsonistic behaviour has been suggested by Calvo and Wellisz (1979), who analysed the effect of a minimum wage in the context of the imposition of a hierarchical wage structure and the payment of efficiency wages within a profit-maximising firm. It is assumed that better-quality workers are assigned to the higher ranks and are paid higher wages than those paid to lower-quality workers, whom the former supervise. The higher wages also represent a bribe to the high-level employees because if a supervisor shirks and, as a result, the supervised workers also shirk, then the firm loses (or suffers a reduction in) the output of the entire team. Thus, the more productive workers are given the higher-level jobs and are offered a wage higher than if based on efficiency considerations alone. In other words, the wage per efficiency unit rises with the hierarchical level; production and lower-level administrative workers are 'exploited' in the sense that they are paid less per effective labour unit than the higher-level workers. In these circumstances the imposition of a minimum wage reduces the propensity to shirk of the lower-level workers and therefore reduces the optimal degree of supervision.

279

Therefore, it becomes profitable to hire more workers although, if there are several supervisory layers the firm may react by reducing the number or the quality of the supervisory staff.

Whatever the source of the monopsonistic power of the firm, in principle a minimum wage in these circumstances can have a positive effect on employment. A number of recent studies in the UK and the US have reported such a positive impact, at least for relatively small changes in the minimum wage: Card (1992) for low-paid workers in California during 1987–89, Katz and Krueger (1992) for workers in the fast-food industry in the US and Machin *et al.*, (1993) for residential care home workers in the UK. Dickens *et al.*, (1994), in a survey of 18 industries covered by Wages Councils during 1978–90, found that minimum wages compressed the distribution of earnings and probably raised employment. Monopsonistic power, it can be argued, may stem from a hierarchical wage structure, which is reinforced by the low bargaining power or the reduced mobility of some kinds of labour. Working mothers and young workers, both highly represented among the minimum wage workers in the industries studied, are probably more likely to possess these latter two characteristics than are other types of employees. The results of these studies can be contrasted with earlier evidence from the US, Canada and the Netherlands which have suggested that employment in general or among certain groups of workers may have been higher without a minimum wage. However it may be that in some of the later studies, minimum wages had fallen to such low levels that they were no longer of much relevance. In both theoretical and empirical terms the employment effects of minimum wages remain contentious.

14.6 THE ECONOMICS OF TRADE UNIONS

As noted in Section 3.5, union membership has declined in most industrialised economies as employment has moved from manufacturing to services and the proportion of part-time workers, who are less likely to be unionised than full-timers, has grown. In the UK the legislation of the 1980s, designed to reduce the power of the unions, has exacerbated these trends. The Employment Acts of 1980, 1982, 1984 and 1988 regulated union activities, reduced the possibilities for strike action and restricted closed shops. There has

been a corresponding fall in the proportion of workers covered by some form of collective bargain; the pay and conditions of 54% of UK employees were so determined in 1992, compared with 71% of workers in 1984. In general, large organisations are more likely to recognise unions than small ones.

Bargaining about pay and work conditions in the UK is decentralised; national bargains supplemented by local deals have been largely replaced by single employer agreements (although these are not usually with single unions). There has also been a spread of new-style human resource management practices, such as performance appraisal, wider employee benefits and greater internal communications, although these are more likely to occur in unionised workplaces and/or in greenfield sites. A similar situation exists in the US, where most union negotiations are at company level, although overall union density is much lower than in the UK, especially in the private sector. This rather fragmented approach towards industrial relations can be contrasted with the more centralised system typical of much of continental Europe. In Germany, for example, highly centralised employers' associations and trade unions negotiate at the industry level, and pay settlements in one region tend to be followed nationwide. The Japanese system, at least among those large firms that recognise unions, is characterised by bargaining between employers and single-enterprise unions that represent all employees in a company below managerial level.

Unions and economic theory

Traditionally, economic theory has stressed the *monopolistic* role of trade unions as sellers of labour. Thus, in a perfectly competitive labour market a union can restrict the supply of labour in order to secure a higher wage or successfully bargain for higher wages above the equilibrium level; either way, the result is a reduction in employment. For example, in Figure 96, page 279, the establishment of a wage rate of W_1 leads to a decline in employment of L_1L^*; in addition, L^*L_2 workers, encouraged to enter the labour market by the higher wage would not be able to find employment. There are also effects on other labour markets, as the unemployed and those not able to secure employment move (assuming that labour is both homogenous and perfectly mobile) with downward consequences for wages in these markets.

In a monopsonistic market, like that shown in Figure 97, page 279, a union would bargain for a higher wage than W_3, the monopsonistic wage; a bilateral monopoly exists and the actual wage rate depends on the relative bargaining strengths of the monopsonist buyer of labour and the union, the monopolist seller of labour. As is the case with the establishment of a minimum wage in a monopsonistic market, if a union were to secure a wage above W_3, say W_2, then this would be accompanied by an increase in employment (which would be the case for any wage up to W_1). The same type of reasoning applies as previously: at W_2, since workers would not be prepared to work below this wage, the supply curve of labour becomes W_2XS_L, the firm's marginal cost curve is given by W_2XYMC_L and employment increases from L_1 to L_2.

The analysis thus far presumes that the monopoly power of the union stems from its control over labour supply to a particular market. However, the fact that an industry or an occupation is highly unionised does not necessarily mean that the union automatically possesses strong market power. The extent of product market competition has to be taken into account, as does the level at which the bargaining is undertaken (whether enterprise, industry or national). The establishment of the Single European Market in 1993, for example, has increased pressure in product markets and, it can be argued, enhanced labour market efficiency. By introducing compulsory competitive tendering (CCT) for many local government services such as catering, cleaning and refuse collection in 1988 (construction and building maintenance work had been put out to tender in 1980) the UK government has tried to use increased competitive pressure in product markets to force down costs in related labour markets. CCT also covers a range of services in the NHS and defence. Private-sector firms bidding for public-sector contracts formerly due in-house must comply with the EU Applied Rights Directive of 1981 and the associated UK Transfer of Undertakings and Protection of Employment Regulations 1981. The effect has been to lower costs in many of these areas, although it is unclear whether the source of these savings has been genuine production efficiencies or lower wages and reduced employment (see Section 15.4). The Equal Opportunities Commission has noted that the marked pressure on the hours worked and hourly rates of pay by part-time council workers has had a disproportionate effect on women workers.

The possibilities for monopolistic wage-setting in a fully unionised economy are reduced when bargaining is conducted at the company level, since workers will be competing indirectly with each other as long as their employers are competing in the product market. An attempt to raise wages above the competitive level in one organisation will result in large job losses as the firm is forced out of business. On the other hand, the monopolistic power of unions is increased when workers producing similar products have identical wages as a result of industry-wide agreements and strong union organisation or because of the extension of collective agreements to third parties.

The traditional monopoly view of unions (whose main purpose is to raise wages) can be contrasted with more recent approaches which emphasise other important purposes that unions may serve. For example, Williamson (1984) has stressed the *efficiency-enhancing* aspect of unions. In their role as agents of labour it is argued that unions can provide employers with information regarding employee requirements of, say, fringe benefits; unions can also help employees to evaluate complex wage and fringe benefit offers by hiring economists and other experts. Unions are also instrumental in establishing the appropriate governance structure (given the nature of labour transactions) and thereby lowering transaction costs by reducing the scope for opportunistic bargaining. This is particularly important where, in situations of high job-specificity, continuity of the employment relation is considered vital by both employers and employees; any investment in human capital undertaken by employers is better protected and employees are provided with a secure work environment for their non-transferable skills. In these circumstances it is claimed that within ILMs, collective bargaining reduces bargaining costs, helps to rationalise the internal wage structure and ensures that investments in specific human capital, which constitute a potential source of monopoly power, are undertaken without risk of exploitation.

The efficiency-enhancing aspect of trade unions has also been explored by Freeman and Medoff (1984), who have referred to their *collective voice* (as opposed to their so-called monopoly 'face') through which it is argued that unions can have a positive impact on productivity. Some of the arguments employed are similar to those expressed by Williamson. Thus, as institutions of collective voice operating in ILMs, unions communicate the preferences of workers directly to employers and participate in the establishment of rules and procedures in ILMs. By providing employees with a voice by which to communicate with employers and by improving internal grievance

Evidence, at least for the UK and the US, indicates that unionised workers receive wage premia (union/non-union differentials between groups of similar workers) over their non-union counterparts, after allowing for human capital characteristics and industry affiliation. Estimates generally reveal quite large union premia in the UK and the US, although the size of the premia in Japan is uncertain. The consensus estimate for the differential in the US in the mid-1980s was about 10–25%, while the estimate for the UK was rather smaller, at around 8–10%. There is also evidence that the premia in the US have remained fairly stable for prime-age workers on average, whereas the premia in the UK appeared to fall by up to 30% between 1984 and 1990, as legislation (particularly that making the closed shop legally unenforceable) accompanied by a reduction in the number of organisations that recognised unions for collective bargaining purposes combined to reduce union power. However, wage premia do not necessarily reflect the monopolistic power of unions; in enterprise-bargaining systems they could reflect rents earned in the product market. They are also not a reliable indicator of the wage-raising power of unions where collective contracts are extended to non-union workers. On the other hand, where company or sector-wide agreements are accompanied by local bargains these may show up as union wage premia.

While there is certainly no consensus on the net productivity effect of unions, in general the results of recent studies imply that unionised workers have become more productive than their non-union counterparts. Evidence on the scale of any differential is hard to come by, but at least one source (Sapsford and Tzannatos, 1993) has suggested that it may be sufficiently large to offset the estimated union/non-union wage differential. As with evidence on the impact of unions on wages it is difficult to disentangle the union impact on productivity from sectoral and other influences, but this evidence indicates that the efficiency effects of unions may be as strong as, if not stronger, than any monopolistic influences.

procedure mechanisms, it is claimed that unions can reduce costly staff turnover or 'exit' rates. Reduced turnover can also be facilitated by seniority rights, which unions can help to establish. Reduced staff turnover and the resulting improvement in employee morale can increase productivity. The fostering of a high level of trust between employers and employees, facilitated by unions, can help in the introduction of new technology, which again can have productivity-enhancing consequences.

Given the conflicting arguments over whether unions act mainly as monopolistic agents or as efficiency-enhancing bodies, it is worthwhile examining the empirical evidence of their impact on wages and productivity (see Box 14.2).

14.7 THE IMPACT OF THE LEGISLATIVE CHANGES IN THE UK DURING THE 1980S ON LABOUR MARKET FLEXIBILITY

In Section 3.5 it was noted that labour market flexibility can take a variety of forms: numerical, functional, flexibility in terms of time and mobility and wage flexibility. The effects of agreements to introduce greater flexibility of work practices into particular plants are considered in the case study at the end of the chapter. This section takes a broader view of flexibility by examining both the aggregate and disaggregated effects of the legislation of the 1980s (the so-called Thatcher reforms) designed to limit institutional intervention in the free market, to promote the 'enterprise culture' and to enhance competition. Many of the reforms related directly to the labour market: industrial relations legislation reduced trade union power, Wages Councils that set minimum wages were largely eliminated, the value of unemployment benefits was reduced relative to wages; there were also lower marginal taxes for individuals, tax incentives to promote the use of private pensions and self-employment and new training initiatives. At the same time, institutional intervention in the labour market was reduced as government-owned businesses were privatised and CCT was introduced into a number of central and local government activities.

The basis of these reforms was to make a more flexible labour market, where labour was more mobile, where wages depended more on company performance and in which market forces predominated. In other words, the idea was to have a labour market resembling the decentralised US market rather than the highly regulated and institutionally structured markets generally found within the EU.

While there is some disagreement about the role of government policies in reducing union density, there is little doubt that the unions suffered a reduction of power in the 1980s: the closed shop was outlawed, single-plant agreements became more common and strikes per worker fell more rapidly than in other countries. As noted in the previous section, concomitant with these changes was a pattern of faster productivity growth for unionised than for non-unionised workers as restrictive practices were reduced. There was also a reduction in the union wage premium. Blanchflower and Freeman (1993) have examined the impact of the reforms on the labour market. On an aggregate basis they estimated that from 1980 to 1988 the relative position of the UK compared with other OECD countries improved in terms of inflation and growth, but for unemployment and employment rates the differences between the UK and the other countries moved in the opposite direction.

At a disaggregated level, the authors calculated transitions for the UK as a whole and for the relatively low unemployment South-east region during 1979–91 (1990, a year of relatively low unemployment, was actually used as an 'after year' in order to minimise cyclical factors). They found that the transition from unemployment to employment for men (although not necessarily for women) worsened. This was despite a large fall in the replacement ratio, the ratio of benefit entitlements to average net earnings. Thus, although the reforms made work more attractive to unemployment for men, they did not work in moving them into jobs more rapidly. There was evidence of greater employment responsiveness by firms plus an increased responsiveness of wages to market conditions, but there was also a large rise in wage inequality (particularly for workers of similar skills) in the period. In fact, it is argued that the reductions in institutional constraints, such as the impact of Wages Councils on low wages and the reduction in the replacement ratio, may have increased labour market segmentation.

In conclusion, while there is some evidence of increased labour market efficiency in terms of improved employment and wage flexibility, there was no corresponding improvement in the transition for men out of unemployment and there was an increase in wage inequality, which is not what is expected from a better functioning labour market. Much of the growth of employment that has occurred in the UK in recent years has stemmed from a growth of part-time jobs, largely filled by women entering the labour market. The effects of CCT have been commented upon in the previous section. The US has certainly been more successful than the EU as a job creator in the past (see Section 3.5) and there is evidence that most new jobs there are full-time and in the more profitable and higher-paying parts of the economy.[4] However, there has also been a huge increase in wage inequality in the US since the late 1970s. There is no

evidence that greater wage flexibility has particularly helped the employment prospects of unskilled workers in the US. In addition, Jacoby and Mitchell (1990) have noted that the groups with the sharpest falls in tenure (with the same employer) in the US between 1983 and 1987 included men aged 45–54, male managers and machine operators in manufacturing, each of which were previously regarded as having had relatively secure employment patterns. Improved labour market flexibility, however defined, offers no panacea for a smoothly functioning and equitable labour market.

14.8 CONCLUSIONS

In a perfectly competitive environment the equilibrium wage and level of employment are determined by the interaction of the forces of market demand and market supply. Wage differentials stem from differences in skills and abilities which result largely from investments in human capital; thus, wages and individual productivity levels are regarded as worker-based. The neoclassical model is capable of some degree of adaptability, although it fails to account for difficulties in quantifying marginal productivity or for the segmentation of labour markets.

The basis of theories of labour market segmentation is that labour markets can be divided into a structured sector, comprising ILMs and ELMs, and a structureless sector, in which pricing and allocating decisions are essentially market-determined; little labour mobility is presumed to take place between the sectors. ILMs have arisen, it is argued, as technological developments have increased the extent of job and human asset specificity, and as productivity and wages have become job- rather than worker-determined. The characteristics of ILMs, such as relatively high wages, secure employment patterns, job ladders and seniority payments, are designed to reduce labour turnover and hiring and firing costs, including the firm's investment in job-specific training; specific IWSs accompany ILMs. The dual labour market hypothesis of a primary/secondary sector dichotomy which increases over time represents the extreme version of labour market segmentation.

According to the new economics of personnel, ILMs are a response to the problems of opportunism and asymmetric information in situations of high human-asset specifity and where individual productivities cannot be measured. In these circumstances, payment incentive systems may be required to reduce shirking and lower monitoring costs. However, an assessment of individual performance may still be used as a proxy for productivity in a firm's wage-setting.

Traditional explanations of educational and training decision-making centre on human capital analysis, in which the individual weighs up the relative costs and benefits of the investment. In principle, individuals should bear the costs and reap the benefits of general training, while specific training is seen as the responsibility of the firm, although in practice the costs and benefits of training are more likely to be shared. Evidence on private and social rates of return to education and training provide some support for human capital explanations, although more recent research has questioned the presumption of a positive experience/productivity relationship. The screening hypothesis assigns a smaller, allocative role to education, while assuming that most skills are acquired through on-the-job training. However, policy-makers are hindered by a lack of precise policy prescriptions resulting from the predictions of economic theory or from the results of empirical investigations.

Some recent evidence, using a monopsonistic analytical framework, has reported positive employment effects of minimum wages; these can be can be contrasted with earlier studies showing a negative impact. Recent theoretical approaches towards trade unions have stressed their efficiency-enhancing impact as opposed to the more traditional role assigned to them as monopolistic suppliers of labour. Evidence from the UK and the US suggests that, compared with their non-unionised counterparts, the productivity differential of unionised workers may be of a similar scale to the wage differential.

An examination of the aggregate effects (the effects at plant-level are discussed in the case study which follows) of legislative changes in the UK during the 1980s relating to the labour market reveals increases in efficiency in terms of improved employment and wage flexibility, but this has been at the expense of increased wage inequality and possibly reduced stability of employment.

Case Study: Changes in Work Practices and Improved Labour Flexibility at the Plant Level

Many manufacturing firms and plants in the UK have introduced greater flexibility into their work practices in recent years. The changes have taken a variety of forms, some of which may have been included under the flexibility umbrella without actually having a great deal of relevance to it; there have also been implications of the changes for other aspects of work organisation, such as training and the role of unions. In many instances the changes in work practices that have been introduced by firms have occurred in times of financial stringency and amidst other organisational and technological developments.

Six examples of changes in plant work practices are examined that vary widely in their scale, timing and nature; they are summarised in Table 69. The changes in work practices have been mainly associated with the removal, or at least reduction in, traditional job demarcation. The changes may have been introduced gradually, in incremental stages, or in a single 'big bang' approach; they have also taken place in new 'greenfield' sites or in established 'brownfield' plants. Most of the agreements have been based on the principle of introducing or improving multi-skilling, especially for craft workers, although in some cases this has been limited by the need for workers to specialise in skills that are plant-specific.

Thus, the additional skills acquired by employees of Babcock Energy and Mobil have been linked to the needs of the job in which the individual specialises. Flexibility for production workers has been limited to them undertaking minor plant maintenance work. CWS at Deeside has probably taken flexibility furthest, but even here it has proved too costly to give all employees all the skills required by the plant. Flexibility deals have been accompanied by (or have contributed to) reductions in the numbers employed by Mobil Oil, Babcock Energy and Rolls-Royce; in the former two cases the contracting out of activities not viewed as core to the operation has been a major factor in the reductions in numbers. The introduction of teamworking has been a common

Table 69 *Labour flexibility agreements at the plant level*

Plant	Product	Nature of site	Date of initial agreement	Type of agreement
Toshiba Consumer Products (TCP), Ernsettle	Colour TVs	Greenfield	1981	Big bang
Mobil Oil, Coryton	Oil refining	Brownfield	1984	Big bang
Co-operative Wholesale Society (CWS), Deeside	Food manuf.	Greenfield	1985	Gradual expansion from broad base
Babcock Energy, Renfrew	Power station plants	Brownfield	1985–87	Incremental
Thorn EMI, Spennymoor	White goods	Brownfield	1988	Incremental
Rolls-Royce, Crewe	Car manuf.	Brownfield	1991	Big bang

Source: *Industrial Relations Review and Reports*, 1992, nos 505 (Feb.), 512(May), 515(July).

feature of the schemes. In general, it would appear that the deals have increased the breadth, but not usually the depth, of skills required by employees, especially those engaged in plant maintenance.

In all cases the flexibility provisions have meant that both new recruits and existing workers have required additional skills training. Cost considerations have usually restricted the training of existing workers to in-house schemes rather than them being able to benefit from schemes run by recruiting outside experts. The effects of the changes on new recruit training have been variable: Babcock has maintained its own apprenticeship scheme, TCP has not provided apprenticeship training and Rolls-Royce and Mobil Oil have reduced the amount of apprenticeship, in Mobil's case quite significantly. In most cases, industrial relations structures have not changed markedly following the introduction of the schemes. Company-wide/multiunion bargains are the norm, although the TCP agreement included one of the earliest single-union deals in the country. The change of culture at Mobil Oil, with its emphasis on individual performance appraisal, is seen as having laid the groundwork for a bargaining system based more on individual performance rather than on collective negotiations, although there is little evidence of a movement to more wage flexibility in general.

The changes in workplace practices have been linked with improved levels of performance in most of the cases cited, and particularly with what have been regarded as more acceptable productivity levels. However, multifunctional flexibility has been fairly limited in several of the cases and cost considerations may sometimes have taken precedence. It is unclear to what extent the productivity improvements have been due to higher and more varied skill levels on the part of the workforce or instead to a reduction in the number of employees; they may also have been the result of the introduction of new technology, irrespective of the new agreements.

FURTHER READING

King, J.E. (1990) *Labour Economics*, 2nd (London, Macmillan), Chapters 1–5.

Sapsford, D. and Tzannatos, Z. (1993) *The Economics of the Labour Market* (London, Macmillan), Chapters 2–5, 10.

Stephen, F.H. (ed.) (1984) *Firms, Organisation and Labour* (London, Macmillan), Chapters 1,6,7.

NOTES

1. See *The Economist*, 17 July 1993, Economic Focus 'Musical Chairs'.
2. See *The Economist*, 6 April 1996, 'Training and Jobs'.
3. See *The Economist*, 6 April 1996, *op. cit.*
4. See *The Economist*, 16 November, 1996, 'Feeling Insecure'.

Questions □ □ □

14.1 'The neoclassical model of the labour market is infinitely adaptable; it is able to account for most, if not all, of the characteristics of modern work practices.' Explain and discuss.

14.2 Account for the existence of ILMs. Explain why wages may differ within the same local labour market for similar groups of workers.

14.3 'Both employers and employees have a vested interest in maintaining the employment contract in situations where human assets are transaction-specific and where marginal productivity cannot be accurately deduced. In these circumstances, however, payment schemes may need to be devised to ensure that workers put in the required amount of effort.' Explain and discuss.

14.4 'Evidence of private rates of return to schooling and training suggest that lifetime earnings' profiles can be more than adequately explained by human capital analysis.' Critically examine this statement and discuss any public policy implications.

14.5 Critically examine the view that firms have little incentive to provide on-the-job training, since other employers will poach the recipients of general training and employees are likely to impose opportunistic threats to quit before firms are able to secure any of the benefits of specific training. Discuss the public policy implications.

14.6 Discuss the view that most training policies are doomed to failure because economic theory does not have much to offer in the way of precise policy prescriptions, and empirical evidence sheds little light on which policies offer the best results.

14.7 Discuss the employment effects of the establishment of a minimum wage for young workers from both a theoretical and an empirical basis.

14.8 Examine the monopolistic and efficiency 'faces' of trade unions. To what extent is either face supported by empirical evidence?

14.9 Discuss the rationale for, and the success of, the policies adopted by the UK government in the 1980s to enhance labour market flexibility.

CHAPTER 15

▶ *Industry Policy and the Firm*

This chapter examines industry policies, with particular reference to competition policy and the privatisation debate, and how they can affect the behaviour and performance of the firm. In so doing, the traditional basis for government intervention is compared with the philosophical stance taken by other schools of thought.

Interventionist policies can be broadly divided into two approaches: a *passive* or *supportive* approach, which is based on the assumption of the superiority of market forces over government directives and in which intervention is limited to relatively neutral policies that support market forces rather than direct them; and an *active* approach that argues for a greater level of government involvement in order to influence the industrial structure more directly by shaping and directing market forces. In practice, in the past most governments in industrial economies have involved themselves vigorously in the affairs of industry, although the degree of success has depended on the philosophical basis from which a particular policy directive is being judged. However, more recently there has been a general move away from an active role towards a more supportive approach by governments.

Most industry policies continue to be directed at the industrial or secondary sector. Manufacturing is especially well targeted, largely for the reasons mentioned in Section 3.4 regarding its importance for an economy. However, the significance of the tertiary sector in industrial economies coupled with the growing interrelationship between services and industry means that future policies are likely to be directed more at both sectors.

The chapter begins by outlining the problems involved in agreeing upon an appropriate theoretical framework for *industry policy*. The theoretical arguments underlying *competition policy* are examined in detail; the particular policy approaches in the UK, the EU and the US are considered. The theoretical and empirical arguments surrounding *state control versus privatisation* are discussed in the next section. The privatisation process in the UK is examined, including the issues of *deregulation* and *franchising*. *Regional, innovation and trade policies* are briefly considered. The *case study* at the end of the chapter investigates the impact of privatisation on British Telecom.

15.1 THE THEORETICAL BASIS FOR INDUSTRY POLICY

The arguments surrounding the appropriate theoretical framework for a policy towards industry have led to confusion and vagueness in its practical implementation. The situation has been highlighted in an EU policy statement:

The debate on the theme of industrial policy is often blurred by the lack of a proper definition and an appropriate conceptual framework. Similarly, the idea of global competitiveness, often put forward as the objective for industrial policy, is vague and ambiguous (CEC, 1990: 1).

Any policy instrument requires sound performance indicators by which it can be judged. At the macroeconomic level these comprise per capita GNP, the rate of inflation, the level of unemployment and the state of the balance of payments. From a microeconomic perspective, performance can be assessed by the use of either profits or productivity, although both suffer from measurement problems. As a result, market models have often been used as the indirect basis for judging performance. The use of market models has been most fully developed in the case of perfect competition, which has been used as a theoretical base for developing performance indicators in more realistic types of market structure. The rationale for this is that perfect competition entails certain key results, i.e. an optimum allocation of resources, which are associated with good performance. However, the neoclassical optimal condition is a theoretical ideal. The firm is regarded as an abstract unit that operates in a static environment under conditions of certainty and with perfect information. In these circumstances, industry policy is based on a comparison of real-world situations with a conceptual abstraction, in which it is assumed that performance is directly attributable to the structural conditions of the market.

In practice, however, firms operate in a dynamic and uncertain world characterised by divergent interests, informational asymmetries and the presence of transaction costs. The disadvantages of monopoly power have to be weighed against the higher relative levels of efficiency of some firms that can lead to the acquisition of market power in the first place. The effectiveness of both actual and potential competition should also be taken into account. In other words, industry policy should consider the *effective level of competition* that actually exists in a particular market.

The absence of a suitable theoretical basis for industry policy underlies the lack of specific directives in policy initiatives. In a recent EU policy report (CEC, 1995) the main 'accelerators' of the structural adjustment required for an efficiently functioning market economy are listed as the following: intangible investments (such as innovation and education and training), industrial co-operation, competition and the modernisation of the role of public authorities. However, there are no details of specific policy measures necessary to achieve the desired aims. Within the OECD as a whole:

Industrial policies in OECD countries have remained focused on improving the underlying competitiveness of firms ... Structural change is being underpinned by policies aimed at improving the business environment, upgrading the infrastructure and enhancing the competence of the labour force, rather than by industry-specific measures (OECD, 1994:13).

Discussion of the implications for particular industrial policies begins with an assessment of competition policy.

15.2 THE RATIONALE FOR COMPETITION POLICY

Many industries in the UK and in other major industrial economies are characterised by high levels of concentration; they are dominated by a small number of firms, each of which has some degree of market power over the price that it can set. If price is set above marginal cost, then in neoclassical terms, market power automatically produces a misallocation of resources and a reduction in the level of economic welfare. The extent to which a profit-maximising firm can maintain price above marginal cost, or the degree

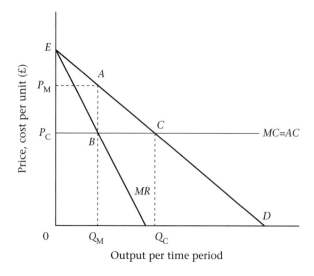

Figure 98   *The deadweight loss of monopoly.*

of its monopoly or market power, can be measured by the Lerner index; this is the equivalent of the markup on price and is equal to the reciprocal of price elasticity of demand (see Note 3, Chapter 10).

The traditional approach to the problem of market power centres on the *deadweight loss* attributable to monopoly. Compared with a perfectly competitive industry, a monopolist is able to restrict output and charge a price above marginal cost. Figure 98 shows the demand and cost conditions (where costs are assumed to be constant) in an industry. If the industry were perfectly competitive the price would be P_C and the output Q_C. However, a monopolist facing the same demand and cost conditions would equate MC and the downward-sloping MR curve; it produces only Q_M and charges a price of P_M. The consequent loss of social welfare can be measured by comparing the sum of the consumer and producer surplus (or excess profit) in each case. When the industry is monopolised, consumer surplus falls from $P_C EC$ to $P_M EA$. However, producer surplus increases from zero (under perfect competition) to $P_C P_M AB$ for a monopolist. Therefore, the triangle ABC represents the net loss of welfare or the deadweight loss.

The extent of the welfare loss depends on the price elasticity of demand for the product and the difference between the prices under monopoly and perfect competition. Harberger (1954) estimated the size of the welfare loss using the following formula:[1]

$$\text{Welfare loss} = \frac{1}{2} e_p P_M Q_M \left(\frac{\Delta P}{P_M}\right)^2 \qquad (15.1)$$

On the basis of this formula and using data aggregated at the industry level, Harberger estimated the welfare loss due to monopoly in US manufacturing to be only 0.1% of GNP. However, this estimate has been subjected to a number of criticisms. The formula requires estimates for price elasticity of demand and for $\Delta P/P_M$, which represents the markup due to monopoly. Harberger assumed unit price elasticity of demand for all industries, but this is inconsistent with profit maximisation because at unit price elasticity marginal revenue is zero, which would imply zero marginal costs. Harberger estimated ΔP by examining the difference between industry rates of return and the average for all manufacturing; however, the average rate of return would probably overstate the competitive rate of return and hence lead to an underestimate of any welfare loss. Monopoly power might also be reflected in higher costs instead of higher profits, a factor not captured by the formula. Finally, there is the problem of using consumer surplus to measure welfare and whether the marginal utility of money can be assumed constant for all individuals at all income levels. Part of the reduction in consumer surplus in Figure 98 is transferred to the monopolist as profit. If the transfer is from consumers to a wealthier monopolist with a lower marginal utility of money, then there is an additional welfare loss. In other words, distributional matters should also be considered.

Cowling and Mueller (1978) estimated welfare loss at the firm level before aggregating. The extent to which a firm with market power can price above the competitive level is given by the Lerner index; therefore, substituting into equation (15.1) gives[2]

$$\text{Welfare loss} = \frac{1}{2} Q_M \Delta P \qquad (15.2)$$

or half the amount of monopoly profit of the firm. On the basis of this formula, Cowling and Mueller estimated the welfare loss of monopoly power to be about 4% of total manufacturing output in the US and about 3.9% in the UK. This method of estimating welfare loss has the advantage that, since it undertakes the analysis at the firm level, it pinpoints more accurately the location of the loss. However, since the analysis is based on the Lerner index it implicitly assumes a short-run profit-maximising objective, thus ignoring both limit pricing behaviour and the pursuit of other objectives by firms.

Most studies that have attempted to measure the welfare losses of monopoly have adopted the Harberger approach; hence the fairly low estimates shown in Table 70. The Kamerschen (1966) study employed a Harberger-type analysis, but used elasticities of demand more consistent with monopoly pricing behaviour for each industry studied. As a result, a much larger estimate of welfare loss was obtained. Estimates at lower levels of aggregation tend to be more reliable (which Cowling and Mueller showed by making comparisons between different levels of aggregation); thus, their results may give a more accurate indication of the actual extent of the welfare loss. It is worth also noting the study by Masson and Shaanan (1984), which distinguished between actual rather than the full profit-maximising social costs of monopoly. The latter would only occur without the existence of either actual and potential competition in a market. By using a limit pricing

Table 70 *Estimates of the welfare loss of monopoly*

Author(s)	Period	Country	Welfare loss[a]
Harberger (1954)	1924–28	USA	0.1
Schwartzman (1960)	1954	USA	0.1
Kamerschen (1966)	1956–61	USA	5.4–7.6
Worcester (1973)	1956–69	USA	0.2–0.7
Cowling and Mueller (1978)	1963–66	USA	4.0–13.1
Masson and Shaanan (1984)	1950–66	USA	2.9
Wahlroos (1984)	1962–75	USA	0.04–0.9
Cowling and Muller (1978)	1968–69	UK	3.9–7.2
Wahlroos (1984)	1970–79	Finland	0.2–0.6
Jenny and Weber (1983)	1967–70	France	0.13–8.85
	1971–74	France	0.21
Oh (1986)	1983	Korea	1.16–6.75

[a] Expressed as a percentage of GDP or total manufacturing output.

model and comparing certain hypothetical outcomes with empirical observations they estimated the deadweight loss for both actual and full monopoly conditions.

The analysis thus far has assumed that costs are identical for both the perfectly competitive industry and the monopolist, which is unlikely. While market power may be identifiable with allocative inefficiency, at least from a traditional viewpoint, there is no reason to assume that *levels of productive efficiency* will be the same under different market conditions. For example, market power might be equated with lower costs due to economies of scale. Using a merger as an example, Williamson (1968) was the first person to formalise the trade-off between the cost savings from economies of scale with the loss of consumer surplus from market power within a social welfare framework.

In Figure 99 average costs in a competitive industry are given by AC_1; the competitive price and output are P_C and Q_C respectively. If the firms merged, costs would fall to AC_2 (which it could be argued might also be achieved through the transaction cost savings of expansion), but the merged firm would produce the monopoly output Q_M and charge the monopoly price P_M. Consumer surplus has been reduced by the area P_MACP_C. Producer surplus has increased by the area P_MAFE. Therefore, since the rectangle P_MABP_C is simply a transfer from consumers to producers, the overall effect on welfare depends on the relative sizes of the cost savings of market power, area A_2, with

the associated deadweight loss, area A_1. In crude terms, if A_2 exceeds A_1, then the merger should be allowed.

However, the situation is not quite so clear-cut. There are a number of qualifications to be made. Even if the merger lowered production costs and the monopolist's gain exceeded the loss of consumer welfare, there is still an opportunity loss to society due to the suboptimal production, Q_MQ_C. The merger may lead to other mergers by competing firms. The distributional effects of the transfer from consumers to producers also need to be considered. A final point to note is that the analysis is a static one. It fails to take into account the effect of the increase in market power associated with the merger on new investment and technical progress. If greater monopoly power is positively related with the degree of innovative activity in a market, then this might provide another reason for lower production costs for the monopolist.

There are conflicting arguments regarding the relative innovative superiority of competition or monopoly. From a traditional perspective it can be argued that monopoly profits are necessary to undertake large-scale R&D, given the costs and risks involved, whereas a monopolist may have little incentive to innovate on its own account (although it may quickly imitate the innovations of competitors). Empirical evidence has found that, at least in those industries where the pace of innovation is less rapid, absolute firm size and market concentration are both positively related to the level of innovative activity, but only up to some threshold level in each case (see Ferguson and Ferguson, 1994; and Devine *et al.*, 1985 for a summary of the evidence). It should be noted that most evidence has failed to consider the possibility (highlighted, for example, by the Austrian school of thought) that reverse causation in either instance may mean that innovation can lead to increases in absolute firm size and/or levels of market concentration.

The opposite argument, that production costs may be higher under monopoly than under competition is mainly associated with Leibenstein (1966). He coined the phrase *X-inefficiency* to describe the production inefficiences associated with monopoly. A firm with market power and protected by barriers to entry lacks the competitive stimulus to employ its resources efficently and hence keep costs to the competitive minimum (see also Section 9.5). In Figure 100 the perfectly competitive industry produces at Q_C and sells at a price of P_C. If it then becomes monopolised and costs rise to AC_I, output will fall to Q_M and price will increase to P_M. In this case the total fall in

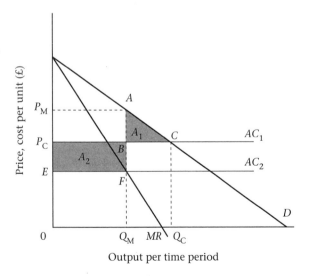

Figure 99 *Monopoly deadweight loss combined with productive efficiency.*

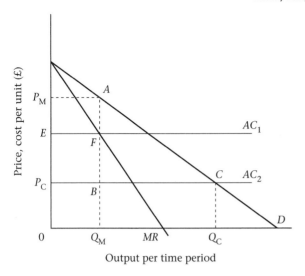

Figure 100 *Monopoly deadweight loss combined with productive Inefficiency.*

consumer surplus is $P_M A C P_C$, of which ABC is the allocative deadweight loss and $EFBP_C$ represents the productive inefficiency of the monopolist. $P_M AFE$ represents a transfer from consumers to producers. Comanor and Leibenstein (1969), on the basis of hypothetical examples, calculated that X-inefficiency represents by far the largest segment (three-quarters) of their welfare loss estimate of monopoly, amounting in total to 12% of net national product. In practice, it is very difficult to measure the extent of X-inefficiency and so empirical evidence is scarce. However, there is anecdotal evidence that the productivity performance of the UK steel industry improved dramatically from the 1970s onwards when it was subjected to greater competitive international forces. The same claim might be made about the UK-based car industry (as well as other Western European and American car manufacturers) following the influx of Japanese producers and techniques from the mid- to late 1980s onwards.

There is one important point to note in the debate about X-inefficiency. Whether the pursuit of personal objectives that do not require cost minimisation, such as security, prestige or leisure, can automatically be regarded as contributing to a net loss of welfare is a moot point. If managers employ excessive staff because it gives them a higher salary, if some of the monopoly profit is transferred to workers in the form of higher wages or if owner-managers opt for a quiet life, then costs are likely to be raised above the competitive level. However, in each case the source

of the so-called X-inefficiency represents a benefit to somebody or some group; therefore, the argument for its removal (at least in traditional welfare terms) is not immediately clear.

The desire for monopoly profits by competing firms may also lead to a wasteful use of resources; Posner (1975) argued that this inefficient resource use should be included as a cost of monopoly. Expenditures incurred in building up and maintaining a monopoly position can take a number of forms: forming a cartel, bribing or lobbying government officials and various types of non-price strategic behaviour which may be carried to an excessive degree and which also may act as barriers to entry, such as advertising and other promotional outlays, product proliferation, pre-emptive patenting, R&D and capital expenditures, building excess capacity, predatory activities and the use of vertical restraints to trade. On this basis Posner concluded that all monopoly profit should count as a social cost of monopoly. In other words, the welfare loss from monopoly in Figure 98, page 288, would be ABC plus $P_C P_M AB$, where the latter represents the resource cost of acquiring and maintaining the monopoly position.

Assuming an average markup in manufacturing and mining of 2% and an average price elasticity of just over one, Posner estimated the social cost of monopoly in the US to be 0.6% of GNP, rising to 1.2% using a 4% markup figure. It was also postulated that government controls and restrictions of various kinds in different markets, although ostensibly designed for consumer protection or for safety reasons, may produce higher markups and lead to an even greater welfare loss in the regulated sector of the economy; this loss was estimated by Posner as 1.7% of GNP. Cowling and Mueller (1978), on the basis of a definition of the social cost of market power which included both advertising expenditures and after-tax profits, estimated the welfare loss of 734 US manufacturing firms as 13.1% and the equivalent for 103 UK manufacturing firms as 7.2% of their respective total outputs.

However, it can be argued that monopoly profits overestimate the wasteful expenditures involved in achieving and maintaining market dominance. Firstly, the social benefits of some of the expenditures are ignored: the spread of information via advertising can lower transaction costs by reducing informational asymmetries; innovation can create cheaper and improved products. Secondly, the various forms of collusive activity associated with market power may reduce any wasteful expenditures. On the other hand, there are other reasons for thinking that monopoly profits will underestimate the relevant welfare losses. Those expenses incurred by firms that do not achieve monopoly power are excluded from the calculations, as are the value of the resources involved in the competition policy process itself.

From a traditional SCP perspective, high profits may be regarded as an inevitable consequence of the effectiveness of collusive policies in highly concentrated markets where barriers to entry are present; hence they are indicative of poor performance. Empirically, the positive relationship between concentration and profits is fairly weak. There is also some empirical support for the notion that market power may be quite transitory (see Section 2.2). In other words, barriers to entry are also required for market power to be effectively implemented. However, there is stronger empirical evidence of a positive, and more persistent, relationship between market share and profitability (see Section 3.2). Very different factors can also lead to the acquisition of market power. These include the technological conditions existing in a market (i.e the shape of LRAC relative to market demand), horizontal and possibly vertical merger activity, collusive and predatory tactics and stochastic influences.

On the other hand, the basis of market power might be the greater relative efficiency of some firms, which is a factor emphasised by various other schools of thought. Transaction cost analysis argues that the existence of specific assets and/or spare capacity can lead to significant transaction cost savings through vertical and horizontal integration. The attainment of monopoly power because of the lower relative costs of some firms or via the efficiency-enhancing effects of innovative activity is an integral part of both the Chicago school and the Austrian approaches. Empirical evidence has so far been unable to ascertain with any degree of certainty whether efficiency or market power plays a larger role in determining profit performance in concentrated industries.

Finally, arguments concerning the relative merits of certain restrictive and anti-competitive practices are relevant to the welfare debate. Arguments in favour of re-sale price maintenance (RPM), whereby the market power of a firm or a group of firms ensures that all retailers set the same price, stem mainly from new industrial organisation theory: RPM does not hinder non-price competition among distributors and their higher markups allow them to offer a better service and to provide more outlets. However, against this is the view that RPM strengthens price agreements among manufacturers and hence facilitates collusive activity. Non-price vertical agreements, such as exclusive dealerships, refusal to supply, tied sales and franchising, may restrict intrabrand competition, but this may not be of particular concern if interbrand competition is widespread.

15.3 COMPETITION POLICY IN PRACTICE

Competition policy is designed to promote or to prevent a reduction in effective competition. In principle, it encompasses policies towards market dominance, the acquisition of dominance via merger activity and the anti-competitive practices associated with dominance and which may lead to a diminution of competition. However, approaches to competition policy can vary between countries (a comprehensive policy was not introduced in Italy until 1990) and over time depending on prevailing economic and political philosophies. The traditional SCP approach implies intervention mainly at the structural and behavioural stages in order to achieve levels of performance more in keeping with a competitive market environment. On the other hand, the Austrian school's belief in the entrepreneurial spur of monopoly profit and the likelihood of an innovative basis for monopoly power places the policy focus on the removal of obstacles to new competition, especially those that are goverment-imposed and which may have the effect of preventing the development of new products and processes.

Competition policy in the UK is basically neutral and pragmatic; a cost–benefit approach to individual cases has usually been adopted, whereby the costs of large size and market dominance are weighed against any possible benefits, such as the attainment of economies of scale and improved overseas competitiveness. Competition policy originated in 1948 with the Monopolies and Restrictive Practices Act, since when it has been revised and updated, notably by the 1965 Monopolies and Mergers Act which included mergers in the policy framework and the Competition Act of 1980 that allowed for investigations of public sector bodies. At present a tripartite system operates in which the Office of Fair Trading (OFT) can investigate and prosecute, the Monopolies and Mergers Commission (MMC) acts as judiciary in disputed cases and the Department of Trade and Industry (DTI) can decide what action, if any, should be taken.

The US has the oldest, and probably the toughest, competition policy regime which is enforced jointly by the Federal Trade Commission and the Antitrust

Division of the Department of Justice. It began with the Sherman Act of 1890 that declared illegal any restraints of trade and attempts to monopolise in trade and commerce. This was followed by the Clayton Act of 1914 and the Robinson–Patman Act of 1936 that outlawed various anti-competitive practices and the Celler–Kefauver Anti-merger Act of 1950. US competition policy has mainly been based within the traditional SCP paradigm, although during the 1980s there was a noticeable easing of the approach and a greater adherence to alternative philosophies that emphasised the more positive aspects of market power. In the 1990s there is some evidence of a more interventionist stance being taken by the authorities once again.

EU policy has generally favoured a more free-market Austrian approach than in the UK or the US. The importance of competition policy was recognised in the Treaty of Rome, the founding treaty of the then EEC. Articles 85–94 provide a system to ensure that 'competition in the Common Market is not distorted'. Policy decisions and rulings are mainly taken by the European Commission (EC), although appeals can be made to the European Court of Justice. The policy has since been updated and new powers have been introduced. An EU-wide merger policy was introduced in 1990 and there are also provisions for the investigation of nationalised firms and industries and state aids (subsidies) to firms.

Policy towards monopoly

Policies towards monopoly hinge essentially on the possible abuse of market power rather than on dominance itself. In the US the use of the term 'to monopolise' suggests that it is the means by which monopoly is attained that is the main area of concern. In fact, there is no statutory definition of market share that constitutes a monopoly in the US, although a threshold criterion of about 60% has often been adopted (which in the 1980s rose to about 80% in a number of cases); instead monopoly power is determined by a combination of the structural and behavioural features existing in a particular market. Thus Eastman Kodak, despite having a clear monopoly position in the relevant market, was declared innocent by the US Supreme Court of having abused its power by introducing the Instamatic camera and cartridge film in 1972; in other words, monopolisation has been allowed if it stems from innovation or from some other form of cost-saving. Where monopoly instances

have been successfully prosecuted, structural remedies have been more eagerly sought than elsewhere. 'Trust-busting' was a particularly popular policy measure until about 1930. In a more recent case that was finalised in 1983–84, the American Telephone and Telegraph Company, AT&T, was divested of its local activities, provided by the Bell Operating Companies (known as the Baby Bells), while being allowed to keep its virtual monopoly of the long-distance telephone service. In 1996 the market was further deregulated when local and long-distance companies were allowed to enter each other's markets. In general, the more interventionist stance of the US administration in the mid-1990s has been reflected in the increase in the number of cases scrutinised by the Justice Department's Antitrust division. They rose from three in the year to September 1992 to 22 two years later.[3]

It is worth noting that, while Japan's Anti-monopoly Law is modelled on US antitrust legislation, its application has tended to be looser. For example, although Eastman Kodak and Fujifilm each have about 70% shares for photographic film and paper in their respective home markets, Eastman Kodak has been subject to substantial scrutiny from the US authorities, while Fujifilm has faced very limited action from Japan's Fair Trade Commission.[4] Part of the reason for this may be the tendency within Japanese society to place co-operation above competition. This is exemplified in the predominance of the *keiretsu* system that has fostered far-reaching and long-lasting industry-wide vertical and horizontal relationships. A stricter enforcement of the law was proposed in 1993 as part of Japan's overall economic package (OECD, 1994).

UK policy is based on an exact legal definition of a monopoly, which is if the market share of a firm (or two or more distinct firms that are felt to be jointly restricting competition) exceeds 25%. (In Germany a monopoly is presumed to exist if a firm has a market share of one-third or more.) The public interest criteria that the authorities are required to take into account include the desirability of maintaining and promoting effective competition, plus effects on the regional balance of resources, innovation and export competitiveness. In each case investigated the onus of proof rests with the MMC to show that US a monopoly operates against the public interest. As with US policy, in each instance the basis of monopoly power is considered relevant to any enquiry, although very few cases are actually investigated. Nestlé was found not to be operating against the public interest despite having a 56% share (by value) of the soluble coffee market and achieving a rate of return on capital of over 100%:

Nestlé has achieved such a market share, and such a degree of profitability, by operating efficiently and by successfully developing products and brands that consumers regard as good value for money (MMC, 1991:107).

In its investigation of the white salt market the MMC (1986) noted that, while both Imperial Chemical Industries (ICI) and British Salt Limited had achieved market dominance monopoly positions (supplying 45% and 50% of the market respectively), both had established their positions through substantial investment in plant and technology. However, the MMC also found that a lack of price competition meant that prices were above effective competition levels and price controls were recommended. Between 1991 and 1994, on average five cases per annum were referred to the MMC for investigation by the Director-General of Fair Trading, the DGFT. The proposed remedies to abuses of monopoly power in the UK are usually along behavioural lines, structural reforms rarely being proposed. An exception was the ruling on brewing (MMC, 1989) which concluded that forward vertical integration in the industry restricted competition and the market power of the major brewers would be reduced if the number of on-licensed premises per brewer was lowered. This led to the eventual divestment of 13 000 premises by the national brewers.

There are three main elements of EU monopoly policy stipulated in Article 86: the establishment of a dominant position, the abuse of that position and the possibility of an effect on trade between member states. There is no precise definition of what constitutes dominance, but previous decisions have suggested that anything under about a 40% market share would not be considered worthy of investigation. In 1994, 16 such cases were launched, as opposed to 27 the previous year.[5] A prime example of the abuse of dominance was the Tetra Pak decision of 1992. Tetra Pak, a Swiss-based firm, had a 95% share of the EU market for supplying cartons for long-life products and for the associated packaging machinery. The European Commission found that it had hindered the competitive process by imposing exclusivity clauses on customers, by practising price discrimination between member states and by engaging in various predatory tactics. It was fined 75 million Ecus and ordered to stop the various practices (CEC, 1992). The emphasis of EU monopoly policy is on those features of market conduct that abuse dominance; hence, remedies are usually conduct-based.

There are important differences in these three approaches to monopoly policy, both in the criteria used to determine dominance and in terms of policy prescriptions. The US and the UK use structural criteria for defining monopolies, but the UK has tended to employ conduct (and performance) standards to rectify particular situations, whereas policies in the US have been more biased towards structural (with some behavioural) solutions. The EU has relied more exclusively on conduct criteria both in definitional and remedial terms. A general problem that has had to be confronted is that of defining the relevant market, both geographically and in product terms. The problems involved in defining markets were discussed in Section 2.1, but it is obvious that the wider the market definition that is adopted the lower the extent of dominance and vice versa. In many EU cases there are obvious implications for the measurement of market dominance should the market comprise national or EU-wide boundaries (or beyond). The European Commission lost a case against Continental Can in 1971 because it had defined the product market too narrowly; as a result it had underestimated competition from substitute products. In general terms, it is also worthwhile noting that the increased internationalisation of production reduces domestic market power and weakens the role of competition policy. On balance and given the current debate about the pros and cons of dominance, the UK case-by-case approach in which specific criteria are put forward as a basis for intervention may be considered preferable. However, it is also very time-consuming, which accounts for the small number of cases investigated.

Policy towards mergers

US policy towards mergers was formalised in 1968 in a set of guidelines referring to all types of merger activity. The promotion of competition was regarded as paramount; improved efficiency was accepted as a mitigating factor only in exceptional circumstances. In 1982, new guidelines were issued which, while continuing to acknowledge that mergers may tighten existing oligopolies and increase the possibility of collusion, recognised the importance of potential as well as actual competition in defining markets. The market definition was further broadened in the 1984 guidelines on horizontal mergers with the inclusion of importers; efficiency considerations were also given greater weight.

The criterion used from 1982 onwards to screen potential horizontal mergers for investigation was based on a variant of the Herfindahl index, HI (see Section 2.3). This is defined as the sum of the squares of market shares of all firms in an industry, although in this context the shares are expressed as percentages rather than in proportionate terms. Thus, the index varies from near zero for a perfectly competitive industry to 10 000 (100^2) for a pure monopoly. Markets with an HI between 1000 and 1800 are defined as being moderately concentrated; mergers would be allowed if other conditions, such as relative ease of entry and no evidence of collusion, prevail. In markets where the HI > 1800, defined as highly concentrated, a merger that increased the index by more than 100 points would usually not be allowed to proceed. The new guidelines represented a softening of attitudes by the US authorities towards all types of mergers, not just horizontal ones. Since 1982, conglomerate mergers have had very few restrictions placed upon them and vertical mergers are now only queried if they are thought likely to facilitate collusion or if potential entrants are forced into more costly two-stage entry.

In the UK the MMC can investigate a proposed merger should it create or enhance a monopoly (leading to a greater than 25% market share) or when the merger involves gross assets of more than a specified threshold amount, currently £70 million. The DGFT chairs a Mergers Panel that screens all mergers that meet either or both of these criteria. The Secretary of State responsible for competition policy can then refer a particular merger to the MMC for investigation. It may be forbidden if it operates, or can be expected to operate, against the public interest. As with monopoly policy, the onus of proof is on the MMC to show that a merger operates against the public interest. Since 1984, successive Secretaries of State have referred mergers mainly on competition grounds. On this criterion it would appear that pure conglomerate mergers are effectively excluded from the legislation and very few are investigated, although such a stance, if taken, would ignore the impact of diversification on the competitive process noted in Section 13.3.

The MMC investigations themselves seem to have become less concerned with market share considerations; several mergers have been allowed to proceed even though they created market shares substantially above 25%. For example, the Gillette/Parker Pen merger was accepted despite creating a 62% market share for refillable pens because it was felt that relative ease of entry combined with retailer power would reduce the scope for any increase in market power by the firms concerned (MMC, 1993a). The main area of interest in the post-1984 investigations has been the possibilities for raising prices following a rise in market power rather than with the increase in market power itself (Morgan and Morgan, 1990). In fact, very few mergers are actually investigated by the MMC and even fewer are banned. Since 1965, less than 3% of eligible mergers have been referred to the MMC, with fewer than 1% being ruled against the public interest (Griffiths and Wall, 1995). In other words, most mergers in the UK are regarded as operating within the public interest.

EU legislation on mergers came into force in September 1990. The regulations apply only to very large mergers that affect more than one member state. There are two qualifying rules: firstly that the merging companies have a combined global turnover of over five billion Ecus and secondly that at least two of the companies involved in the merger each have an EU-wide turnover of over 250 million Ecus (as long as less than two-thirds of the business is in a single member state, otherwise national rules apply). Investigations are conducted for the European Commission by the Mergers Task Force. The major criterion for assessment is the effect on competition: a merger can be banned if it creates or strengthens a dominant position which impairs effective competition in the EU or a substantial part of it; potential efficiency gains are not allowed to outweigh any diminution of competition. Given the restrictive nature of the regulations, only a small number of mergers fall within their scope, and of these very few are actually investigated and even fewer are prohibited. For example, in 1994, 95 mergers were notified to the Commission, but just six were investigated.[6] Only one of these mergers was prohibited on the grounds of creating or strengthening dominance, the proposal by three German firms to establish a joint venture, MSG Media Service, in the market for technical and administrative services for digital pay-TV. In another case, Unilever France was allowed to acquire a majority stake in Safral, despite giving it a 25–50% share of the French ice cream and sorbet markets. It was felt that dominance would be counterbalanced by the growth of the market and the existence of powerful groups among potential new entrants (CEC, 1994).

Both the UK and the EU adopt fairly liberal approaches towards mergers, at least in terms of the small number that are investigated; most mergers presumably are regarded as welfare-enhancing. There has also been a marked easing of the US policy stance during the 1980s, although there has been a sharp rise in the number of merger investigations during the early to mid-1990s. Compared with US policy the British position has been criticised for not having clear guidelines about which mergers might be queried; this has led to inconsistencies in making referrals. EU policy, on the other hand, suffers from employing a size of firm rather than concentration criterion. The attitudes taken by policy-makers in different countries need to be placed squarely alongside the evidence on mergers, which in general finds little support for any welfare-enhancing effects. Many merged firms have proved to be no more profitable and sometimes less profitable than had the individual firms remained separate; this is especially true of horizontal mergers. Some conglomerates have grown quite rapidly and successfully by merger, although there is no justification to exclude them almost entirely from the policy remit, as in the US, or to adopt criteria for investigation which may appear to exclude them, as in the UK. There is also no evidence that hostile takeovers, much more popular in the UK and the US than elsewhere, lead to an overall improvement in managerial efficiency through the operation of an efficient market for corporate control.

Policy towards restrictive and anti-competitive practices

Restrictive practices are agreements between firms that reduce or prevent competition, whereas *anti-competitive practices* are actions undertaken mainly by individual firms that distort or otherwise hinder the competitive process, often through the creation of entry barriers. Restrictive practices either consist of horizontal agreements between firms at the same stage of production, such as price-fixing or market-sharing cartels, sales syndicates and agreements concerning investment plans and patents, or they comprise various vertical price and non-price agreements undertaken at successive stages in the production process. The prime example of a vertical price agreement is RPM; examples of non-price arrangements have been noted previously. Anti-competitive practices usually entail some kind of price or non-price vertical agreement or, alternatively, price discrimination. In many countries, legislation towards these activities represents the most stringent aspect of

competition policy. In general, any such policy implicitly adopts a traditional SCP stance in favour of competition.

US policy in this area shows considerable contrasts. Horizontal restrictive agreements like price-fixing and market-sharing arrangements are declared illegal *per se*; there are considered to be no mitigating circumstances. The same is true of collective RPM, whereby a group of manufacturers combine to charge an identical retail price. Individual RPM is illegal in principle, although since the early 1980s very few examples have been investigated. On the other hand, most non-price vertical arrangements are accepted on the basis that such policies do not increase market power any more than would be achieved through complete vertical integration. However, in 1992 the Supreme Court ruled that even though Eastman Kodak did not possess significant market power in the photocopier market *per se*, it did for repairs and services. It had abused its dominant position in the latter market by effectively tying the sale of its photocopiers to the the purchase of repair and maintenance services, with the effect that independent repair shops could be exploited. It is too early to say whether this is a landmark ruling, but it certainly represents a shift of emphasis in the policy towards non-price vertical strategies (Harbord and Hoehn, 1994).

UK policy originated with the Restrictive Trade Practices Act of 1956, which was followed by several other items of legislation culminating in the Restrictive Trade Practices Act of 1976. Various anti-competitive practices were brought within the scope of the legislation in the 1980 Competition Act. A 'rule of reason' approach is adopted towards restrictive and anti-competitive practices. All restrictive practices have to be registered with the DGFT, the form of the agreement being the main criterion for registration. Registered agreements are presumed to be against the public interest and the onus of proof lies with the firms involved to show that an agreement has net welfare-enhancing effects. This they can do by satisfying one or more of the eight 'gateway' clauses (for example, showing that a restriction protects the public from injury, confers benefits on the public or counterbalances the market power of others). An additional requirement is that an agreement should meet the 'tailpiece' that benefits outweigh any detrimental effects resulting from the practice.

While collective RPM is banned outright, a similar rule of reason approach is used towards individual RPM. The practice is prohibited unless an agreement can meet one or more of various gateway clauses, so that without it the quality of goods, the accompanying services or the number of retail outlets would be reduced, higher retail prices would result or there would be a danger to health. In practice, there have been very few sucessful restrictive practice or individual RPM defences. A neutral stance is taken towards most non-price vertical anti-competitive practices included in the policy remit since 1980. Thus, LRC's exclusive agreements with customers to stock only the company's condoms were considered to operate against the public interest by acting as a barrier to new competition (MMC, 1994), whereas the freezer exclusivity actions of Birds Eye Walls, Nestlé and Mars in the ice-cream market were found not to be against the public interest given the range of alternative options regarding the acquisition of freezers available to retailers (MMC, 1993b).

The EU employs a similar rule of reason approach to restrictive practices as the UK. The practices are prohibited unless they qualify for exemption, which may be the case if an agreement improves production or distribution or promotes innovation. An agreement may be accorded 'negative clearance' if, for example, it does not affect trade between member states. Thus, in the EU it is the effect of any restrictive practice that is considered important rather than its form. In 1994, BT and MCI were given an individual exemption and Fujitsu and Advanced Micro Devices were granted a part exemption and part negative clearance to establish joint ventures in high-technology fields. An exemption was also granted to an agreement to reduce production overcapacity in the Dutch brick industry (CEC, 1994). 'Block exemptions' have also been granted in certain instances, such as agreements concerning R&D and patent licensing. Price-fixing and market-sharing agreements are more or less banned outright. In 1994, large fines were imposed on cartonboard, PVC and cement producers, all having been found guilty of operating cartel agreements (CEC, 1994).

As regards policy towards vertical agreements, collective RPM is banned, but the EU has a more lenient attitude towards individual RPM arrangements than the UK. Individual RPM is allowed as long as retailers retain freedom of purchase. Non-price practices are accepted, given the proviso that effective competition remains unhindered. Thus, in 1992 Hilti, a leading nail gun manufacturer, was found guilty of an abuse of dominance by tying the purchase of cartridge slips for its nail guns to the purchase of nails. This hindered new entry in a market where a number of other barriers to entry already existed (Harbord and Hoehn, 1994). The Tetra Pak case alluded to previously is another example of a dominant firm engaging in various practices that were found to prevent the maintenance of competition (CEC, 1992).

In principle, the *per se* approach of the US (at least towards restrictive practices) necessarily implies a more pro-competitive line than the rule of reason strategy employed by the US and the EU, in which the possibility of net economic benefits are also considered. On the other hand, since very few cases are upheld under the latter system the differences between the approaches may actually be far less marked than they appear. In the US over 1000 restraint of trade investigations took place between 1985 and 1994.[7] Only a dozen or so out of more than 1000 restrictive agreements referred to the Restrictive Practices Court in the UK were upheld between 1956 and 1990. The UK system has been criticised because, without financial penalties for imposition in cases of illegality, it lacks teeth. In addition, under a form-based approach, agreements can avoid the system if carefully written. This has led to pressure for the UK to adopt a general 'prohibition' principle, as in the US, or a system of fines, as in the EU. Rules towards predation are difficult to determine precisely in any system, given the arguments about precise definitions. One other problem that all three systems face is how to legislate against oligopolistic collusive practices. Since the actions of oligopolistic firms are interdependent they have a tendency to collude over price, although much of this behaviour, such as price leadership, may be tacit and therefore difficult to detect. As yet no satisfactory policy solution has been discovered, although the fact that in the UK two or more unconnected firms with a combined market share of more than 25% can be investigated provides some scope for control of anti-competitive practices. In Germany, market dominance is presumed to exist when three firms have a combined market share of at least 50% or when five firms have a market share of over two-thirds; such a legal definition of oligopoly goes further in forming the basis of an effective policy.

15.4 THE PRIVATISATION DEBATE

Privatisation refers to the general removal or diminution of state controls on firms and industries. It covers both the transfer of publicly owned assets to the

Table 71 *Major sales of assets from the public to the private sector in the UK*

Organisation	Date of first sale	Industry
British Petroleum (BP)	1979	Oil
National Enterprise Board Investments	1980	Various
British Aerospace	1981	Aerospace
Cable and Wireless	1981	Telecommunications
Amersham International	1982	Scientific products
National Freight Corporation	1982	Road transport
Britoil	1982	Oil
British Rail Hotels	1983	Hotels
Associated British Ports	1983	Ports
British Leyland (Rover)	1984	Car manufacturing
British Telecom (BT)	1984	Telecommunications
Jaguar	1984	Car manufacturing
Enterprise Oil	1984	Oil
Sealink	1984	Road transport
British Shipbuilders and Naval Dockyards	1985	Shipbuilding
National Bus Company	1986	Transport
British Gas	1986	Gas
Rolls-Royce	1987	Aeroengines
British Airports Authority	1987	Airports
British Airways	1987	Airlines
British Ordnance	1987	Armaments
British Steel	1988	Steel
Water companies	1989	Water
Electricity distribution	1990	Electricity
Electricity generation	1991	Electricity
Trust Ports	1992	Ports
British Coal	1994	Coal
British Rail	1995	Railways
British Energy	1996	Nuclear power

Source: Parker (1994a), updated.

private sector, or *denationalisation*, and to the opening of more activities to competitive pressures by the removal or reduction of regulatory controls, or *deregulation*. The UK was the pioneer of privatisation in the early 1980s; since then the process has become virtually a worldwide phenomenon. The selling of state-owned firms has become a major element of industrial policy in Eastern Europe, Latin America, Australasia, parts of Asia and in Western European countries. France and Italy are committed to large-scale sell-offs, although most sales in Germany have so far been confined to the former East Germany. The transfer of assets in Japan has also been restricted, in this case to the sale of a part of Nippon Telegraph and Telephone (NTT), but further sales are mooted and deregulation has been fairly extensive. In the US

the relatively limited extent of state ownership has meant that privatisation has been mainly confined to deregulatory activities.

In Britain over £60 billion has been raised from the sale of public corporations since 1980. Large chunks of what was previously the public sector have been included in the transfer of resources; more than 650 000 workers have been involved.[8] Sometimes only part of the business has been sold (50.2% of BT initially), whereas in other cases (such as the National Freight Corporation) it has been transferred completely. In some instances, for example British Petroleum (BP), the asset transfer involved the sale of government holdings in private companies. Table 71 lists the major asset transfers since 1979. Most of the public corporations have been floated on the stock market, but there have also been over 150 management and employee buy-outs. As a result, the nationalised industry share of GDP fell from 9% in 1980/81 to about 3% in the early 1990s (Parker, 1994a). In addition, between 1979 and 1991 around 1.4 million council houses were sold to tenants and the 'contracting out' of services has been well established in central and local government as well as in health and education.

Despite the extent of privatisation in the UK, its rationale has never been clearly articulated. Various aims and objectives have been put forward at different times to justify the programme. These include the improvement of economic efficiency in the transferred organisation, the exposure of more activities to the beneficial effects of competition, the need to reduce government interference in the affairs of industry, the reduction of trade union power, the widening of share ownership and the lowering of the Public Sector Borrowing Requirement (PSBR). The last point is significant in that the original justification for privatisation was more political than economic: the sale of public assets was considered to be more popular than cutting public spending. However, the problem with having a range of objectives for a particular policy is that some of them may conflict. Wider and more dispersed share ownership may mean less effective control over managerial behaviour and reduced levels of efficiency in privatised companies.

In fact, while the number of individual shareholders increased from three million in 1979 to 11 million in 1993, including 90% of the employees in the privatised companies, 54% of investors own shares in only one company and only 17% have shares in more than four companies (Parker, 1991). Privatisation may have widened share ownership but it has not deepened it. Concentration of share ownership in the UK actually increased during the 1980s. The percentage of shares held by individuals (rather than institutions) fell from 30% to 20% in the period. Many of the individuals who purchased privatised shares were attracted by the possibility of making fairly substantial capital gains on underpriced issues by selling the shares at a significant profit shortly after purchase (examples being Rolls-Royce, BT, the water companies and the electricity distribution and generating companies). The proceeds from privatisation did help to reduce the PSBR as a percentage of GDP by more than 1.5% during the late 1980s (Griffiths and Wall, 1995), although this figure would have been larger had assets not been sold at discounted prices. It is estimated that the resulting 'cost' to the tax-payer reached £2375 million by the time the electricity generating industry was privatised (Parker, 1991). The government also loses any future income flow from selling profitable assets. Thus, the extent to which the objectives of achieving a wider share ownership and lowering the PSBR have been met remain in dispute. Privatisation has had some impact on industrial relations. Both British Gas and BT have adopted a more assertive management style, although the confrontational attitude has been much more pronounced at BT where changes in the terms and conditions of employees have led to several industrial disputes. In general, however, privatisation has probably only had a limited effect on trade unions and the bargaining process. The fall in trade union membership that occurred during the 1980s was largely confined to industries that at the time were unaffected by privatisation, such as coal, the railways and the civil service.

The main economic debate about privatisation has centred on two objectives: firstly, on the efficiency aspects of the change of ownership and, secondly, on whether competition has been enhanced. These two issues also have implications for other pro-privatisation arguments, like the need to reduce government involvement in industry. These issues will be considered mainly in relation to the policy of transferring assets from the public to the private sector. The deregulation process is discussed later in the chapter.

The ownership debate

It is argued that the move from public to private ownership should improve welfare by stimulating managerial (and other employee) performance, assuming no change in the competitive environment. Thus, if a monopoly were transferred from one sector to the other, its misallocative effects would persist. However, public-sector enterprises in the UK have been expected, at least in principle, to follow pricing and investment rules (such as marginal cost pricing) that would achieve allocative efficiency and maximise social welfare. In Figure 101, page 300, the adoption of marginal cost pricing rules by a single-product natural monopolist gives a lower price, P_C, and a higher output, Q_C, compared with the profit-maximising $P_M Q_M$.

The problem with marginal cost pricing, however, is that it is beset by practical difficulties, not the least of which is the fact that if average costs are falling

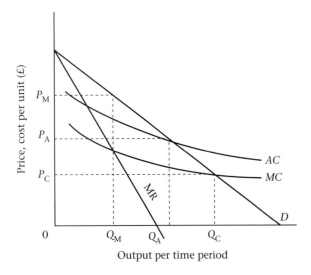

Figure 101 *Price and output outcomes for a natural monopolist.*

(a characteristic of natural monopolies), then losses will result. This is because the marginal cost curve lies below the average cost curve, as shown in Figure 101. As a result, some kind of average cost pricing procedure (shown by $P_A Q_A$ in Figure 101) or a pricing policy based on particular financial targets has usually been implemented.

Assuming an unchanged competitive environment, any improvement in performance in moving from public to private ownership must be based on achieving productive efficiencies in the private sector that could not be gained by operating in the public sector. There are two main reasons why such efficiencies may be achieved. Firstly, the profit motive provides a greater incentive to improve efficiency in private-sector firms because the rewards of managers and other employees are more closely linked to corporate performance through various share ownership and option schemes. As a result, greater levels of investment and innovation in new products and processes may be undertaken. Secondly, the performance of private-sector firms is also influenced by capital market constraints and the ever-present threat of takeover.

Principal–agent relationships exist in both private- and public-sector organisations, in the former between managers and shareholders and in the latter between managers and the government. Manager–employee agency relationships occur within organisations in either sector. However, it may be that the principal–agent problem is more marked in the public sector, since individual performance is less closely tied to the performance of the firm. As a result, it could be argued that under state ownership, managers (as agents) have more freedom to pursue their own objectives, such as the desire for a quiet life or the maximisation of the size of the organisation. Managers as principals may also be more likely to accede to the agency demands of the workforce for improvements in working conditions or higher wages. In addition, changing and inconsistent corporate objectives laid down by successive governments may have contributed towards managerial demoralisation and the pursuit of personal objectives in their stead. Managerial actions may have been further encumbered by the tendency for politicians to place potentially vote-winning policies above public interest considerations.

On the other hand, there is no presumption that large private-sector firms will necessarily pursue or achieve productive efficiency, especially in non-competitive conditions. A divorce between ownership and control coupled with organisational complexities leave plenty of scope for the pursuit of managerial non-profit-maximising objectives, resulting in X-inefficiency. Performance-related remuneration schemes may simply make management more risk averse, actually reducing the incentive for new investment and innovation schemes. A common complaint of 280 middle managers from 36 privatised firms was poor communication between them and senior personnel and, most damning in many eyes, a lack of encouragement of innovation.[9]

The dual disciplines of an efficient capital market and the threat of takeover offer other reasons for the superior efficiency of private-sector firms, at least in principle. However, as has been explained in Section 9.5, an efficient capital market depends on effective monitoring of managerial behaviour by shareholders and they cannot do this if they have access to limited or distorted information. The difficulties of effective monitoring are exacerbated by the free-rider problem. In addition, a belief by management that institutional shareholders adopt a short-term perspective, whether justified or not, may be translated into short-term policy-making by the firms themselves. In consequence, investment and innovation may suffer. The fact that the takeover mechanism does not operate particularly effectively has been previously alluded to in this chapter. There is no evidence that the best-run, and hence most profitable firms, acquire those that are least profitable. In particular, there is a negative relationship between the risk of takeover and size; the largest firms in an industry stand much less chance of being taken over. The size of the very largest privatised firms certainly affords them some measure of protection against takeover, although the acquisition in 1995 of the electricity distribution company Eastern Group, by Hanson, and the hostile bid for a similar concern, Norweb, by North West Water, shows that even utilities are not immune from the threat of capture (or from acquiring other utilities). The fact that a firm feels vulnerable to takeover, on the other hand, may mean that it becomes more concerned with short-term profitability rather than with longer-term investment and innovation plans.

The promotion of competition

Given the conflicting arguments about ownership, it might seem that the main argument in favour of privatisation is the promotion of competition that it may afford. The increase in competition, it is said, should stimulate management to operate their organisations more efficiently. However, relatively few asset transfers have resulted in a marked increase in competition, at least so far. Firms like the National Freight Corporation, Cable and Wireless, and Rover (acquired by BMW in 1994) have continued to operate in a competitive environment, as they did when part of the state sector. The British Airports Authority (BAA) has maintained monopoly ownership of the three largest airports around London (Heathrow, Gatwick and Stansted) since it was privatised in 1987. At the time of its original privatisation in 1984, the management of BT successfully persuaded the government to abandon most its original plans for the liberalisation of the telecommunications industry; BT's management were particularly keen to avoid a break-up of BT, as had happened to AT&T in the US, and to minimise any potential competitive threats. Despite competition from Mercury Communications and more recently from cable-TV companies (any firm can now apply for a telecommunication licence), as well as from cellular and personal communication networks (PCNs), BT still has 86% of the long-distance telephone market and 95% of the local-calling market, although greater competition exists in other telecommunication markets in the UK (see the case on page 309).

Belatedly the government (at the behest of Ofgas, the industry regulator, following the publication of two MMC reports in 1988 and 1993) introduced more competition into gas supply and distribution. As a result, British Gas's share of the industrial and commercial gas supply market fell from 100% in 1990 to about 35% in 1996. The domestic supply market is to be opened to full-scale competition in 1998. In 1996, and in response to the structural changes occurring in the industry, British Gas announced a division of its activities into two new firms, one to concentrate on gas supply in the UK, the other to deal with overseas business, exploration and pipelines. A degree of competition has been introduced into the electricity generating industry by splitting the activities of the Central Electricity Generating Board into three distinct businesses. On the other hand, the electricity distribution companies and the water companies are effectively regional monopolies that now operate in the private rather than in the public sector.

The creation of private-sector monopolies has led to the formation of a series of regulatory bodies, such as Oftel (telecommunications), Ofgas (gas), Ofwat (water) and Offer (electricity); other agencies, such as the MMC, are also involved in the regulatory process. Such a regulatory procedure runs counter to another stated objective of privatisation, to reduce government involvement in the affairs of industry. The basis of the UK approach towards regulation is price limits (as opposed to rate-of-return regulation, as used in the US). Price increases are limited by the RPI $\pm X$ formula, where RPI is the retail price index and X is reset by the regulatory body every few years. Profit increases stemming from reduced costs are allowed. The severity with which the formula has been applied has varied from industry to industry depending on circumstances, although it would appear that X is usually set or reset on the basis of what the regulator considers a satisfactory rate of return in an industry. Thus, BT has faced a series of increases in X (currently placed at -7.5% for a basket of its services, although set at -4.5% from 1997) in the face of rising profits. X for British Gas is currently -5% in order to achieve a desired rate of return of 5–7% on gas supplies. X for the electricity distribution companies was changed to -2% in 1995 from zero, reflecting concern from the regulator about excessive industry profits. The water companies face a positive X in order to finance a large investment programme, although here too, fears about high levels of profitability may herald tighter price controls in the future. The success of the system obviously depends in part on the ability of the regulators to maximise their limited powers, given the fact that they rely on the industry itself for whatever information they can glean.

The performance of the privatised companies

The main problem that most studies face in investigating the performance of the newly privatised companies is separating the effects of competition from ownership. Comparisons between the performance of firms in the public and private sectors, whether on a cross-sectional or time-series basis, also need to adjust for differences in product mix, product quality and objectives (the need for a regulatory framework in the case of the utilities, for example, may dull efficiency). Finally, the question of how performance itself is measured has to be tackled. Most studies have used some indicator of either profitability or productivity (labour or total), but both involve measurement problems.

The evidence on the relative performance of the privatised firms is mixed. Naturally, the longer the time period under investigation, the more useful the evidence, although even recent studies report quite mixed results. Parker (1991) showed that, since privatisation, the return on capital employed has improved marginally in the case of British Gas, BT and Rolls Royce, but has fallen significantly at Associated British Ports, Enterprise Oil and Jaguar cars (now owned by Ford). However, these changes may have occurred in the absence of privatisation, especially as has been pointed out:

The nationalised industries raised their profitability as a percentage of GDP and also increased their productivity faster than the private sector in the 1980s (Parker, 1991: 159).

In a similar vein Bishop and Kay (1988) concluded that the growth in total factor productivity between 1979 and 1988 in the newly privatised firms may have led to their privatisation rather than having been its direct result. Dunsire *et al.* (1991) examined whether change of ownership affected patterns of productivity, profitability and employment in a number of companies, including BT, British Aerospace (BAe), the National Freight Corporation (NFC) and the Royal Ordnance Factories (ROF). Comparing total factor productivity with national trends, only the NFC improved its performance. There was also a marked profitability improvement in only one company, ROF. The NFC and BAe undertook large labour shake-outs, a more limited shake-out took place at BT, whereas there was no significant employment change at ROF. Hunt and Lynk (1995) examined the effects of water privatisation. They showed that the abandonment of the principle of Integrated River Basin Management, whereby individual River Water Authorities controlled and planned all use of water in their catchment area, including environmental functions, denied the industry significant efficiency-enhancing effects through lost economies of scope.

Studies in other countries comparing state and private organisations operating in the same market have had similarly mixed results (see Ferguson and Ferguson, 1994 for an excellent summary of the evidence). Examinations of the relative costs of electricity generators and water utilities in the US and of airlines in Australia and of the relative productivity levels of railway companies in Canada have failed to show that private-sector firms are necessarily more efficient. However, this could be partly explained by the fact that the private-sector organisations are often themselves state-regulated.

A more recent study into the impact of privatisation in the UK (Parker and Martin, 1995) has attempted to take into account the effects on performance of the business cycle and longer-term improvements in performance in the economy. Trends in labour and total factor productivity in eleven privatised firms were compared with trends in the economy, and, where relevant, manufacturing. Changes were measured over five distinct periods, each of which (with the exception of the post-announcement stage) covered about four years. The results for the pre-privatisation, post-privatisation and recession periods are shown in Tables 72 and 73. The figures are four-year annual averages.

Comparing the pre-privatisation period with post-privatisation the results are mixed. In only a minority of cases did privatisation result in an improvement of either labour or total productivity performance relative to the whole economy or to manufacturing. This situation confirms the findings of earlier studies (e.g. Bishop and Kay, 1988) that the run-up to privatisation often tends to be associated with marked improvements in performance as management is spurred into action to improve results. As a result, a deterioration of relative performance post-privatisation is often noted. In two of the cases, Jaguar (because of previous underinvestment) and British Steel (due to increased international competition) the best performance occurred in the nationalisation period prior to pre-privatisation. The recession period, 1989–92, was included in the study to determine how well the privatised firms performed in poor economic conditions, rather than just in the boom period of the mid- to late 1980s. The picture is again

Table 72 *Annual percentage changes in relative labour productivity for selected privatised firms[a]*

	Pre-privatisation		Post-privatisation		Recession	
British Airways	8.0		2.2		4.5	
British Airports Authority	−0.2[b]		−2.2[b]		−5.1[b]	
	3.1[c]		1.5[c]		−2.4[c]	
Britoil	1.1	(0.6)	3.8	(1.2)	n/a[d]	(n/a)[d]
British Gas	4.1	(1.8)	2.9	(−0.2)	1.1	(−1.0)
British Steel	8.8	(6.6)	−1.0	(−2.5)	−0.7	(−2.9)
British Aerospace	−5.1	(1.4)	3.5	(0.3)	14.1	(12.4)
Jaguar	24.3	(21.1)	1.1	(0.9)	−15.7	(−17.5)
Rolls-Royce	4.0	(1.3)	0.7	(−2.6)	4.0	(2.3)
National Freight	4.5		1.5		0.1	
Associated British Ports	1.5		12.9		23.8	
BT	4.1		4.9		8.0	

[a]In comparison with whole economy; figures in parentheses are in comparision with manufacturing only.
[b]Output measure based on number of traffic movements.
[c]Output measure based on real revenue p.a.
[d]Not available.

Source: Parker and Martin (1995), selected data.

Table 73 *Annual percentage change in relative total factor productivity for selected privatised firms[a]*

	Pre-privatisation		Post-privatisation		Recession	
British Airways	2.9		6.3		5.4	
British Airports Authority	−2.7[b]		−8.0[b]		−5.9[b]	
	0.6[c]		4.6[c]		3.5[c]	
Britoil	12.6	(12.0)	7.6	(5.7)	n/a	(n/a)
British Gas	−0.5	(−2.4)	−2.4	(−5.4)	0.3	(−2.1)
British Steel	2.9	(0.6)	−4.2	(−5.8)	−4.0	(−6.7)
British Aerospace	−2.4	(−0.6)	−2.3	(−5.0)	−0.8	(−2.5)
Jaguar	4.0	(1.3)	−1.1	(−3.2)	−14.6	(−16.4)
Rolls-Royce	3.0	(1.1)	0.1	(−3.1)	−0.4	(−2.1)
National Freight	−1.6		2.1		−2.0	
Associated British Ports	6.0		9.4		5.1	
BT	2.0		4.2		5.3	

[a]Notes as for Table 72.

Source: Parker and Martin (1995) selected data.

unclear. British Airways, Associated British Ports and BT performed relatively well in terms of both labour and total factor productivity. British Aerospace, Rolls-Royce and the National Freight Corporation performed relatively well in labour productivity terms only. The British Airports Authority, British Steel and Jaguar performed relatively poorly. Such results provide further confirmation that privatisation does not guarantee good or improved performance.

Deregulation and franchising

Deregulation refers to the removal of regulatory constraints on a market. In principle, this should lead to the opening up of the market to competitive forces and so to improved economic welfare. However, such an argument may not apply in every instance. In the case of a natural monopoly, deregulation may reduce economic welfare, since by definition only one firm can operate efficiently in the industry. Hence, deregulation and the introduction of competition would simply drive up costs, although it may be that not all a firm's operations represent a natural monopoly. It is usually the distribution systems of the utilities that are thus categorised; they also exhibit high sunk costs, which prevent exit and the transformation to a contestable market. Other parts of a utility's activities, such as the generation of electricity, can be opened up to competition.

Alternatively, competition may be enhanced by giving new entrants access to the incumbent's distribution system at low cost. In 1985, Oftel allowed the interconnection of Mercury to BT's national and international network with charges based on BT's cost of provision rather than on the normal higher rate. Competition can also be introduced by divesting a utility of part of its activities, which was the policy used in the US with the stripping of AT&T of its local services in 1982.

Deregulation has occurred in other industries besides the utilities, such as bus and coach services, airlines, legal services (the loss by solicitors of their sole rights to conveyancing) and the dispensing of spectacles for which opticians no longer have a monopoly. The UK local bus market (outside London) was deregulated in 1986, when provision was also made for the privatisation of the National Bus Company. Previously, local operators were granted a licence which gave them a monopoly of a particular route. These operations were usually owned by the local authorities, in which the cross-subsidisation of unprofitable routes (often regarded as socially necessary) by the more profitable ones was an important part of overall policy. The perceived advantages of deregulation were the greater choice and the more innovative policies that competition would bring, plus the improved efficiency from ending cross-subsidisation and by lowering the revenue support in the form of a general subsidy given to operators. Against this it was argued that deregulation would have significant external costs by leading to the duplication of services on the most profitable routes, thereby increasing conges-

tion in urban areas, and by causing a reduction of services on unprofitable routes. The lowering of the general subsidy could also lead to a rise in the level of fares and a fall in total demand.

Competition has also been introduced into certain areas (including some bus and coach operations) via *franchising*. Under this system (which may have particular applicability for natural monopolies, since they can remain within the public sector) a firm is awarded a contract for the sole right of supply (the franchise) for a particular period; the franchise is then usually put up for renewal by *competitive tendering*. In this way, competition *for* the market rather than *in* the market is encouraged. Franchising has also been employed in North Sea oil exploration licences, in radio and television broadcasting, for cleaning, catering and building maintenance services in health, education and other government departments and in local authority activities like refuse collection. Twenty-five passenger and four freight rail franchises were awarded by 1997.

Franchising contracts can be awarded to the firm that bids the highest amount (as has often been the case in cleaning and catering contracts) or to the firm that offers the lowest price. In the former case, productive efficency may be enhanced because the contract-holder has the incentive of reducing costs to boost profits, but at the expense of allocative inefficiency via monopoly pricing; in the latter instance, allocative efficiency may also be improved, although provisos may have to be made in the contract about overall product quality.

There are a number of problems connected with franchising, the first concerning the length of the contract. It has to be sufficiently long to encourage new investment in the business, but not overlong to allow the monopolist supplier to become complacent and inefficient or to conflict with the stated aim of enhancing competition. Some bidders, for example, dropped out of the original train-operating franchise auctions because some of the contracts were considered to be too brief (they are proposed to run from five to 20 years) for adequate investment purposes. A possible solution to this problem is to offer 'operating' rather than 'ownership' franchises. The train operators can rent rolling stock from one of three leasing companies. However, the operating companies may feel that they have insufficient control over their activities, especially since Railtrack owns and manages the railway infrastructure and also has ultimate responsibility for timetabling. Another possible drawback of the franchising procedure is that transaction costs are involved in awarding and monitoring the

---

Box 15.1 *Evidence on the effects of deregulation and compulsory competitive tendering*

Evidence on the effects of deregulation shows mixed results. Deregulation of the bus industry in the UK has led to an increase in bus kilometres travelled (although this could be partly due to rival bus companies shadowing each other's services), but to a fall in passenger journeys of about 4% per annum. Fares in real terms have also increased quite substantially, whereas operating costs from 1985/86 to 1992/93 decreased by 39% (Griffiths and Wall, 1995). Many small bus operators were formed following deregulation, often via management or employee buy-outs, although where incumbents were financially strong and able to reduce prices below those of the entrants and/or increase services, entry was usually short-lived. In fact, a series of mergers and takeovers in the industry has meant that competition is now severely restricted. It is dominated by five large groups (Stagecoach, First Bus, GRT, West Midlands Travel and Go-Ahead), each of which has local monopolies. Evidence of anti-competitive practices has led to several MMC investigations of the industry (see Section 10.2). Winston (1993) found evidence of fairly substantial welfare gains for both consumers (in terms of lower prices and improved services) and producers (via higher profits) in a survey of the evidence on the effects of the deregulation of seven US industries (airlines, railways, road freight, telecommunications, cable television, stockbroking and natural gas) from the late 1970s onwards, although the evidence had little to say about effects on wages and employment. In fact, post-deregulation, wages and jobs suffered in road freight, employment fell in telecommunications, while wages fell substantially in railways and by a smaller amount in the airlines. Employment in airlines increased quite sharply and by a

lesser degree in cable television as output expanded. Overall, Winston judges the welfare impact of these changes to be fairly insubstantial, although further analysis may be necessary to support such a claim.

A survey of the empirical evidence on compulsory competitive tendering (CCT) in public services (Wilson, 1994) concluded that cost-savings have often been secured, although it was not always clear whether the source of the savings was genuine productive efficiencies or lower wages and reduced employment. Wilson points out that evidence on competitive tendering should encompass all costs and benefits to society. In other words, research in this area needs to take into account not just lower costs and prices, but also the external costs of higher unemployment, reduced fringe benefits and the greater use of part-time staff. Furthermore, it was not apparent in every case whether benefits arose from a change of ownership or from a change in the competitive environment. Private contractors have been winning a rising share of CCTs for local government services, although they still only secure about a quarter by value.[10] Most benefits, where they have occurred, have presumably been derived from competition, although this is another area that requires greater research. Taking the evidence as a whole, where deregulation has achieved its desired aim of increasing competition there is some evidence of improved economic performance, although studies probably need to take a more comprehensive view of the relevant costs and benefits involved. A solution to the problem of natural monopoly where only one firm can efficiently supply the market may be franchising, but the problem of an overinvestment in sunk costs by the franchisee needs to be addressed.

---

franchise and these have to be weighed against the perceived benefits of greater competition. The more complex the contract the greater the transaction costs. This is especially true in the case of cable television where a number of variables besides price are involved, such as the number of channels and the variety and quality of programmes offered. Finally, the incumbent firm may be at a significant advantage when a contract is re-offered because it has invested in significant sunk costs. Thus, additional transaction costs, which increase with asset specificity, may have been incurred. This can prove to be a particular problem in the case of natural monopolies where large-scale and long-term investments are often required. Incumbents may also benefit from experience of operating in the industry and from having the financial muscle to combat any attempt at entry, whether deregulation takes the form of franchising or not.

15.5 OTHER INDUSTRY POLICIES

This section briefly assesses other industrial policies, beginning with *regional policies*. In all industrial economies, market forces in the form of changing demand and technological progress lead to the relative decline of some industries and to the rise of others. As a result, because industrial structures vary between regions, disparities in unemployment and levels of per capita income occur. Whether a distinct policy is required to ameliorate such differences depends on how speedily (if at all) it is thought that market forces can rectify the situation. A laissez-faire approach may imply that, since regional disparities are short-term, measures to alleviate them are largely unnecessary. Firms are attracted into the high-unemployment, low-income areas because of their low costs and at the same time labour moves from these regions to the more prosperous ones, leading eventually to a more equitable distribution of income and jobs across regions. However, this scenario assumes no labour and capital market imperfections.

In practice, neither labour nor capital is perfectly mobile. Firms and workers may have imperfect knowledge about the respective opportunities available. There may be high transaction costs involved in any move by labour, such as the breaking of social ties, or in capital movements, like the expenses of having to evaluate different sites for industrial location. Intervention would then be geared towards reducing market imperfections and enhancing the natural tendencies of market forces towards regional convergence. Labour mobility may be promoted by abandoning or restricting the effects of minimum wage agreements. Capital mobility may be enhanced by the establishment of an agency to provide information on the relative costs of different industrial locations, especially given the fact that firms generally prefer to site near their current operations rather than at the lowest-cost site. On the other hand, an active approach towards regional policy is based on the premise that externalities cause regional divergence instead of convergence. For example, labour migration may involve the younger, more qualified sections of the regional labour force, leaving behind a less skilled and less productive workforce, which reduces still further the incentive for firms to set up in the area. Policies, such as grants to firms to locate in problem areas, are needed to counteract market forces according to this approach.

The US has no regional policy *per se*. The UK has had a regional programme of one kind or another since 1934, although there has been a marked change in attitude by the government since the early 1980s with a supportive rather than an active approach being taken. Regional Development Grants were scrapped in 1988 and most assistance for the regions is now discretionary (in the form of Regional Selective Assistance) and is geared towards new firm creation and help for small and medium-sized firms (via Regional Enterprise Grants). EU regional policy is administered and financed through the European Regional Development Fund (ERDF), which is part of the broader Structural Funds. The latter have identified six priority objectives to arrest structural decline, within which three types of problem region have been defined. Objective 1, which is expected to form 70% of the budget of the Structural Funds for 1994–99, covers the economic development of lagging regions. Objective 2 refers to regions in

industrial decline and Objective 5b applies to the development of rural areas. It is essentially a supportive approach to regional problems and issues.

It is difficult to assess the success of regional policy because the actual situation has to be compared with what might have happened had the particular policy not existed. In addition, the opportunity cost of the policy for other regions (in terms of jobs and incomes diverted elsewhere) should be considered. There is some evidence that regional policy in the UK had some success in creating new jobs and establishing new businesses in 'assisted areas', at least during the active period of British policy from about 1960 to 1980. Since then the funding of regional programmes has declined dramatically and, although the cost-effectiveness of policy weapons may have been enhanced, it may be questioned whether the overall level of finance is now sufficient to achieve its desired aims.

Some kind of *innovation policy* may be required because firms do not undertake an 'optimal' amount of R&D, for which there are various reasons. It may be that firms consider that the cost and risk (i.e. the uncertain returns) of some projects are too high; the problem may be all the greater given that most business decision-makers are risk-averse. Secondly, the outcome of R&D expenditure, information or knowledge, exhibits the characteristics of a public good. It is non-excludable because it is very expensive to exclude others from its benefits and it features non-rival consumption, since its use by one person does not reduce its availability to others. Thus, rapid imitation of an invention and the diffusion of information, particularly in the case of new product innovation, diminishes the incentive to undertake R&D. Thirdly, lack of knowledge about rivals' plans may lead to duplication of R&D activity and to an excessive amount of spending on innovation by firms. A supportive approach towards industrial policy is likely to be based on the need to reduce market imperfections and uncertainty by, for example, providing additional information for firms on the latest technical and product developments in their fields and on sources of finance.

There are also externalities involved in R&D expenditures. Consumers may benefit from lower prices and better quality products. The investment in knowledge through R&D activity may also be a major catalyst for economic growth (see Section 3.2). In recognition of these benefits of innovation, an active policy approach may involve financial support for

R&D, the use of patents and the encouragement of joint ventures. Financial support in the form of tax allowances and grants has the advantage that, by being offered at a relatively early stage in the overall process, it may give an incentive to innovate, although it is not dependent on the project being commercially successful. It can be argued that the patent system, on the other hand, stimulates innovation by discouraging imitation and protecting the monopoly profits of invention. However, such a system may give rise to inventions with little economic significance; in addition, it may lead to wasteful expenditures by rivals on similar, but not identical, substitutes. Joint R&D ventures by firms have the benefits of spreading costs and risks and reducing duplication, but they can also create additional transaction costs involving the co-ordination of activities; co-operation at other levels, such as production and distribution, may also be necessary to harness the full effects of any particular project.

Since most industrial economies employ both a patent system and a series of financial measures to aid R&D, it can be assumed that they try to actively promote innovation. In Japan, three R&D programmes have recently been brought together into a new integrated activity called the Science and Technology Frontier Programme that supports a number of different projects in, for example, biotechnology, electronics, new materials and superconductivity (OECD, 1994). This can be contrasted with the fact that, in other countries, the government finances a fairly large proportion of business enterprise R&D itself, but mainly in loss-making activities in the defence, space and nuclear industries. For example, in 1991, 24.8% of US business enterprise R&D was financed by the government, 22.3% in France, 14.6% in the UK, 10.7% in Germany, but only 1.4% in Japan (OECD, 1994).

Both patents and joint ventures in R&D have implications for competition policy. In the UK, patents have generally been regarded favourably, based on the assumption that the beneficial effects on R&D outweigh the restrictions on competition that they entail. In the EU, patents have generally been supported by the authorities, as long as they involve no other restrictions on competition. Joint ventures in the EU can be granted block exemption status, although they are not given any preferential treatment under UK competition policy rules. In the US, the potential advantages of both patents and collaborative R&D ventures are supposed to be given due weight in competition policy rulings.

Trade policy, or the use of tariff and non-tariff barriers to protect selected domestic firms and industries, is used to prevent dumping, to protect infant industries, to slow the decline of a mature industry and to protect strategically important industries. As such, it represents more of an active that a supportive approach to industry policy. A more general protectionist stance was advocated for the UK by the Cambridge Economic Policy Group (see Section 3.2) in the early 1980s to arrest the decline in the manufactured trading balance. Widespread import controls and a fiscal stimulus were recommended as a policy initiative towards deindustrialisation. However, protectionist policies may have adverse welfare implications by raising prices and restricting competition, from which a misallocation of international resources can result (although the size of the effect depends on whether national versus integrated protectionist policies are being considered). The lack of a competitive stimulus may also compound any productive inefficiencies among the protected producers. The World Bank and the OECD have estimated that the Uruguay round of the General Agreement on Tariffs and Trade (GATT) world trade talks, that have taken place since the mid-1980s and which are designed to reform and enlarge GATT, would be worth $213–274 billion each year to the world economy in additional production.[11]

In practice, there has been a general move away from the use of tariffs (especially within regional trading blocks like the EU) towards non-tariff barriers, like voluntary export restraints (VERs), by which exporters agree to restrict the quantity of a product they supply to a particular market for a certain period. Other non-tariff barriers include subsidies and 'health and safety' standards imposed on imports. Such barriers may be imposed on any type of product, although in manufacturing they are mainly confined to textiles, clothing, steel, cars and electronics. VERs, which have become a particularly popular means of protection, have been instigated largely by the US and the EU in recent years to restrict imports from Japan, although since Japan itself has employed them on a number of products since the 1930s (originally textiles and clothing, then steel and finally cars) there is a retaliatory element in the latest round of measures.

Estimates of the effects of non-tariff barriers have usually reported job savings, but at a high cost. For example, de Melo and Tarr[12] found that non-tariff barriers in the textiles, clothing, car and steel industries in the US saved 294 000 jobs, but at a cost of

$72 000 per worker per year. On the other hand, there is also evidence that where an industry is not (as the theoretical arguments in favour of trade usually presume) perfectly competitive but is dominated by a few firms and is subject to economies of scale, then non-tariff barriers may secure net economic benefits, at least at a relatively local level. Neven and Seabright (1995) have pointed out that the subsidies given to Airbus, the European aircraft manufacturing consortium, may be justified because the knowledge that the project enjoys government support affects the strategies of rivals. They may become reluctant to compete in specific areas, for example, which has an impact on relative profitability in the industry. The fact that Boeing, the main producer in the industry at the time already had a rival in McDonnell Douglas, meant that prices were depressed by the arrival of Airbus, but only by a small amount (about 3.5% on average). The consumer surplus argument for subsidy therefore can only be weakly supported. On the other hand, it is argued that the presence of Airbus has reduced the profits of the other two firms (by lowering the potential for economies of scale and scope), while at the same time it is estimated that Airbus itself will make profits of the order of $50 billion over the five decades from the 1970s. Thus, assuming that welfare can be adequately defined as the addition of consumer and producer surplus, Airbus has had a large negative impact on world social welfare, but a significant positive impact on European welfare.

15.6 CONCLUSIONS

A comparison is made between a supportive approach towards industrial policy, in which government intervention is limited to a relatively neutral stance, and an active approach, whereby a more interventionist position is taken. However, whatever approach is adopted there is a lack of a clear theoretical framework with which to guide policy-makers; market models are often used as indirect criteria for assessing performance.

The theoretical basis for competition policy is considered; it is examined mainly from a traditional perspective, although the opinions of other schools of thought are also discussed. The deadweight allocative loss attributable to monopoly is outlined and the arguments concerning the relative productive efficiency levels of competition and monopoly are examined. The transaction cost benefits of integration and the role of innovation as a source of market power are both mentioned.

Competition policy is designed to promote or to prevent a reduction in effective competition. The competition policies of the UK, the US and the EU are compared. In general, the UK has adopted a fairly neutral stance in most aspects of its policy, although since 1984 there has been a narrowing of the basis of reference for mergers, at least until recently. The US has tended to take a stricter, more active approach towards monopoly power, although this has eased in the 1980s as the views of other schools of thought, that emphasise the more positive aspects of monopoly, have been given greater weight. The EU stance has veered more towards a relatively free-market Austrian approach in its policy considerations.

Privatisation refers to the removal or reduction of state controls in firms and industries; it comprises denationalisation, or the transfer of publicly-owned assets to the private sector, and deregulation, which denotes the removal or diminution of regulatory controls. Privatisation has advanced furthest in the UK, although its precise justification has never been fully clarified. The main economic debate has centred on the efficiency aspects of the change of ownership involved in the move from the public to the private sector and on whether competition has been enhanced. Assessments of the performance of denationalised firms face the problem of distinguishing between ownership and competitive effects; evidence of their performance is mixed, although more recent evidence indicates a slightly more positive record.

In principle, the deregulation of a market should open it to greater competition and hence improve economic welfare. Improved competition may be achieved through franchising, in which case competition for the market rather than in the market is encouraged. Studies on the impact of deregulation have again revealed fairly mixed results; where competition has increased there is some evidence of improved performance, but social costs and benefits may also need to be taken into account.

Regional, innovation and trade policies are briefly assessed. Regional policies are rather more supportive than active, while most countries tend to actively encourage R&D via patents and financial inducements. The shift in emphasis in trade policies has mainly been from tariff to non-tariff barrers, such as VERs.

Case Study: The effects of privatisation on the internal structure, conduct and performance of British Telecom (BT)[13]

British Telecom (BT) was privatised in 1984, when 50.2% of the issued shares were sold to the private sector; the remainder were sold in 1991 and 1993. Critics of its privatisation argued that, as a natural monopoly, it would exploit the consumer and that economies of scale and scope would be lost; regulation would either be inadequate or it would inhibit BT's efficiency. Proponents of BT's privatisation, on the other hand, felt that improved efficiency would stem from the change of ownership itself and from the greater competition that would result, in other words from both capital market and product market stimuli.

The impact of the change of ownership on the internal structure of the company has been quite significant. It has become much more consumer-focused. It has also moved from a centralised, functional structure to a more profit-centred divisionalised organisation, with a greater level of local management accountability. Working practices have become more flexible and performance-related pay has become the norm at the managerial level. There has also been evidence of a more assertive managerial style towards the workforce. This has been accompanied by a general weakening of union power within the organisation as various long-standing agreements have been abandoned.

There has also been an increase in product competition, but only in some of BT's markets, such as value-added network services and the supply of telecom apparatus. In its major revenue-gaining markets, long-distance calls and local-calling, BT retains a substantial market share, despite competition from a variety of sources (see Section 15.3). However, in the important City of London market it is estimated that BT is now a much less significant player, with possibly only a 50% share.

Privatisation has had a significant impact on a number of BT's main policies, i.e. on its conduct. The effect of the strict regulatory regime imposed by Oftel (see Section 15.3) is that from 1984 to 1993 the prices of BT fell in real terms by 11%, although there have been wide differences in the relative price changes of particular services, whether or not they have been included in the price-capping formula. For example, prior to privatisation, local calls and exchange-line rentals had been cross-subsidised by the higher charges made for long-distance and overseas calls. Post-privatisation BT has attempted to align its charges more closely to reflect the marginal costs of providing individual services, a process referred to as rebalancing. Thus between 1984 and 1993, national call charges fell by 5.1% per annum, whereas the price of local calls rose by an annual average of 2.7%. Residential connection charges, not covered by the RPI±X formula, rose by an annual average of 7.2% Rebalancing to bring prices more closely in line with costs can be justified in terms of improving economic efficiency, although, as Vickers and Yarrow (1988) note, BT's price changes have involved reducing prices where competition from Mercury has existed and increasing prices where no such competition occurred.

Employment in BT did not show a significant change immediately after privatisation (contrary to the belief that privatisation causes a labour shake-out as wasteful working practices are abandoned). In 1989, BT undertook a large-scale programme of redundances following the tightening of the price cap, its workforce falling from 245 700 in 1990 to 156 000 in 1994. Investment in fixed assets as a share of turnover fell in the early 1980s before rising post-privatisation. More recently it has declined both in relative and in absolute value terms: during 1989/90–1993/94, investment spending fell from over £3.1 billion to about £2.2 billion and from 25.17% of turnover to 15.89%, although by 1995/96 the respective figures had recovered to £2.7 billion and 19.18%. Since 1979/80, R&D spending has risen in nominal terms, but has declined steadily

in terms of turnover (from 2.66% in 1979/80 to 1.76% in 1992/93), before also recovering somewhat to a 1.95% share in 1995/96. The relative decline in both investment and R&D spending
should, however, be placed in the context of the large-scale investment in digital technology
that had occurred during the period and which has now been almost completed: about 88% of
lines are now served by digital exchanges. It is also worth noting that Mercury's interconnection
to BT's network has reduced the need for such an investment in its own system.

The effect of these changes on BT's performance has been variable. Most indicators of quality
of service (network reliability, fault repair times and installation times) have shown improvements,
the majority of these stemming from a highly critical Oftel report in 1987. Profitability, measured
by the rate of return on net assets, has risen from an average of 18.3% in the five years prior to
privatisation to an average return post-privatisation of 20.7%. Labour productivity has also shown
a significant increase, rising from an average growth rate of 3.8% per annum before privatisation
to 6.9% since the change of ownership. The growth rate in total factor productivity, however, is
only around the same as before privatisation (although relative to the whole economy both measures have shown increases since privatisation, as shown in Tables 72 and 73, on page 303).

Overall, there have been improvements in BT's performance in a number of areas, although
it is impossible to say whether some of them might not have occurred in the absence of privatisation. Technological changes that have taken place in the industry, such as the introduction of
digital exchanges, would have had an impact on productivity and profitability whether BT was
under private or public ownership and whatever the level of competition. There is also evidence
(which should be treated with some caution given the problems of comparing like with like)
that BT's total factor productivity performance has been no better than that of the rest of the
European telecommunications industry (Marsh, 1991). Assuming that the changes in performance
of BT are the result of privatisation, it is not always possible to separate the effects of ownership from the effects of competition. The productive efficiencies encompassed in higher labour
productivity growth may have resulted from both the reduction of restrictive working practices
following the change of ownership and from the stimulus of increased competition. The relative
decline of investment and R&D spending suggests that capital market constraints may have been
at least as effective in encouraging short-term attitudes and reducing long-term expenditures as
in producing any cost savings, although their decline occurred at a time when the investment
programme in digital exchanges was reaching its fruition.

FURTHER READING

Beesley, M.E. (ed.) (1992) *Privatisation, Regulation and Deregulation*
(London, Routledge), Chapters 1–4, 9.

de Jong, H.W. (ed.) (1993) *The Structure of European Industry*, 3rd
edn (Dordrecht, The Netherlands, Kluwer Academic
Publishers), Chapter 1.

Ferguson, P.R. and Ferguson, G.J. (1994) *Industrial Economics: Issues
and Perspectives*, 2nd edn (London, Macmillan), Chapters 5,
7–10.

George, K.D., Joll, C. and Lynk, E.L. (1992) *Industrial Organisation:
Competition, Growth and Structural Change*, 4th edn (London,
Routledge), Chapters 12–16.

Vickers, J. and Yarrow, G. (1988) *Privatisation: an Economic Analysis*
(Cambridge, MA, MIT Press).

NOTES

1. The welfare loss formula can be derived as follows (see George
et al., 1992). The size of the welfare loss equals

$$\frac{1}{2}\,(Q_C - Q_M)\,(P_M - P_C) = \frac{1}{2}\,\Delta Q \Delta P$$

In terms of e_p at $(P_M Q_M)$ this can be expressed as

$$e_p = \left(\frac{\Delta Q}{Q_M}\right)\left(\frac{P_M}{\Delta P}\right)$$

$$\Delta Q = e_p Q_M \left(\frac{\Delta P}{P_M}\right)$$

$$\text{Welfare loss} = \frac{1}{2}\,e_p Q_M \left(\frac{\Delta P}{P_M}\right)\Delta P$$

$$= \frac{1}{2}\,e_p Q_M P_M \left(\frac{\Delta P}{P_M}\right)\left(\frac{\Delta P}{P_M}\right)$$

$$= \frac{1}{2}\, e_p P_M Q_M \left(\frac{\Delta P}{P_M}\right)^2$$

where $\Delta P/P_M$ is equal to the proportionate excess of monopoly price over price in perfect competition and $P_M Q_M$ equals the monopolist's revenue.

2. This can be derived as follows:

$$\text{Welfare loss} = \frac{1}{2}\, e_p P_M Q_M \left(\frac{\Delta P}{P_M}\right)^2$$

$$= \frac{1}{2}\, e_p P_M Q_M \left(\frac{\Delta P}{P_M}\right)\left(\frac{1}{e_p}\right)$$

$$= \frac{1}{2}\, P_M Q_M \left(\frac{\Delta P}{P_M}\right)$$

$$= \frac{1}{2}\, Q_M \Delta P$$

3. See *The Economist*, 27 May 1995, 'Rebuffing Microsoft'.
4. See *The Financial Times*, 23 February 1996, 'The Watchdog that Refuses to Bite'.
5. See *The Economist*, 27 May 1995, *op. cit.*
6. See *The Economist*, 27 May 1995, *op. cit.*
7. See *The Economist*, 27 May 1995, *op. cit.*
8. See *The Economist*, 21 August 1993, 'The Privatisation Fashion'.
9. See *The Economist*, 29 April 1995, The Grumbles of Middle Managers'.
10. See *The Economist*, 9 September 1995, 'More Competitive Tendering'.
11. See *The Economist*, 4 December 1993, 'GATT's Last Ditch'.
12. Reported in *The Economist*, 4 December 1993, *op. cit.*
13. This case is based on the article by Parker (1994b), although some of the arguments are my own.

Questions □ □ □

15.1 'The main weakness of industrial policies is a lack of coherent and comprehensive performance indicators by which they can be judged.' Discuss, with particular reference to competition policy.

15.2 In the 1980s, industry policy within the OECD mainly moved away from 'active' policy initiatives towards a more 'supportive' approach. Discuss the theoretical rationale for such a change of attitude.

15.3 Evaluate the Austrian critique of the traditional approach towards monopoly power. To what extent, if at all, do the competition policies of the UK, the US and the EU take into account the views of these two schools of thought in their attitudes towards dominant firms?

15.4 Compare the stance taken by the UK and the EU towards horizontal mergers with US policy, given the welfare implications of market power and the empirical evidence on the effects of mergers.

15.5 'Simply by initiating policies towards restrictive and anti-competitive practices, policy-makers are taking a traditional SCP stance.' Explain this statement and discuss how the policy stance may differ according to alternative schools of thought.

15.6 'Privatisation had a number of different aims, some of which were contradictory ... it is hardly surprising the government has only achieved some' (Marsh, 1991:477). Explain and discuss.

15.7 It has been argued that the main improvements in performance arising from privatisation stem from the productive efficiencies gained in moving from public to private ownership. Explain why this may be so and examine whether empirical evidence supports such an argument.

15.8 'Deregulation should improve economic welfare in most cases. However, for natural monopolies it may have the opposite effect and actually reduce welfare.' Explain and discuss.

15.9 'Where competition *in* the market cannot be adequately obtained, then competition *for* the market may be a better alternative.' Explain this statement and examine some of the difficulties in the promotion of such a policy.

15.10 Discuss the theoretical rationale underlying both the active and the supportive approaches towards regional policy. Examine the regional policies of the UK and the EU in the light of these two approaches.

ANSWERS TO QUESTIONS

mental profit = £28 × 500 000 minus £10 × 500 000 (comprising additional fixed overheads), so accept the new order.

6.1 AP = 12, 15, 16.67, 16.75, 16.2, 15.5, 14.4, 13.25, 12, 10.6.
MP = 12, 18, 20, 17, 14, 12, 8, 5, 2, 2.
(a) 3. (b) 4. (c) 9.

6.3 (a) 40, 82, 46, 17, 8, –4; 40, 61, 56, 45.5, 38, 31. (b) 185 000 per month; about 320L and 220K.

6.4 (a) £550. (b) £3750. (c) £4300. (d) £0.11. (e) £0.75. (f) £0.86. (g) £0.75. (h) £750.

6.5 (a) AVC = £40, £40, £60, £80; ATC = £90, £73.33, £91.25, £107.78.

6.8 (a) AC = £20.5, £17.5, £12.5, £9.8, £9.8; hence the curve is L-shaped. (b) Underutilised (until MES).

6.11 (a) 25 000. (b) 2. (c) Approx 31 250 and 1.71.

7.2 (a) 15. (b) £15. (c) 40/15. (d) 12.

7.5 (a) 66 047.75. (b) P_X = 42.24157 – 0.57143Q_X. (c) –0.011923, 0.10248, 0.02422 and 0.53830.

7.7 (a) –3.579. (b) £4.16.

7.8 (a) 2400. (b) £1. (c) –0.363 and revenue will fall.

7.9 (a) 60 and 55. (b) Inelastic. (c) –0.4783. (d) 0.9166.

7.10 (a) –0.55 and –1.28. (b) Decrease then increase.

8.3 (a) P = £13.4 and Q = 330(000). (b) 21(000). (c) £88 200.

8.4 TR = £18 750 and TVC = £18 850, therefore close.

8.5 (a) P = £210 and Q = 20 000.(b) £2 370 000.

8.6 (a) P = £132.5, Q_A = 412.5(00) and Q_B = 125 (00).(b) £59 303.75. (c) P = £85 and Q_A = 1100(00). (d) Was £44 303.75, now £60 440.

8.8 (a) £6. (b) £8. (c) £10.

8.10 (a) P_L = £64.58 and Q_L = 35 420. (b) Q = 20 270. (c) £1105.2(000). (d) £5.17(000).

10.3 (a) P_1 = £105 and Q_1 = 1900; P_2 = £55 and Q_2 = 1800. (b) £161 500. (c) £90 550.

10.4 (a) P_A = £94 and P_B = £209.5, Q = 810. (b) £64 025.

10.5 (a) P_T = £190 and Q = 3000. (c) £390 000. (d) Demand = 4500 units, 1500 of which is bought from the manufacturing division and 3000 from the open market. (e) Increases to £525 000.

10.7 (a) Markup should be 100%, whereas it is actually 150%. (b) £1.60 and 14(000) units.

11.2 (a) Q = 33 750 and profits = £42 000. (b) 42 550 and £64 240.

2.6 C_5 = 0.85; HI = 0.17.

5.1 (a) Fixed. (b) Variable. (c) Fixed. (d) Fixed. (e) Variable. (f) Variable. (g) Variable (largely) (h) Fixed.

5.2 PV = £4248, hence worthwhile.

5.3 Incremental revenues = £200 000, incremental costs = £145 000, so accept.

Including the effect of the fall in demand for the other product, there is an incremental loss of £55 000, so do not accept.

5.5

Price	Output	TR	TC	π	MR	MC
	0	–	50	–50	50	10
50	1	50	60	–10	40	10
45	2	90	70	20	30	10
40	3	120	80	40	20	10
35	4	140	90	50	10	10
30	5	150	100	50	0	10
25	6	150	110	40	–10	10
20	7	140	120	20	–20	10
15	8	120	130	–10	–30	10
10	9	90	140	–50		

Profit-maximising output = 5 units.

5.6 NPV = £1098, so invest.

5.7 ENPV of business market = £6.82 million and of domestic market = £5.1 million, so serve the business market.

However, the business market is more risky, given that the the standard deviation is £13.27 million compared with £6.39 million for the domestic market.

5.8 Contribution per unit = £28 and yearly incre-

11.5 (a) P = £40 and Q = 100(000), profit = £1400(000); 25% increase in advertising budget raises profits by £125 000.

11.7 £2 million, where the marginal return on the last increment (£1 million spent) of investment equals 6%.

12.2 (a) 3.86 and 4.61 years respectively. (b) 30.4% and 22.3% respectively. (c) NPV = £58 078 (positive), hence IRR should exceed the cost of capital; PI = 1.12, which also implies acceptance.

12.3 On the basis of an 8% money rate of return, the sum of the discounted limit price cash flows equals £12.3433 million against £11.9326 million for the short-run profit-maximising cash flows, so the former strategy should be adopted.

12.4 NPV for the new product (at 4% real discount rate) equals £15.42075 million, whereas the NPV of the old product (at 7% nominal discount rate) comes to £12.57745 million, so introduce the new product.

REFERENCES

Akerlof, G. (1970) The market for lemons: qualitative uncertainty and the market mechanism, *Quarterly Journal for Economics*, **89**(3), 345–64.

Alchian, A.A. and Demsetz, H. (1972) Production, information costs and economic organisation, *American Economic Review*, **62**(5), 777–95.

Alexander, D.L., Flynn, J.E. and Linkins, L.A. (1994) Estimates of the demand for ethical pharmaceutical drugs across countries and time, *Applied Economics*, **26**(8), 821–26.

Amato, L. and Wilder, R.P. (1988) Market concentration, efficiency and antitrust policy: Demsetz revisited, *Quarterly Journal of Business and Economics*, **27**(4), 3–19.

Andrews, P.W.S. (1949) *Manufacturing Business* (London, Macmillan).

Ansoff, H.I. (1965) *Corporate Strategy* (Harmondsworth, Penguin).

Areeda, P. and Hovenkamp, H. (1992) *Antitrust Law: an Analysis of Antitrust Principles and Their Application*, 1992 Supplement (Boston MA, Little Brown).

Areeda, P. and Turner, D. (1975) Predatory pricing and related practices under section 2 of the Sherman Act, *Harvard Law Review*, **88**, 697–733.

Arrow, K. (1962) Economic welfare and the allocation of resources, in K. Arrow (ed.) *The Rate and Direction of Inventive Activity* (Princeton, NJ, Princeton University Press).

Arrow, K. (1973) Higher education as a filter, *Journal of Public Economics*, **2**, 193–216.

Atkinson, A.B., Gomulka, J. and Stern, N.H. (1990) Spending on alcohol: evidence from the Family Expenditure Survey 1970–83, *Economic Journal*, **100**(402), 808–27.

Aylen, J. (1990) Cost curves in the steel industry, *Economic Review*, **8**(1), 2–5.

Bacon, R. and Ellis, W. (1975) *Britain's Economic Problem: Too Few Producers* (London, Macmillan).

Baden-Fuller, C. and Stopford, J.M. (1992) *Rejuvenating the Mature Business: the Competitive Challenge*, 2nd edn (London, Routledge).

Bailey, E.E. and Friedlander, A.F. (1982) Market structure and multiproduct industries, *Journal of Economic Literature*, **20**(September), 1024–48.

Bailey, E.E. and Panzar, J.C. (1981) The contestability of airline markets during the transition to deregulation, *Law and Contemporary Problems*, **44**(Winter), 125–45.

Bain, J.S. (1951) Relation of profit rate to industry concentration: American manufacturing, 1936–40, *Quarterly Journal of Economics*, **65**(3), 293–324.

Bain, J.S. (1956) *Barriers to New Competition* (Cambridge, MA, Harvard University Press).

Bain, J.S. (1959) *Industrial Organisation* (New York, John Wiley).

Bajic, V. (1993) Automobiles and implicit markets: an estimation of a structural demand model for automobile characteristics, *Applied Economics*, **25**(4), 541–51.

Bank of England (1994a) UK trade – long-term trends and recent developments, *Quarterly Bulletin*, **34**(3), 223–32.

Bank of England (1994b) Investment appraisal criteria and the impact of inflation, *Quarterly Bulletin*, **34**(3), 250–55.

Bank of England (1996) How do companies set prices? *Quarterly Bulletin*, **36**(2), 180–92.

Baumol, W.J. (1959) *Business Behaviour, Value and Growth* (New York, Macmillan).

Baumol, W.J. (1982) Contestable markets: an uprising in the theory of industrial structure, *American Economic Review*, **72**(1), 1–15.

Baumol, W.J., Panzar, C. and Willig, D. (1982) *Contestable Markets and the Theory of Industry Structure* (San Diego, CA, Harcourt Brace Jovanovich).

Becker, G.S. (1964) *Human Capital* (New York, National Bureau for Economic Research).

Berger, A.N. (1995) The profit-structure relationship in banking – tests of market power and efficient-structure hypothesis, *Journal of Management, Credit and Banking*, **27**(2), 404–31.

Berger, A.N. and Hannan, T.H. (1989) The price–concentration relationship in banking, *Review of Economic Studies*, **71**, 291–99.

Berle, A.A. and Means, G.C. (1932) *The Modern Corporation and Private Property* (New York, Commerce Clearing House).

Berndt, E.R., Bui, L., Reiley, D.R. and Urban, G.L. (1995) Information, marketing and pricing in the US antiulcer drug market, *American Economic Review*, **85**(2), 100–5.

Berry, T., Capps, T., Cooper, D., Hopper, T. and Lowe, T. (1985) NCB accounts – a mine of dis-information?, *Accountancy*, **96** (January), 10–12.

Bianchi, P. and Forlai, L. (1993) The domestic appliance industry 1945–91, in H.W. de Jong (ed.) *The Structure of European Industry* (Dordrecht, The Netherlands, Kluwer Academic Publishers).

Bishop, M. and Kay, J. (1988) *Does Privatisation Work?* (London, London Business School).

Blanchflower, D. and Freeman, R. (1993) Did the Thatcher reforms change British labour market performance?, *Centre for Economic Performance*, London School of Economics, Discussion Paper Number 168, August.

Blinder, A. (1992) Why are prices sticky? Preliminary results from an interview study, *American Economic Review*, **81**(2), 89–96.

Bowen, H.P. (1991a) Electronic components and semiconductors, in D.G. Mayes (ed.) *The European Challenge* (London, Harvester Wheatsheaf).

Bowen, H.P. (1991b) Consumer electronics, in D.G. Mayes (ed.) *The European Challenge* (London, Harvester Wheatsheaf).

Brewster, D. (1993) Short-termism, stock market efficiency and the takeover mechanism – an overview, *British Review of Economic Issues*, **15**(35), 1–23.

Brozen, Y. (1971) Bain's concentration and rates of return revisited, *Journal of Law and Economics*, **14**(October), 351–69.

Buckley, A. (1972) A profile of industrial acquisition in 1971, *Accounting and Business Research*, **2**, 243–52.

Buckley, A. and Casson, M.C. (1976) *The Future of the Multinational Enterprise* (London, Macmillan).

Cable, J. and Dirrheimer, M.J. (1983) Hierarchies and markets: an empirical test of the multidivisional hypothesis in West Germany, *International Journal of Industrial Organisation*, **1**(1), 43–62.

Calvo, G.A. and Wellisz, S. (1979) Hierarchy, ability and income distribution, *Journal of Political Economy*, **87**(5), 991–1010.

Cambridge Economic Policy Group (1976) *Economic Policy Review*, **2**(March) (Farnborough, Gower Publishing).

Card, D. (1992) Do minimum wages reduce employment? A case study of California, 1987–89, *Industrial and Labour Relations Review*, **46**, 22–37.

Casson, M.C. (1982) *The Entrepreneur: an Economic Theory* (Oxford, Martin Robertson).

Casson, M.C. (1987) Multinational firms, in R. Clarke and T. McGuinness (eds), *The Economics of the Firm*, Oxford, Basil Blackwell.

Caves, R.E. (1980) Industrial organisation, corporate strategy and structure, *Journal of Economic Literature*, **18**(March), 64–92.

Caves, R.E. (1982) *Multinational Enterprise and Economic Analysis* (Cambridge, Cambridge University Press).

Caves, R.E. and Bradburd, R.M. (1988) The empirical determinants of vertical integration, *Journal of Economic Behaviour and Organisation*, **9**, 265–79.

Caves, R.E. and Porter, M.E. (1978) Market structure, oligopoly and the stability of market shares, *Journal of Industrial Economics*, **26**(4), 289–313.

Chamberlin, E.H. (1933) *The Theory of Monopolistic Competition* (Cambridge, MA, Harvard University Press).

Chandler, A.D. (1962) *Strategy and Structure: Chapters in the History of the Industrial Enterprise* (Cambridge, MA, MIT Press).

Chandler, A.D. (1977) *The Visible Hand: the Managerial Revolution in American Business* (Cambridge, MA, Harvard University Press).

Chang, H.S. and Hsing Yu (1991) The demand for residential electricity: new evidence on time-varying elasticities, *Applied Economics*, **23**(7), 1251–56.

Channon, D.F. (1973) *The Strategy and Structure of British Enterprise* (London, Macmillan).

Clark, J.A. and Speaker, P.J. (1992) The impact of entry conditions on the concentration-profit relationship in banking, *Quarterly Review of Economics and Finance*, **82**(4), 45–64.

Clarke, R. (1984) Profit margins and market concentration in UK manufacturing industry, 1970–76, *Applied Economics*, **16**(4), 57–71.

Clarke. R. (1985) *Industrial Economics* (Oxford, Basil Blackwell).

Clarke, R. (1987) Conglomerate firms, in R. Clarke and T. McGuinness (eds), *The Economics of the Firm* (Oxford, Basil Blackwell).

Clarke, R. and Davies, S.W. (1982) Market structure and price-cost margins, *Economica*, **49**(August), 277–88.

Clarke, R. and Davies, S.W. (1983) Aggregate concentration, market concentration and diversification, *Economic Journal*, **93**(March), 182–92.

Cleeve, E. (1994) Transnational corporations and internalisation: a critical review, *British Review of Economic Issues*, **16**(40), 1–25.

Clements, K.W. and Johnson, L.W. (1983) The demand for beer, wine and spirits, *Journal of Business*, 56, part 3, 273–304.

Coase, R.H. (1937) The nature of the firm, *Economica*, New Series, **4**, 386–405; reprinted in G.J. Stigler and V.E. Boulding (eds.), *Readings in Price Theory* (Homewood, IL, Richard D. Irwin), 1952, and in O.E. Williamson and S.G. Winter (eds.), *The Nature of the Firm* (Oxford, Oxford University Press), 1993.

Coate, M.B. (1989) The dynamics of price-cost margins in concentrated industries, *Applied Economics*, **21**(2), 261–72.

Cobb, C.W. and Douglas, P.H. (1928) A theory of production, *American Economic Review*, **16**, 139–62.

Coe, D. and Helpman, E. (1994) International R&D spillovers, *European Economic Review*, **39**(5), 859–87.

Colley, R.H. (1961) *Defining Goals for Measuring Advertising Results* (New York, Association of National Advertisers).

Collins, J. and Porras, J. (1991) Organisational vision and visionary organisations, Research Paper Number 1159, Standford University Graduate Business School.

Collins, N.R. and Preston, L.E. (1968) *Concentration and Price-cost Margins in Manufacturing Industries* (Berkeley CA, University of California Press).

Collins, N.R. and Preston, L.E. (1969) Price-cost margins and industry structure, *Review of Economics and Statistics*, **51**(August), 226–42.

Comanor, W.S. and Leibenstein, H. (1969) Allocative efficiency, X-efficiency and the measurement of welfare losses, *Economica*, **36**, 304–9.

Comanor, W.S. and Wilson, T.A. (1967) Advertising, market structure and performance, *Review of Economics and Statistics*, **49**(4), 423–40.

Commission of the European Communities (CEC) (1990) *Industrial Policy in an Open and Competitive Environment* (Luxembourg, Office for Official Publications of the European Communities).

Commission of the European Communities (CEC) (1992) *Twenty First Report on Competition Policy* (Luxembourg, Office for Official Publications of the European Communities).

Commission of the European Communities (CEC) (1994) *Twenty Fourth Report on Competition Policy* (Luxembourg, Office for Official Publications of the European Communities).

Commission of the European Communities (CEC) (1995) *Action Programme to Strengthen the Industrial Competitiveness of the European Union* (Luxembourg, Office for Official Publications of the European Communities).

Conyon, M. (1994) Corporate governance changes in UK companies between 1988 and 1993, *Corporate Governance: an International Review*, **2**, 87–99.

Conyon, M., Gregg, P. and Machin, S. (1995) Taking care of business: executive compensation in the UK, *Economic Journal*, **15**(430), 704–15.

Cosh, A. and Hughes, A. (1987) The anatomy of corporate control: directors, shareholders and executive remuneration in giant US and UK corporations, *Cambridge Journal of Economics*, **11**(December), 285–313.

Cosh, A., Hughes, A. and Singh, A. (1990) Analytical and policy issues in the UK economy, Institute for Public Policy Research Industrial Policy Paper Number 3, *Takeovers and Short-termism in the UK*, pp. 8–21.

Coulthurst, N.J. (1986) Accounting for inflation in capital investment: the state of the art and science, *Accounting and Business Research*, **17**(65), 33–42.

Cowling, K. and Mueller, D. (1978) The social costs of monopoly, *Economic Journal*, **88**(December), 727–48.

Cowling, K. and Waterson, M. (1976) Price-cost margins and market structure, *Economica*, **43**(August), 267–74.

Cubbin, J. and Geroski, P. (1987) The convergence of profits in the long run: inter-firm and inter-industry comparisons, *Journal of Industrial Economics*, **35**(4), 427–43.

Cubbin, J. and Leach, D. (1983) The effect of shareholder dispersion on the degree of control in British companies: theory and measurement, *Economic Journal*, **93**(2), 351–69.

Cyert, R.M. and March, J.G. (1963) *A Behavioural Theory of the Firm* (Englewood Cliffs, NJ, Prentice Hall).

Dahl, C. (1986) Gasoline demand survey, *The Energy Journal*, 7, 67–82.

Darby, M. and Karni, E. (1973) Free competition and the optimal amount of fraud, *Journal of Law and Economics*, April, 67–88.

Das, B.J., Chappell, W.F. and Shughart, W.F. (1993) Advertising, competition and market share instability, *Applied Economics*, 25(11), 1409–12.

Davies, S.W. (1989) Concentration, in S.W. Davies and B.R. Lyons with H. Dixon and P. Geroski (eds), *Economics of Industrial Organisation* (Harlow, Longman).

Davies, S.W. and Caves, R.E. (1987) *Britain's Productivity Lag* (Cambridge, Cambridge University Press).

Davies, S.W. and Morris, C. (1995) A new index of vertical integration: some estimates for UK manufacturing, *International Journal of Industrial Organisation*, 13, 151–77.

Davis, E.H., Kay, J.A. and Star, J. (1991) Is advertising rational?, *Business Strategy Review*, 2(3), 1–23.

Dean, J. (1950) Pricing policies for new products, *Harvard Business Review*, 28 (November–December), 45–53.

de Jong, H.W. (ed.) (1988) *The Structure of European Industry*, 2nd edn (Dordrecht, The Netherlands, Kluwer Academic Publishers).

de Jong, H.W. (ed.) (1993a) *The Structure of European Industry*, 3rd edn (Dordrecht, The Netherlands, Kluwer Academic Publishers).

de Jong, H.W. (1993b) Market structures in the European Community, in H.W. de Jong (ed.), *The Structure of European Industry*, 3rd edn (Dordrecht, The Netherlands, Kluwer Academic Publishers).

Demsetz, H. (1973) Industrial structure, market rivalry and public policy, *Journal of Law and Economics*, 16(1), 1–9.

Demsetz, H. (1982) Barriers to entry, *American Economic Review*, 72(1), 47–57.

Department of Trade and Industry (DTI) (1989) *Barriers to Takeovers in the European Community* (3 vols), a Study by Coopers and Lybrand for the DTI (London, HMSO).

Department of Trade and Industry (DTI) (1995) *Learning from Japan*, a Study by Andersen Consulting for the DTI (London, HMSO).

Devine, P.J., Lee, N., Jones, R.M. and Tyson, W.J. (1985) *An Introduction to Industrial Economics*, 2nd edn (London, George, Allen and Unwin).

Dickens, R., Machin S. and Manning, A. (1994) The effect of minimum wages on employment: theory and evidence from Britain, Centre for Economic Performance, London School of Economics, Discussion Paper Number 183, January.

Dixit, A. (1980) The role of investment in entry deterrence, *Economic Journal*, 9(March), 95–106.

Dixit, A. (1982) Recent developments in oligopoly theory, *American Economic Review Papers and Proceedings*, 72(2), 12–17.

Doeringer, P.B. and Piore, M.J. (1971) *Internal Labour Markets and Manpower Analysis* (Lexicon, MA, Heath Lexicon Books).

Dorfman, R. and Steiner P.O. (1954) Optimial advertising and optimal quality, *American Economic Review*, 44(December), 826–36.

Downie, J. (1958) *The Competitive Process*, (London, Duckworth).

Doyle, P. (1968) Economic aspects of advertising: a survey, *Economic Journal*, 77(September), 570–602.

Doyle, P. (1989) Building successful brands: the strategic options, *Journal of Marketing Management*, 5(1), 77–95.

Duffy, M. (1987) Advertising and the inter-product distribution of demand: a Rotterdam model approach, *European Economic Review*, 31, 1051–70.

Dunning, J.H. (1993) *The Globalisation of Business* (London, Routledge).

Dunsire, A., Hartley, K. and Parker, D. (1991) Organisational status and performance: summary of the findings, *Public Administration*, 69, 21–40.

Edwards, J. and Fischer, K. (1994) *Banks, Finance and Investment in Germany* (Cambridge, Cambridge University Press).

Egan, C. (1994) Achieving brand potential: the management challenge, *Economics and Business Education*, 2(2), 71–79.

Eichner, A.S. (1973) A theory of the determination of the markup under oligopoly, *Economic Journal*, 63(5), 1184–98.

Evans, D.S. (1987) The relationship between firm growth, size and age: estimates for 100 manufacturing industries, *Journal of Industrial Economics*, 35(4), 567–81.

Fama, E.F. (1980) Agency problems and the theory of the firm, *Journal of Political Economy*, 88(6), 288–307.

Ferguson, P.R. and Ferguson, G.J. (1994) *Industrial Economics: Issues and Perspectives*, 2nd edn (London, Macmillan).

Florence, P.S. (1961) *Ownership, Control and Success of Large Corporations* (London, Sweet and Maxwell).

Freeman, R.B. and Medoff, J.L. (1984) *What Do Unions Do?* (New York, Basic Books).

George, K.D., Joll, C. and Lynk, E.L. (1992) *Industrial Organisation: Competition, Growth and Structural Change*, 4th edn (London, Routledge).

Geroski, P.W. and Jacquemin A. (1988) The persistence of profits: a European comparison, *Economic Journal*, 98(391), 375–89.

Gilson, R.J. and Roe, M.J. (1993) Understanding the Japanese keiretsu: overlaps between corporate governance and industrial organisation, *The Yale Law Journal*, 102(4), 871–906.

Glen, D.R. (1990) The market for beer in the United Kingdom, *UK Economic Studies*, 2(Winter), 15–24.

Green, A. and Steedman, H. (1993) Educational provision, educational attainment and the needs of industry: a review of research for Germany, France, Japan, the USA and Britain, National Institute of Economic and Social Research Report Series Number 5.

Greenhalgh, C. (1994) Why manufacturing still matters, *Economic Review*, 12(1), 11–15.

Greening, L.A., Jeng, H.T., Formby, J.P. and Cheng, D.C. (1995) Use of region, life-cycle and role variables in the short-run estimation of the demand for gasoline and miles travelled, *Applied Economics*, 27(7), 643–57.

Gregg, P. and Wadsworth, J. (1995) A short history of labour turnover, job tenure and job security, 1975–93, *Oxford Review of Economic Policy*, 11(1), 73–90.

Griffiths, A. and Wall, S. (1995) *Applied Economics*, 6th edn (London, Longman).

Grinyer, P.H., Yassai-Ardekani, M. and Al-Bazza, S. (1980) Strategy, structure, the environment and financial performance in 48 United Kingdom companies, *Academy of Management Journal*, 23, 193–220.

Gropper, D.M. (1995) Product-line deregulation and the cost structure of US savings and loans associations, *Applied Economics*, 27(2), 183–91.

Hall, B. (1987) The relationship between firm size and firm growth in the US manufacturing sector, *Journal of Industrial Economics*, 35(4), 583–606.

Hall, R.L. and Hitch, C.J. (1939) Price theory and business behaviour, *Oxford Economic Papers*, 2(May), 12–45.

Hannah, L. and Kay, J.A. (1977) *Concentration in Modern Industry* (London, Macmillan).

Harberger, A. (1954) Monopoly and resource allocation, *American Economic Review Papers and Proceedings*, 44, 77–87.

Harbord, D. and Hoehn, T. (1994) Barriers to entry and exit in European competition policy, *International Review of Law and Economics*, **14**(4), 411–35.

Hart, O.D. (1983) The market mechanism as an incentive scheme, *Bell Journal of Economics and Management Science*, **14**, 366–82.

Hay, D.A. and Morris, D.J. (1979) *Industrial Economics: Theory and Evidence* (Oxford, Oxford University Press).

Hennart, J.F. (1982) *A Theory of Multinational Enterprise* (Ann Arbor, MI, University of Michigan Press).

Hirschman, A.O. (1964) The paternity of an index, *American Economic Review*, **54**(5), 761–2.

Hitiris, T. (1978) Effective protection and economic performance in UK manufacturing industry, 1963 and 1968, *Economic Journal*, **88**(March), 107–20.

Holtermann, S.E. (1973) Market structure and economic performance in the UK manufacturing industry, *Journal of Industrial Economics*, **22**(2), 119–39.

Hood, N. and Young, S. (1979) *The Economics of Multinational Enterprise* (London, Longman).

Household Food Consumption and Expenditure Survey (1989) (London, HMSO).

House of Lords (1985) *Report from the Select Committee on Overseas Trade* (London, HMSO).

Hughes, A. (1993) Mergers and economic performance in the UK: a survey of the empirical evidence, 1950–90, in M. Bishop and J. Kay (eds) *European Mergers and Merger Policy* (Oxford, Oxford University Press).

Hunt, L.C. and Lynk, E.L. (1995) Privatisation in the UK water industry: an empirical analysis, *Oxford Bulletin of Economics and Statistics*, **57**(3), 371–88.

Hymer, S.H. (1960) *The International Operations of National Firms: a Study of Foreign Direct Investment* (Ph.D thesis, Massachusetts Institute of Technology; Cambridge, MA, MIT Press, 1976).

Ingham, H. and Thompson, S. (1994) Wholly owned versus collaborative ventures for diversifying financial services, *Strategic Management Journal*, **15**, 325–44.

Jacoby, S.M. and Mitchell, D.J.B. (1990) Sticky stories: economic explanations of employment and wage rigidity, *American Economic Association*, **80**(2), 33–37.

Jenny, F. and Weber, A.P. (1983) Aggregate welfare loss due to monopoly power in the French economy: some tentative estimates, *Journal of Industrial Economics*, **32**(2), 113–30.

Jensen, M.C. and Meckling, W.H. (1976) Theory of the firm: managerial behaviour, agency costs and ownership structure, *Journal of Finance*, **3**, 305–60.

Jensen, M.C. and Murphy, K.J. (1990) CEO incentives – its not how much you pay, but how, *Harvard Business Review*, **68**(3), 138–53.

Joesch, J.M. and Zick, C.D. (1994) Evidence of changing contestability in commercial airline markets during the 1980s, *Journal of Consumer Affairs*, **28**(1), 1–24.

Jones, A.M. (1989) A systems approach to the demand for alcohol and tobacco, *Bulletin of Economic Research*, **41**, 86–101.

Jones, G. (1996) *The Evolution of International Business* (London, Routledge).

Jones, J.P. (1995) Advertising's impact on sales and profitability, *Institute of Practitioners in Advertising*, March.

Kamerschen, D. (1966) An estimation of the 'welfare losses' from monopoly in the American economy, *Western Economic Journal*, **4**, 221–36.

Kaserman, D.L. and Mayo, J.W. (1991) The measurement of vertical economies and the efficient structure of the electricity utility business, *Journal of Industrial Economics*, **39**(5), 483–503.

Katz, L. and Krueger A. (1992) The effect of the minimum wage in the fast food industry, *Industrial and Labour Relations Review*, **46**, 6–21.

Kerr, C. (1954) The balkanisation of labour markets, in E.W. Bakke *et al.* (eds) *Labour Mobility and Economic Opportunity* (New York, John Wiley).

Kindelberger, C.P. (1969) *American Business Abroad* (New Haven, CT, Yale University Press).

Kirkvliet, J. (1991) Efficiency and vertical integration: the case of mine-mouth electric generating plants, *Journal of Industrial Economics*, **39**(5), 467–83.

Kirzner, I.M. (1979) *Perception, Opportunity and Profit: Studies in the Theory of Entrepreneurship* (Chicago, IL, Chicago University Press).

Klepper, G. (1991) The aerospace industry, in D.G. Mayes (ed.), *The European Challenge* (London, Harvester Wheatsheaf).

Knickerbocker, F.T. (1973) *Oligopolistic Reaction and Multinational Enterprise* (Cambridge, MA, Harvard University Press).

Knight, F. (1921) *Risk, Uncertainty and Profit* (Chicago, IL, Chicago University Press).

Knight, K. (1976) Matrix organisation: a review, *Journal of Management Studies*, **13**, 111–30.

Kotlikoff, L.J. and Gokhale, J. (1992) Estimating a firm's age-productivity profile using the present value of workers' earnings, *Quarterly Journal of Economics*, **107**(November), 1215–42.

Kuehn, D. (1975) *Takeovers and the Theory of the Firm* (London, Macmillan).

Kuznets, S. (1959) *Six Lectures on Economic Growth* (Toronto, Ontario, Free Press).

Lal, R. and Matutes, C. (1994) Retail pricing and advertising strategies, *Journal of Business*, **67**(3), 345–70.

Lancaster, K. (1971) *Consumer Demand: a New Approach* (New York, Columbia University Press).

Larner, R. (1966) Ownership and control in the 200 largest non-financial corporations 1929 and 1963, *American Economic Review*, **56**(4), 777–87.

Lazear, E.P. (1981) Agency, earnings profiles, productivity and hours restrictions, *American Economic Review*, **71**(4), 606–20.

Lazear, E.P. and Rosen, S. (1981) Rank-order tournaments as optimum labour contracts, *Journal of Political Economy*, **89**(5), 841–64.

Leibenstein, H. (1966) Allocative efficiency versus X-efficiency, *American Economic Review*, **56**(3), 392–415.

Leibenstein, H. (1979) A branch of economics is missing: micro-macro theory, *Journal of Economic Literature*, **17**, 477–502.

Leslie, D. (1993) *Advanced Macroeconomics: Beyond IS/LM* (London, McGraw-Hill).

Levine, P. and Aaronovitch, S. (1981) The financial characteristics of firms and theories of merger activity, *Journal of Industrial Economics*, **30**(2), 149–72.

Levy, D.T. (1989) Predation, firm-specific assets and diversification, *Journal of Industrial Economics*, **38**(2), 227–35.

Lieberman, M.B. (1987) Excess capacity as a barrier to entry: an empirical appraisal, *Journal of Industrial Economics*, **35**(4), 607–27.

Lieberman, M.B. (1991) Determinants of vertical integration: an empirical test, *Journal of Industrial Economics*, **39**(5), 451–67.

Littlechild, S.C. (1981) Misleading calculations of the social cost of monopoly power, *Economic Journal*, **91**(June), 348–63.

Lloyds Bank Small Business Research Trust (1995) *Quarterly Small Business Management Report*, Number 4, vol. 3.

Lyons, B.R. (1981) Price-cost margins, market structure and international trade, in D. Currie, D. Peel and W. Peters (eds) *Microeconomic Analysis* (London, Croom Helm).

Lyons, B.R. (1987) Strategic behaviour by firms, in R. Clarke and T. McGuinness (eds) *The Economics of the Firm* (Oxford, Basil Blackwell).

Lyons, B.R. (1989) Barriers to entry, in S. Davies and B.R. Lyons with H, Dixon and P. Geroski (eds) *Economics of Industrial Organisation* (Harlow, Longman).

Machin, S., Manning A. and Woodland S. (1993) Are workers paid their marginal product? Evidence from a low wage labour market, Discussion Paper Number 93–09, University College, London.

Malcolmson, J.M. (1984) Work incentives, hierarchy and internal labour markets, *Journal of Political Economy*, **92**(3), 486–507.

Mann, H.M. (1966) Seller concentration, barriers to entry and rates of return in 30 industries, 1950–60, *Review of Economics and Statistics*, **48**(August), 296–307.

Marsh, P. (1990) Short-termism on trial, Institutional Fund Managers' Association Report.

Marris, R. (1964) *The Economic Theory of Managerial Capitalism* (London, Macmillan).

Marsh, D. (1991) Privatisation under Mrs. Thatcher: a review of the literature, *Public Administration*, **69**(4), 459–80.

Marshall, A. (1890) *Principles of Economics*, (London, Macmillan).

Martin, S. (1988) Market power and/or efficiency, *Review of Economics and Statistics*, **70**(2), 331–35.

Marvel, H.P. (1989) Concentration and price in gasoline retailing, in L.W. Weiss (ed.) *Concentration and Price* (Cambridge, MA, MIT Press).

Mason, E.S. (1939) Price and production policies of large-scale enterprises, *American Economic Review Supplement*, **29**(1), 61–74.

Mason, G. and Wagner, K. (1994) High-level skills and industrial competitiveness: post-graduate engineers in Britain and Germany, National Institute of Economic and Social Report Series Number 6.

Masson, R.T. and Shaanan, J. (1984) Social costs of oligopoly and the value of competition, *Economic Journal*, **94**(September), 520–35.

Masten, S.E., Meehan J.W. Jr. and Snyder, E.A. (1989) Vertical integration in the US automobile industry, *Journal of Economic Behaviour and Organisation*, **12**, 265–73.

Mayer, C. (1987) Financial systems and corporate investment, *Oxford Review of Economic Policy*, **3**, 1–16.

McCauley, R.N. and Zimmer, S.A. (1989) Explaining international differences in the cost of capital, *Federal Reserve Bank of New York Quarterly Review, Summer*, 7–28.

McKillop, D.G. and Glass, C.J. (1994) A cost model of building societies as producers of mortgages and other financial products, *Journal of Business Finance and Accounting*, **21**(7), 1031–46.

Meisel, J.B. (1981) Entry, multi-brand firms and market share instability, *Journal of Industrial Economics*, **29**(4), 375–84.

Mincer, J. (1974) *Schooling, Experience and Earnings* (New York, National Bureau of Economic Research).

Modigliani, F. (1958) New developments on the oligopoly front, *Journal of Political Economy*, **66**(June), 215–32.

Modigliani, F. and Miller, F.H. (1958) The cost of capital, corporation finance and the theory of investment, *American Economic Review*, **48**(3), 261–97.

Modigliani, F. and Miller, F.H. (1963) Corporate income tax and the cost of capital: a correction, *American Economic Review*, **53**(3), 433–43.

Monopolies and Mergers Commission (MMC) (1986) *White Salt*, Cmnd 9778 (London, HMSO).

Monopolies and Mergers Commission (MMC) (1989) *Supply of Beer*, Cmnd 651 (London, HMSO).

Monopolies and Mergers Commission (MMC) (1990) *Plasterboard*, Cmnd 1224 (London, HMSO).

Monopolies and Mergers Commission (MMC) (1991) *Soluble Coffee*, Cmnd 1459 (London, HMSO).

Monopolies and Mergers Commission (MMC) (1992) *New Cars*, Cmnd 1808 (London, HMSO).

Monopolies and Mergers Commission (MMC) (1993a) *The Gillette Company and Parker Pen Holdings Ltd: a Report on the Proposed Merger*, Cmnd 2221 (London, HMSO).

Monopolies and Mergers Commission (MMC) (1993b) *Ice Cream*, Cmnd 2524 (London, HMSO).

Monopolies and Mergers Commission (MMC) (1994) *Contraceptive Sheaths*, Cmnd 2529 (London, HMSO).

Monopolies and Mergers Commission (MMC) (1995) *Supply of Bus Services in the North-east of England*, Cmnd 2933, (London, HMSO).

Morgan, E.V. and Morgan, A.D. (1990) *The Stock Market and Mergers in the United Kingdom*, Hume Occassional Paper No. 24.

Mueller, D.C. (1969) A theory of conglomerate mergers, *Quarterly Journal of Economics*, **83**(3), 643–59.

Mullins, M. and Wadhani, S.B. (1989) The effects of the stock market on investment: a comparative study, *The European Economic Review*, **33**, 939–61.

National Economic Development Council (NEDC) (1991) *Partners for the Long Term: Lessons from the Success of Germany and Japan* (London, NEDC).

Needham, D. (1978) *The Economics of Industrial Structure, Conduct and Performance* (London, Holt, Rinehart and Winston).

Nelson, P. (1974) Advertising as information, *Journal of Political Economy*, **82**(4), 729–54.

Nerlove, M. and Arrow, K.J. (1962) Optimal advertising policy under dynamic conditions, *Economica*, **29**, 129–42.

Neven, D. and Seabright P. (1995) European industrial policy: the Airbus case, *Economic Policy*, **21**(October), 315–48.

Newbold, G.D. (1970) *Management and Merger Activity*, (Liverpool, Gutshead).

Nyman, S. and Silberston, A. (1978) The ownership and control of industry, *Oxford Economic Papers*, **30**(March), 82–9.

O'Connell, B. (1990) Training infrastructure – the industry level, *Employment Gazette* **98**(7), 353–60.

Oh, S.J. (1986) The magnitude of welfare losses in the Korean economy, *Economic Research*, **7**, 219–34.

O'Mahoney, M. (1992) Productivity and human capital formation in UK and German manufacturing, National Institute of Economic and Social Research Discussion Paper Number 128.

O'Mahoney, M, Oulton, N. and Vass, J. (1996) Productivity in market services: international comparisons, National Institute of Economic and Social Research Discussion Paper Number 105.

Organisation for Economic Cooperation and Development (OECD) (1993) *Industrial Policy in OECD Countries, Annual Review* (Paris, OECD).

Organisation for Economic Cooperation and Development (OECD) (1994) *Industrial Policy in OECD Countries, Annual Review* (Paris, OECD).

Oulton N. (1994) Labour productivity and unit labour costs in manufacturing: the UK and its competitors, *National Institute Economic Review*, Number 152, May, 49–60.

Panzar, J. and Willig, R.D. (1981) Economies of scope, *American Economic Review Papers and Proceedings*, **71**, 268–72.

Parker, D. (1991) Privatisation ten years on: a critical analysis of its rationale and results, *Economics*, **27**, 653–68.

Parker, D. (1994a) International aspects of privatisation: a critical assessment of business restructuring in the UK, former Czechoslovakia and Malaysia, *British Review of Economic Issues*, **16**(38), 1–33.

Parker, D. (1994b) A decade of privatisation: the effect of ownership change and competition on British Telecom, *British Review of Economic Issues*, **16**(40), 87–115.

Parker, D. and Martin, S. (1995) The impact of UK privatisation on labour and total factor productivity, *Scottish Journal of Political Economy*, **42**(2), 201–20.

Peacock, M., Reeve, R. and Shaw, H. (1994) 'Spend money on that?' Investment appraisal in the hospitality industry, *International Journal of Contemporary Hospitality Management*, **6**(6), 1–3.

Peltzman, S. (1976) Towards a more general theory of regulation, *Journal of Law and Economics*, **19**, 229–63.

Penrose, E.T. (1959) *The Theory of the Growth of the Firm* (Oxford, Basil Blackwell).

Porter, M. (1980) *Competitive Strategy: Techniques for Analysing Industries and Competitors* (New York, Free Press).

Posner, R.A. (1975) The social costs of monopoly and regulation, *Journal of Political Economy*, **83**, 807–27.

Prais, S.J. (1976) *The Evolution of Giant Firms in Britain* (Cambridge, Cambridge University Press).

Pratten, C.F. (1989) *Research on the Costs of Non-Europe, Vol. 2* (Luxembourg, Office for Official Publications of the European Communities).

Prowse, S.D. (1992) The structure of corporate ownership in Japan, *The Journal of Finance*, **47**(3), 1121–40.

Radice, H. (1971) Control type, profitability and growth in large firms: an empirical study, *Economic Journal*, **81**(Spetember), 547–62.

Ravenscraft, D.J. (1983) Structure-profit relationships at the line of business and industry level, *Review of Economics and Statistics*, **65**(1), 22–31.

Reekie, W.D. (1984) *Markets, Entrepreneurs and Liberty: an Austrian View of Capitalism* (Brighton, Wheatsheaf).

Reid, G. (1987) *Theories of Industrial Organisation* (Oxford, Basil Blackwell).

Riahi-Belkaoui, A. and Bannister, J.W. (1994) Multidivisional structure and capital structure: the contingency of diversification strategy, *Managerial and Decision Economics*, **15**, 267–76.

Robinson, J. (1933) *The Economics of Imperfect Information* (London, Macmillan).

Robinson, P. (1994) The British disease overcome? Living standards, productivity and education attainment, 1979–94, Centre for Economic Performance, London School of Economics, Discussion Paper Number 260, August.

Romer, P. (1986) Increasing returns and long-run growth, *Journal of Political Economy*, **94**(5), 1002–37.

Rose, P.S. (1992) Agency theory and entry barriers, *Financial Review*, **27**(3), 323–53.

Ross, S.A. (1973) The economic theory of agency: the principal's problem, *American Economic Review*, **62**, 134–39.

Rugman, A.M. (1981) *Inside the Multinationals: the Economics of Internal Markets* (London, Croom Helm).

Rumelt, R. (1991) How much does industry matter? *Strategic Management Journal* **12**(3), 167–85.

Salvadori, D. (1991) The automobile industry, in D.G. Mayes (ed.), *The European Challenge* (London, Harvester Wheatsheaf).

Sangster, A. (1993) Capital investment appraisal techniques: a survey of current usage, *Journal of Business Finance and Accounting* **20**(3), 307–30.

Sapsford, D. and Tzannatos, Z. (1993) *The Economics of the Labour Market* (London, Macmillan).

Sass, T.R. and Saurman, D.S. (1995) Advertising restrictions and concentration: the case of malt beverages, *Review of Economics and Statistics*, **77**(1), 66–81.

Sawtelle, B.A. (1993) Income elasticities of household expenditures: a US cross-section perspective, *Applied Economics*, **25**(5), 635–44.

Sawyer, M.C. (1981) *The Economics of Industries and Firms*, 2nd edn (London, Croom Helm).

Scherer, F.M. (1980) *Industrial Market Structure and Economic Performance*, 2nd edn (Chicage, IL, Rand McNally).

Schmalansee, R. (1976) Advertising and profitability: further implications of the null hypothesis, *Journal of Industrial Economics*, **25**(1), 45–54.

Schumpeter, J.A. (1943) *Capitalism, Socialism and Democracy* (London, Unwin University Press).

Schwartzman, D. (1960) The burden of monopoly, *Journal of Political Economy*, **68**, 627–30.

Scott, M. (1989) *A New View of Economic Growth* (Oxford, Clarendon Press).

Selvanathan, E.A. (1991) Cross-country alcohol consumption comparison: an application of the Rotterdam demand system, *Applied Economics*, **23**(10), 1613–22.

Shackle, G.L.S. (1979) *Imagination and the Nature of Choice* (Edinburgh, Edinburgh University Press).

Shepherd, W.G. (1990) *The Economics of Industrial Organisation*, 3rd edn (Englewood Cliffs, NJ, Prentice Hall).

Sibly, H. (1995) Advertising in customer markets, *Scottish Journal of Political Economy*, **42**(1), 66–81.

Simon, H.A. (1957) *Administrative Behaviour* (London, Macmillan).

Singh, A. (1975) Takeovers, economic natural selection and the theory of the firm, *Economic Journal*, **85**(September), 497–515.

Singh, A. (1977) UK industry and the world economy: a case of de-industrialisation?, *Cambridge Journal of Economics*, **1**, 113–36.

Spence, A.M. (1977) Entry, capacity, investment and oligopolistic pricing, *Bell Journal of Economics and Management Science*, **8**, 534–44.

Spence, A.M. and Zeckhauser, R. (1971) Insurance, information and individual action, *American Economic Review*, **61**, 380–87.

Steer, P. and Cable, J, (1978) Internal organisation and profit: an empirical analysis of large UK companies, *Journal of Industrial Economics* **27**(1), 13–30.

Stephen, F. (1994) Advertising, consumer research costs and prices in a professional service market, *Applied Economics* **26**(12), 1177–88.

Stigler, G.J. (1958) The economies of scale, *Journal of Law and Economics*, **1**(October), 54–71.

Stigler, G.J. (1961) The economics of information, *Journal of Political Economy*, **69**, 213–25.

Stigler, G.J. (1968) *The Organisation of Industry* (Homewood, IL, R.D. Irwin).

Stigler, G.J. (1971) The theory of economic regulation, *Bell Journal of Economics and Management Science*, **2**, 3–4.

Strong, N. and Waterson, M. (1987) Principals, agents and information, in R. Clarke and T. McGuinness (eds) *The Economics of the Firm* (Oxford, Basil Blackwell).

Stuckey, J.A. (1983) *Vertical Integration and Joint Ventures in the Aluminum Industry* (Cambridge, MA, Harvard University Press).

Sweezy, P.M. (1939) Demand under conditions of oligopoly, *Journal of Political Economy*, **47**(August), 568–73.

Sylos-Labini, P. (1957) *Oligopoly and Technical Progress* (Cambridge, MA, Harvard University Press).

Syriopoulos, T.C. and Sinclair, M.T. (1993) An econometric study of tourism demand: the AIDs model of US and European tourism in Mediterranean countries, *Applied Economics* **25**(12), 1541–52.

Teece, D.J. (1980) Economies of scope and the scope of the enterprise, *Journal of Economic Behaviour and Organisation*, **1**, 223–47.

Teece, D.J. (1981) Internal organisation and economic performance: an empirical analysis of the profitability of principal firms, *Journal of Industrial Economics*, **30**(2), 173–200.

Teece, D.J. (1982) Towards an economic theory of the multiproduct firm, *Journal of Economic Behaviour and Organisation*, **3**, 39–63.

Teece, D.J. (1986) Transaction cost economics and the multinational enterprise, *Journal of Economic Behaviour and Organisation*, **7**, 21–45.

Uri, N.D. (1995) A note on the estimation of the demand for sugar in the USA in the presence of measurement error in the data, *Applied Economics*, **27**(1), 83–94.

Utton, M.A. (1979) *Diversification and Competition* (Cambridge, Cambridge University Press).

Vernon, J.M. and Graham, D.A. (1971) Profitability of monopolisation by vertical integration, *Journal of Political Economy*, **79**, 924–25.

Vernon, R. (1966) International investment and international trade in the product cycle, *Quarterly Journal of Economics*, **80**, 190–207.

Vernon, R. (1974) The location of economic activity, in J.H. Dunning (ed.) *Economic Analysis and the Multinational Enterprise* (London, George, Allen and Unwin).

Vernon, R. (1979) The product cycle hypothesis in a new international environment, *Oxford Bulletin of Economics and Statistics*, **41**(4), 255–67.

Vickers, J. and Yarrow, G. (1988) *Privatisation: an Economic Analysis* (Cambridge, MA, MIT Press).

von Neuman, J. and Morgenstern, O. (1994) *Theory of Games and Economic Behaviour* (Princeton, NJ, Princeton University Press.

von Weizsacker, C.C. (1980) A welfare analysis of barriers to entry, *Bell Journal of Economics and Management Science*, **11**, 399–420.

Wahlroos, B. (1984) Monopoly welfare loss under uncertainty, *Southern Economic Journal*, **51**, 429–42.

Walsh, B.M. (1982) The demand for alcohol in the UK: a comment, *Journal of Industrial Economics*, **20**(4), 439–47.

Weir, C. (1995) Organisational structure and corporate performance: an analysis of medium and large UK firms, *Management Decision*, **33**(1), 24–32.

Weiss, L.W. (1974) The concentration–profits relationship and antitrust. In: H.J. Goldschmid, H.M. Mann and J.F. Weston (eds), *Industrial Concentration: The New Learning*, (Boston, MA, Little Brown).

Weiss, L.W. (1989) Why study concentration and price? in L.W. Weiss (ed.) *Concentration and Price* (Cambridge, MA, MIT Press).

Williams, K., Haslam, C., Williams, J., Cutler, T. with Adcroft, A. and Johal, S. (1992) Against lean production, *Economy and Society*, **21**(3), 320–54.

Williamson, O.E. (1964) *The Economics of Discretionary Behaviour: Managerial Objectives in a Theory of the Firm* (Englewood Cliffs, NJ, Prentice Hall).

Williamson, O.E. (1968) Economics as an antitrust defense: the welfare trade-offs, *American Economic Review*, **58**, 18–31.

Williamson, O.E. (1975) *Markets and Hierarchies: Analysis and Antitrust Implications* (New York, Free Press).

Williamson, O.E. (1981) The modern corporation: origins, evolution, attributes, *Journal of Economic Literature*, **19**(December), 1537–68.

Williamson, O.E. (1984) Efficient labour organisation. In: F.H. Stephens (ed.) *Firms, Organisation and Labour*, (London, Macmillan).

Williamson, O.E., Wachter, M.L. and Harris, J.E. (1975) Understanding the employment relation: the analysis of idiosyncratic exchange, *Bell Journal of Economics and Management Science*, **6**, 250–78.

Wilson, J. (1994) Competitive tendering and UK public services, *Economic Review*, **11**(40), 31–38.

Winston, C. (1993) Economic deregulation: days of reckoning for microeconomics, *Journal of Economic Literature*, **31**(September), 1263–89.

Womack, J., Jones, D. and Rees, D. (1990) *The Machine that Changed the World* (New York, Rawson Associates).

Worcester, D.A. (1973) New estimates of the welfare loss to monopoly in the United States, 1956–69, *Southern Economic Journal*, **40**, 234–45.

Yen, S.T. (1994) Cross-section estimation of US demand for alcoholic beverage, *Applied Economics*, **26**(4), 381–92.

The present value of £1 due at the end of *n* periods

Period	1%	2%	3%	4%	5%	6%	7%	8%	9%	10%
1	.9901	.9804	.9709	.9615	.9524	.9434	.9346	.9259	.9174	.9091
2	.9803	.9612	.9426	.9246	.9070	.8900	.8734	.8573	.8417	.8264
3	.9706	.9423	.9151	.8890	.8638	.8396	.8163	.7938	.7722	.7513
4	.9610	.9238	.8885	.8548	.8227	.7921	.7629	.7350	.7084	.6830
5	.9515	.9057	.8626	.8219	.7835	.7473	.7130	.6806	.6499	.6209
6	.9420	.8880	.8375	.7903	.7462	.7050	.6663	.6302	.5963	.5645
7	.9327	.8706	.8131	.7599	.7107	.6651	.6227	.5835	.5470	.5132
8	.9235	.8535	.7894	.7307	.6768	.6274	.5820	.5403	.5019	.4665
9	.9143	.8368	.7664	.7026	.6446	.5919	.5439	.5002	.4604	.4241
10	.9053	.8203	.7441	.6756	.6139	.5584	.5083	.4632	.4224	.3855
11	.8963	.8043	.7224	.6496	.5847	.5268	.4751	.4289	.3875	.3505
12	.8874	.7885	.7014	.6246	.5568	.4970	.4440	.3971	.3555	.3186
13	.8787	.7730	.6810	.6006	.5303	.4688	.4150	.3677	.3262	.2897
14	.8700	.7579	.6611	.5775	.5051	.4423	.3878	.3405	.2992	.2633
15	.8613	.7430	.6419	.5553	.4810	.4173	.3624	.3152	.2745	.2394
16	.8528	.7284	.6232	.5339	.4581	.3936	.3387	.2919	.2519	.2176
17	.8444	.7142	.6050	.5134	.4363	.3714	.3166	.2703	.2311	.1978
18	.8360	.7002	.5874	.4936	.4155	.3503	.2959	.2502	.2120	.1799
19	.8277	.6864	.5703	.4746	.3957	.3305	.2765	.2317	.1945	.1635
20	.8195	.6730	.5537	.4564	.3769	.3118	.2584	.2145	.1784	.1486
21	.8114	.6598	.5375	.4388	.3589	.2942	.2415	.1987	.1637	.1351
22	.8034	.6468	.5219	.4220	.3418	.2775	.2257	.1839	.1502	.1228
23	.7954	.6342	.5067	.4057	.3256	.2618	.2109	.1703	.1378	.1117
24	.7876	.6217	.4919	.3901	.3101	.2470	.1971	.1577	.1264	.1015
25	.7798	.6095	.4776	.3751	.2953	.2330	.1842	.1460	.1160	.0923
30	.7419	.5521	.4120	.3083	.2314	.1741	.1314	.0994	.0754	.0573
35	.7059	.5000	.3554	.2534	.1813	.1301	.0937	.0676	.0490	.0356
40	.6717	.4529	.3066	.2083	.1420	.0972	.0668	.0460	.0318	.0221

The present value of £1 due at the end of *n* periods (*continued*)

Period	12%	14%	15%	16%	18%	20%	24%
1	.8929	.8772	.8696	.8621	.8475	.8333	.8065
2	.7972	.7695	.7561	.7432	.7182	.6944	.6504
3	.7118	.6750	.6575	.6407	.6086	.5787	.5245
4	.6355	.5921	.5718	.5523	.5158	.4823	.4230
5	.5674	.5194	.4972	.4761	.4371	.4019	.3411
6	.5066	.4556	.4323	.4104	.3704	.3349	.2751
7	.4523	.3996	.3759	.3538	.3139	.2791	.2218
8	.4039	.3506	.3269	.3050	.2660	.2326	.1789
9	.3606	.3075	.2843	.2630	.2255	.1938	.1443
10	.3220	.2697	.2472	.2267	.1911	.1615	.1164
11	.2875	.2366	.2149	.1954	.1619	.1346	.0938
12	.2567	.2076	.1869	.1685	.1372	.1122	.0757
13	.2292	.1821	.1625	.1452	.1163	.0935	.0610
14	.2046	.1597	.1413	.1252	.0985	.0779	.0492
15	.1827	.1401	.1229	.1079	.0835	.0649	.0397
16	.1631	.1229	.1069	.0930	.0708	.0541	.0320
17	.1456	.1078	.0929	.0802	.0600	.0451	.0258
18	.1300	.0946	.0808	.0691	.0508	.0376	.0208
19	.1161	.0829	.0703	.0596	.0431	.0313	.0168
20	.1037	.0728	.0611	.0514	.0365	.0261	.0135
21	.0926	.0638	.0531	.0443	.0309	.0217	.0109
22	.0826	.0560	.0462	.0382	.0262	.0181	.0088
23	.0738	.0491	.0402	.0329	.0222	.0151	.0071
24	.0659	.0431	.0349	.0284	.0188	.0126	.0057
25	.0588	.0378	.0304	.0245	.0160	.0105	.0046
30	.0334	.0196	.0151	.0116	.0070	.0042	.0016
35	.0189	.0102	.0075	.0055	.0030	.0017	.0005
40	.0107	.0053	.0037	.0026	.0013	.0007	.0002

INDEX

Page numbers in *italics* refer to tables and figures